TALKING ABOUT PEOPLE

TALKING ABOUT PEOPLE

Readings in Contemporary Cultural Anthropology

William A. Haviland
UNIVERSITY OF VERMONT

Robert J. Gordon
UNIVERSITY OF VERMONT
NATIONAL UNIVERSITY OF LESOTHO

Mayfield Publishing Company
Mountain View, California
London • Toronto

Library of Congress Cataloging-in-Publication Data
Talking about people: readings in contemporary cultural anthropology
   / [edited by] William A. Haviland, Robert J. Gordon.
       p.   cm.
   Includes bibliographical references and index.
   ISBN 1-55934-141-6
   1. Ethnology.   I. Haviland, William A.   II. Gordon, Robert J.

   GN316.T34   1992
   306- -dc20   92-35586
                                                                              CIP

Manufactured in the United States of America
10 9 8 7 6 5 4 3 2 1

Mayfield Publishing Company
1240 Villa Street
Mountain View, California 94041

Sponsoring editor, Janet Beatty; production service, The Book Company; manuscript editor, Betty Duncan; text designer, Wendy Calmenson; cover photographer, William Coupon; cover designer, Jeanne M. Schreiber. The text was set in 10/12 Palatino by Fog Press and printed on 50# Finch Opaque by Banta Company.

To Lillian Jahngen,
whose wonderful smile, unfailing good humor,
and incredible patience have meant so much
to us both over the years

Preface

Most anthologies for cultural anthropology courses reproduce with some regularity what we might consider "classic" anthropological articles. While we have nothing against the classics, we do feel that it creates the impression that nothing new has happened in anthropology. We want students to understand what anthropologists are doing *now*. In this reader, we introduce students to some of the more recent and provocative works of anthropologists. In the process, we hope to shake up some of the readers' comfortably ethnocentric beliefs about the world in which they live.

It is no secret that North Americans are surprisingly ignorant about the nature of the "global society" of which they are a part. In an era when the population of North America constitutes but a small minority of the world's people, increasingly dependent on the rest of the world for vital raw materials, manufactured goods, and markets for those products still produced at home, reliable information about other peoples and their lifeways has become ever more important for the survival of North Americans themselves. Anthropology has always been in the forefront of efforts to learn about other peoples, and now more than ever it has a special role to play in bringing college students into the world arena. Thus, the majority of articles in this anthology focus on common global interests. From Kent Redford's examination of the stereotype of the ecologically noble savage in Chapter 1 to Gernot Köhler's analysis of global apartheid in Chapter 13, the volume highlights global concerns.

At the same time, this anthology seeks to show the exotic in the familiar by suggesting new and eye-opening ways of looking at the student's own society. We feel this closer examination is an essential way to combat racism and other invidious distinctions that North Americans like to draw between "us" and "them." From articles such as Alan Dundes' on American foot-

ball in Chapter 4 and James Brain's "Ugly American Revisited" in Chapter 12, readers will gain fascinating insights into their own culture and society.

In keeping with the global perspective of this collection, we include a significant number of articles by authors from outside the United States. Anthropology is not, after all, an exclusively American preserve (and how arrogant we are to call ourselves Americans!). It is an exciting international discipline, whose members are not all white middle-class males. We have tried to reflect the profession more closely by increasing the representation of both foreign (African, British, Canadian, French, Irish, and Mexican, for example) and female contributors, including a number of nonanthropologists. Almost 40 percent of the authors are from outside the United States and one-half are female.

Because anthropology is the study of women as well as of men, we have deemed it important that gender issues be well represented by the articles in this anthology. Considerations of gender enter into virtually everything that people do, so we thought it appropriate to spread the material on gender throughout the book. Notable examples of articles that deal with gender are Alma Gottlieb's "American Premenstrual Syndrome" and Nancy Chodorow's "Being and Doing: A Cross-Cultural Examination of the Socialization of Males and Females" in Chapter 4; Dirk Johnson's "Polygamists Emerge from Secrecy," John Coggeshall's "'Ladies' Behind Bars," Regina Oboler's "Is the Female Husband a Man?" and Juliet Gardiner's "Guys and Dolls" in Chapter 7; Jane Collier, Michelle Rosaldo, and Sylvia Yanagisako's "Is There a Family?" Brett Williams' "Why Migrant Women Feed Their Husbands Tamales," Margery Wolf's "Uterine Families and the Women's Community," and Alice Schlegel's "Male and Female in Hopi Thought and Action" in Chapter 8;

Carol MacCormack's "Women and Symbolic Systems" in Chapter 9; Judith Van Allen's "Sitting on a Man" in Chapter 10; and Silvia Rodgers' "Feminine Power at Sea" in Chapter 11.

USING THIS BOOK

The chapters are arranged by topic in the order typically covered in introductory cultural anthropology courses. (A chart in the Instructor's Manual pairs each article with the appropriate chapters in the most popularly used introductory cultural anthropology texts.) Each chapter begins with a brief introduction written by the editors that serves to tie the articles together and relate them to the chapter topic. Brief biographical sketches of the authors of each article exemplify the international flavor of the volume and contribute further insights into what anthropology is all about. The references and notes for each article will appeal to the student who wants to know more, and the map showing the location of people and places discussed will be helpful to all students. For easy reference, we've included an extensive glossary and index.

A NOTE ABOUT THE ARTICLES

Although many of the articles are reprinted here in their entirety, some have been edited in order to keep the book to a reasonable length. For the most part, the cuts have involved details of methodology, and we have been careful to keep the substance and the spirit of each article intact.

Because most anthropologists from outside the United States who write in English use British spellings and modes of expression, students will find a number of unfamiliar conventions within these pages. Introducing students to other ways of thinking and acting is a significant part of our rationale for this book, so we have retained all these "Britishisms."

ACKNOWLEDGMENTS

A number of people have contributed in one way or another to this book. Those behind the scenes who have made vital contributions include Anita de Laguna Haviland, who, besides riding herd on both editors to meet deadlines, put everything into the computer, caught numerous errors, tracked down a variety of information, and assisted in writing the Instructor's Manual. Rinda Gordon, too, kept one of the editors in line and helped with the Instructor's Manual. Lilo Stainton, a senior anthropology major at the University of Vermont, worked to put together a preliminary version of this reader for "field testing" in the introductory anthropology course in the fall of 1991. To the students in that class, as well as all the others we have taught through the years (Haviland has been teaching introductory students since 1965, Gordon since 1979 in the U.S. and well before that in Papua New Guinea), we are grateful for all we have learned. Finally, we'd like to thank the reviewers, whose comments proved enormously helpful in fine-tuning the final selections: Robert L. Bee, University of Connecticut, Gustav A. Konitzky, Clarion University of Pennsylvania, Jay Sokolovsky, University of Maryland Baltimore County, and Dianne Smith, Santa Rosa Junior College.

Many people at Mayfield Publishing Company have helped bring this project to fruition. First of all, we are grateful to Jan Beatty, who has shown extraordinary patience with us and the delays occasioned as we communicated back and forth from Lesotho to Vermont and then Maine. We appreciate the interest she has shown in our ideas from the outset, as well as for the ideas and advice she has contributed along the way. We are no less grateful to the others at Mayfield who have seen this volume through production.

William A. Haviland
Deer Isle, Maine

Robert J. Gordon
Roma, Lesotho

Contents

2 CULTURE 14

3 LANGUAGE AND COMMUNICATION 39

TALKING ABOUT PEOPLE

1

The Nature of Anthropology

Most anthropologists define **anthropology** as the study of man, claiming that it was derived from the Greek words *anthropos* and *logos* meaning "man study." Thus, many introductory texts bear the title or subtitle "The Study of Mankind, or Humanity." In retrospect, such claims are specious and indeed pretentious. If there is one thing we have learned in our practice of anthropology, it is humility and discretion about what anthropology can claim to do. Indeed, if one probes deeper into the Greek lexicon, *anthropos* and *logos* can also mean "bearer of scandals or tales." This is why Lucy Mair, a pioneering British social anthropologist, would modestly define her discipline in her lectures as simply "talking about people." We pay tribute to her by calling this anthology *Talking About People*. To be sure, such a title will undoubtedly evoke shades of Oprah Winfrey or some other TV talk show, and that gives this book a delightful postmodernist twist. Talking about people, or gossip, is not only a pleasantly informal activity, but as this anthology shows, it can also be a disciplined, engrossing, and enriching experience leading to important personal and social insights. Indeed, as a moment's reflection will show, "talking about people" is a basic social and cultural activity in which we humans engage in order to educate and place ourselves in the world and to make sense of our beings and universe.

We feel that this more modest stance has contributed substantially to the increasing popularity of anthropology in recent years. There are, of course, other reasons as well. Some attribute it to the fact that, of the various social sciences, it has the least amount of jargon—a situation derived from the fact that the people researchers have studied do not read the studies. This has changed, however, in a world that is increasingly becoming a global village. Indeed, the movement toward a global village is probably a much more important reason for anthropology's new-found popularity as there are many more opportunities for cultural misunderstanding and thus the need for an understanding of other cultures. This process of **globalization** has resulted in many of us realizing the importance of the interrelationships between our part of the world and people in other parts of the planet, perhaps most graphically illustrated by our concern for the Amazonian rain forest and how deforestation there will impact our own well-being. Graphic TV images of drought, famine, and pestilence in the Third World have made us conscious of an impending sense of crisis. A growing disillusionment with "development" and the fact that more people are asking penetrating questions about why development has failed have also propelled anthropology to prominence (see readings in Chapters 5 and 13). "Development experts" are starting to realize that possibly one reason for the failure of development has been that they have not understood or talked to local people. Anthropology is the academic discipline that makes it its business to talk to such folks.

Indeed, it is precisely this emphasis on the "Other" that makes the study of anthropology attractive to many. In essence, anthropology is concerned with the study of alternative lifestyles and cultures. It looks at how other people solve common human problems. On a more personal level, people who are generally interested in alternative lifestyles and cultures are those who are dissatisfied with their own society. In short, they suffer from various degrees of alienation; this gives rise to the old joke about the definition of an anthropologist: someone who rejects his or her own society before that society rejects him or her. There is merit in this old joke because, of the various social sciences, anthropology has by far attracted more women and minorities than any other social science. Most first-year students can name some prominent female anthropologists such as the North Americans Margaret Mead and Ruth Benedict or the British Lucy Mair, Audrey Richards, or Monica Wilson. This tradition still continues—over half of all presidents of the American Anthropological Association since World War II have been women. Other social sciences and humanities like sociology, political science, psychology, and history are hard-pressed to even halfway replicate such a distinguished record.

There is nothing deviant or abnormal about being alienated from one's own society. On the contrary, some would argue that it is inevitable given the present condition of modernity. Disciplining one's alienation and using it as a way of seeing can lead to important insights. Indeed, we would argue that this alienated perspective is crucial. When one of the authors first came to the United States, he asked a native what books he should read to understand the United States. He was surprised to be told to read de Tocqueville's *Democracy in America* and Gunnar Myrdal's *An American Dilemma*. In retrospect, what they have in common, apart from providing original and synthetic insights into the workings of the United States, is that both authors were clearly outsiders to the United States. The point was understood by the famous English social historian Eric Hobsbawm when he observed that "it has proved disastrous to leave the history of nationalism to nationalists [just] as that of railways to railway enthusiasts" (1972:397).

So perhaps the most important characteristic of anthropology, then, is that it self-consciously takes an outsider perspective on society and culture. In Robert Burns's immortal words, "Aye wad the giftie gie us, tae see ourselves as others see us." As such, it can be a wonderful antidote to **ethnocentrism** and its various associated myths of **cultural arrogance**. The acquisition of this disciplined outsider perspective is typically gotten by travel, either geographic or imaginary. But as we all know, travel does not necessarily broaden the mind; that only happens if one is predisposed to let it happen, and this is where the anthropological perspective comes in.

A concern with the Other, either real or imagined, leads directly and inevitably into a consideration of difference. What are the implications of difference? Is difference largely in the eye of the beholder? For example, people in a Papua New Guinean village would obey the District Commissioner's instruction to "tidy up the village" by assiduously sweeping up all the dog and pig droppings but leaving all the papers and cans. To them papers and cans are not dirty but a sign of affluence and status. Here is an example of the important role

played by culture in defining difference. Culture is one of the key concerns of anthropology, and in Chapter 2, we concentrate exclusively upon the concept. A concern with difference also raises a host of issues such as how much difference should be tolerated. Should one treat everyone the same or allow for difference? This issue manifests itself in many ways, ranging from the young New Yorker in Papua New Guinea who saw nothing wrong in wearing a scanty bikini among a number of bare-breasted women despite their disapproval of her attire because, she reasoned, in New York she would not object to what they wore, to the explosive issue of **multiculturalism**, which is currently gripping U.S. campuses.

It is this very issue of the Other and cultural differences that is the focus of the article by Marion Benedict. She relates her experiences as an ethnographer in the Seychelles, struggling to understand their lives as *they* live them, yet finding it impossible to be a mere "fly on the wall" herself. Her article not only demonstrates the difficulties of getting to know others, but also the difficulties of accurately writing about a particular culture to an audience with a different cultural background. How does one do this, without the description becoming a caricature?

For the novice, a quick look at any anthropology department would appear to reveal a bewildering array of diverse individuals who appear to have nothing in common with one another, except perhaps a department secretary. This is illusionary, however, because what ties the **linguist**, the **social anthropologist**, the **ethnologist**, the **prehistorian**, and the **physical anthropologist** is precisely an appreciation for the role of culture in the construction of difference. Historically, this arose out of a shared concern for what were originally "tribal people," but the focus is now increasingly on contemporary changes. Anthropologists are increasingly studying segments of their own society, using a distinctive **anthropological perspective**. The article by Judith Okely is a good example of this. Although anthropologists will debate the smaller details, most agree that the following constitute some of the defining characteristics:

1. **Fieldwork** is perhaps the characteristic of which anthropologists are most proud. According to Seligman (quoted in Lewis 1976:27), "What the blood of the martyrs was to the Early Church, Fieldwork was to anthropology." He was perhaps exaggerating only slightly. Indeed, many see this as the most distinctive characteristic and give it the status of a tribal initiation rite: One is not an anthropologist unless one has done fieldwork for an extended period of time.

2. Extended fieldwork leads almost naturally to a focus on local communities and a feel for grass-roots issues.

3. Fieldwork immersion plus the breadth of anthropological training emphasize the **holistic** perspective, that is, examining social relationships in their interrelationships. Whereas other social scientists might spend all their time examining the beauty of the flowers, anthropologists pause from this task to take in the beauty of the fields from the top of the mountain and thus see a broader pattern.

It is from these holistic perspectives that anthropologists can engage in the increasingly important task of debunking myths about the Other. The reading by Kent Redford is but one sample of such an exercise.

REFERENCES

Hobsbawm, E. 1972. "Some Reflections on Nationalism." In *Imagination and Precision in the Social Sciences*. T. J. Nossiter, A. Hauson, and S. Rokkan (eds.). London: Faber.

Lewis, I. M. 1976. *Social Anthropology in Perspective*. Harmondsworth, England: Penguin Books.

Fieldwork in the Home Counties

Judith Okely

Judith Okely has done extensive fieldwork on Gypsies and lectures in social anthropology and sociology at the University of Edinburgh in Scotland and the University of Essex in England.

Malinowski's advice on fieldwork included the famous pleas to learn the indigenous language and to avoid contact with white men. Such advice would have been inappropriate for my fieldwork. Granted, Gypsies in England are respectably exotic as non-literate nomads, not found in the conventional typologies. Yet we shared the same language, apart from the occasional Romani word inserted into English sentences. Fieldwork did not require progress through grammar books, interpreters and mental translations. This apparent concordance with one's own culture masked other differences.

We are always reassuring ourselves that anthropology highlights the contrasts between cultures. These contrasts are rarely experienced within the same space and time as they are during fieldwork at home. Long-term fieldwork in my own country made explicit the contrast with my customary life. The anthropologist abroad has a different relationship with the society within which the group studied is embedded. He or she is usually a stranger to all contexts. By contrast, in my case, I was moving from a specific experience defined by class, gender, race and education into a stigmatized minority about whom I knew almost nothing, beyond the non-Gypsy (Gorgio) stereotypes and representations. Until a community worker drove me to a cluster of modern caravans and lorries just off the M1, I should not have recognised them as members of the exotic category vaguely associated with horses and waggons. Previously, I should have thought I was looking at the caravans of temporary road workers.

You experience the sudden absence of basic amenities like water and a W.C. on a camping holiday, but usually in a depopulated, rural setting. The Gypsies did not live in the woods of the nursery rhyme. The camps were bordered by major roads and sometimes housing estates, lorries thundered along the elevated dual carriageway a few yards away. On one camp we nestled beneath a factory floodlit at night. A costly new site was built on a former sewage farm. Cannibalized car bodies, piles of scrap and smoking tyres were my palm trees and coral strand.

To the Travellers I did not appear as an eccentric foreigner but as a member of the dominant persecuting society, albeit a well-meaning student. In this context, Malinowski's and later Powdermaker's suggestions for a preliminary census were inadvisable at any stage. The Trobriand Islanders may on the face of it have been complimented by attention to their way of life, or perhaps a colonized people has learned to submit to censuses, but nomads everywhere have learned how to evade them. I was warned by one Gypsy friend that I could be burned for writing down a genealogy. Evans-Pritchard and Chagnon have also known difficulties in getting mere names.

Unlike anthropology abroad, fieldwork at home is not a matter of memorizing a new vocabulary; only slowly did I realise that I had to learn another language in the words of my mother tongue. I unlearned my boarding school accent, changed clothing and body movements. Dropping my 'aitches and throwing in swear words, I was doing an Eliza Dolittle in reverse and without Professor Higgins to supervise me. After some months a Traveller said "Judith your speech has improved." Washing and eating became different procedures with the same utensils and food from the same shops up the road (see Okely, 1983). My past identity was slowly dismantled in the home counties I had inhabited since childhood.

The view of a famous provincial town, from the cab of a lorry crammed with Traveller parents and children, looked both familiar and alien. As we drove through districts I had known before, the Travellers would show

"Fieldwork in the Home Counties" by Judith Okely, from *Royal Anthropological Institute News*, 1984, Royal Anthropological Institute. Reprinted with permission.

me another landscape stamped by their past: "That's where I stopped as a kid with our waggon and horses," "we tarmacced that forecourt," "years ago we got loads of scrap from that air base," "Billy rents this field for his horses."

One summer, I was calling for scrap and rags in a sleepy village with my regular Traveller work mate: "Lovely houses these," she said as we passed a desirable Georgian residence. The lilac hung heavy over a white garden seat. I dreamed of a Grantchester tea and imagined the view from a top window; it would make a lovely study, I was thinking. My daydream was fractured by my Traveller companion; "Lovely houses for calling—those rich people'll have a lot to throw out." She had rightly seen them as a resource, a place for acquiring goods not for habitation. If she had pressed her face against the window pane, it would not be with any longing to enter.

Despite my change in clothing, when calling for "any old iron, scrap, batteries or rags," I still couldn't get the demeanour right. The housewives would invariably ask me, but not my Traveller mates, what it was for. Eventually, I found it simpler to say it was for charity than reveal that I was an anthropologist doing participant observation as a Gypsy on Gorgio doorsteps. Some of the Gorgio women looked like myself in another life. I was looking in a distorted mirror. In the company of Travellers, I did experience abuse as a Gypsy at garden gates and in shops, and was chased away where previously I would have been welcome.

An anthropologist abroad does not experience the double knowledge I felt, for example in the following case. My mate Reena persuaded one woman on a private estate to part with an old battery. As it was leaking acid, Reena wrapped it in newspaper. After loading up, Reena's mother Aunt Doll stuffed the newspaper in the hedge, thinking she was being "tidy." The Gorgio woman had been watching us from her gravel drive. Her views on rubbish disposal were as intimately known to me as those of my head-mistress. I shrank at her scorn: "What have you done with that newspaper?" she called out: "It's alright," said Aunt Doll, "I've put it in the hedge." "That's typical of you Gypsies, you like to live among old car bodies in a dust bowl!" Aunt Doll drew herself up to her full height. "Madam. I'm not a Gypsy and I don't live in no dust bowl. If you want to know I give up my time for this work, I'm working for charity." This time it was the Gorgio woman's turn to shrink away. Whereas Aunt Doll was detached from the criticism about rubbish disposal, she resented the stigma attached to the word Gypsy. I was, on the other hand, inwardly free of such identification, but I felt her pain. At the same time, I felt it "wrong" to shove newspaper in that hedge.

The one or two unexpected visits to my camp by Gorgio friends brought into sharper focus the contrast between my two existences and double vision in the same country. Anthropologists abroad may also risk

intrusions from friends back home, but at least the visitors have been partially sobered by the extended journey and the obvious strangeness. My friends, however, drove the same roads as the Travellers.

One afternoon, after an especially dramatic confrontation between Travellers and the police on the camp, a small mini van pulled in. We wondered if this was another "pig" in disguise. Out stepped my college friend Mike in chic Kings Road shirt, tight Levis and dark glasses. I had to emerge from the cluster of confused Travellers and identify myself. I switched to a fellow intellectual tone and became ungainly in my loosely hung attire. Despite his desire to hang around or sit gossiping in my caravan, I told him to drive me to a tea shop in the town. Mike had been given my exact ordnance survey location by a secretary at my London Research Centre.

The other male visitor, well over 60, caused a sensation by greeting me with a slight peck on the cheek. He also anticipated a free and easy conversation in my caravan. Soon we were joined by six children and three women, two of whom had never deigned to visit me before. Their presence was actually a useful protection against any accusation that I fitted the Gypsy stereotype of a free-wheeling Gorgio woman, something I needed to dissociate myself from. My grey-haired "uncle" (the only acceptable category) continued his Hempstead flavoured literary discussion, naively complaining to me later of the "immaturity" of the Travellers' uncontrollable shrieks and giggles. My Gorgio visitors found my prudish demeanour both comical and unnecessary. It was hard to explain that mixed gender encounters are treated as sexual liaisons.

Anthropologists abroad both today and in the past have had to work under the shadow of officials and their policies towards subordinate groups. In my own case, government intervention occurred even before the research began. A senior civil servant wrote to the governor of our independent research centre reminding them of their partial state funding. He then objected to the centre's proposed Gypsy research, all of which he insisted should be conducted within Whitehall. Fortunately a charitable trust had already offered funding. Anthropologists have to negotiate for permits and visas. Similarly, I depended on some official consent to living on a temporary site. In all cases, there is a risk of identification with the officials, whether or not you study them.

Malinowski was also troubled on occasions by a "double vision." He could see the white administrator's view of the Trobriand landscape while he was attempting to understand the Islander's experience of it, or at least while he was attempting to isolate his own view. When accompanied unwillingly by two officials, he wrote "I saw and felt the utter drabness of the Kiriwana villages; I saw them through their eyes (it's fine to have this ability), but I forgot to look at them with my own"

(1967:163). Malinowski, like many other anthropologists, responded to this dilemma by cutting white men out of his research (see Okely 1975). Fieldwork in one's own country may make this separation of suitable research fields even less tenable. Apart from the theoretical and historical necessity of including the wider context, the effects of those same policymakers are lived with daily in the anthropologist's country both before and after fieldwork.

The research project to which I was originally attached included a study of legislation and government reports. Research into officials entering the camps was as problematic as in colonial times. First, because I had had to negotiate with them for my own entry and secondly because they assumed I would identify with their view of the "Gypsy problem." The Travellers also tended at first to identify me with the officials. This identification was hard to throw off. An Officer giving me a lift from the County Hall suddenly stopped the car to ask a Traveller family on the roadside to move on. Predictably, that family never trusted me and spread a story that I collaborated with the police.

I was given free access to files at County Hall because it was assumed, despite my explanations to the contrary, that my research centre was attached to the Ministry and also that my write-up would be wholly favourable. My boarding school accent was useful again. This called for another change of clothing. As a female, I was also seen as harmless. The files proved to be a Pandora's box and when my guarded queries betrayed a lack of consensus, some of the files were mysteriously withdrawn. My double identity had become apparent.

Later, official controls operated in gentlemanly ways, unique to anthropological fieldwork at home. My research centre insisted on sending drafts of our report to the council who sanitized it and inserted a final paragraph which made nonsense of the rest. It was never considered appropriate to send similar drafts to Gypsy representatives.

When publication is in the same country as fieldwork, the anthropologist cannot escape being read or misread by a wide range of interested parties beyond the usual academic constituency. The text will therefore bear the marks of such future scrutiny. If the study includes a minority group, the publication will be read more easily by some of its members. This development is to be welcomed, for the anthropologist cannot avoid the political consequences of his or her research. These consequences remain on the anthropologist's door step. Any latent tendency to treat people as objects or distant curios has to be confronted, not left repressed in a secret diary. The double vision has to be focussed correctly. The fieldworker at home cannot split identities between countries.

REFERENCES

Malinowski, B. 1967. *A Diary in the Strict Sense of the Term*. London: Routledge.

Okely, J. 1975. "The Self and Scientism." In *Journal of the Anthropological Society*, Oxford, Trinity Term.

Okely, J. 1983. *The Traveller-Gypsies*. Cambridge, England: Cambridge University Press.

Fact Versus Fiction

An Ethnographic Paradox Set in the Seychelles

Marion Benedict

Marion Benedict and her husband went to the Seychelles with their young children to do ethnographic fieldwork. She is at present a freelance author living with her anthropologist husband and family in Berkeley, California.

The Seychelles are islands in the middle of the Indian Ocean, where my husband and I went for six months in 1960 and five months in 1975 to do anthropological fieldwork. Once we had decided to go there, I asked about the islands among my friends in London where we then lived. Everyone who had ever heard of the Seychelles had three things to say about them, and these were recited with remarkable agreement of thought and phrasing. First, the islands were breathtakingly beautiful, glittering like a necklace in a sun-splashed sea. Second, it was a land of free love where dark beauties, happy and carefree, all longed for white babies; and third, it was riddled with superstition and black magic.

Right away I wanted to look into that black magic, but my friends warned me not to. It was illegal, they said, and dangerous. Furthermore any investigations into such a subject would be construed as spying for the government, which would queer our fieldwork for good.

So I decided to take a sociological census. I had a notebook, a list of questions to ask, and an informant who could translate the local Creole for me and help me find my way around—and who might drop a few secrets along the way. My aim was to contribute to the world bank of ethnography and ultimately, to get to know people unlike myself—the "not me," the "Other."

Once in the field, in the confusion of new sights, sounds, smells and ways of thinking, I clung to that notebook and those questions as to a lifebelt. It represented the objective truth I was recording. It represented order and system; counting and measurement; collation and comparison; and objective observation. The notebook defined my progress; it promised completion; it rationalized and legitimized my presence in that strange place among those strange people. It connected me to other collectors of ethnography and was a reassuring reminder of my own values, my own logical categories, the way I and my kind think—and, indeed, who I was.

But the facts I was trying to collect by asking questions tended to slide away. It had seemed an easy matter of question and answer, but the answer never came simply and directly, and sometimes never came at all, even after a long discussion of the topic. Lengthy digressions were the rule, and after my frustration wore off, I began to see that the important information lay in those very digressions, and not in the answers I was seeking. Important, I mean, in that my overall purpose was to comprehend these people in their own terms and not in terms of how they answered my questions, or of how they fitted into any ready-made logical categories.

Furthermore, I suspected that many answers to my questions were inventions, and that the more directly the people answered me the more thoroughly they were lying. The vexed problem of what and whom to believe loomed larger and larger until I was forced to consider my own part in the dialogue. Upon what grounds did I decide what was true and what false? Sheerly on intuition, my own gut response based on some private mental/emotional grid far beyond the reach of any available logic.

And on what grounds had I chosen to record some things and not others? How did I sort out the significant from the insignificant? Again, it was on the seemingly illogical basis of intuition. And so the process of altering the text, or tampering with reality—that is, fictionalizing—had begun.

My intuition was at work in other ways, too. For instance, I had begun to think that one informant was paranoid in her fantastic suspicions that people were out to "get" her. But how could I know for sure? And when I began to suspect that people were lying to me and laughing at me, how could I know that I was not catching her paranoia? Although I was able to check up on some facts and some of the answers given me, mostly I had to rely on guesswork.

"Fact Versus Fiction: An Ethnographic Paradox Set in the Seychelles" by Marion Benedict, from *Anthropology Today*, v.1, no.5, October 1985.

I felt that the people were laughing at me and my concern with the tedious exercise of filling my notebook with their lies. I recall, during those first few weeks, bending my head constantly over the pages of my notebook, fingers smudged with ink, shooing away flies, writing up endless little facts that died as I pinned them down while the people around me nudged and winked and whispered and giggled, carrying on their real lives over my head ... I was confronting head-on the difficulty of knowing the "Other." There was also the difficulty of how to write up the material and make it readable. How to begin, and what form to use? It seemed evident that the first step was to determine exactly what I wanted to say and then find the appropriate form in which to say it. In practice, however, there was a constant interchange between those two steps. Considering the form threw me back to reappraising the content, and considering the content threw me back to reappraising the form.

At first I tried the form of the anthropological monograph with its third person narration. That has the benefit of concentrating the reader's attention on the people by eliminating the "I" (except, of course, insofar as the author is always implied). But then I encountered the same difficulty as when collecting the material—without the personal, perceiving "I" the material was dull. In pursuing objectivity I had pushed out the felt life. So the "I" was moved in. But I still wanted to keep out the self: I wanted to write about them, not about me. So I thought of shaping the diary that I had kept in the field into readable form and presenting the material in that way.

The diary form had many advantages. In the first place, it was easy. Keeping my eye on the relations between the people and myself, I had only to shuffle around some times and places, cut irrelevancies, invent some transitions and the job was done. I could thus get rid of distracting disclaimers like "it seemed to me" and "or so I thought" because the personal point of view inhered in the diary form itself. The "I" was squeezed into the form, and so the reader's attention could fix itself upon the people.

The diary form also had the merit of accuracy, in that it was as exact an account of my activities in collecting the material as I could give in a readable form. It gave the sense of the present tense in all its immediacy, and transmitted my response to daily events as I saw them, and left it to the reader to do the work of fitting them into his own mental grid—that is, the work of interpretation.

But the diary had one big disadvantage; it did not have an organizing theme. It was anecdotal, episodic, and didn't go anywhere. There was nothing to carry the reader along; no build up, no suspense. Ultimately there was not enough meaning to make it interesting. It did not lead to any generalizations or argue any theory. So I shoved it into a drawer and did not look at it for several years.

When I did take it out again, I saw clearly that I had not sufficiently digested the material at the time I had written it. It was entertaining—amusing, even—but it didn't explain anything. I had not sufficiently engaged with what, all along, had been my underlying preoccupation.

But now I had digested the material. Now I saw a pattern emerging in my fieldnotes and a theme for my writing up. I saw that, in recording household compositions, behaviour, jokes told by fishermen and priests, schoolteachers and washerwomen, in noting down rituals and even the cost of raising pigs—I had been gathering an understanding about the nature of witchcraft. I had been recording evidence of how it works, and how that working radiates out to illuminate the most intimate and sensitive—and trivial—relations among the people of the Seychelles.

This new theme required a new form. I now saw that the ordering principle of my writing up must be the process of my understanding of witchcraft. In this way the search for content recapitulated the search for form. And the form required that the "I" be moved to centre stage.

This "I" had to be fictionalized. For the sake of coherence and emphasis on the important issues, I pretended to be a more naive observer than I really was. I took the reader by the hand and demonstrated, piece by piece, the evidence I had collected that led to my theory of witchcraft. I didn't actually *say* so, however, because I wanted the reader to go through the process of discovery for himself or herself. Sometimes I even planted clues so that the reader could see what was happening before I did.

Further fictionalizing was done in order to protect my informants. For that, I falsified names and put one person's words into another's mouth. For the sake of clarity and simplification I compressed several people into one. For instance, I really went to four fortunetellers, but I telescoped them into two. My main character herself is a composite of several women whom I had interviewed at length.

In order to clarify the narration I discarded material about whole families who, although they provided complexities and insights that my diary had included, nevertheless would distract the reader from the theme of witchcraft. The insights, however, helped to inform my final conclusions as I rearranged the actual process of discovery.

In order to show rather than to tell, I invented scenes of transition and thus imposed an order upon my narration that was never present in the field.

All this was done in the name of telling the truth and it resulted in a fiction. I had written a continuous narrative with suspense, a plot, fictional characters, a climax and a point—that is, a *novella*.

Fictionalizing continued as I invented another language to convey the rhythm and structure of my informants' diction. Their logic was roundabout; they told the middle first, then left me scrabbling for the subject and the message, so that it seemed a long and meaningless ramble until sometime later when I might have the good fortune to seize the point. But when my favourite informant spoke to her people she did not sound longwinded and tedious. The lilt of her Creole carried the knotty and treacherous structure along in an easy and natural flow that died when literally reproduced in my English on the printed page. Also, there was a freshness in her choice of words and a slyness in her digressions which alerted me to the calculated art that lay behind her kind of organization. But in order to convey the sense of this to my reader, I had to impose my own kind of organization as well as employ a free translation.

Witchcraft was a subject shrouded in secrecy and fraught with hysteria. Asking about it was like asking somebody to take hold of a live wire. The only way to approach it was indirectly. I had to go around in circles, pretending not to be interested in it to get close to it at all.

So my notebook is full of everything from very specific observations related to witchcraft—like accounts of my visits to witches—to the most conjectural. I recorded bits of gossip heavy with innuendo; half-guesses about oblique hints gleaned from informants; conversations with people describing their experiences with witches (or *bonhommes* or *bonnefemmes de bois*, as they called them). I noted behaviour that might be related to witchcraft and kept my eyes and ears open for signs of this hidden but ubiquitous phenomenon.

I was lucky to have, among my informants, an apprentice witch—not that she admitted it until the very end of my stay, by which time I already knew it. But the fieldnotes about my experiences with her became very valuable. They helped me to see, later on, how witchcraft works. I came to see that a witch can do harm simply because people believe that she can. People create the reality of spirits and magic simply by believing in them. They also believe that gossip can hurt them and so give it the power to do so. Gossip then takes on a life of its own, apart from being thoughts in people's minds and words on their tongues, and becomes what I have called gossip power. Gossip, when applied, becomes black magic. And conversely, black magic becomes applied gossip. I go to great pains to demonstrate that in my narration.

It was only through mulling over the material later that these generalizations sprang to mind. I also saw that the phenomenon of witchcraft is a prime example of how one's mental set shapes the world one sees. If somebody expects to see a spirit he will very likely do so. If he believes that his neighbour hates him and is practising black magic against him, he will then act in such a way that the neighbour will do just that. If he believes a fortune-teller's prediction that he will fall ill, he probably will. Thus subjective beliefs become objective reality.

This brings us back to the difficulties of objective truth, in this case of knowing what I now thought of simply as "others." I had wanted to keep myself out of the picture, to watch people interacting while I stood aside, just looking. But that simply did not work. If I stood aside I was ignored; nobody told me anything. It was like being erased. That nearly happened at first, when one of my informants pushed me aside and pursued her own ends at the beginning of my fieldwork. I accepted that for a while and watched from the sidelines, catching what attitudes and words I could as they flew by. But I was missing more than I was catching. Had I been part of their lives—able to help with their illnesses, or with getting jobs, I might have achieved a greater understanding. But as it was, their real lives eluded me because I was not sharing them. I could only achieve a deeper level of understanding through participating in the details and complexities of their everyday lives.

But how could I participate in their lives? The practical difficulties were too many: insufficient time; inadequate grasp of the language; not knowing enough about the people's pasts; not having been there when the important things had happened to them. All these played a part. But most important was the fact that I was an outsider. I was not one of them. I was richer and whiter and I could get out. They were there for life.

Even getting to know one person, as I tried to get to know my favourite informant, turned out to be difficult in a way I had not anticipated. She was watching me as closely as I was watching her. To be her friend required tact, respect, and reciprocity. She was very sensitive to anything I might do that could be construed as a slight. If she caught me in an insincerity she retaliated instantly with some egregious affectation of her own. Any suggestion of patronization maddened her and she would punish me by long absences. I don't think she ever resorted to witchcraft to take revenge upon me, as she did upon others, because she thought white people were not susceptible to black magic. But she could always get her own back by making me, foreigner that I was, a laughing-stock among her people.

She was suspicious of circumspection on my part—perhaps because she herself was so expert at it and knew what it concealed. She despised a doormat and ethnography was, to her, just another name for self-interest. She knew all about trade-offs and was determined to exact her quids-pro-quo.

She would walk all over anyone who let her. She tried it with me, and I called her bluff. It was only then, when I cared enough to show my spite and to pit my wits against hers, only then that I touched the quick of her life as she touched the quick of mine. I had to stand up to her, to talk back in order to win her respect. I could not beg it, or buy it—I had to earn it by becoming vulnerable myself, which involved, among other things, telling her my secrets as she had told me hers. It took my heart as well as my head, my intuition as well as my logic, my whole personality—that watchful, self-concealing ethnographer would never have uncovered her inner life.

There were also epistemological difficulties in knowing others. I had wanted an understanding distinct from self—but what could I know about others except what I could perceive through my own eyes and interpret through my own mental grid? The very cognitive process itself involved an "I" to observe and to know. How could I know anything that was "not me" when my very method of knowing was all me?

It was a paradox. Even though I came back to self when reaching out for the other, nevertheless something of the other did emerge in the process. That is, even though knowing may reside only in the knower, nevertheless some objective knowledge resides in my fictional *novella*.

The Ecologically Noble Savage

Kent H. Redford

Kent H. Redford, who received his Ph.D. (in biology) at Harvard University in 1983, is associate professor of Latin American Studies and director of programs for Studies in Tropical Conservation at the University of Florida.

To live and die with the land is to know its rules. When there is no hospital at the other end of the telephone and no grocery store at the end of the street, when there is no biweekly paycheck nor microwave oven, when there is nothing to fall back on but nature itself, then a society must discover the secrets of the plants and animals. Thus indigenous peoples possess extensive and intensive knowledge of the natural world. In every place where humans have existed, people have received this knowledge from their elders and taught it to their children, along with what has been newly acquired.

The richness of knowledge accumulated in the cultures of indigenous peoples of Latin America has come to light in the Western world through elegant anthropological work by Brent Berlin, Janis Alcorn, William Balee, and Darrell Posey, among others. These same scholars have often led the fight to save this knowledge and the cultures that embody it.

I strongly support the study of indigenous knowledge and the efforts to preserve native cultures. What concerns me is that some investigators justify their work in terms of its relevance to development projects, in effect placing dollar values on indigenous knowledge. If you justify the investigation of indigenous knowledge on economic grounds and your argument is refuted, or your calculations are shown to be inflated, then you have lost the argument, the funding, and potentially the Indian land as well. I have the same concern about shortsighted arguments of biologists who "sell" biodiversity by urging the preservation of plant and animal species on the basis of their potential for yielding useful products.

THE EUROPEAN IDEAL

The economic argument for the investigation of indigenous cultures has its roots in the myth of the noble savage. In its first incarnation, the *noble savage* was a shorthand term for the idealized European vision of the inhabitants of the New World. Early chroniclers noted that among the Indians "the land belonged to all, just like the sun and water. Mine and thine, the seeds of all evils, do not exist for those people. . . . They live in a golden age, . . . in open gardens, without laws or books, without judges, and they naturally follow goodness." Jean-Jacques Rousseau, Thomas More, and others idealized the naked "savages" as innocent of sin. Another chronicler, continuing in this vein, observed that "all are equal in every respect, and so in harmony with their surroundings that they all live justly and in conformity with the laws of nature." For many Europeans, these Indians were dwellers in an earthly Garden of Eden.

It is the latter idea, that Indians lived in conformity with nature, that inspired this century's reincarnation of the noble savage. Writings of several scientists and indigenous rights advocates echo the early chroniclers' assumption that indigenous people lived in "balance" with their environment. Prominent conservationists have stated that in the past, indigenous people "lived in close harmony with their local environment." The rhetoric of Indian spokespersons is even stronger: "In the world of today there are two systems, two different irreconcilable 'ways of life.' The Indian world—collective, communal, human, respectful of nature, and wise—and the western world—greedy, destructive, individualist, and enemy of nature" (from a report to the International NGO Conference on Indigenous Peoples and the Land, 1981). The idealized figure of centuries past had been reborn, as the *ecologically* noble savage.

The recently accumulated evidence, however, refutes this concept of ecological nobility. Precontact Indians were not "ecosystem men"; they were not just another species of animal, largely incapable of altering the environment, who therefore lived within the "ecological limitations of their home area." Paleobiologists, archaeologists, and botanists are coming to believe that most tropical forests have been severely altered by human activities before European contact. Evidence of vast fires in the northern Amazonian forests and of the apparently anthropogenic origins of large areas of forest in eastern Amazonia suggests that before 1500, humans had tremendously affected the virgin forest, with ensuing impacts on plant and animal species. These people behaved as humans do now: they did whatever they had to feed themselves and their families.

"Whatever they had to" is the key phrase in understanding the problem of the noble savage myth in its contemporary version. Countless examples make it clear that indigenous people can be either forced, seduced, or tempted into accepting new methods, new crops, and new technologies. No better example exists than the near-universal adoption of firearms for hunting by Indians in the Neotropics. Shotguns or rifles, often combined with the use of flashlights and outboard motors, change completely the interaction between human hunters and their prey.

There is no cultural barrier to the Indians' adoption of means to "improve" their lives (i.e., make them more like Western lives), even if the long-term sustainability of the resource base is threatened. These means can include the sale of timber and mining rights to indigenous lands, commercial exploitation of flora and fauna, and invitations to tourists to observe "traditional lifestyles." Indians should not be blamed for engaging in these activities. They can hardly be faulted for failing to live up to Western expectations of the noble savage. They have the same capacities, desires, and, perhaps, needs to overexploit their environment as did our European ancestors. Why shouldn't Indians have the same right to dispose of the timber on their land as the international timber companies have to sell theirs? An indigenous group responded to the siren call of the market economy in just this spirit in Brazil in 1989, when Guajajara Indians took prisoners in order to force the government Indian agency, FUNAI, to grant them permission to sell lumber from their lands.

"INHERENT SUPERIORITY"?

Such observed behavior contrasts sharply with the claims made about Indian use of natural resources in the modern world. Despite evidence to the contrary, indigenous people continue to be credited with a natural respect for ecology and a commitment to sustainable methods of resource use under all circumstances. Some Indian groups, reading of the qualities attributed to them by Europeans, have begun to give themselves the same credit. In some cases, Indian spokespersons promise that adoption of "Indian ways" will solve many of the problems created by the ignorant ways of the non-Indians. In the highly publicized Chimane Forest Reserve in Amazonian Bolivia, for example, where indigenous people are protesting lumbering activities by commercial firms, a spokesperson for the Moxo Indians lays claim to some of the land stating: "We have learned to take care and maintain the ecology because we know that it guarantees our existence." The assertion that as Indians these people will be ecologically noble stewards, though unproven, is a trump card in the current world of conservation sensitivities.

The currency of the myth of ecological nobility was demonstrated again in Colombia, when the Colombian government granted Indians rights to more than half of national rainforest territory, arguing that the Indians are the people most likely to protect the biological diversity of the tropical forest. The Indians will administer the territory because, supposedly, as Indians, they will sustainably use and therefore preserve the plant and animal diversity. (Any "serious" exploitation will presumably be turned over to non-Indians, more experienced in nonsustainable resource use. The government has kept the rights to minerals and to commercial extraction of natural resources.)

The belief in the inherent superiority of indigenous resource use systems has reached its twentieth-century apogee in the argument that such systems are ideal models for development. Books, conferences, and learned editorials push the relevance of indigenous knowledge to contemporary development in the tropics. A recent World Wildlife Fund study on indigenous methods of resource use was titled "The Once and Future Resource Managers."

To be sure, several scientists have demonstrated that there are methods used by indigenous peoples that are definitely superior to those used by nonindigenous peoples living in the same habitat. These methods include polycropping, techniques to enhance soil fertility, and sustainable harvesting of forest plants. Other scientists have shown that indigenous groups possess culturally encoded mores that result in preservation of the resource base. But these documented patterns are sustainable only under conditions of low population density, abundant land, and limited involvement with a market economy.

How relevant are such methods and customs to situations where these three conditions no longer exist, as in most places in the Neotropics today? Techniques developed to satisfy subsistence needs are unlikely to work when surpluses are needed for cash. As an example, the Irapa-Yukpa Indians of western Venezuela, who traditionally moved over an extensive area in search of game and plant food, are now stationary. They raise coffee and work as seasonal laborers. The Indian hunters, who for the most part use shotguns, have eliminated most large animals from near their villages and use much of the cash earned growing coffee or working for wages to purchase canned meat or fresh fish. As the anthropologists studying this group note, "Traditional ideology, language, and economic pursuits are rapidly being replaced by the customs and behavioral characteristics of the imposing Venezuelan rural culture." These researchers go on to suggest that what is happening to the Yukpa will soon happen to most other relatively unacculturated tribes. To believe that when confronted with market pressures, higher population densities, and increased sedentism most indigenous peoples will maintain the integrity of their traditional methods is not only to argue against the available evidence, but worse, to fall into the ideological trap that produced the ecologically noble savage.

A MOSAIC OF METHODS

We must face the fact that in many cases, when we dream of the ecologically noble Indian whose knowledge will save us from the consequences of modern development, we dream an old dream, whose roots stretch back to the Garden of Eden and beyond. The future lies not in the discovery of a philosopher's stone long buried in the minds of tropical forest peoples, but in the slow, patient work of assembling solutions from the myriad sources scattered throughout the world.

As part of this effort, we need to learn from Indians. We need to enlist their help and modify their methods—selecting, refining, innovating what is appropriate to a given situation—in order to meet the demands of development in the Neotropics. Not to be ignored are the *mestizos* or *caboclos,* the mixed-blood peoples who for centuries have inhabited some areas of the Amazonian forests. They have already undertaken much experimentation with indigenous methods and are valuable sources of information on sustainable resource use, such as ways to harvest fish from the ecologically complex lacustrine environments.

Indigenous knowledge is tremendously important for many reasons. It reflects the accumulated wisdom of unique cultures; it echoes the experiences of groups whose survival is threatened; it offers fascinating insights of ecological value. And occasionally, only occasionally, it offers methods that, when modified, can be of use to inhabitants, native and nonnative, in the modern Neotropics.

2

Culture

What would happen if a person went into a North American supermarket during rush hour and tried to haggle over the price of a 79-cent tube of toothpaste? Apart from causing considerable embarrassment and probable ejection from the store, such behavior illustrates the dangers of culturally inappropriate behavior. In many parts of the world, haggling constitutes culturally appropriate behavior. As befits its centrality, the notion of culture is problematic and means many different things to different people, even to anthropologists. For example, in 1952 two anthropologists, A. L. Kroeber and Clyde Kluckhohn, published a thick book in which they discussed different anthropological definitions of culture. It is easier, however, to give examples of culture rather than trying to define it.

Culture, in brief, is what gives meaning to the world. It provides the lens through which people interpret and make sense of what they perceive the world to be. As such, it consists largely of knowledge and, like other resources, is not distributed equitably. By "making sense," it gives us a sense of patterning and thus of predictability; predictability is important because it allows us to anticipate events and actions. The importance of people, humans, being able to anticipate one another's social behavior is well illustrated in Luke Rinehart's novel *The Dice Man*. This book is about a psychotherapist who suggests to a client, who was incapable of making a decision, that she roll dice to make her decisions. This manner of decision making slowly starts becoming more and more dominant in his own life; he uses it to decide whether to seduce his secretary and then to murder his wife. The point of the novel is that the police can never catch him because his decisions are all random and no a "motive" can be assigned to his behavior.

Making sense of behavior becomes particularly problematic when one is in a foreign milieu like most anthropologists. As the prominent anthropologist Sir Raymond Firth recalled,

> Even with the pages of my diary before me it is difficult to reconstruct the impressions of that first day ashore—to depersonalize the people I later came to know so well and view them as merely a part of the tawny surging crowd. . . . In his early experience in the field the anthropologist is constantly grappling with the intangible. The reality of native life is going on all around him, but he himself is not yet in focus to see it. He knows that what he at first records will be useless: it will be either definitely incorrect, or so inadequate that it must be later discarded. Yet he must make a beginning somewhere. He realizes that at this stage he is incapable of separating the patterns of custom from the accidentals of individual behavior, he wonders if each slight gesture does not hold some meaning which is hidden from him. . . . At the same time, he is experiencing the delights of discovery, he is gaining an inkling of what is in store; like a gourmet walking round a feast that is spread, he savors in anticipation the quality of what he will later appreciate in full. (Peacock and Kirsch 1980:3)

Culture, in short, provides the patterns for behavior, whereas **society** is the product of patterns of behavior. Perhaps the safest way to define culture is by emphasizing some of its most striking characteristics. Following Roger Keesing (1976), it can be seen as a resource consisting of the sum total of learned accumulated experience that is shared in varying degrees. As an abstraction, it is a generalization—that is, no one has the exact same version. It is also a composite, insofar as no one knows all of it. Finally, it is dialectical—that is, it consists invariably of a number of **subcultures**.

Culture then is an interpretive dimension and knowledge; in making the world we experience more "predictable," it also creates categories. Implicit in such an exercise is the creation of boundaries of class, ethnicity, race, and gender. Boundaries are created when people learn the appropriate rituals and habits of speech and eventually become taken for granted and unproblematic (except for people with a probing anthropological perspective). State borders are a good example, as Robert Thornton, the American South African anthropologist, explains:

> In crossing an "international boundary" we involve ourselves in a complex political ritual which includes elaborate signposts, people wearing austere uniforms with obscure insignia . . . gates and narrow corridors. There is always an element of risk, of interference with personal freedom, even death if the formalities of this particularly powerful political ritual are not acknowledged and complied with. The boundaries between countries in fact, exist only in the imagination. They are created through speech, text and gesture, and are enabled by the complex calculation of latitude and longitude which accurate clocks have made possible. We may see the power of culture in the political boundaries of states—a special kind of cultural category-making—for which most of us today are willing to risk all in modern warfare. (1988:27)

David Maybury-Lewis's article heads this chapter quite deliberately. He brings forth the ethics and passion vital in conveying the message that when a culture dies, a whole people die with it. The readings by Lynn Morgan and Danièle Kintz illustrate the working of the construction and imposition of cultural categories upon our own experience in a striking way.

REFERENCES

Keesing, Roger. 1976. *Cultural Anthropology*. New York: Holt, Rinehart & Winston.

Kroeber, A. L. and Clyde Kluckhohn. 1952. *Culture: A Critical Review of Concepts and Definitions*. Cambridge, Mass.: Harvard University Press (Papers of the Peabody Museum of American Archaeology and Ethnology.)

Peacock, James, and A. Thomas Kirsch. 1980. *The Human Direction: An Evolutionary Approach to Social and Cultural Anthropology*. 3rd edition. Englewood Cliffs, NJ: Prentice Hall.

Thornton, Robert. 1988. "Culture: A Contemporary Definition." In Boonzaier Emiole and John Sharp (eds.), *South African Keywords*. Cape Town: D. Philip.

A Special Sort of Pleading

Anthropology at the Service of Ethnic Groups[1]

David H. P. Maybury-Lewis

David H. P. Maybury-Lewis received his D.Phil. degree from Oxford University in 1960. He has carried out fieldwork among the Shavante and Sherente of central Brazil, whose experience he has followed from independence to their current status as minorities within the Brazilian state. A professor of anthropology at Harvard, he is also president of Cultural Survival, Inc., an organization he founded to defend the interests of indigenous peoples and to help them retain their identity within countries in which they exist.

COMMON MISCONCEPTIONS

Advocacy has a distinctly dubious reputation in the United States and, I suspect, elsewhere. It conjures up images of lobbyists and lawyers and of people whose ethics leave much to be desired. So, if anthropologists are to be cast in the role of advocates, it is important to emphasize the peculiar nature of their advocacy. It has little in common with the hallowed tradition of Anglo-American jurisprudence, according to which truth emerges from the efforts of skilled pleaders who make themselves available to argue the cases of any who can afford their fees. By contrast, anthropologists normally do not possess special skills in advocacy which they can put at the disposal of the peoples they try to assist. In the case of tribal societies and underprivileged ethnic groups, anthropologists usually try to help because of their conviction that such societies are being wronged, often with no very clear idea of how to set about righting a wrong.

The ethical stance is important. It is what impels us to get involved in this work in the first place: but it is not enough. It needs to be supplemented by a rigorous analysis of the nature of the injustices against which we inveigh and the possible strategies for fighting them. Such issues may not be part of the usual anthropological curriculum, although they are increasingly being included in it: but they are directly related to what I consider to be fundamental anthropological precepts. I

shall demonstrate this by referring to data from the Americas, but the argument is applicable to other parts of the world as well.

It is well known that the original conquest of the Americas by European invaders had traumatic consequences for the autochthonous inhabitants of the New World. Many indigenous societies with low population densities were annihilated altogether. Others were driven into remote areas or survived as small pockets of population in regions dominated by aliens. The larger Indian populations of Central and Andean America were decimated, then enslaved, and survive today in a state of virtual peonage in countries which they can hardly call their own.

The conquerors offered justifications for this terrible history. They suggested at first that the indigenous peoples were perhaps not fully human. They did not possess souls. Their barbarous customs placed them beyond the pale. At the very least there were circumstances which made it legitimate to wage just wars on them and to enslave them.[2] Later the mission of conquest tended to be justified in the name of a higher civilization, which would impart peace, scientific thinking and rational institutions to the war-like and illogical natives (Merivale 1861).

These old arguments may seem preposterous, but I repeat them here in order to show their relationship to the modern versions of them that still persist in our conventional wisdom and in much contemporary theorizing. There is something like a second conquest taking place in the Americas today, powered by the worldwide search for resources. This new conquest threatens the Indians with the expropriation of their remaining lands and the total destruction of their way of life. This conquest too has its justification. It is carried out in the name of development. Indigenous peoples are thus stigmatized for clinging to a backward way of life and thereby "standing in the way of development." To the extent that they are reluctant or unable to abandon their separate identities and disappear into the mainstream of the states in which they live, they are also condemned as obstacles to nation-building and therefore to modernization. Hence, the argument runs, they should give up their archaic cultures and join the mainstream. This would not only make development much easier for all concerned but would conveniently remove "ethnic cysts" (to borrow the phrase once used by a Brazilian minister to refer to his country's Indians) from lands which they occupy and which other people covet. Meanwhile the world is assured that this doubtless regrettable disappearance of Indian cultures is inevitable and therefore should not be artificially or sentimentally delayed. This corresponds to the neo-Darwinian view which permeates the thinking of much of what we are pleased to call the developed world, according to which stronger societies are bound to extinguish weaker ones; this is coupled with the implication that there is not much that can be done about this, since it is some sort of natural law.

Such arguments are, of course, the direct descendants of those used by the conquistadors. They are self-serving justifications for the convenient use of power against the relatively powerless and they obscure the fact that indigenous cultures are not extinguished by natural laws so much as by political choices. Moreover, since such arguments make the destruction of indigenous cultures seem not only natural but even beneficial, they preempt any discussion of possible alternatives and thus contribute to the inevitability of that destruction.

Any advocacy of indigenous rights must therefore begin by countering such arguments and reopening the discussion of possible futures for indigenous cultures. We need to remember that it was seriously argued until recently that slavery was a natural part of the human condition. Scholars based their arguments on Aristotle, the Justinian codes and the writings of the French *philosophes* of the eighteenth century as they maintained that the differences in the natural endowments of individuals and races, coupled with the unavoidable differences of power in human affairs, rendered slavery inevitable.[3] We have seen this contention demonstrated as false and we no longer take seriously the nineteenth and even twentieth century arguments about the natural superiority or inferiority of certain races. Pro-indigenous advocates must work to create a similar climate of opinion in which we can look back with bemusement at the plausible falsehoods that were generally and conveniently believed by those who condemned indigenous cultures to extinction.

That is why I have elsewhere (Maybury-Lewis 1984) criticized the mesmeric fascination with which the modern world regards the nation-state. I showed that the divisive effects of ethnic attachments have been systematically over-emphasized and contrasted with the hypothetical benefits of the idealized nation-state. This is done equally by high-minded reformers trying to better the lot of the Indians and by oligarchs trying to break up their communities. The one thing that Simon Bolivar and General Pinochet have in common is the belief that Indians should abandon their traditional ways, should in effect abandon their Indianness, and become solid (preferably property-owning) citizens of their states. For quite different reasons both leaders concluded the persistence of Indian cultures was undesirable, since they weakened the state. If, however, we re-examine the role of ethnic subcultures, particularly in Third World countries, we find that allegations of ethnic divisiveness, backwardness or separatism are often used by governments as cloaks for exploitation, authoritarianism and hegemonic privilege. The cry of "One nation, indivisible" with perhaps added imprecations hurled against tribalists and separatists is all too often used as an ideological weapon against those who wish to alter the *status quo* and to share fully and equally the privileges of citizenship. This is particularly ironic, since our modern fascination with the needs of the state derives from the French revolutionary idea of the state, based on equality and fraternity. Nowadays, in many parts of the world, people are resorting to their ethnicity as a sort of civil rights movement, to achieve the equality of treatment which had previously been denied them in the name of modernization. Yet people do not cling to their cultures merely to use them as inter-ethnic strategies. They cling to them because it is through them that they make sense of the world and have a sense of themselves. We know that when people are forced to give up their culture or when they give it up too rapidly, the consequences are normally social breakdown and personal disorientation and despair. The right of a people to its own culture is therefore derived from a fundamental human need, yet it receives less protection, even in theory, than other human rights because it concerns groups rather than individuals.

The United Nations, for example, has declared its intent to protect the rights of individuals and in practice is most solicitous of the rights of states. But it skirts the issue of the rights of peoples, preferring to assume that peoples who are not part of the mainstream culture of their state should assimilate to it (Claude 1955 and Kuper 1984). There is in fact a world-wide tendency to deny the rights and sometimes even the very existence of ethnic minorities, in order to protect the nation-states. Advocacy of indigenous rights must therefore expose this tendency and develop the arguments for the desirability and viability of multi-ethnic polities.

The right of a people to its own culture is however a complex matter and insistence on it is frequently misunderstood. Let me dispose quickly of two common misunderstandings. The first of these is that the advocacy of the right of peoples to their own cultures entails a total moral and cultural relativism. Anthropologists are sometimes accused of such a relativism, according to which we are supposed to defend the right of any people to engage in any practice, however reprehensible, simply because it is "part of their culture." The charge is absurd but it serves to distract attention from the comfortable and unreasoning ethnocentrism and prejudice of those who make it. It needs therefore to be stressed that what is taken for anthropological relativism is in reality an anthropological insistence on suspending judgment on other peoples' practices; not forever, but only until those practices have been understood in their own cultural terms. This injunction sounds simple enough, but most people (and that includes the majority of the world's planners) find it extremely hard to follow. They tend to pass judgments on other cultures and their practices long before they have any understanding of them and in fact those often unthinking judgments frequently prevent understanding of other cultures in their own terms. An important part of the discipline of an anthropological training is to teach people to recognize and avoid premature judgment on other cultures. It is only where this is done systematically that we can hope to incorporate other people's values into our own thinking, or at least to mediate between our values and theirs. This is a critical matter when our thinking is about the life or death of their cultures. The anthropological stance then is that one does not avoid making judgments, but rather postpones them in order to make informed judgments later.

Another common misconception is that those who defend the right of a people to its own culture are arguing that other societies should remain true to their own traditions. Anthropologists are accused, for good measure, of wanting to keep traditional societies in their backward state in order to study them. The second suggestion is merely a malicious variation on the first, which implies that cultural survival is an antiquarian matter of clinging to tradition and resisting change. It is important to stress therefore that both of these perceptions are quite false. For instance, Cultural Survival, the organization of which I am president, defends the right of tribal societies and ethnic groups to maintain their own cultures, but we do not see this as a matter of maintaining folkways, but rather as a question of a society's having a say in its own affairs and its own future. Our advocacy and our projects therefore aim to create the conditions under which such societies can retain the largest measure of autonomy and power of decision over their own affairs. Ideally we believe that this is best achieved through the creation of appropriate

mechanisms in multi-ethnic states. Furthermore, the advocacy of self-determination for indigenous peoples within such states is often a politically more viable strategy, for it cannot be opposed on the usual grounds that any recognition of the rights of ethnic groups leads inevitably to separatism and the undermining of the state. Nevertheless, we understand the pessimism about multi-ethnic solutions which has led many native peoples to demand that they be recognized internationally as sovereign nations. Independence and separation may be the only solution where justice is denied within the state, which is why it is particularly important to make multi-ethnic solutions work.

It is worth stressing that the sort of cultural survival for which we work is defined in the last analysis by the societies which we assist. We do not urge them to be true to their traditions; partly because such a stance would be intolerably paternalistic, but also because we assume that all societies are constantly changing and some are abandoning their traditions of their own accord. We therefore offer our help to tribal societies and ethnic groups who need it to maintain those aspects of their culture which they consider important.

This brings me at last from theory to the practicalities of advocacy in action. I make no apology for spending so much of this short paper on theoretical questions, for I am convinced that useful action must flow logically from a clear understanding of theoretical issues. Much project action, in the Americas and elsewhere, revolves around land and access to material resources. These issues are particularly acute in the Americas since it was the invading Europeans who set up the systems of law and land titling which everywhere form the basis of valid claims to land ownership. The indigenous inhabitants were outside these systems, which were then manipulated to their detriment, so that they have been engaged in a constant struggle to force or persuade their unsympathetic conquerors to grant them title to any part of the lands which they originally considered theirs.

This continues to be extremely difficult for most indigenous peoples. Although most nations in the Americas recognize in theory that their aboriginal inhabitants have some rights to land, the gap between that theoretical recognition and actual granting of title is wide and all too often permanent. Most native land claims are disputed by interests with the power to block them. Even when they are not, the process of demarcating, registering and titling lands has often proved impossible for indigenous groups to complete.

Such a situation recently posed a cruel dilemma for pro-Indian organizations in Paraguay. In the late 1970s few Indian societies in Paraguay had legal title to the lands they occupied and Paraguayan law did not recognize collective title to land, even for indigenous peoples. The two major organizations working for the Indians in Paraguay responded to this problem in different, even conflicting ways. AIP (the Paraguayan Indigenist Association) insisted that Indians had inherent rights of ownership in their lands and was lobbying to persuade the government to recognize this, by passing a law enabling Indian societies to hold lands collectively, and by putting this law into effect. Meanwhile, API (the Association of Indian Peoples) also insisted on Indian rights to land; but it had concluded that the situation of many Indian groups was so desperate that it had begun to buy lands for them from Paraguayans. AIP complained that their campaign to get the government to recognize Indian land rights was being undercut by the willingness of their sister organization to buy lands for the Indians. API responded that it was trying to help groups which would starve or disband or both if they waited for the success of AIP's strategy (see Maybury-Lewis and Howe 1980).

PROBLEMS OF LAND

Land is the key to the cultural and often even the physical survival of indigenous peoples. Tribal societies that have traditionally supplied their own wants from their own environment can be physically annihilated if forced off their own lands. Cast adrift, with no marketable skills, to fend for themselves in an alien society, whose language they do not speak and whose economy they do not understand, such peoples face a grim future or no future at all. It is their plight, as the nations of the Americas have stepped up their efforts to explore and exploit their own hinterlands, that has recently been arousing world-wide concern. Yet peoples who are long settled and have centuries of contact with settler society are still traumatically threatened by the prospect of losing their lands.

Such losses are a constant threat, because the indigenous society's title is usually unclear and because it is usually unable to protect its holdings against powerful interests in settler society. Meanwhile there is constant pressure on indigenous societies to break up their communal lands and to treat them as individual (and saleable) holdings. A variety of factors combine to produce this pressure. The laws of most American countries do not recognize communal land holdings or make it extremely difficult to register them. Meanwhile, even liberal reformers have traditionally thought that the individual ownership of land was the means by which indigenous peoples could modernize and join the mainstream. At the same time, those who wish to eliminate Indian societies altogether find that insistence on individual landholding is an effective way to do it and one which does not incur the opprobrium which is occasionally visited nowadays on nations that resort to genocide. So Chile's new land law, making it obligatory to subdivide the lands left to the Mapuche Indians if only one person living on them requests such subdivision, may achieve the final elimination of Mapuche society and culture which has survived incredible pressures for more than four hundred years.[4] Meanwhile, in an entirely different spirit, the Alaskan Native Claims Settlement Act, which is regarded as a reasonably generous settlement of indigenous land claims may have similar results. In the 1990s Alaskan native communities will legally become joint stock corporations, in which individuals who received shares at the time of the act will hold stock. This is an entirely different notion of community from the one the indigenous peoples are accustomed to and the one which most of them still live by. It is becoming clear that the majority of them have not realized the implications of what is likely to happen in ten years time when individuals can sell their stock in the "community," and shares in the "community" can be bought on the open market (see Arnold 1976).

Here then is one of the critically important aspects of pro-indigenous advocacy. The advocate can help native communities to analyze not only the consequences of their own actions, but also the possible effects of processes which affect them. This is a vital matter in the negotiation of land rights. A normal and natural reaction on the part of tribal communities whose land is threatened for the first time is to insist that they should be left alone to enjoy what has traditionally been theirs. Advocacy in such a case involves helping the indigenous community realize that it is unlikely to be left alone, that it will have to fight (but not physically) for its lands and that it is unlikely to be able to hold onto all of them. At the same time it involves persuading the powers-that-be that native rights should be taken seriously and, if necessary, creating administrative or public pressure to see that this is done. In the Pichis-Palcazu area of Amazonian Peru, for example, advocacy involved persuading the Peruvian government which was sponsoring a scheme of massive colonization for the area and US AID (Agency for International Development) which was about to finance it, that the valleys were already occupied by native peoples and that the project would be a disaster. Cultural Survival took a leading role in this campaign, which ultimately succeeded in changing the original colonization scheme into the Central Selva Resource Management project. The new project is more sensibly designed to protect not only the Indian inhabitants of the area but also the local environment and the interests of the future occupants, both Indian and non-Indian, of the region as a whole. As a preliminary to the implementation of the project, survey teams were sent out and they enabled the Amuesha Indians to gain formal title to their lands for the first time. This is no more than a reprieve, however. The project as originally designed has yet to be put into effect and it is not clear whether it will be, now that the economic and political climate in Peru is becoming more and more uncertain.[5]

Ideally, native lands should be titled and guaranteed before development projects are planned for their areas but, as we have seen, the native land situation in the Americas is far from ideal. There are therefore twin strategies which should be followed by pro-Indian organizations. One is to exert constant pressure for the regularization of all native land titles. The other is to try and turn the threat posed to native peoples by development projects into an opportunity to create pressure for the protection of indigenous lands. Cultural Survival used the latter strategy when the Brazilian government asked the World Bank for a loan to improve the road system in its northwestern region and thus encourage colonization of a vast area where scores of small Indian tribes are known to live. Cultural Survival urged the bank to make the demarcation of Indian lands and the protection of their cultures a condition of the loan. In response to years of pressure the bank finally adopted, prior to the signing of the loan agreements, its own policy guidelines making it mandatory in the future to insist on guarantees for tribal peoples and ethnic minorities in areas where loans are contemplated (World Bank 1981). I believe that these are the only such guidelines at present contained in the policies of any international lending agency. Naturally, the policies are only as effective as their enforcement and the preliminary reports from Brazil indicate that this leaves much to be desired, but having such policies and laws on the books is not unimportant as I shall argue in a moment.[6]

The defence of native land rights is a complex matter, even when they are not threatened by ruthless and unscrupulous interests. The view that native peoples have a dubious claim to land if other people can make better (i.e., more productive) use of it is very common in developmental circles. The moral and legal absurdity of such a view is readily exposed if one asks the earnest planner whether he or she would be willing to apply the same precepts to his or her own piece of property. Does another person have a superior claim to that property to plant vegetables on it, if the present owner manages only flowers and crab-grass? Yet governments regularly use such arguments when moving to take native lands by eminent domain. They act, they insist, for the greater good of the greatest number, to make better use of the land and they imply that it is somehow selfish of native peoples to want to sit on resources which should rightfully be distributed throughout the entire populace. Such arguments can usually be exposed as flimsy justification for exploitation.

PROBLEMS OF DEVELOPMENT

In Brazil, for example, this type of argument has regularly been used by successive military governments, all claiming to give development the highest priority and insisting that small Indian tribes should not be allowed to stand in the way of it. The argument only holds, however, if development promotes equity and Indian peoples are obstacles to it. Yet neither contention is true. The Brazil model of development, which was so highly touted in the sixties and seventies (though not by those of us who were working at the grass roots) is no longer regarded as a miracle. In fact it is closer to being regarded as a disaster for the entire Western banking system. This is not due to bad luck, like the rise in the price of oil, which Brazil has still been unable to find within her own capacious land, but rather to a policy which has paid insufficient attention to structural change and modernization within Brazilian society. The years of the "Miracle" produced enormous profits for some but they did little to solve the problems of Northeastern Brazil (the largest pocket of poverty in the western hemisphere) or of the increasing numbers of urban poor or of the landless rural labourers. The latter are constantly moved off their patches of land in much the same way as the state has intermittently sought to move the Indians off theirs. The argument from equity thus breaks down.[7] Hypothetically, such an argument could be made in other places, but it would in any case come down to a question of what compensation should be made to native peoples (or others) who are asked to give up a resource for the common good.

At the same time it is important to insist that native peoples are not inherently "obstacles to development." This is only true if "development" is defined in such a way to exclude their participation. There are innumerable examples to show that indigenous peoples whose land base and cultural survival are guaranteed can make productive contributions to the local economy. Advocacy here becomes a matter of persuading the powers-that-be that this is so, and getting them to include indigenous representatives in the development planning for a given region. Cultural Survival has recently succeeded in doing this, for example, in Ecuador. There the Ecuadorian government established a commission consisting of representatives from Cultural Survival, the National Agrarian Reform Institute, the Forestry and National Parks Department, a regional development agency and 22 Indians representing three groups. The commission studied the land needs of Ecuador's most seriously threatened Indian groups, the Siona-Secoya, Cofan and Huaorani. It documented their land requirements and recommended specific borders to satisfy their needs. It also recommended that Indian lands should be titled at the borders of national parks. The Indians would have access to the parks for subsistence hunting and fishing and their lands would act as buffers to protect the parks from settler incursion. Meanwhile these newly titled Indian lands were incorporated into a large forestry development and management project (see Macdonald 1980 and in press, and Uquillas 1982).

Another dramatic example of such a project is one which I have recently been observing in Brazil. This is the project sponsored in the midst of bitter controversy by the Brazilian Indian Agency (FUNAI) and which has transformed many communities of Shavante Indians into extensive, tractor-driven rice farmers. The project was put into effect over the violent protests of the local landowners who complained to the President of the Republic that FUNAI was trying to turn the State of Mato Grosso into a vast Indian reserve. This was hyperbole, even by settler standards, considering that Mato Grosso was so large—larger than Bolivia or Colombia and only slightly smaller than Peru—that it has now been divided into two states; moreover its population is still tiny. The project was finally put into effect because the Shavante were tough enough to threaten the local landowners and force them off Indian lands and astute enough to visit Brasilia regularly to present their demands to the government. These visits also served to rally their supporters among anthropologists and the Brazilian public at large and received great publicity. The publicity reached its peak when a delegation of Shavante chiefs threatened to defenestrate the general in charge of FUNAI, and escaped reprisals since the threat was carried out with the cameras of the major TV networks waiting to record the consequences (Maybury-Lewis 1983a and 1985).

PROBLEMS OF REPRESENTATION

The Shavante affair highlights another dilemma of pro-Indian advocacy. Whom do pro-Indian advocates represent and how do they relate to the Indians who are being their own advocates? Initially, of course, such advocates may not represent any more than their own consciences. They are people who are willing to speak out to denounce what they perceive as injustice. The pro-Indian commissions which were formed all over Brazil at the end of the 1970s came into existence because of the outcry raised by anthropologists over the government's proposal to "emancipate" the Indians. It was concerned anthropologists who pointed out that such emancipation would abolish the FUNAI and its tutelary role towards the Indians. It would thus do away with the legal requirement to demarcate and defend Indian lands and the agency which was supposed to carry it out. The newly "emancipated" Indians would then be able to take their chances on their own and as individuals against whichever interests happened to be threatening them in their part of the country. When these consequences were pointed out to the Indians, they themselves opposed emancipation unreservedly and, backed by the newly formed pro-Indian commissions, insisted that the government, rather than abolish FUNAI, should press it to do its job on behalf of the Indians (see Maybury-Lewis 1979 and Comissão Pro-Indio 1979).

Later the pressure and publicity generated by such commissions were instrumental in helping the Shavante gain their objectives. The campaign on behalf of the Shavante launched one of their number into national prominence. Mario Juruna, the chief of a small Shavante community, had spent years in his youth traveling and working his way around Brazil and learning the ways of the white man. He endeared himself to the Brazilian media as "the Indian with the tape-recorder," because he carried around his own recording machine and insisted on recording the promises made to him and his people, so that they could not later be blandly forgotten or denied. In 1982 he was elected to Congress as the first Indian ever to become a federal deputy. Needless to say he was elected to represent Rio de Janeiro, not his native Mato Grosso, a state which is hardly ripe yet for an Indian candidacy. It is not even clear that he would have been elected in a solely Shavante constituency, if such a one were to exist. He has nevertheless become a leader who speaks for Brazilian Indians in general and is recognized by most of them as their spokesman (Maybury-Lewis 1983b).

The question of who really represents indigenous peoples has led to some confusion among those who deal with them or seek to assist them. It is of course a question which is often debated with reference to other societies as well. When the representative of a nation state speaks on behalf of its people, we know that he or she is unlikely to represent the views of all of them; but we also know how he or she came by his or her credentials and we normally have a good deal of information about which groups are represented by the official view and which groups are not. It is precisely this kind of information which is usually lacking for indigenous societies. The world at large does not normally know much about their internal politics, nor does it know whom their representatives do and do not speak for, nor how the representatives came to be chosen in the first place. Indeed, the situation is so fluid that individuals can and do appear at international gatherings and claim to represent indigenous societies, without those societies being aware that they are being so represented and in some cases without those societies even knowing the individuals who claim to represent them. Obviously this makes for considerable misunderstanding and political manipulation (see Richard Chase Smith 1982).

Even when there are no such uncertainties concerning the leaders or representatives of an indigenous group, there is no guarantee that its leadership will speak with a single voice. It is a form of naive romanticism to believe that political disagreements do not exist among indigenous peoples or to suppose that they always achieve consensus on every issue, even though such claims are sometimes made on their behalf, especially when their way is being contrasted with the white man's way. Both the record and ordinary common sense would lead us instead to expect a certain amount of politicking in indigenous societies. One deals with this in much the same way as one does with politicking in any other society, by being as well informed as possible about the divisive issues and how people stand on them. Cultural Survival, for example, tries hard to get opinions from its own network of contacts on the politics of indigenous societies in order to discover which leaders enjoy a sufficient base of support for them to represent their peoples with some legitimacy. Where a people or a community is so badly divided that they cannot be so represented, then Cultural Survival would not normally consider collaborating with them on a project. Since all of our field projects are designed and carried out in collaboration with the people they are intended to help, this means in effect that we would not consider a project to assist these people until the political situation was clarified.

PROBLEMS OF DISAGREEMENT

A more difficult question is what to do when the indigenous society and its recognized leaders insist on pursuing a course of action which we, as advocates, believe to be disastrous. Let me give two examples to illustrate this sort of dilemma. In southern Brazil an Indian society was offered what seemed to them to be a vast sum of money by lumber companies in return for the right to cut down trees on Indian land. The Indians, who had no idea of the ecological devastation which uncontrolled lumbering can cause, felt that they were being offered a small fortune for the depletion of an essentially inexhaustible resource. They were anxious to accept. Anthropologists from the University of Santa Catarina, who have been very active in the pro-Indian cause, tried hard to dissuade them. In the meantime they also worked to prevent the start of the lumbering operation. Eventually however they failed to convince the Indians, abandoned their active opposition to the lumbering project, and withdrew as advisers to these particular Indians. It seems to me that that was the correct thing to do. The lumbering project was being carried out with the informed consent of the Indians and the anthropologists had done what they could to make the harmful consequences of it known to the people it was going to harm. It would have been the worst sort of paternalism to try to prevent the project from being put into effect over the wishes of the Indians themselves.

Even more difficult is the issue of what to do when indigenous leaders espouse what we consider to be the harmful rhetoric of settler society. Mario Juruna, the Shavante deputy in the Brazilian congress, learned for example that Brazilian farmers could raise money by mortgaging their land. He therefore argued at one time that Indians should be allowed to do the same. They are normally unable to do so because their land (when it is legally theirs at all) is held in trust for their communities by FUNAI. Juruna wanted the government to get off the backs of the Indians by making it possible for them to own their own land individually and to do what they like with it. Here again there is only one course of action open to an advocate who believes, as I do, that such a policy would be disastrous for the Indians. That is to try and persuade both Juruna himself and the Indians in general of the reasons why this is so and to encourage them to support a different point of view. This may not be so difficult. I have heard many Indian leaders lecture me eloquently about their people's attitude to land as a common and sacred good and their revulsion against the white man's insistence on treating it as a commodity that may be individually owned, bought and sold. The Mapuche, for example, are desperately aware of what individual land holding is likely to do to their way of life and have requested help to try and hold their society together in what they see as a last do or die effort. Yet if it came to the point that an Indian people was fully aware of the likely consequences of dividing up the land and still wanted to do it, then it should have the right to do so.

ADVOCACY IN A SUPPORTING ROLE

It follows from this that I see no particular problem posed for pro-Indian groups by the fact that Indians are increasingly doing their own advocacy. On the contrary, it should be the desired aim of such groups to assist indigenous peoples to conduct their own advocacy. The form of this assistance will change as a function of the relations between the Indians being assisted and the outside world. A tribal society which has had little contact with settler society needs advocates to speak for it in the nation at large. It also needs people who are able to help its members understand the national and regional forces with which it must henceforward cope. Eventually, one hopes, such a society will be able to negotiate on its own behalf or at least to join with others in indigenous associations which can do such negotiating. Even at this stage, however, indigenous associations which speak for their own people can be well served by friendly advocates in the world at large. Such advocates can provide them with expertise which it is difficult and unnecessary for them to acquire on their own. Cultural Survival can, for example, document what happens to Indian societies whose land is divided into individually owned parcels and make this information available to the Indians themselves. We can tell Indians in Brazil about the techniques used in successful projects that have benefitted Indians in, say, Ecuador. We can put Indian societies in touch with each other both at a national and international level. Above all, indigenous advocacy normally depends for its success on a favourable or at least not resolutely hostile climate of opinion in the country concerned. The role of national and international advocates of the indigenous cause, in creating this climate and keeping up the pressure to maintain it, should not be underestimated.

This brings me back to the point I made earlier about the importance of good laws and policies, even when they are ineffectively enforced. Settler societies are everywhere unscrupulous about the rights of the autochthonous peoples whom they dispossess. The frontiersmen and their supporters in the metropolis can always be relied upon to be resolutely anti-Indian or anti any other native people. It is when these elements receive the wholehearted support of the metropolis that indigenous peoples suffer most. It is no accident that the tribal Indians of Brazil suffered most acutely in the late sixties, at a time when the military regime in power was at its most repressive and was insisting on development without regard to human costs. When liberal elements gain a hearing in the metropolis, they are unlikely ever to eliminate the anti-Indian factions and are certainly unlikely to change the minds of the frontiersmen. But they can and do provide a counterweight to the sentiments of the frontiersmen, and it is this tension that provides indigenous peoples with the opportunity to have their rights respected and to establish themselves in the wider society. It is thus critical to keep up the pressure for good laws. They represent the conscience of the society and can thus be appealed to when they are not being properly enforced. The link between good laws and effective enforcement has to be the focus of advocacy efforts on behalf of indigenous peoples.

UNUSUAL ADVOCACY: ORDINARY ANTHROPOLOGY

I hope these comments have served to show that although work on behalf of tribal peoples and ethnic groups may be a peculiar form of advocacy it is not a very strange sort of anthropology. It only seems strange at times because it abandons old anthropological habits that were once so much part of anthropological practice that they acquired ritual, if not actually canonical status. Anthropologists used to see themselves as lone scientists who dissected exotic cultures and presented the truth of their systems to a scholarly audience. They now know that they are not alone in their work, that the truth of another culture is never monolithic, that better and better approximations to it emerge from rigorous analysis and vigorous debate, in which the members of the cultures studied increasingly participate. Anthropologists used to think that advocacy was "unscientific" and would undermine their scholarly credibility. Many of us now believe that it is precisely the most rigorous

anthropological analysis which impels us toward advocacy and provides us with the tools to engage in it. Indeed the credibility of anthropologists and their work in many parts of the world is nowadays more threatened by an unwillingness to engage in any form of advocacy than the reverse.

The kind of advocacy discussed in this paper requires the classic skills of anthropology. It requires the ability to suspend judgment while analyzing societies very unlike our own. It also requires the ability to study our own society (or other "modern industrial societies") with a detachment similar to that we strive for in studying the exotic. It requires the ability to analyze national policies, developmental ideologies and the workings of bureaucracies with a detachment that enables us to see beyond their familiar obfuscations and self-deceptions. It then requires the advocate to combine these analyses dialectically in order to understand and eventually influence the complex processes which affect underprivileged ethnic groups. The rest is politics and the extent to which the advocate is willing or effectively able to get involved in that depends very much on temperament, circumstance and opportunity. Even at the political stage of advocacy an anthropological training is not a bad preparation, though an anthropological temperament may well be. Above all, this type of advocacy is intimately related to what I consider to be perhaps the most important impulse behind anthropology itself—the interest in social theory and moral philosophy. Boas and Durkheim, to mention the apical ancestors of what used to be thought of as the American and British styles of anthropology, did not devote themselves to their professions just to do science. This misreading of their efforts was a distortion introduced by their disciples, one that reduced anthropology to a kind of functionalist trick which was soon proclaimed not to work. In fact, Boas and Durkheim, while extremely concerned that their work should be properly scientific, both felt strongly that they were engaged in researches which would help to improve the human conditions. They practised, as Boas once put it, "science in the service of a higher tolerance." Boas devoted his science to the fight against racism. We could do worse than to devote ours to the battle against ethnocentrism in the struggle to shape a world where people can live together in multi-ethnic societies on the basis of mutual tolerance and respect.

N O T E S

1. I wish to acknowledge the assistance of Dr. Theodore Macdonald and Dr. Jason Clay, my colleagues in Cultural Survival, in preparing this paper. It should be clear to the reader that in writing about the advocacy undertaken by our organization, I am describing something which is very much a collective effort.
2. See Hanke 1959 for a discussion of the famous debates on these issues at the Spanish court between Las Casas and Sepulveda.
3. For a discussion of these ideas, see D. B. Davis 1966.

4. See the report of the Interchurch Committee on Human Rights in Latin America (1980) and Barreiro and Wright (1982:60–63).
5. See Cultural Survival 1981a and Richard Chase Smith 1979, 1982.
6. For a discussion of the World Bank project in northwestern Brazil, see Cultural Survival 1981b.
7. There is voluminous literature on the Brazilian "miracle," but especially relevant to the points made here are Furtado 1982, Fishlow 1973, Foweraker 1981 and Velho 1976.

REFERENCES

Arnold, Robert. 1976. *Alaska Native Land Claims.* Anchorage: The Alaska Native Foundation.

Barreiro, Jose, and Robin Wright (eds.) 1982. *Native Peoples in Struggle: Russell Tribunal and Other International Forums.* Boston: Anthropology Resource Center, Inc.

Claude, Inis L. 1955. *National Minorities: An International Problem.* Cambridge: Harvard University Press.

Comissão Pro-Indio. 1979. *A Questão da Emancipação.* São Paulo, Brazil: Comissão Pro-Indio. Caderno No. 1.

Cultural Survival. 1981a. "Development Planning in Peru's Amazon—the Palcazu." *Cultural Survival Newsletter,* 5(3).

Cultural Survival. 1981b. *In the Path of Polonoroeste: Endangered Peoples of Western Brazil.* Cambridge: Cultural Survival Occasional Paper No. 6.

Davis, David Brion. 1966. *The Problem of Slavery in Western Culture.* Ithaca: Cornell University Press.

Fishlow, Albert. 1973. "Some Reflections on Post-1964 Brazilian Economic Policy." In Alfred Stepan (ed.), *Authoritarian Brazil.* New Haven: Yale University Press.

Foweraker, Joe. 1981. *The Struggle for Land: A Political Economy of the Pioneer Frontier in Brazil from 1930 to the Present Day.* Cambridge: Cambridge Latin American Studies No. 39.

Furtado, Celso. 1982. *Analise do "Modelo" Brasileiro.* Rio de Janeiro: Civilizaçao Brasileira.

Hanke, Lewis. 1959. *Aristotle and the American Indians: A Study in Race Prejudice in the Modern World.* Bloomington: University of Indiana Press.

Interchurch Committee on Human Rights in Latin America. 1980. *Mapuches: People of the Land.* Toronto: ICCHRLA.

Kuper, Leo. 1984. "International Protection Against Genocide in Plural Societies." In David Maybury-Lewis (ed.), *The Prospects for Plural Societies.* Washington, D.C.: Proceedings of the American Ethnological Society (1982).

Macdonald, Theodore. 1980. "Ecuador Land Demarcation." *Cultural Survival Newsletter,* 4(4).

Maybury-Lewis, David (ed.). 1979. *Brazil.* Special Report No. 1. Cambridge: Cultural Survival.

Maybury-Lewis, David. 1983a. "The Shavante Struggle for Their Lands." *Cultural Survival Quarterly,* 7(1).

Maybury-Lewis, David. 1983b. "Brazilian Indians Find Their Voice." *Cultural Survival Quarterly,* 7(1).

Maybury-Lewis, David. 1984. "Living in Leviathan: Ethnic Groups and the State." In David Maybury-Lewis (ed.), *The Prospects for Plural Societies.* Washington, D.C.: Proceedings of the American Ethnological Society (1982).

Maybury-Lewis, David. 1985. "Brazilian Indianist Policy: Some Lessons from the Shavante Project." In Theodore Macdonald, Jr. (ed.), *Native Peoples and Economic Development: Six Studies from Latin America.* Cambridge: Cultural Survival Occasional Paper No. 16.

Maybury-Lewis, David, and James Howe. 1980. *The Indian Peoples of Paraguay: Their Plight and Their Prospects.* Cambridge: Cultural Survival Special Publication No. 2.

Merivale, Herman. 1861. *Lectures on Colonization and Colonies.* London: Green, Longman and Roberts.

Smith, Richard Chase. 1979. *The Multinational Squeeze on the Amuesha People of Central Peru.* Copenhagen: International Work Group for Indigenous Affairs, Document No. 35.

Smith, Richard Chase. 1982. *The Dialectics of Domination in Peru: Native Communities and the Myth of the Vast Amazonian Emptiness.* Cambridge: Cultural Survival Occasional Paper No. 8.

Uquillas, Jorge E. (ed.). 1982. *Informe para la Delimitacion de Territorios Nativos Siona Secoya, Cofán y Huaorani.* Quito: Ediciones INCRAE #039.

Velho, Otavio. 1976. *Capitalismo Autoritário e Campesinato.* São Paulo, Brazil: DIFEL.

World Bank 1981. *Economic Development and Tribal Peoples: Human Ecologic Considerations.* Washington, D.C.: World Bank.

Formal Men, Informal Women

How the Fulani Support Their Anthropologists

Danièle Kintz

Danièle Kintz is a researcher at l'Université de Paris X-Nanterre. She has spent more than twenty years doing research in West and Central Africa.

The term *formal* alludes primarily to form or appearance as opposed to matter or content. But in English (and increasingly in French, too) the word "informal" *(informel)* has taken on the secondary meaning of "unofficial"; and we can describe persons, and not simply acts or situations, as being formal or informal. The distinction helps me to explain how my informants, male and female, in the Central African Republic in 1988 managed to present me with their society on a plate.

Fulani societies, spread as they are throughout the Sahel from Mauretania and Senegal to Sudan, and also in all the coastal countries of West Africa as well as in part of Central Africa, are similar but different, showing a strong unity but no uniformity. It is as if certain Fulani groups, but not all of them—that would be too simple—had decided to help their anthropologists, who would otherwise be lost, by proposing to them a model of Fulani society set out clearly, perfectly visible, including also an explanatory notice for those who would like to investigate the functioning of the model. To make things even clearer, it is the men who have a look quite different from that of the women, admitting of no error—who present the model and the women who provide the notice.

THE CHIC OF SEGREGATION

All societies provide some form of segregation, social in general and by gender in particular, even those which deny and disclaim it. (In France, examples are legion, one of the best I know being that of a woman such as myself going to buy spare parts for a car. The scale of the transgression is measurable from the movements and the words of rejection and quasi-refusal from the so-called salesman. Try it . . .)

"Formal Men, Informal Women: How the Fulani Support Their Anthropologists" by Danièle Kintz, from *Anthropology Today*, Vol. 5, No. 6, 1989, Royal Anthropological Institute. Reprinted with permission.

The Fulani have developed their segregative system with a hierarchy of social value. To each given social position corresponds some degree of gender segregation; if one increases this, one can receive in exchange an equivalent in social esteem. But watch out! You must know up to what point you can exaggerate: adopting the segregative attitudes of chiefs when one is not a chief leads only to ridicule.

Gender segregation among the Fulani presents the following traits which I shall analyse in turn:

1. It must be proportional to social position, each influencing the other.

2. It is always ostentatious, for why put on airs when there are no witnesses?

3. It governs everyday behaviour and organizes its space according to complicated procedures whereby everyone's art of living is expressed.

In all Fulani groups, there exist forms of organized segregation, at least among the chiefs and, to a less systematically marked degree, among the marabouts. For segregation is chic, elegant, important. However, the wives of chiefs have, like their husbands, more prestige than most of their fellow-citizens and they receive many visitors of both sexes. One cannot therefore take the view that they are hidden from the domains of political power. Nor do they present themselves as constrained by men to keep their distance: I have never heard this opinion, and we must beware of the ethnocentrism of Northern countries which is so quick to interpret phenomena against its own grid. How does gender segregation become chic? A high-status Fulani woman will sometimes say, with visible satisfaction, "I never go out of my courtyard."

That shows three things. First, in fact she does go out of her courtyard less than most other women do, but there is nobody who never goes out: there are always *some* opportunities to go out: for religious duties, or for health (one's own or other people's), or for visits of congratulation and condolence, or the organization of social, economic or family activities. Second, there are people who can carry out obligatory visits for her—to the well or the market—and so she has a large domestic entourage of descendants of captives, servants, dependents, children. And finally, her social status is such that others visit her at her home, and there are very few visits that she must make herself.

Let us add that in the hot countries where the Fulani live, countries where much time is spent out of doors night and day (even if only in one's own courtyard), European notions of "taking the air," "going for a walk" or "going out" have no meaning or interest. Value is given to showing oneself only on rare occasions and in certain conditions, and above all to not having to go out to do the vulgar tasks which the majority of people under the sun of Africa are tied to.

Whatever the Fulani group under consideration, it always includes at least some women who "never" leave their courtyards. But these women are more numerous among the urban or wealthy Fulani or among fervent (or ostentatious) Muslims, and especially among Fulani who possess two or three of these characteristics.

In the Central African Republic, where I did my most recent fieldwork, the Fulani are rich in cattle and trade compared to either the Fulani of the Sahel or the other peoples of the CAR. Fulani women in villages or towns, sometimes rich in cattle themselves on their own account, have their domestic staff. Thus it is possible to cross a Fulani village in the CAR without ever seeing a single Fulani woman. The only Fulani women whom one sees there sometimes in the streets, markets or villages are those who have come from the encampments to sell milk where there are some customers. These women are the most peasant-like in their way of life and their economic activity, and also in the attitude of the other women towards them. They can in some cases be rich in cattle themselves but their tradition is not urban: they follow directly the circuits of animal production in the countryside.

How to make gender segregation apparent? How to be sure that it escapes nobody's attention? It is not enough that women avoid being seen in public: they must be seen not to be seen. For example, if surprised, they make off in an agitated manner, not furtively as they would if they hoped not to be seen. When a woman's husband entertains male friends, he does so in a room used for that purpose opening onto the outside, so that the wife brings food to the limit of her segregative space, and her husband serves it to the guests. The husband *could* go and fetch the food from right inside the courtyard, the wife *could* decide not to show herself at all but to send a child to announce that the dishes have been put

down behind the fence. Generally she chooses to show just a little of herself so that it escapes none of her guests' attention that she disappears immediately.

It is important that the practice of segregation is visible because it is a sign of social prestige: for the whole family, men and women. The more numerous and highly regarded the guests, and the larger the village, in other words the more there is of a public, the more segregation is practised and ostentatiously underlined. It is a way of life where protocol matters, and in the absence of a public it loses its meaning and utility in terms of social prestige. The less this public is known, and the less frequent its visits, the less strong are bonds of kinship and alliance, and the more carefully put into practice is segregation. Certain members of the family are honoured by an identical treatment to that given to strangers, especially a man or a woman's parents-in-law: for when these are present, one has to show them how well-brought-up and so how segregated one is.

DOUBLE CIRCUITS

Segregation is certainly not more difficult to live with than mixing of the sexes (and of course, these very notions are culturally determined), but it is more complicated to organize, especially in space. Double channels of circulation for individuals must be provided for: this duplication being required for women who "never" go out and who cannot be seen in public, on roads and paths or in markets.

So a small Fulani village in the CAR (or the Fulani part of a polyethnic village, the Fulani part being called "Hausa," which in this case means "trader") is generally crossed by a road or path along which are found public places: shops, mosques, communal wells, markets. All Fulani courtyards include a shelter, a place for conversation, a shop or porch giving onto a road: you only see men there and it is they who receive visitors, Fulani and other, who are generally men. When a Fulani woman has to come by way of this male space, for instance when she arrives by car, she crosses as quickly as possible—ostensibly—and those men who know her, or are related to her, and can pay her a visit, do so afterwards inside the courtyard.

This men's space is separated from the rest of the family courtyard by a fence of plaited straw, much more rarely by a cob wall, which is more socially prestigious. Of the building materials, straw is the least valued, having a peasant look, then comes cob, but cement blocks are the most prestigious of the three. In the courtyard, each woman has a personal house for herself and her children. Normally a Fulani man does not have his own house. He stays in his wife's house—in peasant surroundings where the houses are straw huts, these are built by women, but the cob and cement houses are put up by men—or in his wives' houses if he is polygynous. However, sometimes men, especially the oldest and richest ones, build a personal house for themselves as well.

All courtyards have a way out on the side of the open countryside (opposite the way out that leads into the road) and women use it when they have to devote themselves to occupations of an agricultural, pastoral, domestic or social kind. These ways out leading to the countryside are sometimes also used by men who do not wish people to see from the road where they are going. Thus, if a man uses these ways out, it is clear that he wants to be discreet, which results in discussion inside the courtyard about where he may be going.

Moreover, the courtyards all communicate with one another and women go frequently to one another's houses by a circuit parallel to that of the road. If the village is grouped on the two sides of the road, there are two circuits parallel to the road, which hence must sometimes be crossed. This is done furtively, or *apparently* furtively, at a half-run, or for preference at night (if one is not seen, there is no crossing).

Gender segregation results then in a particular organization of the way individuals circulate, to which both men and women bring a good deal of care, and which gives everyone an evident pleasure in the form of a social game, where good upbringing is expressed in the art of knowing how to play it and how to break the rules when the opportunity arises.

The material form of the distinction between the men's domain and the women's is a fence. This is never a hermetic closure: you can see very well between two blades of straw, and walls of cob or cement rapidly develop faults, which can be expanded. Moreover, you hear everything on either side of the fence, and that is why women go away from it when speaking to one another.

But the fence is at the same time a materialization of (among other things) distinct social and intellectual behaviours and of modes of expression which are also inverted.

THE SUPPORT THAT THE FULANI GIVE TO THEIR ANTHROPOLOGISTS

Men are committed to a social façade, a serious demeanour, a stereotyped discourse about their society: these are the phenomena which one has access to from the road and which are shown externally. Here we find descriptions of chiefships, their official role, the organization of a society and its methods of production. Here we find ideological notions of patrilinearity, virilocality, the *essential* function of men in their society. Anthropologists must begin with these themes and affirmations and, when the anthropologist is a woman, she will be perceived above all as an anthropologist.

By contrast, the anthropologist can shoulder her status as a woman, and cross the fence—when everything changes. Joking and warmth win the day. On the women's side of the fence, we learn that patrilinearity is modified by the fact that lineal and familial endogamy is very strong, so that all individuals claim a lineage from their fathers which is also that of their mothers. Virilocality is much called into question too because it is not unusual for women to refuse to follow their husbands in their moves, whether seasonal or permanent. As for the necessity of the male role in every society, it provides an inexhaustible topic of conversation. And among the Fulani, both men and women, it is often said that family and society can function only where the women are intelligent.

The Fulanis in the CAR are not the only group to champion gender segregation, which is also found in northern Nigeria, for example, and in certain restricted circles in every Fulani society. It would be tempting for the Western or westernized anthropologist, man or woman, to study this segregation from a feminist angle which values highly either mingling or equal opportunities for both sexes. CAR Fulani society, and especially its more prestigious parts, sets a high value on the opposite: a maximum of gender segregation which everyone strives for, at least in public, giving much effort to it, for avoidance is probably more difficult to cater for than meeting.

Whatever opinion one many have on gender segregation in general or the Fulani's in particular, two linked points seem to me clear. First, Fulani women are not economically exploited. They possess their own cattle which is [*sic*] at their disposal, whereas they have far fewer economic obligations than men. Second, this kind of dichotomization of society, with its contrastive discourses and attitudes, is a precious aid to the anthropologist. Our female informants devote themselves to explaining the real functioning of the ideological model provided by our male informants outside the fence. During the Muslim *ramadan* in 1988 I spent whole nights on the other side of the fence discussing human societies and their complications, without which the anthropologist's job would lose its interest. Isn't it exactly the role of the anthropologist to go [to] the other side of the fence?

When Does Life Begin?

A Cross-Cultural Perspective on the Personhood of Fetuses and Young Children

Lynn M. Morgan

Lynn M. Morgan has a Ph.D. in medical anthropology, awarded jointly by the University of California, Berkeley, and the University of California, San Francisco, in 1987. An assistant professor at Mount Holyoke College, she has carried out fieldwork in Latin America; besides medical anthropology, her interests include development and political economy.

Participants in the U.S. abortion debate have argued about life and personhood from philosophical, religious, moral, biological, and political points of view, yet very few have examined the cultural dimensions of when life begins. Because they have overlooked the relevance of comparative cultural information, it has been difficult for participants in the debate to acknowledge the extent to which human life and personhood are culturally constructed. Perhaps a reflexive, cross-cultural perspective on personhood is an unaffordable luxury now, with the 1973 landmark *Roe v. Wade* Supreme Court decision legalizing abortion under fire from anti-abortion groups. Because the legality of abortion is seriously threatened, the subtleties and ambiguities about abortion are rarely acknowledged for fear of muddying the central policy issue.[1] In spite of the political stakes, however, I will argue that the discourse on personhood should be expanded to include perspectives from other cultures, thus encouraging Americans to confront and challenge the myriad culture-bound assumptions which permeate the U.S. debate over reproductive health policy.

The social recognition of fetuses, newborns, and young children is embedded within a wider social context. This observation is not new: a burgeoning literature illuminates the links between abortion, childrearing, women's status, social stratification, child welfare, ethnic and gender discrimination, and changing relations between the sexes. The process through which young

human lives come to be valued is derived in part from these factors, but personhood is also a function of cultural divisions of the life cycle, attitudes toward death, the social organization of descent and inheritance, and social systems of authority and achievement. Anthropologists such as Mauss, Fortes, and La Fontaine[2] have documented a rich and remarkable range of variation showing the relationship among notions of self, body imagery, social organization, and ideational features such as consciousness and individuality. The cross-cultural evidence shows that the early thresholds of human life and personhood are just one issue in the larger question of whom society allows to become a person, under what circumstances, and why.

Every human being is potentially at risk of being aborted, miscarried, stillborn, or killed by natural cause or human agency before being accepted into a social community and labelled a person, yet there has been no recent systematic attempt to examine when other cultures come to value human life. . . .

Viewing the issue of personhood from a cross-cultural perspective helps to illustrate inconsistent and contradictory features of reproductive ethics debates in the United States. The ethnographic data show that the parameters of the U.S. abortion debate as presently constituted do not exhaust the realm of possibilities found among the earth's inhabitants. A close reading of the ethnographic evidence shows that killing neonates is often not regarded as murder, especially when the killing occurs before an infant is recognized as a human or person. Infanticide, then, with all the moral repugnance it evokes in the West, is a cultural construct rather than a universal moral edict. Apart from Tooley's influential *Abortion and Infanticide*,[3] few theorists have seriously considered the moral justifications for infanticide, yet the comparative cultural data indicate that this question deserves far more attention than it receives.

The cross-cultural evidence reveals two culturally-constructed concepts used widely to divide the human life cycle continuum at its earliest stages: human-ness and personhood. In order to be granted status as a person, a fetus or neonate must first be recognized as a member of the human species. In some societies the decision to call a fetus "human" is not made until biological birth when the newborn's physical attributes can be assessed. Personhood, in contrast, is a socially-recognized moral status. Neonates may not be labeled as persons until social birth rites are performed, often several days or months after biological birth. Social birth gives the neonate a moral status and binds it securely to a social community. Biological and social birth are not recognized as separate events in Western societies, even though they structure the onset of personhood in many non-Western societies. The U.S. abortion debate thus replicates Western divisions of the life cycle, overlooking the fact that even the human developmental cycle is socially patterned.

The attribution of personhood is a collective social decision, for the legal and ethical boundaries of personhood can only be negotiated within social settings. The limits of personhood are not decided by individuals, but by the entire society acting on shared cultural beliefs and values. For this reason, personhood—the value placed on human life—is not a concept which will be altered by religious mandate, nor by radical legislation by either the Right or the Left. Yet consensus is obviously eluding us, and seems destined to elude us as long as North Americans feel personal ambivalence and the compulsion to engage in increasingly polarized struggles over the issues surrounding abortion. Perhaps by reflecting on the social context of personhood and the value of fetuses and young children in other cultural contexts, we will be better able to understand how they are valued in our own.

"HUMAN" VERSUS "PERSON"

The furor over abortion in the United States has been waged in part through the manipulation of highly emotional symbols, resulting in a great deal of semantic confusion (a fetus may be called a "baby," an "unborn child," or "the product of conception"[4]). I will make only one semantic distinction while examining the cross-cultural evidence: between the concepts of "human," and "person.". . .

Although "human" generally refers to a biological designation, the term is still subject to cultural influence and negotiation. In the United States, most people assume that the product of a human pregnancy will be

human, yet the cross-cultural evidence shows greater variety. Among the Arunta of Central Australia, "[if] a child is born at a very premature stage, nothing will persuade the natives that it is an undeveloped human being, for it is nothing like a *Kuruna* [spirit] or a *retappa* [newborn]; 'they are perfectly convinced that it is the young of some other animal, such as a kangaroo, which has by mistake got inside the woman.'"[5] In Bang Chan, Thailand, women related episodes of "giving birth to 'gold,' 'jewels,' 'a monkey,' 'a fish's stomach,' and a mouse-like 'Golden Child.'"[6] In aboriginal Australia and Thailand, the products of conception are not assumed *a priori* to be human, for human status must be empirically verified.

In societies where humanity and personhood are defined separately, the determination of humanity always precedes the determination of personhood. On the island of Truk, for example, people waited until biological birth to see whether the newborn could be categorized as human. They did not take for granted the anthropomorphic character of the creature which would emerge from the womb. Abnormal or deformed infants were labelled as ghosts and burned or thrown into the sea: "Culturally this is not defined as infanticide and the suggestion of infanticide horrified the Trukese; a ghost is not a person and cannot be killed in any case."[7] This case, in which humanity itself was denied, is characteristic of the justification given for killing twins in some societies. Among the Tallensi in Africa, Fortes reports that twins were regarded suspiciously, because they may have been "malicious bush spirits" in human guise. After the first month of birth, a twin would be treated as any other child, but "only when it reaches the age of about four, and is placed under the spiritual guardianship of an ancestor spirit, is a twin definitely regarded as a complete social being."[8] A turn-of-the-century account of childhood in southern Africa noted that twins were regarded as more animal than human, and thus dangerously unpredictable: "No woman would care to marry a twin, for she would say that he was not a proper human being, and might turn wild like an animal, and kill her."[9] In these societies the neonate is not assumed to be born human, but is "anthropomorphized" after birth on the basis of physical characteristics which may or may not subsequently be endowed with moral significance. The criteria used to anthropomorphize newborns in different cultural contexts vary with caretakers' perceptions of the status of neonates.

DEFINING PERSONHOOD

Personhood is contingent on social recognition, and a person is recognized using established sociocultural conventions. Persons possess a special moral stature within their societies, yet in specific historical circumstances this status has been denied to certain groups, including women, children, slaves, prisoners of war, lepers, countless subordinate ethnic groups, and the insane. In all cultures, persons are living human entities whose killing is classed as murder, that is, the killing invokes some degree of moral condemnation and social retribution. The social construction of personhood varies according to the environmental, cosmological, and historical circumstances of different societies. What this means, in sum, is that "people are defined by people."[10] There can be no absolute definition of personhood isolated from a sociocultural context.

Burial customs may provide one source of data on cultural definitions of personhood, since only "persons" are buried. The data show a range of variation sufficient to highlight some of the contradictions in current U.S. policy. For example, on one extreme, a Chippewa Amerindian woman:

> knew her baby was two or three months along when she lost it . . . You could tell that it was just beginning to form. They cleaned it just like a child that is born and wrapped it. They gave a feast for it just like for a dead person and buried it in the same way. They believe that a child is human when it is conceived.[11]

Such behavior contrasts strikingly with burial practices in the United States, where fetuses weighing less than 500 grams are not buried, even in Roman Catholic hospitals where stated policy professes to respect human life from the time of conception.[12] On the other extreme, Ashanti children of Ghana who died before adolescence were reportedly thrown on the village midden heap,[13] indicating that burial rites and the full status of personhood were adult perquisites. In the U.S., "fetuses ex utero over 500 grams are considered premature newborns, and therefore birth certificates must be issued for them and they must be buried,"[14] yet U.S. burial customs for children depend on more than the weight or size of the body. In New York City, a study revealed that many indigent children under one year of age were buried in unmarked graves in Potter's Field, where parents were not permitted to visit the gravesites.[15] Apparently child burial customs and the parents' right to graveside grieving are at least in part a function of social class in the U.S., suggesting that the lives of poor children are valued less than those from wealthier families.

SOCIAL BIRTH

In Western industrialized societies, people generally believe that biological birth marks the entrance of a new being into the social community. The tenacity of this belief results from the cultural conviction that biological events have social significance. Unconsciously but relentlessly, Westerners have imbued that biological act of birth with profound importance, to the extent that legal and civil institutions confer personhood instantly when an infant is born alive. The social status of personhood is thus granted concurrently with a biological act: emerging from the womb. In several non-Western societies, however, members observe a period of transitional, liminal time between biological birth—when the infant can be seen, inspected, and evaluated—and social birth, when the infant is formally accepted into its social community. This is a stage of the life cycle which acknowledges and reinforces the cultural and cognitive divisions between the marginal, uncertain status of the fetus and the secure, protected status of a person. As a clearly bounded life cycle division, this period between biological and social birth so characteristic of many non-Western societies is unknown in 20th century Western societies.

Until abortion became such a contentious issue, most people in the United States rarely stopped to question whether the social status of an infant could be separated from its biological status. It would be thought inappropriate to refer to the unborn fetus as a person complete with social identity (in part because the sex of the individual is essential to the construction of an individual's social identity). At birth the healthy child was automatically endowed with a social identity: as soon as the umbilical cord was cut, the neonate became a person. Biological birth was the major moral dividing line along the life cycle continuum: every individual who had passed the line was granted the rights and social status of persons,[16] while every individual shy of the line was not. Biological and social birth were inextricably intertwined in legal and medical institutions as well as in popular consciousness. This has changed only recently. In 1973, for example, *Roe v. Wade* established "viability" as the moral dividing line between fetuses which could be legally aborted and those which merited the protection of the State. Amniocentesis and other advances in medical technology have also altered the idea that persons could be distinguished from nonpersons only at birth.

Many non-industrial societies, on the other hand, do not endow biological facts with the same degree of social importance. They separate the purely physiological act of birth from the social acceptance of the newborn. Social birth is marked by a ritual held sometime after biological birth, during which the newborn is granted a place in the social world. Social birth rituals often introduce the newborn formally for the first time to significant members of the community such as parents, siblings, godparents, other relatives, and community elders. The infant may also be presented to non-human entities considered important by the community, for example, sacred animals, natural entities, or supernatural beings. Social birth may be the occasion for some symbolically important event such as naming, hair cutting, depilation,[17] ear piercing,[18] removing incisor teeth,[19] or circumcision. Social birth may take place anywhere from a few days to several years after biological birth. It can be a one-time occurrence or it may be a gradual process involving a number of socially significant events: crying, suckling, or weaning for the first time, or learning—as a small child—to perform certain chores.[20] Long, gradual transitions to personhood, sometimes lasting an entire lifetime are common in non-Western societies,[21] yet a crucial induction into personhood often occurs early in life, with social birth. In a society where social birth rites are essential to personhood, an infant who dies before social birth has died before it was born.

DIVIDING THE LIFE CYCLE

Models of an individual life cycle, from the moment of conception to death and afterlife, are constructed differently from one society to the next. Societies divide the developmental cycle into segments, and mark transitions from one stage to the next by birthdays, marriage, parenthood, and religious rites of passage. Life cycle divisions are one way in which societies categorize their members. Life stages allow status to be monitored and evaluated by other members of society who look for age- and status-related cues to determine their attitudes and behavior toward those around them. Stages of life which North Americans take for granted, such as childhood, adolescence, and middle age, are in fact cultural constructions which have evolved in response to demographic, economic, and social factors. Anthropologists have been acutely aware of the social nature of the life cycle since Margaret Mead wrote about the nature of adolescence in Samoa. In the twentieth century United States, she said, adolescence had become known "as the period in which idealism flowered and rebellion against authority was strong, a period during which difficulties and conflicts were absolutely inevitable."[22] In Samoa, however, teenagers did not pass through an analogous period of turmoil. Mead used the ethnographic evidence to show that adolescence was a phase of life unique to Western culture, specifically to the United States.

Childhood is another stage of life with a discernible social history, as Aries demonstrates for Western Europe. By analyzing European literature and iconography, Aries shows that children were not accorded the unique status they now occupy in the West until well after the advent of institutionalized schooling in the 16th and 17th centuries. Around that time, moralists began to argue that children needed to be trained, reformed, and subjected to "a kind of quarantine" before they would be fit company for adults.[23] The concept of infancy did not arise in western Europe until much later. British vital statistics did not distinguish among

miscarried, stillborn, or infant deaths until late in the 19th century.[24] Until the mid-19th century, the French had no word for "baby."[25] During the first few months of life, when an infant could not interact with or respond to adult stimuli, it "simply 'did not count.'"[26] As the concept of childhood evolved in modern Europe, so did parents' ideals of the number and quality of children they desired, and society's expectations of the appropriate behaviors characterizing ideal adults and children.

Middle-age, in addition to adolescence and childhood, is also a socially constructed life stage category. Brandes has shown that the American mid-life crisis (often associated with the fortieth birthday) is not a biological or developmental phenomenon, but cultural.[27] The turmoil and anxiety one feels on approaching the fortieth year is a reflection of our society's success in continuing the process of socialization through the adult years. Adults as well as children internalize society's popular wisdom and myths, one of which is that mid-life crisis is inevitable, natural, and almost genetically programmed. This relentlessly repeated message is deeply encoded in many realms of social life, including Western number symbolism. As a result, the American mid-life crisis has become a self-fulfilling prophecy: "the expectation of change at certain key times along the life course—especially if such expectation is elevated to the position of a shared, transmitted cultural norm—is likely actually to produce a change that might not otherwise occur."[28]

If the ethnographic evidence shows that the human developmental cycle is divided differently according to cultural and historical contingencies, then non-Western cultures can be expected to have divisions of the life cycle unfamiliar to Westerners. One well-known example is the clearly marked transition from childhood and adulthood celebrated by adolescent initiation rites in parts of Africa and Melanesia. Another such stage occurs early in life, during the period between biological birth and social birth.

PERSONHOOD, A CROSS-CULTURAL VIEW

When viewed in cross-cultural perspective, the criteria for personhood are widely divergent: in one society personhood may be an ascribed status, conferred automatically when an infant is born alive or given a name; in another society the status may be achieved only through a very long, gradual process of socialization. In Java "the people quite flatly say, 'To be human [i.e., a "a person" in my terms] is to be Javanese.' Small children, boors, simpletons, the insane, the flagrantly immoral, are said to be *ndurung kjawa*, 'not yet Javanese'" and hence, not yet persons.[29] Evans-Pritchard reported that among the Nuer of the Nilotic Sudan, the death of a small child was not considered the death of a person:

People do not mourn for a small child, for "a small child is not a person (*ran*). When he tethers the cattle and herds the goats he is a person. When he cleans the byres and spreads the dung out to dry and collects it and carries it to the fire he is a person." A man will not say he has a son till the child is about six years of age.[30]

A 1950s ethnographic account of Korea reported that the death of a newborn would receive "scarcely more deference than any other animal. If it lives only through a long course of learning and ceremonies will it obtain the position of a recognized personality."[31] Personhood is not a "natural" category or a universal right of human beings, but a culturally and historically constructed assemblage of behaviors, knowledge, and practices. For societies which observe social birth rites, biological birth and the recognition of humanity are only early indications of what an individual may become. Biological birth acknowledges potential, but carries no guarantee of eventual acceptance into the social community. . . .

LIMINALITY, DANGER, AND THE FATE OF THE NEONATE

In many societies, the period between biological and social birth is treated socially and symbolically as an extension of being in the womb. The newborn is kept in seclusion, sheltered indoors away from the view of all save its mother (and perhaps a midwife or other female caretaker). Danger is minimized by recreating and maintaining a womb-like environment in which the infant resides until social birth. In the rural Philippines, for example, the newborn must be kept in strict seclusion for two weeks after biological birth, behind closed windows and above a well-sealed floor.[32] An ethnographer reporting on the Yavapai Amerindians of central Arizona wrote that mother and newborn stayed isolated and immobile for six days after parturition, resting on a bed of warm coals and earth and covered with grass.[33]

In society's terms none of these children have yet been born. They have emerged from their mother's uterus to a womb-like waiting room for pre-persons; their liminal status is perhaps analogous to a transitory phase at the other end of the life cycle known to Christians as purgatory.

Seclusion of infants is sometimes justified by citing the many perceived threats to their existence. Peoples of the Ghanaian Northern Territories told ethnographers that the infant may be reclaimed by spirits during the first seven days after biological birth:

> [A] newborn baby may in fact be a spirit-child, and not a human child at all. If it is a spirit, it will return to the world of spirits before a week is out, so for the first seven days after the birth the mother and child are confined to the

room in which the birth took place, or at any rate to the house. If the child dies during that time, it is assumed that it was in fact a spirit-child. The body is mutilated and buried in a pot, to prevent its return in similar circumstances. The parents are not allowed to mourn its loss, but should show signs of joy at being rid of such an unwelcome guest.[34]

If the infant survives its first seven days outside the biological womb, it will be allowed to emerge from the symbolic social womb as well. At that point, "it is considered that the child is human, and it is 'out-doored,' or brought into the open for the first time."[35] Supernatural threats to the newborn also justify an eight day hiatus between biological and social birth among the Ashanti of western Africa. Ashanti beliefs about conception and early infancy are known to anthropologists because of the *ntoro* concept, a spiritual bond passed from father to child in a society structured around matrilineal descent. At biological birth the Ashanti question whether the newborn is meant to stay in the human world or whether it is a wandering ghost who will soon return to the spirit world. For eight days the mother and child remain indoors, with no special efforts made to bind the child to the human world: "It is given any kind of old mat or old rag to lie upon; it is not addressed in any endearing terms; water or pap, if given to it, is administered out of an old banana skin or ground-nut husk. It is true it is permitted to feed at the mother's breast, but it is hardly encouraged."[36] If the child is still alive after eight days, a *Nteatea* rite is performed, "when the child is named for its senior *ntoro* relative, and it is then for the first time regarded as a member of the human family."[37]

Similar "out-dooring" ceremonies have been recorded in other parts of the world. In the Nilgiri hills in south India, the Toda keep the newborn indoors for three months after biological birth. The sun is not allowed to touch the child's face. One morning after three months have passed, a "face opening" ceremony is held at dawn. The infant is brought outdoors with its face covered, and unveiled when the first bird sings. During this social birth rite the infant is introduced to the temple, to nature, to buffaloes, and to its clansmen. The infant is not considered a person until the ceremony has been performed.[38] Greeting the sun was also a feature of social birth among the Hopi Amerindians a century ago. On the twentieth day after birth, a ceremony was held to purify the new mother, name the baby, and present the child to the sun. Great care was taken by the father to announce the precise moment the sun rose above the horizon. At that instant, the "godmother throws the blanket from the face of the baby" and presents a cornmeal offering to the sun.[39] All those present, including the newborn, then ate a ritual breakfast marking the entrance of a new person into the community.[40]

The above are quintessential examples of social birth rites: the newborn is kept indoors and out of sight for a specified period of time while the larger society remains symbolically unaware of its presence. This is a period of trial. The infant must "prove" it is worthy of personhood; first by managing to survive, then by exhibiting the vigor, health, and affect of one destined to become a functioning member of the community. If it survives and thrives, it is ready to pass through the social birth canal, to be ceremoniously welcomed as a person into the community. Completion of social birth rites ties the individual to the kin group and to the mortal world, granting it a moral status designed to protect it from harm by placing it under the protection of the group. If any of these criteria are not satisfied, the infant is classed as a nonperson (and may in fact be labelled as non-human and hence not eligible for personhood, as with witches, ghosts and spirit-children). If it does not die of its own accord, it may be neglected until it does die, or it may be killed.

Infanticide is murder by definition, but most societies punish only the killing of human persons. It is problematic, then, to apply the label of infanticide to killing neonates before they are recognized as human or granted personhood. We might rather think of this as post-partum abortion, an image more applicable to the American experience. Induced abortion in the U.S. is rationalized (in part) by regarding the fetus as a pre-person, not yet accorded the same sanctity of life applied to "babies." Societies without safe and effective means of inducing abortion at early gestational stages may delay valuing the infant until well after biological birth. During this interim between biological and social birth the unwanted fetus (and it *is* still regarded as a fetus by that society) can be killed while its caretakers remain immune from punishment. Infanticide is condemned in most societies, but only after the newborn has been accorded human status or recognized as a person:

> [I]nfanticide is most readily condoned if it occurs before the infant is named and has been accepted as a bona fide member of its society. It seems that the primary and fundamental restriction in most societies is the taboo on murder, i.e., killing a member of the ingroup. The less eligible a child is for membership in the group, the less seriously the act of killing the child is viewed.[41]

Thus the Bariba of Benin believe that some babies will be born witches, who may endanger their mothers' health and bring misfortune to the entire community. Witch babies can be identified at biological birth and should ideally be killed at that time to prevent future havoc.[42] In many societies the decision to expose or kill a neonate is made immediately at biological birth or within a few hours afterward. Among the Mohave Amerindians, if a newborn "was permitted to live long enough to be put to the breast, it was no longer subject to being killed."[43]

Post-partum abortion becomes infanticide if it is practiced after social birth rites are performed: "Thus in Athens the child could be exposed before the Amphidromia, a family ceremony at which the child was carried by its nurse around the hearth and thus received the religious consecration and its name."[44] In England during the 17th and 18th centuries, infanticide was practiced even though newborns were socially recognized as persons.[45] In those cases, however, personhood was granted incrementally, and infants were considered to be less significant persons than older children and adults. Under civil and religious law, killing a baby was a sin and a crime, but as practiced by the populace infanticide was less heinous than murdering an adult.

Becoming a person sometimes involves a long period of nurturing and socialization by the mother. This makes the infant's right to personhood in some societies contingent on the mother's survival and well-being. For example, an ethnographer reported that, among the Toba Amerindians of the Bolivian Gran Chaco, if a woman died in childbirth the newborn would be buried alive with her body. If both lived, personhood was granted only when the infant gained physical autonomy from the mother after weaning. Before that time, neither abortion nor infanticide was considered immoral: "A new-born child is no personality and has not an independent existence; its parents, and particularly the mother, have full right to decide over its life."[46] Yanomamo infants, also living in lowland South America, were considered appendages of their mothers until weaned at the end of their third year. When nursing ended, "the child, which hitherto belonged to the flesh and blood of the mother, has become an independent human being."[47] The personhood of the newborn in these two societies was predicated, at least in part, on attaining physical independence from the mother.

Ethnographic accounts cite a wide range of socially significant events which mark the end of liminality and the beginning of personhood. Weaning is one example, but naming is by far the most common. A nameless infant, in many cases, is not considered a person. The social function of naming is discussed in Ford's cross-cultural study of reproductive behavior:

> Naming probably has derived its extremely widespread acceptance from the manifest advantages which result from the practice. A name facilitates social intercourse . . . Naming a child helps to pull him into the framework of his society as an accepted member of the group. By virtue of being named the infant becomes a person like everyone else in the society; he is no longer a nameless outsider.[48]

Killing a child prior to naming was acceptable among certain societies, while killing a child after it was named would be tantamount to murder.[49] This was apparently the case among the Atayal aborigines of Formosa, where an early ethnographer reported "there is no punishment for the killing of an as yet nameless—i.e., less than two-or-three-year-old—child."[50] Among Arctic coast peoples, an ethnographer noted that infants were named after the deceased, thereupon reincarnating their ghosts: "naming may have restrained infanticide . . . because killing a named child could offend the reincarnated ghost."[51] Countless similar cases are found in the literature, where the name is a symbol of having become a person, and where a child who died prior to receiving a name was not regarded as a person.[52] Cherokee Amerindian babies were generally named a few days after birth. If the birth were prolonged or difficult, however, the child would be named during birth "so as to have something 'material' by which to exercise an influence upon it."[53] In the contemporary United States, where biological and social birth occur simultaneously, most newborns have names already chosen for them, which allows them to move directly from the womb into a permanent social identity.

Not everywhere, however, is a name the dominant symbol of the value placed on a newborn's life. Naming is delayed in many societies, but this behavior can have completely different meanings according to the social and environmental context. In northeast Brazil, where infant mortality is high, delayed naming is one of the emotional defenses which poor mothers use to shield themselves from the devastating psychological impact of frequent infant death. These Brazilian women view their children "as human, but [as] significantly less human than the grown child or adult."[54] Extreme poverty, widespread hunger, and high infant mortality rates affect the mother's emotional investment in her children: emotional deprivation is, in this context, a product of material scarcity.[55] Conversely in the Himalayas, where infant mortality is also high, children are not called their names precisely because their vulnerable young lives are highly valued. There Hindu children are named by a Brahmin priest on the tenth day after birth, but no one calls a child by this name for fear of making the child susceptible to the perils of "evil eye." Although not calling a child by its name may correspond with a denial of personhood in some societies, among the Hindus it is a "strong expression of the value and vulnerability placed on early lives, already begun but somehow requiring more protection."[56]

DISCUSSION

The ethnographic literature offers no universal consensus about who or what constitutes a person, for personhood is evaluated and bestowed on the basis of moral criteria which vary tremendously among and within different sociocultural contexts. The value placed on the lives of fetuses, neonates, and young children is determined according to a complex constellation of cultural factors, and cannot be determined simply by asking, "When does life begin?" Without a more general understanding of what it means to be a person in a given society, the beginnings of personhood can never be fully understood. An awareness of beginnings affords us only rudimentary insights into the social construction of personhood, which depends on the social relevance of gender, age, and material conditions and is in many contexts a gradual process. An example from West Africa will illustrate the point.

The Ashanti were mentioned earlier in connection with social birth rites which occur eight days after birth, but apparently these rites did not complete the transition to personhood. According to Rattray personhood was sometimes not solidified until adolescence: "In times not so very remote, persons dying before they reached adolescence were in no case accorded the ordinary funeral rites, and were often merely buried on the village midden heap. They were classed with the 'ghost children' who had not even survived eight days."[57] Not until passing through adolescent initiation rites did an Ashanti youngster become a complete person. As reflected in burial rites, children were not as highly valued as adults. This can be understood by examining the context and significance of personhood within Ashanti society. Among the Ashanti, differentiation between the sexes was an essential feature of adulthood, but sexual differentiation was insignificant until a child reached puberty and acquired the capacity to reproduce. Because reproduction was crucial to the perpetuation of the socio-political order, adolescent initiation rites symbolized the growth not only of the individual physical body but of the collective social body as well. Adolescents embodied society's hopes for its future. This point is made in Comaroff's discussion of healing among the Tshidi; there adolescent initiation rites "linked the natural maturation of the physical body to the reproduction of the socio-political system."[58] The importance of continuing the social formation is underscored by rites which grant personhood to adolescents: in La Fontaine's terms, "The concept [of person] serves to fuse the finite span of a human life with the unlimited continuity of social forms, by identifying personhood with self reproduction."[59] For the Ashanti child, to be a person meant to enjoy bodily autonomy with few corresponding social obligations, but to be an adult person meant that one's social responsibilities were multiplied, intensified, and enmeshed more tightly within the body politic.

So far we have been concerned with the valuation of fetuses and children cross-culturally, yet societal norms affect the personhood of the mother as well as the fetus, newborn, and young child. The mother's status as a person depends in most societies on her reproductive condition, the reproductive choices she makes, and her society's attitudes toward childbearing and childrearing. Feminist scholars writing in the United States argue that the abortion debate has focused too exclusively on fetal rights, virtually ignoring the role of women in society.[60] Recent attempts to reverse this trend include books by Luker, who demonstrates that U.S. women's opinions about abortion are conditioned by their life circumstances and perceived career options,[61] and Petchesky, who argues that the reproductive choices available to women must be understood within the broad socio-economic and political framework affecting the role of women.[62] Certainly these insights are applicable cross-culturally as well. Throughout the world women are primarily responsible for decisions affecting the lives and well-being of fetuses, neonates, and young children, and the choices women make in this regard are contingent on their own assessments of available options. The options change with the social tides, alternately restricting and expanding women's responsibilities for their born and unborn offspring. Such changes can be seen in a California lawsuit where a woman was charged with the wrongful death of her newborn child because she took illicit drugs and had sexual relations late in pregnancy, disregarding her doctor's orders. If this trend continues, American women will be increasingly held responsible for prenatal child abuse and neglect, even though fetuses have not been granted the rights of persons under the U.S. Constitution.

The ethnographic and historical literature is filled with accounts illustrating that a woman's status—even her claim to personhood and life itself—is contingent on her reproductive choices. In 15th century England, for example, mothers known to have destroyed their newborn children were punished by death while wet nurses guilty of the same crime were not punished.[63] Piers argues that the reason for differential treatment was class bias, since wealthy women could afford to hire wet nurses for their children while poor women could not. Wet nurses were not executed for infanticide because breast milk was a rare and valuable commodity and wet nurses were scarce: "society simply could not have afforded to kill her."[64] Indigent natural mothers, in contrast, were relatively expendable, and these were the women most often found guilty of murdering their babies. The 15th century criminal sentence for murdering an infant depended not on the value of the infant's life, but on the social class of the accused. The hierarchy of values ranked the lives of wet nurses above the lives of "natural" mothers, obscuring the fact that wet nurses were themselves natural mothers. While Christian moralists railed against child murder, society's response

reflected how certain classes of women were so devalued and oppressed that their execution was condoned. Their crime was in reality the inability to afford a wet nurse.

A woman's status within society can be heightened, undermined, or made ambiguous by pregnancy. Generally if the pregnancy results in a healthy newborn (in some patrilineal societies only a healthy newborn boy is satisfactory) her status will be enhanced but, if the pregnancy outcome is viewed as negative, she may suffer irreparable damage or even death. Devereux cites at least two societies where women could reportedly be killed with impunity for inducing an abortion.[65] The mother's status in such cases was rendered ambiguous by the liminal status of the fetus. Whereas before the pregnancy her murder would have been a punishable crime, in pregnancy her life was valued less than that of the fetus she carried.

Most often the woman making reproductive decisions is held directly responsible for her own actions, as interpreted through societal mores and prejudices. In some cases, though, the lives of several people may be affected by a woman's decision. The Azande of central Africa have a polygamous, patrilocal social structure which allowed a woman's reproductive decisions to have far-reaching repercussions:

> If the husband learns that his wife has used an abortifacient plant, he considers this tantamount to the assassination of his child. He therefore asks his father-in-law for a second wife, or else, in vengeance, he kills the wife of his father-in-law or one of his father-in-law's children.[66]

In this case, the woman's relatives paid the consequences of her actions, demonstrating the links between fetal status, female status, and the status of other members of society. A similar issue can be seen in the United States abortion debates: should the decision to induce abortion be made in private between a woman and her physician, or should the permission of the father also be required? To what extent is the personhood of the woman contingent on her relationship to others in her sphere of social relations? Anthropologists have shown that in some societies one's social identity and personhood is completely, inextricably embedded in the social structure, to the point where individuals cannot envision having relationships not dictated by social structural roles and statuses.[67] The very essence of personhood is negotiated, manipulated, bestowed, and denied in accordance with the tacit or considered approval of society's members.

In the United States, the abortion debate has been foreshortened by a culture-bound discourse on personhood. The discussion of fetal personhood and abortion legislation has been limited almost exclusively to the period between conception and biological birth, largely as a result of a shared, cultural belief that biological birth is the event which distinguishes persons from non-persons. Consequently, the only space left to negotiate the boundaries of personhood is prior to biological birth. We have framed the debate over abortion in such a way that we argue whether it would be defensible to push the dividing line earlier, toward conception, but not later, toward early childhood. In the process of limiting debate to this realm, we have largely ignored the expansive, multiple meanings of personhood in American society, including the implications for adult women and men of the social context which determines our life decisions.

How can the range of cultural variability discussed here affect the U.S. abortion policy debates? In spite of the relativist stance presented here, I will not argue that Americans should weigh the merits of post-partum abortion—that would be ignoring a fundamental U.S. cultural reality which gave us the term "infanticide." Nonetheless Americans have felt forced to construct convoluted philosophical justifications for their positions on these issues, even when contorted logic theoretically could be avoided by admitting the existence and relevance of cultural variation. Debates over fetal personhood would be more honest, although undoubtedly more agonizing, if it were easier to admit that the moral dividing of life between persons and non-persons at biological birth or "viability" is a cultural construction. The question is whether we can tolerate knowing that our beliefs and values are remarkably malleable, arbitrary products of our cultural milieu.

NOTES

1. Daniel Callahan, "How Technology Is Reframing the Abortion Debate," *Hastings Center Report* (February 1986): 33–42, esp. 41.
2. Marcel Mauss, "A Category of the Human Mind: The Notion of Person, The Notion of Self," in *The Category of the Person*, ed. M. Carrithers, S. Collins, and S. Luke (Cambridge: Cambridge University Press, 1985), 1–25; Meyer Fortes, "On the Concept of the Person Among the Tallensi," in *La Notion de la Personne en Afrique Noire*, ed. G. Dieterlen (Paris: Editions du Centre National de la Recherche Scientifique, 1973); J. S. La Fontaine, "Person and Individual: Some Anthropological Reflections," in *The Category of the Person*, ed. M. Carrithers, S. Collins, and S. Luke (Cambridge: Cambridge University Press, 1985), 123–140.
3. Michael Tooley, "Abortion and Infanticide," *Philosophy and Public Affairs* 2 (1972): 37–65.
4. Leonard Kovit, "Babies as Social Products: The Social Determinants of Classification," *Social Science & Medicine* 12 (1978): 347–351.
5. Ashley Montagu, *Coming Into Being Among the Australian Aborigines* (London: Routledge & Kegan Paul, 1974), p. 31.
6. Jane Richardson Hanks, *Maternity and Its Rituals in Bang Chan* (Ithaca: Cornell Thailand Project, 1963), esp. 34–35.
7. Thomas Gladwin and Seymour B. Sarason, *Truk: A Man in Paradise* (New York: Wenner-Gren Foundation, 1953), p. 133; quoted in George Devereux, *A Study of Abortion in Primitive Societies* (New York: International University Press, 1955), p. 344.
8. Meyer Fortes, *The Web of Kinship Among the Tallensi: The Second Part of an Analysis of the Social Structure of a Trans-Volta Tribe* (London: Oxford University Press, 1949), p. 271.
9. Dudley Kidd, *Savage Childhood: A Study of Kaffir Children* (London: Adam and Charles Black, 1906), p. 45.
10. Andie L. Knutson, "The Definition and Value of a New Human Life," *Social Science & Medicine 1* (1967): 7–29.
11. Devereux 1955, pp. 207–208.
12. Caroline Whitbeck, "The Moral Implications of Regarding Women as People: New Perspectives on Pregnancy and Personhood," in *Abortion and the Status of the Fetus*, ed. William B. Bondeson et al. (Dordrecht, Holland: D. Reidel Publishing Company, 1983), 247–272, esp. 258.
13. Robert S. Rattray, *Religion and Art Among the Ashanti* (Oxford: Clarendon Press, 1927).
14. Whitbeck, p. 258.
15. Peter Kerr, "Groups Fault City Policy on Burial of Poor Infants," *New York Times* (May 25, 1986), p. 30.
16. H. Tristram Engelhardt, Jr., "Viability and the Use of the Fetus," in *Abortion and the Status of the Fetus*, ed. William B. Bondeson et al. (Dordrecht, Holland: D. Reidel Publishing Company, 1983), 183–208, esp. 191.
17. Among the Siriono of eastern Bolivia, see Allan R. Holmberg, *Nomads of the Long Bow* (New York: Natural History Press, 1969).
18. Among the Argentine Araucanians, see M. Inez Hilger, *Araucanian Child Life and Its Cultural Background* (Washington: Smithsonian Miscellaneous Collections, Volume 133, 1957).
19. Performed among the Nuer when a child reached seven or eight years of age, see E. E. Evans-Pritchard, *Nuer Religion* (Oxford: Clarendon Press, 1956).
20. See Mead and Newton, p. 154, for examples.
21. La Fontaine, p. 132.
22. Margaret Mead, *Coming of Age in Samoa* (New York: American Museum of Natural History, 1928).
23. Philippe Aries, *Centuries of Childhood* (New York: Vintage Books, 1962), p. 412.
24. David Armstrong, "The Invention of Infant Mortality," *Sociology of Health and Illness 8* (1986): 211–232, p. 214.
25. Aries, p. 29.
26. Aries, p. 128.
27. Stanley H. Brandes, *Forty: The Age and the Symbol* (Knoxville: University of Tennessee Press, 1985).
28. Brandes, p. 126.
29. Clifford Geertz, *The Interpretation of Cultures* (New York: Basic, 1973), p. 52.
30. Evans-Pritchard, p. 146.
31. Cornelius Osgood, *The Koreans and Their Culture* (New York: Ronald Press, 1951).
32. J. Landa Jocando, *Growing Up in a Philippine Barrio* (New York: Holt, Rinehart and Winston, 1969).
33. E. W. Gifford, "Northeastern and Western Yavapai," *University of California Publications in American Archaeology and Ethnology 34* (1937): 247–354, esp. 300.
34. Barrington Kaye, *Bringing Up Children in Ghana* (London: George Allen & Unwin Ltd., 1962), pp. 56–57.
35. Kaye, p. 57.
36. Rattray, p. 59.
37. Edith Clarke, "The Sociological Significance of Ancestor Worship in Ashanti," *Africa 3* (1930): 431–470, esp. 431.
38. David G. Mandelbaum, Department of Anthropology, University of California, Berkeley, personal communication.
39. J. G. Owens, "Natal Ceremonies of the Hopi Indians," *Journal of American Ethnology and Archaeology 2* (1892): 163–75, esp. 170–73.

40. See Tilly E. Stevenson, "The Religious Life of a Zuni Child," *Fifth Annual Report of the Bureau of Ethnology* (1883–84): 539–555, esp. 546, for an account of a similar social birth rite which took place among the Zuni of western New Mexico.

41. Clelland S. Ford, "Control of Contraception in Cross-Cultural Perspective," *Annals of the New York Academy of Sciences 54* (1952): 763–768; cited in Mildred Dickeman, "Demographic Consequences of Infanticide in Man," *Annual Review of Ecology and Systematics 6* (1975): 107–137, esp. 115.

42. Carolyn Fishel Sargent, *The Cultural Context of Therapeutic Choice* (Dordrecht, Holland: D. Reidel Publishing Company, 1982), esp. 89–91.

43. George Devereux, "Mohave Indian Infanticide," The *Psychoanalytic Review 35* (2, 1948): 126–139, esp. 127.

44. Glanville Williams, *The Sanctity of Life and Criminal Law* (New York: Knopf, 1957), p. 14.

45. Peter C. Hoffer and N. E. H. Hull, *Murdering Mothers; Infanticide in England and New England 1558–1803* (New York: New York University Press, 1981).

46. Rafael Karsten, *The Toba Indians of the Bolivian Gran Chaco* (Oosterhout N. B., The Netherlands: Anthropological Publications, 1967 [1923]), pp. 24–25; thanks to Beth Ann Conklin for providing me with this reference.

47. Hans Becher, *Die Surara und Pakidai, swei Yanonami Stamme in Nordwestbrasilien* (Hamburg: Mirseum fur Voklerkinde, Mitteilunger 26, 1960).

48. Clelland S. Ford, *A Comparative Study of Human Reproduction* (New Haven: Human Relations Area Files Press, 1964), p. 77.

49. Clelland S. Ford, *Field Guide to the Study of Human Reproduction* (New Haven: Human Relations Area Files Press, 1964).

50. O. Wiedfeldt, "Wirtschaftliche, rechtliche, und soziale Grandtatsachen und Grandformen der Atayalen auf Formosa," *Deutsche Geselschaft fur Natur—und Volkerkunde Ostasiens*, Witteilungen 15 (Teil C, 1914): 1–55, esp. 23.

51. Asen Balicki, "Female Infanticide on the Arctic Coast," *Man 2* (1967): 615–25, esp. 619.

52. Devereux 1955, p. 232; Mead and Newton, p. 154; and Gerald T. Perkoff, "Toward a Normative Definition of Personhood," in *Abortion and the Status of the Fetus*, ed. William B. Bondeson et al. (Dordrecht, Holland: D. Reidel Publishing Company, 1983), 159–166, esp. 162.

53. James Mooney and Frans M. Olbrechts, "The Swimmer Manuscript: Cherokee Sacred Formulas and Medicinal Prescriptions," *Smithsonian Institution Bureau of American Ethnology 99* (1932): 127.

54. Nancy Scheper-Hughes, "Culture, Scarcity and Maternal Thinking: Maternal Detachment and Infant Survival in a Brazilian Shantytown," *Ethos 13* (1985): 291–317, esp. 312.

55. Scheper-Hughes, p. 292.

56. Lois McCloskey, School of Public Health, University of California, Los Angeles, personal communication.

57. Rattray, p. 61.

58. Jean Comaroff, "Medicine: Symbol and Ideology," in *The Problem of Medical Knowledge*, eds. P. Wright and A. Treacher (Edinburgh: Edinburgh University Press, 1982), 49–68, esp. 52.

59. La Fontaine, p. 132.

60. See Whitbeck, 1983.

61. Kristin Luker, *Abortion and the Politics of Motherhood* (Berkeley: University of California Press, 1984).

62. Petchesky, Rosalind P., *Abortion and Women's Choice: The State, Sexuality and Reproductive Freedom* (Boston: Northeastern University Press, 1985).

63. Maria W. Piers, *Infanticide* (New York: W. W. Norton & Company, 1978).

64. Piers, p. 51.

65. Devereux, 1955, pp. 58, 248.

66. Devereux, 1955, p. 188.

67. La Fontaine, 1985, p. 129.

REFERENCES

Aries, Philippe. 1962. *Centuries of Childhood*. New York: Vintage Books.

Armstrong, David. 1986. "The Invention of Infant Mortality," *Sociology of Health and Illness* 8: 211–232.

Balicki, Asen. 1967. "Female Infanticide on the Arctic Coast," *Man 2*: 615–25.

Becher, Hans. 1960. *Die Surara und Pakidai, swei Yanonami Stamme in Nordwestbrasilien*. Hamburg: Mirseum fur Voklerkinde, Mitteilunger 26.

Brandes, Stanley H. 1985. *Forty: The Age and the Symbol*. Knoxville: University of Tennessee Press.

Callahan, Daniel. 1986. "How Technology Is Reframing the Abortion Debate," *Hastings Center Report* (February 1986): 33–42.

Clarke, Edith. 1930. "The Sociological Significance of Ancestor Worship in Ashanti," *Africa 3*: 431–470.

Comaroff, Jean. 1982. "Medicine: Symbol and Ideology," in *The Problem of Medical Knowledge*, eds. P. Wright and A. Treacher. Edinburgh: Edinburgh University Press, pp. 49–68.

Devereux, George. 1948. "Mohave Indian Infanticide," The *Psychoanalytic Review 35* (2): 126–139.

Engelhardt, H. Tristram, Jr. 1983. "Viability and the Use of the Fetus," in *Abortion and the Status of the Fetus*, eds. William B. Bondeson et al. Dordrecht, Holland: D. Reidel, pp. 183–208.

Evans-Pritchard, E. E. 1956. *Nuer Religion*. Oxford: Clarendon Press.

Ford, Clelland S. 1952. "Control of Contraception in Cross-Cultural Perspective, "*Annals of the New York Academy of Sciences 54*: 763–768; cited in Mildred Dickeman, "Demographic Consequences of Infanticide in Man," *Annual Review of Ecology and Systematics 6* (1975): 107–137.

Ford, Clelland S. 1964. *A Comparative Study of Human Reproduction*. New Haven: Human Relations Area Files Press.

Ford, Clelland S. 1964. *Field Guide to the Study of Human Reproduction*. New Haven: Human Relations Area Files Press.

Fortes, Meyer. 1949. *The Web of Kinship Among the Tallensi: The Second Part of an Analysis of the Social Structure of a Trans-Volta Tribe*. London: Oxford University Press.

Fortes, Meyer. 1973. "On the Concept of the Person Among the Tallensi," in *La Notion de la Personne en Afrique Noire*, ed. G. Dieterlen. Paris: Editions du Centre National de la Recherche Scientifique.

Geertz, Clifford. 1973. *The Interpretation of Cultures*. New York: Basic.

Gifford, E. W. 1937. "Northeastern and Western Yavapai," *University of California Publications in American Archaeology and Ethnology 34*: 247–354.

Gladwin, Thomas, and Seymour B. Sarason. 1953. *Truk: A Man in Paradise*. New York: Wenner-Gren Foundation, p. 133; quoted in George Devereux, 1955. *A Study of Abortion in Primitive Societies*. New York: International University Press, p. 344.

Hanks, Jane Richardson. 1963. *Maternity and Its Rituals in Bang Chan*. Ithaca: Cornell Thailand Project.

Hilger, M. Inez. 1957. *Araucanian Child Life and Its Cultural Background*. Washington, D.C.: Smithsonian Miscellaneous Collections, Volume 133.

Hoffer, Peter C., and N. E. H. Hull, 1981. *Murdering Mothers; Infanticide in England and New England 1558–1803*. New York: New York University Press.

Holmberg, Allan R. 1969. *Nomads of the Long Bow*. New York: Natural History Press.

Jocando, J. Landa. 1969. *Growing Up in a Philippine Barrio*. New York: Holt, Rinehart and Winston.

Karsten, Rafael. 1967 [1923]. *The Toba Indians of the Bolivian Gran Chaco*. Oosterhout N.B., The Netherlands: Anthropological Publications, pp. 24–25.

Kaye, Barrington. 1962. *Bringing Up Children in Ghana*. London: George Allen & Unwin.

Kerr, Peter. 1986. "Groups Faults City Policy on Burial of Poor Infants," *New York Times* (May 25), p. 30.

Kidd, Dudley. 1906. *Savage Childhood: A Study of Kaffir Children*. London: Adam and Charles Black.

Knutson, Andie L. 1967. "The Definition and Value of a New Human Life," *Social Science & Medicine* 1: 7–29.

Kovit, Leonard. 1978. "Babies as Social Products: The Social Determinants of Classification," *Social Science & Medicine* 12: 347–351.

La Fontaine, J. S. 1985. "Person and Individual: Some Anthropological Reflections," in *The Category of the Person*, eds. M. Carrithers, S. Collins, and S. Luke. Cambridge: Cambridge University Press, pp. 123–140.

Luker, Kristin. 1984. *Abortion and the Politics of Motherhood*. Berkeley: University of California Press.

Mandelbaum, David G. Department of Anthropology, University of California, Berkeley, personal communication.

Mauss, Marcel. 1985. "A Category of the Human Mind: The Notion of Person, The Notion of Self," in *The Category of the Person*, eds. M. Carrithers, S. Collins, and S. Luke. Cambridge: Cambridge University Press, pp. 1–25.

McCloskey, Lois. School of Public Health, University of California, Los Angeles, personal communication.

Mead, Margaret. 1928. *Coming of Age in Samoa*. New York: American Museum of Natural History.

Mead, Margaret, and Niles Newton. 1967. "Cultural Patterning of Perinatal Behavior," in *Childbearing: Its Social and Psychological Aspects*, eds. S. A. Richardson and A. F. Guttmacher. New York: Williams and Wilkins, p. 153.

Montague, Ashley. 1974. *Coming Into Being Among the Australian Aborigines*. London: Routledge & Kegan Paul.

Mooney, James, and Frans M. Olbrechts. 1932. "The Swimmer Manuscript: Cherokee Sacred Formulas and Medicinal Prescriptions," *Smithsonian Institution Bureau of American Ethnology* 99: 127.

Osgood, Cornelius. 1951. *The Koreans and Their Culture*. New York: Ronald Press.

Ovens, J. G. 1982. "Natal Ceremonies of the Hopi Indians," *Journal of American Ethnology and Archaeology* 2: 163–175.

Perkoff, Gerald T. 1983. "Toward a Normative Definition of Personhood," in *Abortion and the Status of the Fetus*, eds. William B. Bondeson et al. Dordrecht, Holland: D. Reidel, pp. 159–166.

Petchesky, Rosalind P. 1985. *Abortion and Women's Choice: The State, Sexuality and Reproductive Freedom*. Boston: Northeastern University Press.

Piers, Maria W. 1978. *Infanticide*. New York: Norton.

Rattray, Robert S. 1927. *Religion and Art Among the Ashanti*. Oxford: Clarendon Press.

Sargent, Carolyn Fishel. 1982. *The Cultural Context of Therapeutic Choice*. Dordrecht, Holland: D. Reidel.

Scheper-Hughes, Nancy. 1985. "Culture, Scarcity and Maternal Thinking: Maternal Detachment and Infant Survival in a Brazilian Shantytown," *Ethos* 13: 291–317.

Stevenson, Tilly E. 1883–84. "The Religious Life of a Zuni Child," *Fifth Annual Report of the Bureau of Ethnology*: 539–555.

Tooley, Michael. 1972. "Abortion and Infanticide," *Philosophy and Public Affairs* 2: 37–65.

Turner, Victor. 1964. "Betwixt and Between: The Liminal Period in Rites of Passage," in *Symposium on New Approaches to the Study of Religion*, ed. J. Helm. Seattle: American Ethnological Society, p. 5.

United States Senate Subcommittee on Separation of Powers. (1981). *Report to the Committee on the Judiciary*. The Human Life Bill—S. 158. 97th Congress. Washington, D.C.: U.S. Government Printing Office, p. 12.

Van Gennep, Arnold. 1960 [1908]. *The Rites of Passage*. Chicago: University of Chicago Press.

Whitbeck, Caroline. 1983. "The Moral Implications of Regarding Women as People: New Perspectives on Pregnancy and Personhood," in *Abortion and the Status of the Fetus*, eds. William B. Bondeson et al. Dordrecht, Holland: D. Reidel, pp. 247–272.

Wiedfeldt, O. 1914. "Wirtschaftliche, rechtliche, und soziale Grandtatsachen und Grandformen der Atayalen auf Formosa," *Deutsche Geselschaft fur Natur—und Volkerkunde Ostasiens, Witteilungen* 15 (Teil C., 1914): 1–55.

Williams, Glanville. 1957. *The Sanctity of Life and Criminal Law*. New York: Knopf.

3

Language and Communication

One of the things that people spend a great deal of time doing is talking to one another. The reason they do so is simple—they have a great deal to communicate. For one thing, as social creatures, they need to let one another know how they are feeling and what they are up to at a given moment. People do this so that they can adjust their behavior in appropriate ways so as not to antagonize one another or operate at cross purposes. For another, because people rely so heavily for their survival on the learned body of knowledge we call culture, there is an extraordinary amount of information that must be passed from one person to another and from one generation to the next. Of course, humans are not alone in their need to communicate, nor are they the only animals for whom learning plays an important role in their survival. For example, in the past few decades, studies of both captive and free-living monkeys and apes have shown the importance of learned behavior in their lives and revealed unsuspected communicative abilities among them. Indeed, so highly developed are these abilities that several captive apes have been taught to converse with humans using such systems as American Sign Language; some have even taught this to others of their kind. Yet, the sheer complexity of what humans must learn in order to function on an adequate level requires some means of **communication** surpassing those normally used by monkeys and apes. Although these primates can be taught to "talk" in a variety of nonverbal ways, they do not normally do so on their own. Humans, by contrast, are "programmed" by their biology to talk, and it is virtually impossible to prevent them from doing so. All normal individuals, growing up in appropriate social environments, will learn to talk at the proper time; precisely which language they learn to speak depends upon the one spoken by the people among whom they live.

Although **language**—a system of sounds that, when put together according to certain rules, conveys meanings intelligible to all its speakers—is the primary means by which humans communicate, it is not their sole means of communication. Two others that accompany language are **paralanguage**, a system of extralinguistic noises that have meaning, and **kinesics**, a system of body motions used to convey messages. Both represent survivals of systems relied upon heavily by other primates, such as monkeys and apes, to communicate their current states of being (contented, irritated, uncomfortable, sleepy, restless, and so forth) as well as their immediate intentions. Among humans, kinesics, or "body language," has received a good deal of attention and even popular interest. Paralanguage has received less attention despite our awareness of its importance, as signified by the phrase "It's not so much what she said but how she said it." As anthropologists William O'Barr and John Conley point out, in courtroom proceedings, *how* things are said are often more important than *what* is said.

Naturally enough, because humans rely primarily on language to communicate their hopes and aspirations, their upsets and concerns, and to transmit their accumulated wisdom from one generation to the next, specialists in the field of **linguistic anthropology** have devoted a great deal of time to its study. Besides their analyses of the structure of languages (**structural linguistics**) and their historical development (**historical linguistics**), they have investigated the important relation between language and culture; for instance, how social **variables** such as class, gender, and status of the speaker will influence his or her use of a language (**sociolinguistics**). Such interests are represented in this chapter by educator Dorothy Seymour, who looks at the nature of so-called Black English. The importance of such studies is indicated by Seymour's demonstration that Black English is not the "defective" version of Standard English it is all too often taken to be but shows the same sort of structure exhibited by any fully developed language. To be properly understood, like any language, it must be examined in its historical and social context.

The example of Black English serves to introduce another important point: Besides enabling us to communicate with one another, language also serves other important purposes. For one thing, it establishes boundaries between **social groups**, the members of which speak different languages or dialects of a particular language. Conversely, the imposition of one group's language or dialect upon another group has served as a means by which one people has asserted its dominance over another. The importance of language as an ethnic marker cannot be overestimated and raises important issues of human rights. The fact is, to deprive a people of their language does more than rob them of their identity, for a people's language is uniquely tailored to express their particular culture's view of the world and facilitate their customary ways of thinking. These issues are discussed by the Mexican scholar Rodolfo Stavenhagen, excerpted from a presentation at a 1989 Geneva seminar organized by the United Nations Centre for Human Rights.

Language and Social Identity

Rodolfo Stavenhagen

Rodolfo Stavenhagen, who has an international reputation as a development anthropologist, is on the faculty of El Colegio de Mexico. He is also coordinator of the United Nations university project on ethnic minorities and human and social development.

Languages shape culture and society in many important ways. They are, for example, the vehicles for literary and poetic expressions, the instruments whereby oral history, myths and beliefs are shared by a community, and transmitted from generation to generation. Just as an Indian without land is a dead Indian (as the World Council of Indigenous Peoples states), so also an ethnic community without a language is a dying community. This was well understood by the romantic nationalists of the 19th and 20th centuries who strove for a revival of "national" languages as part of the politics of nationalism.

On the other hand, language has always been an instrument of conquest and empire. Nebrija, a 15th century Castillian grammarian and adviser to Queen Isabella I of Spain, published his Spanish grammar the same year Columbus reached America, and he advised his queen to use the language as an instrument for the good government of the empire. Both the Spanish Crown and the Church took the advice to heart—and Spanish became one of the universal languages of the modern world. So did English, of course, for the British Empire knew well the power of the word as an instrument of world power.

In the process of colonization, the languages of the colonized peoples—especially if unwritten—were usually downgraded to mere "dialects," a term which connotes something less than a full-fledged structured language, and therefore casts doubt on the status of the culture which uses it. Thus indigenous and tribal peoples are still widely considered today to speak only dialects and not languages—a position frequently shared by government bureaucrats.

This is, of course, linguistic nonsense, but it carries a political message. As some anonymous wit has expressed it: a language is a dialect with an army. Or, to put it in another way, a dominant group is able to impose its language on subordinate groups. Linguistic dominance is more often than not an expression of political and economic domination. To be sure, there are exceptions: in Africa, Asia and the Caribbean, there are a number of *linguae francae*, vehicular languages used for trade and commerce which do not necessarily denote political domination.

In the predominant statist view, stressing national unity, assimilation and development, the languages of indigenous and tribal peoples have usually been destined to disappear. Government policies have generally been designed to help this process along. In most countries, indigenous languages are not given legal recognition, are not used in official administrative and judicial dealings, and are not taught in schools. The people who do use them are discriminated against and treated by the nonindigenous as outsiders, foreigners, barbarians, primitives, and so on.

Very often, the men of a tribe or indigenous community, who move around in the outside world for economic reasons, learn the official or national language of a country and become bilingual. Women tend to be more monolingual, which increases their isolation and the discrimination which they suffer. Small children, before school age, speak the maternal language—but often, as soon as they start school, are not allowed to speak it in class. Observers have noted that this can create serious psychological and learning problems among the school-age children of many indigenous and tribal peoples. Indeed because of language and other forms of discrimination, families sometimes avoid sending their children to official or missionary schools at all.

A United Nations examination of language practices noted that the policies followed by a great many governments were based on earlier assumptions that "indigenous populations, cultures and languages would disappear naturally or by absorption into other segments of

"Language and Social Identity" by Rodolfo Stavenhagen, from United Nations *Work in Progress*, Vol. 13, No. 2, December 1990.

the population and the national culture." Now, however, judging by their effects, such policies are beginning to be recognized as not well-grounded; public schooling directed toward the achievement of these policies has been severely questioned.

As a result of policies of persecution and general attitudes of discrimination against them, many indigenous peoples have internalized the negative attitudes of the dominant society against their languages and cultures. Particularly when they leave their communities, they tend to deny their identity and feel ashamed of being "aboriginal, or "native" or "primitive."

But hiding an identity is not always possible, given that many ethnic and cultural differences are accompanied by biological distinctions. This has been particularly the case in European settler societies where the biological differences between the upper classes and the indigenous populations are particularly visible. It is less so in societies which have undergone a process of racial intermarriage and mixing, as in many Asian and Latin American countries.

In recent years, indigenous and tribal peoples have begun to resist the forced disappearance of their languages and cultures. And there has been a slow but growing awareness among social scientists, humanists, educators and even politicians that the maintenance of indigenous languages within the concept of cultural pluralism is not necessarily undesirable for a given country.

One of the questions being debated currently among linguistic specialists is whether language rights should be considered human rights. Article 27 of the International Covenant on Civil and Political Rights establishes that persons belonging to ethnic, religious or linguistic minorities shall not be denied the right to use their own language. However, organizations of indigenous peoples around the world refuse to be categorized among "ethnic minorities." This is one of the reasons why a specific declaration of indigenous rights is being prepared in the specialized UN bodies.

Language rights certainly seem to be a major issue among indigenous organizations. At the regional level, for example, periodic inter-American indigenist congresses (which are affiliated with the Organization of American States) have reaffirmed for several years the linguistic rights of the indigenous populations in the Western Hemisphere. UNESCO has also underlined the importance of the use of vernacular languages as an integral part of the cultural policies of states, particularly as regards education for minority groups. A number of countries have recently changed their traditional postures of discrimination against, and the neglect of, indigenous and tribal minority languages, and have designed policies to protect and promote these languages.

In a number of countries, indigenous organizations—and sometimes sympathetic governments—are experimenting with new linguistic and educational policies which take indigenous claims into account. In order to teach the vernacular language, however, many unwritten indigenous languages have had to be turned into written tongues. Alphabets have had to be prepared; educational materials in the vernacular have had to be provided, and teachers have had to be trained.

But this can be a lengthy and complicated process, and among educators and government officials the debates continue as to the relative merits of one or another kind of educational system—monolingual or multilingual. In countries where there exist myriad small indigenous linguistic groups, governments argue that such educational innovations are costly and basically inefficient. In addition, it is often feared that fragmenting the educational systems along linguistic lines is a potential threat to national unity. In these countries, if a majority national language exists, government policy tends to favour teaching only the national or official language.

In other countries, where the indigenous communities are large—and particularly if they have a certain amount of political clout—the education in indigenous languages is more likely to become accepted. In most countries where indigenous language schooling is taking root, bilingual education tends to be the norm. The indigenous language is taught together with the official or national language.

Just what the pedagogical mix between the various languages is depends on local conditions. Some authors consider formal schooling in an indigenous language as merely a step towards the appropriation of the official or national language. Others consider it as an end in itself—which is what the indigenous peoples themselves claim. In most countries, the teaching of an indigenous language is carried out only at the lower levels of elementary schooling. In others it also covers up through secondary levels and higher technical schools.

A linked, but much more complicated, educational problem is making bilingual schooling truly bicultural or intercultural. School children in urban industrial environments formally learn about their own larger "national" culture. Children in indigenous schools must take the reverse path: learning about their own particular cultures and identities, along with what they are taught about their "total society." This poses a formidable task for educational planners as to curriculum development, preparation of textbooks, reading and audio-visual materials, and so forth.

Indigenous peoples have been claiming the right to establish and control their own educational institutions, which means exercising control over their own curriculum, and educational contents. In some countries this is being achieved, and, in many areas, interesting educational experiments are taking place. In other countries—and particularly in the poorer third world countries—this must be the government's responsibility. But, as I have noted, governments are not always eager to undertake such innovation, particularly because they have been identified so long with assimilationist approaches.

The individual human rights spelled out in the Universal Declaration of Human Rights are now, forty years after their proclamation, generally accepted as international *customary* law. Obviously, indigenous peoples enjoy these same rights. There is a growing consensus, however, that the various international human rights instruments are not enough to guarantee the survival and protection of indigenous peoples around the world—particularly in the face of accelerated economic, social and cultural change. Thus the need for the definition of *collective* economic, social and cultural human rights is now becoming increasingly recognized.

When a Juror Watches a Lawyer

William M. O'Barr and John M. Conley

William M. O'Barr has a joint professorship in the departments of cultural anthropology and sociology at Duke University and is adjunct professor of law at the University of North Carolina. He received his Ph.D. from Northwestern University in 1969. His research has involved peoples of Africa as well as the United States, and his interests include legal anthropology, sociolinguistics, and discourse analysis. He also researches the anthropology of advertising.

John M. Conley is a professor of law at the University of North Carolina where he currently holds the Ivey Research Chair. He is also an adjunct professor in anthropology at Duke and practiced trial law for a number of years. His recent book, *Fortune and Folly*, is an anthropological look at institutional investors on Wall Street. Conley received his J.D. from Duke in 1977 and his Ph.D. in anthropology from Duke in 1980.

How things are said in court, as any successful trial lawyer knows, may be much more important than what is actually said.

Not only in the court, but in our everyday language, all of us have an intuitive notion that subtle differences in the language we use can communicate more than the obvious surface meaning. These additional communication cues, in turn, greatly influence the way our spoken thoughts are understood and interpreted. Some differences in courtroom language may be so subtle as to defy precise description by all but those trained in linguistic analysis. No linguistic training is necessary, however, to sense the difference between an effective and an ineffective presentation by a lawyer, a strong and a weak witness or a hostile versus a friendly exchange. New research on language used in trial courtrooms reveals that the subliminal messages communicated by seemingly minor differences in phraseology, tempo, length of answers and the like may be far more important than even the most perceptive lawyers have realized.

Two witnesses who are asked identical questions by the same lawyer are not likely to respond in the same way. Differences in manner of speaking, however, are usually overlooked by the court in its fact-finding quest. Once an initial determination of admissibility has been made, witnesses may follow their own stylistic inclinations within the broad bounds of the law of evidence.

"When a Juror Watches a Lawyer" by William M. O'Barr and John M. Conley, from *Barrister*. Reprinted with permission.

Scrutinize carefully the following pairs of excerpts from trial transcripts, and consider whether, as the law of evidence would hold, they are equivalent presentations of facts.

EXAMPLE 1

Q. What was the nature of your acquaintance with her?
A_1. We were, uh, very close friends. Uh, she was even sort of like a mother to me.
A_2. We were very close friends. She was like a mother to me.

EXAMPLE 2

Q. Now, calling your attention to the 21st day of November, a Saturday, what were your working hours?
A. Well, I was working from, uh, 7 a.m. to 3 p.m. I arrived at the store at 6:30 and opened the store at 7.

Compare this answer to the following exchange ensuing from the same question.

A. Well, I was working from 7 to 3.
Q. Was that 7 a.m.?
A. Yes.
Q. And what time that day did you arrive at the store?
A. 6:30.
Q. 6:30. And did, uh, you open the store at 7 o'clock?
A. Yes, it has to be opened.

EXAMPLE 3

Q. Now, what did she tell you that would indicate to you that she . . .
A. (interrupting) She told me a long time ago that if she called, and I knew there was trouble, to definitely call the police right away.

Compare the above with the slightly different version, where the lawyer completes his question before the witness begins answering.

Q. Now, what did she tell you that would indicate to you that she needed help?

A. She told me a long time ago that if she called, and I knew there was trouble, to definitely call the police right away.

Two years of study of language variation in a North Carolina trial courtroom, sponsored by the National Science Foundation, have led us to conclude that differences as subtle as these carry an impact which is probably as substantial as the factual variation with which lawyers have traditionally concerned themselves.

POWER LANGUAGE AND GETTING POINTS ACROSS

The three examples of differences in testimony shown here are drawn from separate experiments which the team has conducted. The study from which Example 1 is taken was inspired by the work of Robin Lakoff, a linguist from the University of California at Berkeley.

Lakoff maintains that certain distinctive attributes mark female speech as different and distinct from male styles. Among the characteristics she notes in "women's language" are:

- a high frequency of *hedges* ("I think . . . , it seems like . . . ." "Perhaps . . . ." "If I'm not mistaken . . .");

- *rising intonation* in declarative statements (e.g., in answer to a question about the speed at which a car was going, "Thirty, thirty-five?" said with rising intonation as though seeking approval of the questioner);

- *repetition* indicating insecurity;

- *intensifiers* ("very close friends" instead of "close friends" or just "friends");

- high frequency of *direct quotations* indicating deference to authority, and so on.

We studied our trial tapes from the perspective of Lakoff's theory and found that the speech of many of the female witnesses was indeed characterized by a high frequency of the features she attributes to women's language. When we discovered that some male witnesses also made significant use of this style of speaking, we developed what we called a "power language" continuum. From powerless speech (having the characteristics listed above), this continuum ranged to relatively more powerful speech (lacking the characteristics described by Lakoff).

Our experiment is based on an actual ten-minute segment of a trial in which a prosecution witness under direct examination gave her testimony in a relatively "powerless" mode. We rewrote the script, removing most of the hedges, correcting intonation to a more standard declarative manner, minimizing repetition and intensifiers, and otherwise transforming the testimony to a more "powerful" mode.

From the point of view of the "facts" contained in the two versions, a court would probably consider the two modes equivalent. Despite this factual similarity, the experimental subjects found the two witnesses markedly different. The subjects rated the witness speaking in the powerless style significantly less favorably in terms of such evaluative characteristics as believability, intelligence, competence, likability and assertiveness.

To determine whether the same effects would carry over for a male witness speaking in "power" and "powerless" modes, we took the same script, made minor adjustments for sex of witness, and produced two more experimental tapes. As with females, subjects were less favorably disposed toward a male speaking in the powerless mode.

These results confirm the general proposition that how a witness gives testimony may indeed alter the reception it gets. Since most juries are assigned the task of deciding upon relative credibility of witnesses whose various pieces of testimony are not entirely consistent, speech factors which may affect a witness' credibility may be critical factors in the overall chemistry of the trial courtrooms.

These findings are not limited to a single study. Similar patterns have been discovered with other kinds of variation in presentational style.

Example 2 comes from a study of differences in the length of answers which a witness gives in the courtroom. Treatises on trial practice often advise allowing the witness to assume as much control over his testimony as possible during direct examination. Implicit in such advice is an hypothesis that relative control of the questioning and answering by lawyer versus witness may affect perception of the testimony itself.

To test this hypothesis we again selected a segment of testimony from an actual trial. The original testimony was rewritten so that, in one version, the witness gave short attenuated answers to the lawyer's probing questions. In the other version, the same facts were given by the witness in the form of longer, more complex answers to fewer questions by the lawyer.

BUT THEN, HOW LONG SHOULD A WITNESS SPEAK?

Contrary to our expectations, the form of answer did not affect the subjects' perception of the *witness*, but it did have a significant influence on the judgments about the *lawyer*. When the lawyer asked more questions to get the same information, subjects viewed him as more manipulative and allowing the witness less opportunity to present evidence.

The subjects' perceptions of the lawyer's opinion of his witness were also colored by the structure of the witness' answers; however, the differences were significant only when the witnesses were male. When more questions were asked by the lawyer, subjects believed the lawyer thought his witness was significantly less intelligent, less competent and less assertive.

On this point, then, standard trial practice theory is confirmed indirectly. The lawyer who finds it necessary to exert tight control over his witness will hurt his presentation by creating a less favorable impression of himself and suggesting that he has little confidence in the witness.

A LOT DEPENDS ON WHO INTERRUPTS WHOM

Example 3 is part of a study of interruptions and simultaneous talk in the courtroom. We wanted to know what effect a lawyer's interrupting a witness or a witness' interrupting a lawyer would have. Preparing a witness for a courtroom examination often includes an admonishment against arguing with the opposition lawyer during cross-examination, and a lawyer often advises his own witness to stop talking when he interrupts what the witness is saying.

To study some aspects of this complex phenomenon, we focused on the relative tendency of the lawyer and the witness to persist in speaking when the other party interrupts or begins to speak at the same time. This is one of the most subtle factors of language variation in the courtroom which we have studied, but, like the other differences, this too alters perception of testimony.

Working from the same original testimony, four experimental tapes were prepared: one in which there were no instances of simultaneous talk by lawyer and witness, one in which the witness primarily yielded to the lawyer during simultaneous talk by breaking off before completion of his statement, one in which the lawyer deferred to the witness by allowing the witness to talk whenever both began to talk at once, and finally one in which the frequency of deference by lawyer and witness to one another were about equal.

All four tapes are clearly "hostile" and "unfriendly" in tone. The three containing simultaneous speech, or overlaps between lawyer and witness, would be difficult to distinguish by a person untrained in linguistic analysis of sequencing of questions and answers. Yet these subtle differences in patterns of deference in overlapping speech can be and are perceived differently by experimental subjects.

Findings from this study, like those from the second experiment, show significant effects on the perception of the lawyer. Subject-jurors rate the lawyer as maintaining most control when no overlapping speech occurs. The lawyer's control over the examination of the witness is perceived to diminish in all those situations where both lawyer and witness talk at once.

Comparing the situation in which the lawyer persists to the one in which the witness persists, interesting results also emerge. When the lawyer persists, he is viewed not only as less fair to the witness but also as less intelligent than in the situation when the witness continues. The lawyer who stops in order to allow the witness to speak is perceived as allowing the witness significantly more opportunity to present his testimony in full.

The second and third experiments thus show speech style affecting perceptions of lawyers in critical ways. Modes of speaking which create negative impressions of lawyers may have severe consequences in the trial courtroom. In all adversarial proceedings, lawyers assume the role of spokesmen for their clients. Impressions formed about lawyers are, to some degree, also impressions formed about those whom they represent.

The implications of these findings may be most severe in those criminal trials where the defendants elect not to testify, but they apply as well to all situations where lawyers act as representatives of their clients.

THE FACT IS: A FACT MAY BE MORE THAN A FACT

While the results of these particular experiments are undoubtedly important for the practicing lawyer, we feel that the true significance of the project lies in its broader implications. In a variety of settings, we have shown that lay audiences pay meticulous attention, whether consciously or unconsciously, to subtle details of the language used in the trial courtroom.

Our results suggest that a fact is not just a fact, regardless of presentations; rather, the facts are only one of many important considerations which are capable of influencing the jury.

As noted earlier, the law of evidence has traditionally concerned itself primarily with threshold questions of admissibility. The guiding principles have always been held to be ensuring the reliability of evidence admitted and preventing undue prejudice to the litigants. If it is true that questions of style have impact comparable to that of questions of fact, then lawyers will have to begin to read such considerations into the law of evidence if they are to be faithful to its principles.

As judges and lawyers become increasingly sensitized to the potentially prejudicial effects of speech style, one remedy might be to employ cautionary instructions in an effort to control jury reactions. For example, might it not be appropriate for a court confronted with a witness speaking in an extreme variant of the powerless mode to instruct the jury not to be swayed by style in considering the facts?

Additionally, lawyers themselves might begin to give greater recognition to stylistic factors while addressing the jury during voire dire, opening statement and closing argument.

Lawyers are already accustomed to calling jurors' attention to such presentational features as extreme emotion in urging on them particular interpretations of the evidence. What we suggest is merely an extension of a familiar technique into newly explored areas. . . .

REFERENCES

Lakoff, Robin T. 1976. *Language and Woman's Place*. New York: Octagon Books.

Lakoff, Robin T. 1990. *Talking Power: The Politics of Language in Our Lives*. New York: Basic Books.

Black Children, Black Speech

Dorothy Z. Seymour

Dorothy Z. Seymour received an M.A. in 1952 from Case Western Reserve and then did further graduate study. Her early interest was in using linguistics to facilitate her work as a reading instructor to elementary school students for seventeen years. Now she is a writer, literary agent, and senior editor for Stillpoint Publishing in Walpole, New Hampshire.

"Cmon, man, les git goin'" called the boy to his companion. "Dat bell ringin'. It say, 'Git in rat now!'" He dashed into the school yard.

"Aw, f'get you," replied the other. "Whe' Richuh? Whe' da' muvvuh? He be goin' to schoo'."

"He in de' now, man!" was the answer as they went through the door.

In the classroom they made for their desks and opened their books. The name of the story they tried to read was "Come." It went:

Come, Bill, come
Come with me.
Come and see this.
See what is here.

The first boy poked the second. "Wha' da' wor'?"

"Da' wor' *is*, you dope."

"*Is*? Ain't no wor' *is*. You jivin' me? Wha' da' wor' mean?"

"Ah dunno. Jus' *is*."

To a speaker of Standard English, this exchange is only vaguely comprehensible. But it's normal speech for thousands of American children. In addition it demonstrates one of our biggest educational problems: children whose speech style is so different from the writing style of their books that they have difficulty learning to read. These children speak Black English, a dialect characteristic of many inner-city Negroes. Their books are, of course, written in Standard English. To complicate matters, the speech they use is also socially stigmatized. Middle-class whites and Negroes alike scorn it as low-class poor people's talk.

"Black Children, Black Speech" by Dorothy Z. Seymour, from *Commonweal*, 1972. Reprinted with permission.

Teachers sometimes make the situation worse with their attitudes toward Black English. Typically, they view the children's speech as "bad English" characterized by "lazy pronunciation," "poor grammar," and "short jagged words." One result of this attitude is poor mental health on the part of the pupils. A child is quick to grasp the feeling that while school speech is "good," his own speech is "bad," and that by extension he himself is somehow inadequate and without value. Some children react to this feeling by withdrawing; they stop talking entirely. Others develop the attitude of "F'get you, honky." In either case, the psychological results are devastating and lead straight to the dropout route.

It is hard for most teachers and middle-class Negro parents to accept the idea that Black English is not just "sloppy talk" but a dialect with a form and structure of its own. Even some eminent black educators think of it as "bad English grammar" with "slurred consonants" (Professor Nick Aaron Ford of Morgan State College in Baltimore) and "ghettoese" (Dr. Kenneth B. Clark, the prominent educational psychologist).

Parents of Negro school children generally agree. Two researchers of Columbia University report that the adults they worked with in Harlem almost unanimously preferred that their children be taught Standard English in school.

But there is another point of view, one held in common by black militants and some white liberals. They urge that middle-class Negroes stop thinking of the inner-city dialect as something to be ashamed of and repudiated. Black author Claude Brown, for example, pushes this view.

Some modern linguists take a similar stance. They begin with the premise that no dialect is intrinsically "bad" or "good," and that a nonstandard speech style is not defective speech but different speech. More important, they have been able to show that Black English is far from being a careless way of speaking the Standard; instead, it is a rather rigidly constructed set of speech patterns, with the same sort of specialization in sounds, structure and vocabulary as any other dialect.

THE SOUNDS OF BLACK ENGLISH

Middle-class listeners who hear black inner-city speakers say "dis" and "tin" for "this" and "thin" assume that the black speakers are just being careless. Not at all; these differences are characteristic aspects of the dialect. The original cause of such substitutions is generally a carryover from one's original language or that of his immigrant parents. The interference from that carryover probably caused the substitution of /d/ for the voiced *th* sound in *this*, and /t/ for the unvoiced *th* sound in *thin*. (Linguists represent language sounds by putting letters within slashes or brackets.) Most speakers of English don't realize that the two *th* sounds of English are lacking in many other languages and are difficult for most foreigners trying to learn English. Germans who study English, for example, are surprised and confused about these sounds because the only Germans who use them are the ones who lisp. These two sounds are almost nonexistent in the West African languages which most black immigrants brought with them to America.

Similar substitutions used in Black English are /f/, a sound similar to the unvoiced *th*, in medial word-position, as in *birfday* for *birthday*, and in final word-position, as in *roof* for *Ruth* as well as /v/ for the voiced *th* in medial position, as in *bruvver* for *brother*. These sound substitutions are also typical of Gullah, the language of black speakers in the Carolina Sea Island. Some of them are also heard in Caribbean Creole.

Another characteristic of the sounds of Black English is the lack of /l/ at the end of words, sometimes replaced by the sound /w/. This makes words like *tool* sound like *too*. If /l/ occurs in the middle of a Standard English word, in Black English it may be omitted entirely: "I can hep you." This difference is probably caused by the instability and sometimes interchangeability of /l/ and /r/ in West African languages.

One difference that is startling to middle-class speakers is the fact that Black English words appear to leave off some consonant sounds at the end of words. Like Italian, Japanese and West African words, they are more likely to end in vowel sounds. Standard English *boot* is pronounced *boo* in Black English. *What* is *wha*. *Sure* is *sho*. *Your* is *yo*. This kind of difference can make for confusion in the classroom. Dr. Kenneth Goodman, a psycholinguist, tells of a black child whose white teacher asked him to use *so* in a sentence—not "sew a dress" but "the other *so*." The sentence the child used was "I got a *so* on my leg."

A related feature of Black English is the tendency in many cases not to use sequences of more than one final consonant sound. For example, *just* is pronounced *jus*, *past* is *pass*, *mend* sounds like *men* and *hold* like *hole*. *Six* and *box* are pronounced *sick* and *bock*. Why should this be? Perhaps because West African languages, like Japanese, have almost no clusters of consonants in their speech. The Japanese, when importing a foreign word, handle a similar problem by inserting vowel sounds between every consonant, making *baseball* sound like *besuboru*. West Africans probably made a simpler change, merely cutting a series of two consonant sounds down to one. Speakers of Gullah, one linguist found, have made the same kind of adaptation of Standard English.

Teachers of black children seldom understand the reason for these differences in final sounds. They are apt to think that careless speech is the cause. Actually, black speakers aren't "leaving off" any sounds; how can you leave off something you never had in the first place?

Differences in vowel sounds are also characteristic of the nonstandard language. Dr. Goodman reports that a black child asked his teacher how to spell rat. "R-a-t," she replied. But the boy responded "No ma'am, I don't mean rat mouse, I mean rat now." In Black English, *right* sounds like *rat*. A likely reason is that in West African languages, there are very few vowel sounds of the type heard in the word *right*. This type is common in English. It is called a glided or dipthongized vowel sound. A glided vowel sound is actually a close combination of two vowels; in the word *right* the two parts of the sound "eye" are actually "ah-ee." West African languages have no such long, two-part, changing vowel sounds; their vowels are generally shorter and more stable. This may be why in Black English, *time* sounds like *Tom*, *oil* like *all*, and *my* like *ma*.

LANGUAGE STRUCTURE

Black English differs from Standard English not only in its sounds but also in its structure. The way the words are put together does not always fit the description in English grammar books. The method of expressing time, or tense, for example, differs in significant ways.

The verb *to be* is an important one in Standard English. It's used as an auxiliary verb to indicate different tenses. But Black English speakers use it quite differently. Sometimes an inner-city Negro says "He coming"; other times he says "He be coming." These two sentences mean different things. To understand why, let's look at the tenses of West African languages; they correspond with those of Black English.

Many West African languages have a tense which is called the habitual. This tense is used to express action which is always occurring and it is formed with a verb that is translated as *be*. "He be coming" means something like "He's always coming," "He usually comes," or "He's been coming."

In Standard English there is no regular grammatical construction for such a tense. Black English speakers, in order to form the habitual tense in English, use the word *be* as an auxiliary: *He be doing it. My Momma be working. He be running.* The habitual tense is not the same as the present tense, which is constructed in Black English without any form of the verb to be: *He do it. My Momma working. He running.* (This means the action is occurring right now.)

There are other tense differences between Black English and Standard English. For example, the non-standard speech does not use changes in grammar to indicate the past tense. A white person will ask, "What did your brother say?" and the black person will answer, "He say he coming." (The verb *say* is not changed to *said*.) "How did you get here?" "I walk." This style of talking about the past is paralleled in the Yoruba, Fante, Hausa, and Ewe languages of West Africa.

Expression of plurality is another difference. The way a black child will talk of "them boy" or "two dog" makes some white listeners think Negroes don't know how to turn a singular word into a plural word. As a matter of fact, it isn't necessary to use an *s* to express plurality. In Chinese and Japanese, singular and plural are not generally distinguished by such inflections; plurality is conveyed in other ways. For example, in Chinese it's correct to say "There are three book on the table." This sentence already has two signals of the plural, *three* and *are*, why require a third? This same logic is the basis of plurals in most West African languages, where nouns are often identical in the plural and the singular. For example, in Ibo, one correctly says *those man*, and in both Ewe and Yoruba one says *they house*. American speakers of Gullah retain this style; it is correct in Gullah to say *five dog*.

Gender is another aspect of language structure where differences can be found. Speakers of Standard English are often confused to find that the nonstandard vernacular often uses just one gender of pronoun, the masculine, and refers to women as well as men as *he* or *him*. "He a nice girl," even "Him a nice girl" are common. This usage probably stems from West African origins, too, as does the use of multiple negatives, such as "Nobody don't know it."

Vocabulary is the third aspect of a person's native speech that could affect his learning of a new language. The strikingly different vocabulary often used in Negro nonstandard English is probably the most obvious aspect of it to a casual white observer. But its vocabulary differences don't obscure its meaning the way different sounds and different structure often do.

Recently there has been much interest in the African origins of words like *goober* (peanut), *cooter* (turtle), and *tote* (carry), as well as others that are less certainly African, such as *to dig* (possibly from the Wolof *degan*, "to understand"). Such expressions seem colorful rather than low-class to many whites; they become assimilated faster than their black originators do. English professors now use *dig* in their scholarly articles, and current advertising has enthusiastically adopted *rap*.

Is it really possible for old differences in sound, structure, and vocabulary to persist from the West African languages of slave days into present-day inner-city Black English? Easily. Nothing else really explains such regularity of language habits, most of which persist among black people in various parts of the Western Hemisphere. For a long time scholars believed that certain speech forms used by Negroes were merely leftovers from archaic English preserved in the speech of early English settlers in America and copied by their slaves. But this theory has been greatly weakened, largely as the result of the work of a black linguist, Dr. Lorenzo Dow Turner of the University of Chicago. Dr. Turner studied the speech of Gullah Negroes in the Sea Islands off the Carolina coast and found so many traces of West African languages that he thoroughly discredited the archaic-English theory.

When anyone learns a new language, it's usual to try speaking the new language with the sounds and structure of the old. If a person's first language does not happen to have a particular sound needed in the language he is learning, he will tend to substitute a similar or related sound from his native language and use it to speak the new one. When Frenchman Charles Boyer said "Zees ees my heart," and when Latin American Carmen Miranda sang "Souse American way," they were simply using sounds of their native languages in trying to pronounce sounds of English. West Africans must have done the same thing when they first attempted English words. The tendency to retain the structure of the native language is a strong one, too. That's why a German learning English is likely to put his verb at the end: "May I a glass beer have?" The vocabulary of one's original language may also furnish some holdovers. Jewish immigrants did not stop using the word *bagel* when they came to America; nor did Germans stop saying *sauerkraut*.

Social and geographical isolation reinforces the tendencies to retain old language habits. When one group is considered inferior, the other group avoids it. For many years it was illegal to give any sort of instruction to Negroes, and for slaves to try to speak like their masters would have been unthinkable. Conflict of value systems doubtless retards changes, too. As Frantz Fanon observed in *Black Skin, White Masks*, those who take on white speech habits are suspect in the ghetto, because others believe they are trying to "act white." Dr. Kenneth Johnson, a black linguist, put it this way: "As long as disadvantaged black children live in segregated communities and most of their relationships are confined to those within their own subculture, they will not replace their functional nonstandard dialect with the nonfunctional standard dialect."

Linguists have made it clear that language systems that are different are not necessarily deficient. A judgment of deficiency can be made only in comparison with another language system. Let's turn the tables on Standard English for a moment and look at it from the West African point of view. From this angle, Standard English: (1) is lacking in certain language sounds, (2) has a couple of unnecessary language sounds for which others may serve as good substitutes, (3) doubles and drawls some of its vowel sounds in sequences that are unusual and difficult to imitate, (4) lacks a method of forming an important tense, (5) requires an unnecessary number of ways to indicate tense, plurality and gender, and (6) doesn't mark negatives sufficiently for the result to be a good strong negative statement.

Now whose language is deficient?

How would the adoption of this point of view help us? Say we accepted the evidence that Black English is not just a sloppy Standard but an organized language style which probably has developed many of its features on the basis of its West African heritage. What would we gain?

The psychological climate of the classroom might improve if teachers understood why many black students speak as they do. But we still have not reached a solution of the main problem. Does the discovery that Black English has pattern and structure mean that it should not be tampered with? Should children who speak Black English be excused from learning the Standard in school? Should they perhaps be given books in Black English to learn from?

Any such accommodation would surely result in a hardening of the new separatism being urged by some black militants. It would probably be applauded by such people as Roy Innis, Director of C.O.R.E., who is currently recommending dual autonomous education systems for white and black. And it might facilitate learning to read, since some experiments have indicated that materials written in Black English syntax aid problem readers from the inner city.

But determined resistance to the introduction of such printed materials into schools can be expected. To those who view inner-city speech as bad English, the appearance in print of sentences like "My mama, he work" can be as shocking and repellent as a four-letter word. Middle-class Negro parents would probably mobilize against the move. Any stratagem that does not take into account such practicalities of the matter is probably doomed to failure. And besides, where would such a permissive policy on language get these children in the larger society, and in the long run? If they want to enter an integrated America they must be able to deal with it on its own terms. Even Professor Toni Cade of Rutgers, who doesn't want "ghetto accents" tampered with, advocates mastery of Standard English because, as she puts it, "if you want to get ahead in this country, you must master the language of the ruling class." This has always been true, wherever there has been a minority group.

The problem then appears to be one of giving these children the ability to speak (and read) Standard English without denigrating the vernacular and those who use it, or even affecting the ability to use it. The only way to do this is to officially espouse bidialectism. The result would be the ability to use either dialect equally well—as Dr. Martin Luther King did—depending on the time, place, and circumstances. Pupils would have to learn enough about Standard English to use it when necessary, and teachers would have to learn enough about the inner-city dialect to understand and accept it for what it is—not just a "careless" version of Standard English but a different form of English that's appropriate in certain times and places.

Can we accomplish this? If we can't, the result will be continued alienation of a large section of the population, continued dropout trouble with consequent loss of earning power and economic contribution to the nation, but most of all, loss of faith in America as a place where a minority people can at times continue to use those habits that remind them of their link with each other and with their past.

4

Culture and Personality

In 1925 a young anthropology graduate student named Margaret Mead set out for Samoa in order to test a theory widely accepted at the time: The biological changes of adolescence could not be accomplished without a great deal of psychological and social stress. Three years later, she published a book that was to become a classic, *Coming of Age in Samoa: A Study of Primitive Youth for Western Civilization*. (See "Guys and Dolls" in Chapter 7.) Although the work has been the subject of some criticism, it is generally credited as establishing culture and personality as a specialty within **cultural anthropology**. Originally concerned with the effects of different child-rearing practices on the formation of adult personalities, the specialty has since developed into the broader one of **psychological anthropology**.

Because culture is learned rather than biologically inherited, it is only natural that anthropologists should have become interested in *how* culture is learned. Initially, anthropologists thought that the different ways in which societies reared their children ought to result in adult personalities that differed in distinctive ways from one culture to another. Perhaps the most famous (and extreme) statement of this point of view was Ruth Benedict's attempt to categorize whole cultures in terms of certain personality types. In her best-selling book *Patterns of Culture*, published in 1934 (and still in print), she characterized the Kwakiutl Indians of North America's Northwest Coast as "Dionysian," the Zuni Indians of the southwestern United States as "Apollonian," and the Dobuans of New Guinea as "Paranoid." Aside from the fact that her labels reflect the biases of Western culture, what she overlooked was the range of variation to be seen in any culture. For example, to characterize the Zuni as "Apollonian," she

focused on their distrust of individualism and rejection of excess and disruptive psychological states, while ignoring such seemingly "Dionysian" practices as sword swallowing and walking over hot coals.

What we now know is that no culture can be characterized in terms of a single personality structure exhibited by all or even a majority of adults. Because each individual is born with a particular genetic potential and because no two individuals have *precisely* the same childhood experiences, as adults their personalities show considerable variability. On the other hand, it is true that each culture does hold up a particular ideal toward which individuals should aspire. Often, these are not the same for men as they are for women. Nancy Chodorow looks at the gender-related ideals of contemporary North American culture, how they are promoted, and some of the problems that ensue from this effort. Her conclusion is that significant numbers of men wind up unsure of their sexual identity and so must "prove" to themselves who they are by exaggerating approved masculine traits. The problem for women is that a more easily accepted identity is devalued, all too often leading to feelings of inferiority.

Alma Gottlieb's paper, too, focuses on the feminine "ideal" of modern North American culture. She shows how the constraints associated with this ideal, in tandem with the belief of Western culture that women have a dual nature—quiet, considerate, and "giving" on the one hand, but seductive, selfish, and capable of leading men astray on the other—predisposes women to a regular rejection of the stringent expectations placed on their behavior. What our culture has done is to take a perfectly normal occurrence in the reproductive cycle of women, menstruation, used it as an excuse for women to periodically escape the constraints of "acceptable" behavior, and labeled this an "illness." In doing so, a "guilt trip" is laid on women, pressuring them to conform to "normal" behavior. Thus, we see how illnesses are not always physical disorders but may be created by culture itself.

Given their interest in the relation between childhood experiences and personality, it was inevitable that anthropologists early on would develop an interest in **psychoanalytic theory**, with its emphasis on the importance of early childhood experiences. One problem with psychoanalytic theory, however, is that its concepts have often been based in assumptions of Western culture. Another is that, clinical studies to the contrary not withstanding, psychoanalytic theorists have done little systematic testing through recourse to cross-cultural data. Hence, many of the early culture and personality studies carried out by anthropologists were explicit tests of psychoanalytic theory. Among some anthropologists, interest in a psychoanalytic approach continues today; it is represented in this chapter by anthropologist/folklorist Alan Dundes. He sees football as a kind of ritual **homosexuality** in which sexual acts are carried out in symbolic form by males against other males. Thus, he likens the game to adolescent **male initiation rites** in many non-Western cultures that involve homosexual activity.

REFERENCES

Benedict, Ruth. 1934. *Patterns of Culture*. Boston and New York: Houghton Mifflin.

Mead, Margaret, 1928. *Coming of Age in Samoa: A Psychological Study of Primitive Youth for Western Civilization*. New York: Morrow.

American Premenstrual Syndrome

A Mute Voice

Alma Gottlieb

Alma Gottlieb is assistant professor of anthropology at the University of Illinois, Urbana–Champaign, having received her Ph.D. at the University of Virginia in 1983. She has carried out fieldwork in West Africa, and her research interests include such diverse topics as interpretive theory, religion, gender issues, kinship, and epistemology of fieldwork.

In America there is much talk these days about "premenstrual syndrome," or PMS, heralded as the most important women's health issue of the 80s (Witt 1984:27). The medical community increasingly claims PMS as a biological fact: with organic causes, it can be diagnosed and cured, especially with hormones (progesterone) (e.g., Dalton 1979). But some feminists are raising a wary eyebrow at this development, which has an eerie ring of the nineteenth century (for other critiques, see Sommer 1982, 1985; Koeske 1985; Rome 1986). Only last century a woman's entire being was seen as ruled by her uterus (Ehrenreich and English 1978). Now, women's mental states are said to be at the mercy of their hormones. Both models derive the nature of the feminine psyche from bodily processes, and both confirm what *Genesis* first proposed: that it is women's nature to suffer.

Emily Martin (1987) has recently offered a provocative analysis of American PMS along Marxist lines. She argues convincingly that the late industrial workplace, demanding of the body ever-increased work efficiency, is responsible for labelling as an illness the reduction in work energy that often accompanies the premenstrual time. PMS may well have become a means, however unconscious, whereby women rebel against excessive demands placed on them in the workplace as well as the home.

I take as a given that PMS fits into late industrial society in the ways Martin has proposed; but rather than emphasizing political and economic aspects I stress the symbolic nature of American PMS complaints in relation to accepted ideologies of the female personality.[1] I assume that there is a normative personality to which women feel they should aspire, with the construction of

"American Premenstrual Syndrome: A Mute Voice" by Alma Gottlieb, from *Anthropology Today*, Vol. 4, No. 6, 1988, Royal Anthropological Institute. Reprinted with permission.

self shaped deeply by culture (cf. Rosaldo 1984, Lutz 1986). While I acknowledge that many women do not fit or even aspire to the cultural ideal (nor is PMS experienced by all American women),[2] I suggest that individual variability does not negate the ideal.

My analysis does *not* take PMS as an "imagined" disease—as Western doctors have tended to see women's medical problems, a "case of female nerves," or something that is "all in the head" (Brown and Zimmer 1986). I accept any symptom identified by a sufferer as real enough. What I focus on is the cultural construction of such symptoms (cf. Helman 1987).

While comparative studies of the menstrual experience remain underdeveloped, there are hints that a culturally meaningful category of disease whose contours would be roughly those of PMS are absent in at least some of the world's cultures. Earlier this century Margaret Mead (1928:113) wrote that Samoan women may feel some bodily discomfort while menstruating but do not associate menstruation with other emotional changes. More recently, Marjorie Shostak has written of !Kung women that despite having hormonal cycles similar to Western women (1981:353–4),

> The !Kung did not have any expectation or belief comparable to that held in the west of a premenstrual or menstrual syndrome. Nor did they recognize any effect of the menstrual cycle on women's moods or behavior . . . They did associate physical discomfort with menstruation, especially with its onset, but this . . . was described only in practical terms, not in terms of wider psychological ramifications (1981:353).

Other societies in which the psychological component of PMS would appear unlikely to find a place include the Rungus of Borneo, the Beng of Côte d'Ivoire and the Yurok of California (Buckley and Gottlieb 1988). Because the physical changes associated with menstruation (abdominal cramps, lower back pain, etc.) appear to be very widespread if not universal, while the mood changes that are associated with PMS in America do not seem to be found cross-culturally, I focus exclusively on the psychological dimension, leaving aside as a more purely biological matter the physical discomforts.[3]

I will be deliberately vague about delimiting the duration of PMS. In varying accounts its duration has ranged in scope from one day to two weeks before the onset of menses but in any case it begins after ovulation occurs. I take "premenstrual" to encompass that amount of time that is *perceived to be relevant* by those women who report PMS symptoms. In other words, I take PMS as a native category with a great deal of flexibility in its application.

Before the current rage over PMS, it was the menstrual period itself that was blamed for the negative mood changes that we associate nowadays with PMS. Nevertheless, many women—and men—still associate menstruation itself with those negative mood changes. Thus I am really discussing "paramenstruum": the time both preceding and encompassing the menstrual period (typically lasting about ten days). But because in contemporary America "PMS" has emerged as the core term by which menstrual-related psychological distress can be explained, I echo current usage.[4]

To anticipate my analysis, I shall propose that every month the PMS sufferer inverts the explicitly valued form of feminine personality to enact its opposite. This monthly reversal is certainly disapproved of by the culture, yet it is intrinsic to Western understanding of womanhood. Together, the two extreme styles of feminine personality, as exhibited during the time preceding (and encompassing) the menstrual period and during the rest of the month, combine to produce a whole conception of femaleness that is deeply embedded in ambivalence.

Women who suffer from PMS say that they lose control, are seized with overpowering urges. What shape do these urges take? As Martin has pointed out, certain themes emerge, especially with married women, who by far predominate among PMS sufferers and are therefore the focus of this paper. Almost uniformly, these urges are seen as negative traits both by the women themselves and by the wider society (but for creative reshaping of these urges, see Martin 1987; Witt 1984:149–152; Rome 1986:146; and especially Shuttle and Redgrove 1978). The urges have been grouped by one doctor (Guy Abraham) into two clusters, "Type A" (anxiety) and "Type D" (depression) (in Trupin 1985:22), each encompassing several related symptoms. As Type A moods seem by far to predominate (Abraham's estimate is 80%), I concentrate on those.

During PMS "attacks," married women who are Type A say that they "rant and rave," especially to their families. They become angry and "lash out," particularly at their husbands but also their children. They are critical and edgy for what they, and those around them, perceive as no reason other than "the time of the month." *Irritability* and *hostility* are terms that recur in descriptions of PMS.

Let us consider the following statement by a PMS sufferer (in Witt 1984:133):

> About once a month, I'd become a different person. I would yell, pick fights, become unbelievably aggressive. It terrifies me. I don't like to think that's the way I am. I'm a nice, quiet person the rest of the month. But the days before my period I feel like a monster.

In this lament, typical of descriptions of PMS attacks, the woman reports that premenstrually she behaves in an opposite manner to how women should behave normally according to mainstream Western standards. Of what does this series of expectations consist? In the words of the woman just quoted, women are—or long to be seen as—"nice" and "quiet." Implied in "nice" is that they should be kind, considerate of others, even altruistic (Adams 1971, Bardwick and Douvan 1971). That these expectations are not merely cultural stereotypes but actively internalized is borne out by studies that show, for example, that American women smile more than men do and interrupt men more rarely than the reverse (in Anderson 1983:48; also Lakoff 1975). In the private sphere, it is women who are supposed to hold together the family, who "make the house a home" (Ehrenreich and English 1978).[5] "The home," identified with women, even partakes of the sacred: a sanctuary to which men can escape after being polluted by the symbolic dirt of the workaday world (Rybczynski 1986:160). Correspondingly, in the public sphere, it is women who conduct the vast majority of volunteer work (Smith 1975:125).

There are many reasons for this, including economic and political factors, but these are surely grounded in the general tendency for women's "nature" to be defined around giving to others for the sheer pleasure of compassion (Gold 1971).

During most of the month, women should embody the positive virtues just summarized; yet during the paramenstruum they are permitted to play out what are perceived widely as disapproved modes of behaviour, not only suffering but also causing others to suffer by revoking their normal compassion. In effect, they reverse their "normal" role. The typical woman is permitted—even encouraged—to oscillate between two personality extremes, which have been temporalized into specific chunks of the month.[6] (One woman in a PMS workshop I observed brought up the film *Dr. Jekyll and Mr. Hyde*, though she insisted that this bifurcation of personality was more extreme than her own.) While we may see women during this time as acting "abnormally," this model of behaviour is nevertheless very much written into a cultural script. Taken together, the two ends of the female personality spectrum offer a complete range of experience considered acceptable for women in America.

These attitudes are taught to women when quite young: there is evidence that the expectation that girls will embody this set of ideals appears as early as birth. The new mother in some American hospitals may be given an information sheet entitled either "What is a Girl?" or "What is a Boy?", as I was in April 1987, detailing the nature of her baby.[7]

With this in mind, let us examine a portion of the text for "What is a Girl?", with its list of traits that American females should embody. To put it at its most succinct:

> Who else can cause you more grief, joy, irritation, satisfaction, embarrassment and genuine delight than this combination of Eve, Salome and Florence Nightingale?

Here we have combined the extremes of feminine allure: purity, seduction, plus selfless dedication to others. The publication admits, delicately, that girls have their imperfections, but these are relatively harmless:

> Little girls are the nicest things that happen to people. They are born with a little bit of angel-shine about them and though it wears thin sometimes, there is always enough left to lasso your heart—even when they are sitting in the mud, or crying temperamental tears, or parading up the street in mother's best clothes.

Here we have the most positive image possible of girls: the angelic. This, in spite of the occasional moodiness or cute sources of exasperation they might be. But let us continue:

> A little girl can be sweeter (and badder) oftener than anyone else in the world. She can jitter around, and stomp, and make funny noises that frazzle your nerves, yet just when you open your mouth, she stands there demure with that special look in her eyes. A girl is Innocence playing in the mud, Beauty standing on its head, and Motherhood dragging a doll by the foot.

Now, a negative note is introduced. The girl can be "bad"—but note this is in parentheses, subsidiary as it were to sweetness. "Motherhood dragging a doll by the foot" is a compelling image: she can be irresponsible as a mother, but it's in innocence, and she can't be blamed. By means of these tropes, the dual images of extreme goodness and extreme badness are introduced to girls literally at birth, via the expectations of their new parents, who will be socializing them. But always the Good should subsume the Bad, as in the grammatical construction used in the handout.

If socialization into this script begins at birth, it continues through a woman's life. Let us explore briefly two examples of how instruction about PMS, specifically, teaches women about anticipated mood shifts from the "nice" to the "irritable."

At adolescence a girl is intensely curious about her changing body and seeks information about the transformations. One source is her doctor's office. Widely available in American pediatricians' offices are booklets on various subjects, including menarche. One such booklet, called "To answer your questions about your teenage menstrual cycle" (printed by Personal Products Company) is in a question-and-answer format. Here is one section:

> Sometimes I feel tired and moody. Does this have anything to do with my cycle?
> *It may. Many things influence the way you feel. In some cases your moods may be affected by your cycle. For example, some girls and women feel tired and irritable a week or so before their periods. This may be related to the levels of hormones in your blood during the premenstrual phase.*
>
> (Anonymous 1986).

This publication not only puts physical ("tired") and mental ("irritable") symptoms on the same level, but it posits a direct, causal association between biological processes (hormones) and mental states (moods). In so doing, this booklet, teaching young girls what to expect from the (pre-) menstrual experience, in effect instructs them that "PMS" (unnamed in the present instance) is a natural occurrence.

Socialization into psychological changes during paramenstruum continues through a woman's adulthood. On a first visit to a gynecologist's office an American woman is usually asked to fill out a personal history sheet. Included in one sheet collected is the question:

> Do you have moodiness, depression, irritability, swelling or bloating prior to your menstrual period?

As with the previous case, this question implies that "moodiness," "depression" and "irritability" might be normal or common during the premenstrual time. Secondly, it puts these personality changes on a par with the physical changes of "swelling" and "bloating," thereby medicalizing the personality changes with an implied biological foundation.[8] In filling out forms such as these in their daily lives, American women are in effect told by "experts" (who presumably construct such forms) that negative moods experienced premenstrually are indeed a medical problem and therefore perhaps to some degree inevitable. Further study of other widely distributed pamphlets and questionnaires (as well as school textbooks teaching about the female body) is sorely needed to discover the extent to which these attitudes are explicitly taught throughout wide sectors of the culture.

In any case, individual women have come to see certain states of mind as being due to PMS even when there is no evidence to support this in their own particular histories. One woman in a PMS workshop I observed complained of headaches before, during and after her menstrual period, but blamed them all on PMS. Such attributions of any negative states to PMS are apparently made by women quite commonly. Sommer reports that women complained of negative moods associated with the premenstrual time, but later investigation of the women's own diaries of their moods and menstrual cycles revealed no such association (parallel findings are cited in Frieze et al. 1978:201). On the other hand there is a tendency among both men and women to blame the menstrual cycle for negative moods that do occur during the paramenstruum while blaming other factors for negative moods that occur during other times (Sommer 1982:62). In other words, the menstrual cycle is held responsible for as much as possible even when it cannot possibly be held accountable for all negative moods. Sommer confirms that negative moods are taught to American women (and men) as a "natural" component of the paramenstrual time.

I have suggested how the negative moods that define PMS constitute the opposite of what is "normally" expected of women in America. During PMS, the idealized attributes are reversed temporarily. What is the purpose of such a reversal, and what can it accomplish?

In writing of rituals of reversal, the historian Natalie Zemon Davis has pointed out (1978:152–153) that anthropological analyses have emphasized the stabilizing force that, paradoxically, they represent. In many African and other rituals of reversal, no real rebellion is effected or even attempted (e.g., Gluckman 1963, 1965). The goal of the typical ritual of reversal as presented by anthropologists is not to topple the underlying structure but to affirm it. During the ritual, the arbitrariness of the structure may be acknowledged, implicitly or even explicitly (Turner 1967); but once the ritual is over, life reverts to its prior state and continues as if uninterrupted.

Davis's own analysis of sexual reversals in early modern European literature, art and street festivals offers a contrasting perspective, as she shows the potentially subversive nature of at least some sexual reversals. In the case of American PMS, is the reversal of personality that I have outlined, which might be termed a "ritual,"[9] essentially conservative or potentially radical? Does it maintain the existing ideals of feminine behavior (and, by extension, the configuration of power relations between women and men), or might it serve to undermine that system of representations and create a new set of images and ideals to which women of the future might aspire? I suggest that at present PMS has an essentially conservative effect because the hallmark of PMS is to turn women's experience against themselves. By inflicting them-

selves on others, they themselves suffer. In terming their domestic acts of rebellion "irritability," women are made to feel guilty for reversing the normal expectations of them (Martin 1987:134).

To what extent might PMS be seen as an "escape valve," a means whereby American women "let off steam" from the enervating machine of the daily domestic grind? To some extent this explanation is valid, but it tells only part of the story. It ignores the specific contours of PMS and its predictable trajectory; moreover it puts PMS in a place that is peripheral to the American vision of womanhood, whereas my contention is that the current understanding of PMS (and, before its creation, of the menstrual period itself) is integral to how we view femininity. Even if it occupies a small portion of women's lives (although some women may see the paramenstruum as occupying half the month), and even if not all women suffer from it, I contend that the contemporary vision of PMS is so much a part of general cultural consciousness that it constitutes, qualitatively, half the female story. It combines with the other part of the month to produce a bifurcated vision of femininity whose two halves are asymmetrically valued.

Married women who suffer from PMS report that during the "normal" phase of the month they allow their husbands myriad irritating acts to go uncriticized. But while premenstrual they are hyper-critical of such acts, sometimes "ranting and raving" for hours over trivial annoyances. Unable to act "nice" continually, women break down and are regularly "irritable" and even "hostile." Their protest is recurrent but futile, for they are made to feel guilty about it, or, worse, they, are treated condescendingly. "We both know you're going to have your period tomorrow so why don't we just go to bed?" one husband regularly tells his wife at the first sign of an argument, thereby dismissing any claim to legitimate disagreement. Without legitimacy, as Weber taught us long ago, protests are doomed to failure; and so it is with PMS.

I suggest that these women in effect choose, however unconsciously, to voice their complaints at a time that they know those complaints will be rejected as illegitimate. If complaints were made during the non-premenstrual portion of the month, they would have to be taken seriously. But many American women have not found a voice with which to speak such complaints and at the same time retain their feminine allure. They save their complaints for that "time of the month" when they are in effect permitted to voice them yet by means of hormones do not have to claim responsibility for such negative feelings. In knowing when their complaints will not be taken seriously yet voicing them precisely during such a time, perhaps women are punishing themselves for their critical thoughts. In this way, and despite the surface-level aggression they display premenstrually, women continue to enact a model of behavior doomed to failure, as is consistent with what some feminists have argued is a pervasive tendency among American women in other arenas (Horner 1972).

So long as American society recreates its unrealistic expectations of the female personality, it is inevitable that there will be a PMS, or something playing its role: a regular rejection of the stringent expectations of female behavior. But PMS masks the protest even as it embodies it: for, cast in a biological idiom, PMS is made to seem an autonomous force that is often uncontrollable (see Martin 1987:132–3); or if it can be controlled, it is only by drugs not acts of personal volition. Thus women's authorship of their own states of mind is denied them. As women in contemporary America struggle to find their voices, it is to be hoped that they will be able to reclaim their bodies as vehicles for the creation of their own metaphors, rather than autonomous forces causing them to suffer and needing to be drugged.

NOTES

1. I aim my analysis of PMS at American society but suggest that the general conception of feminine personality sketched here is pervasive in Western cultures (for Italy see Giovannini 1981). Though it exists as a public category, I have not researched the specific question of PMS in Europe (but see, for example, Dalton 1980, d'Orban and Dalton 1980).
2. Estimates vary considerably, from 25%–100% (Janiger et al. 1973:226). A recent television report (on News Information Weekly Service, a Division of Lorimar-Telepictures, as seen on the Champaign, Illinois CBS affiliate station, WCIA, 20 April 1988) claimed that "nearly half" of all American women have some PMS symptoms.
3. Janiger et al. (1973:232) suggest tentatively that "Premenstrual distress is a universal phenomenon" but acknowledge that their field data were gathered in less than optimal ways (p. 229) and, in any case, among only five non-American culture groups. I do not take their conclusion as definitive.
4. Sceptical observers of the recent PMS phenomenon may inquire, What did women do before PMS was named? My answer is that the symbolic place occupied by PMS in women's lives nowadays, as I analyze it in this article, was previously occupied by the menstrual period itself. A historical analysis of the origins of that relationship to the menstrual period is surely needed but beyond the scope of the present essay.
5. A trivial but telling example of this attitude is imprinted on a Hallmark cup with "Mom sweet Mom" on a background of flowers, as a play on the old saw, "Home sweet Home."
6. For related Italian conceptions of femininity oscillating between the virgin/Madonna and the prostitute, see Giovannini (1981).
7. This was first printed by the New England Mutual Life Insurance Co. The company ceased distributing it about ten years ago but private individuals and other agencies continue to reprint and distribute it in large quantities. When New England Life was distributing the handouts, the intention was that they would "pull on the heartstrings" of new parents, making enough cultural sense to them that they would purchase life insurance (Laura Lock, Advertising Department, New England Life Insurance Company: personal communication, 9 Nov. 1987).
8. A strikingly parallel example of somatization of psychological symptoms is exhibited in the following description of a PMS sufferer: "She had breast pain, bloatedness, and frequently started arguments with her husband" (Witt 1984:41).

9. As outlined by Turner (1967:95) the essential feature of ritual is that the identity of the participants is transformed permanently, the most famous instance being rituals of initiation. By this definition, PMS as I understand it would not be a ritual, as *its* hallmark is that the monthly transformation is both regular and reversible: few women would like to become permanently the women they are during the premenstrual (and/or menstrual) phase. Yet I suggest there is an intermediate form of ritual in which personal identity is transformed, but only temporarily, and then reverts to earlier structures (Gottlieb n.d.). As I have analysed it, PMS would seem to be a perfect example of such an intermediary form of ritual.

REFERENCES

Ablanalp, J. 1985. Premenstrual syndrome: a selective review. In S. Golub (ed.) *Lifting the Curse of Menstruation*. Pp. 107–123. New York: Harrington Park Publishers.

Adams, M. 1971. The compassion trap. In V. Gornick and B. K. Moran (eds.) *Woman in Sexist Society*. Pp. 555–575. New York: Basic Books.

Anderson, M. L. 1983. *Thinking About Women*. New York: Macmillan.

Anon. 1986. *To Answer Your Questions About Your Teenage Menstrual Cycle*. Milltown, NJ: Personal Products Co. Rev. ed.

Bardwick, J. M. and E. Douvan. 1971. Ambivalence: The socialization of women. In V. Gornick and B. K. Moran (eds.) *Woman in Sexist Society*. Pp. 225–241. New York: Basic Books.

Brown, M. A. and P. A. Zimmer. 1986. Help-seeking for premenstrual symptomology: A description of women's experiences. In V. L. Olesen and N. F. Woods (eds.) *Culture, Society and Menstruation*. Pp. 173–184. Washington: Hemisphere Publishing Corp./New York: Harper & Row.

Buckley, T. and A. Gottlieb, eds. 1988. *Blood Magic: The Anthropology of Menstruation*. Berkeley: University of California Press.

Dalton, K. 1979. *Once a Month*. Pomona, CA: Hunter House.

Dalton, K. 1980. Cyclical criminal acts in premenstrual syndrome. *The Lancet* 8203 (II) (Nov. 15):1070–1071.

Davis, N. Z. 1978. Women on top: Symbolic sexual inversion and political disorder in early modern Europe. In B. Babcock (ed.) *The Reversible World*. Pp. 147–190. Ithaca: Cornell U. P. (Essay originally published 1975.)

d'Orban, P. T. and J. Dalton. 1980. Violent crime and the menstrual cycle. *Psychological Medicine* 10:353–359.

Ehrenreich, B. and D. English. 1978. *For Her Own Good*. New York: Doubleday.

Freize, I. H. et al. 1978. *Women and Sex Roles*. New York: Norton.

Giovannini, M. 1981. Woman: A dominant symbol within the cultural system of a Sicilian town. *Man* 16:408–426.

Gluckman, M. 1963. *Order and Rebellion in Tribal Africa*. New York: Free Press.

Gluckman, M. 1965. *Custom and Conflict in Africa*. Glencoe, IL: Free Press.

Gold, D. B. 1971. Women and voluntarism. In V. Gornick and B. K. Moran (eds.) *Woman in Sexist Society*. Pp. 533–554. New York: Basic Books.

Gottlieb, A. n.d. Between "ritual" and "ceremony." Unpublished ms.

Helman, C. G. 1987. Heart disease and the cultural construction of time: The Type A behaviour pattern as a Western culture-bound syndrome. *Social Science and Medicine* 25(9):969–979.

Horner, M. 1972. Toward an understanding of achievement-related conflicts in women. *Journal of Social Issues* 28:157–175.

Janiger, O., R. Riffenburgh and R. Kersh. 1973. Cross cultural study of premenstrual symptoms. *Psychosomatics* 13:226–235.

Koeske, R. D. 1985. Lifting the curse of menstruation: Toward a feminist perspective on the menstrual cycle. In S. Golub (ed.) *Lifting the Curse of Menstruation*. Pp. 1–16. New York: Harrington Park Publishers.

Lakoff, R. 1975. *Language and Woman's Place.* New York: Harper & Row.

Lutz, C. 1986. Emotion, thought and estrangement: Emotion as a cultural category. *Cultural Anthropology* 1(3):287–309.

Martin, E. 1987. *The Woman in the Body.* Boston: Beacon.

Rome, E. 1986. Premenstrual syndrome (PMS) examined through a feminist lens. In V. L. Olesen and N. F. Woods (eds.) *Culture, Society and Menstruation.* Pp. 145–151. Washington: Hemisphere Publishing Corp./New York: Harper & Row.

Rosaldo, M. Z. 1984. Toward an anthropology of self and feeling. In R. A. Shweder and R. A. Levine (eds.) *Culture Theory.* Pp. 137–157. New York: C.U.P.

Rybczynski, W. 1986. *Home: A Short History of an Idea.* New York: Viking.

Shostak, M. 1981. *Nisa.* Cambridge: Harvard U.P.

Shuttle, P. and P. Redgrove. 1978. *The Wise Wound.* London: Gollancz.

Smith, L. M. 1975. Women as volunteers: The double subsidy. *Journal of Voluntary Action Research* 4 (3–4):119–136.

Sommer, B. 1982. Menstrual distress. In G. C. Hongladarom, R. McCorkle and N. F. Woods (eds.) *The Complete Book of Woman's Health.* Pp. 59–73. Englewood Cliffs, NJ: Prentice Hall.

Sommer, B. 1985. How does menstruation affect cognitive competence and psychophysiological response? In S. Golub (ed.) *Lifting the Curse of Menstruation.* Pp. 53–90. New York: Harrington Park Publishers.

Trupin, S., M.D. 1985. PMS: A Personal Workbook. Champaign, IL: Privately printed and circulated; 2nd ed.

Turner, V. 1967. Betwixt and between: The liminal period in rites of passage. In *The Forest of Symbols.* Pp. 93–111. Ithaca: Cornell U. P.

Witt, R. L. 1984. *PMS: What Every Woman Should Know About Premenstrual Syndrome.* New York: Stein & Day. Rev. ed.

Into the Endzone for a Touchdown

A Psychoanalytic Consideration of American Football

Alan Dundes

Alan Dundes received his Ph.D. in 1962 from Indiana University and is now professor of anthropology at the University of California in Berkeley. Best known as a folklorist, his research interests include structural analysis, symbolism, worldview, and psychoanalysis.

In college athletics it is abundantly clear that it is football which counts highest among both enrolled students and alumni. It is almost as though the masculinity of male alumni is at stake in a given game, especially when a hated rival school is the opponent. College fund raisers are well aware that a winning football season may prove to be the key to a successful financial campaign to increase the school's endowment capital. The Rose Bowl and other postseason bowl games for colleges, plus the Super Bowl for professional football teams have come to rank as national festival occasions in the United States. All this makes it reasonable to assume that there is something about football which strikes a most responsive chord in the American psyche. No other American sport consistently draws fans in the numbers which are attracted to football. One need only compare the crowd-attendance statistics for college or professional baseball games with the analogous figures for football to see the enormous appeal of the latter. The question is: what is it about American football that could possibly account for its extraordinary popularity?

In the relatively meager scholarship devoted to football, one finds the usual array of theoretical approaches. The ancestral form of football, a game more like Rugby or soccer, was interpreted as a solar ritual—with a disc-shaped rock or object supposedly representing the sun[1]—and also as a fertility ritual intended to ensure agricultural abundance. It had been noted, for example, that in some parts of England and France, the rival teams consisted of married men playing against bachelors.[2] In one custom, a newly married woman would throw over the church a ball for which married men and bachelors fought. The distinction between the married and the unmarried suggests that the game might be a kind of ritual test or battle with marriage signifying socially sanctioned fertility.[3]

The historical evolution of American football from English Rugby has been well documented,[4] but the historical facts do not in and of themselves account for any psychological rationale leading to the unprecedented enthusiasm for the sport. It is insufficient to state that football offers an appropriate outlet for the expression of aggression. William Arens has rightly observed that it would be an oversimplification "to single out violence as the sole or even primary reason for the game's popularity."[5] Many sports provide a similar outlet (e.g., wrestling, ice hockey, roller derby), but few of these come close to matching football as a spectacle for many Americans. Similarly, pointing to such features as a love of competition, or the admiration of coordinated teamwork, or the development of specialists (e.g., punters, punt returners, field-goal kickers, etc.) is not convincing since such features occur in most if not all sports.

Recently, studies of American football have suggested that the game serves as a male initiation ritual.[6] Arens, for example, remarks that football is "a male preserve that manifests both the physical and cultural values of masculinity,"[7] a description which had previously been applied, aptly it would appear, to British Rugby.[8] Arens points out that the equipment worn "accents the male physique" through the enlarged head and shoulders coupled with a narrowed waist. With the lower torso "poured into skintight pants accented only by a metal codpiece," Arens contends that the result "is not an expression but an exaggeration of maleness." He comments further: "Dressed in this manner, the players can engage in hand holding, hugging, and bottom patting, which would be disapproved of in any other context, but which is accepted on the gridiron without a second thought."[9] Having said this much, Arens fails to draw any inferences about possible ritual homosexual aspects of football. Instead, he goes on to note that American football resembles male rituals in other cultures insofar as contact with females is discouraged if not forbidden. The argument usually given is one of "limited good."[10] A man has only so much energy and if he uses it in sexual activity, he will have that much less to use in hunting, warfare, or in this case, football. I believe Arens and others are correct in calling attention to the ritual and symbolic dimensions of American football, but I think the psychological implications of the underlying symbolism have not been adequately explored.

Football is one of a large number of competitive games which involve the scoring of points by gaining access to a defended area in an opponent's territory. In basketball, one must throw a ball through a hoop (and net) attached to the other team's backboard. In ice hockey, one must hit the puck into the goal at the opponent's end of the rink. In football, the object is to move the ball across the opponent's goal into his endzone. It does not require a great deal of Freudian sophistication to see a possible sexual component in such acts as throwing a ball through a hoop, hitting a puck across a "crease" into an enclosed area bounded by nets or cage, and other structurally similar acts. But what is not so obvious is the connection of such sexual symbolism with an all-male group of participants.

Psychologists and psychoanalysts have not chosen to examine American football to any great extent. Psychologist G. T. W. Patrick, writing in 1903, tried to explain the fascination of the game: "Evidently there is some great force, psychological or sociological, at work here which science has not yet investigated"; but he could offer little detail about what that great force might be.[11] Similarly, psychoanalyst A. A. Brill's superficial consideration of football in 1929 failed to illuminate the psychodynamics of the game.[12] Perhaps the best known Freudian analysis of football is the parody written originally in 1955 in the *Rocky Mountain Herald* by poet Thomas Hornsby Ferril, using the pseudonym Childe Herald, but the essay is more amusing than analytic. Actually his interpretation tends to be more inclined towards ritual than psychoanalytic theory. He suggests "football is a syndrome of religious rites symbolizing the struggle to preserve the egg of life through the rigors of impending winter. The rites begin at the autumn equinox and culminate on the first day of the New Year with great festivals identified with bowls of plenty; the festivals are associated with flowers such as roses, fruits such as oranges, farm crops such as cotton and even sunworship and the appeasement of great reptiles such as alligators."[13] While he does say that "football obviously arises out of the Oedipus complex," he provides little evidence other than mentioning that college games are usually played for one's alma mater, which he translates

as "dear mother." Actually, a more literal translation would be "nourishing mother" (and for that matter, *alumnus* literally means nursling.)

A more conventional psychoanalytic perspective is offered by Adrian Stokes in his survey of ball games with special reference to cricket. Stokes predictably describes football (soccer) in Oedipal terms. Each team defends the goal at their back. "In front is a new land, the new woman, whom they strive to possess in the interest of preserving the mother inviolate, in order, as it were, to progress from infancy to adulthood: at the same time, the defensive role is the father's; he opposes the forward youth of the opposition."[14] Speaking of Rugby football, Stokes proposes the following description: "Ejected out of the mother's body, out of the scrum, after frantic hooking and pushing, there emerges the rich loot of the father's genital." According to Stokes, both teams fight to possess the father's phallus, that is, the ball, in order to "steer it through the archetypal vagina, the goal."[15] Earlier, Stokes had suggested the ball represented semen though he claimed that "more generally the ball is itself the phallus."[16] Folk speech offers some support for the phallic connotation of a ball. One thinks of "balls" for testicles. A man who has "balls" is a man of strength and determination. To "ball" someone is a slang expression for sexual intercourse.[17] On the other hand, while one might agree with the general thesis that there might be a sexual component to both soccer and American football, it is difficult to cite concrete evidence supporting Stokes's contention that the game involves a mother figure or a father surrogate. If psychoanalytic interpretations are valid, then it ought to be possible to adduce specific details of idiom and ritual as documentation for such interpretations. It is not enough for a psychoanalyst to assert ex cathedra what a given event or object supposedly symbolizes.

I believe that a useful way to begin an attempt to understand the psychoanalytic significance of American football is through an examination of football folk speech. For it is precisely in the idioms and metaphors that a clear pattern of personal interaction is revealed. In this regard, it might be helpful first to briefly consider the slang employed in the verbal dueling of the American male. In effect, I am suggesting that American football is analogous to male verbal dueling. Football entails ritual and dramatic action while verbal dueling is more concerned with words. But structurally speaking, they are similar or at least functionally equivalent. In verbal dueling, it is common to speak about putting one's opponent "down." This could mean simply to topple an opponent figuratively, but it could also imply forcing one's adversary to assume a supine position, that is, the "female" position in typical Western sexual intercourse. It should also be noted that an equally humiliating experience for a male would be to serve as a passive receptacle for a male aggressor's phallic thrust. Numerous idioms attest to the widespread popularity of this pattern of imagery to describe a loser. One speaks of having been screwed by one's boss or of having been given the shaft. Submitting to anal intercourse is also implied in perhaps the most common single American folk gesture, the so-called *digitus impudicus,* better known in folk parlance as "the finger." Giving someone the finger is often accompanied by such unambiguous explanatory phrases as "Fuck you!" "Screw you!" "Up yours!" or "Up your ass!"

Now what has all this to do with football? I believe that the same symbolic pattern is at work in verbal dueling and much ritual play. Instead of scoring a putdown, one scores a touchdown. Certainly the terminology used in football is suggestive. One gains yardage, but it is not territory which is kept in the sense of being permanently acquired by the invading team. The territory invaded remains nominally under the proprietorship of the opponent. A sports announcer or fan might say, for example, "This is the deepest *penetration* into (opponent's team name) territory so far" [my emphasis]. Only if one gets into the endzone (or kicks a field goal through the uprights of the goalposts) does one earn points.

The use of the term *end* is not accidental. Evidently there is a kind of structural isomorphism between the line (as opposed to the backfield) and the layout of the field of play. Each line has two ends (left end and right end) with a "center" in the middle. Similarly, each playing field has two ends (endzones) with a midfield line (the fifty-yard line). Ferril remarked on the parallel between the oval shape of the football and the oval shape of most football stadiums,[18] but I submit it might be just as plausible to see the football shape as an elongated version of the earlier round soccer or Rugby ball, a shape which tends to produce two accentuated ends of the ball. Surely the distinctive difference between the shape of a football and the shape of the balls used in most other ball games (e.g., baseball, basketball, soccer) is that it is not perfectly spherical. The notion that a football has two "ends" is found in the standard idiom used to describe a kick or punt in which the ball turns over and over from front to back during flight (as opposed to moving in a more direct, linear, spiraling pattern) as an "end over end" kick.

The object of the game, simply stated, is to get into the opponent's endzone while preventing the opponent from getting into one's own endzone. Structurally speaking, this is precisely what is involved in male verbal dueling. One wishes to put one's opponent down; to "screw" him while avoiding being screwed by him. We can now better understand the appropriateness of the "bottom patting" so often observed among football players. A good offensive or defensive play deserves a pat on the rear end. The recipient has held up his end and has thereby helped protect the collective "end" of the entire team. One pats one's teammates' ends, but one seeks to violate the endzone of one's opponents!

The trust one has for one's own teammates is perhaps signalled by the common postural stance of football players. The so-called three-point stance involves bending over in a distinct stooped position with one's rear end exposed. It is an unusual position (in terms of normal life activities) and it does make one especially vulnerable to attack from behind, that is, vulnerable to a homosexual attack. In some ways, the posture might be likened to what is termed *presenting* among nonhuman primates. *Presenting* refers to a subordinate animal's turning its rump towards a higher ranking or dominant one. The center thus presents to the quarterback—just as linemen do to the backs in general. George Plimpton has described how the quarterback's "hand, the top of it, rests up against the center's backside as he bends over the ball—medically, against the perineum, the pelvic floor."[19] We know that some dominant nonhuman primates will sometimes reach out to touch a presenting subordinate in similar fashion. In football, however, it is safe to present to one's teammates. Since one can trust one's teammates, one knows that one will be patted, not raped. The traditional joking admonitions of the locker room warning against bending over in the shower or picking up the soap (thus presumably offering an inviting target for homosexual attack) do not apply since one is among friends. "Grabass" among friends is understood as being harmless joking behavior.

The importance of the "ends" is signalled by the fact that they alone among linemen are eligible to receive a forward pass. In that sense, ends are equivalent to the "backs." In symbolic terms, I am arguing that the end is a kind of backside and that the endzone is a kind of erogenous zone. The relatively recently coined terms *tight end* and *split end* further demonstrate the special emphasis upon this "position" on the team. The terms refer to whether the end stays close to his neighboring tackle, e.g., to block, or whether he moves well away from the normally adjacent tackle, e.g., to go out for a pass. However, both *tight end* and *split end* (cf. also *wide receiver*) could easily be understood as possessing an erotic nuance.

I must stress that the evidence for the present interpretation of American football does not depend upon just a single word. Rather, there are many terms which appear to be relevant. The semantics of the word *down* are of interest. A down is a unit of play insofar as a team has four downs in which to either advance ten yards or score. A touchdown, which earns six points, refers to the act of an offensive player's possessing the ball in the opponent's endzone. (Note it is not sufficient for the player to be in the endzone; it is the ball which must be in the zone.) In a running play, the ball often physically touches the endzone and could therefore be said to "touch down" in that area. However, if an offensive player catches a pass in the endzone, the ball does not actually touch the ground. The recent practice of "spiking" the ball, in which the successful offensive player hurls the ball at the ground as hard as he can, might be construed as an attempt to have the football physically touch down in the endzone. In any case, the use of the word *touch* in connection with scoring in football does conform to a general sexually symbolic use of that term. The sexual nuances of *touch* can even be found in the Bible. For example, in I Corinthians 7:1–2, we find "It is good for a man not to touch a woman. Nevertheless to avoid fornication, let every man have his own wife" (cf. Genesis 20:6; Proverbs 6:29). Touching can be construed as an aggressive act. Thus to be touched by an opponent means that one has been the victim of aggression. The game of "touch football" (as opposed to "tackle" football) supports the notion that a mere art of touching is sufficient to fulfill the structural (and psychological) requirements of the basic rules. No team wants to give up a touchdown to an opponent. Often a team on defense may put up a determined goal-line stand to avoid being penetrated by the opponent's offense. The special spatial nature of the endzone is perhaps indicated by the fact that it is not measured in the one hundred yard distance between the goal lines. Yet it is measured. It is only ten yards deep; a pass caught by an offensive player whose feet are beyond the end line of the endzone would be ruled incomplete.

Additional football folk speech could be cited. The object of the game is to "score," a term which in standard slang means to engage in sexual intercourse with a member of the opposite sex. One "scores" by going "all the way." The latter phrase refers specifically to making a touchdown.[20] In sexual slang, it alludes to indulging in intercourse as opposed to petting or necking. The offensive team may try to mount a "drive" in order to "penetrate" the other team's territory. A ball carrier might go "up the middle" or he might "go through a hole" (made by his linemen in the opposing defensive line). A particularly skillful runner might be able to make his own hole. The defense is equally determined to "close the hole." Linemen may encourage one another "to stick it to 'em," meaning to place their helmeted heads (with phallic-symbolic overtones) against the chests of their opposite numbers to drive them back or put them out of the play.

A player who scores a touchdown may elect to "spike" the ball by hurling it down towards the ground full force. This spiking movement confirms to all assembled that the enemy's endzone has been penetrated. The team scored upon is thus shamed and humiliated in front of an audience. In this regard, football is similar to verbal dueling inasmuch as dueling invariably takes place before one or more third parties. The term *spike* may also be germane. As a noun, it could refer to a sharp-pointed long slender part or projection. As a verb, it could mean either "to mark or cut with a spike" (the football would presumably be the phallic spike) or "to thwart or sabotage an enemy." In any event, the ritual act of spiking serves to prolong and accentuate the all-too-short moment of triumph, the successful entry into the enemy's endzone.

The sexual connotations of football folk speech apply equally to players on defense. One goal of the defensive line is to penetrate the offensive line to get to the quarterback. Getting to the offensive quarterback and bringing him down to the ground is termed "sacking the quarterback." The verb *sack* connotes plunder, ravage, and perhaps even rape. David Kopay, one of the few homosexuals in professional football willing to admit a preference for members of the same sex, commented on the nature of typical exhortations made by coaches and others:

> The whole language of football is involved in sexual allusions. We were told to go out and "fuck those guys"; to take that ball and "stick it up their asses" or "down their throats." The coaches would yell, "knock their dicks off," or more often than that, "knock their jocks off." They'd say, "Go out there and give it all you've got, a hundred and ten per cent, shoot your wad." You controlled their line and "knocked" 'em into submission. Over the years I've seen many a coach get emotionally aroused while he was diagramming a particular play into an imaginary hole on the blackboard. His face red, his voice rising, he would show the ball carrier how he wanted him to "stick it in the hole."[21]

The term *rape* is not inappropriate and in fact it has been used to describe what happens when an experienced player humiliates a younger player: "That poor kid, he was raped, keelhauled, he was just *destroyed*. . . ."[22] Kopay's reference to *jock* as phallus is of interest since *jock* is a term (short for *jockstrap*, the article of underapparel worn to protect the male genitals) typically used to refer generally to athletes. Calling an athlete a *jock* or a *strap* thus tends to reduce him to a phallus. A *jocker* is used in hobo slang and in prison slang to refer to an aggressive male homosexual.[23] (The meaning of *jock* may well be related to the term *jockey* insofar as the latter refers to the act of mounting and riding a horse.)

Some of the football folk speech is less obvious and the interpretation admittedly a bit more speculative. For example, a lineman may be urged to "pop" an opposing player, meaning to tackle or block him well. Executing a perfect tackle or block may entail placing one's helmet as close as possible to the middle of the opponent's chest. The use of the verbs strongly suggests defloration, as in the idiom "to pop the cherry" referring to the notion of rupturing the maidenhead in the process of having intercourse with a virgin."[24] In Afro-American folk speech, "pop" can refer to sexual penetration.[25] To "pop" an opponent thus implies reducing him to female-victim status. Much of the sexual slang makes it very clear that the winners are men while the losers are women or passive homosexuals. David Kopay articulates this when he says, "From grade school on, the curse words on the football field are about behaving like a girl. If you don't run fast enough to block or tackle hard enough you're a pussy, a cunt, a sissy."[26] By implication, if a player succeeds, he is male. Thus in the beginning of the football game, we have two sets or teams of males. By the end of the game, one of the teams is "on top," namely the one which has "scored" most by getting into the other team's "end zone." The losing team, if the scoring differential is great, may be said to have been "creamed."

It is tempting to make something of the fact that originally the inner portion of the football was an inflated animal bladder. Thus touching the enemy's endzone with a bladder would be appropriate ritual behavior in the context of a male homosexual attack. However, it could be argued that the bladder was used simply because it was a convenient inflatable object available to serve as a ball.

If the team on offense is perceived in phallic terms, then it is the quarterback who could be said to be nominally in charge of directing the attack. In this context, it may be noteworthy that a quarterback intending to pass often tries to stay inside of the "pocket," a deployment of offensive players behind the line of scrimmage designed to provide an area of maximum protection.[27] A pants pocket, of course, could be construed as an area where males can covertly touch or manipulate their genitals without being observed. "Pocket pool," for example, is a slang idiom for fondling the genitals,[28] an idiom which incidentally may suggest something about the symbolic nature of billiards. The quarterback, if given adequate protection by his "pocket," may be able to "thread the needle," that is, throw the ball accurately, past the hands of the defensive players, into the hands of his receiver. The metaphor of threading the needle is an apt one since getting the thread through the eye of the needle is only preparatory for the act of "sewing." (Note also that "to make a pass" at someone is a conventional idiom for an act of flirtation.) Once the ball is in his possession, the receiver is transformed from a passive to an active role as he tries to move the ball as far forward as possible.

While it is possible to disagree with several of the interpretations offered of individual items of folk speech cited thus far, it would seem difficult to deny the overall sexual nature of much of football (and other sports) slang. The word *sport* itself has this connotation and has had it for centuries. Consider one of Gloucester's early lines in *King Lear* when he refers to his bastard son Edmund by saying "There was good sport at his making" (I,i,23) or in such modern usages as "sporting house" for brothel"[29] or "sporting life" referring to pimps and prostitutes.[30] In the early 1950s, kissing was commonly referred to by adolescents as a "favorite indoor sport" presumably in contrast to outdoor sports such as football. It should also be noted that *game* can carry the same sexual connotation as *sport*.[31]

I have no doubt that a good many football players and fans will be skeptical (to say the least) of the analysis proposed here. Even academics with presumably less personal investment in football will probably find implausible, if not downright repugnant, the idea that American football could be a ritual combat between groups of males attempting to assert their masculinity by penetrating the

endzones of their rivals. David Kopay, despite suggesting that for a long time football provided a kind of replacement for sex in his life and admitting that football is "a real outlet for repressed sexual energy,"[32] refuses to believe that "being able to hold hands in the huddle and to pat each other on the ass if we felt like it" is necessarily an overt show of homosexuality.[33] Yet I think it is highly likely that the ritual aspect of football, providing as it does a socially sanctioned framework for male body contact—football, after all, is a so-called body contact sport—is a form of homosexual behavior. The unequivocal sexual symbolism of the game, as plainly evidenced in folk speech, coupled with the fact that all of the participants are male, make it difficult to draw any other conclusion. Sexual acts carried out in thinly disguised symbolic form by, and directed towards, males and males only, would seem to constitute ritual homosexuality.

Evidence from other cultures indicates that male homosexual ritual combats are fairly common. Answering the question of who penetrates whom is a pretty standard means of testing masculinity crossculturally. Interestingly enough, the word *masculine* itself seems to derive from Latin *mas* (male) and *culus* (anus). The implication might be that for a male to prove his masculinity with his peers, he would need to control or guard his buttocks area while at the same time threatening the posterior of another (weaker) male. A good many men's jokes in Mediterranean cultures (e.g., in Italy and in Spain) center on the *culo*.

That a mass spectacle could be based upon a ritual masculinity contest should not surprise anyone familiar with the bullfight. Without intending to reduce the complexity of the bullfight to a single factor, one could nonetheless observe that it is in part a battle between males attempting to penetrate one another. The one who is penetrated loses. If it is the bull, he may be further feminized or emasculated by having various extremities cut off to reward the successful matador. In this context, we can see American football as a male activity (along with the Boy Scouts, fraternities, and other exclusively male social organizations in American culture) as belonging to the general range of male rituals around the world in which masculinity is defined and affirmed. In American culture, women are permitted to be present as spectators or even cheerleaders, but they are not participants. Women resenting men's preoccupation with such male sports are commonly referred to as football widows (analogous to golf widows). This too suggests that the sport activity is in some sense a substitute for normal heterosexual relations. The men are "dead" as far as relationships with females are concerned. In sport and in ritual, men play both male *and* female parts. Whether it is the verbal dueling tradition of the circum-Mediterranean[34] in which young men threaten to put opponents into a passive homosexual position, or the initiation rites in aboriginal Australia and New Guinea (and elsewhere) in which younger men are subjected to actual homosexual anal intercourse by older members of the male group,[35] the underlying psychological rationale appears to be similar. Professional football's financial incentives may extend the playing years of individuals beyond late adolescence, but in its essence American football is an adolescent masculinity initiation ritual in which the winner gets into the loser's endzone more times than the loser gets into his!

NOTES

1. W. Branch Johnson, "Football, A Survival of Magic?" *The Contemporary Review* 135 (1929):228.
2. Johnson, 230–31; Francis Peabody Magoun, Jr., "Shrove Tuesday Football," *Harvard Studies and Notes in Philology and Literature* 13 (1931):24, 36, 44.
3. Johnson, 230.
4. David Riesman and Reuel Denney, "Football in America: A Study in Cultural Diffusion," *American Quarterly* 3 (1951): 309–25.
5. William Arens, "The Great American Football Ritual," *Natural History* 84 (1975):72–80. Reprinted in W. Arens and Susan P. Montague, eds., *The American Dimension: Cultural Myths and Social Realities* (Port Washington, 1975), 3–14.
6. Arnold R. Beisser, *The Madness in Sports* (New York, 1967); Shirley Fiske, "Pigskin Review: An American Initiation," in *Sport in the Socio-Cultural Process*, ed. M. Marie Hart (Dubuque, 1972), 241–58; and Arens, 72–80.
7. Arens, 77.
8. K. G. Sheard and E. G. Dunning, "The Rugby Football Club as a Type of `Male Preserve': Some Sociological Notes," *International Review of Sport Sociology* 3–4 (1973):5–24.
9. Arens, 79.
10. George M. Foster, "Peasant Society and the Image of Limited Good," *American Anthropologist* 67 (1965):293–315.
11. G. T. W. Patrick, "The Psychology of Football," *American Journal of Psychology* 14 (1903):370.
12. A. A. Brill, "The Why of the Fan," *North American Review* 228 (1929):429–34.
13. Childe Herald [Thomas Hornsby Ferril], "Freud and Football," in *Reader in Comparative Religion*, eds. William A. Lessa and Evon Z. Vogt (New York, 2nd ed., 1965), 250–52.
14. Adrian Stokes, "Psycho-Analytic Reflections on the Development of Ball Games, Particularly Cricket," *International Journal of Psycho-Analysis* 37 (1956):185–92.
15. Stokes, 190.
16. Stokes, 187.
17. Bruce Rodgers, *The Queens' Vernacular: A Gay Lexicon* (San Francisco, 1972), 27; Dennis Wepman, Ronald B. Newman, and Murray B. Binderman, *The Life: The Lore and Folk Poetry of the Black Hustler* (Philadelphia, 1976), 178.
18. Herald, 250.
19. George Plimpton, *Paper Lion* (New York, 1965), 59.
20. Kyle Rote and Jack Winter, *The Language of Pro Football* (New York, 1966), 102.
21. David Kopay and Perry Deane Young, *The David Kopay Story* (New York, 1977), 53–54.
22. Plimpton, 195, 339.
23. Harold Wentworth and Stuart Berg Flexner, *Dictionary of American Slang* (New York, 1967), 294; Rodgers, 155.
24. Vance Randolph, *Pissing in the Snow & Other Ozark Folktales* (Urbana, 1976), 9.
25. Wepman, Newman, and Binderman, 186.
26. Kopay and Young, 50–51.
27. Rote and Winter, 130.
28. Rodgers, 152.
29. Wentworth and Flexner, 511.
30. Wepman, Newman, and Binderman, *The Life*.
31. Rodgers, 92; Wepman, Newman, and Binderman, 182.
32. Kopay and Young, 11, 53.
33. Kopay and Young, 57.
34. Cf. Alan Dundes, Jerry W. Leach, and Bora Özkök. "The Strategy of Turkish Boys' Verbal Dueling Rhymes," *Journal of American Folklore* 83 (1970):325–49.
35. Cf. Alan Dundes, "A Psychoanalytic Study of the Bullroarer," *Man* 11 (1976):220–38.

REFERENCES

Arens, William. 1975. "The Great American Football Ritual," *Natural History* 84 (1975):72–80. Reprinted in W. Arens and Susan P. Montague, eds. 1975. *The American Dimension: Cultural Myths and Social Realities*. Port Washington, 3–14.

Beisser, Arnold R. 1967. *The Madness in Sports*. New York.

Brill, A. A. 1929. "The Why of the Fan," *North American Review* 228:429–34.

Childe, Herald [Thomas Hornsby Ferril]. 1965. "Freud and Football," in *Reader in Comparative Religion*, eds. William A. Lessa and Evon Z. Vogt. New York, 2nd ed., 250–52.

Dundes, Alan. 1976. "A Psychoanalytic Study of the Bullroarer," *Man* 11:220–38.

Dundes, Alan, Jerry W. Leach, and Bora Özkök. 1970. "The Strategy of Turkish Boys' Verbal Dueling Rhymes," *Journal of American Folklore* 83:325–49.

Fiske, Shirley. 1972. "Pigskin Review: An American Initiation," in *Sport in the Socio-Cultural Process*, ed. M. Marie Hart. Dubuque, 241–58.

Foster, George M. 1965. "Peasant Society and the Image of Limited Good," *American Anthropologist* 67:293–315.

Johnson, W. Branch. 1929. "Football, A Survival of Magic?" *The Contemporary Review* 135:228.

Kopay, David and Perry Deane Young. 1977. *The David Kopay Story*. New York.

Magoun, Francis Peabody, Jr. 1931. "Shrove Tuesday Football," *Harvard Studies and Notes in Philology and Literature* 13:24, 36, 44.

Patrick, G. T. W. 1903. "The Psychology of Football," *American Journal of Psychology* 14:370.

Plimpton, George. 1965. *Paper Lion*. New York.

Randolph, Vance. 1967. *Pissing in the Snow & Other Ozark Folktales*. Urbana.

Riesman, David and Reuel Denney. 1951. "Football in America: A Study in Cultural Diffusion," *American Quarterly* 3:309–25.

Rodgers, Bruce. 1972. *The Queens' Vernacular: A Gay Lexicon*. San Francisco.

Rote, Kyle and Jack Winter. 1966. *The Language of Pro Football*. New York.

Sheard, K. G. and E. G. Dunning. 1973. "The Rugby Football Club as a Type of `Male Preserve': Some Sociological Notes," *International Review of Sport Sociology* 3–4:5–24.

Stokes, Adrian. 1956. "Psycho-Analytic Reflections on the Development of Ball Games, Particularly Cricket," *International Journal of Psycho-Analysis* 37:185–92.

Wentworth, Harold and Stuart Berg Flexner. 1967. *Dictionary of American Slang*. New York.

Wepman, Dennis, Ronald B. Newman, and Murray B. Binderman. 1976. *The Life: The Lore and Folk Poetry of the Black Hustler*. Philadelphia.

Being and Doing

A Cross-Cultural Examination of the Socialization of Males and Females

Nancy Chodorow

After graduating from Radcliffe College in 1966, Nancy Chodorow pursued advanced study in sociology at Harvard and then at the London School of Economics. She took her Ph.D. at Brandeis University in 1974 and is now professor of sociology at the University of California, Berkeley. She has done fieldwork in a highland Maya community in Mexico and is well known for her writings on gender-related issues.

There are two crucial issues that people concerned about the liberation of women and men from rigid and limiting sex roles must consider. One is whether there is any basis to the claim that there are biologically derived (and therefore inescapable) psychological or personality characteristics which universally differentiate men and women. The other is to understand why it is that in almost every society women are physically, politically, and/or economically dominated by men and are thought to be (and think themselves to be) inferior to men. This essay refutes the claim for universal and necessary differentiation, and provides an explanation based on a comparison of cultures and socialization practices to account for such differences where and when they occur. It then examines the development of identity in males and females and shows how this development, and in particular the socialization and development of males, leads to and perpetuates the devaluation and oppression of women.

CROSS-CULTURAL RESEARCH

Cultural Personality

Cross-cultural research[1] suggests that there are no absolute personality differences between men and women, that many of the characteristics we normally classify as masculine or feminine tend to differentiate *both* the

males and females in one culture from those in another, and in still other cultures to be the reverse of our expectations.

Margaret Mead's studies describe societies in which both men and women are gentle and unaggressive (the Arapesh); in which women dislike childbearing and children and both sexes are angry and aggressive (the Mundugumor); in which women are unadorned, brisk and efficient, whether in childrearing, fishing, or marketing, while men are decorated and vain, interested in art, theater, and petty gossip (the Tchambuli); in which adult sex roles follow conventional expectations, but both boys and girls are initially raised alike—to be alternately gentle and nurturant or assertive—following which boys undergo severe initiation ceremonies "and claim to forget" any feminine-type experiences or reactions (the Iatmul).[2] Mead's suggestion, typifying the approach of culture and personality theorists, is that cultures emphasize and reinforce behavior according to many sorts of criteria. Although one culture may have different expectations for male and female behavior, the criteria of differentiation may bear no relation to the criteria of differentiation in other cultures. Male and female personality in one culture may be poles along one continuum of behavior, which is itself differentiated from the continua of behavior of other cultures. . . .

The Whitings [Beatrice B. and John W. M.] . . . have compared "egoistic" ("seeks attention," "seeks dominance," "seeks help"—typically masculine) and "altruistic" ("offers support," "offers help," "suggests responsibly"—typically feminine) behavior among children of six cultures. Although the amount of "egoistic" and "altruistic" behavior observed was about equal..., a comparison of the two kinds of behavior within each society reveals that in three societies, children's behavior is much more "altruistic"... and that in the other three, children are clearly "egoistic".... Thus, "masculine" behavior seems to characterize certain societies, and "feminine" behavior others.

Sex Differences Within Cultures

This is not to claim that within most cultures, male and female differences do not generally conform to our traditional expectations.... [D]ata on the division of labor by sex indicate that most work is divided regularly between men and women, along conventional lines. Men's work, for instance, is "strenuous, cooperative, and ... may require long periods of travel";[3] women's work is mainly associated with food gathering and preparation, crafts, clothing manufacture, child care, and so forth.

The extent of these differences between the sexes may be large or small. Although in American society we can recognize clear differences between boys' and girls' socialization and between adult sex roles, these differences are relatively small in comparison to many other societies. The Whitings found that the boys and girls in their New England community showed no statistically significant differences in any of the twelve types of behavior that they were measuring, whereas boys and girls in each of the other cultures differed significantly on at least three of the twelve types....[4]

The Whitings compare girls and boys within each culture and find that in five of the six cultures, boys are more "egoistic" than girls, and girls more "altruistic" than boys.... Specifically, tendencies towards "egoism" and "altruism" change with age. Young girls, three to six, "seek help" and "suggest responsibly" more than young boys, while young boys "seek dominance" more than young girls. All these differences disappear with age. However, while there is no difference in the other three behavior types between young boys and girls, older boys, seven to eleven, "seek attention" more than older girls, while older girls "offer help" and "support" more than older boys. These changes make sense: young girls, used to relying on older siblings and adults ("seeking help"), soon give this help ("offer help and support") to younger children. Their not necessarily successful attempts to "suggest responsibly" to other children turn into actual instances of aid and direction. On the other hand, boys, who are allowed as very young children to be demanding ("seek dominance") to adults (especially women) and older children socializers, often lose this privilege as they get older, without receiving instead a well-defined role in the economy or division of labor. The still growing boy is then reduced to more "illegitimate" demands (to "seeking attention") that are often ignored by the people performing their work around him—people unlikely to be aware of his "roleless" status and therefore unsympathetic to his bothering them.[5] In sum, the Whitings find that while there is no statistically significant difference in "egoism" or "altruism" between boys and girls of three to six years old, boys from seven to eleven years old are significantly more "egoistic" than girls, and girls significantly more "altruistic" than boys."[6]

Explanations of Cultural and Sexual Differences: Nature or Culture?

These behavioral tendencies should not be taken to reflect "biological" (hence, "necessary") bases of sex roles and the sexual division of labor. The fact that in The Six Cultures Study (where an equal number of children of each sex were observed for equal amounts of time in each culture, and where the total amount of each type of behavior is almost exactly equivalent), 96 percent of egoistic-altruistic behavior in one society was "egoistic," while in another 93 percent was "altruistic," and that similarly extreme tendencies characterize the other four societies, proves that sex differences could not be responsible. An examination of the explanations offered for these cultural differences and for sexual differences of behavior substantiates the claim that personality and behavior are culturally determined and learned and provides insight into the apparent parallels between cultural and sexual differences.

I have already mentioned one indication that sex roles are learned and related to adult values and work: the Whitings find that young boys and girls exhibit less differentiated behavior than older children, that children, as they *learn* the actual work expected of them (or are unable to learn this work, and thus temporarily not integrated meaningfully into the culture), also learn the more general personality and behavioral characteristics which facilitate this work (or which fill time for those without work).[7]

... In societies that depend on constant care of animals, or on regular tending of crops, it is necessary to teach children to be obedient and responsible, since disobedience or irresponsibility can endanger or eliminate a food supply for a long period to come. Similarly, experimentation and individual achievement cannot be risked because of the great potential cost. On the other hand, in societies that rely totally or partially on hunting and fishing, disobedience or lack of responsibility is not so crucial; it means missing one day's catch, perhaps, but not a food supply for months to come. In this kind of economy it is worthwhile to be daring, to try new ways of doing things, since success may bring great reward and failure only temporary loss, and perhaps no greater loss than otherwise.

It is clear, however, that those qualities required by the economy in a "high accumulation" society are similar, and for the same reasons, to those normally required by woman's work, especially the requirements of child care, but also those of feeding and clothing a family.[8] Because of these more or less constant requirements, girls' socialization in societies of "low accumulation" cannot be too variable. Although girls are pressured to act "assertively" as are boys, it is noticeable that in those societies exhibiting pressures toward "masculine" behavior, ranked differences in the strength of socialization of the different kinds of behavior for girls is quite small, whereas the difference for boys between pressure toward "assertion" and pressure toward "compliance" is relatively large. The reverse is also true: in those societies which require "feminine" ("compliant") behavior, girls' socialization tends to diverge more widely among different kinds of behavior than boys', although the difference is not so extreme.[9]

These differences are accounted for by the fact that men's and boys' work in the two kinds of society can be more radically different than women's and girls' work. Men may *either* hunt, or fish, or farm, or herd. For instance, in societies with animal husbandry, it is often boys who tend livestock, and who thus from an early age must learn to be responsible in the same way that potential childrearers must learn responsibility.[10] But in societies with hunting and fishing, although women may fish, they still have to take care of children and cook food. Although reliance on gathering and general uncertainty about food supply, along with irregularity of meals and instability of living place, may contribute to differences in female behavior, these regularities remain.

. . . As far as I know [from general ethnographic knowledge], men are the only hunters of large animals in any society; they also generally tend large domestic animals and pastoral herds. Both women and men, on the other hand, may fish and participate in various agricultural activities. . . . [I]n societies with hunting, herding, and animal husbandry with large animals and without fishing, the largest sex differences in socialization are found.[11] What seems characteristic of this type of society is not so much that there is specific men's work, but that this work tends to take the men away from the women and children. I would hypothesize that not only is sex-role training most different in these societies, but that they are the ones most characterized by boys' lacking continuous and regular development toward a clearly defined role.

This suggests a possible problem in studies of the relation between socialization and adult economy or culture. While girls are probably consistently and regularly trained to perform a woman's role, much of (what is viewed as) the training that boys receive in nurturant behavior particularly, but also in other "feminine" behavior, may not be indicative of or preparatory to an adult role at all, but a reflection of the fact that the normal societal organization groups women, girls, and boys in opposition to adult men; since boys are not taught actual woman's work, a natural lot that falls to them is sibling care. This difference may also be true of the Whitings' findings on "egoism" and "altruism";

while "altruistic" behavior in girls is preparatory to an adult role, in boys it may either be this (as, for example, in herding societies) or a time filler where training for an adult male role is unavailable. Egoistic behavior in both sexes may also simply be an indication that these children have little "real" place in the surrounding adult world.

In the preceding consideration of the effect of economy on cultural personality and sex-role distinctions, I was often led to "explanations" of correlations in terms of the "logical" division of labor, or of familial organization and socialization patterns which a particular economy would entail. It is useful to look at these variables by themselves. The Whitings attempt to explain differences between cultures where children behave "egotistically" and those where they behave "altruistically."[12] They find that with one exception (New England), cultures with "altruistic" children have either nuclear or mother-child households, while cultures with "egoistic" children tend to have households and courtyards inhabited by extended families. . . . [Others have found that] large sex differences in socialization are correlated with large family groups with cooperative interaction— either extended families or polygynous families in which co-wives help each other. The Whitings find further that more complex societies (societies with occupational specialization, a centralized political system, class or caste differentiation, and a complex settlement and land-use pattern) tend to produce "egoistic" children.

Both household structure and complexity of society would seem to entail similar tendencies in child training. In households with few adults, it is likely that more contributions are required from children, both regularly and as temporary substitutes for the mother, than in extended households in which adult substitutes are much more available. In such households as well, it is likely that a man and a woman must be prepared to take each other's role when the other is sick or away; therefore, there cannot be a very large difference in the socialization of sex roles.

Similarly, in less complex societies, children from a very young age can be and are trained toward their already known adult roles; they are usually functioning members of the economy. Whatever work they do is a necessary and expected contribution. Furthermore, children in this situation can usually understand the reasons for what they are learning and see tangible results of their work—that they took part in producing the meal which they eat. In these societies it is also more likely that women participate in the producing economy, making it necessary for children to take care of younger children and to do things at home while their mother is out working. On the other hand, in more complex societies, children cannot be as certain of their future role in the division of labor, nor can "work" for them seem as immediately contributory to family welfare as in simpler societies. Crucially, however, these characteristics would probably apply even more to boys than to girls, for whom there is always some basic household and child-care work that they can understand and expect to do, and whose relevance is immediately perceptible.

Differences in the Genesis and Meaning of Masculine and Feminine Behaviors

Similar sex-role socialization and less sex differentiation in adult work are primarily a reflection of the extent to which boys are socialized to perform more (traditionally) feminine behavior and work, although the reverse may sometimes be true (for example, ... boys in societies stressing "compliance" are much more "compliant" according to their ratings than are girls "assertive" in societies stressing "assertion"). This is partially a result of the fact that variations in "economy" still leave women with one element of their "economic" role certain, thus one aspect of their training assured.

There seem to be differences in how compliant and assertive behavior are learned. All children have the basic experience of being raised primarily by women. In societies that stress masculine behavior, women, however resentful, must perform tasks that require reliability, responsibility, and nurturance. And if both children learn to be more independent, assertive, and achievement-oriented, girls still learn this from women, whereas it is likely that boys learn much of this behavior from men. There is a lack of symmetry in the childrearing situations of the two kinds of society. Both boys and girls learn "compliant," "altruistic" behavior from women, but while boys may learn "assertive" behavior from men, girls still learn it from women.

There also seem to be different situational and cultural reasons for pressure toward "assertion" and actual "egoistic" behavior than for pressure toward "compliance" and actual "altruistic" behavior. In the latter case, "altruistic" behavior seems to relate to actual learning of role ("offering help," "offering support," and so forth) and is thus directly supported by pressure toward "compliant" behavior, toward responsibility and obedience. Boys and girls who exhibit these behavioral characteristics are actually doing things—are taking care of siblings, being responsible for livestock, perhaps helping in agricultural work.

"Egoistic" behavior, as pointed out, is likely to be a time filler for someone who does not have a definite role. There is no necessary relation between "egoistic" behavior and adult role, although "egoism" may be an adult personality characteristic. Similarly, it would seem that in societies with pressure toward "assertive" behavior, the usefulness of this behavior is greater in activities which only older people can do well—hunting, warring, successfully competing in business, and the like—and cannot

seem immediately relevant to a child, nor so tied to successful fulfillment of work role for children. Pressure toward "assertion" and "egoistic" behavior seems to exist in societies where there is no "obvious" and simple relation between children's role and adult role, societies in which "characters are formed" rather than "roles learned." This seems to be *the* major characteristic of what it means to be trained to be "masculine," to perform a (typically) "male" role.

In most societies, to the extent that an economy or household structure requires that children learn real work as children, they learn what are normally thought of as female patterns of behavior. To the extent that there is no obvious continuity between childhood and adulthood, children learn what are normally male behaviors. Societies in which sex differences in socialization are small might be simple societies in which all children learn early to be responsible, obedient, and nurturant in the performance of real work, or they may be complex societies, such as ours, in which the socialization of both sexes is not perceptibly and immediately contributory to the society's economy and social organization. The extent to which sex-role socialization differs in ways we would expect, whether differentiation is great or small, reflects the difference in the extent to which boys wait, while girls do not, to be integrated into the adult world of work.

What accounts for "feminine nature," then, is that a certain part of woman's work in all societies requires feminine kinds of behavior, even when the attitude to this behavior is only disdain: women who hate childbearing must bear children and nurse them regularly in nontechnological societies where there are no contraceptives nor bottles. Men's work, on the other hand, varies across cultures both in actual type and in the kinds of personality characteristics it requires. What is "biological necessity" is biological necessity: women bear and in most societies must nurse children. However, it is clear that all those characteristics that constitute this "feminine" nature may also characterize men where other sorts of work or role expectations require them. Beyond this biological minimum, for which even girls can be socialized more or less "appropriately," girls' socialization can produce women whose adult personality can range among all those characteristics which we consider "male" and "female." It is easy to confuse statistical predominance with norms, and to explain norms as being "only natural." This is inaccurate and unnecessary; a convincing explanation considers specific facts, not normative generalizations or desires. This consideration of specific facts provides a logically consistent and empirically complete accounting for sexual and cultural differences which does not need to rely on a universal and therefore in some sense nonexplanatory truth.

IDENTITY AND SEX ROLE

Female and Male Identity: Being and Doing

There are many ways of characterizing the differences in the processes and goals of female and male socialization. Without trying to evaluate the exactness of these sorts of characterizations, I will describe them briefly. Distinctions can be drawn both between the degree of immediacy of (sex) roles for the child in primitive as opposed to Western societies and between boys and girls in each.

Anthropologists contrast the continuity and clarity of socialization in most primitive societies with modern society. In simpler societies the economic system is relatively understandable to a child. Work training constitutes gradual initiation into different kinds of work that will be expected of the child as an adult. Mothers' work is usually performed near children, and fathers' work, even if it is away, is liable to be a concretely describable, if not observable task—hunting game or planting and harvesting corn in the lowlands—rather than abstract thinking or assembly-line work to understand which involves understanding the whole process of production in a factory of bureaucratic paper work. In addition, in societies that are less complex, more parents (especially fathers) do the same kind of work. For an American child, even if his or her father does something concrete and complete, like running a small grocery store or farming, a comparison with other fathers indicates immediately that this particular work cannot be easily equated with *the* "male" role.

Biological differences too are less apparent. In modern society children's sexuality is played down . . . , and adult sex and childbearing are hidden. Clothes do their best to hide bodies and bodily differences. Primitive societies often approach bodies and sex differently: children and often adults wear much less clothing; families may all sleep in the same room; and childbirth takes place in the home. Children's sexual behavior may be either ignored or encouraged rather than actively repressed.

While these distinctions mean that the learning of adult sex roles is easier for children in less complex societies, it is also probably true that within each of these types of society, similar distinctions insure that a girl's development into a woman is more continuous and understandable than a boy's development into a man. In some sense "feminine identity" is more easily and surely attainable than "masculine identity." Margaret Mead claims that from the time of birth, girls can begin to take on feminine identity through identification with their mothers, while for little boys, masculine identification comes through a process of differentiation, because what would be his "natural" identification—identification with the person he is closest to and most dependent upon—is according to cultural values "unnatural," this

works against his attainment of stable masculine identity. The boy's "earliest experience of self is one in which he is forced, in the relationship to his mother, to realize himself as different, as a creature unlike the mother, as a creature unlike the human beings who make babies in a direct, intelligible way by using their own bodies to make them."[13] This seems to be the paradigmatic situation which describes many of the more general sex-role problems considered below.

I have already described how in many non-Western societies, a girl's development and learning of her adult female role is more regular and continuous than a boy's development. Although the case is not so clear in our society (especially because there are more cross-pressures on the girl), it would seem that here also, pressure on girls, and the development of "feminine" identity, is not as difficult for the girl to understand. Talcott Parsons claims that it is "possible from an early age to initiate girls directly into many important aspects of the adult feminine role."[14] At least part of their mother's work is around the home, and the meaning of this activity is tangible and easily understandable to the child. Children can also participate in this work or imitate it. For a girl this is direct training in her adult role; for a boy it is often that part of his socialization which most complicates his development.

In contrast, an urban child's father works away from his home, where his son cannot participate in or observe his work. In addition, masculine functions are "of a relatively abstract and intangible character such that their meaning must remain almost wholly inaccessible to a child."[15] Thus, boys are deprived of the possibility of modeling themselves meaningfully after tangible adult male roles or of being initiated gradually into adult work. Parsons wonders about boys in rural areas, whose fathers' work is closer to home and more available to children, and suggests that these boys tend to be "good" in a sense not typical of urban boys (and like boys in societies where children of both sexes can be gradually integrated into the economy).

This suggests that in both [simple] and [complex] societies, girls seem to have an easier time learning their adult role: their socialization is less conflicted, less irregular, more continuous, than the socialization of boys. However, socialization for both sexes is more continuous, and thus identity more stable, in [simple] than in complex societies.

A distinction reiterated in many different sources which both characterizes and explains this difference in the relative difficulty of girls' and boys' attainment of sex-role identity is that girls and women "are," while boys and men "do": feminine identity is "ascribed," masculine identity "achieved." . . . [E]ven biological differences reflect this distinction: "the man is actually obliged to go on proving his manhood to the woman. There is no analogous necessity for her: even if she is frigid, she can engage in sexual intercourse and conceive and bear a child. She performs her part by merely *being*, without any *doing*. . . .The man on the other hand has to do something in order to fulfill himself."[16] Mead claims that the little boy's period of "simple sureness" about his sexuality is short—the period during childhood when he knows he has a penis, the potential to be manly, like other "men," but before he finds out that he will not be big or strong enough for a number of years to act like a man.[17] This period is the little girl's only period of doubt about her sexuality; on either end is sureness about this identity, first through identification with her mother and then because she herself has borne a child.

Culturally, too, "maleness . . . is not absolutely defined, it has to be kept and re-earned every day."[18] Parsons suggests that women have an attainable goal—to marry and have children—and that how well they do this may bear on how people judge them, but not on their fundamental female status.[19] He contrasts this with male status, which is constantly dependent in a basic way on a man's success at work, at getting promotions, and as a provider.

The need to differentiate himself continues throughout the boy's childhood. Mead points out that the boy "is trained by women to be a male, which involves no identification of the self with the mother-teacher (and when it does, I would add, this identification is harmful to his attainment of identity). He is to be a boy by doing the things Mother says but doing them in a manly way."[20] His upbringing, and the attainment of any kind of success, is characterized by its conditional nature: success is always temporary—a failure wipes it out—and love and approval are dependent upon success.

Simone de Beauvoir sees positive rather than negative effects on boys from this differentiation.[21] She describes girls' upbringing and contrasts it with boys', rather than attempting to explain how these contrasts have arisen. For her, boys' "doing" becomes men's transcendence: men are artists, creators, risk their lives, have projects. Women, on the other hand, are carefully trained to "be." A girl's natural inclination would also be to "do," but she learns to make herself into an object, to restrict herself to the sphere of immanence. Female destiny is foreordained and repetitive; men can choose their destiny:

> The young boy, be he ambitious, thoughtless, or timid, looks toward an open future; he will be a seaman or an engineer, he will stay on the farm or go away to the city, he will see the world, he will get rich; he feels free, confronting a future in which the unexpected awaits him. The young girl will be wife, grandmother; she will keep house just as her mother did, she will give her children the same care she herself received when young—she is twelve years old and already her story is written in the heavens. She will discover it day after day without ever making it.[22]

The Cultural Universal: Socialization by Females

The common fact in all socialization situations I have mentioned is that women are the primary socializers. Men may also help in child care, but their "work" is elsewhere; for women it is the reverse. I have indicated certain effects that this seems to have on children's development in terms of primary identity, and on the differences between the development of identity in boys and girls. One result for children of both sexes is that, since "it is the mother's and not the father's voice that gives the principal early approval and disapproval, the nagging voice of conscience is feminine in both sexes."[23] Thus, as children of either sex attempt to gain independence, to make decisions on their own, different from their upbringing, they must do this by consciously or unconsciously rejecting their mother (and people like her) and the things she is associated with. This fact, and the cultural institutions and emphases that it seems to entail, has different consequences for boys and for girls.

Effects on Boys: The Dread of Women

One consequence of the fact that women are primary socializers for boys (who later become men) is what Horney calls the "dread of women."[24] This has both psychological and cultural aspects. Psychologically, Horney believes that fear of the mother (women) in men is even greater and more repressed than fear of the father (men). The mother initially has complete power over the child's satisfaction of needs and first forbids instinctual activities and therefore encourages the child's first sadistic impulses to be directed against her and her body. This creates enormous anxiety in the child. Fear of the father, on the other hand, is not so threatening. For one thing, it develops later in life, as a result of specific processes which the child is more "aware" that he is experiencing, and not in reaction to the father's total and incomprehensible control over the child's livelihood: "dread of the father is more actual and tangible, less uncanny in quality."[25] For another, it does not entail a boy's admitting fear of a different sort of being, and "masculine self-regard suffers less in this way."[26] Because all men have mothers, these results are to a greater or lesser degree universal: "the anxiety connected with his self-respect leaves more or less distinct traces in every man and gives to his general attitude to women a particular stamp which either does not exist in women's attitude to men, or, if it does, is acquired secondarily. In other words, it is no integral part of their feminine nature."[27]

Individual creations, as well as folk legends and beliefs, are often attempts to cope with this dread. For instance, there are poems and ballads that talk about fears of engulfment by whirlpools, allurement by sirens who entice the unwary and kill whom they catch. Women and symbols of women in these creations and fantasies are for grown men what the all-powerful mother is for the child. But if this power can be named and externalized, it can possibly be conquered. Another way of coping with dread is to glorify and adore women—"There is no need for me to dread a being so wonderful, so beautiful, nay, so saintly"—or to debase and disparage them—"It would be too ridiculous to dread a creature who, if you take her all round, is such a poor thing."[26]

Culturally, this means that in general it is important for men to gain power and to insure that the attributes of power and prestige are masculine, or, more precisely, that whatever cultural role accrues to the male is then accorded power and prestige: "If such activities [like cooking and weaving] are appropriate occupations of men, then the whole society, men and women alike, votes them as important. When the same occupations are performed by women, they are regarded as less important."[29] It also becomes necessary to reserve many of these activities for men, to believe that women are unable to do many of the "important" things that contribute to society—to exercise political power, to be artistic or creative, to play an equal role in the economy—and at the same time to devalue whatever it is that women do—whether they are housewives, teachers, or social workers. In fact, "cultures frequently phrase achievement as something that women do not or cannot do, rather than directly as something which men do well."[30]

Melford Spiro's work on the kibbutz indicates that this "causal" argument is valid.[31] He makes it clear that this happens even in a community that is specifically trying to eliminate sexual inequalities, but in which women continue to be the main socializers of children.[32] On the kibbutz where Spiro lived, it seems clear that women's work is not as prestigious as men's work. This is particularly evident in the socialization institutions most affecting children. Until children are twelve or thirteen, all their nurses and teachers are women; when they reach thirteen and begin high school—are more clearly doing "serious work" and not just being brought up—their teachers and supervisors are all men. "Nurses" in the high school perform mainly menial functions—clean buildings and bathrooms, clean and repair clothing—and take care of children only when they are sick. Serving "as an important transitional buffer from an all-female to an all-male [sic! These children are boys *and* girls, growing into a male *and* female world] adult environment,"[33] nurses, from being the most important adults in the child's world (parents are visited several hours a day and are loving and warm, but are not really the child's "socializers"), cede this status to men and become maids, for some reason incapable of continuing to play an important socializing role in the child's life.

Around this time, girls (for reasons not apparent to, or at least not mentioned by, Spiro) cease to be moral leaders of the students and become less intellectual and

artistic than boys, when before they had been more so. Boys become more interested in their work and more politically interested. Among the adult kibbutz members, women do not serve on important committees, rarely speak up at meetings—and when they do, are not listened to with the same seriousness as men—and do not participate in the economic administration or intellectual life of the kibbutz. Although they work harder and longer than most men in order to "prove" themselves and their worth, the men continue to find it necessary not to recognize the value of this work or to accord women equal status.[34]

Dread and Bisexuality

Thus, institutionally and culturally, men have often managed to overcome this "dread" of women through a devaluation of whatever women do and are. But the dread continues within the men themselves, a perfectly understandable, if errant, product of socialization by women: a retention of feminine qualities, partial identification with women, desire to be a woman like one's mother. Freud calls this bisexuality and considers that all people, both men and women, contain traits of both sexes. Without pursuing what these "traits" as universal "constituents" could mean, we can deal with the same concept by examining the fact that all people within a culture contain within themselves both what are considered (and tend to be) masculine and what are considered feminine characteristics in that culture. I would suggest that in most cultures, the earliest identity for any child is "feminine," because women are around him and provide (and do not provide) him with the necessities of life. This identification is probably more threatening to the boy, because more basic, than the elements of masculine identification that a little girl acquires. Several kinds of evidence attest to the existence (and repression) of "bisexual" or "feminine" elements in boys and men.

An indication of the continuing threat of "femininity" to males in our culture is the strength of both external and internal pressure on little boys to conform to masculine ideals, to reject identification with or participation in anything that seems "feminine." Initially, this pressure is generated by socializers of both sexes, but it is soon rigidly internalized by young boys, who hold both themselves and their peers to account over it.

The narrowness and severity of this training is far greater than comparable "training" for femininity in girls. Girls can be tomboys, wear jeans and other men's clothing, fight, climb trees, play sports, ride bikes. Their mothers may become somewhat anxious about them, but this behavior will not be cause for great alarm, nor will it be forbidden or cruelly ridiculed. Similarly, they will be considered "strange" or "unfeminine" if they continue to be active, to succeed academically or professionally; however, many women do so nonetheless, without feeling a fundamental challenge to their identity. The training and subsequent behavior of boys is not so flexible. It would be unheard of for boys to wear dresses; if they want to cook or play with dolls, do not like sports, or are afraid to fight, this is cause for panic by parents, educators, and psychologists. And in fact, boys do conform closely to the male goals and behavior required of them. They learn early not to exhibit feminine personality traits—to hide emotions and pretend even to themselves that they do not have them, to be independent participants in activities rather than personally involved with friends. Later, as men, they are careful never to choose women's careers unless they are prepared to bear enormous stigma.

The extent and strength of boys' training not to have or admit "feminine" traits is indicated by Daniel Brown's studies on sex-role preference in children.[35] From kindergarten age, boys are much less likely to claim a preference for anything feminine than girls to prefer masculine roles or objects. The extent of this difference is demonstrated by some of Brown's data: of girls $3\frac{1}{2}$ to $5\frac{1}{2}$ about half tend to prefer "feminine" and half to prefer "masculine" toys, roles, and activities; at this age, 70 percent to 80 percent of boys express "masculine" preferences. The differences increase as children get older. From six to nine years old, boys become even more strongly masculine in their preferences, and girls' preferences become less feminine, that is, more girls from six to nine make "masculine" choices than "feminine" choices.

The extent of boys' masculine "preferences," particularly in contrast to the willingness of girls to claim cross-sexual preferences, is striking. Clearly, part of the reason may be that it is apparent to both boys and girls, and becomes more apparent as they grow older, that in our society "male" roles and activities are more prestigious and privileged than "female" roles and activities. However, another interpretation is that the extreme unwillingness of boys to make cross-sex choices indicates that they have been taught very early, and have accepted more or less completely, that it is right for them to prefer masculine things; therefore, they are extremely reluctant to make feminine choices. More important, it would seem that these boys, in contrast to the girls, believe that making such choices helps to insure their masculinity, and, alternatively, that different choices would not just be different choices among a number of possible alternatives, but rather threatening in the deepest sense.

This latter explanation, in terms of fear and attempts to insure masculinity, seems to account better for the regularity with which even very young boys—boys who spend most of their time in a world of female privilege with their mother or female teachers, and who

play with children of both sexes—refuse to choose those things that are associated with females, and that thus might give them some of the feminine attributes of power. Studies of parental orientation in young boys also support such an interpretation. At ages when boys are already making strongly "masculine" choices of objects and playmates, they still do not identify with their fathers or male figures as strongly as girls, who are not making "feminine" choices, identify with their mothers.[36]

Fear of the feminine may not be so well absorbed and repressed: according to some interpreters, certain cultural or subcultural phenomena attest to direct jealousy of women and attempt to appropriate female roles. In Plains Indian cultures, for example, which stressed extreme bravery and daring for men, transvestism was an institutionalized solution for those men who did not feel able to take on the extremely masculine life required of them. A more important example are cultures in which *all* men perform certain rituals identifying with women. The most obvious of these rituals is the *couvade*. Roger Burton and John Whiting hypothesize that in cultures with both early mother-child sleeping arrangements and matrilocal residence—that is, a world controlled by the child's mother and other female relatives[37]—a boy child will have both primary and secondary feminine optative identity ("those statuses a person wishes he could occupy but from which he is disbarred").[38] In this situation, "the society should provide him some means to act out, symbolically at least, the female role."[39] Their data suggest that an institution that serves this purpose in a large number of societies of this type is the *couvade*.

Initiation rites have been variously interpreted as attempts to appropriate or incorporate the feminine role, or, on the other hand, to exorcise it. On the basis of both anthropological and psychological evidence, Bettelheim claims that male initiation rites, which often involve subincision, and in general include some kind of cutting or wounding of the genitals, are means for symbolically acquiring a vagina, "to assert that men, too, can bear children."[40] At the same time, circumcision and other tests of endurance, strength, and knowledge are ways of proving masculine sexual maturity, of asserting and defining maleness.[41]

Burton and Whiting's cross-cultural evidence provides the explanation of this jealousy that we are looking for, in terms of the maternal role in socialization.[42] In certain ("father-absent") societies, children sleep exclusively with their mother during their first two years, and there is a long postpartum sex taboo. All children in such societies develop a "primary feminine optative identity." These societies contrast with ones in which the father and mother continue to sleep together and in which both parents give and withhold resources to some extent; in such societies children's primary optative identity is "adult."[43] Further, among "father-absent" societies, there is a contrast between matrilocal and patrilocal societies. In the latter, a boy's secondary identity—which develops when he becomes a "yard child" and observes that in the society at large, it is males who have higher status and power—is masculine; boys thus develop a "cross-sex identity." Burton and Whiting demonstrate that initiation ceremonies tend to occur in societies whose sleeping arrangements and residence patterns produce cross-sex identity in boys; the function of these ceremonies is "to brainwash the primary feminine identity and to establish firmly the secondary male identity."[44] In many societies with male initiation rites, sex-identity terms, rather than being the equivalent of "male" and "female" in our society, are instead differentiated so that one term refers to women, girls, and uninitiated boys, while the other refers only to men who have already been initiated.

Evidence from more [complex] societies also suggests that "father-absence" or "low father-salience" in childhood may lead to "compulsively masculine" behavior which entails the same rejection, although not in a ritual context, of the female world and feminine behavior. Gang and delinquent behavior among American lower-class men often includes compulsive, and strong denial of anything feminine with corresponding emphasis on masculinity—risk and daring, sexual prowess, rejection of home life, physical violence—as well as severe "tests" (which might be seen as forms of "initiation rites") as requirements of gang membership. Similar behavior also seems characteristic of Caribbean men raised in "father-absent" households.[45]

Beatrice Whiting shows that criminal and other violent behavior occurs more frequently in those two out of the six cultures in which husband and wife may neither sleep nor eat together and seldom work or play together. Sex-identity conflict seems to develop differently in the two societies, however. One is an Indian Rajput caste community, in which children of both sexes score high in "egoistic" behavior. Boys are around women, perhaps desire their role, and have no role of their own until they grow up. Children in the other community, Nyansongo, Kenya, score highest in "altruistic" behavior. Here, boys from a quite young age are herders. Since they are being taught "feminine" behavior of responsibility and nurturance, and eat and sleep only with women, it is probable that their identity is even more strongly "feminine" than that of the Rajput boys. Like violent behavior, male narcissism, pride, and phobia toward mature women—other indications of compulsive assertion of masculinity—seem to be prevalent in societies in which boys spend their earlier years exclusively or predominantly with women, and in which the "degree of physical or emotional distance between mother and father as compared with that between mother and child" is great.[46]

All this evidence—of cultural institutions that exorcise or attempt to gain control of feminine powers for men; of institutions that provide for the assertion of compulsively masculine behavior; of the threats of bisexuality or femininity to boys and men—suggests that it is not sufficient to attribute the devaluation of female work roles and personality to external and conscious "dread of women," to known fear of woman's power. Rather, it must be attributed to fear of that womanly power which has remained *within* men—the bisexual components of any man's personality. This is so threatening because in some sense, there is no sure definition of masculinity, no way for the little boy to know if he has really made it, except insofar as he manages to differentiate himself from what he somehow vaguely defines as femininity. "For maleness in America [and, I would suggest, elsewhere] is not absolutely defined, it has to be kept and re-earned every day, and one essential element in the definition is beating women in every game that both sexes play, in every activity in which both sexes engage.[47]

Although the reasons for the difficulty in defining male identity are very complicated, I have tried to indicate one direction which may provide some answers. This direction is based on an examination of how children attain sureness of themselves, of an "identity" which is theirs, and of what it means for one sex that there are no people "like me" who are there—and as important as people "not like me"—from earliest infancy, as nurturers, as models, as providers and deniers of resources. What it means, according to Mead, is that "the recurrent problem of civilization is to define the male role satisfactorily enough,"[48] both for societies and for individuals who must live up to these undefined roles.

Feminine Development: Identity Versus Preference

In this section I will examine comparatively the development of "feminine identity" in girls, studying especially how the problems of male socialization seem to affect this development and sex-role preference in girls and women.

Most of the evidence presented so far indicates that girls should have an easier time than boys developing a stable sexual identity: they are brought up primarily by women; their socialization is fairly gradual and continuous in most societies; the female role is more accessible and understandable to the child. I will not be able to evaluate or examine cross-cultural evidence about feminine identity and about how women or girls in other (non-Western) cultures view their feminine role. For the purposes of this or any specific investigation about the psychological effects of female socialization, evidence on conflict about the feminine role and its causes, comparable to that on cross-sex identity in males, is so scanty that even hypothesizing about what must "logically" be the case seems unacceptable. I will be primarily concerned with the different forms (and "secondary" psychological importance) which female envy of males seems to take in Western society.

In contrast to non-Western societies, Western female socialization is not so clear or unambiguous, just as the adult feminine role is not so clearly an essential or important part of the society. The universal, and not just sexually defined, "superiority" of men and masculinity in the "important" realms of the culture means that women get trained partially for traditionally feminine roles (childrearing, housekeeping) and personality (passivity, compliance, "goodness"); at the same time in school they are taught goals of achievement and success, and it is made clear to them that their other (feminine) role and its values are less desirable, less highly valued, in the progress of humanity and the world.

This situation is comparable to the problem of cross-sex identity for boys. Girls are initially brought up in a feminine world, with mothers all-powerful and all-prestigious, where it is desirable to acquire a feminine identity. They later go into a world where male power is clearly important (even if, as in school, its values are transmitted by women), where males dominate society and its important resources. Beauvoir (in a somewhat culturally limited and dated, but still suggestive, way) describes this situation:

> If the little girl at first accepts her feminine vocation, it is not because she intends to abdicate; it is, on the contrary, in order to rule; she wants to be a matron because the matrons' group seems privileged; but, when her company, her studies, her games, her reading, take her out of the maternal circle, she sees that it is not the women but the men who control the world. It is this revelation—much more than the discovery of the penis—that irresistibly alters her conception of herself.[49]

However, this does not seem to present the same challenge to fundamental identity as a shift from a female to a male world presents for boys, because in the little girl's case, her primary identity is feminine.

It is apparently the case as well that just that kind of maternal behavior most conducive to greater sex conflict in boys, to less easy attainment of a sense of masculinity—for example, general nonpermissiveness, pressures toward inhibition and nonaggression, use of physical punishment and ridicule, high sex anxiety, and severity of toilet training—is also (not surprisingly) that behavior which encourages the development of "feminine" qualities and femininity in girls.[50] This maternal behavior, according to Slater, develops especially in those kinds of societies or subcultures where the marriage relationship is "distant" and where family patterns usually entail most extreme masculine insecurity and compulsive masculine behavior.[51] I have suggested, however, that these tendencies are probably present to some extent in all childrearing situations; the mother has major responsibility for children, and this situation, in which a mother's whole life and sense of self depends on rearing "good" or "successful" children, always produces anxiety over performance and over-identification with children.[52]

This perpetuates a childrearing cycle. As long as these "feminine" qualities are produced in a socialization situation in which mothers are anxious and conflicted—as they must be in Western society—they must necessarily involve girls' resentment and conflicts over their acceptance, and thus anxious and resentful behavior toward children in the next generation. It should be emphasized, however, that these "conflicts" do not seem to be a reflection of a girl's uncertainty about whether she has attained a "feminine" identity; childhood environment and pressures on both sexes toward "feminine" compliance probably ensure that she has. Her conflicts, rather, are about whether or not she wants this identity that relies on her own ability to inhibit herself and to respond to the demands of others, eventually leading her to an adult fate where her role and her dependence upon it doom her to bring up sons and daughters resentful of her and the "femininity" she represents.

It seems clear to the whole society, and especially to the little girl, that this identity and its future leave much to be desired. Brown's findings indicate that not only do small girls "prefer" a masculine role with much more frequency than small boys "prefer" a feminine role, but that this preference for a masculine role increases with age from kindergarten to fourth grade: after the age of five, more girls prefer a masculine role than prefer a feminine role. Lawrence Kohlberg claims that one reason for the huge discrepancy in male and female same-sex and opposite-sex choices and the huge increase in female opposite-sex choices is that, in fact, Brown's "it" figure is more masculine than feminine, and that girls become with age less self-projective and increasingly oriented to this reality aspect of the test.[53] A finding of Brown's that would seem to mitigate this criticism is that in his fifth-grade sample, girls show a strong reversal from their previous masculine choices and a strong preference for feminine role choices.

Kohlberg, however, also presents data from several other preference studies of activities, toys, and peer choices which, although they do not show the extreme differences that Brown found between boys and girls, or extreme masculine preferences in girls, do show that for boys, masculine preferences of activities and peers either begin and remain very high, or begin relatively high and increase with age. In contrast, girls' same-sex preferences are never so high as boys' and tend to be more erratic—to show no consistent or increasing pattern of preference for feminine activities and peers.[54] He also mentions studies which indicate that not only are girls' sex-typed preferences of activities and playmates lower than boys', but also that "girls make fewer judgments than boys that their own sex is better . . . and girls' preferential evaluations of their own sex decrease with age."[55] Girls also tend to make more "feminine" judgments or preferences when they are asked directly "which do you like?" than they do when asked "which do girls like?"[56] My guess is that the former question puts girls more on the line—they are afraid of not being "good" whereas the latter is a way for them to express their real preferences and judgments of value, without indicating to the interviewer that they do not know or believe in what they really "ought" to like or do.

All of these preferences seem to reflect the clear cultural evaluation of masculine pursuits and characteristics as superior, an evaluation that is probably made more evident to the girl as she grows up and learns more about the world around her. Karen Horney calls this the development of the girl's "flight from womanhood." "In actual fact a girl is exposed from birth onwards to the suggestion—inevitable, whether conveyed brutally or delicately—of her inferiority, an experience which must constantly stimulate her masculinity complex."[57] Horney attributes this both to unconscious psychological motives and to cognitive assessment of the world around her. The girl's unconscious motives stem from an attempt to deny an Oedipal attachment to her father by recoiling from femininity and therefore these feminine desires. This is in contrast to the boy, whose fear of his attachment to his mother leads to increased compensatory masculinity. Importantly, these unconscious motives "are reinforced and supported by the actual disadvantage under which women labour in social life."[58] Horney, writing from within the psychoanalytic tradition, seems more defensive about emphasizing the cultural components of the "flight" than we would be today; however, she still describes those components accurately. While these latter reasons may be partially a form of "rationalization" for less acceptable unconscious motives, "we must not forget that this disadvantage is actually a piece of reality," that there is an "actual social subordination of women."[59] This "flight" is not from an unsureness of feminine identity, but from a knowledge of it and its implications.

Partially because of this social subordination of women and cultural devaluation of feminine qualities, girls are allowed and feel themselves free to express masculine preferences and to have much greater freedom than boys—to play boys' games, dress like boys and so forth. For this reason, they are encouraged to achieve in school, and it is considered "only natural" that they would want to do so. In neither case does the girl or her socializers doubt that her feminine identity is firm, that she will eventually resign herself to her feminine adult role, and that at this time, this role will come naturally to her.

As she gets older, however, her peers and the adults around her cease such tolerance of this envy of males and of these attempts to engage in male activities or to achieve like men: "any self-assertion will diminish her femininity and her attractiveness."[60] She is supposed to begin to be passive and docile, to become interested in her appearance, to cultivate her abilities to charm men, to mold herself to their wants. This is not a one-sided requirement, however. At the same time she is supposed to continue to do well in school, but must expect to be stigmatized or reproved if she does. In American society she continues in school to be instilled with "American" (masculine) goals—success, achievement, competition. She fails as a good citizen, as a successful human being, if she does not succeed, and as a woman if she does. Mead sums up the girl's position:

> We end up with the contradictory picture of a society that appears to throw its doors wide open to women, but translates her every step towards success as having been damaging—to her own chances of marriage, and to the men whom she passes on the road [whom she must pass, in a society where success is defined only by beating other people].[61]

And it does seem that the society succeeds in imposing its demands. We can recall Brown's finding that fifth-grade (prepubertal and pubertal) girls make a dramatic switch and all of a sudden develop strong "preferences" for feminine activities and objects; we remember the "unexplainable" fact that girls on the kibbutz, formerly creative and interested in their work, moral and social leaders and organizers in their children's group, suddenly in high school become uninterested in intellectual activities, unconcerned about politics, uncreative and unartistic. We know that in general, as children grow up, girls become less successful in school and drop out of the role of equal participant in activities that they once held.

CONCLUSION

Sex-role ideology and socialization for these roles seem to ensure that neither boys nor girls can attain both stable identity and meaningful roles. The tragedy of woman's socialization is not that she is left unclear, as is the man, about her basic sexual identity. This identity is ascribed to her, and she does not need to prove to herself or to society that she has earned it or continues to have it. Her problem is that this identity is clearly devalued in the society in which she lives. This does not mean that women too should be required to compete for identity, to be assertive and to need to achieve—to "do" like men. Nor does it suggest that it is not crucial for everyone, men and women alike, to have a stable sexual identity. But until male "identity" does not depend on men's proving themselves, their "doing" will be a reaction to insecurity, not a creative exercise of their humanity, and woman's "being," far from being an easy and positive acceptance of self, will be a resignation to inferiority. And as long as women must live through their children, and men do not genuinely contribute to socialization and provide easily accessible role models, women will continue to bring up sons whose sexual identity depends on devaluing femininity inside and outside themselves, and daughters who must accept this devalued position and resign themselves to producing more men who will perpetuate the system that devalues them.

NOTES

Note: I am grateful to Susan Contratto Weisskopf for first suggesting to me certain severe problems in male-identity development which led me to the particular comparative approach taken in this essay.

1. I am aware of many potential drawbacks in "cross-cultural" studies: their dubious reliability; in many cases, the relatively incomparable nature of much of the data used for cross-cultural comparisons, particularly those comparisons based on material from the Human Relations Area Files or other large-scale comparisons in which the original gathering of data was not under the control of the person using this data; the difficulty of rating cultures according to nonculturally defined variables; and the tenuous nature of causal explanations based on statistical correlation or comparison. Although it is beyond the scope of this essay to offer a specific criticism of such studies and beyond the scope of my abilities to evaluate statistical methods and results, I have attempted to avoid reliance on minute statistical differences for proof, and to attribute adequacy to explanations according to their logical and experiential plausibility, rather than their statistical reliability.

2. Margaret Mead, *Male and Female* (New York: William Morrow, 1949).

3. Roy D'Andrade, "Sex Differences and Cultural Institutions," in E. Maccoby, ed., *The Development of Sex Differences* (Stanford: Stanford University Press, 1966), p. 176.

4. Beatrice B. Whiting and John W. M. Whiting, "Egoism and Altruism," *Children of Six Cultures, Part 1: Egoism vs. Altruism* (forthcoming), p. 32.

5. Zinacantan, a highland Indian community in Mexico where I did fieldwork, perfectly exemplifies this hypothetical description. Men's agricultural work is done in the lowlands, away from the community, and boys, depending on whether or not they are in school, do not work with their fathers until they are nine to eleven. They perform a certain amount of "helping" work when they are young—fetching things, and so forth—but this is not seen as "real" work for them. They remain without real work training from their mothers, while their sisters as they grow up learn progressively how to tend fires, cook, and weave. As the boy's role in his house seems to become less and less relevant, and he is less and less able to fill time meaningfully, he turns increasingly to antics to get attention from his all-too-busy mother and sisters.

6. Whiting and Whiting, "Egoism and Altruism," p. 35.

7. *Ibid.*

8. Beatrice Whiting told me in a conversation that their data indicate that girl children stay closer to their mothers, and receive more numerous and frequent commands than boys. She suggests that this is training specifically useful for childrearing and household work, in which a woman has to expect to be interrupted irregularly in whatever tasks she is doing, and cannot detach herself from her surrounding situation nor try many new ways to work. This seems to relate to typical "feminine" intellectual characteristics—nonabstract thinking, field dependence, etc.—and also to be closer to the kind of training boys would get in economics where they are generally trained and given specific work to do.

9. Herbert Barry III, Margaret Bacon, and Irvin L. Child, "Relation of Child Training to Subsistence Economy," *American Anthropologist* 61 (1959): 51–63.

10. Beatrice B. and John W. M. Whiting, "Task Assignment and Personality: A Consideration of the Effect of Herding on Boys," paper presented at the Social Science Conference, University of East Africa, Dar-es-Salaam, 1968.

11. Herbert Barry III, Margaret K. Bacon, and Irvin L. Child, "A Cross-Cultural Survey of Some Sex Differences in Socialization," *Journal of Abnormal Psychology* 55 (1957): 330.

12. Whiting and Whiting, "Egoism and Altruism."

13. Mead, *op. cit.*, p. 167.

14. Talcott Parsons, "Age and Sex in the Social Structure of the United States," *American Sociological Review* 7 (1942): 604–616. I would like to note here that the fact that these are "important aspects" does not necessarily mean that they are important in actual economic or social fact or in a society's, or the little girl's, evaluation of them. I will go into the implications of this fact for female development below.

15. *Ibid.*

16. Karen Horney, "The Dread of Women," *International Journal of Psychoanalysis* 13 (1932): 359.

17. Mead, *op. cit.*, p. 167.

18. *Ibid.*, p. 303.

19. Parsons, *op. cit.*

20. Mead, *op. cit.*, p. 295.

21. Simone De Beauvoir, *The Second Sex* (New York: Bantam Books, 1968).

22. *Ibid.*, p. 278.

23. Mead, *op. cit.*, p. 298.

24. Horney, *op. cit.*

25. *Ibid.*, p. 351.

26. *Ibid.*

27. *Ibid.*, p. 357.

28. *Ibid.*, p. 351.

29. Mead, *op. cit.*, p. 168.

30. *Ibid.*

31. Melford E. Spiro, *Children of the Kibbutz: A Study in Child Training and Personality* (New York: Schocken Books, 1965).

32. The following interpretation was not made by Spiro, but seemed to me to explain fairly clearly many differences between men and women which Spiro did not seem to understand.

33. Spiro, *op. cit.*, p. 291.

34. *Ibid.*, p. 352.

35. Daniel G. Brown, "Sex-Role Preference in Young Children," *Psychological Monographs* 70 (1956): 1–19; "Masculinity-Femininity Development in Children," *Journal of Consulting Psychology* 21 (1957): 197–202; "Sex Role Development in a Changing Culture," *Psychological Bulletin* 55 (1958): 232–242.

36. Brown, "Sex Role Development in a Changing Culture," pp. 237–238; Lawrence Kohlberg, "A Cognitive-Developmental Analysis of Children's Sex Role Concepts and Attitudes," in Maccoby, *op. cit.*

37. The dynamics of this are not as clear as Burton and Whiting suggest. In most "matrilocal" societies (usually also matrilineal), "control" or "power" still rests in the hands of men, although these men are now "mother's brothers" or "mother's maternal uncles" rather than fathers and grandfathers (see David Schneider and Kathleen Gough, eds., *Matrilineal Kinship* [Berkeley: University of California Press, 1967], for the most extensive treatment of matrilineal societies). Although these men may spend a lot of time with their own wives, thus away from the maternal residence, it is not clear how the exercise of power is then distributed:

whether it is given to the women of the lineage, exercised only on special occasions by men of the lineage, or entrusted to in-marrying men. In-marrying men may control the day-to-day operation of the economy, even though they are not owners of the lands or their produce. I do not wish to discount Burton and Whiting's theory, but simply to point out that to understand it, the relation between matrilocal residence and the operation of control and power both in lineage theory and in everyday life (perhaps the instability of what men control what and are around when) would have to be examined more closely than their initial hypothesis would lead us to believe.

38. Roger V. Burton and John W. M. Whiting, "The Absent Father and Cross-Sex Identity," *Merrill-Palmer Quarterly* 7 (1961): 85–95. It is not within the scope of this essay to evaluate Whiting's status-envy hypothesis as a learning theory, although, clearly, the extent to which we would want to accept his conclusions depends largely on this evaluation.

39. *Ibid.*, p. 91.

40. Bruno Bettelheim, *Symbolic Wounds: Puberty Rites and the Envious Male* (Glencoe: The Free Press, 1954), p. 45.

41. Bettelheim does not restrict this interpretation to male initiation rites only, but claims that female initiation rites may equally be expressions of envy for the masculine role. He emphasizes male initiation and envy of the female because he feels that female envy of male sex functions—penis envy—has been overemphasized at the expense of the other. He suggests that this is because "in any society, envy of the dominant sex is the more easily observed [and] more readily admitted, more openly expressed and more easily recognized." (Bettelheim, *op. cit.*, p. 56). It is also true that female initiation rites are not nearly so widespread nor so complex as male rites. Bettelheim suggests, rightly, I think, that this is because while women can express their jealousy of men openly in most societies and it is considered only natural that they should be jealous—"the consensus is that it is desirable to be a man" (*ibid.*)—men's jealousy is not so admissible and "can be expressed only in ritual" (*ibid.*). This is in accordance with reasons for differences in the strictness of male and female socialization which I discussed earlier.

42. Burton and Whiting, *op. cit.*

43. I would maintain that even in these societies, mothers have more control of resources and spend more time with children, so that boys would still have a harder time than girls in developing a sex-role identity.

44. Burton and Whiting, *op. cit.*, p. 90.

45. *Ibid.*; Beatrice B. Whiting, "Sex Identity Conflict and Physical Violence: A Comparative Study," unpublished paper.

46. Philip and Dori I. Slater, "Maternal Ambivalence and Narcissism: A Cross-Cultural Study," *Merrill-Palmer Quarterly* 2 (1965): 241–259. . . .

47. Mead, *op. cit.*, p. 303.

48. *Ibid.*, p. 168.

49. Beauvoir, *op. cit.*, p. 267.

50. Kohlberg, *op. cit.*, p. 162.

51. Slater and Slater, *op. cit.*, pp. 249–250.

52. Beauvoir, *op. cit.*, pp. 249–497; Betty Friedan, *The Feminine Mystique* (New York: Dell Publishing Co., 1963).

53. Kohlberg, *op. cit.*, p. 117.

54. *Ibid.*, pp. 118–119.

55. *Ibid.*, p. 120. . . .

56. *Ibid.*, p. 121.

57. Karen Horney, "The Flight from Womanhood: The Masculinity Complex in Women, as Viewed by Men and by Women," *International Journal of Psychoanalysis* 7 (1926): 324–339.

58. *Ibid.*, p. 337.

59. *Ibid.*, p. 338.

60. Beauvoir, *op. cit.*, p. 314.

61. *Ibid.*, p. 301.

REFERENCES

Barry III, Herbert, Margaret K. Bacon, and Irvin L. Child. 1957. "A Cross-Cultural Survey of Some Sex Differences in Socialization," *Journal of Abnormal Psychology* 55: 327–332.

Barry III, Herbert, Margaret Bacon, and Irvin L. Child. 1959. "Relation of Child Training to Subsistence Economy," *American Anthropologist* 61: 51–63.

Bettelheim, Bruno, 1954. *Symbolic Wounds: Puberty Rites and the Envious Male.* Glencoe: The Free Press.

Brown, Daniel G. 1956. "Sex-Role Preference in Young Children," *Psychological Monographs* 70: 1–19. 1957. "Masculinity-Femininity Development in Children," *Journal of Consulting Psychology* 21: 197–202. 1958. "Sex Role Development in a Changing Culture," *Psychological Bulletin* 55: 232–242.

Burton, Roger V. and John W. M. Whiting. 1961. "The Absent Father and Cross-Sex Identity," *Merrill-Palmer Quarterly* 7: 85–95.

D'Andrade, Roy. 1966. "Sex Differences and Cultural Institutions," in E. Maccoby, ed., *The Development of Sex Differences.* Stanford: Stanford University Press.

De Beauvoir, Simone. 1968. *The Second Sex.* New York: Bantam Books.

Friedan, Betty. 1963. *The Feminine Mystique.* New York: Dell Publishing Co.

Horney, Karen. 1926. "The Flight from Womanhood: The Masculinity Complex in Women, as Viewed by Men and by Women," *International Journal of Psychoanalysis* 7: 324–339. 1932. "The Dread of Women," *International Journal of Psychoanalysis* 13: 359.

Kohlberg, Lawrence. 1966. "A Cognitive-Developmental Analysis of Children's Sex Role Concepts and Attitudes," in E. Maccoby, ed., *The Development of Sex Differences.* Stanford: Stanford University Press.

Mead, Margaret. 1949. *Male and Female.* New York: William Morrow.

Parsons, Talcott. 1942. "Age and Sex in the Social Structure of the United States," *American Sociological Review* 7: 604–616.

Schneider, David and Kathleen Gough, eds. 1967. *Matrilineal Kinship.* Berkeley: University of California Press.

Slater, Philip and Dori I. 1965. "Maternal Ambivalence and Narcissism: A Cross-Cultural Study," *Merrill-Palmer Quarterly* 2: 241–259.

Spiro, Melford E. 1965. *Children of the Kibbutz: A Study in Child Training and Personality.* New York: Schocken Books.

Whiting, Beatrice B. n.d. "Sex Identity Conflict and Physical Violence: A Comparative Study," unpublished paper.

Whiting, Beatrice B. and John W. M. Whiting. 1968. "Task Assignment and Personality: A Consideration of the Effect of Herding on Boys," paper presented at the Social Science Conference, University of East Africa, Dar-es-Salaam. 1968. "Egoism and Altruism," *Children of Six Cultures, Part 1: Egoism vs. Altruism* (forthcoming.)

5

Subsistence

With images of famine and drought very much at the forefront of the media, the question of how people subsist takes on an added urgency. American society has ritually affirmed the importance of this issue by proclaiming World Food Day on October 16 and Earth Day on April 22. **Subsistence** at its most elementary entails the production of food and other necessities, requiring the application of human labor, techniques, and technologies to natural resources. In sum, it is a process in which energy is expended in order to produce energy in different forms. The way in which a society produces energy—preeminently in the form of food, but including fire, animal power, and fossil fuels—obviously has a significant impact in shaping the way people live because neither features of the environment nor technology can be changed limitlessly. At the same time, the environment will obviously impose constraints upon the type of subsistence people will practice.

Most anthropology textbooks discuss the various subsistence practices used globally; thus, they will not be discussed in-depth here. Typically, they include the following:

1. Foraging
    a. Pedestrian
    b. Equestrian
    c. Aquatic
2. Swidden/slash and burn/extensive agriculture
3. Pastoralism
    a. Transhumance
    b. Nomadism
4. Intensive/large-scale agriculture

There is much debate about which of these systems are the most energy efficient, an issue dramatized during the regular "energy crises" the United States undergoes. It is important to emphasize that these are generally ideal types and that in reality most people, especially in the current world society, practice a mix of these strategies. (Even the most isolated **hunter-gatherers** like the Bushmen have access on occasion to Coca-Cola!) The point that must be stressed is that in the current world situation, more and more people are being locked together in ties of interdependence. Although officially the United States became involved in removing Iraq from Kuwait because of international law, most people realized that the need for Middle Eastern oil was the major unspoken factor. We have also begun to realize how one form of subsistence—for example, large-scale agriculture as practiced in the United States—can have an irreversible impact on people practicing, say, **foraging** in the Amazon and vice versa. At the same time, these types of subsistence can interpenetrate or encapsulate each other. What, for example, is homelessness in the United States but a form of foraging? This is in sharp contrast to some of the ideal types of subsistence where people had a larger degree of **autonomy** and were not so dependent upon other people. As people believe that they can produce energy and goods more cheaply by specialization, ties of interdependence increase. Don Stephen Rice and Prudence Rice make this point in their article on the Maya. Even in the past, subsistence systems consisted of a number of interlocking institutions, and to change one can have a calamitous impact on the whole of society.

At the same time, in seeming contradiction, at another more local level, Polly Hill shows the poor have a need to be indebted in order to survive. Hill suggests that one of the reasons why we have misunderstood and misinterpreted the battle for survival by the poor in the southern countries of this globe has been because of our belief that the epitome of success is to be an independent, self-reliant person. On the contrary, Hill, a prominent **development economist**, argues that from the local grass-roots perspective, village credit granting should be regarded as a sign of a lively economy.

From the vantage point of the closing of the twentieth century, the important anthropological question is not how do these different systems function, but why are they seemingly inadequate and why do all the development programs ostensibly designed to help feed people fail. Increasingly, this is becoming the focus of attention. Vulnerability to famine has been generally explained by reference to failures of production and exchange, but neither is adequate to explain the vulnerability of poor people to famine. One way in which this issue has been approached is to examine the status and trends in household assets—that is, investments and stocks of food and of value and the claims households and communities can exert on others (see, for example, the Hill article). One factor that forms an obvious point of departure is that as the world population increases, more and more people are going to become landless. How does this affect their strategies of subsistence? Judith Heyer provides important insights in this regard in her analysis of the asset strategies of landless people in Tamil Nadu, India. The options for landless agricultural laborers include changing patterns of consumption, "investment strategies" (for example, in marriage), and labor strategies. Antipoverty programs for landless agricultural laborers will fail because these programs do not address the real problem preventing the poor from acquiring more assets. The problem is not so much a lack of finances but a lack of incentives that limit the investments of poor people.

Lessons from the Maya

Don Stephen Rice and Prudence M. Rice

Don and Prudence Rice received their Ph.Ds from Pennsylvania State University in 1976 and have carried out extensive fieldwork in Guatemala. Prudence Rice, now professor in the department of anthropology at Southern Illinois University at Carbondale, is an archaeologist with interests in ceramics, craft specialization, and physicochemical analysis. Don Rice, professor of anthropology also at Southern Illinois University, is also an archaeologist with interests in ethnohistory, ecology, and the development of complex societies.

In 1977 concern for the long-range effects of policy-making prompted President Carter to direct the U.S. Council on Environmental Quality and the Department of State to study the "probable changes in the world's population, natural resources, and environment through the end of the century." The projections of that commission, as detailed in *The Global 2000 Report to the President* (Barney et al. 1981), foresee a growth in the world's population of as much as 70 percent, combined with staggering increases in demand for the world's resources of water, minerals, soils, and forest products. The report concludes that

> the most serious environmental development will be an accelerating deterioration and loss of resources essential for agriculture. This overall development includes soil erosion; loss of nutrients and compaction of soils; increasing salinization of both land and water used for irrigation; loss of high-quality cropland to urban development; . . . extinction of local and wild crop strains needed by plant breeders for improving cultivated varieties; and more frequent and more severe regional water shortages—especially . . . where forest losses are heavy and the earth can no longer absorb, store and regulate the discharge of water. (p. 32)

This sobering assessment underscores the serious implications of present trends for the future of the world environment. At the same time, it dramatically highlights the intricate balance between human exploitation

This article has been edited for inclusion in this book. The reader is referred to the original article for the complete data and methods on which the authors' interpretations are based. "Lessons from the Maya" by Don Stephen Rice and Prudence M. Rice, from *Latin American Research Review*, Vol. 19, No. 3, 1984, pp. 7–34. Reprinted with permission.

of resources and the cycles and processes of natural ecosystems. Nowhere is the precariousness of this situation more evident than in tropical lowland forests.

More than one-half of the world's "closed" or mature forests, which comprise over seven hundred million hectares worldwide, are located in tropic and subtropic regions, and they are being rapidly cleared for farmland, fuel, and economic development (Persson 1974; UNESCO 1978). In Latin America, where closed forest occupies approximately one-third of the total land area, deforestation is proceeding at rates as high as 4 percent per year. It is projected that the great tropical moist forest of the Amazon will cover less than one-half of its present area by the year A.D. 2000 (Barney et al. 1981, 127).

Agriculture, ranching, lumbering, and community expansion are moving tropical forests to the brink of wholesale destruction through the removal of trees. But the problem of uncontrolled modern extractive development of tropical forests is far more complex than this simple statement would suggest. Its real significance may be appreciated only through considering some of the biological characteristics of tropical forests, especially as they are distinguished from temperate forests. The distinctions hinge on the structure of the productivity of a forest ecosystem, which is a function of mineral storage, nutrient cycling, and biomass. The essential components are soil and standing vegetation, and in tropical forests, these components are in a fragile and delicate balance.

In a forest of temperate regions, the soil contains the major proportion of nutrients to sustain production and growth. When a temperate forest is cut, the soil retains most of those nutrients and stores them until they are extracted by forest regeneration or agriculture (Odum

1971, 102–3). Temperate forest regeneration is slow, however, taking as much as one hundred years to reach maximum biomass (Farnworth and Golley 1974, 76).

In tropical forests, by contrast, the vegetation cover, rather than the soil, holds the key to overall productivity. Tropical lowland forests are characterized by extremely high biomass and rapid rates of nutrient cycling (Richards 1952; Stark 1971; UNESCO 1978). More than 75 percent of the nutrients in the ecosystem are tied up in living vegetation and dead organic matter on the forest floor (Golley 1975; Whittaker and Likens 1975). Under the high heat and rainfall conditions of the tropics, the dead forest litter rapidly decomposes and is quickly recycled into vegetation growth rather than enriching the soil. Recent agronomic research indicates that tropical soils are highly variable in their nutrient status and can be quite fertile (Sánchez and Buol 1975), but because of the high ambient temperatures, heavy precipitation, and the thinness of the soils, they do not store nutrients as effectively as do temperate forest soils. Most nutrients in tropical forest soils are contained in the upper thirty centimeters of the profile, and correspondingly, it is here that 65 to 80 percent of the forest vegetation's root system is also found (Greenland and Kowal 1960).

When treefalls or limited clearings are created in tropical forests, vegetation can quickly reestablish itself; the forest rapidly accumulates nutrients from the soil and has the capacity to attain as much as 90 percent of its total original biomass in ten years or less (Sánchez 1976, 351). If a large section of the forest is cut and burned, however, as is typical in clearing operations for agriculture or settlement in tropical regions, nutrients are immediately released to the soil in the absence of vegetation to recapture them. Expanses of unprotected soils subsequently are exposed to heavy rainfall, with consequent deterioration of the soil structure, erosion, and the leaching of soluble nutrients deeper into the subsoils beyond the effective reach of crops or vegetation. Prolonged or repeated exposure dramatically accelerates alteration of the soil matrix and the hydrological regime, further diminishing the already restricted capacity of the ecosystem to store and cycle nutrients. In these situations, the process of regrowth and recovery after forest clearance is a long and slow one. Ultimately, the consequences of extractive exploitation of tropical forests are not only soil erosion, destabilization of water flows, and nutrient loss, but elimination of a fabulously rich capital resource in the form of stored photosynthetic energy and biological diversity.

The Global 2000 Report acknowledges that at present there are no successful methods by which to analyze the balance between the benefits and these relative costs of transforming tropical forest land to other uses (Barney et al. 1981, 132). The failure of resource planners for tropical regions to develop long-range strategies for present and future use of tropical forests that would prevent such losses is linked in part to the inability to evaluate the long-term impact of human exploitation of tropical forests until irreversible damage already has occurred. Unfortunately, few modern societies can serve as models for such assessments because they have replaced forests after clearance and do not continue to use them.

This lack of foresight—an inability to translate from the present to the future—that underlies rampant consumption is matched by a concomitant failure of hindsight—an inability to learn from the past. Large, wasteful, and exploitive populations are not exclusively modern phenomena: cities and civilizations have come and gone for millennia, and in their histories lie many lessons as to the nature of this uneasy balance between society and environment. Ancient civilizations in theory could provide a long time span for investigating human impact on tropical environments, but most ancient civilizations—Sumer, Egypt, Teotihuacan, Mohenjo-Daro—arose in arid valleys, rather than in lowland forests. Rarely did an ancient civilization call a tropical forest "home." Instead, tropical forests seem to have been viewed in both the past and the present as impenetrable "jungles" of strangling vegetation, with a reputation for limited agricultural potential and a concomitantly retarded cultural development (Meggers 1954).

At least one ancient civilization belies this view. The Maya civilization arose in the lowland tropical forests of Belize, Guatemala, and Mexico, where it flourished from approximately 1000 B.C. to A.D. 1525. During the period from A.D. 300 to 900, the Maya attained what is considered to have been a pinnacle of "Classic" development (Culbert 1974). Their superlative achievements are known to archaeologists through their architecture, art, and artifacts, which include huge temple pyramids, sumptuous burials, carved stone monuments, painted pottery, murals, and trade in exotic goods. These and other lines of evidence illuminate the Classic Maya as a hierarchically organized, theocratic society with an agricultural base, a complex calendrical system, elaborate ceremonial and religious activities, and a powerful political and economic leadership.

In the ninth century, the Maya star began to wane over much of the lowland region. The rapid cultural decline and population loss that is thought to have occurred is referred to by archaeologists as the "collapse" of the Classic Maya (Culbert 1973). The causes for this decline have puzzled archaeologists for decades, and such factors as malnutrition, disease, foreign invasion, and internal civil uprising have been suggested as possible explanations. Other hypotheses concern the relationship of the Maya to their environment, positing soil exhaustion, crop failure, and famine as underlying causes of the "collapse." The basis of the whole Maya agricultural system as well as the methods by which the society sustained itself agriculturally up to the ninth century are being increasingly investigated (Flannery 1982; Harrison and Turner 1978), and they raise nagging questions about the long-term interactions between a complex society and its fragile lowland forest environment. Mayanists long have been interested in the question of the relevance of the Classic Maya "collapse" to modern society (Sabloff 1971) because these questions surpass mere academic interest, given the modern threat to the remaining reserves of tropical forest.

THE CENTRAL PETÉN HISTORICAL ECOLOGY PROJECT

In order to understand better these interactions between society and environment through time, a continuing historical ecology research project was initiated in Guatemala in 1972. The location chosen for this study was the Department of Petén in northern Guatemala, the heartland of Lowland Maya cultural development. By means of geochemical, biological, and archaeological studies, this project set out to investigate the effect of Maya occupation on a tropical forest ecosystem.

The investigation was structured around an unusual research perspective. In many sciences, including ecology and archaeology, research often must proceed without the controlled laboratory experimentation that characterizes other sciences such as physics or chemistry. Large environmental and social systems are not usually amenable to experimental manipulation; instead, the situations already provided by time and history must be viewed by the scientist as the "experiments." In such cases, the objectives of the research are to define the "experimental conditions" within which the events of history took place (Deevey 1969).

From this perspective, the Maya provide a laboratory for the study of long-term environmental impact and resource management. The two thousand years of development of Classic Maya civilization in Petén can be regarded as one of the few large-scale "experiments" in the use of tropical forest by a complex society. The conditions of that experiment—that is, its cultural and environmental parameters—are largely unknown to scholars, however, which is the reason why the outcome—the collapse and its causes—are still being debated.

Among other considerations, the debate concerns the degree to which this agricultural society may have affected its environment adversely so as to undermine subsistence productivity and contribute to its own decline. In the terms of our research project, if the Maya did severely alter the forest ecosystem, the strain should be identifiable both demographically (by measurement of human population dynamics) and through paleoenvironmental characterization (including evidence of vegetation history, hydrological relations, soil integrity, and nutrient cycling).

The thirty-six thousand square kilometers of lowland forests of the Department of Petén constitute modern Guatemala's last reserve of virtually uninhabited land. The area has been underpopulated since the decline in the ninth and tenth centuries of the Classic Maya populace, which is estimated to have numbered in the millions (Adams, Brown, and Culbert 1981). This condition of sparse settlement is rapidly ending, however. The Petén is currently experiencing a flow of new farmers and ranchers from the heavily populated highlands to the south, a movement stimulated by recent governmental land-granting policies. Rapid in-migration has pushed the Petén's population from a level of 25,910 inhabitants in 1964 to almost 200,000 by the close of the 1970s (Castellanos Lopez 1980; Schwartz 1977). . . .

The relative lack of perennial water sources in Petén is relieved in the central portion of the department, where a chain of lakes formed at the close of the Pleistocene (Deevey, Brenner, and Binford 1983) along an east-west fault fracture roughly coinciding with seventeen degrees north latitude. This lake region is significant as a research locale for our investigation of long-term adaptations of an agricultural society to a lowland tropical forest environment. . . .

A pair of lakes at the eastern end of the chain, Yaxha and Sacnab, was selected as the location for beginning efforts at correlating Maya population history with natural history. Subsequent archaeological and paleolimnological investigations by our team in the region have studied Lakes Macanche, Salpetén, Quexil, and Petenxil, but we are focusing here on Yaxha and Sacnab to demonstrate the efficacy and results of the approach. The two lakes are separated by a narrow isthmus and differ in size, Yaxha having a shoreline of twenty kilometers and a maximum depth of twenty-seven meters, while Sacnab has a shoreline of twelve kilometers and a maximum depth of thirteen meters. Previous archaeological work suggested that these two lakes diverged in their occupation histories as well (Bullard 1960, 1970). The differences in size and population of the two lakes established the variation within the "experimental parameters" of the historical ecology project: the sediments of each lake could be investigated for conditions before, during, and after Maya occupation, and the two lakes' sedimentary histories could be compared in terms of the effects of high versus low occupation intensities.

Archaeological Research

The objectives of the archaeological research program were to locate settlement remains in the basins of Lakes Yaxha and Sacnab in order to determine the size and density of human populations in each basin as well as changes in such occupation through time. These determinations allowed comparison of the similarities and differences in settlement between the two lakes, as well as evaluation of the effect of changing human-settlement characteristics on the history of the lacustrine environment. This phase of the research consisted of two steps: the survey and mapping of settlement remains within defined areas and a program of test excavations.

Because it was physically impossible to survey the entire pollen- and sediment-producing area of each lake basin, surveys were restricted to rectangular sampling units (transects) radiating out north and south from the shore of each lake for a distance of two kilometers (the approximate limit of the hydrographic basins). Each transect was searched for structural remains, which were mapped, and then approximately 25 percent of these were excavated by small, one-meter-by-two-meter test-pits. Broken pieces of pottery and stone tools recovered from these excavations allowed estimates of the date of building of the structures because of a peculiar Maya construction practice. Maya builders apparently gathered up available household refuse at the time of construction and mixed this debris with the rubble and dirt that comprised the bulk of the fill of walls and floors. In addition, it was common practice to remodel earlier structures, thus incorporating previous constructions into the new edifice. Centuries later, archaeologists excavating a structure can determine the approximate time or times of construction by the latest pottery styles that are incorporated into one or more rubble fills.

It was known from earlier archaeological work that Lake Yaxha was heavily settled from the Preclassic (1000 B.C.–A.D. 250) through Classic periods (A.D. 250–900) and also in the Postclassic period (A.D. 900–1697) of Maya history in Petén. Lake Sacnab, on the other hand, was more lightly occupied during the Preclassic and Classic periods. Lake Yaxha was further distinguished by the presence of a large Classic period civic-ceremonial center with numerous temples and carved stelae (erect stone monuments that were often sculptured), the site of Yaxha, on its northern shore. Following the collapse, the Yaxha basin saw sizeable Postclassic settlement focused on the Topoxte Islands, located off the southwestern shore of that lake. Lake Sacnab, smaller and to the east, had no comparable large Classic period centers and no Postclassic occupation at all.

The archaeological investigations of the historical ecology project in Petén filled in the details of this broad outline of settlement in the Yaxha-Sacnab basins. The distribution and dates of construction of structures on the Yaxha-Sacnab transects suggest that the basins were first occupied by about 1000 B.C. (P. Rice 1979). Within the sampled zones, early communities in the Middle Preclassic (1000–250 B.C.) and Late Preclassic (250 B.C.–A.D. 250) periods were generally located on the well-drained uplands and may have been oriented around small special-function areas with temples or civic structures and plazas. Initial settlement in our sampled areas was denser around Lake Sacnab than

Lake Yaxha, although the latter exhibited a greater number of structures because of its larger basin area. During the Middle Preclassic, several settlement loci on the south shore of Lake Sacnab exhibited monumental architecture, as did the center of Yaxha on the north shore of that lake. By the end of the Late Preclassic period, however, the architectural growth of the site of Yaxha had far exceeded that of others in our transects (D. Rice 1976). . . .

Settlement growth peaked in the basins between A.D. 700 and 900 and was followed by a dramatic population loss and change in settlement location. The Sacnab basin remained uninhabited in succeeding centuries, while the Topoxte Islands in Lake Yaxha were occupied as a node of Postclassic residence and civic-ceremonial activity (Rice and Rice n.d.). This Postclassic focus on the islands in Lake Yaxha is part of a broader overall settlement retrenchment to the lake basins of central Petén after the tenth century (D. Rice n.d.; P. Rice n.d.).

The size of Preclassic and Classic occupation in the basins can be shown to have increased approximately exponentially through time. This growth can be demonstrated by means of a demographic curve, which is constructed from the combined survey strip-settlement figures by plotting the maximum number of structures built or occupied during each phase as an end-of-phase estimate of population size. In so doing, we assume that by the end of each phase, the structures constructed during the phase were contemporaneous (Haviland 1970, 191). Although the chronological intervals are rather coarse and the dynamics of growth within any period, or from one period to the next, are likely to have been highly variable, the slope of the line indicating log-linear growth suggests a growth rate on the order of 0.17 percent per year, or a doubling time of 408 years.

The settlement growth curve for structures can be converted to a population profile by a formula in which the total number of structures per phase is adjusted to reflect the actual number of residences, and the resulting figure then is multiplied by an estimated constant population per residence (D. Rice 1978, 42–46). In computing population figures, it was assumed that approximately 84 percent of the total number of structures occupied during a phase were actual residences (Haviland 1970, 193) and that 5.4 persons per structure is a stable average for Preclassic and Classic population estimates (Puleston 1973, 183). Although it is doubtful that these constants were invariant from area to area or through time, they do allow us to propose an approximate magnitude of population density per square kilometer within the basins, per time period. Such a conversion adds no new information on the rate of demographic change, but these population estimates become significant for estimating the approximate per capita impact of exponential growth within the lacustrine ecosystem.

From an average of 25 persons per square kilometer by the close of the Middle Preclassic period, the population in the Yaxha-Sacnab basins rose to an average of 211 persons per square kilometer in the Late Classic. Population sizes and densities are more difficult to project for Postclassic populations, whose residences were apparently largely confined to the site of Topoxte. Between 750 and 1000 people may have lived on the island we sampled (the second largest of the four "island" loci of Topoxte), but Postclassic densities for the entire Yaxha-Sacnab basins would have been low, perhaps as low as Middle Preclassic levels. Although fluctuations of population cannot be identified over short periods of time, the overall Preclassic-to-Classic demographic trend suggests no factors limiting growth until the end of the Late Classic period (the collapse), or at least no constraints that could not be overcome by technological or social means. Nonetheless, the continued growth of agrarian population in the basins during the two thousand years of Maya occupation preceding the collapse undoubtedly had some effect on the environment. The paleoecological aspect of the historical ecology project was designed to measure that impact.

Paleolimnological Research

Because lakes act as traps for erosional materials and for nutrients and chemical elements being cycled by the terrestrial plants and animals within the system, they are excellent indicators of human activities in their watershed. Forest clearance for agriculture and architectural construction is a major source of such disturbance. Deforestation, establishment of agricultural crops, field abandonment, and natural succession, for example, are all reflected in the kinds and amounts of pollen that find their way into the lakes. As landscape is put into production for long periods of time, protracted manipulation and exposure contribute to structural degeneration of the soil and altered local water flow, the products of which ultimately find their way to the lake sediments.

Soils under vegetation cover are relatively deep, benefiting from the buildup of an organic-rich horizon with open structure and good permeability. By breaking the impact of raindrops on the soil surface, vegetation permits more gradual interception of rainfall by the soil; surface depressions fill and infiltration of water into the subsoils begins apace. This infiltration contributes to soil moisture storage and deep percolation of water to saturated zones of ground water, as well as to downhill water flow *within* soil layers (called "throughflow"), where the permeability of those layers decreases with depth (Chorley 1969). Where rainfall intensities exceed infiltration rates, overland flow or runoff of rainwater occurs, which moves much more rapidly and differs physically from the throughflow moving through subsurface soil pores. Within basins of well-structured soils under mature forest, runoff is minimized and tends to occur uniformly throughout the basin (Kirkby 1969).

The contribution of standing vegetation to soil structure and to the amount of rainfall intercepted depends on the types of plants and their stage of growth. Prolonged deflection of forest to crop plants, successional species, or exposed earth leads to breakdown of soil structure, soil compaction, increased impermeability of the soil surface, and reduced infiltration. These conditions contribute to increased overland flow at the expense of soil moisture and ground water recharge as well as to throughflow. The heightened volumes and velocities of runoff accelerate erosion of the products of structural deterioration of soil. Under corn plants, for example, which are relatively poor at holding soil, gently sloping terrain can lose around twenty tons of soil per acre per year (Barney et al. 1981, 281).

Physical manipulation of the landscape surface, such as in cropping and construction activities, further exaggerates erosion and waterborne transport of soils (slopewash). Mechanical breakdown or removal of soils decreases the contextual integrity of surfacial organic and inorganic materials, while the covering of the landscape with impervious architectural surfaces further increases the rates of removal and downhill deposition of those materials. In lake basins, these terrestrial outputs eventually enter the aquatic zone, altering the chemistry of lake waters and influencing the kinds and growth characteristics of aquatic flora and fauna. There they become incorporated into the accumulating lacustrine sediments, forming a stratified record of the natural and cultural history of the catchment.

A major portion of the ecological research program in the Yaxha-Sacnab basin was a paleolimnological study that was undertaken to recover quantitative evidence of the sequence of sedimentary, palynological, chemical, and microzoological and microbotanical inputs into the lakes. The sediments were sampled for study by drilling into the floor of the lakes to remove a column or core of the sequentially deposited sediment layers. . . .

The major constituent of the sediments of both lakes was found to be a thick layer of silty montmorillonite clay, with increasing proportions of limestone inclusions in the upper reaches of the cores. This layer is an erosional deposit of sediments moved downhill by gravity (colluvium) or by water (slopewash) as a result of Maya disturbance. Above this "Maya clay" deposit lies an organic layer corresponding to the last few centuries of modern, post-Maya occupation. The heavy clay in Lake Sacnab was underlain by a pre-Maya layer of similar, highly organic mud. In Lake Yaxha, the clay sediments were so thick that the coring apparatus could not penetrate below the section into the pre-Maya layer. . . .

Chronological zoning of the cores involved the assignment of archaeological dates to various sediment levels within the inorganic layer based on the identification of discrete pollen assemblages. The basic assumption of this procedure is that the degree of deforestation reflected in the regional pollen profiles will track population densities projected from the archaeological data. The resulting temporal sequence for the section of "Maya clay" commences with a progressive decline of arboreal or high-forest pollen from Preclassic through Classic periods. Accompanying this decline is an increase in the weedy or "disturbance" species associated with human agricultural activity and forest clearance. An interruption in this trend—a decline in cultivation weeds and an indication of reforestation—is correlated with the Classic Maya collapse (Vaughan, Deevey, and Garrett-Jones n.d.). Subsequent increases in grasses and decline in arboreal pollen reflect Postclassic Maya activity in the basin, which is followed by a rise in successional species and modern reforestation (Vaughan 1979).

The correlation of pollen zones with archaeological periods of Maya prehistory links a relative environmental stratigraphy to absolute time. This step permits evaluation of relative rates of chemical inputs to the lakes during these periods as indicators of human impact on the lacustrine environment. In determining the effect of growth of Maya settlement in the basins, we are particularly interested in two elements, silicon and phosphorus. Unlike other elements critical to plant growth (such as carbon, nitrogen, or sulfur), silicon and phosphorus lack atmospheric components to their biogeochemical cycles. Their net flow is unidirectional to the lakes and their rates of delivery to lacustrine sediments reflect their rates of extraction and movement within the basins.

As silica (SiO_2, quartz) or as alumino-silicate clay minerals, silicon is important as the main constituent of soil. Most silicates in lake sediments were originally terrestrial soils, transported and redeposited from shores as mineral fragments (clastics), and their accumulations reflect the impact of architecture and agricultural engineering on the environment.

The high rate of silica deposition in Lakes Yaxha and Sacnab is signalled by the thick montmorillonite clay sediments corresponding to the period of Maya occupation. The differential thickness of these clay layers in the two basins reflects the relative degree of human disturbance on their shores. Lake Yaxha, which was more heavily settled and experienced more intense engineering activities, has a clay deposit more than one meter thicker than that of Lake Sacnab, despite the fact that the Yaxha core is an incomplete sample of the Maya period sediments. In both lakes, the quantity of clay deposition was such that to this day, the waters of the lakes continue to be effectively sealed or insulated from ground waters.

Phosphorus, on the other hand, is a biological element that is geochemically scarce but essential to support life in all ecosystems. Phosphate ions are made available to plants through the slow process of the weathering of rock during soil formation, and they are not abundant in the geological materials of limestone regions such as Petén. In addition, phosphate ions are highly reactive with other chemicals and may become incorporated into insoluble compounds in sediments if not taken up as nutrients by plants. Because phosphorus is limited in the Petén environment and because tropical forests are rapid converters of soluble nutrients, the movement of phosphorus at levels above normal minimums results primarily from human deflection of the element to surface soils through deforestation, sewage and waste disposal, the use of fertilizers, and interments. Thus, phosphorus, like silicon, is a direct indicator of human activity on the lakeshore, and its rate of deposition is a measure of environmental impact.

Inputs of phosphorus into the lakes, like those of silica, rise through the time of Maya occupation, increasing nearly exponentially. In Lake Sacnab, the influx peaks in the Early Classic period and then declines; in Lake Yaxha, the rate climbs from Preclassic through Classic periods and into the Postclassic before declining after the time of final abandonment of the basin (Brenner 1978). High correlations between rates of delivery of silica and phosphorus suggest that both are derived from outside the lake (anochthonous) and that the latter was deposited as an insoluble component of the particulate sediments, rather than the "throughflow" of soluble phosphate ions (Deevey et al. 1979, 303).

MAYA IMPACT ON THE LACUSTRINE ENVIRONMENT

It appears that Maya architectural and agro-engineering activities released phosphorus from vegetation and concentrated it in surface soils. This process involved the direct release of phosphorus to soils through clearing and burning as well as the intermediate cycling in which humans consume plant tissues, utilize the captured phosphorus in their organic processes, then cast off excess or incorporated phosphorus through excretion and death. Much of the released phosphorus was locked in insoluble compounds by limestone-derived soils and removed from the terrestrial environment through erosion, then buried in lake sediments. There it was made permanently unavailable in any form to support forest growth, crops, or human populations (Deevey and Rice 1980). Because bulk transport of soil was apparently the mechanism by which phosphorus reached the lakes, it is impossible to determine the actual percentage of phosphorus that was physically cycled through human bodies.

The inference of phosphorus fixation, translocation, and loss is supported by the results of terrestrial soil testing within the Petén lake basins. Soil profiles sampled in excavations of residence structures or those sampled in the vicinity of Maya construction exhibited extremely high levels of phosphorus, suggesting a human-induced source for the nutrient in these enriched soils (Brenner 1983a). The concentration of phosphorus in surficial soils, in contrast to the homogeneous distribution of highly soluble sodium or potassium throughout the soil profiles, argues against mobilization of phosphorus and rapid leaching. Rather, continued high influxes of phosphorus (alone among the soluble elements) to post-Maya lacustrine sediments, during a period when nutrient loss should have been diminished by forest regrowth, suggest that sediment and phosphorus entered the lakes together as erosional sediments. . . .

Lacustrine changes have their origin in the terrestrial component of the forest-lake ecosystem, and the environmental strain of the growing Maya settlement would have been felt there even more directly. The pollen sequence reflects a progressive deforestation of the region, while accelerated removal of soils and deposition of erosional sediments indicate technological manipulation of the basin surfaces. These modifications would have diminished natural habitats and affected terrestrial resources for the hunting or collecting of wild food supplements, as well as for the collection of botanical resources for construction, crafts, and particularly fuel. The latter strain is often underestimated; approximately one-third of the modern world's population uses wood for fuel, with the average user consuming about one ton of wood per year (Lawless 1978, citing United Nations 1967). The Maya consumption rate was probably comparable.

Moreover, increasing amounts of terrain were being covered by buildings and plazas, which effectively removed some of the well-drained lands from production, in addition to altering local hydrology and promoting erosion. Maya farmers in the Yaxha and Sacnab basins thus had to cope with declining access to upland soils, progressive deterioration of the structure of those available, destabilization of water flows and storages, and constant diminution of essential nutrients within the system.

LESSONS FROM THE MAYA

The Maya, like other large developing societies, made increasing demands upon their environment in order to feed, shelter, and otherwise support their growing populations. It is clear from the Yaxha-Sacnab data that, in this area at least, the Maya drastically altered the terrestrial and aquatic components of their tropical forest ecosystem. Deforestation, agricultural cultivation, and urban construction are known to enhance erosion rates by one, two to three, and three to four orders of magnitude respectively (Deevey and Rice 1980); and the Yaxha-Sacnab data follow a similar trend. Compounding the strain is the related phenomenon of "nutrient sequestering," a process that results in essential nutrients being permanently removed from the terrestrial system. Information from other Petén lakes (Cowgill and Hutchinson 1966a; Binford 1983; Brenner 1983b; Deevey, Brenner, and Binford 1983), other areas of Petén (Cowgill and Hutchinson 1966b; Olson 1969; Olson and Puleston 1972; Wiseman, cited in Turner and Miksicek 1981), and nearby Belize (Wiseman 1982, 1983) suggests the degradation was similar and regional in scope.

The measurement of such alterations confirms the concerns and projections of *The Global 2000 Report to the President,* identifies the processes involved, and provides preliminary estimates of critical rates of change in essential components of the ecosystem. There is more to be gleaned from the outcome of the Maya "experiment" than verification of the fragility of tropical environments, however. The Maya were conspicuously successful in harnessing the productivity of such a landscape for two millennia, and the details of that adaptation constitute positive lessons to be learned for future tropical forest exploitation.

Tropical forests are diverse—in their topography, soil characteristics, and hydrology. As a result, numerous exploitive responses are possible. The Maya of Yaxha-Sacnab functioned within a broader pan-Maya community, and it is on this regional level that the varied strategies of adaptation to the tropical-forest zone become apparent. Both explicit and implicit evidence exists showing that the Maya were aware of the heterogeneity and fragility of their environment and of the impact of their practices on the inherent processes and productivity of the exploited terrain. This recognition is reflected in direct evidence of sophisticated agrotechnologies throughout the Maya area, which include terraces (Healy, Van Waarden, and Anderson 1980; D. Rice 1982; Turner 1974, 1979) and systems of raised fields and canals (Adams 1980; Adams, Brown, and Culbert 1981; Siemens and Puleston 1972; Turner and Harrison 1981). The locations of these relic agricultural features indicate effective use of a number of different microhabitats, while their structure, contents, and ecological contexts suggest specific cropping procedures instituted as conservation measures within these varied loci.

Terraces are prominent on upland terrain and gradual planations of exterior drainage, where they check the downhill movement of materials and water. In so doing, they impede the effects of erosion and chemical weathering and build up thick soils. In addition, soils containing fixed phosphorus are held in situ, rather than being lost from the cropping area, and thus allow the slow release of phosphorus ions from insoluble compounds to soil solution over a period of years. In this manner, terracing prolongs the viability of arable land through preservation of soil structure and nutrient content and increases the actual quantity of land that can be considered arable.

Like agricultural terraces, canal-field systems allow for expansion of the cropping area by incorporating inundated zones, such as depressions of internal drainage (bajos) and lacustrine or riverine locations. In these zones, which are not encumbered by architecture and not contested by urbanization, the canal-field constructions provide an improved soil medium for cultivation in which waterlogged soils are essentially recycled. That is, intact soils are either drained through channelization or dug and piled onto a platform to enhance drainage, with water relegated to the resultant adjacent canals. The plots may extend out from the higher ground of depression edges, lakeshores, or river banks, or they may be situated toward the centers of swampy zones with fluctuating, perched water tables. The variability in field construction and placement reflects an understanding of seasonal variability in moisture regimes and the likelihood of scheduling more than one crop per year. Wet-season cropping is feasible on the higher and drier raised fields, while dry-season crops may be sown in the higher canals and on the raised fields in depression interiors (Gliessman et al. 1981).

The investment in permanent agro-engineering implies that these systems were foci of intensive production, although the intensity undoubtedly varied, with increased frequency of cropping and heightened labor input per cropping period. Both terraced fields and raised plots require maintenance, tillage, weeding, and fertilization. Investigations of raised-field construction have revealed the presence of vegetal detritus from upland and wetland species (Miksicek 1980, 1982), which served as mulch, and the presence of night soil and manure (Pohl 1982; Turner and Harrison 1978, 350–52). Such applications increase supplies of organic matter, contributing to a rejuvenation of soil structure, and they supplement the supplies of available nutrients, thus compensating for the removal or loss of essential elements through harvest, leaching, or fixation into relatively insoluble compounds (Lal et al. 1975).

Another method of enhancing utilization of soil nutrients is through reliance on a large number of plant species and varieties with wide ranges of physical needs and tolerances for the limiting nutrient elements such as nitrogen, phosphorus, and sulphur. The evidence is less direct regarding the degree to which the Maya intensified the use of cropping time and space through the simultaneous or sequential growing of two or more different crops in the same field. Botanical materials recovered from structure and field contexts do indicate that the Maya utilized a multitude of plant forms, including both domesticated crops and wild species (Fish 1978, n.d.; Miksicek 1982; Miksicek et al. 1981; Turner and Miksicek 1981). Ethnohistoric descriptions of sixteenth-century Maya subsistence practices and analogies drawn from modern Maya agricultural techniques also suggest that a given production area may have supported a variety of usable species at any one time and that multicropping of various species was common (Barrera Marin, Barrera Vásquez, and Lopez Franco 1976; Lundell 1933; Marcus 1982).

The integration of economically important botanical materials apparently took place on a number of different scales, which included open fields, perennial gardens, and orchards (Marcus 1982, 249). The mix of plant species implies an effective field or garden structure that to varying degrees avoids the diseases, pests, and soil problems associated with monocultures of genetically identical crops (Harris 1972; Netting 1977). In such systems, it is the vegetative structure—a complex pattern of foliage distributions, canopy heights, and nutrient demands—that reduces the impact of physical forces on the soil surfaces and maximizes the utilization and cycling of soil nutrients.

Although deforestation during the Maya periods is an undeniable fact and the diversity of native vegetation was undoubtedly reduced, the presence of many wild species in the paleobotanical record indicates that the Maya were well aware of that variety and its useful components. Some genetic stores were maintained, and the biological diversity of cropping systems was enhanced by the selective use of local species. Animal populations, like plant communities, become less plentiful and less diverse as forests are destroyed, and in the face of massive habitat destruction, the Maya may have practiced selective protection of some animal populations as well. Several terrestrial species may have constituted semidomesticated sources of protein that were maintained in the proximity of residential areas (Hamblin n.d.; Harris 1978; Rice and Rice 1979; Turner and Harrison 1978); pisciculture could have been practiced in some aquatic habitats in the vicinities of raised fields (Thompson 1974; Dahlin 1979).

In sum, it is apparent that the Maya initiated practices to reduce the regionwide processes of nutrient loss, deterioration of soil structure, destabilization of water flows, soil erosion, and loss of productive components of their environment. The results of the Maya "experiment" demonstrate that tropical forests are neither zones of unbounded fertility nor homogeneous zones in which cultivation redundancy is in order (Turner 1980). Theirs was a multihabitat and multitechnology system that was labor intensive, a system that relied on a primary motivation for increased production—a growing population—as the source of energy to run the system. Relatively speaking, it was an ecologically efficient regime that met increased demands for production through increased labor intensity and an increased agricultural land base.

The Maya adapted to the tropical forest environment over a long period, and a key to their success was undoubtedly the opportunity for sustained experimentation and evaluation. In the Yaxha-Sacnab basins, the environmental strains caused by soil depletion and alteration of the lacustrine ecosystem developed slowly, in tandem with low rates of population growth, too slowly to act as a mechanism to reduce overall population increase until at least Late Classic times. This statement is not meant to suggest that the Maya did not suffer constraints. Their growth, expansion, and intensification forced the Maya to consider more closely the processes of degradation. No data exist at present, however, indicating that the Maya agricultural system had reached its productive limits or that reduced productivity caused the civilization's "collapse." Certainly, some habitats or technologies were more vulnerable to strain than others, and the circumstantial juxtaposition of degradation and cultural decline in the Yaxha-Sacnab basins is theoretically enticing. But Maya responses to production problems were not only technological but social, religious, and political, and effective maintenance of an agro-economic infrastructure depended on cultural forces in addition to environmental ones. Both require further investigation.

The unresolved issue of the Maya "collapse" and the long-term success of the Maya civilization may foster spurious—and dangerous—complacency toward future economic development of the tropics if the relative rates of change are not kept in perspective. Current population trends in tropical areas engender a real sense of urgency about the work ahead. Tropical environments such as the Petén must be evaluated before modern populations obscure the details of ecosystem history so that pertinent information on successful, long-term adaptive strategies can be made available while it still might have some impact on future land use.

REFERENCES

ADAMS, R. E. W.
1980   "Swamps, Canals, and the Locations of Ancient Maya Cities." *Antiquity* 54:206–14.

ADAMS, R. E. W., W. E. BROWN, JR., AND T. P. CULBERT
1981   "Radar Mapping, Archaeology, and Ancient Maya Land Use." *Science* 213:1457–63.

BARNEY, G. O., ET AL.
1981   *The Global 2000 Report to the President: Entering the Twenty-First Century*, Vols. 1 and 2. Council on Environmental Quality and the Department of State. Charlottesville: Blue Angel.

BARRERA MARIN, A., A. BARRERA VÁSQUEZ, AND R. M. LOPEZ FRANCO
1976   *Nomenclature etnobotánica Maya: Una Interpretación Taxonómica. Colección Científica 36 (Ethnology)*. Mexico: Institute Nacional de Antropología e Historia, Centro Regional del Sureste.

BINFORD, M.
1983   "Paleolimnology of the Petén Lake District, Guatemala, I: Erosion and Deposition of Inorganic Sediment as Inferred from Granulometry." *Hydrobiologia* (The Hague) 103:199–203.

BRENNER, M.
1978   "Paleolimnological Assessment of Human Disturbance in the Drainage Basins of Three Northern Guatemalan Lakes." Master's Thesis, University of Florida, Gainesville.
1983a   "Paleolimnology of the Maya Region." Ph.D. diss., University of Florida, Gainesville.
1983b   "Paleolimnology of the Petén Lake District, Guatemala, II: Mayan Population Density and Sediment and Nutrient Loading of Lake Quexil." *Hydrobiologia* (The Hague) 103:205–10.

BULLARD, W. R., JR.
1960   "Maya Settlement Patterns in Northeastern Petén, Guatemala." *American Antiquity* 25:355–72.
1970   "Topoxte, a Postclassic Maya Site in Petén, Guatemala." In *Monographs and Papers in Maya Archaeology*, edited by W. R. Bullard, Jr. Papers of the Peabody Museum of Archaeology and Ethnology, vol. 61. Cambridge: Harvard University.

CASTELLANOS LOPEZ, J. E.
1980   "Consideraciones Sobre el Desarrollo de Petén." *Petén-Itza* 21:15.

CHORLEY, R. J., ED.
1969   "The Drainage Basin as the Fundamental Geomorphic Unit." In *Introduction to Physical Hydrology*. London: Methuen.

COWGILL, U. M., AND G. E. HUTCHINSON
1966a   "The Chemical History of Laguna de Peténxil." *Memoirs of the Connecticut Academy of Arts and Sciences* 17:121–26.
1966b   "La Aguada de Santa Ana Vieja: The History of a Pond in Guatemala." *Polskie Archiwum Hydrobiologii* 623:335–72.

CULBERT, T. P.
1974   *The Lost Civilization: The Story of the Classic Maya*. New York: Harper & Row.

CULBERT, T. P., ED.
1973   *The Classic Maya Collapse*. Albuquerque: University of New Mexico Press.

DAHLIN, B.
1979   "Cropping Cash in the Protoclassic: A Cultural Impact Statement. In *Maya Archaeology and Ethnohistory*, edited by N. Hammond and G. R. Willey. Austin: University of Texas Press.

DEEVEY, E. S.
1969   "Coaxing History to Conduct Experiments." *Bioscience* 19:40–43.

DEEVEY, E. S., M. BRENNER, AND M. BINFORD
1983   "Paleolimnology of the Petén Lake District, Guatemala, III: Late Pleistocene and Gamblian Environments of the Maya Area." *Hydrobiologia* (The Hague) 103:211–16.

DEEVEY, E. S., AND D. S. RICE
1980   "Coluviación y Retención de Nutrientes en el Distrito Lacustre del Petén Central, Guatemala." *Biótica* 5:129–44.

DEEVEY, E. S., D. S. RICE, P. M. RICE, H. H. VAUGHAN, M. BRENNER, AND M. S. FLANNERY
1979   "Maya Urbanism: Impact on a Tropical Karst Environment." *Science* 206:298–306.

FARNWORTH, E., AND F. GOLLEY
1974   *Fragile Eco-Systems: Evaluation of Research and Applications in the Neotropics*. New York: Springer-Verlag.

FISH, S.
1978   "Palynology of Edzna and Aguacatal: Environment and Economy." Paper presented at the Forty-Third Annual Meeting of the Society for American Archaeology, Tucson.
n.d.   "Palynology of Edzna: Environment and Economy." In *The Economic Basis for Maya Civilization*, edited by M. Pohl. Cambridge: Harvard University Press.

FLANNERY, K. V., ED.
1982   *Maya Subsistence: Studies in Memory of Dennis E. Puleston*. New York: Academic Press.

GLIESSMAN, S. R., B. L. TURNER, F. J. ROSADO, AND M. F. AMADOR
1981 "Ancient Raised-Field Agriculture in the Maya Lowlands of Southeastern Mexico." Paper presented at the Conference on Prehistoric Intensive Agriculture in the Tropics, Australian National University, Canberra.

GOLLEY, F. B.
1975 "Productivity and Mineral Cycling in Tropical Forests." In *Productivity of World Ecosystems,* Proceedings of a symposium at the Fifth General Assembly of the Special Committee for the International Biological Program, National Academy of Sciences, Washington, D.C.

GREENLAND, D. J. AND J. KOWAL
1960 "Nutrient Content of the Moist Tropical Forest of Ghana." *Plant Soil* 12, no. 2:154–74.

HAMBLIN, N.
n.d. "Isla Cozumel Archaeological Avifauna." In *The Economic Basis for Maya Civilization,* edited by M. Pohl. Cambridge: Harvard University Press.

HARRIS, D.
1972 "Swidden Systems and Settlement." In *Man, Settlement, and Urbanism,* edited by P. J. Ucko, R. Tringham, and G. W Dimbleby. London: Duckworth.
1978 "The Agricultural Foundations of Lowland Maya Civilization: A Critique." In *Pre-Hispanic Maya Agriculture. See* Harrison and Turner 1978.

HARRISON, P. D., AND D. L. TURNER, EDS.
1978 *Pre-Hispanic Maya Agriculture.* Albuquerque: University of New Mexico Press.

HAVILAND, W. A.
1970 "Tikal, Guatemala, and Mesoamerican Urbanism." *World Archaeology* 2:186–98.

HEALY, P. F., C. VAN WAARDEN, AND T. J. ANDERSON
1980 "Nueva Evidencia de las Terrazas Mayas en Belice." *América Indígena* 40:773–96.

KIRKBY, M. J.
1969 "Infiltration, Throughflow, and Overland Flow." In *Introduction to Physical Hydrology, See* Chorley 1969.

LAL, R., B. T. KANG, F. R. MOORMAN, A. S. R. JUO, AND J. C. MOOMAW
1975 "Soil Management Problems and Possible Solutions in Western Nigeria." In *Soil Management in Tropical America,* edited by E. Bornemisze and A. Alvarado. Raleigh: North Carolina State University.

LAWLESS, R.
1978 "Deforestation and Indigenous Attitudes in Northern Luzon." *Anthropology* 2, no. 1:1–17.

LUNDELL, C.
1933 "The Agriculture of the Maya." *Southwest Review* 19:65–77.

MARCUS, J.
1982 "The Plant World of the Sixteenth- and Seventeenth-Century Lowland Maya." In *Maya Subsistence. See* Flannery 1982.

MEGGERS, B. J.
1954 "Environmental Limitation on the Development of Culture." *American Anthropologist* 56:801–24.

MIKSICEK, C.
1980 "Archaeobotanical Aspects of the Excavations." In *Maya Raised-Field Agriculture and Settlement at Pulltrouser Swamp, Northern Belize.* Report of the 1979–80 University of Oklahoma National Science Foundation Pulltrouser Swamp Project.
1982 "Plant Macrofossils from Northern Belize: A 3000-Year Record of Maya Agriculture and Its Impact on Local Environment." Paper presented at the conference on Lowland Maya Environment and Agriculture, University of Minnesota, Minneapolis.

MIKSICEK, C., R. M. BIRD, B. PICKERSGILL, S. DONAGHEY, J. CARTWRIGHT, AND N. HAMMOND
1981 "Preclassic Lowland Maize from Cuello, Belize." *Nature* 289: 50–59.

NETTING, R. M.
1977 "Maya Subsistence: Mythologies, Analogies, Possibilities." In *The Origins of Maya Civilization,* edited by R. E. W. Adams. Albuquerque: University of New Mexico Press.

ODUM, E.
1971 *Fundamentals of Ecology.* Philadelphia: Saunders.

OLSON, G. W.
1969 "Description and Data on Soils of Tikal, El Petén, Guatemala, Central America." Mimeo 69–2, Department of Agronomy, Cornell University.

OLSON, G. W., AND D. E. PULESTON
1972 "Soils and the Maya." *Americas* 24:33–39.

PERSSON, R.
1974 *World Forest Resources.* Stockholm: Royal College of Forestry.

POHL, M.
1982 "New Evidence from Albion Island, Belize." Paper presented at the symposium on Lowland Maya Environment and Agriculture, University of Minnesota, Minneapolis.

PULESTON, D. E.
1973 "Ancient Maya Settlement and Environment at Tikal, Guatemala: Implications for Subsistence Models." Ph.D. diss., University of Pennsylvania.

RICE, D. S.
1976 "The Historical Ecology of Lakes Yaxha and Sacnab, El Petén, Guatemala." Ph.D. diss., Pennsylvania State University.
1978 "Population Growth and Subsistence Alternatives in a Tropical Lacustrine Environment." In *Pre-Hispanic Maya Agriculture. See* Harrison and Turner 1978.
1982 "The Central Petén Grasslands: Genesis, Dynamics, and Land Use." Paper presented at the conference on Lowland Maya Environment and Agriculture, University of Minnesota, Minneapolis.
n.d. "The Petén Postclassic. A Settlement Perspective." Paper prepared for the School of American Research Advanced Seminar Series, *Late Lowland Maya Civilization: Classic to Postclassic,* edited by J. A. Sabloff and E. W. Andrews V. Albuquerque: University of New Mexico Press.

RICE, P. M.
1979 "Ceramic and Non-Ceramic Artifacts of Yaxha-Sacnab, El Petén, Guatemala, Part I: The Ceramics, Section A, Middle Preclassic. *Cerámica de Cultura Maya* 10:1–36.
n.d. "Perspectives on the Petén Postclassic." Paper prepared for the School of American Research Advanced Seminar Series, *Late Lowland Maya Civilization: Classic to Postclassic,* edited by J. A. Sabloff and E. W. Andrews V. Albuquerque: University of New Mexico Press.

RICE, P. M., AND D. S. RICE
1979 "Home on the Range: Aboriginal Maya Settlement in the Central Petén Savannas." *Archaeology* 32:16–25.
n.d. "Topoxte, Macanche, and the Central Petén Postclassic. In *The Lowland Maya Postclassic,* edited by A. Chase and P. Rice. Austin: University of Texas Press.

RICHARDS, P. W.
1952 "The Tropical Rain Forest." Cambridge: Cambridge University Press.

SABLOFF, J. A.
1971 "The Collapse of Classic Maya Civilization." In *The Patient Earth,* edited by J. Harte and R. Socolow. New York: Holt, Rinehart and Winston.

SÁNCHEZ, P. A.
1976 *Properties and Management of Soils in the Tropics.* New York: John Wiley and Sons.

SÁNCHEZ, P. A., AND S. W. BUOL
1975 "Soils of the Tropics and the World Food Crisis." *Science* 188:598–603.

SCHWARTZ, N. B.
1977   *A Milpero of Petén, Guatemala: Autobiography and Cultural Analysis.* University of Delaware Latin American Studies Program Occasional Papers and Monographs no. 2.

SIEMENS, A. H., AND D. E. PULESTON
1972   "Ridged Fields and Associated Features in Southern Campeche: New Perspectives on the Lowland Maya." *American Antiquity* 37:228–39.

STARK, N. M.
1971   "Nutrient Cycling II: Nutrient Distribution in Amazonian Vegetation." *Tropical Ecology* 12, no. 2:177–201.

THOMPSON, J. E. S.
1974   "Canals of the Rio Candelaria Basin, Campeche, Mexico." In *Mesoamerican Archaeology: New Approaches,* edited by N. Hammond. Austin: University of Texas Press.

TURNER, B. L.
1974   "Prehistoric Intensive Agriculture in the Mayan Lowlands." *Science* 185:118–24.

1979   "Prehispanic Terracing in the Central Maya Lowlands: Problems of Agricultural Intensification." In *Maya Archaeology and Ethnohistory,* edited by N. Hammond and G. R. Willey. Austin: University of Texas Press.

1980   "La Agriculture Intensive de Trabajo en las Tierras Mayas." *América Indígena* 15, no. 4: 653–70.

n.d.   "Issues Related to Subsistence and Environment Among the Ancient Maya." In *The Economic Basis for Maya Civilization,* edited by M. Pohl. Cambridge: Harvard University Press.

TURNER, B. L., AND P. D. HARRISON
1978   "Implications from Agriculture for Maya Prehistory." In *Pre-Historic Maya Agriculture. See* Harrison and Turner 1978.

1981   "Prehistoric Raised-Field Agriculture in the Maya Lowlands." *Science* 213:399–405.

TURNER, B. L., AND C. MIKSICEK
1981   "Economic Species Associated with Prehistoric Agriculture in the Maya Lowlands." Paper presented at the Thirteenth International Botanical Congress, Sydney.

UNESCO
1978   *Tropical Forest Ecosystems: A State-of-Knowledge Report.* Natural Resources Research 14. Paris: UNESCO.

UNITED NATIONS
1967   *Wood: World Trends and Prospects.* Basic Study no. 16. Rome: United Nations.

VAUGHAN, H. H.
1979   *Prehistoric Disturbance of Vegetation in the Area of Lake Yaxha, Petén, Guatemala.* Ph.D. diss., University of Florida, Gainesville.

VAUGHAN, H. H., E. S. DEEVEY, AND S. E. GARRETT-JONES
n.d.   "Pollen Stratigraphy of Two Cores from the Petén Lake District, with an Appendix on Two Deep-Water Cores." In *The Economic Basis for Maya Civilization,* edited by M. Pohl. Cambridge: Harvard University Press.

WHITAKER, R. H., AND G. E. LIKENS
1975   "The Biosphere and Man." In *Primary Productivity of the Biosphere,* edited by H. Lieth and R. H. Whittaker. New York: Springer-Verlag.

WISEMAN, F.
1982   "Palynology in Northern Belize." Paper presented at the conference on Lowland Maya Environment and Agriculture, University of Minnesota, Minneapolis.

1983   "Palynological Studies of Raised Fields and Canals at Pulltrouser Swamp." In *Pulltrouser Swamp: Preliminary Study of Habitat, Land Use, and Settlement of the Prehistoric Maya,* edited by B. L. Turner and R. D. Harrison. Austin: University of Texas Press.

The Need to Be Indebted

Polly Hill

Polly Hill is a Fellow of Clare Hall, Cambridge, in England. She has achieved renown for being both an economist and an anthropologist of agrarian systems. She has done fieldwork in Ghana.

With a recent notable exception, the literature on credit-granting and debt (or, as I often prefer to put it, lending and borrowing) in the rural tropical world has tended *either* to be very crude, being tainted with the colonial prejudices that "poor people" should be protected from their helpless, foolish recklessness (and so forth) and that most creditors are wicked, rapacious scoundrels; *or* to be very sophisticated, being largely taken up with the intricate personal relationships between the parties and with the interesting sequences of borrowing and lending which, in certain circumstances, are apt to be involved. (The recent notable exception is provided by the younger generation of historians of India originally based in Cambridge—see *The Imperial Impact.* Dewey *et al.* 1978). This paper is something different: it is an endeavour to "decolonialise the attitude to debt" on the basis of the assumption that borrowing and lending are as necessary to the economic health of any rural community as are buying and selling—so that desirable, i.e. non-exploitative, types of credit-granting deserve encouragement, whereas exploitative types should be stifled, so far as possible. It cannot be sufficiently emphasised that lending either cash or produce such as grain is an activity with no more inherent moral overtones than selling something for cash and that, indeed, there are many circumstances when the two types of transactions are logically indistinguishable.

> Throughout the colonial empire rural indebtedness was ignorantly prudishly and invariably regarded as a moral problem, a sign that "natives" lacked the virtues of thrift, self-reliance ... Village credit-granting was never seen as the converse of stultification or a sign of a lively economy (Hill, 1982: 216).

"The Need to Be Indebted" by Polly Hill, from *African Seminar Collected Papers*, Vol. 4, 1984, M. Hall (ed.) Reprinted with permission.

The colonial attitude to debt was extremely moral—resembling the attitude of missionaries to "adultery." This was partly a matter of semantics. In the home country "debt was bad"—so bad that one might land up in a debtors' prison; so, it followed that it was "even worse" in the colonies. But had the colonialists employed "borrowing" rather than "debt," they might have reflected that in their own country it was the richer and more secure members of society who were in a position to borrow from the bank or in other ways—and that something similar might happen to apply in rural tropical communities. There was, therefore, a strong tendency (one which has persisted as a colonial hangover until the present day) *to regard debt as a problem*—almost as a kind of illness, for which a cure should be found. Here again we only have to replace "debt" by "borrowing" to realise that no necessary moral connotations are involved.

Another semantic obstacle was the colonial tendency to identify creditors with moneylenders—a word with many unpleasant associations. In West Africa, and elsewhere, "moneylender" has a quite specific meaning. He is a man who makes a profession of lending money to others at cash interest—and the colonialists sought to control his activities by means of legislation involving licensing and control of interest rates. But the point in this context (and all the time I am thinking of West Africa or south India as representing the rural tropical world) is that all the licensed moneylenders were in the really large towns and cities—there were none in the countryside where most of the local creditors were themselves richer farmers, who naturally preferred to put their surplus cash to work. Such local men were not much given to lending at interest: their loans took multifarious forms, one of the most interesting of which was the loan granted on the security of farmland—the farm mortgage. Of course a particular mortgagee (a creditor) may impose wicked, crippling terms on his mortgager (the debtor) and may be all too inclined to foreclose: on the other hand he may be a reasonable man—a possibility which is in no wise conveyed by the emotive "moneylender."

Although I tend to regard the prevailing moral attitude to village generated credit (as distinct from credit emanating from banks and other official institutions) as a kind of colonial hangover, one must be clear that other ideologies may be involved—for example the official Muslim attitude to usury in Hausaland in northern Nigeria. This Hausa case is interesting as demonstrating the unavoidability of borrowing in inegalitarian cash economies. The villagers are sincere and active Muslims, who would wish to avoid "usury," as defined by legal texts and scholars, were this remotely practicable—and did they understand the complex texts! But they find this to be an impossible ideal. (On the absurdity of any strict application of concepts of usury to the countryside see Hill, 1972).

I am, of course, concerned with cash economics—i.e. with economies such that any kind of produce, even cow dung for use as manure, might happen to be bought and sold. These economics being *innately inegalitarian* (it is a grave and common error to suppose that inequality invariably emanates from the outside world, though it may be exacerbated by it), it is inconceivable that borrowing and lending (as well as buying and selling) would happen not to occur, for it is in the interests of all concerned. Besides, it is erroneous to believe that lending and borrowing necessarily lead to the establishment of personal relationships (which are often exploitative) between the parties—for, as with buying and selling, they may do so or they may not.

One reason for the provocative title of this paper is my need to emphasise that many poorer people have no hope of bettering themselves unless they borrow: in other words, if (as is commonly the case) people cannot borrow *because they are too poor*, then there is no hope for them. I also wish to stress that owing to the pronounced seasonality of many rural economies, especially in savannah West Africa (but also in south India where, although there are two annual monsoons, there is only one annual dry grain crop), a large proportion of households may be obliged to borrow in the pre-harvest months merely to meet their household living requirements. Evidently, since I am laying so much stress on the inevitability of rural borrowing and lending, I really need some such title as "Credit as the Life Blood of Rural Economics." The creditors need the debtors (though usually not so urgently) as the debtors need the creditors. The flow of credit is analogous to a natural physiological function rather than to an illness.

In densely populated rural conditions it is mistaken to assume that a richer man is necessarily able to apply all his capital productively without the help of a poorer man—who may then be a debtor. I will take a very simple example relating to south India. If a rich man finds it difficult to provide for all his cattle, because grazing is scarce and family labour limited, it may very

well suit his convenience to lend a cow to a poor man who has the time to take it out grazing—under a system such that the borrower is rewarded with the first calf. Is this relationship any more deplorable than if the rich man sold the cow to the poor man?

I now list, in rather arbitrary order, a few more of the postulates on which this paper is based:

1. The terms and conditions involved in credit-granting vary on a continuum from very harsh to lenient—only by studying the type of credit involved can we begin to assess the situation.

2. Poorer borrowers often, but by no means always, obtain worse terms than richer people, if only because of the higher risk of default. (Poorer people are likewise apt to pay more for what they buy—they buy in smaller [more expensive] quantities and at the wrong times, this being a worldwide phenomenon).

3. However, it is usually inappropriate to think in terms of annual interest rates, both because borrowing is apt to be timeless and because partial default is almost a rule in some circumstances.

4. In different connections, fairly high proportions of country people are both borrowers and lenders. For all sorts of practical reasons, such people do not think in terms of *the net balance of debt or credit*—indeed they may very well not know whether the balance is positive or negative, which makes the bald terms *debtor* and *creditor* very misleading. This is one of many reasons why that condition known as "indebtedness" cannot be measured by any questionnaire approach (see Hill 1984).

5. As I have said, many poorer people have no hope of bettering themselves except by means of borrowing. One of the main ways in which richer people help the poorer is by granting them non-cash loans which enable them to set themselves to work. Thus, in Hausaland, local traders may receive farm produce which they pay for after sale, transport donkeys may be borrowed on credit, grain may be granted to farm-labourers who repay, over a period, in terms of work, or payment for the use of a temporarily-borrowed farm plot may be made after harvest.

6. Although some creditors have bad reputations in their villages (because, for example, they are apt to foreclose on mortgages in cruel fashion), the general attitude to local men who are lenders is that they are being helpful. To be a rich man and not to help anybody by lending—and "help" is used in such a context—is to indulge in conspicuous waste. All are agreed that it is improper not to make money work as hard as possible.

7. The high incidence of extreme poverty in many communities *is seldom the consequence of debt as such*, unless there are many men who have mortgaged all their farms under a system such that they commonly fail to redeem them; the misfortune of inheriting too little land is a much commoner cause of extreme poverty.

8. Only richer people are in a position to borrow from banks and other credit institutions such as co-operatives, since they alone have sufficient security of the right type; poorer people are necessarily dependent on credit granted by local people, who know that they are dependable from personal experience. Yet, sad to say, village credit is frowned on in both Hausaland and south India—the regions where I have worked most recently.

9. Most large village lenders are, to some degree, engaged in re-lending money which they borrowed from outsiders: they are the necessary link with the outside world.

10. The bashfulness of the ordinary creditor about his detailed activities is liable to misinterpretation, for as much secrecy may be associated with selling as with lending. Thus, in Hausaland the sale of grain by one householder to another is commonly wrapped in secrecy, either because the seller is frightened of taunts that he is neglecting his family by selling grain they need for themselves or because he is afraid of appearing to be "too rich" on village standards. (The act of lending is more embarrassing than that of borrowing.)

I conclude this summary by dealing in a cursory way with four types of "lending" which may be mainly responsible for giving credit-granting such a bad name: these are the credit-granting activities of the Indian shopkeeper or trader, share-cropping, farm-mortgaging and bonded labouring.

Before I went to south India in 1977, I had heard so much about moneylenders in that continent that I was very much surprised to find that, as in West Africa, the main village lenders were farmers. The historian C. J. Baker (see Dewey *et al.* 1978), when writing about Madras in 1929–36, insisted that it was the rich local agriculturists who, as he put it, "performed the important function of guaranteeing control over the liquidity of the local economy." The Madras government's attempts between 1934 and 1938 to provide legislative machinery for scaling down debts merely exacerbated the situation. The word *bania* in north India (but not in the south) means a trader or a creditor or both; many of the contributors to Dewey (*ibid.*) were concerned to decry his significance, if only because he is a semi-urban creature, and most people live in the deep countryside.

Systems of share-cropping proper (and land-renting systems such that the rent is a share of the crop do not fall in this category unless other inputs besides land are provided) are basically farm-borrowing systems. As we all know, share-cropping has a bad name; I had hoped to study it in India, as it is found but rarely in West Africa. But in my research area (south-eastern Karnataka) there was no share-cropping worth mentioning—and the records in the State Archives showed that this was nothing new. There is much that might be said about share-cropping here, but I confine myself to the following points: first, there is no inherent reason why share-cropping is more disadvantageous to the tenant than renting—all depends on the actual terms; second, no one, so far as I know, has explored the question of the conditions in which share-cropping, rather than renting, is likely to exist; third, share-cropping *may* be more advantageous to the tenant than renting if it involves the loan of plough animals, which he does not himself possess and could not afford to hire.

Turning to mortgaging, I think (but I cannot be sure) that, in both Hausaland and in the Karnataka villages, high proportions of those who mortgage their farmland fail to redeem it—so that mortgaging is an act of desperation, almost tantamount to forced selling at a low price. Given my experience in southern Ghana, which I shall shortly relate, I was very much surprised to find that the agreed terms of mortgage were seldom (if ever) recorded in a written document, so I do not know whether the Harijans (those formerly known as untouchables) who complained to me that their farms had been unlawfully seized by their creditors had right on their side, especially as the creditors refused all information. The creditors (a few of whom were identified for my benefit by third parties) purport to believe that mortgaging is prohibited by Karnataka land reform legislation—as it is not. Although I am sure that legislative control is required, I am also convinced that prohibition of mortgaging is out of the question—the practice would merely be driven underground.

But the point I am seeking to emphasise is that mortgaging is not, in all circumstances, an undesirable way of raising money and I hope that I shall not now confuse the reader by suddenly switching from the grain farmers of Hausaland and south India to the cocoa farmers of southern Ghana (see Hill 1956, 1963). The cocoa farmers are able to mortgage their farms (and they often need only to mortgage one of a set of farms) under a system such that there is no risk of losing them, since the cocoa, which is received by the creditor, automatically goes towards liquidating the debt, the farm ultimately being restored to the borrower.

The colonial conviction that debt was necessarily wicked was inherited by the Nkrumah government which, in 1953, shortly before Ghana's independence in 1957, determined to relieve the cocoa farmers of their indebtedness by means of an absurd procedure which involved paying the creditor a lump sum down which the debtor then owed to the government. (Never mind that the creditor might immediately lend this windfall to someone else; at least the government would have done it's best to purify the economic atmosphere!)

What the government did not know was that creditor and debtor, far from being enemies, were usually friends (as is often the case in villages), so that they acted collusively from the outset, dividing the new official loan between them, and having no intention of repaying it. (That the Ghanaian officials regarded the creditors as villains is vouched for by my having once heard one of them referring to a creditor, at a loan-liquidating session, as "a black Shylock"—the official, of course, being black himself.) The farmers being astute enough, it was not long before they outwitted the bureaucrats by applying for the relief of non-existent indebtedness; all that was necessary was for the play-acting creditor and debtor to persuade a local letter-writer (a kind of petty village lawyer) to draw up a convincing document specifying the terms of their "indebtedness" which would then be duly "relieved." The farmers also outwitted the bureaucrats by neglecting to repay the great bulk of the sum of nearly 3 million pounds which had been paid out in this way before the operation ended, in chaos, in 1956.

I have earlier mentioned that impoverished people are commonly too poor to borrow. But at that point I did not mention the possibility that they might offer the services of themselves or their children as security for the loan, my reason being that neither in Hausaland nor, to any significant degree, in the south Indian villages was "bonded labouring," as it is commonly called, a significant institution. Just as in the case of share-cropping, I do not think that any proper study has been made of the circumstances in which this institution is apt to exist. In 1975, as part of her Twenty Points Programme, Mrs. Gandhi had declared that bonded labouring was illegal but by 1977–78 Harijan fathers were increasingly gaining the courage to borrow money on the security of the labour of their unmarried sons, the debt being automatically liquidated after about two years. But any system of bonded labouring such that the labourer can never hope to escape from the clutches of his employer (perhaps because he has borrowed money from him to meet his marriage expenses) is a different case, which may need to be prohibited by legislation.

So I hope I have demonstrated that village borrowing (as such) is necessary, to the degree that it does something to reduce household inequality—and that it is only in some circumstances that the particular terms and arrangements are exploitative.

REFERENCES

Dewey, C. and Hopkins, A. G. (eds.), 1978. *The Imperial Impact: Studies in the Economic History of Africa and India.* London: The Athlone Press.

Hill, Polly, 1956. *The Gold Coast Cocoa Farmer.* Oxford University Press.

———, 1963. *The Migrant Cocoa Farmers of Southern Ghana.* Cambridge.

———, 1972. *Rural Hausa: A Village and a Setting.* Cambridge.

———, 1982. *Dry Grain Farming Families: Hausaland (Nigeria) and Karnataka (India) Compared.* Cambridge.

———, 1984. "The poor quality of official socioeconomic statistics relating to the rural tropical world: with special reference to South India." *Modern Asian Studies*, 18, 3.

Landless Agricultural Labourers' Asset Strategies

Judith Heyer

Judith Heyer is a Fellow of Somerville College, Oxford. She has extensive research experience in Kenya and more recently in South India.

INTRODUCTION

Asset strategies of the poor are a neglected area in India as elsewhere, despite the fact that since the early 1970s there has been a substantial programme of government intervention to improve the asset positions of India's poor. Some of the reasons why asset strategies of the poor have not been taken seriously are (a) because the poor are thought of as basically assetless; (b) because increasing the assets of the poor is thought to be a relatively low priority; (c) because increasing the assets of the poor is thought to be fruitless; (d) because it is felt that it is obvious what is needed—there is no need for further studies of the situation. But (a) the poor do have assets that are often quite crucial to them, and to understanding their behaviour and their predicament; (b) there may be higher priorities, but assets may be a priority too; (c) there have been some notable successes with policies designed to increase the assets held by the poor; (d) what seems obvious is often wrong. Some of these points are addressed in this article.

There has been a good deal of debate in the Indian literature on the array of policies aimed at strengthening the position of landless agricultural labourers. One of the debates has centred on the relative merits of employment generation versus schemes to improve landless agricultural labourers' asset positions. Another has revolved around the argument about whether more fundamental changes in the structure of both production itself and production relations are essential to produce the massive increases in employment and labour productivity that are needed to make serious inroads into the problem of landless agricultural labourer poverty.[1]

"Landless Agricultural Labourers' Asset Strategies" by Judith Heyer, from *IDS Bulletin*, Vol. 20, No. 2, Institute of Development Studies. Reprinted with permission.

Agricultural labourer households made up an estimated 31 per cent of all rural households in India in 1983 and the proportion has been increasing (Unni 1988). It is important to consider how the position of agricultural labourers can be improved as labourers, as well as what can be done to enable agricultural labourers to move into other occupational categories. Increases in the demand for labour are crucial. Supply side factors are also important, however, and these have received less attention. This article concentrates on some of the supply side factors, more specifically on what individual labourers can do through investment strategies to strengthen their positions.[2] Looking at the investment behaviour of landless agricultural labourers in South India raises questions relevant to the strategies of poor people in general. There are parallels between the situation of these landless agricultural labourers and poor people more generally.

An examination of the asset positions of landless agricultural labourers, and the priorities that landless agricultural labourers attach to the acquisition of more of particular kinds of assets, helps to explain why the results of many of the Indian government programmes designed to help poor people to acquire more assets have been so disappointing, at least as far as landless agricultural labourers are concerned. One can take the view that these programmes were never intended as more than weak palliatives in the first place, or even that they were designed to make it possible to continue to exploit the poor more effectively. But if one takes the view that they were intended to achieve at least some improvement, the lack of understanding of the roles that (particular) assets play, and the lack of appreciation of the difficulties that landless agricultural labourers face in using the assets available to them, must be seen as real obstacles to the effectiveness of the government interventions.

The most important asset as far as landless agricultural labourers are concerned is labour power. The quantity and quality of labour power is influenced by investments, some of which are not normally recognised as "productive." Investment in housing may be crucial, as also investment in education. Investment in marriages and health can be important too. These often compete with investments that are more commonly recognised as "productive."

The more obviously "productive" assets with which landless agricultural labourers in India are concerned are livestock, carts and ploughs, and tools and equipment associated with the supply of services and petty manufacturing. There is a whole range of government programmes designed to help landless labourers, among others, to make more of these investments. However, landless agricultural labourers often have rather limited access to these programmes, and even when they do get access it can be difficult for them to generate returns from the investments they undertake.

In a 1981–82 study of villages in Coimbatore district in Tamil Nadu, I looked at the major expenditures of landless agricultural labourers. One of the questions that arose was why they were not spending their "surpluses" on more obviously productive investments, but spending them instead on so many investments that appeared to be less productive. There is always a certain amount of differentiation, even among landless labourers, if only through variations in dependency ratios. Some landless agricultural labourers in the Coimbatore villages were markedly better off than others. But they seemed to be making no attempt to acquire assets such as livestock, tools, equipment or land. They seemed to be doing better as agricultural labourers, "investing" in their agricultural labouring, than they would by acquiring land or other assets that might enable them to establish different occupational positions. Many of the conventionally recognised "productive" investments seemed not to be productive for them.

THE CONTEXT

The evidence discussed in this paper comes from villages in an area in which agriculture is relatively dynamic, and there are nearby urban areas in which employment growth has been considerable. The villages are 40–60km north-east of Coimbatore, an industrial town of around one million people, dominated by textile mills and light engineering. There are also several smaller towns in the neighbourhood. An enormous variety of crops is grown on well-fed land, on which sugar and cotton predominate. Groundnuts and sorghum are grown quite widely on rain-fed land as well. There is a shortage of water, which makes paddy a very minor crop. Agriculture is very commercialised, with high levels of application of purchased inputs, a large amount of wage labour, and up to date crop varieties and production techniques. It is an area in which livestock play an important role. There is very little mechanical cultivation, but irrigation is virtually all electrified.

The villages are dominated by groups of larger farmers from Gounder and Naidoo castes, with up to 30 acres of land each. The landless agricultural labourers, who made up 31 per cent of the 1981–82 population, are chakkiliyans, panadis, and lower caste individuals. Agricultural labourers are employed almost exclusively within their own villages. The exception is sugar-cane crushing on which groups of agricultural labourers spend several weeks at a time in other parts of the district.

The fieldwork on which much of the evidence in this article is based involved interviewing a 20 per cent random sample of 233 households of all occupational categories in six hamlets over a period of six months. There were 73 landless agricultural labourer households in the sample (and a further 14 agricultural labourers with very small areas of land). A number of non-sample households were also interviewed.

There was no attempt to emphasise the position of women, as opposed to men, in the original study. The whole discussion is thus somewhat male centred.

Landless agricultural labourers in these villages are not as poor as in some parts of Tamil Nadu and the rest of India. The relatively tight labour market is reflected in relatively high earnings. Daily wage rates are low: they were Rs.6–7 for men, and Rs.2–3 for women in 1982, roughly equivalent to 2 kgs of rice for men and less than 1 kg of rice for women for a day's work. But earnings are higher than these figures suggest because there is relatively little seasonal unemployment. Permanent agricultural labourers were getting between Rs.1800 and Rs.2400 per year in 1982. This would have been the equivalent of 300–400 days of work at a daily rate of Rs.6 over a year. Despite these earnings however, less than 10 per cent of the households had bicycles, virtually none had bullocks, none had ploughs or carts, and very few had even tiny pieces of land.

Differentiation still follows caste lines very closely. All chakkiliyans and all panadis are agricultural labourers, except those with official government positions. No chakkiliyan or panadi household has more than a very small piece of land; most have no land at all. Political alliances are vertical, and collective action runs along vertical, not horizontal lines. It is easy to see why agricultural labourers are unwilling to risk straining relationships with employers: wages are virtually their only sources of income, help from employers in times of adversity is crucial, perks from employers are important. Employers are the only route to the administration. But it is not easy to explain why in other areas, apparently quite similar, landless agricultural labourers are so much more politically conscious and organised.[3]

The villages were originally chosen for study because they had some of the highest uptakes of Small Farmer Development Agency (SFDA) loans in Coimbatore district. They were villages with relatively high levels of direct intervention in the late 1970s and early 1980s. In the event, however, there was a conspicuous absence of interventions that reached agricultural labourers, and there was not much evidence of interventions reaching other disadvantaged groups either. There was a Rural Employment programme project in the neighborhood in 1981–82, but none of the beneficiaries were agricultural labourers. Only small or marginal farmers gained access to the relatively favourable employment that this offered in 1981–82. Small and marginal farmers were also the main beneficiaries of the SFDA programme.

LABOUR OPTIONS

Variations in dependency ratios mean that some households have the potential to earn a "surplus" over and above what they survive on. Thus some households have room for manoeuvre, albeit at a very basic level. This room for manoeuvre is reflected in more leisure or less arduous work: more consumption; and/or more investment. Evidence of "surpluses" includes (1) decisions to work fewer days or fewer hours per day, or on less arduous forms of work; (2) substantial expenditures on marriages, housing, etc. for which some landless agricultural labourer households manage to mobilise relatively large sums; and (3) relatively advantageous dependency ratios.

There are a number of different wage labour options, and there are important differences in the way these are used by chakkiliyans, panadis and caste hindus. Thus there is a high incidence of pannayal labour among chakkiliyans, and of sugar-cane crushing labour among panadis. Pannayal labour "attached" by the year, at the beck and call of the employer, with no fixed hours or holidays, is the most arduous, least desirable, and best paid. It is something a lot of chakkiliyans do for a while when they are young. A few take it up again when they are older, often for a particular purpose or because they are in difficulty. It is unusual for panadis or caste hindus to take up pannayal labour, though there are those who do. Similarly, while sugar-cane crushing is something that many panadis do, it is much less common among chakkiliyans or caste hindus. The earnings are relatively high, but it involves going away for weeks at a time, and a large proportion of the earnings get spent on the job. The other alternative is casual labouring ostensibly on a daily basis, although often in practice negotiated and paid by the week. This is associated with the lowest earnings: an adult man earning the top rate of pay would have to work for 343 days to get the equivalent of the top pannayal earnings per year. Casual labourers never work as many days as this.

Other important variables as far as employment is concerned are the age at which children start wage work, and the intensity with which they do this, and the amount of wage work women do. Virtually all women's wage work is casual. There are considerable variations for women at different stages of the life cycle. They may work for a higher or lower proportion of their time at any stage, and they may stop work for longer or shorter periods when they are pregnant, or have young children, or have children that can earn. Women's wages are very much lower than men's Rs.2–3 per day in 1981–82 compared with Rs. 6–7, only partly because they work shorter days. This puts less pressure on them to work, or continue working when there are reasons for them not to do so, and vice versa (Jose 1988; Unni 1988; Bardhan 1985).

Boys, particularly chakkiliyan boys, are sent out to work as pannayals when they are as young as seven years, but more commonly from the age of 10 or 12. They start by herding livestock, and then move gradually to more strenuous work, with higher rates of pay, as they get older and more experienced. Those that do not work as pannayals start casual work, or sugar-cane crushing, a little older. They often herd household livestock before that. Girls start casual work as young as 8 or 10 years, and by the age of 12 or so they earn a full female casual worker's wage.

How much a particular household earns depends a great deal on its labour strategy. Chakkiliyans tend to earn most, per adult-equivalent. Panadis' earnings are quite high too, but a substantial proportion of these are consumed away sugar-cane crushing. Caste hindus earn least. There are substantial variations within each group, though.

INVESTMENT

"Investment" is defined very broadly here to include anything involving the acquisition or purchase of assets that will bring future returns. It thus includes expenditures on marriage and kinship relationships, ceremonial expenditures, as on temple visits; health expenditures; expenditures on education, training and skills; expenditures on migration; on physical assets, such as land, livestock, tools, equipment, machinery, housing and other buildings, bicycles and other consumer durables; and even expenditures on financial assets and jewelry. Seeing all of the above as important and substantial alternative "investments" brings out the fact that considerable "investment" is being undertaken by agricultural labourer households, and it plays an important role.

There are some important distinctions to be made however. Some "investment" does not augment productive potential in the aggregate, although it may do so for individuals. Much marriage expenditure is of this kind. Other "investment" augments productive potential, possibly by transferring it from one group to another in the society. Some of the livestock acquired by agricultural labourers might otherwise have been maintained by others. This is even more obviously true of land. The question then becomes whether in the hands of agricultural labourers these assets are more productive. Equipment often represents a clearer addition to productive capacity for the society as well as the individual. The same is true of housing, in so far as it is associated with health improvements, for example.

Investment may make a direct contribution to quality of life or standard of living. It may also strengthen the bargaining positions of landless agricultural labourers by diversifying their income sources or improving their ability to survive periods of adversity. The vulnerability of landless agricultural labourers in these villages needs to be emphasised. This still makes for extremely dependent employer-employee relationships. Relationships with employers are crucial in times of adversity: employers can be called upon to pay medical expenses, to help with access to medical care, to provide food and other essential needs, and to help with access to the administration. These can all be critical in times of adversity.

There are noticeable differences between chakkiliyans, panadis and caste hindu labourers in household and other social relationships which have an important bearing on investment decisions and strategies. Thus young chakkiliyan men tend both to contribute to and to benefit from the income of the parental household for much longer in their life-cycles than panadis. Young chakkiliyan men tend to stay at home, earning substantial sums, much of which they contribute to the income of their parental households. They then get help with marriage expenses, and sometimes also with housing, before setting themselves up in independent households. Panadis, on the other hand, do not contribute much to the household in their teenage and early adult years. In turn they seem not to get much help with marriage, or housing, from their parental households. This has important implications for the amount of accumulation that takes place: the additional earnings of teenage and young adult chakkiliyans seem to result in relatively good housing standards, and good marriages, as compared with those of panadis in these villages. They also result in relatively strong asset positions that have a bearing on the living conditions of the families that they sustain.

Other social relationships seem to be important where caste hindus are concerned. Caste hindus benefit from connections with relatively better off households in their castes, and from generally less restricted access to the village community, as compared with chakkiliyans and panadis. They also benefit from the inheritance of better housing. Thus some members of caste hindu labourer households have got jobs in textile mills, set up shops, and even acquired substantial amounts of land in the past. These options do not seem to have been open to members of chakkiliyan or panadi households. Caste and kin connections widen the range of opportunities quite considerably.

LANDLESS AGRICULTURAL LABOURERS' "INVESTMENTS"

I will now summarise the evidence on some of the major categories of "Investment" among landless agricultural labourers in the Coimbatore villages.

Marriage

In common with people from all castes and classes in India, agricultural labourers in the Coimbatore villages go to tremendous lengths to finance marriage outlays. These are important for obtaining access to kin relationships, which bring a whole range of advantages including some forms of insurance. They are also important for obtaining able-bodied wives. Even agricultural labourers that one would think had barely any "surplus" at all manage to mobilise substantial sums where marriages are concerned. The upper ranges of expenditure for a groom are roughly equivalent to the annual wage of a permanent adult male agricultural labourer. They are also equivalent to the purchase of a milch animal or bullock, an acre of dry land, an average house or a substantial house improvement. For a bride, the expenditure is somewhat less. Only a handful of these agricultural labourer households are involved in a dowry system. Those that are, are almost all caste hindus.

Those who cannot mobilise a substantial sum for marriage postpone, marry a social outcast or a physically disabled person, or marry within a family or kinship network where some reciprocal arrangement is possible. None remain unmarried beyond the age of 40, but some wait until they are in their late 30s, and this is regarded as a considerable hardship. Late marriage makes adverse dependency ratios more likely. It can also make it difficult for the couple to recover its financial position in the years after marriage. There was a marked contrast between chakkiliyans who all married early, and panadis who all married later, some much later, in the study villages. Caste hindus came somewhere in between.

Money is raised for marriage by fathers, mothers, brothers, grooms, or some combination of these, with other close relatives helping as well in some cases. People work more intensively, or under a more arduous but more remunerative contract for a while; sell livestock purchased earlier for the purpose; sell other assets; borrow. Some of the loans are repaid, and asset holdings rebuilt, in the early years of marriage, before children are born, when the wife can contribute substantially to earnings. How much remains to be repaid and by whom, and how much asset holdings are rebuilt before the children are born, substantially influences the prospects of the household. How much marriage is a family rather than an individual undertaking obviously makes a great deal of difference. This varies considerably within as well as between social groups.

Housing

Housing (house sites, houses, house improvements) is the other major investment in which a large number of landless agricultural labourer households are involved. Landless agricultural labourers spend up to twice as much on housing as they spend on a good marriage. In theory agricultural labourers are entitled to government housing subsidies, but no one in these villages had been able to take these up.[4]

Agricultural labourers mobilise resources for housing in similar ways to the mobilisation of resources for marriages, but where housing is concerned the onus is entirely on the young couple. Whether they have to consider investing in housing and when, makes a great deal of difference to the long term opportunities of the couple and their children. If a young couple has to invest in housing this can put them in a difficult net asset position from which it may not be easy to recover as dependency ratios deteriorate with the arrival of children. The risk of serious indebtedness is then very real. The availability of inherited housing makes it unnecessary for them to suffer a deterioration in their net asset position at a time when it may be particularly risky to do this.

There is a dramatic contrast between the housing standards of chakkiliyans and panadis in the Coimbatore villages. Chakkiliyans have been investing very considerably in housing and this is reflected in the relatively well-built, *pucca* housing they nearly all have as a result. Their house sites and surrounds are crowded, but there are very few dilapidated or cheap houses and there is relatively little overcrowding within the houses themselves. Panadis, in contrast, have cheap thatched houses with mud walls, many very dilapidated, and many very crowded inside. Caste hindu labourers' housing, most of it inherited, is somewhat better than chakkiliyans'.

Livestock

Livestock play a relatively important role in this area: bullocks are used very extensively for ploughing and for transport, and milch animals are widespread. Livestock have been an important means of strengthening the position of agricultural labourers and others in India in the 1970s and 1980s. Agricultural labourers in the Coimbatore villages keep buffaloes, sheep and goats, pigs and chickens, but not bullocks, and very seldom milch animals. Many of the landless agricultural labourers who have most experience with cattle are considered unclean from the point of view of handling milk. Their cattle have to be milked by others if their milk is to be sold. Bullocks and carts and milch animals were the focus of the SFDA programmes in these villages in the late 1970s and the early 1980s. Landless agricultural labourers were effectively excluded from these programmes. However this was partly because they were judged by the local cooperative leadership to be ineligible, also because the investments for which they might have been eligible were

of little use in their circumstances (Heyer 1981). Unlike in some parts of India, agricultural labourers do not hire themselves out with bullocks and carts, or bullocks and ploughs in these villages. The terms of employment, the relatively easy availability of fodder and grazing on farms, and the discriminatory access to veterinary and other services, all undoubtedly play a part in making it attractive for farmers to keep their own bullocks, ploughs and carts instead.

Most agricultural labourers involved with livestock either rear buffaloes and cattle on a small scale, many on a share ownership basis, or keep sheep and goats. Sixty per cent of the agricultural labourer households in the sample had kept livestock at some stage; 44 per cent had some at the time of the study; half of these had some on a share basis.

Livestock are used as a means of accumulating savings over the medium term. They give some return, although they also involve an element of risk; and they are relatively liquid. They are more remunerative if there is some room for manoeuvre over when they are sold: thus they are better for financing marriage or housing expenditures which can be planned ahead, than for insurance against unforeseen emergencies such as illnesses or accidents. They appear to compare well with alternative savings instruments: financial assets, and gold and silver jewelry. The only "financial assets" that these agricultural labourers have are loans out, and these only to a very small extent. They have very little jewelry. Consumer durables play a minor role as savings: few have good second-hand value in these communities.

Land

Agricultural labourers in these villages are not investing in land. Irrigated land, and the more productive rain-fed land is beyond their reach. Moreover, although one acre of land costs less than a good marriage, much less than a new house, and less than an agricultural labourer's annual wage, it is quite costly to operate. Land may also limit agricultural labourers' ability to participate in the most lucrative wage labouring at peak seasons; and it may limit agricultural labourers' mobility.

It seems to have been possible for some landless households in the right caste groups to make a success of acquiring land in the past, but not now. Some agricultural labourers, all panadis, have very small amounts of land inherited from the past. They are not selling these: none are buying land either, however.

Non-Agricultural Self-Employment

Non-agricultural self-employment opportunities open to most households in these villages are limited to produce, trading, retail trading, hotels, and bicycle shops. The traditional services of barbers, washermen, carpenters, blacksmiths, stonemasons, and potters are strictly limited to those of the right caste group, and there is a declining demand for these. Two of the self-employed outside the traditional services in the sample were ex-agricultural labourers, both caste hindus, one a petty shopkeeper, the other running a tea shop. Most non-agricultural self-employed came from landed families though none were from chakkiliyan or panadi house-holds. There are opportunities being provided within the Integrated Rural Development Programme (IRDP), one of the successors to the SFDA, which helps under-employed rural people to start up in non-agricultural self-employment. There was no evidence of any of this in the study villages in 1981–82 however.

Education

Access to education is a real problem for agricultural labourers, despite the fact that there are primary schools in all the villages, and a secondary school in one. Few boys from agricultural labourer households go to pri-mary school for more than one or two years, and girls almost never go at all. Only 25 per cent of school-age boys in the landless agricultural labourer households in the sample had ever been to school; eight per cent had reached Standard V; four per cent had gone on to, but none had completed, secondary school. There were fewer in older age groups who had gone beyond the first few years of primary school. The free noon meals scheme introduced by the Tamil Nadu state government in 1981–82 is reported to have brought in large numbers hitherto excluded from school, but this was not yet in evidence at the time of the study. Nor is it clear that it is getting children much more access to education, even where it is bringing them in for the free meals (Harriss 1986).

Many agricultural labourers are entitled to some government financial support if they get beyond Stan-dard V, and they get preferential access to a range of government jobs that require secondary or higher edu-cational qualifications. However, there is no system of preferential treatment for agricultural labourers in the lower levels of the educational system, or in jobs that require primary education or less. Fifteen out of a total of 98 sons of agricultural labourer households in the sample who were 15 years or over had been to school. Six of these had found their education of some use in obtaining employment. The remaining nine were all agricultural labourers.

It is a major problem for the child of an agricultural labourer to get as far as Standard V or beyond in the Coimbatore villages. Children of agricultural labourers are not very successful when they get to school, and as soon as they are old enough to be sent out to work most are taken away. Many will already have given up before this. (Reasons for leaving school were variously given as because the child had had a try and proved not to be making a success of it: because the child concerned was reluctant to continue: and/or because the child con-cerned was needed to work.)

The costs of schooling, implicit or explicit, even at the primary level, are large relative to the earning capacities of agricultural labourer households. The pe-riod over which they have to be borne is long, and the risks of failure along the way are very substantial. One person from an agricultural labourer household (not in the sample) in one of the study villages managed to complete secondary school and beyond. He is now an agricultural assistant. The household concerned made tremendous sacrifices over a period of 10 years or more before the son obtained employment that reflected the qualifications he had acquired. It was easy to see why others were unable or unwilling to emulate this.

What needs explaining is the fact that in other parts of India the situation appears to be better (Subbarao 1987; Kumar 1983; Saradamoni 1981). In the Coimbatore vil-lages the extreme social differentiation may help to ex-plain why it's so difficult for chakkiliyan or panadi chil-dren to succeed in school. The relatively good agricultural labour market also makes the opportunity cost of school high, and agricultural labouring, a reasonable option, for those who do not go to school. Furthermore, there is the very low level of political mobilisation. All of these cer-tainly contribute to an appallingly low level of education where agricultural labourers' children are concerned.

Migration

Migration also appears to provide limited opportunities for agricultural labourers in these villages. Of the 98 sons of agricultural labourers in the sample who were 15 years or over, 10 were living or working away. These include an unskilled labourer in Coimbatore, a water-seller and two petty traders in smaller nearby towns, someone who migrated near Ootacamund in the Nilgiris Hills where he could make a success of owning land, three people work-ing in textile mills, and a clerk with the Coimbatore Elec-tricity Board. The majority of these are from caste hindu households. It is rare for sons from chakkiliyan or panadi households to move away. The relatively plentiful oppor-tunities for agricultural labour in these villages tip the balance in favour of staying, rather than moving away.

General Points

Thus, for these agricultural labourers, in a relatively "progressive" area, the obviously high priority invest-ments are marriage and housing. A few have invested in migration; a few in education; very few in non-agricultural self-employment; none recently in land. Few of these investments make landless agricultural labourers dramatically better off, in either the short or long term. Housing and marriage investments may increase the quality of labour, sometimes rather indi-rectly. Education investments increase the quality of labour of the very tiny minority. Direct investments in health hardly feature at all. There is very little that is obviously directly productive. It may be that better health, less vulnerability, etc. are improving the quality of labour, but this is not obvious. The situation in these villages is not notably different from that elsewhere in India in this respect (Jose 1988). And to the extent that there is any improvement, what is happening on the demand side is probably more important than what is happening to supply. However, the gradual increase in quality of labour that's taking place may play some role in determining the earning possibilities of labourers; it is also of some benefit in its own right. Small gains that accumulate almost imperceptibly are easy to underestimate.

Alternative ways of improving the situation of some of these landless agricultural labourers may include nonagricultural opportunities. But the problem is not just, or even always primarily, a problem of finance, as so many government programmes seem to assume. It is as much a problem of weak incentives. More efforts need to be made to create an environment in which landless agricultural labourers' assets can be more productive. More efforts also need to be made to enable the children of landless agricultural labourers to get something of real substance, with real content, from the educational system. Government programmes need to put more emphasis on these other aspects if their existing emphasis on finance is to be successful where landless agricultural labourers are concerned.

CONCLUSIONS

Even in India, where direct government intervention has put a strong emphasis on improving the asset positions of landless agricultural labourers and others among the poor, landless agricultural labourer investment strategies are poorly understood. The failure to take seriously what landless agricultural labourers are doing leads to missed opportunities, and poor policy performance. Asset strategies are misunderstood by outsiders, who ignore them because they think they are unimportant, and/or try to change them because they think they know which investments are "better" for landless agricultural labourers and for society more generally. But here, as in other areas, one needs to understand to intervene successfully. Studies of what people do, and why their priorities are as they are, even if they seem perverse, are a necessary starting point. Building on what is already there may have a better chance of success than more radical intervention based on tabula rasa assumptions.

NOTES

1. See, for example, Guhan 1980, 1986; Rath and Hatao 1985; Dantwala and Hatao 1985; Hirway and Hatao 1985; Subbarao 1985; Parthasarathy 1985; Prasad 1985; Kurian 1987; Rao and Erappa 1987; Bandophadhyay 1988.

2. There is of course some work on assets and asset strategies of the poor in India, notably the work by N. S. Jodha. (For example, Jodha forthcoming). See also Sivakumar 1978; Chambers and Leach 1987.

3. There is an extensive Indian literature on this question. See Rudra 1987 for a specific example of the point.

4. Hirway (1987) has a good discussion of the situation.

REFERENCES

Bandophadhyay, D., 1988. "Direct intervention programmes for poverty alleviation: an appraisal." *EPW*, vol 23, no 26, June 25.

Bardhan, K., 1985. "Women's work, welfare and status." *EPW*, vol 20, no 50, December 14.

Chambers, R. and Leach, M., 1987. "Trees to meet contingencies: a strategy for the rural poor," *Discussion Paper 228*. IDS. Sussex. January.

Dantwala, M. L., 1985. "Garibi hatao: strategy options." *EPW*, vol 20, no 11, March 16.

Guhan, S., 1980. "Policy and play acting," *EPW*, vol 15, no 47, November 22.

———. 1986. "Reaching out to the poor." *Economic Times* December 19.

Harriss, B., 1986. "Meals and noon meals in South India: food and nutrition policy in the rural food economy of Tamil Nadu State." *Occasional Paper 31*, School of Development Studies. University of East Anglia.

Heyer, J. 1981. "Attempting to reach the rural poor? the Small Farmer Development Agency in Varandur Village, Coimbatore." *Working Paper No. 22*. Madras Institute of Development Studies.

Hirway, I., 1985. "Garibi hatao: Can IRDP do it?" *EPW*, vol 20, no 13, March 30.

———. 1987. "Housing for the rural poor," *EPW*, vol 22, no 34, August 22.

Jodha, N. S., forthcoming. "Social science research on rural change: some gaps." In P. Bardhan (ed.), *Rural Economic Change in South Asia: Methodology of Measurement*.

Jose, A. V., 1988. "Agricultural wages in India," *EPW*, vol 23, no 26, June 25.

Kumar, K., 1983. "Educational experience of scheduled castes and tribes." *EPW*, vol 18, no 36–37, September 3–10.

Kurian, N. J., 1987. "IRDP: how relevant is it?," *EPW*, vol 22, no 52, December 26.

Parthasarathy, G., 1985. "Reorientation of rural development programmes: a note on some basic issues." *EPW*, vol 20, no 48, November 30.

Prasad, P. H., 1985. "Poverty and agricultural development," *EPW*, vol 20, no 50, December 14.

Rao, V. M. and Erappa, S., 1987. "IRDP and rural diversification: a study in Karnataka." *EPW*, vol 22, no 52, December 26.

Rath, N., 1985. "Garibi hatao: can IRDP do it?" *EPW*, vol 20, no 6, February 9.

Rudra, A., 1987. "Labour relations in agriculture: a study in contrasts," *EPW*, vol 22, no 17, April 25.

Saradamoni, K., 1981. "Education, employment, and land ownership, role of caste and economic factors." *EPW*, vol 16, no 36, September 5.

Sivakumar, S. S., 1978. "Aspects of agrarian economy in Tamil Nadu: a study of two villages. Part III." *EPW*, vol 13, no 20, May 20.

Subbarao, K., 1985. "Regional variations in impact of anti-poverty programmes: a review of evidence." *EPW*, vol 20, no 43, October 26.

———. 1987. "Some aspects of access to education in India." Workshop on Poverty in India. Queen Elizabeth House. Oxford. September.

Unni, J., 1988. "Agricultural labourers in rural labour households, 1956–6 to 1977–8: changes in employment, wages and incomes." *EPW*, vol 23, no 26, June 25.

6

Economic Systems

Generally, two meanings are attached to the word **economics**. On the one hand, it refers to maximizing behavior, as when we have to economize; on the other hand, it refers to a system of how production is organized, exchanged or distributed, and consumed. Although we like to think of economic behavior as rational, values, tastes, fads, and other idiosyncrasies play a role in our decision making in such a way that bedevils any apparent rationality. How many parents would charge their children interest for a loan? Why do we grow our own vegetables when it would be much cheaper to purchase them at the local supermarket?

At the same time, we have an institution known as the national economy in which we feel as if we are passive recipients of forces beyond our control. Although these two economies seem to be disparate and distinct, they share a number of common characteristics; most important, because very few people directly consume what they produce, both of them have to do with **exchange**.

Marshall Sahlins (1972), who has defined the various types of exchange, distinguishes between reciprocal, redistributive, and market exchanges. Reciprocity is of three types. First is **generalized reciprocity** where there is no expectation of an immediate counterflow of equal value. Two typical examples are the following:

- Bushmen foragers share the spoils of a hunt with other camp followers in the expectation that their generosity will be reciprocated in some distant time.

- Parents will spoil children in the hope that when they are old, the children will feel obligated to help them.

In these types of exchanges, the participants will deny that they are economic and will couch them in terms of kinship or friendship obligations. Second, there is **balanced reciprocity**, or trade, where one has a direct obligation to reciprocate in order to continue the social relationship. Again, it need not be a single commercial transaction. For example, it might be cheaper for me to buy groceries at the supermarket, but I often prefer to use my local corner store, even though it is more expensive, because on occasion they will provide me with credit and other favors. Similarly, as most members of a social drinking group know, where one buys a round, everyone reciprocates. If one member does not drink beer, however, but prefers whiskey, very soon that person gets left out or changes his or her taste because the reciprocity becomes unbalanced and this somehow "spoils the atmosphere." Finally, one has **negative reciprocity**, which is impersonal, barter-based, and centered on one's own ends. In terms of economic behavior, it is the "most economic" and ranges from theft to exploitation. It has very little morality in it and is typically practiced on people separated by great social distance.

All types of reciprocity can be found in one relationship, as in the case of a marital relationship in which one's spouse is unfaithful. Even socially frowned-upon practices like corruption can be analyzed in terms of exchange, as is made clear by Sean Cush McNamara's case study of how to bribe a policeman.

The second type of exchange that Sahlins mentions is **redistributive**, and it is more coercive and entails the produce of labor from several individuals being brought to a central place where it is sorted, counted, and reallocated. Such forms of redistribution can take two forms:

egalitarian or stratified. A good example of **egalitarian redistribution** would be among the Yanomami where the headman/redistributer simply has to work harder than anyone else and gets nothing in return immediately, except perhaps admiration. In stratified redistribution, the redistributer withholds his or her own labor, retains the largest share, and ends up with more material wealth. Typically, these exchanges are clothed in a rhetoric of kinship obligations.

Market exchange is the final type and is by far the most dominant; its most important form of exchange is buying and selling. Closely related to the capitalist system in which the idea of a market is central, market exchange is not, however, the sole mechanism for subsistence in a capitalist society. Prices on the market are determined by supply and demand. In the market, loyalties and values are not supposed to enter, but they often do.

One of the great contributions of anthropology has been in the discovery of the *informal sector*, or *dual economy*, of the market. This notion, first pioneered by the anthropologist Keith Hart in 1973, has had a major impact on our understanding of how people survive economically. It refers essentially to people's innumerable economic activities that are not recorded in such government statistics as tax returns or licenses. In many parts of the world, this vibrant sector was usually ignored by economists, principally because it is so difficult to track. Philippe Bourgois's study, "Crack in Spanish Harlem," is representative of this type of economic activity. In many parts of the world, the informal sector is more important than the formal sector.

Another contribution anthropologists have made is in their "discovery" of the obvious, namely, the crucially important role of children in the economy. Victoria Goddard's article shows how important children can be in Naples. In many parts of the world, preteenage children can average easily up to thirty hours a week, working often for no wages. It behooves us to remember that children currently form the silent majority of Earth's population.

Most textbooks and lectures end their discussions of **economic anthropology** with consumption, but as anthropologists we should go further. This is what William Rathje does when he examines peoples' legacy to their successors, the postconsumption phase that in our society is dismissed as garbage. This integration of the study of garbage, archaeology, current practices, and history has come to be known as **garbology** and reveals the truth about what we actually do as compared to what we are told we do!

REFERENCES

Sahlins, Marshall. 1972. *Stone Age Economics*. Chicago: Aldine.

Child Labour in Naples

The Case of Outwork

Victoria Goddard

Victoria Goddard is a lecturer in anthropology at Goldsmith College, University of London. She has done extensive fieldwork in Europe on child labor.

In January 1981 the Anti-Slavery Society held a workshop on child labour at the Institute of Development Studies. The intention of this workshop was to bring together social scientists and policy-makers to discuss a problem which has proved to be elusive. In particular, it was hoped that the contribution of anthropologists and historians would help to rectify a weakness which runs through much of the political and social literature on the subject of child labour: a tendency to take a moralistic standpoint which universalizes the category "child" and uncritically transposes European urban middle-class expectations to this category wherever and whenever it may be found.

It was agreed at the workshop that both the category "child" and the category "work" were culturally and historically specific. In the attempt to develop more rigorous frameworks, it was important to rid oneself of mystifications and romanticizations, both those associated with extending "European" concepts and values and also those associated with the idealization of "traditional" or "primitive" society and its institutions—which is equally dangerous (Cf. IDS, 1981).

The social scientist studying child labour is faced bluntly with her or his preconceptions and sentiments. A satisfactory treatment of the subject has to go beyond the boundaries of sociological categories. Concepts which in other contexts have been powerful tools of analysis, such as "exploitation," fall short of dealing with the various ways in which the time and labour of children is used and appropriated. With these points in mind, I will briefly look at the question of child labour in the organization of outwork in Naples, Southern Italy.

"Child Labour in Naples: The Case of Outwork" by Victoria Goddard, from *Anthropology Today*, Vol. 1, No. 5, 1985. Royal Anthropological Institute. Reprinted with permission.

CHILDREN AND WORK IN NAPLES

Even the briefest visit to Naples will reveal to the often surprised tourist the existence of child workers. As you sit in any café you will see a nine or ten-year-old boy flit in and out of office buildings carrying his tray of cups of coffees, or hanging around during his workbreak, with a cigarette dangling from his mouth in expert fashion. A more adventurous visitor, exploring the narrow streets of the old quarters of the city, will see small boys covered in grease helping out at a car mechanic's workshop or bicycle-shop. And there are the small groups of boys practising guerrilla warfare tactics on tourists, as well as those windscreen cleaners who make their services necessary by taking the precaution of wiping a dirty cloth over your windscreen as soon as the traffic lights turn red (Cf. Anti-Slavery Society, 1980 & 1981).

I was not in Naples to study child labour, but my search for outworkers in different trades led to one particular sector of the child labour-market. Outworkers are the last link in the chain of subcontracting, whereby industrial or commercial enterprises hand out all or part of the process of production to smaller units or individual workers who provide goods or services in their own homes.[1] This system operates worldwide and for good reason. It presents many advantages to the entrepreneur: it reduces costs, since often (and in the Neapolitan case almost always) the machines used belong to the workers and they shoulder the costs of repair, electricity and sometimes the secondary material, such as thread, as well. The outwork system allows the entrepreneur a greater degree of flexibility in the use of labour, because the worker is paid on a piece-rate basis, so that the oscillations of demand can be handled without a paid workforce standing idle at times when demand is low. Usually, labour-power on piecework systems is cheaper because the workers so employed are not unionized and, being scattered and usually isolated, are in a more vulnerable position than most factory workers. They can thus be paid lower rates of pay.

The entrepreneur escapes not only the limitations imposed on his business by trade unions but also taxes and various conditions of employment imposed by the state—one of these being the prohibition against employing minors.[2] Many enterprises do employ people under the legal age limit, but large-scale companies, sensitive to public opinion and state intervention, fight shy of doing this. Being defined as illegal, child workers are pushed out of those work-places where labour relations are better regulated and where safety and hygiene conditions may be more adequate. Instead, it is in the small workshop or sweatshop, unnoticed by either public or State, and cramped into unhygienic conditions by its lack of capital, that we find the bulk of minors employed in industrial work.

The Neapolitan outworker is usually a woman. The productive work she may carry out for a shoe, glove or toy factory will be interspersed with her household chores. It is the assumption that her responsibility as housewife and mother (either in the present or projected into the future) which is usually given as a justification for her working in the home rather than in a factory (Goddard, 1977).

Households in Naples differ in their composition, and their boundaries fluctuate; but in all cases there is a clear division between the sexes in respect of tasks and responsibilities. Domestic tasks are the women's concern. This means that little girls start work in the home, helping their mothers at a younger age than most boys start to work. In fact, if a mother has to work outside the home, her daughter(s) take over most of her household duties, and if the mother works at home, she or they may start housework when still very young.

There is also a division of labour by age in the household, which may take many forms, according to the needs and aspirations of parents. An elder son or daughter may start work at a very young age, to ease the burden on the parents while the brothers and sisters are still young. An elder child may even work to help put his/her siblings through the education system, even through university. A younger daughter on the other hand runs the risk of taking over more and more household responsibilities, thus freeing the labour of her mother and older sisters who can earn more—and older sisters are likely to marry and leave the household anyway. Of course older daughters can also meet this fate. Whatever the case, it is frequent to find a "specialization" within the household whereby the women allocate different tasks to each other. Thus some young women are specialist paid workers, having worked in production from a very early age. Their skills in the domestic sphere are hence very limited. Others are

specialist housewives and can run a household but have no other skills. This specialization in the household from an early age has important consequences for their future lives. Where the girl starts paid work at an early age—especially factory work—she is likely to have problems in adapting to her role as wife at marriage. Where, however, a girl specializes as a domestic worker, she is likely to join the ranks of the most poorly paid unskilled category of outworkers when the economic situation of the household which she has formed at marriage forces her to make a monetary contribution.

Children's paid work is usually parallel to schooling. Where there is a family workshop or other business, the children will almost certainly be expected to spend many hours helping out after school. Where the mother only is involved in production in the home, there may be less pressure but it is usual for little girls to help their mothers. Not so little boys, who help only (and this very casually) when they are quite young. As they grow older the sexual division of labour establishes itself: the mother is doing a woman's job and the women and girls around her should help her and learn her skills. But both boys and girls may be apprenticed out to a neighbour or kin to learn a trade. The burden of carrying out two activities—or more in the case of little girls who may help in the home and work for money and go to school— is a heavy one. Absenteeism from school is high in certain areas of Naples and there is a tendency for numbers to drop progressively from the first grade onwards.[3]

TRAINING VERSUS EDUCATION

In order to consider why parents may impose such a burden on their children it is important to take into account the economic structure of Naples and the Italian South as a whole. Naples is a city of contrasts in its production profile as well as in so many other aspects. The giant steelworks at Bagnoli was established when the Italian State experimented with the concept of "poles of development" to reverse the poverty of the South; there is also the large Alfa Sud car plant in Pomigliano d'Arco and a few medium-sized enterprises. A privileged few will find jobs in such places and will try to keep them; in fact many pass them on to their children. The majority of working-class Neapolitans, however, will be competing for jobs in small factories and tiny workshops, which characteristically emerge and disappear almost overnight. Unemployment is massive. In spite of certain actions which have been taken by Neapolitans, such as electing a Communist mayor and organizing combative leagues of unemployed workers, complex problems relating to insufficient work opportunities remain unsolved.

Given this backdrop, it is important to point out that neither the Neapolitan working-class nor the lumpen-proletariat are homogeneous. Not only are there important variations in terms of their occupational status; there are also differences in attitude and expectations, for example regarding their children. Thus, many Neapolitan couples opt for having two or no more than three, children so that they can provide for them adequately and give them a solid basis for their adult lives. They look down upon couples who have many children, considering them uncaring and selfish. Many such do not wish their own fate on their children: they find their own work tiring and dull, and want something better for their offspring. Most would consider a graduate, professional status for their children to be over-ambitious and seem happy to settle for a white-collar or secretarial job. Some however do hope to get at least one of their children through university, and with the joint efforts of both themselves and other offspring they may achieve this. But there has been growing disaffection with education as a solution and as a way out of the hard life of the working class, now that more and more university graduates join the ranks of the unemployed, to the extent of forming their own league of "organized unemployed."

As a result of the economic conditions in Naples and disillusion with formal education, most parents prefer to play both alternatives: sending their children to school for as long as this is feasible, while at the same time inserting them in the economic structure of the city, preferably as an apprentice in a trade. In the case of a daughter, apprenticing her out to an outworker in the shoe trade is considered a wise move. Women, some of whom are very highly skilled, can always find work in this traditional Neapolitan export industry. In addition it is a skill which they can use either in a factory or at home, so that the factory can be left on marriage. Thus the sexual division of labour, and the values which dictate a preference for women to be at home, are protected. So training, that is, preparing a child for his or her adult responsibilities, is an important objective of parents who put their children in paid work.

THE ECONOMIC CONTRIBUTION OF CHILDREN

The financial motive is important as well. Very few children after a certain age can get away with living in a household without making some contribution, however small and erratic. In the case of young girls working with outworkers, their earnings are negligible for the first years of their training. Daughters working with their mothers are unlikely to get any wages at all, and their contribution to the household is made directly through their labour.

In the shoe trade, the task of the young apprentice is to place glue on the rim of pieces of leather which will form the upper part of the shoe. Another, more difficult task, is to fold the edges of the leather onto the glue and hammer them down without distorting the shape. To do this really well requires a lot of practice, and there are many adult workers who specialize in the folding task rather than move on to the machine work which will render them a fully-fledged *orlatrice*. This in turn means higher rates of pay and better opportunities both for factory workers and outworkers. It is to such women, usually a kinswoman or neighbour, that a young girl will be apprenticed out at about the age of 10 or 12 (if she is learning from a mother this could start much earlier, say at the age of 7).

From the point of view of the teacher, initially, such an apprentice may not help very much; but, as the child becomes more skilful she allows her to increase her output, since the more glued and folded pieces there are, the more a machinist can sew—which is of course very significant in piece-rate work. It is difficult to say to what extent, if at all, these apprentices are exploited by their teachers. In any case the situation will be acceptable to the girl's parents and often to the girl herself, since after such a period of training she will be in a position to enter a factory or workshop at about the age of 14, when her wages will increase considerably.

A girl's earnings are usually handed over to her mother. She may take them as a contribution towards the costs of keeping the family fed and dressed, or she may use them to pay for the needs of this particular daughter. As the daughter gets older, the mother may subtract a certain amount each week from this income for the girl's *corredo*: the various items such as bed linen which a girl should have when she marries. The *corredo* can in some cases be the major reason for a girl's employment, once she is engaged to marry. So earnings are important economically but not necessarily for immediate purposes: that is to say, earnings must be seen in relation to longer-term and more general objectives.

THE QUESTION OF CONTROL

Girls in general, because of the forms their work takes, and those boys who are apprenticed out or work in a family business, are very much under adult control. But those children, mostly boys, who are involved in various "street activities" can obtain a greater degree of autonomy from their parents and other adults as well. It is unlikely that they can totally escape adult authority, or the "seniority system" as Diane Elson has called it (Elson, 1982) but they have a better chance than others to keep or spend a part of their takings without having to consult adults. Children who work in the context of a family or kinship-based unit of production are under much greater control, and there may well be a compounding of the authority of work relations with the authority of parent-child relations.

Machado Neto (1981, 1982), writing on her research in Bahia, Brazil, points out that the work children carry out in the household or neighbourhood is closely controlled by the family or the neighbourhood. As the child grows older, s/he is likely to venture further afield than the neighbourhood—girls usually being employed as domestic servants and boys more probably involved in various street activities. Street activities take place far from the neighbourhood, which allows these boys considerable freedom, although various adult figures will attempt to control their labour and their incomes. Interestingly those who are most successful in escaping adult control are those who are most likely to join up with gangs involved with petty crime, who are both feared and respected.

So it appears that boys have more opportunities of becoming relatively autonomous and wide-ranging in their movements than girls, who are in most cases restricted to the home and its immediate surroundings, or are employed in conditions where strong control is exercised over them. In the City of Mexico, on the other hand, although boys dominate many street activities, both boys and girls engage in petty vending or begging away from the home. This difference between the Mexican and Neapolitan situations could be related in part to ideological differences related to the degree of control considered necessary for girls; but given the importance attributed to female virginity in Mexico, it is more likely that the explanation will be found in Mexico City's larger "floating population" and in the economic organization of Naples which may provide opportunities for women's economic pursuits to take place in the home or the neighbourhood.

It would appear that adult Mexican women are more likely than their Neapolitan counterparts to be involved in street activities in which they also involve their children, whether male or female. There is an important link to be considered here between the activities of children and those of women. The conditions which determine women's status also shape the lives of children (for an interesting example of this see Schildkrout, 1978 and 1979).

CONCLUSION

To sum up:

1. Child labour has to be located within the context of social and economic relations and to understand it we must take into account ideological factors.

2. Although economic necessity is a central motive for child labour, in the case of the child outworkers of Naples this must be understood in a broad context. Furthermore this economic necessity must be seen to be shaped and conditioned by ideological factors which emphasize control over women's sexuality, and therefore movement from an early age, the importance of marriage, the institution of the *corredo* and the relative importance of formal education in comparison to other forms of preparation for adulthood.

3. The division of labour between adult men and women and the position allocated to women in a given society have important repercussions for children: especially, and more enduringly, for girl children. In other words, the activities of mothers (and of women generally) largely determine the activities of children, and the sexual division of labour which holds for both adult men and women can also be seen to operate at the level of childhood.

4. Although a child may be more "protected" when working within the context of a family or kinship-based enterprise, this does not necessarily mean that the child is better off from the point of view of health or finances. In fact, the child working in such a situation is liable to suffer much stricter control and exploitation than do many "street" children and may fall under the dual authority structures of kinship and work relations.

5. Legislation is a double-edged sword. By declaring child workers to be illegal the State enhances children's already existing social vulnerability. Because of their illegality, child workers are concentrated in small, unsafe work-places where their working conditions cannot be monitored. This has, in fact, resulted in more than one tragedy such as the episode when three girls died in a fire in a Casavatore workshop in 1976, because all exits were blocked with boxes and machinery. Furthermore, the glues used in the leather trades can be very toxic. This is especially true of the cheaper glues which because of the pressures on small workshops and factories are used widely. The toxic elements from these glues cause a neuromuscular disease which affect women workers and working and non-working children alike, since babies and toddlers play close to their outworker-mothers' machines and materials (Cf. Berlinguer *et al*, 1977).

6. We should be cautious when appraising the significance of formal education. Education in this sense should not be considered only in institutional terms; but rather its forms and content must be related to its socioeconomic context. Thus the negative attitude of some Neapolitans towards schooling can be seen either as a failure to appreciate the value of formal education or as an accurate assessment of the local labour-market.

NOTES

1. For a survey of the outwork system for Italy as a whole see Frey, L. *et al* (1975). For the informal sector, including outwork in Naples see De Marco & Talamo 1976.
2. According to the 1967 Act the minimum age for admission to employment (including apprentices) is 15 years.
3. According to a survey carried out in 1977 (quoted in ASS 1981) 74% of the children interviewed said they had left school because of work; 45% of children left school before the final year of primary education. 15% left during the final year and 19% left during the first year of middle school (at the ages of 10 and 12 respectively).

REFERENCES

Allum, P. 1973. *Politics and Society in Post-War Naples*, Cambridge.

Anti-Slavery Society 1980. *Child Labour in Italy—Report for 1980 to the United Nations Working Group Experts on Slavery*.

Anti-Slavery Society 1980. *Child Labour: Published and Unpublished Material* compiled by A. Hill Black.

Anti-Slavery Society 1981. *Child Labour in Italy*, Report No. 5 by Marina Valcarenghi.

Belmonte, T. 1979. *The Broken Fountain*, Columbia University Press, N.Y.

Berlinguer, G., L. Cecchini, & F. Terranova 1977. *Gli Infortuni sul lavaro dei Minori*. Il Pensiero Scientifico Editore, Rome.

Challis, J., & D. Elliman 1979. *Child Workers Today*, Quartermaine House.

De Marco, C., & M. Talamo 1976. *Lavoro Nero*, Gabriele Mazzotta editore.

Elson, D. 1982. The Differentiation of Children's Labour in the Capitalist Labour Market, in *Development and Change*, Vol. 13, No. 4.

Frey, L., G. De Santis, & R. Livraghi 1975. *Lavoro a domicilio e decentramento dell'attivita produttiva nei settori tessili e dell'abbigliamento in Italia*, Franco Angelo Ed., Collana ISVET, No. 30, Milano.

Goddard, V. 1977. Research Note: Domestic Industry in Naples in *Critique of Anthropology*, Vol. 3, No. 9 & 10.

Goddard, V. 1981. *Child Labour—An Introduction to Some of the Issues*, mimeo Child Labour Workshop, I.D.S., Sussex.

Institute of Development Studies 1981. *Working Children—An International Perspective*, Report of a Child Labour Workshop at the I.D.S., Sussex.

Machado Neto, Z. 1981. See I.D.S. 1981.

Machado Neto, Z. 1982. Work, Poverty, Starvation, in *Development and Change*, Vol. 13, No. 4.

Mendelievich, E. 1979. Italy, in *Children at Work*, ed. by Mendelievich, I.L.O., Geneva.

Rouard, D. 1979. Enfants au Travail, in *Le Monde de L'Education*, No. 53, Sept. Paris.

Schildkrout, E. 1978. Age and Gender in Hausa Society: Socio-Economic Roles of Children in Urban Kano, in *Sex and Age as Principles of Social Differentiation*, ASA Monograph No. 7, ed. by J. S. LaFountaine, Academic Press.

Schildkrout, E. 1979. Women's Work and Children's Work: Variations Among Moslems in Kano, in *Social Society of Work*, ASA Monograph No. 19, ed. by S. Wallman, London, Academic Press.

Learning How to Bribe a Policeman

Sean Cush McNamara

Sean Cush McNamara is a British anthropologist who has carried out fieldwork in Bolivia.

There has been some discussion by social scientists interested in development studies on the use of public office for private gain. Although this question has had general interest for me, I never thought I would have any experience to contribute to the discussion. Indeed, as for many law-abiding people in Britain, such interests appear rather exotic. It was therefore rather a surprise, during a recent visit to Bolivia, to find myself inside a prison and bribing my way out again. What was immediately interesting was that I did not know how to bribe someone. This does not seem to have been part of my education in life skills and I had to learn about the process.

How did I find myself in this situation? Well, with a friend I had just arrived in Santa Cruz from La Paz. Santa Cruz is of interest as one of the last remaining "frontier" regions of the world. This frontier has been created first of all by discovery of oil and the subsequent immigration this has stimulated. The sleepy town surrounded by forest of the early 1970s is now a bustling centre from which the forest has receded. It has the feel of the Wild West to match its situation but with new pick-up trucks, not horses, in the streets. Two hours after arrival in Santa Cruz we were in the central plaza looking at an exhibition of handicrafts, and about a quarter of an hour later we were in the police station. Later, out again and back in our hotel, we overheard an American couple talking of their brush with the law and of their near-imprisonment. So this was not an isolated incident. In order to understand the system which gives rise to harassment of foreigners in Santa Cruz there is a need to describe the most salient features of the local economy.

"Learning How to Bribe a Policeman" by Sean Cush McNamara, from *Anthropology Today*, Vol. 2, No. 2, 1986. Royal Anthropological Institute. Reprinted with permission.

THE CONTEXT

In Bolivia there is an inflation rate variously estimated between 500 and 2,000% per year. This means salaries erode rapidly and rises granted every quarter or even every month cannot keep pace. Daily paid workers obtain rises daily. There are two exchange rates in operation: in early June 1985 the official rate was 75,000 pesos to the dollar while the parallel rate was rising rapidly from about 300,000 to 400,000 pesos. This means that there is a great desire among salaried people, including the police, to obtain dollars in order to retain the value of "savings" (i.e. cash that has not been spent today but which will be needed tomorrow). The general importance of these factors in the bribery of policemen will be seen later. I should stress that these are not sufficient conditions: there are special features of Santa Cruz which make it different from the rest of the country. Whilst the national economy is struggling, the economy of Santa Cruz is buoyant. Santa Cruz is the area where oil, cocaine, and contraband play major roles in the economy. The resultant dollar wealth has two consequences which are relevant here. First, there is an extremely unequal distribution of dollars. Second, every foreigner is a potential supply, as are street money changers, and small-time cocaine dealers.

THE PROTECTION OF THE LAW

The general objective for a salaried policeman is to ensure his subsistence for the whole month. In June 1985 it was reckoned that his salary of approximately $28 would last about a fortnight. Other cash must be obtained from other sources. The operational problem to be resolved by many policemen (without access to other funds) is how to ensure a reasonable flow of cash. Here the policeman's duty of upholding the law is very useful as it can be used to generate further funds.

Dealing in cocaine or contraband is illegal. There is mounting international pressure to reduce the flow of cocaine from Bolivia, and the Bolivian Government is itself concerned about increasing domestic drug addiction. However it is common knowledge in Santa Cruz that some drug dealers are very wealthy and powerful and manage to evade the law. The same cannot be said of small-time dealers with few connections. Such small-timers populate the local prison.

Currency transactions in the street are also illegal but can be considered almost a necessity if the illegal dollar earnings are to be used within the Santa Cruz economy. Perhaps in recognition of this, money changers continue to operate in the street but have been moving away from the central plaza to the ring road.

Because of the intense interest in drugs there is a justification for taking an interest in foreigners: every one is a potential drug smuggler. However there must usually be some pretext for questioning a foreigner. Such pretexts are easy to find: talking to a known money changer; not carrying passports; driving a foreign vehicle. Once contact has been established, the game plan is as follows:

- talking to someone *is* changing money illegally;
- not carrying passport *is* being a suspected drug smuggler;
- parking a vehicle *is* parking illegally.

All these pretexts enable the law to be used to gain a top-up of salary. In our case we were talking in the plaza when a policeman asked for proof of identity. Our passports were in the hotel—theft of passports is quite common—and a driving licence was not considered sufficient.

At this point there are three options for a foreigner:

1. Walk away immediately and with determination;
2. Pay bribe on the spot;
3. Accompany officer to the police station.

The problem of the second option is that foreigners do not know how to do it, and the first option does not come to mind. The third option has the consequence that a senior officer is involved and he wishes to receive the bribe. However, in front of many people in the outer offices of the police station it will probably appear even more difficult to bribe a policeman. The opportunity is offered by the senior officer requesting all pockets to be emptied. Having cash in pesos and dollars is further

"evidence" of illegal money changing. We had the impression that confiscation of dollars was possible at this stage, except that since we were carrying travellers' cheques in the main this was less likely.

Not resolving the issue at this stage brings about an escalation in police pressure. The protest of innocence to the first policeman is now interpreted as "threatening behaviour," and the suspect is removed to the inner courtyard. This is inhabited by minor drug dealers and others serving a range of sentences or simply being held in custody. The economy of this part of the prison involving sale of clothing to buy food, negotiations between guards and women also held there—would be an interesting study in its own right.

Once in the courtyard the charge is rumoured to have increased again to assaulting a policeman, and an even more senior officer (who never appears in person) is involved. The immediate prospect seems to be a few hours or days in this courtyard; this is clearly designed as a softening up until the bribe is paid.

LEARNING HOW TO PAY A BRIBE

In the courtyard the minor drug dealers know the rules. One, who had been in the main prison elsewhere, had secured his own transfer to the relative comfort of the courtyard. A laid-back character who has now kicked his own habit but with 20 years still to serve officially (having completed 5), he makes himself useful talking to newcomers and passing on information received. We had the feeling our story was being checked informally and we heard how the charges were escalating. Through this intermediary it was made known that a bribe could be made and initial negotiations began over the amount. At the same time a CID man was sent to the hotel to collect the passports. Also the police heard that it was difficult for us to give a "bribe."

The final arrangements were made by the officer from the outer offices. The charges about hitting a policeman were forgotten but a "fine" was to be paid for keeping the passports safely in the hotel. We were asked how much we would like to pay. Working on the basis that $1 would have probably been acceptable to the very first policeman and that $50 obtains an internal transfer for a drug dealer according to our new friend, a sum of approximately $15 was offered in pesos to compensate for the inconvenience we had caused the police. This was agreed. Possibly a lower "fine" would have been acceptable in dollars.

As a sidelight on the affair, the CID man who had collected the passports had to accompany us back to the hotel where the staff had made him sign a receipt for the passports. He asked for $2 for his inconvenience.

CONCLUSIONS

The experience brings out a number of points:

1. If a bribe is a "fine," cross-cultural difficulties are resolved.

2. The amount increases as the centre of the prison is approached, and more senior officers are involved. A visitor should avoid accompanying the officer to the police station.

3. The police require their own justifications—for making the first contact and for raising the "fine" and these are found by reference to the law.

4. Police harassment is determined in this situation by economic factors; the incidence of harassment increases as the month progresses (and the salary diminishes in value).

5. The contempt with which local people treated the local police almost amounted to counter-harassment, except that locals were very aware of how and when to walk away from confrontation.

Ironically we had been trying to obtain cash dollars in order to pay the airport tax but were not able to find any legally so on the way to the airport the ring road money changers proved useful—though they were reluctant to buy pesos. This was an illustration of how a system of law not founded in economic reality—i.e. having to pay airport tax in dollars but there being none offered legally for purchase—creates a necessity for illegality.

Finally, although the experience is unique, I hope it adds some local colour to the recent debate on the use of public office for private gain.

Crack in Spanish Harlem

Culture and Economy in the Inner City

Philippe Bourgois

Philippe Bourgois, an assistant professor at San Francisco State University was awarded the Ph.D. by Stanford University in 1985. Bourgois has carried out fieldwork in the Caribbean and Central America as well as in Spanish Harlem and has research interests in political economy, ethnicity, immigration, and the work process.

The heavy-set, white undercover policeman pushed me across the ice-cream counter, spreading my legs and poking me around the groin. As he came dangerously close to the bulge in my right pocket I hissed in his ear "It's a tape recorder." He snapped backwards, releasing his left hand's grip on my neck and whispering a barely audible "Sorry." Apparently, he thought he had clumsily intercepted an undercover from another department because before I could get a close look at his face he had left the *bodega* grocery-store cum numbers-joint. Meanwhile, the marijuana sellers stationed in front of the *bodega* that Gato and I had just entered to buy 16-ounce cans of Private Stock (beer), observing that the undercover had been rough with me when he searched through my pants, suddenly felt safe and relieved—finally confident that I was a white drug addict rather than an undercover.

As we hurried to leave this embarrassing scene we were blocked by Bennie, an emaciated teenager high on angel dust who was barging through the door along with two friends to mug us. I ran to the back of the *bodega* but Gato had to stand firmly because this was the corner he worked, and those were his former partners. They dragged him onto the sidewalk surrounding him on all sides, shouting about the money he still owed, and began kicking and hitting him with a baseball bat. I found out later that Gato owed them for his share of the supply of marijuana confiscated in a drug bust last week... After we finished telling the story at the crack/*botanica*[1] house where I had been spending most of my evening hours this summer, Chino, who was on duty selling that night with Julio (pronounced Jew-Lee-oh), jumped up excitedly calling out "what street was that

on? Come on, let's go, we can still catch them—How many were they?" I quickly stopped this mobilization for a revenge posse, explaining that it was not worth my time, and that we should just forget about it. Chino looked at me disgustedly sitting back down on the milk crate in front of the *botanica's* door and turned his face away from me, shrugging his shoulders. Julio, whom I knew better and had become quite close to for a number of weeks last year, jumped up in front of me raising his voice to berate me for being "pussy." He also sat back down shortly afterwards feigning exasperated incredulity with the comment "Man you still think like a *blanquito*." A half dozen spectators—some of them empty-pocketed ("thirsty!") crack addicts, but most of them sharply dressed teenage drug-free girls competing for Chino's and Julio's attentions—giggled and snickered at me.

CULTURE AND MATERIAL REALITY

The above extract from sanitized fieldwork notes is merely a personalized glimpse of the day-to-day struggle for survival *and for meaning* by the people who stand behind the extraordinary statistics on inner city violent crime in the United States. These are the same Puerto Rican residents of Spanish Harlem, New York City, that Oscar Lewis in *La Vida* declared to be victims of a "culture of poverty" enmired in a "self-perpetuating cycle of poverty" (Lewis 1966: 5). The culture of poverty concept has been severely criticized for its internal inconsistencies, its inadequate understanding of "culture" and ethnicity, its ethnocentric/middle class bias, its blindness to structural forces, and its blame-the-victim implications (cf. Leacock ed. 1971; Valentine 1968; Waxman 1977; Stack 1974). Despite the negative

"Crack in Spanish Harlem: Culture and Economy in the Inner City" by Philippe Bourgois, from *Anthropology Today*, Vol. 5, No. 4, 1989. Royal Anthropological Institute. Reprinted with permission.

scholarly consensus on Lewis's theory, the alternative discussions either tend towards economic reductionism (Ryan 1971; Steinberg 1981; Wilson 1978) or else ultimately minimize the reality of profound marginalization and destruction—some of it internalized—that envelop a disproportionate share of the inner city poor (cf. Stack 1974; Valentine 1978; see critiques by Maxwell 1988; Wilson 1987). More importantly, the media, public policy-makers and a large proportion of inner city residents themselves continue to subscribe to a popularized blame-the-victim/culture of poverty concept that has not been adequately rebutted by scholars.

The inner city residents described in the ethnographic vignette above are the pariahs of urban industrial US society. They seek their income and subsequently their identity and the meaning in their life through what they perceive to be high-powered careers "on the street." They partake of ideologies and values and share symbols which form the basis of an "inner city street culture" completely excluded from the mainstream economy and society but ultimately derived from it. Most of them have a few direct contacts with non-inner city residents, and when they do it is usually with people who are in a position of domination: teachers in school, bosses, police officers, and later parole or probation officers.

How can one understand the complicated ideological dynamic accompanying inner city poverty without falling into a hopelessly idealistic culture of poverty and blame-the-victim interpretation? Structural, political economy reinterpretations of the inner city dynamic emphasize historical processes of labour migration in the context of institutionalized ethnic discrimination. They dissect the structural transformations in the international economy which are destroying the manufacturing sector in the United States and are swelling the low wage, low prestige service sector (cf. Davis 1987; Sassen-Koob 1986; Steinberg 1981; Tabb and Sawers, eds. 1984; Wilson 1978, 1987). These analyses address the structural confines of the inner city dynamic but fall prey to a passive interpretation of human action and subscribe to a weakly dialectic interpretation of the relationship between ideological processes and material reality, or between culture and class.

Although ultimately traceable directly to being products of international labour migrations in a transnational world economy, street-level inner city residents are more than merely passive victims of historical economic transformations or of the institutionalized discrimination of a perverse political and economic system. They do not passively accept their fourth-class citizen fate. They are struggling determinedly—just as ruthlessly as the railroad and oil robber-barons of the previous century and the investment-banker "yuppies" of today—to earn money, demand dignity and lead meaningful lives. Tragically, it is that very process of struggle against—

yet within—the system which exacerbates the trauma of their community and which destroys hundreds of thousands of lives on the individual level.

In the day-to-day experience of the street-bound inner city resident, unemployment and personal anxiety over the inability to provide one's family with a minimal standard of living translates itself into intra-community crime, intra-community drug abuse, intra-family violence. The objective, structural desperation of a population without a viable economy, and facing systematic barriers of ethnic discrimination and ideological marginalization, becomes charged at the community level into self-destructive channels.

Most importantly, the "personal failure" of those who survive on the street is articulated in the idiom of race. The racism imposed by the larger society becomes internalized on a personal level. Once again, although the individuals in the ethnographic fragment at the beginning of this paper are the victims of long-term historical and structural transformations, they do not analyse their difficult situation from a political economy perspective. In their struggle to survive and even to be successful, they enforce on a day-to-day level the details of the trauma and cruelty of their lives on the excluded margins of US urban society.

CULTURAL REPRODUCTION THEORY

Theorists of education have developed a literature on processes of social and cultural reproduction which focus on the ideological domination of the poor and the working class in the school setting (cf. Giroux 1983). Although some of the social reproduction approaches tend towards an economic reductionism or a simple, mechanical functionalism (cf. Bowles and Gintis 1977), the more recent variants emphasize the complexity and contradictory nature of the dynamic of ideological domination (Willis 1983). There are several ethnographies which document how the very process whereby students resist school, channels them into marginal roles in the economy for the rest of their lives (cf. Willis 1977; Macleod 1987). Other ethnographically-based interpretations emphasize how success for inner city African-American students requires a rejection of their ethnic identity and cultural dignity (Fordham 1988).

There is no reason why these theories of cultural resistance and ideological domination have to be limited to the institutional school setting. Cultural reproduction theory has great potential for shedding light on the interaction between structurally induced cultural resistance and self-reinforced marginalization at the street-level in the inner city experience. The violence, crime and substance abuse plaguing the inner city can be understood as the manifestations of a "culture of resistance" to mainstream, white racist, and economically exclusive society.

This "culture of resistance," however, results in greater oppression and self-destruction. More concretely, refusing to accept the outside society's racist role playing and refusing to accept low wage, entry-level jobs, translates into high crime rates, high addiction rates and high intra-community violence.

Most of the individuals in the above ethnographic description are proud that they are not being exploited by "the White Man," but they feel "like fucking assholes" for being poor. All of them have previously held numerous jobs in the legal economy in their lives. Most of them hit the street in their early teens working odd jobs as delivery boys and baggers in supermarkets and *bodegas*. Most of them have held the jobs that are recognized as among the least desirable in US society. Virtually all of these street participants have had deeply negative personal experiences in the minimum-wage labour market, owing to abusive, exploitative and often racist bosses or supervisors. They see the illegal underground economy as not only offering superior wages, but also a more dignified work place. For example, Gato had formerly worked for the ASPCA cleaning out the gas chambers where stray dogs and cats are killed. Bennie had been fired six months earlier from a night shift job as security guard on the violent ward for the criminally insane on Wards Island; Chino had been fired a year ago from a job installing high altitude storm windows on skyscrapers following an accident which temporarily blinded him in the right eye. Upon being disabled he discovered that his contractor had hired him illegally through an arrangement with a corrupt union official who had paid him half the union wage, pocketing the rest, and who had not taken health insurance for him. Chino also claimed that his foreman from Pennsylvania was a "Ku Klux Klanner" and had been especially abusive to him as he was a black Puerto Rican. In the process of recovering from the accident, Chino had become addicted to crack and ended up in the hospital as a gunshot victim before landing a job at Papito's crack house. Julio's last legal job before selling crack was as an off-the-books messenger for a magazine catering to New York yuppies. He had become addicted to crack, began selling possessions from out of his home and finally was thrown out by his wife who had just given birth to his son, who carried his name as Junior the IIIrd, on public assistance. Julio had quit his messenger job in favour of stealing car radios for a couple of hours at night in the very same neighbourhood where he had been delivering messages for ten hour days at just above minimum wage. Nevertheless, after a close encounter with the police Julio begged his cousin for a job selling in his crack house. Significantly, the sense of responsibility, success and prestige that selling crack gave him enabled him to kick his crack habit and replace it by a less expensive and destructive powder cocaine and alcohol habit.

The underground economy, consequently, is the ultimate "equal opportunity employer" for inner city youth (cf. Kornblum and Williams 1985). As Davis (1987: 75) has noted for Los Angeles, the structural economic incentive to participate in the drug economy is overwhelming:

> With 78,000 unemployed youth in the Watts-Willowbrook area, it is not surprising that there are now 145 branches of the rival Crips and Bloods gangs in South L.A., or that the jobless resort to the opportunities of the burgeoning "Crack" economy.

The individuals "successfully" pursuing careers in the "crack economy" or any other facet of the underground economy are no longer "exploitable" by legal society. They speak with anger at their former low wages and bad treatment. They make fun of friends and acquaintances—many of whom come to buy drugs from them—who are still employed in factories, in service jobs, or in what they (and most other people) would call "shitwork." Of course, many others are less self-conscious about the reasons for their rejection of entry-level, mainstream employment. Instead, they think of themselves as lazy and irresponsible. They claim they quit their jobs in order to have a good time on the street. Many still pay lip service to the value of a steady, legal job. Still others cycle in and out of legal employment supplementing their bouts at entry-level jobs through part-time crack sales in an almost perverse parody of the economic subsidy of the wage labour sector by semi-subsistence peasants who cyclically engage in migratory wage labour in third world economies (cf. Meillassoux 1981; Wallerstein 1977).

THE CULTURE OF TERROR IN THE UNDERGROUND ECONOMY

The culture of resistance that has emerged in the underground street-level economy in opposition to demeaning, underpaid employment in the mainstream economy engenders violence. In the South America context of extreme political repression and racism against Amerindians and Jews, anthropologist Michael Taussig has argued that "cultures of terror" emerge to become "... a high powered tool for domination and a principal medium for political practice (1984: 492)." Unlike Taussig's examples of the 1910s Putumaya massacres and the 1970s Argentine torture chambers, domination in the case of the inner city's culture of terror is self-administered even if the root cause is generated or even imposed externally. With the exception of occasional brutality by policemen or the bureaucratized repression of the social welfare and criminal justice institutions (cf. Davis 1988), the physical violence and terror of the inner city are largely carried out by inner city residents themselves.

Regular displays of violence are necessary for success in the underground economy—especially at the street-level drug dealing world. Violence is essential for maintaining credibility and for preventing rip-off by colleagues, customers and hold-up artists. Indeed, upward mobility in the underground economy requires a systematic and effective use of violence against one's colleagues, one's neighbours and, to a certain extent, against oneself. Behaviour that appears irrationally violent and self-destructive to the middle class (or the working class) outside observer, can be reinterpreted according to the logic of the underground economy, as a judicious case of public relations, advertising, rapport building and long-term investment in one's "human capital development."

The importance of one's reputation is well illustrated in the fieldwork fragment at the beginning of this paper. Gato and I were mugged because Gato had a reputation for being "soft" or "pussy" and because I was publicly unmasked as *not being* an undercover cop: hence safe to attack. Gato tried to minimize the damage to his future ability to sell on that corner by not turning and running. He had pranced sideways down the street, though being beaten with a baseball bat and kicked to the ground twice. Significantly, I found out later that it was the second time this had happened to Gato this year. Gato was not going to be upwardly mobile in the underground economy because of his "pussy" reputation and he was further cementing his fate with an increasingly out of control addiction to crack.

Employers or new entrepreneurs in the underground economy are looking for people who can demonstrate their capacity for effective violence and terror. For example, in the eyes of Papito, the owner of the string of crack franchises I am currently researching, the ability of his employees to hold up under gunpoint is crucial as stick-ups of dealing dens are not infrequent. In fact, since my fieldwork began in 1986, the *botanica* has been held up twice. Julio happened to be on duty both times. He admitted to me that he had been very nervous when they held the gun to his temple and had asked for money and crack. Nevertheless, not only did he withhold some of the money and crack that was hidden behind the bogus *botanica* merchandise, but he also later exaggerated to Papito the amount that had been stolen in order to pocket the difference.

On several occasions in the midst of long conversations with active criminals (i.e. once with a dealing-den stick-up artist, several times with crack dealers, and once with a former bank robber) I asked them to explain how they were able to trust their partners in crime sufficiently to ensure the longevity and effectiveness of their enterprise. To my surprise I was not given any righteous diatribes about blood-brotherhood trustworthiness or any adulations of boyhood loyalty. Instead, in each case, in slightly different language I was told somewhat aggressively: "What do you mean how do I trust him? You should

ask 'How does he trust me?'" Their ruthlessness is their security: "My support network is me, myself and I." They made these assertions with such vehemence as to appear threatened by the concept that their security and success might depend upon the trustworthiness of their partner or their employer. They were claiming—in one case angrily—that they were not dependent upon trust: because they were tough enough to command respect and enforce all contracts they entered into. The "How can they trust me?" was said with smug pride, perhaps not unlike the way a stockbroker might brag about his access to inside information on an upcoming hostile takeover deal.

At the end of the summer Chino demonstrated clearly the how-can-I-be-trusted dynamic. His cocaine snorting habit had been degenerating into a crack addiction by the end of the summer, and finally one night he was forced to flee out of state to a cousin's when he was unable to turn in the night's receipts to his boss Papito following a binge. Chino also owed Papito close to a thousand dollars for bail that Papito had posted when he was arrested for selling crack at the *botanica* a few months ago. Almost a year later when Papito heard that Chino had been arrested for jumping bail he arranged through another associate incarcerated in the same prison (Rikers Island) to have Chino beaten up before his trial date.

My failure to display a propensity for violence in several instances cost me the respect of the members of the crack scene that I frequented. This was very evident when I turned down Julio and Chino's offer to search for Bennie after he mugged Gato and me. Julio had despairingly exclaimed that I "still [thought] like a *blanquito*," genuinely disappointed that I was not someone with common sense and self-respect.

These concrete examples of the cultivation of violent public behaviour are the extreme cases of individuals relying on the underground economy for their income and dependent upon cultivating terror in order to survive. Individuals involved in street activity cultivate the culture of terror in order to intimidate competitors, maintain credibility, develop new contacts, cement partnerships, and ultimately to have a good time. For the most part they are not conscious of this process. The culture of terror becomes a myth and a role model with rules and satisfactions all its own which ultimately has a traumatic impact on the majority of Spanish Harlem residents—who are drug free and who work honestly at poorly remunerated legal jobs, 9 to 5 plus overtime.

PURSUING THE AMERICAN DREAM

It is important to understand that the underground economy and the violence emerging out of it are not propelled by an irrational cultural logic distinct from that of mainstream USA. On the contrary, street participants are frantically pursuing the "American dream."

The assertions of the culture of poverty theorists that the poor have been badly socialized and do not share mainstream values is wrong. On the contrary, ambitious, energetic, inner city youths are attracted into the underground economy in order to try frantically to get their piece of the pie as fast as possible. They often even follow the traditional US model for upward mobility to the letter by becoming aggressive private entrepreneurs. They are the ultimate rugged individualists braving an unpredictable frontier where fortune, fame and destruction are all just around the corner. Hence Indio, a particularly enterprising and ambitious young crack dealer who was aggressively carving out a new sales point, shot his brother in the spine and paralyzed him for life while he was high on angel dust in a battle over sales rights. His brother now works for him selling on crutches. Meanwhile, the shooting has cemented Indio's reputation and his workers are awesomely disciplined: "If he shot his brother he'll shoot anyone." Indio reaffirms this symbolically by periodically walking his turf with an oversized gold chain and name plate worth several thousand dollars hanging around his neck.

The underground economy and the culture of terror are experienced as the most realistic routes to upward mobility. Entry-level jobs are not seen as viable channels to upward mobility by high school dropouts. Drug selling or other illegal activity appear as the most effective and realistic options for getting rich within one's lifetime. Many of the street dealers claim to be strictly utilitarian in their involvement with crack and they snub their clients despite the fact that they usually have considerable alcohol and powder cocaine habits themselves. Chino used to chant at his regular customers "Come on, keep on killing yourself; bring me that money; smoke yourself to death; make me rich."

Even though street sellers are employed by the owner of a sales point for whom they have to maintain regular hours, meet sales quotas and be subject to being fired, they have a great deal of autonomy and power in their daily (or nightly) routine. The boss only comes once or twice a shift to drop off drugs and pick up money. Frequently, it is a young messenger who is sent instead. Sellers are often surrounded by a bevy of "thirsty" friends and hangers-oners—frequently young teenage women in the case of male sellers—willing to run errands, pay attention to conversations, lend support in arguments and fights and provide sexual favours for them on demand because of the relatively large amounts of money and drugs passing through their hands. In fact, even youths who do not use drugs will hang out and attempt to befriend respectfully the dealer just to be privy to the excitement of people coming and going, copping and hanging; money flowing, arguments, detectives, and stick-up artists—all around danger and excitement. Other non-users will hang out to be treated to an occasional round of beer, Bacardi or, on an off night, Thunderbird.

The channel into the underground economy is by no means strictly economic. Besides wanting to earn "crazy money," people choose "hoodlum" status in order to assert their dignity at refusing to "sling a mop for the white man" (cf. Anderson 1976: 68). Employment or better yet self-employment—in the underground economy accords a sense of autonomy, self-dignity and an opportunity for extraordinary rapid short-term upward mobility that is only too obviously unavailable in entry-level jobs. Opulent survival without a "visible means of support" is the ultimate expression of success and it is a viable option. There is plenty of visible proof of this to everyone on the street as they watch teenage crack dealers drive by in convertible Suzuki Samurai jeeps with the stereo blaring, "beem" by in impeccable BMWs, or—in the case of the middle-aged dealers—speed around in well waxed Lincoln Continentals. Anyone can aspire to be promoted to the level of a seller perched on a 20-speed mountain bike with a beeper by their side. In fact, many youths not particularly active in the drug trade run around with beepers on their belts just pretending to be big-time. The impact of the sense of dignity and worth that can accompany selling crack is illustrated by Julio's ability to overcome his destructive addiction to crack only after getting a job selling it: "I couldn't be messin' up the money. I couldn't be fucking up no more! Besides, I had to get respect."

In New York City the insult of working for entry-level wages amidst extraordinary opulence is especially painfully perceived by Spanish Harlem youths who have grown in abject poverty only a few blocks from all-white neighbourhoods commanding some of the highest real estate values in the world. As messengers, security guards or xerox machine operators in the corporate headquarters of the Fortune 500 companies, they are brusquely ordered about by young white executives who sometimes make monthly salaries superior to their yearly wages and who do not even have the time to notice that they are being rude.

It could be argued that Manhattan sports a *de facto* apartheid labour hierarchy whereby differences in job category and prestige correlate with ethnicity and are often justified—consciously or unconsciously—through a racist logic. This humiliating confrontation with New York's ethnic/occupational hierarchy drives the street-bound cohort of inner city youths deeper into the confines of their segregated neighbourhood and the underground economy. They prefer to seek out meaning and upward mobility in a context that does not constantly oblige them to come into contact with people of a different, hostile ethnicity wielding arbitrary power over them. In the underground economy, especially in the world of substance abuse, they never have to experience the silent subtle humiliations that the entry-level labour market—or even merely a daily subway ride downtown—invariably subjects them to.

In this context the crack high and the rituals and struggles around purchasing and using the drug are comparable to the millenarian religions that sweep colonized peoples attempting to resist oppression in the context of accelerated social trauma—whether it be the Ghost dance of the Great Plains Amerindians, the "cargo cults" of Melanesia, the Mamachi movement of the Guaymi Amerindians in Panama, or even religions such as Farrakhan's Nation of Islam and the Jehovah's Witnesses in the heart of the inner city (cf. Bourgois 1986, 1989). Substance abuse in general, and crack in particular, offer the equivalent of a millenarian metamorphosis. Instantaneously users are transformed from being unemployed, depressed high school dropouts, despised by the world—and secretly convinced that their failure is due to their own inherent stupidity, "racial laziness" and disorganization—into being a mass of heart-palpitating pleasure, followed only minutes later by a jaw-gnashing crash and wideawake alertness that provides their life with concrete purpose: get more crack—fast!

One of the most dramatic illustrations within the dynamic of the crack economy of how a cultural dynamic of resistance to exploitation can lead contradictorily to greater oppression and ideological domination is the conspicuous presence of women in the growing cohort of crack addicts. In a series of ten random surveys undertaken at Papito's crack franchises, women and girls represented just under 50% of the customers. This contrasts dramatically to the estimates of female participation in heroin addiction in the late 1970s.

The painful spectacle of young, emaciated women milling in agitated angst around crack copping corners and selling their bodies for five dollars, or even merely for a puff on a crack stem, reflects the growing emancipation of women in all aspects of inner city life, culture and economy. Women—especially the emerging generation which is most at risk for crack addiction—are no longer as obliged to stay at home and maintain the family. They no longer so readily sacrifice public life or forgo independent opportunities to generate personally disposable income. This is documented by the frequent visits to the crack houses by pregnant women and by mothers accompanied by toddlers.

A more neutral illustration of the changed position of women in street culture outside the arena of substance abuse is the growing presence of young women on inner city basketball courts. Similarly, on the national level, there are conclusive statistics documenting increased female participation in the legal labour market—especially in the working class Puerto Rican community. By the same token, more women are also resisting exploitation in the entry-level job market and are pursuing careers in the underground economy and seeking self-definition and meaning through intensive participation in street culture.

Although women are using the drug and participating intensively in street culture, traditional gender relations still largely govern income-generating strategies in the underground economy. Most notably, women are forced disproportionately to rely on prostitution to finance their habits. The relegation of women to the traditional street role of prostitution has led to a flooding of the market for sex, leading to a drop in the price of women's bodies and to an epidemic rise in venereal disease among women and newborn babies.

Contradictorily, therefore, the underlying process of emancipation which has enabled women to demand equal participation in street culture and to carve out an expanded niche for themselves in the underground economy has led to a greater depreciation of women as ridiculed sex objects. Addicted women will tolerate a tremendous amount of verbal and physical abuse in their pursuit of a vial of crack, allowing lecherous men to humiliate and ridicule them in public. Chino, who is married and is the father of nine children, refers to the women who regularly service him with oral sex as "my moufs" [mouths]. He enjoys calling out to these addicted women from across the street. "Yo, there goes my mouf! Come on over here." Such a public degradation of a cohort of women who are conspicuously present on the street cannot be neutral. It ultimately reinforces the ideological domination of women in general.

DE-LEGITIMIZING DOMINATION

How can one discuss and analyse the phenomenon of street-level inner city culture and violence without reproducing and confirming the very ideological relationships that are its basis? In his discussion of the culture of terror, Taussig notes that it is precisely the narratives about the torture and violence of the repressive societies which ". . . are in themselves evidence of the process whereby a culture of terror was created and sustained (1984: 279)." The superhuman power that the media has accorded to crack serves a similar mythical function. The *New York Times* has run articles and interviews with scientists that portray crack as if it were a miraculous substance beyond the power of human beings to control (cf. 25 June, 1988: 1). They "prove" this by documenting how quickly rats will ecstatically kill themselves when provided with cocaine upon demand. Catheterized rats push the cocaine lever to the exclusion of the nutrient lever until they collapse exhausted to die of thirst.

The alleged omnipotence of crack coupled with even the driest recounting of the overpowering statistics on violence ultimately allows US society to absolve itself of any real responsibility for the inner city phenomena. The mythical dimensions of the culture of terror push economics and politics out of the picture and enable the US to maintain in some of its larger cities a level of ethnic segregation and economic marginalization that are unacceptable to any of the other wealthy, industrialized nations of the world, with the obvious exception of South Africa. Worse yet, on the level of theory, because of the continued domination—even in their negation—of the North America-centered culture of poverty theories, this discussion of the ideological implications of the underground economy may take readers full circle back to a blame-the-victim interpretation of inner city oppression.

NOTE

1. A *botanica* is a herbal pharmacy and *santeria* utility store.

REFERENCES

Anderson, Elijah. 1976. *A Place on the Corner*. Chicago: University of Chicago Press.

Bourgois, Philippe. 1986. The Miskitu of Nicaragua: Politicized Ethnicity. *Anthropology Today* 2:2: 4–9.

Bourgois, Philippe. 1989. *Ethnicity at Work: Divided Labour on a Central American Banana Plantation*. Baltimore: Johns Hopkins University Press.

Bowles, Samuel and Herbert Gintis. 1977. *Schooling in Capitalist America*. New York: Basic Books.

Davis, Mike. 1987. *Chinatown, Part Two?* The "Internationalization" of Downtown Los Angeles. *New Left Review* 164: 65–86.

Davis, Mike, with Sue Ruddick. 1988. Los Angeles: Civil Liberties Between the Hammer and the Rock. *New Left Review* 1970: 37–60.

Fordham, Signithia. 1988. Racelessness as a Factor in Black Students' School Success: Pragmatic Strategy or Pyrrhic Victory? *Harvard Educational Review* 58:1: 54–84.

Giroux, Henry. 1983. Theories of Reproduction and Resistence in the New Sociology of Education: A Critical Analysis. *Harvard Educational Review* 53:3: 257–293.

Kornblum, William and Terry Williams. 1985. *Growing Up Poor*. Lexington, MA: Lexington Books.

Leacock, Eleanor Burke. ed. 1971. *The Culture of Poverty: A Critique*. New York: Simon & Schuster.

Lewis, Oscar. 1966. The Culture of Poverty. In *Anthropological Essays*. Pp. 67–80. New York: Random House.

Macleod, Jay. 1987. *Ain't No Makin' It*. Boulder, CO: Westview Press.

Maxwell, Andrew. 1988. The Anthropology of Poverty in Black Communities: A Critique and Systems Alternative. *Urban Anthropology* 17:2&3: 171–191.

Meillassoux, Claude. 1981. *Maidens, Meal and Money*. Cambridge: Cambridge University Press.

Ryan, William. 1986 [1971]. Blaming the Victim. In *Taking Sides: Clashing Views on Controversial Social Issues*. Pp. 45–52. Ed. Kurt Finsterbusch and George McKenna. Guilford, CT: Dushkin Publishing Group.

Sassen-Koob, Saskia. 1986. New York City: Economic Restructuring and Immigration. *Development and Change* 17:1: 87–119.

Stack, Carol. 1974. *All Our Kin: Strategies for Survival in a Black Community*. New York: Harper & Row.

Steinberg, Stephen. 1981. *The Ethnic Myth: Race, Ethnicity and Class in America*. New York: Atheneum.

Tabb, William and Larry Sawers. eds. 1984. *Marxism and the Metropolis: New Perspectives in Urban Political Economy*. New York: Oxford University Press.

Taussig, Michael. 1984. Culture of Terror-Space of Death, Roger Casement's Putumayo Report and the Explanation of Torture. *Comparative Studies in Society and History* 26:3: 467–497.

Valentine, Bettylou. 1978. *Hustling and Other Hard Work*. New York: Free Press.

Valentine, Charles. 1968. *Culture and Poverty*. Chicago: University of Chicago Press.

Wallerstein, Emanuel. 1977. Rural Economy in Modern World Society. *Studies in Comparative International Development* 12:1: 29–40.

Waxman, Chaim. 1977. *The Stigma of Poverty: A Critique of Poverty Theories and Policies*. New York: Pergamon.

Willis, Paul. 1983. Cultural Production and Theories of Reproduction. In *Race, Class and Education*. Pp. 107–138. Eds. Len Barton and Stephen Walker. London: Croom-Helm.

Willis, Paul. 1977. *Learning to Labor: How Working Class Kids Get Working Class Jobs*. Aldershot, England: Gower.

Wilson, William Julius. 1978. *The Declining Significance of Race: Blacks and Changing American Institutions*. Chicago: University of Chicago Press.

Wilson, William Julius. 1987. *The Truly Disadvantaged: The Inner City, the Underclass and Public Policy*. Chicago: University of Chicago Press.

Rubbish!

William L. Rathje

William Rathje, who is best known today for his long-term study of garbage (and founding of the field of "garbology"), began his career in Maya archaeology with a study of prehistoric burials from Guatemala and Belize. He received his Ph.D. from Harvard University in 1971 and is now professor of anthropology at the University of Arizona, as well as head of the refuse section of that university's Bureau of Applied Research in Anthropology. Besides his research into modern material culture, he retains his interest in early civilizations.

. . . . To get some perspective on garbage let's review a few fundamentals. For most of the past two and a half million years human beings left their garbage where it fell. Oh, they sometimes tidied up their sleeping and activity areas, but that was about all. This disposal scheme functioned adequately, because hunters and gatherers frequently abandoned their campgrounds to follow game or find new stands of plants. Man faced his first garbage crisis when he became a sedentary animal—when, rather than move himself, he chose to move his garbage. The archaeologist Gordon R. Willey has argued, only partly in fun, that *Homo sapiens* may have been propelled along the path toward civilization by his need for a class at the bottom of the social hierarchy that could be assigned the task of dealing with mounting piles of garbage.

This brings us to an important truth about garbage: There are no ways of dealing with it that haven't been known for many thousands of years. These ways are essentially four: dumping it, burning it, converting it into something that can be used again, and minimizing the volume of material goods—future garbage—that is produced in the first place ("source reduction," as it is called). Every civilization of any complexity has used all four methods to varying degrees.

From prehistory through the present day dumping has been the means of disposal favored everywhere, including in the cities. The archaeologist C. W. Blegen, who dug into Bronze Age Troy in the 1950s, found that floors had become so littered that periodically a fresh supply of dirt or clay had been brought in to cover up the refuse. Of course, after several layers had been applied,

"Rubbish!" by William L. Rathje, from *Atlantic Monthly*, December 1989. Reprinted with permission.

the doors and roofs had to be adjusted upward. Over time the ancient cities of the Middle East rose high above the landscape on massive mounds, called tells. In 1973 a civil engineer with the Department of Commerce, Charles Gunnerson, calculated that the rate of uplift owing to the accumulation of debris in Bronze Age Troy was about 4.7 feet per century. If the idea of a city rising above its garbage at this rate seems extraordinary, it may be worth considering that "street level" on the island of Manhattan is fully six feet higher today than it was when Peter Minuit lived there.

At Troy and elsewhere, of course, not all trash was kept indoors. The larger pieces of garbage and debris were thrown into the streets. There semi-domesticated animals (usually pigs) ate up the food scraps, while human scavengers, in exchange for the right to sell anything useful that they might find, carried much of what was left to vacant lots or to the outskirts of town, where the garbage was burned or simply left.

In most of the Third World a slopping-and-scavenging system that Hector and Aeneas would recognize remains in place. The image of sulfurous "garbage mountains" in the Third World may be repellent, but the people who work these dumps, herding their pigs even as they sort out paper and plastic and metal, are performing the most thorough job of garbage recycling and resource recovery in the world. The garbage mountains point up another important (and often overlooked) truth about garbage: efficient disposal is not always completely compatible with other desirable social ends, such as human dignity and economic modernization. In a liberal democracy these other ends compete for priority and more often than not win.

Dumping, slopping, and scavenging were the norm in Europe and the United States until the late 1800s. It is difficult for anyone alive now to comprehend how appalling, as recently as a century ago, were the conditions of daily life in all the cities of the Western world, even in the wealthiest parts of town. The stupefying level of filth accepted as normal from the Middle Ages through the Enlightenment was augmented horribly by the Industrial Revolution. As the historian Martin Melosi has noted in his book *Garbage in the Cities* (1981), one of the ironies of laissez-faire capitalism is that it gave rise to a kind of "municipal socialism," as cities were forced, for the first time since antiquity, to shoulder responsibility for such duties as public safety and sanitation. Taking the long view reminds us of one more often-overlooked truth about garbage: Ever since governments began facing up to their responsibilities, the story of the garbage problem in the West has been one of steady amelioration, of bad giving way to less bad and eventually to not too bad. To be able to complain about the garbage problems that persist is, by past standards, something of a luxury.

AN UNKNOWN QUANTITY

What most people call garbage, professionals call solid waste. The waste that we're most familiar with, from the households and institutions and small businesses of towns and cities, is "municipal solid waste," or MSW. Professionals talk about what we all throw away as entering the "solid-waste stream," and the figure of speech is apt. Waste flows unceasingly, fed by hundreds of millions of tributaries. While many normal activities come to a halt on weekends and holidays, the production of garbage flows on. Indeed, days of rest tend to create the largest waves of garbage. Christmas is a solid-waste tsunami.

One might think that something for which professionals have a technical term of long standing should also be precisely calibrated in terms of volume. As we shall see, this is not the case with MSW. Nonetheless, there has been a good deal of vivid imagery relating to volume. Katie Kelly, in her book *Garbage* (1973), asserted that the amount of MSW produced in the United States annually would fill five million trucks; these, "placed end to end would stretch around the world twice." In December of 1987 *Newsday* estimated that a year's worth of America's solid waste would fill the twin towers of 187 World Trade Centers. In 1983 *The Baltimore Sun* claimed that Baltimore generates enough garbage every day to fill Memorial Stadium to a depth of nine feet—a ballpark figure if ever there was one.

Calculating the total annual volume or weight of garbage in the United States is difficult because there is, of course, no way one can actually measure or weigh more than a fraction of what is thrown out. All studies have had to take shortcuts. Not surprisingly, estimates of the size of the U.S. solid-waste stream are quite diverse. Figures are most commonly expressed in pounds discarded per person per day, and the studies that I have seen from the past decade and a half give the following rates: 2.9 pounds per person per day, 3.02 pounds, 4.24, 4.28, 5.0, and 8.0. My own view is that the higher estimates significantly overstate the problem. Garbage Project studies of actual refuse reveal that even three pounds of garbage per person per day may be too high an estimate for many parts of the country, a conclusion that has been corroborated by weight-sorts in many communities. Americans are wasteful, but to some degree we have been conditioned to think of ourselves as more wasteful than we truly are—and certainly as more wasteful than we used to be.

Evidence all around us reinforces such perceptions. Fast-food packaging is ubiquitous and conspicuous. Planned obsolescence is a cliché. Our society is filled with symbolic reminders of waste. What we forget is everything that is no longer there to see. We do not see the 1,200 pounds per year of coal ash that every American generated at home at the turn of the century and that was usually dumped on the poor side of town. We do not see the hundreds of thousands of dead horses that once had to be disposed of by American cities every year. We do not look behind modern packaging and see the food waste that it has prevented, or the garbage that it has saved us from making. (Consider the difference in terms of garbage generation between making orange juice from concentrate and orange juice from scratch; and consider the fact that producers of orange-juice concentrate sell the leftover orange rinds as feed, while households don't.) The average household in Mexico City produces one third more garbage a day than does the average American household. The reason for the relatively favorable U.S. showing is packaging—which is to say, modernity. No, Americans are not suddenly producing more garbage. Per capita our record is, at *worst*, one of relative stability.

WHAT'S IN A LANDFILL?

A sanitary landfill is typically a depression lined with clays, in which each day's deposit of fresh garbage is covered with a layer of dirt or plastic or both. A great deal of mythology has built up around the modern landfill. We have stuffed it with the contents of our imaginations. It is a fact, however, that there is an acute shortage of sanitary landfills for the time being, especially in the northeastern United States. From 1982 to 1987 some 3,000 landfills have been filled up and shut down nationwide. The customary formulation of the problem we face (you will find it in virtually every newspaper or magazine article on the subject) is that 50 percent of the landfills now in use will close down within five years. As it happens, that has always been true—it was true in 1970 and in 1960—because most landfills are designed to be in use for only about ten years. As noted, we are not producing more household garbage per capita (though we are probably producing more garbage overall, there being more and more of us). The problem is that old landfills are not being replaced. Texas, for example, awarded some 250 permits a year for landfills in the mid-seventies but awarded fewer than fifty last year.

The idea persists nevertheless that we are filling up landfills at an exponential rate, and that certain products with a high public profile are disproportionately responsible. I recently ran across articles in two different newspapers from Oregon in which the finger of blame was pointed at disposable diapers; one of them claimed that disposable diapers accounted for a quarter of the contents of local landfills and the other put the figure at "five percent to thirty-two percent." A recent editorial in *The New York Times* singled out fast-food packaging for straining the capacity of the nation's landfills. Fast-food packaging is, perhaps not surprisingly, almost everyone's villain of choice. I have over the years asked many people who have never seen the inside of a landfill to estimate what percentage of the contents consists of fast-food packaging, and the answers I have gotten have ranged from five to 35 percent, with most estimates either 20 or 30 percent.

The physical reality inside a landfill is considerably different from what you might suppose. I spent some time with The Garbage Project's team over the past two years digging into seven landfills: two outside Chicago, two in the San Francisco Bay area, two in Tucson, and one in Phoenix. We exhumed 16,000 pounds of garbage, weighing every item we found and sorting them all into twenty-seven basic categories and then into 162 subgroupings. In those eight tons of garbage and dirt cover there were fewer than sixteen pounds of fast-food packaging; in other words, only about a tenth of one percent of the landfills' contents by weight consisted of fast-food packaging. Less than one percent of the contents by weight was disposable diapers. The entire category of things made from plastic accounted for less than five percent of the landfills' contents by weight and for only 12 percent by volume. The real culprit in every landfill is plain old paper—non-fast-food paper, and mostly paper that isn't used for packaging. Paper accounts for 40 to 50 percent of everything we throw away, both by weight and by volume.

If fast-food packaging is the Emperor's New Clothes of garbage, then a number of categories of paper goods collectively deserve the role of Invisible Man. In all the hand-wringing over the garbage crisis, has a single voice been raised against the proliferation of telephone books? Each two-volume set of Yellow Pages distributed in Phoenix last year—to be thrown out this year—weighed 8.63 pounds, for a total of 6,000 tons of wastepaper. And competitors of the Yellow Pages have appeared virtually everywhere. Dig a trench through a landfill and you will see layers of phone books, like geological strata or layers of cake. Just as conspicuous as telephone books are newspapers, which make up 10 to 18 percent of the contents of a typical municipal landfill by volume. Even after several years of burial they are usually well preserved. During a recent landfill dig in Phoenix, I found newspapers dating back to 1952 that looked so fresh you might read one over breakfast. Deep within landfills, copies of that *New York Times* editorial about fast-food containers will remain legible until well into the next century.

As the foregoing suggests, the notion that much biodegradation occurs inside lined landfills is largely a popular myth. Making discards out of theoretically biodegradable materials, such as paper, or plastic made with cornstarch, is often proposed as a solution to our garbage woes (as things biodegrade, the theory goes, there will be more room for additional refuse). Laboratories can indeed biodegrade newspapers into gray slime in a few weeks or months, if the newspapers are finely ground and placed in ideal conditions. The difficulty of course, is that newspapers in landfills are not ground up, conditions are far from ideal, and biodegradation does not follow laboratory schedules. Some food and yard debris does degrade, but at a very, very slow rate (by 25 to 50 percent over ten to fifteen years). The remainder of the refuse in landfills seems to retain its original weight, volume, and form. It is, in effect, mummified. This may be a blessing, because if paper did degrade rapidly, the result would be an enormous amount of inks and paint that could leach into groundwater.

The fact that plastic does not biodegrade, which is often cited as one of its great defects, may actually be one of its great virtues. Much of plastic's bad reputation is undeserved. Because plastic bottles take up so much room in our kitchen trash cans, we infer that they take up a lot of room in landfills. In fact by the time garbage has been compressed in garbage trucks (which exert a pressure of up to fifty pounds per square inch on their loads) and buried for a year or two under tons of refuse, anything plastic has been squashed flat. In terms of landfill volume, plastic's share has remained unchanged since 1970. And plastic, being inert, doesn't introduce toxic chemicals into the environment.

A new kind of plastic that is biodegradable may in fact represent a step backward. The definition of "biodegradable" plastic used by most manufacturers focuses on tensile strength. Plastics "totally" degrade when their tensile strength is reduced by 50 percent. At that point—after as long as twenty years—a biodegradable plastic item will have degenerated into many little plastic pieces, but the total volume of plastic will not have changed at all. The degeneration agent used in biodegradable plastic, usually mostly cornstarch, makes up no more than 6 percent of a biodegradable plastic item's total volume; the 94 percent that's left represents more plastic than would be contained in the same item made with nonbiodegradable plastic, because items made with biodegradable plastic have to be thicker to compensate for the weakening effect of the degenerating agent.

The potentially toxic legacy of landfills that may long ago have been covered over by hospitals and golf courses illustrates one of the terrible ironies of enlightened garbage management: an idea that seems sensible and right is often overtaken by changes in society and in the contents of garbage. The idea of the sanitary landfill was advanced by civil engineers who lived in a simpler age. Industries used very toxic chemicals, yes, but most households lacked the array of pesticides, cleansers, and automotive fluids that one can find today in virtually every American home. Moreover, the landfill movement that matured after the Second World War, though hardly messianic was led by people who had a vision. They believed that in the disposal of garbage two birds could almost always be killed instead of one.

This is a historically peculiar trait of garbage science in the United States. The safe and efficient disposal of garbage has never been deemed a high enough end in itself by the professionals here. The goal has always been to get rid of garbage and do something else—create energy, make fertilizer, retrieve precious metals. In the case of sanitary landfills, their proponents hoped not only to dispose of mountains of garbage but also to reclaim thousands of acres of otherwise "waste" land and, literally to give something back to America. The ideal places for landfills, they argued, were the very places that most scientists now believe to be the worst places to put garbage: along rivers or in wetlands. It is in unlined landfills in places like these that, not surprisingly the problem of chemical "leachates" has been shown to be a matter of grave concern.

Environmental scientists believe that they now know enough to design and locate safe landfills, even if those landfills must hold a considerable amount of hazardous household waste such as motor oil and pesticides. The State of Delaware seems to be successful at siting such landfills now. But places like Long Island, where the water table is high, should never have another landfill. In the congested northeastern states there may simply be no room for many more landfills, at least not safe ones. Some 1,550 twenty-ton tractor trailers laden with garbage now leave Long Island every week bound for landfills elsewhere. But the country at large still has room aplenty. The State of New York recently commissioned an environmental survey of 42 percent of its domain with the express aim of determining where landfills might be properly located. The survey pinpointed lands that constitute only one percent of the area but nevertheless total 200 square miles.

The obstacles to the sanitary landfill these days are monetary—transporting garbage a few hundred miles by truck may cost more than shipping the same amount to Taiwan—and, perhaps more important, psychological: no one wants a garbage dump in his backyard. But they are not insuperable, and they are not fundamentally geographic. Quite frankly, few nations have the enormous (and enormously safe) landfill capabilities that this one has. . . .

THE TECHNOLOGICAL FIX

Americans have never been content to do things the old-fashioned way, and when garbage has been involved, they have always been receptive to any new, state-of-the-art means of disposal—especially if it promises savings in money, or, better, a tidy profit. The very first technological fixes in this country were a technique known as reduction, which heralded the age of recycling, and the incinerator, a device whose popularity has enjoyed enormous ups and suffered enormous downs.

In reduction, which was imported from Europe but never widely adopted there, wet garbage and dead animals were stewed in large vats in order to produce grease and a substance called residuum. The grease was sold for three to ten cents a pound and was used in the manufacture of soap, candies, glycerine, lubricants, and perfume. The residuum brought five to ten cents a ton and was used for fertilizer. The negative side of this process was that the reduction plants emitted pungent odors and a black, molten runoff that polluted nearby streams. By the 1920s most plants had been deemed impossibly disgusting and shut down, leaving a vacancy that was quickly filled by incinerators.

By 1920 there were incinerators in twelve American cities, including Topeka and Berkeley, and on the eve of the Second World War some 700 incinerators were in operation. Then, rather abruptly, incinerators fell into a period of decline. The advantages of incinerators were plain (they burned garbage up), but so were the disadvantages (they discharged foul odors, noxious gases, and gritty smoke). For aesthetic reasons rather than reasons of health or the environment (this was decades before anyone had heard of "risk factors" or acid rain) municipalities in the 1950s began shutting down their incinerators and focusing on sanitary landfills.

Then came the energy crisis. Amid skyrocketing fuel costs and a fear of resource shortages, incinerators were reinvented and renamed. The idea behind the "resource-recovery" plant was simple: not only would it burn trash to cinders but also it would garner from it any valuable materials and at the same time provide heat and electricity to customers nearby. By 1977 some twenty new resource-recovery plants were in use, another ten were being built, and about thirty-five were on the drawing board.

But resource-recovery plants tried to accomplish too much. A surfeit of variables had to be factored into their operations. For one thing, the machinery was complicated. The plants were dependent for their profitability on sales of recovered materials, but the secondary-materials markets are exceedingly erratic. Overestimates of the waste stream meant that many plants had difficulty just getting enough garbage to operate. Some operators ended up importing garbage from out of state. Today only a few resource-recovery plants remain in operation.

The newest means of incineration, a European import called mass burn, will have more staying power, because it is simple. Garbage is fed into a furnace, where it falls onto moving grates that tumble it at temperatures up to 2400° F. The burning mass heats water, and the steam drives a turbine to generate electricity, which is sold to a utility. To curb pollution, the waste gases are blown into electrostatic precipitators, or acid scrubbers, and then through fabric filters called baghouses. The ash residue is extracted, cooled, and, generally, dumped in a municipal landfill, where it takes up roughly ten percent of the room it would have taken as raw garbage. There are more than a hundred mass-burn incinerators in operation today in the United States, and there may be about 300 by 1995, when perhaps a quarter of America's garbage will go through their doors.

The main drawback to mass-burn incinerators is that for all their pollution controls, they can release into the atmosphere small amounts of certain metals, acid gases, and also classes of chemicals known as dioxins and furans, which have been implicated in birth defects and several kinds of cancer. No one really knows what the long-term risks are from the emissions released by incinerators. A portion of the ash produced by mass-burn plants is also toxic, containing dangerous levels of lead and cadmium, and some cities have had difficulty finding landfills for this ash. Quite apart from health issues, mass-burn incinerators are hugely expensive—they cost as much as $400 million apiece—and the task of getting one sited and built attracts the kind of pork-barrel chicanery and eco-bravado that one might expect, with best-case scenarios pitted against worst-case ones. Plants can usually be operated safely for a time. But plants get old, and performance begins to decline. Nevertheless, incineration is a big piece of the future, and environmentalists—at least mainstream environmentalists—seem more or less resigned to mass-burn plants as the only conceivable alternative to a heavier reliance on landfills, many of which, as noted, are old and unsafely located.

DEMAND-SIDE ECONOMICS

The yards of America's wastepaper and scrap-metal dealers are located near interstates and in warehouse districts, and they contain piles of crushed automobiles, railroad cars filled with cans, and baled newspaper and cardboard stacked several stories high. These are the trading pits of the recycled-materials markets. There is a big split between those who would recycle to make money and those who would recycle to do good, and I was made painfully aware of it one night at an Association of Recycling Industries convention, where I was scheduled to speak. Talking to a wastepaper dealer, I described with satisfaction the municipal newspaper-recycling program that the city of Tucson had just begun. The dealer looked at me in horror. He said, "You're telling me how well the competition is doing—the ones who are subsidized by the taxpayers to take away our livelihood. Don't you understand there never has been a shortage of recycled newspapers. The shortage is in demand. Markets fill up just like landfills. There are just so many car panels and cereal boxes that need to be made. I suppose you believe GM's going to say, 'Hey, great! Here's a bunch more newspapers for door panels. Let's make some more cars.' The more Tucson recycles, the less I do."

Twelve years later I count wastepaper dealers and other for-profit recyclers among my friends and also among the most valuable resources available to the United States for dealing with garbage. The champions of municipal recycling, who in communities across the country have been crying to move in on bottles, newspapers, and cans in the belief that recyclable commodities represent virgin territory, have found that the territory is already inhabited. Recycling by anyone should be encouraged, in my view, but it is important to understand at the outset what kind of recycling works and what kind may end up doing more harm than good.

Newsprint illustrates one potential problem. Only about ten percent of old newspapers go on to be recycled into new newspapers. What newspapers are really good for is making cereal and other boxes (if it's gray on the inside, it's from recycled stock), the insides of automobiles (the average car contains about sixty pounds of recycled newsprint), wallboard, and insulation. All these end uses are near saturation. Scrap dealers are in the precarious position of being able to obtain enough newsprint to supply demand completely but not daring to sell so much that the price of newsprint plummets and puts them out of business. What happens when the market is suddenly flooded with newsprint? Last year the State of New Jersey implemented new legislation requiring every community to separate at curbside, and collect, three categories of recyclables. As a result, in recent months the price of used newspaper in most parts of New Jersey has plummeted from up to $40 a ton to $25 a ton—in other words, you have to pay to have it taken away. If legislation like this became widespread, without complementary measures to increase demand for recycled-paper products, the effects could be precisely opposite those intended.

The fact is that for the time being, despite the recriminations and breast-beating, we are recycling just about as much paper as the market can bear. As noted, the marker for recyclable paper is glutted; expansion is possible only overseas. The demand for recyclable plastic and aluminum has not yet been fully met, but Americans have been doing a pretty good job of returning their plastic bottles and aluminum cans, and the beverage industry which hates it when states pass bottle bills, has pre-empted the issue in most places by opening up successful recycling centers.

Suppose there were a lot of room for growth and that the demand for recycled paper, plastic, and aluminum were insatiable. How much garbage would Americans be prepared to recycle? The only factor that could conceivably drive a systematic recycling effort is money. Money is the reason why junk dealers pay attention to some kinds of garbage and not to others, and it is the reason why most people return cans to supermarkets, and newspapers to recycling centers.

I belabor that point because it is so often lost sight of, and because there are studies that seem to suggest—erroneously, I think—that for noble motives alone people would go to considerable lengths to make recycling a basic feature of American life. Barry Commoner, the biologist and environmentalist, recently conducted a study of a hundred households in Easthampton, Long Island, in which participants were asked to separate their garbage into four containers: one for food debris and soiled paper (to be composted into fertilizer), one for clean paper, one for metal cans and glass bottles, and one for all the rest. Commoner found that because the garbage was rationally discarded, a stunning 84 percent of it could be sold or recycled. Only 16 percent had to be deposited in a landfill. Of course, this experiment lasted only a few weeks, and the households surveyed had actively volunteered to take part. Recognizing that his results were perhaps a little skewed, Commoner conducted a survey in Buffalo, New York, and ascertained that a reassuring 78 percent of all respondents said, sure, they'd be willing to separate their garbage into four containers. However, only 26 percent of the respondents said that they thought their neighbors would be willing to do so. This "What would the neighbors do?" question has a special resonance for Garbage Project researchers. We have found over the years, by comparing interview data with actual trash, that the most accurate description of the behavior of any household lies in that household's description of the behavior of a neighboring household.

There have been studies that have claimed that the people most likely to recycle are those with the most money and the most education, but all these studies are based on people's "self-reports." A look through household garbage yields a different picture. From 1973 to 1980 The Garbage Project examined some 9,000 loads of refuse in Tucson from a variety of neighborhoods chosen for their socioeconomic characteristics. We carefully sorted the contents for newspapers, aluminum cans, and glass bottles (evidence that a household is not recycling), and for bottle caps, aluminum pop-tops, and plastic sixpack holders (possible evidence, in the absence of bottles or cans, that a household *is* recycling). A lot of complicated statistical adjustments and cross-referencing had to be done, but in the end we made three discoveries. First, people don't recycle as much as they say they do (but they recycle just about as much as they say their neighbors do). Second, household patterns of recycling vary over time; recycling is not yet a consistent habit. Third, high income and education and even a measure of environmental concern do not predict household recycling rates. The only reliable predictor is the price paid for the commodity at buyback centers. When prices rose for, say, newsprint, the number of newspapers found in local garbage suddenly declined.

If there is a prosperous future for recycling it probably lies in some sort of alliance between wastepaper and scrap dealers and local governments. Where recycling is concerned, municipalities are good at two things: collecting garbage and passing laws to legislate monetary incentives. Wastepaper and scrap-dealers are good at something different: selling garbage. Local programs run by bureaucrats and tied to strict cost-accounting measures need predictable prices. Stability in a commodities' market is rare. Secondary-materials dealers thrive on daily, hourly fluctuations.

LIFE-STYLE OVERRIDE

Not long ago I stopped in Berkeley, where a ban was being considered on the use of expanded polystyrene foam—the substance that is turned into coffee cups and hamburger boxes and meat trays. The ban had originally been proposed because chlorofluorocarbons are used in the blowing of foam objects and are believed to contribute to the depletion of atmospheric ozone, and because foam objects are aesthetically repugnant to many people and symbolize the garbage problems we have. At the Berkeley campus of the University of California, I passed Sproul Plaza. It was lunchtime, and the plaza was filled with some 700 or 800 students in various forms of repose; virtually all of them held on their laps what first appeared to be pairs of white wings. The wings turned out to be large foam clamshells, which held hot food. I asked one group of lunchers what they thought about a ban on polystyrene foam. Great idea, they said between mouthfuls, and without irony. The ban has since gone into effect, even though the major producers and users of chlorofluoro-carbons agreed to a phase-out.

Source reduction is to garbage what preventive medicine is to health: a means of eliminating a problem before it can happen. But the utility of legislated source reduction is in many respects an illusion. For one thing, most consumer industries already have—and have responded to—strong economic incentives to make products as compact and as light as possible, for ease of distribution and to conserve costly resources. In 1970 a typical plastic soda bottle weighed sixty grams; today it weighs forty-eight grams and is more easily crushed. For another, who is to say when packaging is excessive? We have all seen small items in stores—can openers, say—attached to big pieces of cardboard hanging on a display hook. That piece of cardboard looks like excessive packaging, but its purpose is to deter shoplifting.

Finally, source-reduction measures don't end up eliminating much garbage; hamburgers, eggs, and VCRs, after all, will still have to be put in *something*.

Most source-reduction plans are focused on a drastic reduction in the use of plastic. And yet in landfills foams and other plastics are dormant. While some environmentalists claim that plastics create dioxins when burned in incinerators, a study by New York State's Department of Energy Conservation cleared the most widely used plastics of blame. The senior staff scientist of the National Audubon Society, Jan Beyea, contends that plastics in landfills *are fine* so long as they don't end up in the oceans. There plastic threatens marine animals, which can swallow or become enmeshed in it. Beyea's big complaint is against paper, whose production, he believes, creates large volumes of sulfur emissions that contribute to acid rain.

Ultimately the source-reduction question is one of lifestyle override. The purists' theory is that industry is forcing plastics and convenience products on an unwilling captive audience. This is nonsense. American consumers, though they may in some spiritual sense lament packaging, as a practical matter depend on the product identification and convenience that modern packaging allows. That's the reason source reduction usually doesn't work.

Our "wasteful" life-style is a product of affluence; disregard for the environment is not. Indeed, our short-term aesthetic concerns and long-term practical concerns for the environment are luxuries afforded us only by our wealth. In Third World countries, where a job and the next meal are significant worries, the quality of the environment is hardly a big issue in most people's minds. Concern for the environment can be attributed in major part to the conveniences—and the leisure time they afford—that some activists seem to want to eliminate.

None of this makes us unique. For all our new-fangled technologies, Americans are not that different from those who inhabited most of the world's other great civilizations. Our social history fits neatly into the broader cycles of rise and decline that other peoples have experienced before us. Most grand civilizations seem to have moved, over time, from efficient scavenging to conspicuous consumption and then back again. It is a common story, usually driven by economic realities.

In their beginnings most civilizations, both ancient and recent, make efficient use of resources. The Preclassic Maya, who inhabited the rain forests of the southern Yucatan from 1200 to 300 B.C., seem to have lived relatively simple farming lives. They built a few small temples, constructed large houses out of thatch on low dirt platforms, and interred their dead with one or two monochrome pots. Around 300 B.C. something extraordinary happened. A Classic Maya life-style of conspicuous consumption was born. The Classic Maya went in for excessive display: fancy ceremonial clothes and feathered headdresses; tall temples with intricately carved facades; cache offerings of jade and shell mosaics; and lavish burials. This cult of conspicuous consumption spread throughout southern Mesoamerica. Toward the end of major civilizations things are usually quite different. During the Decadent Period temples were small, tombs were reused, and caches contained only a few pieces of broken pottery or chipped obsidian knives. Whatever the stimulus, that which archaeologists in the 1950s saw among the ancient Maya as decadence we can see today as efficient resource utilization. Among the Decadent Maya everything was recycled or reused, and virtually no resources were put away beyond easy retrieval. The Decadent Maya were living on the edge. They had no choice.

The United States is still well within a Classic phase, at least in terms of its disposal habits. And I am not worried that even if present trends continue, we will be buried in our garbage. To a considerable extent we will keep doing what other civilizations have done: rising *above* our garbage. (One of the great difficulties I have met in excavating landfills is finding municipal sites that have not already been covered by new facilities.)

A rough consensus has emerged among specialists as to how America can at least manage its garbage, if not make it pretty or go away. Safely sited and designed landfills should be employed in the three quarters of the country where there is still room for them. Incinerators with appropriate safety devices and trained workers can be usefully sited anywhere but make the most sense in the Northeast. And states and municipalities need to cut deals with wastepaper and scrap dealers on splitting the money to be made from recycling. This is a minimum. Several additional steps could be taken to reduce the biggest component of garbage: paper. Freight rates could be revised to make the transport of paper for recycling cheaper than the transport of wood for pulp. Also, many things could be done to increase the demand for recycled paper. For example, the federal government, which uses more paper by far than any other institution in America, could insist that most federal paperwork be done on recycled paper. Beyond confronting the biggest-ticket item head-on, most garbage specialists would recommend a highly selective attack on a few kinds of plastic: not because plastic doesn't degrade or is ugly or bulky but because recycling certain plastics in household garbage would yield high-grade costly resins for new plastics and make incineration easier on the furnace grates, and perhaps safer. Finally, we need to expand our knowledge base. At present we have more reliable information about Neptune than we do about this country's solid-waste stream. . . .

7

Sex and Marriage

Why is it that the worst swearwords in our society are utterances that refer to reproduction or the sexual organs and incest? Although there are no ready answers to this question, it does underline the importance of the rules we attach to sexual activity, in particular incest.

The literature on **incest** is voluminous and cannot be summarized here. Suffice to say that there are at present two main camps, the Freudians and the evolutionary theorists. The psychoanalytically oriented Freudian interpreters try to explain how individual development blocks the possibility of incest. Freud argued that the child normally represses erotic feelings toward the opposite-sex parent or sibling out of fear of reprisal from the same-sex parent (the **Oedipus complex**). In short, familiarity breeds attempt, and thus incest came into being to prevent this rivalry.

The evolutionary theorists take as their founding father Edward Westermarck, the Finnish anthropologist who in 1891 suggested that **natural selection** had endowed humans with a tendency to avoid inbreeding and its harmful effects on offspring. It was, in effect, a question of familiarity breeds contempt or "marry out or die out." In recent years, this view has been supported by findings from sociobiologists like Robert Trivers, who maintains that children generally covet more attention from parents, especially mothers, when more siblings are added; this results in even the most tranquil families having occasional sibling rivalries and child–parent flare-ups. An analysis of intrafamily homicides shows that there is no evidence for a preponderance of same-sex bias that one would expect from a Freudian interpretation. Moreover, an analysis of incest in the United States, or at least of those cases that reach the courts, shows that it is usually stepfathers who have not had extended contact with the youthful victim, not biological fathers, who initiate the incest.

The most recent contribution to this debate is by anthropologist Nancy Thornhill (reported by *Science News*, Vol. 140:249, 1991) who argues that

> [M]any scholars . . . erred in assuming that all human societies retain explicit taboos against incest within the immediate family. . . . Incest rules primarily exist to regulate mating behavior between in-laws and cousins rather than close genetic relatives, who show little interest in incest. . . .
>
> Thornhill tracked information on mating and marriage rules in the ethnographies of 129 societies . . . . Only 57 of the societies—less than half—specified rules against nuclear family incest, whereas 114 societies designated rules to control mating or marriage with cousins, in-laws or both. . . .
>
> Rules regulating mating between in-laws serve as checks on paternity and obstacles to female adultery, mainly in societies that require a woman to live with her husband and his relatives upon marriage . . . Only 14 of the ethnographies describe societies that require a man to live with his wife and her relatives upon marriage, and most of these societies either lack rules regarding in-law mating or mete out mild punishments for an infraction of the rules.
>
> Rulers of stratified societies enforce sanctions against cousin marriage and inbreeding in order to secure their lofty positions by discouraging the concentration of wealth and power within families other than their own. . . . In nonstratified societies, with no central rulers and relatively equal distribution of food and other resources, dictums against cousin unions foil the accumulation of wealth in extended families and maintain the level playing field trod by most men.

Clearly, the last word on incest has not been said, and anthropologists bedevil the discussion by pointing out the large degree of variations in cultural practices, even those as basic as incest and marriage. Indeed, anthropology goes further. If there is one thing that we have shown, it is how even the most basic behavior of those whom we define as male and female is very much a cultural production. John Coggeshall very clearly brings this out in "'Ladies' Behind Bars." Biology is not necessarily destiny, and Regina Smith Oboler further underlines this. Moreover, even sexual practices are culturally constructed and can change over time.

Theories and explanations of procreation, incest, marriage, and sex are interrelated and closely related to the wider worldview of people. From such a broader perspective, the power of women has been substantially underestimated in many societies. Consider, for example, the following quote from Nisa, a Bushman woman:

> Women are strong; women are important. Zhun/twa men say that women are the chiefs, the rich ones, the wise ones. Because women possess something very important, something which enables men to live: their genitals. A woman can bring a man life even if he is almost dead. She can give him sex even if he is almost dead. She can give him sex and make him alive again. If she were to refuse, he would die! If there were no women around, their semen would kill men. Did you know that? If there were only men, they would all die. Women make it possible for them to live. (Shostak 1981)

Reproduction involves more than just sex; it also includes **marriage**, the **family**, and kinship. Marriage provokes many questions. Why do different arrangements occur, and why and how are they socially recognized?

Marriage does not have a single function. It ties a bundle of rights and obligations into one of several packages creating economic units, relating the individual to other kin groups and defining social status. It is a political instrument as royal marriages in Europe show or even the once popular soap opera "Dynasty" showed; it regulates sex and creates a social security network. Seen from such a broad perspective, sex might have nothing to do with marriage, as every teenager knows. It is for this reason that one can find woman–woman marriages and even Ghost marriages. The range of marriage types is also extraordinary as Dirk Johnson clearly shows in his article on **polygamy**.

Because of its multifunctionality, some anthropologists see marriage as the basis for human society as we know it. It is also a relatively conservative institution in that it tends to preserve the status quo. Although most American youth might believe in the illusion of falling in love and marrying anyone, chances are high that they will marry someone similar to them. Juliet Gardiner poignantly recaptures the hazards and thrills of cross-cultural dating and mating, based on an early example of **applied anthropology** done by Margaret Mead during World War II. In short, we marry within acceptable limits, a phenomenon known as **endogamy**. Marriage by itself does not really produce society but rather **exogamy**: the cultural prescriptions that force people to marry beyond their own group, which can be seen as an intensification of the incest taboo.

REFERENCES

Shostak, Marjory, 1981. *Nisa: The Life and Words of a !Kung Woman.* Cambridge, Mass.: Harvard University Press.

Polygamists Emerge from Secrecy, Seeking Not Just Peace but Respect

Dirk Johnson

Dirk Johnson received his B.A. from the University of Wisconsin in 1981 and went to work for the *New York Times*. He served first in New York City, then went on to become a national correspondent in Chicago. Since January 1991, he has been regional bureau chief of the Rocky Mountain Bureau.

COLORADO CITY, Ariz.—With arms full of groceries, three women in long, flowered dresses emerged from the general store here on a sun-splashed afternoon. After rounding up their playful children, they climbed into a car and headed back down the gravel road to the house, and the husband, they share.

Until recently theirs was a world that shunned outsiders, who were often stopped on the outskirts of town by police officers from the community who protected their legally forbidden way of life. The practice of polygamy has thrived quietly for generations in places like this small desert town, where fundamentalist Mormons settled after their church turned away from the practice of plural marriages a century ago.

But in recent years, as state law-enforcement officials have adopted an unwritten policy of leaving them alone, polygamists have gone public.

Indeed, they have begun a virtual public relations campaign to achieve tolerance, respect, a greater following, and ultimately legal protection. They are speaking at university forums, granting interviews to reporters and forming alliances with groups they once condemned. One such group, the state branch of the American Civil Liberties Union, has petitioned its parent organization to make legal recognition of polygamy a national cause like gay and lesbian rights.

"In this liberal age, with all the alternative life styles that are condoned," said Mayor Dan Barlow, who has five wives, "it is the height of folly to censure a man for having more than one family."

In an official endorsement of such arguments, the Utah Supreme Court ruled in March that polygamy, while still illegal, did not by itself make a family ineligible for adoption.

About 50,000 people in the Rocky Mountain states live in households made up of a man and two or more wives, and experts believe that the number of these households has been growing. Around Colorado City, a town of about 6000 people in northwest Arizona, the population has roughly doubled in every decade since it was founded in the 1930's. Most of the people in the area are polygamists or believe in the practice.

"Without any real threat from the law, these communities have begun to feel much freer about opening a public dialogue," said Martha Bradley, a professor at Brigham Young University who studies the polygamy movement. "It's really been apparent in the last three years or so. It's almost like a P.R. campaign. They want the world to know they're not a threat. And they want to continue to attract new people."

Most of the polygamists consider themselves fundamentalist Mormons, many of them descendants of people who split from the Church of Jesus Christ of Latter-day Saints.

According to early Mormon teaching, Joseph Smith, the founder of the church, learned in a revelation from God that he should take more than one wife, as some prophets in the Old Testament had done.

"The only justification was that it was commanded by God," said Ronald K. Esplin, the director of the Joseph Fielding Smith Institute for Church History, which studies the history of Mormonism.

The Mormon Church officially abandoned polygamy 101 years ago after it was forbidden by Utah law in a deal required by Congress for the territory to become a state. The church now excommunicates members for polygamy.

Among polygamists and their wives, the degree of religious influence varies significantly.

"I see it as the ideal way for a woman to have a career and children," said Elizabeth Joseph of Big Water, a

Utah town near the Arizona border. She is a lawyer and one of the nine wives of Alex Joseph. "In our family, the women can help each other care for the children. Women in monogamous relationships don't have that luxury. As I see it, if this life style didn't already exist, it would have to be invented to accommodate career women."

Her husband takes a more biblical view. "Every writer in the Old Testament, except for Daniel, was a polygamist," said Mr. Joseph, 54 years old. "The way I see it, if you're going to get a degree in electrical engineering, then you have to learn a little something about engineering. And if you're going to understand the Bible, you have to adopt the life style of those who wrote it."

SHIFT BY LAW OFFICIALS

The position among legal authorities toward polygamy has changed drastically in the past generation. In 1953, the Governor of Arizona ordered the National Guard to raid this community. Many men were jailed for bigamy, and some children were taken from their mothers and placed in foster homes.

Today law-enforcement officials generally take a "live and let live" attitude toward polygamists. Except in a few celebrated cases recently in which polygamists have committed violent acts, law-enforcement officials do not intervene.

"We all know what's going on," said Paul Van Dam, Utah's Attorney General. "But trying to do anything about it legally would be opening one Pandora's box after another."

It is a matter of legal interpretation whether this way of life technically constitutes polygamy, since the men do not typically take out more than one marriage license. In the eyes of the law, the men would be considered to be legally married to one woman, and cohabiting with one or more others.

And although laws against cohabitation or adultery may be applicable against such families, prosecutors are very reluctant to use them. "Once you start going after people for cohabitation, or adultery, where do you stop?" Mr. Van Dam asked.

Indeed, the fundamentalists, who have long rejected being grouped with other people who have adopted nontraditional living arrangements, like homosexual couples, now see society's greater tolerance as grounds to call for their own legitimacy.

It was the desire to live a more open life that led Don Cox and his wives, Katie and Earlean, to settle in Colorado City. Nearly 25 years ago, they were living in Salt Lake City and keeping their family arrangement a secret. "We told people that I was a friend of the family," Katie said.

When Katie's first child reached school age, the family moved to the polygamous community here, but they have since split with the fundamentalist church, which they feel restricts their lives too greatly. Although Mr. Cox built the family house, he does not have the property deed. It belongs to a trust controlled by the fundamentalist Mormon sect in Colorado City.

"It's a cult," Mr. Cox, a large white-haired man in suspenders, said bitterly. "They own a lot of property and they own a lot of people."

The Coxes and several other dissidents have filed a Federal suit in Salt Lake City to win the deeds for their homes. And in another sign of new openness here, the church authorities in Colorado City welcomed the suit as a way to settle the differences.

NO CHOICE IN A MARRIAGE

The Coxes live in an 11 bedroom home with a dining table long enough to accommodate them and most of their 19 children. But compared with some households here, the Cox family is relatively small. One man in town has 80 children.

In Colorado City, which straddles the Utah-Arizona border, the church faithful are expected to adopt a modest manner. Girls and women wear dresses that cover their knees, and shirts that cover their necks. They use no makeup.

Marriage partners are not a matter of choice. When individuals decide to marry, they "turn themselves in" to the church president. He is regarded as a prophet with powers of divine revelation. And he decides who marries whom. In some cases, the people have never met.

The Coxes said they did not advise their children to enter plural marriages, but left the choice to them. Only one of the children, a daughter, has chosen the polygamous way.

"It's a difficult life," Mr. Cox said. "You get competition between the sets of kids and their mothers. And you sometimes get jealousy between the wives."

In Kane County, Utah, which has a land mass as large as Connecticut and a population of about 5000 people, some polygamists found a place where they could live undisturbed.

One town in the county is Big Water, a tiny isolated settlement of weather-beaten houses and dirt roads on the Colorado Plateau. Mr. Joseph, the mayor, lives there with his 9 wives and 20 children. He shares a rambling house with 7 wives and their children; 2 other wives and their children live in a smaller house across the road.

Like Elizabeth Joseph, the lawyer, most of Mr. Joseph's wives have careers. One is a graphic designer. Another is a real estate broker.

"The only hassle I get is from men who cheat on their wives and get outraged about my life style," he said. "Sexual variety is part of it, I guess. But I know a dozen men who have more interesting sex lives than I do."

Mr. Joseph and his wives say their children experience no problems with the living arrangement. They never get teased about it at school, they said, in part because they account for about 10 percent of the enrollment. And it helps that their father is the Mayor.

One of the children, Stonewall, 11 years old, said he referred to the other women in the family as aunts, if asked where they fit in the family. But he said he did not give it much thought.

DREAMS OF BEING 3RD WIFE

Stonewall's mother, Margaret Joseph, was the only one of the wives who was raised in a polygamous family. As a child, she said, she had always dreamed that she would grow up to be a man's third wife.

"The first wife doesn't like it when the second wife comes along," she explained. "And the second wife doesn't care for the wife who came first. So you can get some fighting and bad feeling. But the third wife, she's the tie that holds it all together."

When she met Mr. Joseph, who had only two wives at the time, she was delighted to be able to become the third.

"The hard part of this arrangement is measuring up," said another wife, Bodicca Joseph, the real estate broker. "You're surrounded by all these intelligent, successful women. So you feel like you always have to be your best."

"Since you only spend a limited amount of time with Alex, things always stay fresh," she added. "In this house, things never get boring."

"Ladies" Behind Bars

A Liminal Gender as Cultural Mirror

John M. Coggeshall

John M. Coggeshall, an assistant professor of anthropology at Clemson University in South Carolina, has carried out fieldwork in two medium-security prisons in Illinois. He received his Ph.D. in 1984 from Southern Illinois University.

"You here to see the show?" the inmate leered. The focus of attention was the tall blond then receiving her food in the prison cafeteria. The workers filled her plate with polite deference, and as she walked between the tables her fine blond hair bounced over her shoulders. "Make you want to leave home?" the guard next to me teased. His joke clarified the significance of the episode I had just witnessed. The object of attention was genetically a male, reconstructed as female according to the perception of gender within the cultural rule system of prison. Behind bars, certain males become redefined as "ladies." I have not been able to discern any correlation between assigned gender and the type of crime for which an inmate was sentenced. The process by which this transformation occurs reveals not only clues about gender construction in prison culture, but also suggests perceptions of gender identity in American culture in general.

Prison culture involves one predominant theme: control. To establish identity, males profess a culturally-defined image to defend themselves from oppression by guards and other inmates. Men define themselves as males by juxtaposing maleness with femaleness, fabricating gender identity from the reflection. For inmates, the concept of female emerges from the concept of male. To borrow a well-known metaphor, the rib for Eve's creation is taken from Adam's side, and draws both its cultural significance and social status from the extraction. Woman is defined in contrast to man, and takes a lesser place at his side. In prison, males create females in their image, and by doing so, dominate and subjugate them.

The fieldwork upon which this study is based was conducted in two medium-security prisons in southern Illinois between 1984 and 1986. Within that time span I taught three university-level courses to about thirty

"'Ladies' Behind Bars: A Liminal Gender as Cultural Mirror" by John M. Coggeshall, from *Anthropology Today*, Vol. 4, No. 4, 1988. Royal Anthropological Institute. Reprinted with permission.

adult inmates, constituting a range of racial group and criminal record diversity representative of the overall prison population. Their perceptions provided a portion of the field data, supplemented by my observations of and conversations with guards and staff. After having received some instruction on ethnographic data collection, a former student and then resident inmate, Gene Luetkemeyer, volunteered to collect additional information on "ladies" behind bars. His nine detailed interviews of various categories of inmates, identified in the text by pseudonyms, significantly enhanced the scope and detail of the study.

Prison culture is extremely complex, and deserves much more detailed study by anthropologists (see for example the treatment by Goffman 1961, Davidson 1983, and Cardozo-Freeman 1984).[1] Even my relatively brief "incarceration" has suggested numerous leads for future research. Gender identity in prison could be explored in much greater detail, describing for example the abusive context whereby young males might become pawns by an administration concerned with pacifying gangs. Another productive line of inquiry might explore the overall cultural context of gender identity in prison culture, for themes of sexuality pervade prison, indicating its cultural significance for staff as well as inmates.

GENDER PERCEPTIONS OF CONVICTS

Here the research concentrates on the gender perceptions of convicts, i.e. the long-term residents (Davidson 1983). Convict attitudes toward homosexual behaviour vary considerably from one individual to the next. Not all participate, and not all do so with the same self-perception or with the same purposes. A subtle distinction is made by many inmates between individuals who engage entirely in submissive, recipient homosexual intercourse, and those who participate in mutual exchange of pleasure. Further distinctions also exist. Certain types or categories of homosexuals, some of which are discussed below, provide a ranking of these attitudes. Despite intra-cultural variation, widespread agreement prevails on cultural definitions of masculine and feminine gender identities.

Inmates have provided various estimates for the amount of homosexual activity in prison.[2] All agree that long-timers are more likely to engage in such practices, for they have less of a future to anticipate, more opportunities for sexual pleasure to utilize, and relatively lenient punishments for violations. For example, Paul and Sandy, homosexual lovers, and Frank, Paul's straight friend, believe that about 65% of their prison population engages in homosexual activity, an estimate supported by Dr. B, an incarcerated medical doctor. While such numbers reveal the amount of control and coercion in prisoner culture, they also reveal the "need for love, affection, [and] intimate relationships" denied by the system, another inmate observes. Some ties are based on affection, but these are relatively rare.[3] Homosexual behaviour fulfills numerous functions in the social and cultural system of prison. Thus most inmates see it as at worst a repugnant necessity and at best a tolerable alternative.

Despite varying views on prevalence, prisoners agree on the general gender constructs in prisoner culture. Males in prison adopt a "masculine role," inmates assert. Robert describes "a big . . . macho weight-lifting virile Tom Selleck type guy" as typical of the stereotype. Weight lifters, in fact, seem to predominate in the category, for strength suggests masculinity. Real men vigorously protest sexual advances from other males by exhibiting a willingness to fight. Men are also seen as preoccupied with sexual gratification, and will obtain it at all costs.

Real men in prison are perceived as those who can keep, satisfy, and protect "women." The dominant sex partner is termed a "daddy," who watches out for and protects his "kid" or "girl." For some men, the acquisition of sex partners strongly resembles courting, where the pursuer flirts with and purchases commissary (snack foods, cosmetics, and similar items) for the object of his interest. Others acquire submissive sex partners by force. Ultimately, with either type, sexual partnerships are based on power and control, the complete domination of one person and one gender by another. In fact, domination defines the structure of the relationship which distinguishes the genders in prison.

However, in prison, since the culturally-defined females had been males at one time, this presents "real" men with a gender identity problem: reconciling having sexual intercourse with males while maintaining a masculine self-concept. This adjustment is accomplished by means of a unique folk explanation of the origins of gender development and orientation. Basically, males in prison redefine selected males as females.

In direct contrast to these self-perceptions of males, men portray women in a painting of their own creation. Males see females as passive, subordinate, sexual objects. According to Robert, women are "sweet and charming," "fluid of movement," with "seductive gestures." Dr. B believes that he himself exhibits such effeminate qualities as "mild manners" and a "passive demeanour." Women are also viewed as attractive, and they use that allure to their advantage by feigning helplessness; this allows women to maintain a "certain power" over men, Paul feels. A woman might "use her charms" to "get what she wanted," while at the same time she might not "put out" sexually, according to Dr. B. Women often tease to coerce men, and sometimes withhold what had apparently been promised, he adds.

Of course, nearly all female staff in prison culture do not meet these stereotypes. By inmate definition, then, they must not be women. Such "non-women" do not challenge gender constructs but reinforce them further. Female guards and staff occupy positions of power and authority over inmates, decidedly atypical for women from a prisoner's perspective. Moreover, most of these women dress in ways to deliberately de-accentuate anatomical differences and to resemble their male counterparts uniformly. Because these women dress as "non-women" and control men, they cannot be women and must therefore be homosexuals or "dykes," as the convicts term them. To inmates, this can be the only explanation for women who do not act like women. Cultural reality persists as potentially disruptive anomalies disappear through redefinition.

TRAPPED BETWEEN MALE AND FEMALE ROLES

The process by which certain males become redefined as females in prison provides an example of Victor Turner's (1969) concept of liminality. Prisoner culture perceives certain males as being trapped in between male and female, thus necessitating the release of their true gender identities. The period of incarceration provides the "time out of time" necessary for the transfiguration to occur. In fact, inmate terms for the metamorphosis reveal this gender ambiguity: males "turn out" these non-males, transforming them into the cultural equivalent of females. The liminal gender is actually "male as female," betwixt and between both. Such individuals figuratively "turn out" to be females, reconstructed according to the prisoner cultural stereotypes of "female." They thus become their "true" selves at last.

This duality creates additional complications in self-identity for such men. Goffman (1961) noted the struggle inmates have in reconciling the staff's perception of them from their own self-concept. Inmates readjusting a sexual orientation share a similar problem. Dr. B explains that individuals who make the transition from male to female must reconcile past heterosexual behaviour with their present homosexual identity. The homosexual in prison must convince herself that this new self-perception had been her true identity all along. Thus she now has adapted the normal role befitting her identity and gender adjustment.

Vindication for the transformation comes as those forced to become homosexuals remain as such. The acceptance by the homosexual of her new gender identity and associated behaviour justifies the conversion in the eyes of the rest of the prison population. If the "male becoming female" had no natural proclivity or had not been submissive by nature and thus also female, she would never have agreed to have adopted a feminine identity. As Frank (an inmate) explains, those who surrender are weak, and females are weak. Therefore those who surrender must be female by nature.

Folk conceptions of the origins of gender further support this perspective. Tommy (another inmate) notes that all humans are "conceived as female, then either, as foetuses, develop genitalia or not." Some individuals perpetuate, even unconsciously, this dualistic foetal identity into adulthood: they can be transformed or "turned out." Not resisting, or not resisting aggressively enough, merely validates this gender liminality. In a sense, it is only appropriate that those trapped betwixt and between be released, to unfetter their true natures. Even coercive gender conversion restores the natural order.

Prisoner culture divides homosexuals into several types, each defined on the basis of degree of sexual promiscuity, amount of self-conceptual pride, and severity of coercion used to turn them out. Generally, status declines as sexual promiscuity increases, self-concept decreases, and the types and intensity of coercion used in the conversion process increase.

The highest status category of homosexuals in prison is that of "queens" or "ladies," those who had come out both voluntarily and willingly. Prisoner cultural belief suggests that these individuals had been homosexual on the outside but may have lacked the freedom to have been themselves. Prison has provided them with a treasured opportunity to "come out," and they have accepted the freedom gratefully. Such individuals maintain a high status by remaining in control of their own lives and of their own self-concept.

Other individuals volunteer to be females, transforming themselves in order to acquire material comforts or social prestige. Terms for this general category vary, depending on the amount of coercion or force needed to "turn out" the female image. "Kids," "gumps," or "punks" describe individuals who in effect have sold their male identities, surrendering their culturally-defined masculinity to be redefined as females.

Many other inmates, however, are forced to become homosexuals against their initial will. According to Wadley (another inmate):

[E]veryone is tested. The weak—of personality, personal power, willingness to fight, physical frailty, timidity—are especially susceptible.

"Respect is given to one who can control the life of another," he adds. Those unwilling or unable to control others are thus themselves controlled. According to the cultural rules of gender identity in prison, those who dominate, by natural right, are males, and those who submit, by natural temperament, are females.

A FORCED FEMALE ROLE

Individuals forced to adopt a female role have the lowest status, and are termed "girls," "kids," "gumps," or "punks." Kids are kept in servitude by others, as a sign of the owner's power and prestige. Gumps are generally owned or kept by a gang, which collects money by prostituting the sexual favours of the unfortunate inmate. A gump may at one time have volunteered to come out to her feminine identity, but due to lack of personal status or power she has been forced to become sexually promiscuous for money or her physical survival. A punk, most agree, initially hesitates, and is turned out by coercion.

However transformed, most homosexuals in prison take on a feminine persona and appearance, even assuming a feminine name and requesting feminine pronouns as referents. The external transformation from male to female often is remarkable. Despite the formal restrictions of a dress code in prison, clothing styles may be manipulated rather patently to proclaim gender identity. Hair is often styled or curled and worn long. Even cosmetics are possible: black felt-tip pens provide eye liner and shadow; kool-aid substitutes for blush; and baby powder disguises prominent cheekbones. The personal appearance of homosexuals enhances their identity by demarcating them as obviously different from men.

Homosexuals perform numerous functions depending upon their status and relative freedom. Generally, the higher the status the more control one has over one's activities and one's life. High status individuals such as Sandy select their own lovers. These couples live as husbands and wives, with the "little woman" providing domestic services such as laundry, cell cleaning, grooming, and sex.

Those with less status perform much the same tasks, but less voluntarily and with less consideration from their daddies. Once an inmate has been forced to adopt a submissive lifestyle, the nightmare of domination becomes more intense. For example, gumps might be forced to pleasure a gang chief, or may be passed down to soldiers in the gang for enjoyment. A particularly attractive kid might be put "on the stroll," forced to be a prostitute, for the financial benefit of the gang. Business may prove to be so lucrative that some homosexuals must seek protective custody (solitary confinement) to get some rest.

According to Dr. B, some homosexuals actually prefer to be dominated. The prevalent value system in prison suggests that those "females" who resist sexual attacks vicariously enjoy being dominated physically and sexually by more powerful individuals.

Hated and abused, desired and adored, ladies in prison occupy an important niche: they are the women of that society, constructed as such by the male-based perception of gender identity. In prison, females are termed "holes" and "bitches," reflecting the contempt of what Dr. B believes to be characteristic of society's view of lower-class women in general. In prison, he adds, a homosexual "is likely to receive much of the contempt [and] pent-up hostility that would otherwise be directed at women." Herein lies the key to unlocking the deeper significance of gender construction in prisoner culture.

GENDER CONSTRUCTION IN PRISON

Recall the general inmate perception of this liminal gender in prisoner culture. Homosexuals are owned and protected by daddies, who provide for their material and social comfort. In exchange, they provide sexual gratification. They often sell themselves and their bodies for material objects, promiscuously using their allure to manipulate men and to improve their social status. They feign helplessness in order to control their men. Ladies are emotional, helpless, and timid, while at the same time petulant, sassy, and demanding, nagging their men for attention. Best suited for certain tasks, homosexuals provide domestic and personal services for their daddies, serving their every whim.

Most fundamentally, homosexuals are sexual objects, to be used, abused, and discarded whenever necessary. Passive recipients of male power, they even enjoy being dominated and controlled. Males do them favours by releasing their "true" female identities through rape. In prison, sexuality equals power. Males have power, females do not, and thus males dominate and exploit the "weaker sex."

Ultimately, in whose image and likeness are these "males as females" created? Genetically female staff and administrators do not fit the stereotypical view, and thus provide no role models for ladies in prison. Males themselves draft the image of female in prison, forming her from their own perceptions. Males "turned out" as females perform the cultural role allotted to them by males, a role of submission and passivity. In actuality, males produce, direct, cast, and write the script for the cultural performance of gender identity behind bars.

In prison, woman is made in contrast to the image and likeness of man. Men define women as "not men," establishing their own self-identity from the juxtapositioning. Gender as a cultural construct is reflexive; each pole draws meaning from a negation of the other. As in Monteros (Brandes 1980:205, 207), folk concepts reinforce the differences, emphasizing maleness at the expense of femaleness and the powerful at the expense of the powerless. By means of sexual domination, women remain in a culturally-defined place of servitude and submission.

PRISON CULTURE AS A DISTORTING MIRROR

It is precisely this concept of gender identity that has proven most disquieting about the status of homosexuals in prison. Granted, prison culture fosters a terribly distorted view of American culture.[4] Nevertheless, one sees a shadowy reflection in the mirror of prisoner culture which remains hauntingly familiar. As ladies are viewed by males in prison culture, so are females perceived by many males in American culture. Gender roles and attitudes in prison do not contradict American male values, they merely exaggerate the domination and exploitation already present. In prison gender constructs, one sees not contrasts but caricatures of gender concepts "on the street." Thus, the liminal gender of ladies behind bars presents, in reality, a cultural mirror grotesquely reflecting the predominant sexism of American society in general, despite initiatives by women to redefine their position and change gender relationships.

N O T E S

1. In my other writings I have discussed various ways in which inmates successfully retaliate to maintain a sense of identity. Much more could be explored, but space constrains discussion.
2. There are obvious implications for study of the spread of the AIDS virus. From my research it seems that most inmates had not yet thought about acquiring AIDS, probably on account of a low self-concept paralleling that of intravenous drug users. Since homosexual behaviour in prison cannot be eliminated, education and protection should be stressed.
3. I do not mean to suggest that homosexual relationships in society at large are similar. In this article, I do not deal with homosexuality outside of prison, nor with affectional homosexual inside prison, which does exist.
4. Racial distinctions become exaggerated in prison. Some research indicates that prison administrations sometimes deliberately exacerbate racial antagonism to "divide and conquer" gangs by rewarding leaders with homosexuals of the opposite "race."

R E F E R E N C E S

Brandes, Stanley. 1980. *Metaphors of masculinity: sex and status in Andalusian folklore.* Publications of the American Folklore Society (n.s.) Vol. 1, Philadelphia: University of Pennsylvania Press.

Cardoza-Freeman, Inez. 1984. *The joint: language and culture in a maximum-security prison.* Springfield, Ill.: Thomas.

Davidson, R. Theodore. 1983. *Chicano prisoners: the key to San Quentin.* Prospect Heights, Ill.: Waveland Press.

Goffman, Erving. 1961. *Asylums: essays on the social situation of mental patients and other inmates.* Garden City, N.Y.: Anchor Books.

Turner, Victor. 1969. *The ritual process.* Chicago: Aldine.

Is the Female Husband a Man?

Woman/Woman Marriage Among the Nandi of Kenya

Regina Smith Oboler

Regina Smith Oboler has taught at Temple University in Philadelphia where she earned her Ph.D. in 1982 and has been a research associate of the Institute for Development Studies, University of Nairobi, Kenya. She is known for her fieldwork among the Nandi of highland Kenya. She is currently assistant professor of anthropology at Ursinus College.

No, I don't (carry things on my head). That is a woman's duty and nothing to do with me. I became a man and I am a man and that is all. Why should I assume women's work anymore?

—Taptuwei, a Nandi female husband

The institution of woman/woman marriage as practiced by the Nandi of western Kenya presents an example of how one society deals with a problem of sexual classification. In a cultural system in which certain important attributes of the category "man" versus the category "woman" are well defined, a woman who functions in certain ways as only a man can (e.g., exchanging cattle for a wife, transmitting property to heirs) represents an anomaly. In the Nandi case, the anomaly is resolved by the frequently reiterated public dogma that the female husband is a man. I will show that in specified sociocultural domains it is crucial that the female husband adopt male gender. Within these domains, she makes every attempt to conform to male role behavior and informants go out of their way to rationalize any deviation therefrom by a female husband. Within other sociocultural domains, the assertion that the female husband is a man masks the fact that the role adopted by the female husband is sexually ambiguous and occupies an intermediate position between male and female roles.

A female husband is a woman who pays bridewealth for, and thus marries (but does not have sexual intercourse with) another woman. By so doing, she becomes the social and legal father of her wife's children. The basic institution of woman/woman marriage is widespread in African patrilineal societies, although the way

"Is the Female Husband a Man? Woman/Woman Marriage Among the Nandi of Kenya" by Regina Smith Oboler, from *Ethnology*, Vol. 19, No. 1, pp. 69–88. Reprinted with permission.

it functions varies from society to society. In Nandi, a female husband should always be a woman of advanced age who has failed to bear a son. The purpose of the union is to provide a male heir.

The argument presented here is that the key to the question of the female husband's gender lies in her relationship to the property that is transmitted through her to the sons of her wife.[1] The exact status of this property will be discussed in greater detail below. For now, let it be said that it is an extremely important canon of Nandi ideology that the most significant property and primary means of production—livestock and, in the modern setting, land—should be held and managed exclusively by men. I will argue that the strength of the female husband's identification as a male is dependent on the social context in which the identification is made. In contexts which directly implicate the issues of property and heirship, Nandi informants are unanimous in considering it of the utmost importance to insist that the female husband is a man and behaves in exact accordance with the ideal model of the male role. Such areas are the management of family property, legitimate authority over the wife and children and the responsibility to provide for the wife and children in a material sense. The further one moves away from these issues into other aspects of the cultural definition of the male role the weaker become both the female husband's own attempts to conform to male role behavior and informants' dogmatic insistence that they in fact do so. To say that a female husband is a man in certain contexts but not in others lends a degree of clarity to the situation which is not present in fact.

The cultural definition of the category "man" is not limited to the relation to property. Once the ideological statement that the female husband is a man has been made, Nandi informants feel that they have to carry through on this idea in terms of the total cultural definition of this category. This leads them to make assertions about female husbands' behavior that observation shows to be untrue: that female husbands completely adopt the male role in the sexual division of labor, that they participate in public political discussions, that they do not carry things on their heads, and that they attend men's circumcision rites as a result of their male status. In fact, most female husbands do attend male initiation, but not because they are now considered to be men. The situation is one of rationalization and selective perception such as is typical of defensive strategies attempting to maintain important but precarious dogmas.

WOMAN/WOMAN MARRIAGE IN AFRICA

The question of the gender of the female husband has been raised, but hardly resolved, in recent publications.[2] Its resolution bears on the problem of the conditions under which sex role barriers may be transcended, and a cross-culturally valid definition of marriage. Is the role of female husband an instance of some individuals crossing sex role boundaries and, as it were, changing sex? Or is the cultural role "man" not an inevitable concomitant of the husband role, in which case marriage cannot be defined as a transaction between the categories male and female? Riviere (1971) asserts that female husbands are invariably culturally recoded as male and take on other aspects of the male role; husband is a subcategory of male, and marriages in all societies must be viewed as transactions between the male and female cultural categories. Krige (1974) rejects this view, at least for the Lovedu, and argues that the husband role in Lovedu society may be either male or female. Moreover, she maintains, Riviere's formulation reflects a misunderstanding of the nature of African marriage, in which relationships created by a marital union other than those of husband and wife may be of paramount importance. According to Krige, it is the intrinsic right of a woman (the mother of the "female husband") to the services of a daughter-in-law that is the basis of Lovedu woman marriage. O'Brien (1977) has examined accounts of woman marriage in southern Bantu societies and concluded that where female husbands may also be political leaders they are regarded as social males. The Nandi female husband is clearly culturally recoded as a man, though it is by no means clear that this is the case in all African societies (Huber 1969). Her assignment to the male gender does not mean that she easily and automatically assumes male role behavior in all spheres, however. Her position, as will be shown, is far from unambiguous and unproblematic.

The data reported here result from a study of nine woman/woman marriages in one Nandi community.[3] Nine of ten known cases of female husbands living in the community, and wherever possible their wives, were interviewed extensively. A few female husbands and wives from other communities were also interviewed with varying degrees of thoroughness. Information was also obtained through observation, and a large number of informants who were not participants in woman/woman marriages were interviewed on the subject.

THE ETHNOGRAPHIC SETTING

The Nandi are a section of Kenya's Kalenjin-speaking peoples, whom Sutton (1970) calls Highland Nilotes. Huntingford (1953) classifies them as a pastoral people. They are well-known for their military organization and aggressive cattle raiding practices and their culture during the nineteenth and early twentieth centuries was marked by a pastoral ideology. Cultivation, however, has always played a major role in their economy (Gold 1977). The Nandi at present are prosperous mixed economy farmers producing maize, milk, tea and a variety of vegetables for the national market as well as for home consumption. Maize is the staple subsistence crop.

The research community is located in the north-central part of Nandi District, where elevation varies between 6,200 and 6,800 feet and rainfall, distributed over the entire year, averages between 60 and 75 inches annually. Selected for its typicality, the community is neither the most traditional nor the most modernized in Nandi District. The average household (based on a random sample community census)[4] contains 8.1 people and 9.1 adult cattle and holds 20.6 acres of land; 76.4 per cent of households grow tea, and 61.9 per cent hire a tractor for at least part of their annual plowing. Over 60 per cent of household heads are at least nominal Christians; most of them adherents of the Africa Inland Church, a fundamentalist body. Almost 51 per cent have had some primary education, 33.9 per cent perform some sort of part-time cash-gaining activity, and 16.8 per cent of ever-married male household heads are polygynous.

Traditional Nandi social organization was crosscut by a system of seven rotating age-sets (ibinwek) for men, localized military units (pororosiek), patrilineal clans (but not corporate patrilineages), and patrilocal extended families. While land was plentiful, every Nandi man was entitled to move with his family and herds to reside effectively wherever he wished. The most important unit was the local community (kokwet). It was the unit within which ceremonies were performed and disputes settled in most cases and within which day-to-day interaction took place. Today these functions take place at the level of the sublocation, an administrative unit made up of several traditional local communities and presided over by a government-appointed chief. It is the locus of political interaction. At its center is a group of shops, businesses, public buildings, and a community gathering place (the settlement pattern is otherwise one of scattered homesteads). The sublocation is overwhelmingly endogamous, whereas the *kokwet* is not. Patrilocal extended families are still important in today's social organization. Married couples reside patrilocally unless the husband buys a farm away from his father's homestead. The sole (but weak) function of patrilineal clans is the regulation of marriage.

THE PROPERTY SYSTEM AND WOMAN/ WOMAN MARRIAGE

In Nandi ideology, women's rights in land and cattle are very limited. A girl may be given a heifer by her father if she is a virgin at her initiation and a woman may keep one cow as bridewealth for each of her daughters. Animals held by either spouse form the family estate but the bulk of the herd consists of animals a man receives from his father through inheritance or as gifts. This is augmented by cattle the family acquires through proceeds from their cash crops, as bridewealth for their daughters, etc. Husband and wife should jointly control those cattle in which the wife's rights predominate, though the husband has the right to control independently those cattle in which his rights predominate. If a woman leaves her husband, she has no right to take any animals with her. Many informants say that it is also better that she take no property with her to her husband so that this can never be a bone of contention between them.

Management of land and cattle is a male prerogative, although informants will admit that when the husband is incapable of administering the family estate it would not be wrong for the wife to assume responsibility. The exception to the rule that women do not manage property is the case of widows. Widows can hold property in their own right and make decisions regarding the property which they hold in trust for their minor sons. The lack of congruence with public ideology that this fact presents is dealt with by the typical male claim (contrary to observable events) that effective control of the family estate is held not by the widow but by the deceased man's brother. This man may or may not be the woman's levirate husband.

Women—wives and mothers—though supposedly barred from administering the family estate are critical in its transmission. A woman's "house" (patrilineal descendants) is automatically endowed with a share of her husband's property at the time of her marriage. The system is that which Gluckman (1950) has called the house-property complex. All property held by a polygynous family is ideally divided evenly among sets of full siblings, each set receiving exactly the same share regardless of how many children the mother has. A man

can marry only by using those of his father's cattle which were allotted to his mother's house, or those which came as bridewealth for his own full sisters; he should not use his half-sister's bridewealth cattle, nor may his father allot him cattle from the herd of one of his mother's co-wives. Although the effective share of the family estate to which each wife's house is entitled obviously changes as each additional wife is added to her husband's menage, the basic principle that her house is entitled to an equal share is never abrogated. Marriage is considered to be a once in a lifetime event for a Nandi woman. Though a traditional divorce proceeding existed, and while it is possible now to obtain a legal divorce through the courts, both these options are so rarely invoked that divorce may be said to be absent. Separation, however, does occur. A woman may leave her husband for a period of many years or even for life. She may live with a man in the meantime and have children by him. She may go to a town and become a prostitute. All this does not change her marriage and property rights. She remains the legal wife of the man who first married her, and her children remain his legal heirs. She can return, with children, after an absence of many years, and her husband will take her back. She can even return and take up her rights to her husband's property after his death. A woman retains throughout her life a right to live on the land of her father and brothers, but she can in no way transmit any rights to this land. A woman is incorporated into her husband's family at marriage, she takes his clan identity, and her children's only legitimate rights to filiate are with his family. Illegitimacy is a new phenomenon in Nandi, and though it would seem that there must be cases on record of children affiliating matrilaterally in exceptional circumstances, I found none in the course of the research. It is possible, however, for women to transmit to their sons property which they themselves have acquired.

Traditionally, the property of a woman's house could only be transmitted to male heirs. As it was inappropriate for a woman to hold property, it could not be passed to daughters. If an heir was completely lacking, the property would have to revert to a man's sons by other wives or to his brothers, but it was considered wrong and very unfortunate if this should happen. The demographic reality is that not every woman gives birth to a son. Woman/woman marriage is one solution to this problem. The intention is that the wife of a female husband should bear sons who will become their female father's house's male heirs in the property system.

A woman who has taken a wife is said to become a man. It is said that she has been promoted to male status (*kagotogosta komostab murenik*). She can no longer have sexual intercourse with a man (nor with a woman). She has all the nonsexual prerogatives of a male husband with regard to her wife, and is supposed to abandon all women's work. She theoretically acquires certain public prerogatives of men; for example, the right to speak in public meetings. In the past, she would also be expected to adopt to some extent male dress and adornment. She normally stops attending female initiation and in most cases will already have been admitted to male initiation in hopes of curing her infertility or inability to bear a son. (In Nandi, an infertile person of either sex is admitted to the opposite sex's initiation rituals in the hope that the infertility will thereby be cured.) Female husbands, like their male counterparts, are required to observe procedures for avoiding contamination by ritual pollution with regard to their wives and children.

Although property is the crux of the institution of woman/woman marriage, and although informants cite the advantages of being married to a wealthy woman rather than a poor man, female husbands are not exceptionally rich. In fact, those on whom data are available are not as wealthy as the community average, with average land holdings of 15.8 (versus 20.6) acres and herds of 7 (versus 9.1) adult cattle.

MOTIVATIONS OF THE PRINCIPALS IN WOMAN/WOMAN MARRIAGES

The motivation of a woman who becomes a female husband is fairly clear-cut; it is the acquisition of a male heir for her property. But why does she choose this means to her end rather than another?

There are two options other than woman/woman marriage available to a woman whose house has no heir. First, she may adopt or "buy" a male child by the payment of a large sum (these days, normally, money) to the parents of the child, who relinquish all ties to him. The children bought by Nandi women usually come from the neighboring Abaluhyia. It is difficult to find any child, particularly a Nandi child available for sale. In the past, children born to unwed mothers were killed unless requested for adoption by a barren woman who happened to be present at the birth. Thus it was easier to adopt a child in the past than presently, as barren women would be sure to know of the approaching confinement of any pregnant girl. Today, although infanticide has been eliminated, unwed mothers usually raise their own children. Moreover, by the time a woman resigns herself to the fact that she will not bear a son, she is often too old for adoption to be a realistic option. Thus, adoption is relatively rare.

Another option is the institution known as "marrying the house" or "marrying the center post" (*tunisiet ab got, kitunis toloita*). In this form of marriage, the sonless woman's youngest daughter is retained at home and her "husband" is said to be the house or its center post. This daughter will have children by self-selected sexual partners and her sons will inherit the house's property.

The custom is said to be a recent innovation but has not gained much popularity relative to woman/woman marriage.

It seems that woman/woman marriage is the most commonly adopted of these options in the case of lack of a male heir but only a minority of women who are eligible to become female husbands actually do so. From a large-scale survey of marital and fertility histories, it was found that among women over 40 years of age, only 4.3 per cent of those ever married and 24.5 per cent of those who bore no sons ultimately became female husbands. This includes women of the youngest age cohort over 40, among whom many who are candidates to be female husbands have not yet made the decision to marry. For the older two age cohorts, 39 per cent and 27 per cent, respectively, of women with no male heir married; 6.8 per cent and 6 per cent, respectively, of ever-married women ultimately became female husbands. In the community intensively studied, at least ten out of a total of 286 households were headed by female husbands. The rate for female husbands as household heads, then, is just under 3 per cent.[5]

Several factors may prevent a sonless woman from becoming a female husband. First, her house's property may not be large enough to warrant an heir, especially if her house lacks enough bridewealth cattle to acquire a wife. Second, a woman who is prepared to take a wife may have difficulty in finding one. This was the reason most commonly given by women who were prime candidates for becoming female husbands. They point out that they will not marry anyone and maintain that they will marry as soon as they find willing girls who are hard-working, well-mannered, and from good families. Occasionally sonless old women who have not become female husbands cite personal reasons for their failure to marry; e.g., the difficulty of adjusting to another person in the household. It has been suggested to me that some women may resist becoming female husbands because of the prohibition on sexual intercourse which the role entails.

Why should a woman choose to marry a wife in favor of other options? Two female husbands said that they would have adopted sons but could find no available male children. Two did adopt sons but both children were sickly. One died in infancy and the other turned out to be simple-minded and thus not a suitable heir to the property. Another female husband explained that it is bad economics to pay money equivalent to a bridewealth payment for just one infant son who might not even survive to reproductive age when, for the same amount, one can acquire a grown woman who will reproduce herself several times over in a few years. Three female husbands have daughters who wished to marry their boyfriends and refused to "marry the house." Still others provided various personal and idiosyncratic reasons for choosing woman/woman marriage. Over and above all these explanations, there is the general reason that woman/woman marriage entails a rise in status for the female husband.

Why do women become wives of female husbands? They are usually girls who for one reason or another— for example, a physical or mental defect—fail to attract a male husband. These days, the most common reason why a girl is considered unmarriageable by men is that she already has a child or is pregnant by a man who refuses to marry her. Such girls quite often become the wives of female husbands.

Some informants maintain that a girl will always prefer marriage to a man if it is possible, while others claim that there are many girls who choose to be married by female husbands as a matter of preference. The wives of female husbands are themselves divided on this score. Several said that they had received offers of marriage from men but they and their families preferred to accept an offer for woman/woman marriage. Most informants agree that it is better to be married by a wealthy woman than by a poor man. As one informant put it, "When you actually live with a man the love may fade, but the property will always be there." Second, informants cite greater sexual and social freedom for the wife as a reason to prefer woman/woman marriage. Female husbands are said to be less-likely to question their wives' comings and goings. Third, informants say that female husbands are less likely than men to quarrel with their wives and beat them. Another possible motivating factor is the slight tendency of female suitors, being very anxious to marry, to give bridewealth of higher value than that given by men. Males in my sample who married between 1970 and 1977 gave bridewealth ranging between four and six adult cattle, one sheep or goat, and money ranging between none and 500 shillings. During the same period, out of seven cases of woman/woman marriage, the amounts given in five cases fell within the range of the amounts given by the men, but one female husband gave seven cattle and 500 shillings, and another gave seven cattle, 600 shillings and three sheep; an extremely high amount for Nandi bridewealth.

DOMESTIC RELATIONS IN FEMALE HUSBAND–HEADED HOUSEHOLDS

Female husbands, their wives and children, are real people living together in actual household situations. What, then, are the typical patterns of interaction in these female husband-headed households? Besides the husband, wife and children, other parties—such as the female husband's male husband, her co-wives and their children—are frequently significant in these interactions. Another significant party is the wife's consort, who may or may not be a regular visitor in the compound.

The wife and her children ideally occupy a separate dwelling from that of the female husband to facilitate the wife's relationship with her consort.[6] The dwellings of the female husband and wife should, however, be within the same compound and in close proximity. I know of at least one case in which both a barren woman and her husband married young wives at the same time, divided their plot, and lived side by side with their new families as brothers might. In several cases, female husbands and their wives are found living together in a common dwelling. The female husband, in these cases, maintained that she had not yet had an opportunity to provide separate housing arrangements for the wife but would do so soon.

The division of labor is said by informants to be much the same as in male husband-headed households. Cooking, washing utensils, carrying water and collecting firewood, sweeping, plastering the house, and washing clothes are supposed to be exclusively female chores. Jobs technically reserved for men include plowing, inoculating cattle, clearing bush, digging drainage ditches, fencing, house-frame building, thatching, and slaughtering. Both sexes engage in herding, cultivation, and making (see Oboler 1977 for a detailed description of the division of labor by sex). In the main, female husbands avoid female tasks, although with less rigidity than do men. Because of their advanced age, they are not often observed doing heavy work reserved for men but employ men to do such work for their households. Most female husbands take an active role in tasks which are not sexually coded.

Informants maintain that, except for the absence of the sex act, the relationship between a female husband and her wife should be no different from that between a male husband and his wife. They should go to the fields together in the morning, like any other married pair, and in the afternoon the female husband is free to "go for a walk" while the wife takes care of household chores. Female husbands do typically behave as men in reserving most of their afternoons for socializing but they differ little from other old women in this respect. Female husbands and their wives also behave exactly as male husbands and their wives when entertaining visitors. As one informant put it, "When a visitor comes, I sit with him outside and converse with him. My wife brings out maize-porridge, vegetables, and milk. When we have finished eating I say, `Wife, come and take the dishes.' Then I go for a walk with the visitor." Observation confirms this description.

The wife of a female husband probably has more opportunity than the wife of a male husband to be relieved of her domestic responsibilities such as in the case of illness or a family crisis which causes her to return temporarily to her parents' home. The female husband is more able and willing to fend for herself in the domestic domain than is the typical male husband. If the two women are on good terms, the female husband will usually sympathize with the problems of her wife, having been a wife herself. Women often cited the tendency of female husbands to be less harsh and demanding as one of the advantages of woman/woman marriage.

In terms of informal interaction, it seems that female husbands and their wives enjoy more casual companionship than do ordinary couples. More opportunities for friendly and companionable conversation between female husband and wife arise since the female husband spends more time in her compound than a male husband. This is partly the result of preference and partly the result of habit. Female husbands are supposed to spend most of their time socializing with men and most of them claim that they do, but observation does not support this claim. One informant confided what is probably true for many other female husbands as well, "Men like fighting, and I don't like being with them most of the time."

No female husband would admit that she is not totally in charge of important household decisions (e.g., farm management and money allocation) but several women stated that another advantage of marriage to a female husband is the opportunity to participate more equally in household decisions.

The female husband is technically in the same position of authority over her wife as a male husband. All wives agreed that they must ask permission from their female husbands to go away from the compound, except for local, short-term activities such as marketing and visiting neighbors. The husband supervises the wife's behavior and has the right to beat her if she errs. It is agreed, however, that female husbands rarely invoke this right. This is not to say that female husbands never beat their wives, but on the whole wives of female husbands see their domestic situations as atypically harmonious. "A man who finds a mistake with his wife only wants to beat her. A woman just scolds and that is enough."

Traditionally, the female husband appointed a man to act as consort to her wife. This man would most likely be a younger clan-mate of the female husband's husband—possibly his younger brother, his brother's son, or the son of one of his other wives. It could never be the female husband's husband himself nor could it be any of her own patrilineal kin.[7] These days, however, wives are insistent on choosing their own consorts, and usually make sure that the female husband agrees in advance to this arrangement before consenting to the marriage. Where the female husband tries to appoint a consort for her wife against the wife's will, the latter remains adamant. The wife sees her sexual autonomy as one of the chief advantages to her of woman/woman marriage and will not surrender it lightly.

Nevertheless, the wives of female husbands and other observers confirm, that they are not promiscuous, but have one long-standing relationship with a male friend (*sandet*). This man visits the wife in her house on a more or less regular basis. His responsibility is to give her children and nothing else. He may occasionally give her a gift of friendship, but he is not obligated to do so. The consort may or may not be acquainted with the rest of the household, including the female husband. Some informants implied that it would be bad form for the latter to acknowledge him, while others said that he could visit the compound openly and be treated as a friend of the family. The consort has no rights of any kind in the wife or her children. He cannot demand her sexual fidelity or any wifely services, although she usually cooks for him when he visits her. He has no right to beat her if she displeases him. If he should do so, she can have him fined by the village elders. Most female husbands vigorously denied that they would ever request money or services from the wife's consort in times of difficulty. Agreement is complete that pollution connected with the wife's child cannot harm her consort, the biological father, because he is not the legal father.

Female husbands assume the formal role of father to their wive's children. The relationship between fathers and their young children is normally reserved and distant and the relationship between female fathers and their children is no different.[8] Female husbands believe that they can be harmed by pollution connected with the wife's children and treat them with the same cool aloofness displayed by male fathers. In relation to their other kin, for example, their daughters' children, they maintain the same kinship role behavior as before. It is quite remarkable to watch a female husband treat her daughter's child in the warm affective style of a grandmother at one moment and her wife's child with the reserve of a father at the next.

Female fathers, like male fathers, are responsible for the discipline of their wives' children and children reportedly respect and fear female fathers as much as they would male fathers. One of the most important areas of significance of the father role is the father's responsibility to care for the wife's children materially. That they meet this requirement was constantly stressed by female husbands.[9]

Cases of separation and estrangement occur between female husbands and their wives, just as they occur in ordinary marriages. In the beginning of my inquiries on this subject, some highly acculturated informants told me that girls do not want to be married by women and usually run away if such a marriage is arranged for them. Subsequent contacts and interviews with the principals in woman/woman marriages have convinced me that this is not the case. The usual pattern in woman/woman marriage is one of harmony and mutual respect between husband and wife which, as in ordinary marriages, often develops into real affection. As one wife said, "I respect Kogo as I would have respected a man if he had married me."

Both the female husband and her wife gain status in the community through a stable marriage. The female husband gains descendants and promotion to male status, after spending years in the unenviable status of a barren or sonless wife. The wife is likely to be a girl for whom getting married has been difficult. If she already has children, she gains inheritance and clan status for them. Otherwise, she is licensed to bear legitimate children. If she has made the mistake of premarital pregnancy and thus lost face in the community and the chance to make a good marriage with a man, she is able to recoup her position through marriage with a woman. Most wives of female husbands believe that their situation compares favorably with that of ordinary wives in many respects. . . .

IS THE FEMALE HUSBAND A MAN?

Nandi informants know very well that the female husband is not a man in the sense that she has changed her physiological sex or all her sex typed behaviors. The impossibility of completely changing the habitual actions of a lifetime is recognized. Everyone is of course aware that the female husband is not really a man but it is a grave insult for anyone to call attention to this fact. What, then, is the claim that the female husband is a man intended to encode? What does the female husband have in common with a man that makes it essential for her to be defined as such? The oft reiterated statement of the female husband's masculine identity is a cultural dogma (Leach 1969). It is an ideological assertion which masks the fact that the female husband is an anomaly: she is a woman who of necessity behaves as no woman in her culture should. Her situation forces her to assume male behavior in certain areas that are crucial to the cultural definition of the differences between the sexes. These areas have to do with the management and transmission of the family estate.

Behaviors associated with men are not all equally important in the attempt to maintain the ideological fiction that the woman who has taken a wife is now a man. Some are essential, and the female husband insists that for these her behavior conforms to the masculine ideal. Others can be more or less ignored. Female husband is thus a category which, in some sense, occupies an intermediate position between male and female.

Unanimity about the norms to which the female husband's behavior must conform is greatest in those areas that are closest to her role in the management and transmission of the family estate: her role in the domestic division of labor, as husband to her wife and father to the wife's children, and the cessation of sexual intercourse. There is less agreement regarding other aspects of the male role such as conversing primarily with men, speaking in public meetings, attending men's initiation, refraining from carrying things on the head, and the manner of relating to children other than those of the wife and other women.

Female husbands tend to avoid such feminine chores as household maintenance, laundry, and wood and water carrying, although typically with less rigidity than do men. Several female husbands said that they can help with the milking, as many young men do nowadays. Cooking is the most indispensable domestic job and ideally should be done by the wife. Even informants who say that it is possible for a female husband to cook under unusual circumstances insist that she should never do so at her wife's hearth, which she may not approach for any purpose. This is an example of the contextuality of the female husband's gender status; in relation to female symbols connected with her wife she is quintessentially a man.

A female husband should not see her wife naked because in relation to her she is a husband and therefore a man, but she may see any other woman naked. A female husband is never present during her wife's labor. It is generally believed that the female husband can be affected by feminine/child pollution (*kerek*) due to close contact with the wife's child. The effect is reportedly at least partly the result of magic performed during the traditional wedding ceremony. This explains why it is not felt by the genitor. Since *kerek* is believed to have a negative effect on those manly qualities which insure success as a warrior, some informants say that this is naturally of little concern to a female husband and that she can therefore take these prohibitions less seriously than do men. Others assert that female husbands take *kerek* very seriously because it can induce rapid aging and skin disease.

If the male husband of a female husband is still alive, and does not have another wife living in the compound, the wife of the female husband may be responsible for providing nonsexual domestic services to both of them, or the female husband may continue to provide some or all of these to her male husband while herself being provided them by her wife. She will not wash her own clothes because in relation to her wife she is a man (husband); but she can still wash clothes for her male husband because in relation to him she is a wife and therefore a woman. In this situation it is perhaps easiest to see the ambiguity and contextuality of the female husband's gender position.

Female husbands are rarely observed doing work that is technically reserved for men. This they rationalize, when challenged, on the grounds that they are old and no longer able to engage in such strenuous activity. Female husbands are active in types of work appropriate to both sexes—cultivation and herding—but reinterpret it as male work in order to affirm their male status. Since female husbands were occasionally observed fencing, the claim that they do male tasks is not a complete fallacy. In general, however, this is a situation in which people now conceptually defined as men have never learned to perform certain aspects of the male role and it is now too late to change the behavior patterns of a lifetime. In spite of this, female husbands are considered to have assumed the male role in the division of labor. On the one hand, informants make it a point to argue that female husbands are doing the work of men when they are in fact doing work that is equally appropriate to men or women. On the other, their taking responsibility for having male tasks done is coded as the equivalent of personally doing them.

In extradomestic contexts it is less important that female husbands conform to male role behavior. Nevertheless, since female husbands are said to be men, many informants find it necessary for the sake of logical consistency to insist that they behave as men in areas important to the cultural definition of this category. This leads people to make claims that are sometimes contrary to observation. For example, female husbands say they typically converse with men rather than women, but the observational evidence is to the contrary. All say they can participate in public meetings and political discussions but admit that they have never done so. All but one attend men's initiation. It was revealed, however, that in all cases this is due to the woman's barrenness or failure to bear a son and preceded her decision to marry a wife. Yet female husbands all implied that they attend male initiation as the result of their status as female husbands, therefore men. There is disagreement as to whether it is possible for female husbands to continue attending female initiation but it is agreed that it is at least not usual, since they are now regarded as men. Neither is there unanimity as to whether a female husband can carry things on her head, act as midwife to women other than her wife, or hold another woman's baby. Many informants say that there is nothing wrong in the latter two behaviors but some deny that a female husband should ever be present at a birth or hold any young baby because she is a man. Thus in many areas of action the female husband's gender position is ambiguous.

The female husband makes her greatest attempt to conform to male behavior, and informants rationalize any deviation from such behavior, in contexts that are closely connected with the management of the heirship to the family estate. Though issues such as avoidance of *kerek* and close physical contact with the wife's children are not immediately relevant to the management of property, they are relevant to the issue of heirship. They are the categories of thought and action through which the relationship between the property holder and heir is acted out. With regard to heirship,

the insistence that the female husband abandon her sex life is also noteworthy. Though she is presumed to be unable to conceive, there is still the danger that the impossible will somehow occur. If she should conceive, both the issue of inheritance and the dogma that she is a man would be too thoroughly confounded to be withstood.

The issue of heirship and property is also relevant to the strength with which informants maintain the ideology that the female husband is a man in the area of kinship terminology. It has been shown above that there is a great deal of ambiguity about the female husband's gender as encoded in the kinship terminology appropriately used between principals in woman/woman marriages and their respective relatives. Most uniformity exists in the areas where property transmission within patrilineal families and property exchange between patrilineal families are involved. Thus the major factor which distinguishes a female husband from a woman and makes her the same as a man is the legitimate right to hold and manage land and livestock and transmit them to heirs.

Particularly in contexts less immediately relevant to issues of property and heirship, female husband is an intermediate category between man and woman. While this is not made explicit in the cultural ideology, the recognition of this situation is often implicit. An old man explained it this way: "It is just like getting a promotion. Always when you are promoted there is still that person who does the promoting, which means that you are still under somebody. So women who have married wives have limited prerogatives. They are more nearly equal to men than are other women, but men are always ahead of them."

CONCLUSION

Among the Nandi, only men can hold and manage land and livestock, the means of production, but these are transmitted through women and rights therein devolve to a woman's house at marriage and can never be revoked. The argument developed in the preceding pages is essentially that woman marriage is the outcome of this contradiction between men's and women's rights in the house-property complex. Moreover, some of the most important attributes of the category "man" in Nandi culture have to do with management of the family estate.

These two facts taken together explain why the female husband is culturally conceptualized as a man. She must manage property because of her special circumstances, but a female holder, manager, and exchanger of property is an extremely anomalous being. Thus she is culturally recoded as a man to reduce the contradiction implicit in her role with regard to property.

This explains why informants insist that the female husband is a man, and why her attempts to behave as a man are most pronounced in the areas of life that have most bearing upon the family estate and heirship to it. The degree to which the status, role, and behavior of a female husband approximates that of an actual man in various areas of ideology and activity has been reviewed in an attempt to show that the closer one gets to issues of property and heirship the stronger is the dogma that the female husband is a man, the further the remove from these issues the more this dogma is diminished.

Once articulated, the ideology that the female husband is a man has an independent existence. Informants strive for logical consistency and thus extend this ideology, which is so important in the domain of property relations, into other domains. In some senses, the female husband becomes an intermediate category between male and female. In areas removed from the realm of property relations, thus not crucial to the female husband's male status but generally important to the cultural construct man, the ambiguity is greatest. It is in these areas (e.g., political participation, male initiation) that the dogma that the female husband is a man comes to be defended with an impressive edifice of evasion, rationalization, and selective perception.

NOTES

1. For assistance in arriving at this interpretation, I am indebted to Cathy Small, Lorraine Sexton, Denise O'Brien and Diane Freedman, although I remain solely responsible for any errors of logic in its development. I am further indebted to Jennifer Jeptoo Kosut, who assisted in the collection of the data.

    The term "woman marriage" is commonly used in the anthropological literature to denote the institution I am discussing. This term is somewhat confusing, since all marriages involve women. O'Brien (1977: 110) prefers to drop the term "woman marriage" in favor of "female husband." The Nandi institution clearly belongs in the context of the entire range of institutions found in African societies in which a woman can pay bridewealth to acquire predominant rights in a wife. In some of these societies, the relationship between the two women is not that of "husband" and "wife." Therefore, I choose to use "woman/woman marriage" as a general term for the institution, and "female husband" as the term for a woman who takes a wife and is considered to stand as "husband" to her according to the rules of their culture.

2. Although the existence of woman/woman marriage in a large number of African societies has been briefly noted in various ethnographic sources (summarized by O'Brien 1972), it has received very little detailed anthropological study. A handful of ethnographic accounts by Herskovits (1937) on Dahomey; Krige and Krige (1943) and Krige (1974) on Lovedu; van Warmelo and Phophi (1948) on Venda; Evans-Pritchard (1951) on Nuer; Huber (1969) on Simbiti; and Obbo (1976) on Kamba contain more than passing references to woman/woman marriage. The most complete accounts are those of Krige (1974) and Huber (1969).

3. This study was funded by grants from the National Institute for Mental Health, the National Science Foundation, and the Woodrow Wilson National Fellowship Foundation. It was carried out during my tenure as a Research Associate of the Institute for Development Studies, University of Nairobi, Kenya. To all of the above, I wish to express my appreciation for making the research possible.

4. The census included 116 households, or a 40 per cent sample of the approximately 286 households in Kaptel sublocation. The list of 286 households from which the random sample was selected was compiled from lists provided by sublocation Chief Paulo arap Lelei and *kokwei* elders. This was the most accurate information available.

5. Woman/woman marriage is not declining in popularity at present, but several factors may ultimately work against it. For example, there are the opposition of Christians and the growing idea that daughters as well as sons should be eligible to inherit family property. Woman/woman marriage will probably continue as an option for completely childless women and girls with children who have not inherited property. The institution of woman/woman marriage is in the process of diffusing from the Nandi to other Kenyan societies.

6. In Nandi, dwelling structures are of two kinds, *got* and *sigiroinet*. The former is traditionally the dwelling of a family, with cooking hearth, overhead storage compartment, and a room for sheep and goats. The latter is usually a smaller one-room dwelling which traditionally served as sleeping quarters for warriors and their girlfriends and now houses adolescent boys and unmarried men or a man who wishes a place to sleep away from the family. The most significant distinction is that the fireplace of the *sigiroinet* is not generally used as a cooking hearth. The wife's house is consistently referred to as *got*, the female husband's fairly consistently as *sigiroinet*.

7. Langley (1979) says that the female husband "raised children either to her own or her husband's clan," that some of her informants believed that the wife's consort should belong to the female husband's own kin group and that the consort had to be approved by the female husband's own kin group as well as that of her male husband. All these points are vehemently and unanimously denied by the scores of informants I interviewed about woman/woman marriage in various areas of Nandi District and other areas of Nandi settlement.

8. The distance between father and child stems to a large degree from traditional pollution beliefs. *Kerek* is the Nandi word for a polluting substance believed to emanate from newborn infants and from women due to their close association with babies. Its effect on a man, particularly the child's own father, is to weaken his *murenotet*, or manly qualities. He loses his prowess in warfare and becomes stupid, weak, and indecisive. At the birth of a child, a husband leaves his wife's house and is not completely reincorporated into the household until the child is eight to twelve months old. Today, the period of avoidance has been shortened to about a month, in most cases, and most young people do not admit to believing in *kerek*.

9. Readers may wonder whether a male child raised in a female husband-headed household will not have a gender identity problem as the result of lacking a male role model. This concern is needless on two grounds. First, the father's relationship with the child is ordinarily distant. Second, some male adult relative is always living in or in close proximity to the female husband's compound and this man, be he the female husband's brother-in-law, the son of her co-wife, or whoever, serves as a male role model. The question of the absence of a male role model is specifically restricted to a nuclear family socialization context.

REFERENCES

Evans-Pritchard, E. E. 1951. *Kinship and Marriage Among the Nuer.* Oxford.

Gluckman, M. 1950. "Kinship and Marriage Among the Lozi of Northern Rhodesia and the Zulu of Natal." *African Systems of Kinship and Marriage*, ed. A. R. Radcliffe-Brown and D. Forde, pp. 166–206. London.

Gold, A. E. 1977. *Cultivation and Herding in Southern Nandi ca. 1840–1914.* University of Nairobi Staff Seminar Paper.

Herskovits, M. 1937. A Note on "Woman Marriage" in Dahomey. *Africa* 10: 335–341.

Huber, H. 1969. "Woman Marriage" in Some East African Societies. *Anthropos* 63/64: 745–752.

Huntingford, G. W. B. 1953. *The Nandi of Kenya: Tribal Control in a Pastoral Society.* London.

Krige, E. J. 1974. Woman Marriage with Special Reference to the Lovedu—Its Significance for the Definition of Marriage. *Africa* 44: 11–36.

Krige, E. J., and J. D. Krige. 1943. *The Realm of a Rain Queen.* London.

Langley, M. S. 1979. *The Nandi of Kenya: Life Crisis Rituals in a Period of Change.* New York.

Leach, E. R. 1969. Virgin Birth. *Genesis as Myth and Other Essays.* London.

Obbo, C. 1976. Dominant Male Ideology and Female Options: Three East African Case Studies. *Africa* 46: 371–389.

Oboler, R. S. 1977. "Work and Leisure in Modern Nandi: Preliminary Results of a Study of Time Allocation." Working Paper No. 324. Institute for Development Studies, Nairobi.

O'Brien, D. 1972. "Female Husbands in African Societies." Paper presented at the 71st Annual Meeting of the American Anthropological Association, Toronto.

O'Brien, D. 1977. Female Husbands in Southern Bantu Societies. *Sexual Stratification: A Cross-Cultural View*, ed. A. Schlegel, pp. 109–126. New York.

Riviere, P. G. 1971. *Marriage: A Reassessment. Rethinking Kinship and Marriage*, ed. R. Needham, pp. 57–74. London.

Sutton, J. E. G. 1970. Some Reflections on the Early History of Western Kenya. *Hadith 2: Proceedings of the 1968 Conference of the Historical Association of Kenya*, ed. B. Ogot, pp. 17–29. Nairobi.

van Warmelo, N. J., and W. N. D. Phophi. 1948. "Venda Law." Ethnological Publication No. 23. Department of Native Affairs. Pretoria.

Guys and Dolls

Juliet Gardiner

After reading history at the University College, London, Juliet Gardiner became an editor at *History Today*, which led to her editing the book *What Is History Today . . . ?* She most recently has been the academic director at Weidenfield and Nicholson, publishers.

The bombing of Pearl Harbor by the Japanese on December 7, 1941, the act that brought a reluctant and isolationist US into the Second World War, had a special significance for the American anthropologist Margaret Mead and her British husband, fellow anthropologist Gregory Bateson. It meant an end to their fieldwork in the Pacific islands where Mead had made her name when she was 26 with her (then) widely acclaimed study, *Coming of Age in Samoa*.

In the nine months Mead had allowed herself to study pubescent girls in Samoa (staying part of the time in the ramshackle, tin-roofed hotel in Pago Pago that Somerset Maugham had made famous in his short story, "Rain"), she had become convinced that these "primitive peoples" had a lesson for modern American youth. She was confident that her data told her—and she lost no time in telling the world—that it was not innate physiological changes that made adolescents "difficult," rather it was "the civilisation in which they grew up."

When war broke out in Europe in 1939 for the second time in little over 20 years, it seemed to many American anthropologists that they should redirect their investigations from the Pacific and other "primitive" areas towards the "civilised world" which was currently tearing itself apart again. Margaret Mead was resolute: "In 1939, I came home to a world on the brink of war, convinced that the next task was to apply what we knew, as best we could, to the problems of our own society."

In 1942 Mead was seconded from her job as assistant curator at the American Museum of Natural History in New York and headed for Washington, another expert

willingly mobilised in the service of the war. She and four other anthropologists were recruited for the Committee for National Morale where they were given a general brief to investigate "national character."

Mead had been a student of America's most influential anthropologist, Franz Boas, who had spearheaded the opposition to the school of eugenics and biological determinism associated with Francis Galton, and insisted on the primacy of culture as an explanation for "national characteristics." As Mead herself explained, "Anthropological studies have shown that it isn't race but the way in which people are brought up, that makes them behave the way they do."

By 1943, it had become obvious that there was an urgent need for some practical work and Margaret Mead set off on a field trip (or "mission") to England that summer. The problem once more was the sexual behaviour of the young. In January 1942 the first GIs had arrived in the UK, the vanguard of over one and a half million of a predominantly young conscript that would be stationed in Britain by May 1944 on the eve of D-Day. The British government, only too aware not only of the need for US military aid in wartime, but acutely conscious, too, of the inevitability of Britain's post-war economic and political dependence, was very anxious that Anglo-American relations should be of the most cordial. The US government, aware that the majority of its citizens were at a loss to understand why their boys should be over here fighting Europe's war again, were of the same mind.

Both agreed: the GIs were mixing with the "wrong sort" of British girls—and many of the girls attracted by the GIs' smart uniforms "which fit in all the right places unlike our boys' drab, thick, khaki felt," relative affluence (a US private was paid five times more than a British private), and confident charm, were, in the language of the time "drifting" into collaboration with the Yanks and abandoning their British servicemen husbands and boyfriends, away at war. The spectre of disaffected British soldiers and thousands of illegitimate babies haunted the British, while the Americans were forced to contemplate a bevy of "good time girls" earning their right to US citizenship by ensnaring a GI husband, and both were appalled by the dramatic rise in cases of VD.

It wasn't that either the Americans or their British hosts were short on advice on how to understand each other. On disembarkation each GI was issued with *A Short Guide to Great Britain*. It was written by Eric Knight, author of the best-selling war novel, *This Above All*, and its tone was brisk: "If you come from an Irish-American family, you may think of the English as persecutors of the Irish, or you may think of them as enemy Redcoats who fought against the American Revolution and the war of 1812. But there is no time today to fight old wars over again . . . the most evident truth of all is that in their major ways of life the British and American people are much alike. They speak the same language . . . but each country has minor national characteristics which differ. It is by causing misunderstandings over these minor differences that Hitler hopes to make his propaganda effective."

The British had their own handbook to the GIs, *Meet the Army*, written by the poet Louis MacNeice. His prose was rather more reflective with several pages sketching out "the country they come from" since he found it "impossible to answer . . . succinctly and comprehensively," when he asked himself the question "If America is not like Britain, what is it like?"

Margaret Mead had made her contribution too, in a book she wrote while commuting between New York and Washington in 1942, called *And Keep Your Powder Dry*. It was published in Britain, as *The American Character*. But that was before she had "sat in an English garden." Now with the arrival of the GIs she was over here for some work in the field. The diminutive anthropologist (Mead was only just over five feet tall) spent four months in Britain living among the natives, learning to speak their language, and studying their strange propensity to form a queue or to dig their gardens at every opportunity. She had "driven through the little sunken roads of Devon . . . seen a Town Clerk waiting in the rain with a rolled umbrella . . . and seen the harvest standing in patterns as formal as a musical notation in the frosty fields of Scotland." And all the while she had been "lecturing, lecturing in canteens and public meetings, visiting aircraft factories and mines, responding to the ceremonious welcome accorded me by officials and official hosts." But amid all this, she had "been listening to and watching the ordinary life of Britain," and by the end of her trip she had cracked the problem: it came down to a simple misunderstanding of courtship rituals.

The report Margaret Mead wrote for the Office of War Information, the agency that had dispatched her to the war zone, was immediately recognised by the British Foreign Office as "an admirable document—though it does rather concentrate on one rather special aspect of relations—i.e. boy meets girl." The FO appreciated that this was "perhaps rather natural since Miss Mead is an anthropologist of a school notable for its studies into the mating habits of certain aboriginal tribes in the SW Pacific." And, they made sure that the report was available to "Organisers of local, voluntary bodies, concerned with the entertainment of the American forces" in a threepenny pamphlet, *The American Troops and the British Community*, which also served very nicely as a *vade mecum* for any British girl venturing into the camp of the "friendly invaders." Mead's text was instructive from the first sentence: "Usually foreigners are described as being rather like ourselves but having a few funny customs, wearing different clothes, using odd expressions, eating some strange foods. . . ." But, faithful to her training, Mead explained the "weakness in this approach." It was the society in which they were raised that conditioned young people's social responses—and there were serious misunderstandings when it came to boy/girl relations when the foreigners seemed anything but "rather like ourselves."

The demographic fact that underlay these misapprehensions was that "Britain has a great surplus of women and it has been up to the women or their mothers to find husbands. The great disapproval of the community falls on the man who plays fast and loose with a girl's affection. But in America, there have always been more men than women, and it was felt difficult for the man to find himself a wife. Social disapproval falls heaviest, not on the man who deceives the girl, but on the girl who uses unfair methods to make a man marry her . . . there is a lot of room for misunderstanding."

As Mead elaborated, "British boys don't go out with girls unless they have what one British boy described to me as 'an ulterior purpose good or bad.' If they want to spend a pleasant evening, more often they spend it with other boys. Even when the boys and girls do go to the same school in Britain, they act as 'if they were still going to separate schools.' To an American eye, the absence of flirting and backchat among secondary school boys and girls is astonishing. American boys and girls start having dates with each other in the early teens long before they are emotionally mature enough to be interested in each other for anything really connected with sex."

It was this concept of the "date" that was the key to the problem. Apparently, it was "quite a different sort of thing from an evening spent with someone whom one hopes to marry. It exists for itself, just as an evening in time, in which two people dance or go to the cinema, of soft drinks together while they talk to each other in a gay, wise-cracking style, the metaphors and similes changing every week."

But the rules of this pre-courtship ritual must have seemed totally impenetrable to the average British girl, used to evenings of neglect punctuated with talk of sport or cars. For a start, it was important to an American boy that his date "should be a very popular girl." No right-thinking male wanted to be lumbered with what Mead categorised as "a 10 minute girl"—someone who you might dance with for nearly a quarter of an hour without anyone cutting in to try to take her from you. But she mustn't be too popular or that might denote someone who gained her popularity by "giving sex favours" and that would make her stock fall, and soon, Mead suggested darkly, the girl would find herself having to "pay more heavily for each date."

Whereas no American prom queen would want to compromise her popularity by giving "sex favours," the way an American boy maximised his popularity was precisely by asking for them. In this way "each was flattered ... the line obviously becomes for the boy to ask for as much as possible, thus displaying his estimate of himself—and the girl to give as little as possible, thus displaying her estimate of herself." And this "subtle battle of invitation and refusal goes on as a framework to the normal activities of an evening, a cinema, a dance, a soda at the corner drugstore, etc."

But as Mead diagnosed, British girls just weren't playing according to Yankee rules. They were either "rebuffing (the boy) curtly" which left him "hurt and affronted" and apt to feel that "Britain is a cold—and then he will add little—country."

Or: "Pattern two, the girl does not rebuff the boy when he makes his first advances"—thinking from her understanding of American movies that that's how they do things over there, or she "may simply be too shy and inexperienced and tongue-tied (what with single sex education and no opportunity to practice 'gay wise-cracks') to know how to halt his advances."

Anyway, whatever the reason, the "American will go on increasingly surprised and decreasingly flattered by his progress" until "the episode ends in a seduction which neither wanted," and the "folklore floating about of the American who seduces girls with a single tin of fruit juice, is confirmed."

Then there is "pattern three"—perhaps the most deadly—when the "girl does not rebuff the boy completely for this first advance, but she is able to hold him somewhat at arm's length ... which gives him a familiar and comfortable feeling, this is like home, this is a girl who knows what a date ought to be, this is a girl who a fellow can be proud to go out with." But this time it is the boy who has misunderstood the signals. For the girl, fed a diet of American movies where the heroine ends up marrying the hero, is soon taking him home to meet her father. "Then after a few dates, he finds to his horror and amazement that the girl feels that he is committed to marrying her ... he feels entrapped in a totally false situation."

Of course, the habitat didn't help. Margaret Mead despaired at the lack of public places where all this badinage could take place. The pub was "quite unsuitable," no British street corner had a drugstore or soda fountain, and the design of British homes was inimical to successful early courtship rites. For a start, British houses, unlike American ones, rarely had a front porch, that ambiguous cultural space sited both within and yet without the home territory, and the lack of central heating meant that all members of a family clustered round the fire and "could not be shooed out." So an invitation home meant that a GI was catapulted straight in the heart of the family circle with his feet under the table, whether or not that is where he wanted them to be.

The answer, Mead prescribed, lay in education—cartoons, circulars, talks and film shows—all showing how "misunderstandings" arose, teaching the GIs that British girls "really know as little as your 14-year-old sister at home" and that they are likely "either to give nothing at all or—more than you wanted and it's up to you to teach her how to play the American game."

It also lay in moving the goal posts, creating little outposts of America in Britain where the culture of the drugstore could be replicated with "a sort of light refreshment room and soft drinks, preferably with ice, low lights, continuous dance music and a pleasant atmosphere."

Mead's work represented "a social scientist's contribution to winning the war and establishing a just and lasting peace" and fully justified her claim that "the whole world is my field. It is all anthropology." Her friend and fellow anthropologist, Rhoda Metraux, recalled that "everything got straightened out ... and we got some nice English wives." Nearly 70,000 in fact.

8

Family and Kinship

Like apple pie, everyone, especially politicians on the stump, is in favor of The Family, yet few people specify what they mean by it and why they believe it to be the bedrock of North American society. Many anthropologists have also followed this line of reasoning. For example, George Murdock (1965), in a survey of some 250 societies that all had a form of **nuclear family** (a married couple with dependent offspring), claimed that the family served a number of functions such as preventing disruptive sex, being essential for enculturation and the sexual division of labor, and protecting females during their reproductive years. In short, the family is seen as providing the domestic sphere in which the focus is on such essentials as food preparation, discipline, sex, and grooming. Of course, all these activities can be and are undertaken in some societies by other institutions; for example, among the Mae Enga of Papua New Guinea, men and women sleep in separate men's and women's houses. Sex is frequently a matter of coupling in the fields. In some societies where the household is organized around a group of related women, men eat at their sisters' house. Similarly, in British society, much **enculturation** of boys takes place away from home at "exclusive public schools" like Eton and Harrow.

Recently, the conventional approach has been increasingly questioned, and the paper by Jane Collier, Michelle Rosaldo, and Sylvia Yanagisako is a typical example of this "revisionist" thinking. They argue that the family is not a concrete institution designed by God or even people to satisfy human needs; rather, it is an ideological construct tied up with the development of the state. They conclude that families, "a sphere of human relationships," are the product of various social forms shaped by a state that recognizes families as property and welfare units; however, the family is sanctified, ironically, as the last stronghold against the state. Such a view obviously has crucial political implications even for countries like the United States where the debate on social welfare has been brought to the fore by the riots in Los Angeles. Ideologically, we feel that what happens in the family is of no concern to the state. As Collier and her colleagues point out, domestic violence is tolerated to a far greater extent than other forms of violence. Indeed, whereas most of us would not hesitate reporting a theft by a stranger to the police, we probably would have doubts about reporting the same theft if it were committed by a family member. Even though we might personally dislike family members, we feel a sense of obligation to them.

Revisionist thinking is also evident in Brett Williams's article on migrant farm workers. In the United States, we hear a great deal about the breakdown of families among the poor; yet among Hispanic migrants, marital relationships show a strength that is often lacking in middle- and upper-class families. Looking at the wives in migrant communities, who are quite submissive to their husbands, one might conclude that they are oppressed and without power; yet the same women are sisters, mothers, grandmothers, aunts, and godmothers, all of whom in fact have considerable authority over men. Hence, the glib stereotype of the "oppressed woman" in migrant families needs rethinking.

Williams's paper also challenges another stereotype held by many North Americans: that families constitute independent social units. As she shows, the women in migrant Hispanic communities work long and hard at gathering and binding relations so that their families are firmly embedded in a wider network of kin—what anthropologists would call a **kindred**. These are the relatives on whom an individual can call in time of need, and in migrant communities, they are crucial in helping people cope with the exigencies of life.

In most human societies, families (where they exist) are likewise embedded within larger networks of kin. In **agrarian societies**, there often exists a whole hierarchy of groups based on descent, with some form of extended, multigenerational family at the base. In traditional China, for example, upon marriage, a woman would leave the family into which she had been born to go live with her husband in the family into which he had been born. Thus, all men in the family shared a common male ancestor, and as older members died off, younger members were born into the family. Several families together whose men could trace their descent through men back to a more distant common male ancestor constituted a larger male descent group that anthropologists would call a **lineage**. Finally, lineages sharing a common ancestry—**clans** in anthropological parlance—were also recognized.

The Chinese case just cited constitutes an example of patrilineal descent, a common device for specifying group membership in societies in which men perform the bulk of productive work and hold political authority. In societies without centralized political organization, in which much of the productive work is done by women, descent is apt to be reckoned matrilineally, exclusively through women. The Hopi Indians of the North American Southwest (and the subject of Alice Schlegel's article) are one example. An important correlate of how descent is reckoned is the way family relationships are structured. As Margery Wolf shows in her article, in **patrilineal societies**, a woman is apt to be isolated from her kin and must defer to the dictates of the men in her husband's family, in which she is something of an outsider. Under such conditions, women must show great resourcefulness if they are to find ways to protect their own self-interests. By contrast, although patrilineal societies are generally patriarchal, **matrilineal societies** are not matriarchal. As Schlegel's essay shows, relations between men and women are apt to be less skewed in favor of one sex over the other. In Hopi society, for example, men are not isolated from their blood kin as women are in a patrilineal society. But although they cannot be dominated by women, neither can they do anything of which women disapprove.

REFERENCES

Murdock, George P. 1965 *Social Structure*. New York: Free Press.

Is There a Family?

New Anthropological Views

Jane Collier, Michelle Z. Rosaldo, and Sylvia Yanagisako

Jane F. Collier and Michelle Z. Rosaldo are professors and Sylvia Yanagisako is an associate professor in the anthropology department at Stanford University. Collier, who has done fieldwork in Mexico, received her Ph.D. from Tulane University in 1971 and is particularly interested in legal anthropology. Rosaldo, whose regional interests are in Latin America and island Southeast Asia and whose topical research interests include religion, society, and history, was awarded her Ph.D. in 1971 by Harvard University. Yanagisako, who received her Ph.D. from the University of Washington in 1976 has done fieldwork in the United States and specializes in family and kinship, social and cultural change, urban anthropology, and ethnicity.

This essay poses a rhetorical question in order to argue that most of our talk about families is clouded by unexplored notions of what families "really" are like. It is probably the case, universally, that people expect to have special connections with their geneaologically closest relations. But a knowledge of genealogy does not in itself promote understanding of what these special ties are about. The real importance of The Family in contemporary social life and belief has blinded us to its dynamics. Confusing ideal with reality, we fail to appreciate the deep significance of what are, cross-culturally, various ideologies of intimate relationship, and at the same time we fail to reckon with the complex human bonds and experiences all too comfortably sheltered by a faith in the "natural" source of a "nurture" we think is found in the home.

This essay is divided into three parts. The first examines what social scientists mean by The Family. It focuses on the work of Bronislaw Malinowski, the anthropologist who first convinced social scientists that The Family was a universal human institution. The second part also has social scientists as its focus, but it examines works by the nineteenth-century thinkers Malinowski refuted, for if—as we shall argue—Malinowski was wrong in viewing The Family as a universal human institution, it becomes important to

explore the work of theorists who did not make Malinowski's mistakes. The final section then draws on the correct insights of nineteenth-century theorists to sketch some implications of viewing The Family, not as a concrete institution designed to fulfill universal human needs, but as an ideological construct associated with the modern state.

MALINOWSKI'S CONCEPT OF THE FAMILY

In 1913 Bronislaw Malinowski published a book called *The Family Among the Australian Aborigines*,[1] in which he laid to rest earlier debates about whether all human societies had families. During the nineteenth century, proponents of social evolution argued that primitives were sexually promiscuous and therefore incapable of having families because children would not recognize their fathers.[2] Malinowski refuted this notion by showing that Australian aborigines, who were widely believed to practice "primitive promiscuity," not only had rules regulating who might have intercourse with whom during sexual orgies but also differentiated between legal marriages and casual unions. Malinowski thus "proved" that Australian aborigines had marriage, and so proved that aboriginal children had fathers, because each child's mother had but a single recognized husband.

Malinowski's book did not simply add data to one side of an ongoing debate. It ended the debate altogether, for by distinguishing coitus from conjugal relationships, Malinowski separated questions of sexual behavior from questions of the family's universal existence. Evidence of sexual promiscuity was henceforth irrelevant for deciding whether families existed. Moreover, Malinowski argued that the conjugal relationship, and therefore The Family, had to be universal because it fulfilled a universal human need. As he wrote in a posthumously published book:

> The human infant needs parental protection for a much longer period than does the young of even the highest anthropoid apes. Hence, no culture could endure in which the act of reproduction, that is, mating, pregnancy, and childbirth, was not linked up with the fact of legally-founded parenthood, that is, a relationship in which the father and mother have to look after the children for a long period, and, in turn, derive certain benefits from the care and trouble taken.[3]

In proving the existence of families among Australian aborigines, Malinowski described three features of families that he believed flowed from The Family's universal function of nurturing children. First, he argued that families had to have clear boundaries, for if families were to perform the vital function of nurturing young children, insiders had to be distinguishable from outsiders so that everyone could know which adults were responsible for the care of which children. Malinowski thus argued that families formed bounded social units, and to prove that Australian families formed such units, he demonstrated that aboriginal parents and children recognized one another. Each aboriginal woman had a single husband, even if some husbands had more than one wife and even if husbands occasionally allowed wives to sleep with other men during tribal ceremonies. Malinowski thus proved that each aboriginal child had a recognized mother and father, even if both parents occasionally engaged in sexual relations with outsiders.

Second, Malinowski argued that families had to have a place where family members could be together and where the daily tasks associated with child rearing could be performed. He demonstrated, for example, that aboriginal parents and their immature children shared a single fire—a home and hearth where children were fed and nurtured—even though, among nomadic aborigines, the fire might be kindled in a different location each night.

Finally, Malinowski argued that family members felt affection for one another—that parents who invested long years in caring for children were rewarded by their own and their children's affections for one another. Malinowski felt that long and intimate association among family members fostered close emotional ties, particularly between parents and children, but also between spouses. Aboriginal parents and their children, for example, could be expected to feel the same emotions for one another as did English parents and children, and as proof of this point, Malinowski re-

counted touching stories of the efforts made by aboriginal parents to recover children lost during conflicts with other aborigines or with white settlers and efforts made by stolen aboriginal children to find their lost parents.

Malinowski's book on Australian aborigines thus gave social scientists a concept of The Family that consisted of a universal function, the nurturance of young children, mapped onto (1) a bounded set of people who recognized one another and who were distinguishable from other like groups; (2) a definite physical space, a hearth and home; and (3) a particular set of emotions, family love. This concept of The Family as an institution for nurturing young children has been enduring, probably because nurturing children is thought to be the primary function of families in modern industrial societies. The flaw in Malinowski's argument is the flaw common to all functionalist arguments: Because a social institution is observed to perform a necessary function does not mean either that the function would not be performed if the institution did not exist or that the function is responsible for the existence of the institution.

Later anthropologists have challenged Malinowski's idea that families always include fathers, but, ironically, they have kept all the other aspects of his definition. For example, later anthropologists have argued that the basic social unit is not the nuclear family including father but the unit composed of a mother and her children: "Whether or not a mate becomes attached to the mother on some more or less permanent basis is a variable matter."[4] In removing father from the family, however, later anthropologists have nevertheless retained Malinowski's concept of The Family as a functional unit, and so have retained all the features Malinowski took such pains to demonstrate. In the writings of modern anthropologists, the mother-child unit is described as performing the universally necessary function of nurturing young children. A mother and her children form a bounded group, distinguishable from other units of mothers and their children. A mother and her children share a place, a home and hearth. And, finally, a mother and her children share deep emotional bonds based on their prolonged and intimate contact.

Modern anthropologists may have removed father from The Family, but they did not modify the basic social science concept of The Family in which the function of child rearing is mapped onto a bounded set of people who share a place and who "love" one another. Yet it is exactly this concept of The Family that we, as feminist anthropologists, have found so difficult to apply. Although the biological facts of reproduction, when combined with a sufficiently elastic definition of marriage, make it possible for us, as social scientists, to find both mother-child units and Malinowski's conjugal-pairs-plus-children units in every human society, it is not at all clear that such Families necessarily exhibit the associated features Malinowski "proved" and modern anthropologists echo.

An outside observer, for example, may be able to delimit family boundaries in any and all societies by identifying the children of one woman and that woman's associated mate, but natives may not be interested in making such distinctions. In other words, natives may not be concerned to distinguish family members from outsiders, as Malinowski imagined natives should be when he argued that units of parents and children have to have clear boundaries in order for child-rearing responsibilities to be assigned efficiently. Many languages, for example, have no word to identify the unit of parents and children that English speakers call a "family." Among the Zinacantecos of southern Mexico, the basic social unit is identified as a "house," which may include from one to twenty people.[5] Zinacantecos have no difficulty talking about an individual's parents, children, or spouse; but Zinacantecos do not have a single word that identifies the unit of parents and children in such a way as to cut it off from other like units. In Zinacanteco society, the boundary between "houses" is linguistically marked, while the boundary between "family" units is not.

Just as some languages lack words for identifying units of parents and children, so some "families" lack places. Immature children in every society have to be fed and cared for, but parents and children do not necessarily eat and sleep together as a family in one place. Among the Mundurucu of tropical South America, for example, the men of a village traditionally lived in a men's house together with all the village boys over the age of thirteen; women lived with other women and young children in two or three houses grouped around the men's house.[6] In Mundurucu society, men and women ate and slept apart. Men ate in the men's house, sharing food the women had cooked and delivered to them; women ate with other women and children in their own houses. Married couples also slept apart, meeting only for sexual intercourse.

Finally, people around the world do not necessarily expect family members to "love" one another. People may expect husbands, wives, parents, and children to have strong feelings about one another, but they do not necessarily expect prolonged and intimate contact to breed the loving sentiments Malinowski imagined as universally rewarding parents for the care they invested in children. The mother-daughter relationship, for example, is not always pictured as warm and loving. In modern Zambia, girls are not expected to discuss personal problems with, or seek advice from, their mothers. Rather, Zambian girls are expected to seek out some older female relative to serve as confidante.[7] Similarly, among the Cheyenne Indians who lived on the American Great Plains during the last century, a mother was expected to have strained relations with her daughters.[8]

Mothers are described as continually admonishing their daughters, leading the latter to seek affection from their fathers' sisters.

Of course, anthropologists have recognized that people everywhere do not share our deep faith in the loving, self-sacrificing mother, but in matters of family and motherhood, anthropologists, like all social scientists, have relied more on faith than evidence in constructing theoretical accounts. Because we *believe* mothers to be loving, anthropologists have proposed, for example, that a general explanation of the fact that men marry mother's brothers' daughters more frequently than they marry father's sisters' daughters is that men naturally seek affection (i.e., wives) where they have found affection in the past (i.e., from mothers and their kin).[9]

LOOKING BACKWARD

The Malinowskian view of The Family as a universal institution—which maps the "function" of "nurturance" onto a collectivity of specific persons (presumably "nuclear" relations) associated with specific spaces ("the home") and specific affective bonds ("love")—corresponds, as we have seen, to that assumed by most contemporary writers on the subject. But a consideration of available ethnographic evidence suggests that the received view is a good deal more problematic than a naive observer might think. If Families in Malinowski's sense are *not* universal, then we must begin to ask about the biases that, in the past, have led us to misconstrue the ethnographic record. The issues here are too complex for thorough explication in this essay, but if we are to better understand the nature of "the family" in the present, it seems worthwhile to explore the question, first, of why so many social thinkers continue to believe in Capital-Letter Families as universal institutions, and second, whether anthropological tradition offers any alternatives to a "necessary and natural" view of what our families are. Only then will we be in a position to suggest "new anthropological perspectives" on the family today.

Our positive critique begins by moving backward. In the next few pages, we suggest that tentative answers to both questions posed above lie in the nineteenth-century intellectual trends that thinkers like Malinowski were at pains to reject. During the second half of the nineteenth century, a number of social and intellectual developments—among them, the evolutionary researches of Charles Darwin; the rise of "urban problems" in fast-growing cities; and the accumulation of data on non-Western peoples by missionaries and agents of the colonial states—contributed to what most of us would now recognize as the beginnings of modern social science. Alternately excited and perplexed by changes in a rapidly industrializing world, thinkers as diverse as socialist Frederick Engels[10] and bourgeois apologist Herbert Spencer[11]—to say nothing of a host of mythographers, historians of religion, and even feminists—attempted to identify the distinctive problems and potentials of their contemporary society by constructing *evolutionary* accounts of "how it all began." At base, a sense of "progress" gave direction to their thought, whether, like Spencer, they believed "man" had advanced from the love of violence to a more civilized love of peace or, like Engels, that humanity had moved from primitive promiscuity and incest toward monogamy and "individual sex love." Proud of their position in the modern world, some of these writers claimed that rules of force had been transcended by new rules of law,[12] while others thought that feminine "mysticism" in the past had been supplanted by a higher male "morality."[13]

At the same time, and whatever else they thought of capitalist social life (some of them criticized, but none wholly abhorred it), these writers also shared a sense of moral emptiness and a fear of instability and loss. Experience argued forcefully to them that moral order in their time did not rest on the unshakable hierarchy—from God to King to Father in the home—enjoyed by Europeans in the past.[14] Thus, whereas Malinowski's functionalism led him to stress the underlying continuities in all human social forms, his nineteenth-century predecessors were concerned to understand the facts and forces that set their experiential world apart. They were interested in comparative and, more narrowly, evolutionary accounts because their lives were torn between celebration and fear of change. For them, the family was important not because it had at all times been the same but because it was at once the moral precondition for, the triumph of, and the victim of developing capitalist society. Without the family and female spheres, thinkers like Ruskin feared we would fall victim to a market that destroys real human bonds.[15] Then again, while men like Engels could decry the impact of the market on familial life and love, he joined with more conservative counterparts to insist that our contemporary familial forms benefited from the individualist morality of modern life and reached to moral and romantic heights unknown before.

Given this purpose and the limited data with which they had to work, it is hardly surprising that the vast majority of what these nineteenth-century writers said is easily dismissed today. They argued that in simpler days such things as incest were the norm; they thought that women ruled in "matriarchal" and peace-loving states or, alternatively, that brute force determined the primitive right and wrong. None of these visions of a more natural, more feminine, more sexy, or more violent primitive world squares with contemporary evidence about what, in technological and organizational terms, might be reckoned relatively "primitive" or "simple" social forms. We would suggest, however, that whatever their mistakes, these nineteenth-century

thinkers *can* help us rethink the family today, at least in part because we are (unfortunately) their heirs, in the area of prejudice, and partly because their concern to characterize difference and change gave rise to insights much more promising than their functionalist critics may have thought.

To begin, although nineteenth-century evolutionary theorists did not believe The Family to be universal, the roots of modern assumptions can be seen in their belief that women are, and have at all times been, defined by nurturant, connective, and reproductive roles that *do not change* through time. Most nineteenth-century thinkers imaged social development as a process of differentiation from a relatively confused (and thus incestuous) and indiscriminate female-oriented state to one in which men fight, destroy their "natural" social bonds, and then forge public and political ties to create a human "order." For some, it seemed reasonable to assume that women dominated, as matriarchs, in the undifferentiated early state, but even these theorists believed that women everywhere were "mothers" first, defined by "nurturant" concerns and thus excluded from the business competition, cooperation social ordering, and social change propelled and dominated by their male counterparts. And so, while nineteenth-century writers differed in their evaluations of such things as "women's status," they all believed that female reproductive roles made women different from and complementary to men and guaranteed both the relative passivity of women in human history and the relative continuity of "feminine" domains and functions in human societies. Social change consisted in the acts of men, who left their mothers behind in shrinking homes. And women's nurturant sphere was recognized as a complementary and necessary corrective to the more competitive pursuits of men, not because these thinkers recognized women as political actors who influence the world, but because they feared the unchecked and morally questionable growth of a male-dominated capitalist market.

For nineteenth-century evolutionists, women were associated, in short, with an unchanging biological role and a romanticized community of the past, while men were imaged as the agents of all social process. And though contemporary thinkers have been ready to dismiss manifold aspects of their now-dated school of thought, on this point we remain, perhaps unwittingly, their heirs. Victorian assumptions about gender and the relationship between competitive male markets and peace-loving female homes were not abandoned in later functionalist schools of thought at least in part because pervasive sexist biases make it easy to forget that women, like men, are important actors in all social worlds. Even more, the functionalists, themselves concerned to understand all human social forms in terms of biological "needs," turned out to strengthen earlier beliefs associating action, change, and interest with the deeds of men because they thought of kinship in terms of biologically given ties, of "families" as units geared to reproductive needs, and finally, of women as mere "reproducers" whose contribution to society was essentially defined by the requirements of their homes.

If most modern social scientists have inherited Victorian biases that tend ultimately to support a view uniting women and The Family to an apparently unchanging set of biologically given needs, we have at the same time failed to reckon with the one small area in which Victorian evolutionists were right. They understood, as we do not today, that families—like religions, economies, governments, or courts of law—are *not* unchanging but the product of various social forms, that the relationships of spouses and parents to their young are apt to be different things in different social orders. More particularly, although nineteenth-century writers had primitive society all wrong, they were correct in insisting that *family* in the modern sense—a unit bounded, biologically as well as legally defined, associated with property, self-sufficiency, with affect and a space "inside" the home—is something that emerges not in Stone Age caves but in complex state-governed social forms. Tribal peoples may speak readily of lineages, households, and clans, but—as we have seen—they rarely have a word denoting Family as a particular and limited group of kin; they rarely worry about differences between legitimate and illegitimate heirs or find themselves concerned (as we so often are today) that what children and/or parents do reflects on their family's public image and self-esteem. Political influence in tribal groups in fact consists in adding children to one's home and, far from distinguishing Smith from Jones, encouraging one's neighbors to join one's household as if kin. By contrast, modern bounded Families try to keep their neighbors out. Clearly their character, ideology, and functions are not given for all times. Instead, to borrow the Victorian phrase, The Family is a "moral" unit, a way of organizing and thinking about human relationships in a world in which the domestic is perceived to be in opposition to a politics shaped outside the home, and individuals find themselves dependent on a set of relatively noncontingent ties in order to survive the dictates of an impersonal market and external political order.

In short, what the Victorians recognized and we have tended to forget is, first, that human social life has varied in its "moral"—we might say its "cultural" or "ideological"—forms, and so it takes more than making babies to make Families. And having seen The Family as something more than a response to omnipresent, biologically given needs, they realized too that Families do not everywhere exist; rather, The Family (thought to be universal by most social scientists today) is a moral and ideological unit that appears, not universally, but in particular social orders. The Family as we know it is not

a "natural" group created by the claims of "blood" but a sphere of human relationships shaped by a state that recognizes Families as units that hold property, provide for care and welfare, and attend particularly to the young—a sphere conceptualized as a realm of love and intimacy *in opposition* to the more "impersonal" norms that dominate modern economies and politics. One can, in nonstate social forms, find groups of genealogically related people who interact daily and share material resources, but the contents of their daily ties, the ways they think about their bonds and their conception of the relationship between immediate "familial" links and other kinds of sociality, are apt to be different from the ideas and feelings we think rightfully belong to families we know. Stated otherwise, because our notions of The Family are rooted in a contrast between "public" and "private" spheres, we will not find that Families like ours exist in a society where public and political life is radically different from our own.

Victorian thinkers rightly understood the link between the bounded modern Family and the modern state, although they thought the two related by a necessary teleology of moral progress. Our point resembles theirs not in the *explanations* we would seek but in our feeling that if we, today, are interested in change, we must begin to probe and understand change in the families of the past. Here the Victorians, not the functionalists, are our rightful guides because the former recognized that *all* human social ties have "cultural" or "moral" shapes, and more specifically, that the particular "morality" of contemporary familial forms is rooted in a set of processes that link our intimate experiences and bonds to public politics.

TOWARD A RETHINKING

Our perspective on families therefore compels us to listen carefully to what the natives in other societies say about their relationships with genealogically close kin. The same is true of the natives in our own society. Our understanding of families in contemporary American society can be only as rich as our understanding of what The Family represents symbolically to Americans. A complete cultural analysis of The Family as an American ideological construct, of course, is beyond the scope of this essay. But we can indicate some of the directions such an analysis would take and how it would deepen our knowledge of American families.

One of the central notions in the modern American construct of The Family is that of nurturance. When antifeminists attack the Equal Rights Amendment, for example, much of their rhetoric plays on the anticipated loss of the nurturant, intimate bonds we associate with The Family. Likewise, when pro-life forces decry abortion, they cast it as the ultimate denial of nurturance. In a sense, these arguments are variations of a functionalist view that weds families to specific functions. The logic of the argument is that because people need nurturance, and people get nurtured in The Family, then people need The Family. Yet if we adopt the perspective that The Family is an ideological unit rather than merely a functional unit, we are encouraged to subject this syllogism to closer scrutiny. We can ask, first, What do people mean by nurturance? Obviously, they mean more than mere nourishment—that is, the provision of food, clothing, and shelter required for biological survival. What is evoked by the word nurturance is a certain kind of relationship: a relationship that entails affection and love, that is based on cooperation as opposed to competition, that is enduring rather than temporary, that is noncontingent rather than contingent upon performance, and that is governed by feeling and morality instead of law and contract.

The reason we have stated these attributes of The Family in terms of oppositions is because in a symbolic system the meanings of concepts are often best illuminated by explicating their opposites. Hence, to understand our American construct of The Family, we first have to map the larger system of constructs of which it is only a part. When we undertake such an analysis of The Family in our society, we discover that what gives shape to much of our conception of The Family is its symbolic opposition to work and business, in other words, to the market relations of capitalism. For it is in the market, where we sell our labor and negotiate contract relations of business, that we associate with competitive, temporary, contingent relations that must be buttressed by law and legal sanctions.

The symbolic opposition between The Family and market relations renders our strong attachment to The Family understandable, but it also discloses the particularity of our construct of The Family. We can hardly be speaking of a universal notion of The Family shared by people everywhere and for all time because people everywhere and for all time have not participated in market relations out of which they have constructed a contrastive notion of the family.

The realization that our idea of The Family is part of a set of symbolic oppositions through which we interpret our experience in a particular society compels us to ask to what extent this set of oppositions reflects real relations between people and to what extent it also shapes them. We do not adhere to a model of culture in which ideology is isolated from people's experience. On the other hand, neither do we construe the connection between people's constructs and people's experience to be a simple one of epiphenomenal reflection. Rather, we are interested in understanding how people come to summarize their experience in folk constructs that gloss over the diversity, complexity, and contradictions in their relationships. If, for example, we consider the

second premise of the aforementioned syllogism—the idea that people get "nurtured" in families—we can ask how people reconcile this premise with the fact that relationships in families are not always this simple or altruistic. We need not resort to the evidence offered by social historians . . . of the harsh treatment and neglect of children and spouses in the history of the Western family, for we need only read our local newspaper to learn of similar abuses among contemporary families. And we can point to other studies . . . that reveal how people often find more intimacy and emotional support in relationships with individuals and groups outside The Family than they do in their relationships with family members.

The point is not that our ancestors or our contemporaries have been uniformly mean and nonnurturant to family members but that we have all been both nice and mean, both generous and ungenerous, to them. In like manner, our actions toward family members are not always motivated by selfless altruism but are also motivated by instrumental self-interest. What is significant is that, despite the fact that our complex relationships are the result of complex motivations, we ideologize relations within The Family as nurturant while casting relationships outside The Family—particularly in the sphere of work and business—as just the opposite.

We must be wary of oversimplifying matters by explaining away those disparities between our notion of the nurturant Family and our real actions toward family members as the predictable failing of imperfect beings. For there is more here than the mere disjunction of the ideal and the real. The American construct of The Family, after all, is complex enough to comprise some key contradictions. The Family is seen as representing not only the antithesis of the market relations of capitalism; it is also sacralized in our minds as the last stronghold against The State, as the symbolic refuge from the intrusions of a public domain that constantly threatens our sense of privacy and self-determination. Consequently, we can hardly be surprised to find that the punishments imposed on people who commit physical violence are lighter when their victims are their own family members.[16] Indeed, the American sense of the privacy of the things that go on inside families is so strong that a smaller percentage of homicides involving family members are prosecuted than those involving strangers.[17] We are faced with the irony that in our society the place where nurturance and noncontingent affection are supposed to be located is simultaneously the place where violence is most tolerated.

There are other dilemmas about The Family that an examination of its ideological nature can help us better understand. For example, the hypothesis that in England and the United States marriages among lower-income ("working-class") groups are characterized by a greater degree of "conjugal role segregation" than are marriages among middle-income groups has generated considerable confusion. Since Bott observed that working-class couples in her study of London families exhibited more "segregated" conjugal roles than "middle-class" couples, who tended toward more "joint" conjugal roles,[18] researchers have come forth with a range of diverse and confusing findings. On the one hand, some researchers have found that working-class couples indeed report more segregated conjugal role-relationships—in other words, clearly differentiated male and female tasks, as well as interests and activities—than do middle-class couples.[19] Other researchers, however, have raised critical methodological questions about how one goes about defining a joint activity and hence measuring the degree of "jointness" in a conjugal relationship.[20] Platt's finding that couples who reported "jointness" in one activity were not particularly likely to report "jointness" in another activity is significant because it demonstrates that "jointness" is not a general characteristic of a relationship that manifests itself uniformly over a range of domains. Couples carry out some activities and tasks together or do them separately but equally; they also have other activities in which they do not both participate. The measurement of the "jointness" of conjugal relationships becomes even more problematic when we recognize that what one individual or couple may label a "joint activity," another individual or couple may consider a "separate activity." In Bott's study, for example, some couples felt that all activities carried out by husband and wife in each other's presence were

> similar in kind regardless of whether the activities were complementary (e.g. sexual intercourse, though no one talked about this directly in the home interview), independent (e.g. husband repairing book while the wife read or knitted), or shared (e.g. washing up together, entertaining friends, going to the pictures together). It was not even necessary that husband and wife should actually be together. As long as they were both at home it was felt that their activities partook of some special, shared, family quality.[21]

In other words, the distinction Bott drew among "joint," "differentiated," and "autonomic" (independent) relationships summarized the way people thought and felt about their activities rather than what they were observed to actually do. Again, it is not simply that there is a disjunction between what people say they do and what they in fact do. The more cogent point is that the meaning people attach to action, whether they view it as coordinated and therefore shared or in some other way, is an integral component of that action and cannot be divorced from it in our analysis. When we compare the conjugal relationships of middle-income and low-income people, or any of the family relationships among different class, age, ethnic, and regional sectors of American society, we must recognize that our comparisons rest on

differences and similarities in ideological and moral meanings as well as on differences and similarities in action.

Finally, the awareness that The Family is not a concrete "thing" that fulfills concrete "needs" but an ideological construct with moral implications can lead to a more refined analysis of historical change in the American or Western family than has devolved upon us from our functionalist ancestors. The functionalist view of industrialization, urbanization, and family change depicts The Family as responding to alterations in economic and social conditions in rather mechanistic ways. As production gets removed from the family's domain, there is less need for strict rules and clear authority structures in the family to accomplish productive work. At the same time, individuals who now must work for wages in impersonal settings need a haven where they can obtain emotional support and gratification. Hence, The Family becomes more concerned with "expressive" functions, and what emerges is the modern "companionate family." In short, in the functionalist narrative The Family and its constituent members "adapt" to fulfill functional requirements created for it by the industrialization of production. Once we begin to view The Family as an ideological unit and pay due respect to it as a moral statement, however, we can begin to unravel the more complex, dialectical process through which family relationships and The Family as a construct were mutually transformed. We can examine, for one, the ways in which people and state institutions acted, rather than merely reacted, to assign certain functions to groupings of kin by making them legally responsible for these functions. We can investigate . . . the manner in which the increasing limitations placed on agents of the community and the state with regard to negotiating the relationships between family members enhanced the independence of The Family. We can begin to understand the consequences of social reforms and wage policies for the age and sex inequalities in families. And we can elucidate the interplay between these social changes and the cultural transformations that assigned new meanings and modified old ones to make The Family what we think it to be today.

Ultimately, this sort of rethinking will lead to a questioning of the somewhat contradictory modern views that families are things we need (the more "impersonal" the public world, the more we need them) and at the same time that loving families are disappearing. In a variety of ways, individuals today *do* look to families for a "love" that money cannot buy and find; our contemporary world makes "love" more fragile than most of us hope and "nurturance" more self-interested than we believe.[22] But what we fail to recognize is that familial nurturance and the social forces that turn our ideal families into mere fleeting dreams are *equally* creations of the world we know *today*. Rather than think of the ideal family as a world we lost (or, like the Victorians, as a world just recently achieved), it is important for us to recognize that while families symbolize deep and salient modern themes, contemporary families are unlikely to fulfill our equally modern nurturant needs.

We probably have no cause to fear (or hope) that The Family will dissolve. What we can begin to ask is what we *want* our families to do. Then, distinguishing our hopes from what we have, we can begin to analyze the social forces that enhance or undermine the realization of the kinds of human bonds we need.

NOTES

1. Bronislaw Malinowski, *The Family Among the Australian Aborigines* (London: University of London Press, 1913).
2. Lewis Henry Morgan, *Ancient Society* (New York: Holt, 1877).
3. Bronislaw Malinowski, *A Scientific Theory of Culture* (Chapel Hill: University of North Carolina Press, 1944), p. 99.
4. Robin Fox, *Kinship and Marriage* (London: Penguin, 1967), p. 39.
5. Evon Z. Vogt, *Zinacantan: A Maya Community in the Highlands of Chiapas* (Cambridge, Mass.: Harvard University Press, 1969).
6. Yolanda and Robert Murphy, *Women of the Forest* (New York: Columbia University Press, 1974).
7. Ilsa Schuster, *New Women of Lusaka* (Mountain View, Calif.: Mayfield, 1979).
8. E. Adamson Hoebel, *The Cheyennes: Indians of the Great Plains* (New York: Holt, Rinehart and Winston, 1978).
9. George C. Homans and David M. Schneider, *Marriage, Authority, and Final Causes* (Glencoe, Ill.: Free Press, 1955).
10. Frederick Engels, "The Origin of the Family, Private Property and the State," in *Karl Marx and Frederick Engels: Selected Works*, vol. 2 (Moscow: Foreign Language Publishing House, 1955).
11. Herbert Spencer, *The Principles of Sociology*, vol. 1, *Domestic Institutions.* (New York: Appleton, 1973).
12. John Stuart Mill, *The Subjection of Women* (London: Longmans, Green, Reader and Dyer, 1869).
13. J. J. Bachofen, *Das Mutterecht* (Stuttgart, 1861).
14. Elizabeth Fee, "The Sexual Politics of Victorian Social Anthropology," in *Clio's Banner Raised*, ed. M. Hartman and L. Banner (New York: Harper & Row, 1974).
15. John Ruskin, "Of Queen's Gardens," in *Sesame and Lilies* (London: J. M. Dent, 1907).
16. Henry P. Lundsgaarde, *Murder in Space City: A Cultural Analysis of Houston Homicide Patterns* (New York: Oxford University Press, 1977).
17. Ibid.
18. Elizabeth Bott, *Family and Social Network: Roles, Norms, and External Relationships in Ordinary Urban Families* (London: Tavistock, 1957).
19. Herbert J. Gans, *The Urban Villagers* (New York: Free Press, 1962); C. Rosser and C. Harris, *The Family and Social Change* (London: Routledge and Kegan Paul, 1965).

20. John Platt, "Some Problems in Measuring the Jointness of Conjugal Role-Relationships," *Sociology* 3 (1969): 287–97; Christopher Turner, "Conjugal Roles and Social Networks: A Re-examination of an Hypothesis," *Human Relations* 20 (1967): 121–30; and Morris Zelditch, Jr., "Family, Marriage and Kinship," in A *Handbook of Modern Sociology*, ed. R. E. L. Faris (Chicago: Rand McNally, 1964), pp. 680–707.
21. Bott, *Family and Social Network,* p. 240.
22. Rayna Rapp, "Family and Class in Contemporary America: Notes Toward an Understanding of Ideology," *Science and Society* 42 (Fall 1978): 278–300, republished in this volume.

REFERENCES

Bachofen, J. J. 1861. *Das Mutterecht.* Stuttgart.

Bott, Elizabeth. 1957. *Family and Social Network: Roles, Norms, and External Relationships in Ordinary Urban Families.* London: Tavistock.

Engels, Frederick. 1955. The Origin of the Family, Private Property and the State, in *Karl Marx and Frederick Engels: Selected Works*, vol. 2. Moscow: Foreign Language Publishing House.

Fee, Elizabeth. 1974. "The Sexual Politics of Victorian Social Anthropology," in *Clio's Banner Raised*, ed. M. Hartman and L. Banner. New York: Harper & Row.

Fox, Robin. 1967. *Kinship and Marriage.* London: Penguin.

Gans, Herbert J. 1962. *The Urban Villagers.* New York: Free Press.

Hoebel, E. Adamson. 1978. *The Cheyennes: Indians of the Great Plains.* New York: Holt, Rinehart and Winston.

Homans, George C. and David M. Schneider. 1955. *Marriage, Authority, and Final Causes.* Glencoe, Ill.: Free Press.

Lundsgaarde, Henry P. 1977. *Murder in Space City: A Cultural Analysis of Houston Homicide Patterns.* New York: Oxford University Press.

Malinowski, Bronislaw. 1913. *The Family Among the Australian Aborigines.* London: University of London Press.

Malinowski, Bronislaw. 1944. *A Scientific Theory of Culture.* Chapel Hill: University of North Carolina Press.

Mill, John Stuart. 1869. *The Subjection of Women.* London: Longmans, Green, Reader and Dyer.

Morgan, Lewis Henry. 1877. *Ancient Society.* New York: Holt.

Murphy, Yolanda and Robert. 1974. *Women of the Forest.* New York: Columbia University Press.

Platt, John. 1969. "Some Problems in Measuring the Jointness of Conjugal Role-Relationships," *Sociology* 3: 287–97.

Rapp, Rayna. 1978. "Family and Class in Contemporary America: Notes Toward an Understanding of Ideology," *Science and Society* 42: 278–300, republished in this volume.

Rosser, C. and C. Harris. 1965. *The Family and Social Change.* London: Routledge and Kegan Paul.

Ruskin, John. 1907. "Of Queen's Gardens," in *Sesame and Lilies.* London: J. M. Dent.

Schuster, Ilsa. 1979. *New Women of Lusaka.* Palo Alto, Calif.: Mayfield.

Spencer, Herbert. 1973. The Principles of Sociology, vol. 1, *Domestic Institutions.* New York: Appleton.

Turner, Christopher. 1967. "Conjugal Roles and Social Networks: A Re-examination of an Hypothesis," *Human Relations* 20: 121–30.

Vogt, Evon Z. 1969. *Zinacantan: A Maya Community in the Highlands of Chiapas.* Cambridge, Mass.: Harvard University Press.

Zelditch, Morris, Jr., 1964. "Family, Marriage and Kinship," in *A Handbook of Modern Sociology*, ed. R. E. L. Faris, pp. 680–707. Chicago: Rand McNally.

Why Migrant Women Feed Their Husbands Tamales

Foodways as a Basis for a Revisionist View of Tejano Family Life

Brett Williams

Brett Williams is associate professor of anthropology and director of American studies at American University, Washington, D.C. She received her Ph.D. from the University of Illinois in 1975. Her fieldwork has been done in the United States, among migrant workers of Mexican descent from Texas, in a mixed ethnic neighborhood of a northeastern city (see Chapter 9), and among waitresses. She has written on all of these topics, as well as on southern folklife and on the African-American hero, John Henry. Her research interests include poverty, the media, folklore, and politics and culture.

In the array of artifacts by which Tejano migrant farmworkers identify themselves, the tamale has no serious rival.[1] It is a complicated culinary treat demanding days of preparation, marking festive—sometimes sacred—occasions, signalling the cook's extraordinary concern for the diners, and requiring a special set of cultural skills and tastes to appreciate and consume appropriately. Tamales are served wrapped in corn husks which hold a soft outer paste of *masa harina* (a flour) and a rich inner mash prepared from the meat of a pig's head.

Only women make tamales. They cooperate to do so with domestic fanfare which stretches through days of buying the pigs' heads, stripping the meat, cooking the mash, preparing the paste, and stuffing, wrapping, and baking or boiling the final tamale. Women shop together because the heads are very bulky; they gather around huge, steaming pots to cook together as well. Tamales are thus labor-intensive food items which symbolize and also exaggerate women's routine nurturance of men. The ritual and cooperation of tamale cookery dramatically underscore women's shared monopoly of domestic tasks.

For middle-class women, such immersion in household affairs is generally taken as a measure of a woman's oppression. We often tend to equate power

and influence in the family with freedom from routine family tasks and find such tamale vignettes as those below disconcerting:

- At home in Texas for the winter, an elderly migrant woman, with her daughters-in-law, nieces, and goddaughter, spends several weeks preparing *200 dozen* tamales to distribute to friends, relatives, and local taverns for Christmas. The effort and expense involved are enormous, but she regards this enterprise as a useful and rewarding way to commemorate the holiday, to obligate those she may need to call on later, and to befriend the tavern owners so that they will watch over her male kin who drink there.

- In Illinois for six months a year, migrant women take precious time out from field labor to prepare elaborate feasts, with many tamales, commemorating the conclusion of each harvest (in asparagus, peas, tomatoes, pumpkins, and corn) as well as dates of biographical significance to others in the camp. An especially important day is the *quinceñiera* or fifteenth birthday, on which a young girl who will most likely spend her life in field labor is feted with tamales, cakes, and dancing all night, just as though she were a debutante.

- A young migrant, with the full support of his wife's kin as well as his own, sues his wife for divorce in a smalltown Illinois court. His grounds are that she refuses to cook him tamales and dances with other men at fiestas. A disconcerted Illinois judge refuses to grant a divorce on such grounds and the migrant community is outraged: women argue with special vehemence that to nurture and bind her husband a proper wife should cook him tamales.[2]

Incidents like the last, focused on women, their husbands, elaborate domestic nurturance, and the jealous circumscription of sexuality in marriage, again seem to reveal the most repressed and traditional of females. Because migrant women are so involved in family life and so seemingly submissive to their husbands, they have been described often as martyred purveyors of rural Mexican and Christian custom, tyrannized by excessively masculine, crudely domineering, rude and petty bullies in marriage, and blind to any world outside the family because they are suffocated by the concerns of kin.[3] Most disconcerting to outside observers is that migrant women seem to embrace such stereotypes: they argue that they *should* monopolize their foodways and that they should *not* question the authority of their husbands. If men want tamales, men should have them. But easy stereotypes can mislead; in exploring the lives of the poor, researchers must revise their own notions of family life, and this paper argues that foodways can provide crucial clues about how to do so.[4]

The paradox is this: among migrant workers both women and men are equally productive wage earners, and husbands readily acknowledge that without their wives' work their families cannot earn enough to survive. For migrants the division of labor between earning a living outside the home and managing household affairs is unknown; and the dilemma facing middle-class wives who may wish to work to supplement the family's income simply does not exist. Anthropologists exploring women's status cross-culturally argue that women are most influential when they share in the production of food and have some control over its distribution.[5] If such perspectives bear at all on migrant women, one might be led to question their seemingly unfathomable obsequiousness in marriage.

Anthropologists further argue that women's influence is even greater when they are not isolated from their kinswomen, when women can cooperate in production and join, for example, agricultural work with domestic duties and childcare.[6] Most migrant women spend their lives within large, closely knit circles of kin and their work days with their kinswomen. Marriage does not uproot or isolate a woman from her family, but rather doubles the relatives each partner can depend on and widens in turn the networks of everyone involved. The lasting power of marriage is reflected in statistics which show a divorce rate of 1 percent for migrant farmworkers from Texas, demonstrating the strength of a union bolstered by large numbers of relatives concerned that it go well.[7] Crucial to this concern is that neither partner is an economic drain on the family, and the Tejano pattern of early and lifelong marriages establishes some limit on the whimsy with which men can abuse and misuse their wives.

While anthropology traditionally rests on an appreciation of other cultures in their own contexts and on their own terms, it is very difficult to avoid class bias in viewing the lives of those who share partly in one's own culture, especially when the issue is something so close to home as food and who cooks it. Part of the problem may lie in appreciating what families are and what they do. For the poor, public and private domains are blurred in confusing ways, family affairs may be closely tied to economics, and women's work at gathering and obligating or *binding* relatives is neither trivial nor merely a matter of sentiment. Another problem may lie in focusing on the marital relationship as indicative of a woman's authority in the family. We too often forget that women are sisters, grandmothers, and aunts to men as well as wives. Foodways can help us rethink both of these problematic areas and understand how women elaborate domestic roles to knit families together, to obligate both male and female kin, and to nurture and bind their husbands as well.

THE SETTING FOR FAMILY LIFE

To understand migrant family foodways, it is important to explore first the economic circumstances within which they operate. The two thousand Tejano migrants who come to Prairie Junction, Illinois, to work in its harvest for six months a year are permanent residents of the Texas Rio Grande Valley, a lush and tropical agricultural paradise.[8] Dominating that landscape are great citrus and truck farms, highly mechanized operations which rely on commuters from across the Mexican border for whatever manual labor they need. Lacking jobs or substantial property at home, Tejanos in the valley exit for part of each year to earn a living in the north. Agricultural pay is low and employment is erratic, guaranteeing no income beyond a specific hourly wage and offering no fringe benefits in the event of unemployment or disability.[9] As a consequence, migrant workers must be very flexible in pursuing work and must at the same time forge some sort of security on their own to cushion frequent economic jolts. Migrants use kinship to construct both the security and the flexibility they need to manage a very marginal economic place.

In extended families, all members are productive workers (or at the very least share in childcare duties), and migrants find a great deal of security within families whose members are mutually committed to stretching scarce resources among them. Kin call on kin often for material aid, housing, and emotional support; they cooperate in field labor and domestic tasks and freely share food, money, time, and space. Because resources are only sporadically available to individuals, depending on kin eases hard times. In turn, most persons are sensitive to their relatives' needs not only because they care about them but also because they recognize the great value of reciprocity over time.

Migrant families are not easily placed in a convenient anthropological category for they implicate relatives in binding ways while allowing husbands and wives a great deal of freedom to move and settle when they need to, and to return whenever they like. This relative independence of nuclear families allows them to scatter and regroup when pursuing erratic opportunities to work, but always underlying their travels is a sense of a long-term place within a wider circle of kin. I call migrant families *convoys*, for they should be conceptualized as a process rather than a structure; they literally join persons in travel, in work, and through the life course, sharing food as well as the most intimate of concerns.

In the rural Texas settlements (*colonias*) where most migrants spend jobless winters, and in the stark barracks of Prairie Junction where they work each summer, convoys come together (1) to produce and share food for economic survival, (2) to surround food with ritual in order to save one another's dignity in degrading situations, (3) to reaffirm their cultural identity through marking and crossing boundaries with outsiders, and (4) to gather and bind kin, including spouses, to accompany them through life.

STRATEGIES FOR SURVIVAL: ROUTINE

Just as tamales ritually underscore women's domestic commitments, the everyday preparation and sharing of food routinely reaffirms family ties and allows families to work as efficiently and profitably as possible. Especially in emergencies, the sharing of food attests to migrants' visions of their lives as closely, mutually intertwined. The discussion which follows explores the foodways of the Texas *colonias* and the Prairie Junction migrant camps, the routines which surround them, and the ways they mobilize in crisis.

A newcomer to the Texas *colonias* is struck first by the appalling poverty in which migrants live there. Most are too far from the valley's urban centers to share in such amenities as running water, sewage disposal, or garbage collection. Hand-constructed shacks usually surround a primitive central area where fruits and vegetables grow, goats and chickens roam, and children play. The homes have many hastily-constructed additions and ill-defined rooms, attesting to the mobility of the individual family members and seemingly indicating an impermanence to domestic life. This feeling of

impermanence is belied, however, by the ongoing family-scale agricultural and pastoral system through which kin produce and share their own food over the Texas winters. Individuals may come and go; but through the extended family migrants adapt as peasants to those times when there is no income. The *colonias* offer evidence of creative domestic cooperation in stretching and sharing food within families and in the continuing migration of family members north from Mexico and back and forth to Illinois to work. These kin know that they can always find food from the winter gardens in Texas.

It is in this context that one can appreciate Sra. Compartida's great Christmas feasts of 200 dozen tamales for relatives, friends, and people she considers resources or contacts. She has worked for most of her life to allow her relatives in Mexico to join her, and in her old age she finds herself surrounded by kin who help her and whom she can count on. She feeds them still and is known especially for the beans and flour tortillas which she always cooks for those she welcomes home. She is clearly at the center of a convoy of cooperating kin whom she has organized and continues to remind of their obligations to one another.[10]

Sra. Compartida has worked for wages throughout her life and continues to do part-time housework when it is available. But, like other migrant women, she is a wife who appears much too submissive to her husband: she offers him extraordinary care, cooks everything he eats, and quietly abides his beer-drinking although she disapproves of it. On the other hand, her efforts on behalf of her family have compelled Sra. Compartida to learn English and cultivate respectable skills at negotiating bureaucracies such as immigration service. Her husband clearly depends on her as his ambassador, not only among kin but also with the outside Anglo world. They cooperate in setting their particular relationship apart through constructing roles in which he pretends to be boss, proclaiming extreme jealousy and expecting that she nurture him in elaborate ways. Yet one cannot dismiss their interaction by stereotype, for Sra. Compartida's authority and influence as mother, aunt, god-mother, sister, and grandmother are so definite that she simply will not fit a category. Tamales help her maintain that influence, and she uses them to express affection and obligate others, as well as gather a network of tavern owners who watch out for her husband when she cannot be there.

Domestic cooperation extends to the Illinois migrant camps, long barracks of small single rooms originally designed to accommodate prisoners of war. The camps offer domestic convoys highly inappropriate living situations, for they allot these single rooms to conjugal families, and through separating kin dramatically defy their routine commitment to shared domestic tasks. Because observers often prefer that each family convene in a tidy still-life world, migrant family life in the camps has been portrayed by some as very chaotic.[11] Kin realign in this inappropriate space to share domestic duties, care for children, cook cooperatively, allow husbands and wives conjugal privacy, and meet recurring emergency needs. While a conjugal family might remain basically committed to a particular room, kin move in and out of one another's rooms throughout the day, often carrying pots of food or other supplies. Children gather with elderly caretakers in a central outdoor spot (for the small rooms are stifling), and it is sometimes difficult to identify their mothers and fathers. Other kin who have settled temporarily in town visit the camp frequently, bringing food and children back and forth with them.

Women cook together routinely, sharing and stretching short supplies, combining scarce ingredients to preserve what they can of traditional Tejano tastes. They transport clay pots, tortilla presses, and chilies from their homes to the camps each year, and replenish short supplies throughout the summer as kin travel back and forth to Texas. Thus, surrounded by Illinois cornfields, women simmer beans in the barracks, save tomatoes from the fields for sauces when they can, and do their best to stretch the family's wages to support a large group of relatives.

STRATEGIES FOR SURVIVAL: CRISIS

If the tamale symbolizes elaborate celebration and nurturance, the tortilla is probably the most symbolic of the last bit of food a woman has to share. Simply, quickly, expertly made by migrant women, tortillas are treated very much like bread. Women roll a dough from *masa harina* or plain white flour, lard, salt, and water, flatten it with a press or by hand, and fry it on a dry griddle for just a few minutes. It is the least expensive and most basic of their food items, and when women worry (as they often do) that their supplies have dwindled to the ingredients for tortillas, they are speaking of real want. Tortillas stand for emergencies and it is through such crises that one can see perhaps most clearly how migrant family foodways work.

One family which has weathered many crises typical of migrant life is the Gomas. Their domestic convoy stretches through four generations and across several marriages, and their members are dispersed in Texas and Illinois but remain closely involved in one another's lives. The woman most central to this family is middle-aged and lives with her husband and their teenaged children off-and-on in Prairie Junction. Joana Goma and her husband have never been able to last for long in Illinois, for it is difficult for them to find work there, and they move back and forth to Texas often, sometimes leaving one of their children there for a time or returning with other young relatives so, as she puts it, "I won't

have to be lonesome for them all winter." Each summer some two dozen of the Goma's relatives arrive to work through the migrant season, and during that time Sra. Goma mobilizes on their behalf the resources of her Illinois networks—legal aid, public assistance, transportation, and a less formal example, a service station owner who will cash paychecks. She has worked hard to stretch and secure this network, often initially obligating friends through food. By sharing her locally famous taco dinners, Illinois residents act as though they are kin, and through time she finds that she can call on them for help as if they really were.

Although Joana Goma's marriage also appears quite traditional, with food and sex recurring metaphors for conjugal loyalty, she is the center of a world on which her husband and his kin depend.[12] When her sister-in-law was disabled because her hands were poisoned by pesticides, Sra. Goma saw to it that her own sister assumed the woman's cooking and housekeeping tasks. When her sister's nephew was stricken with hepatitis, Sra. Goma untangled the complicated legal procedures whereby a local hospital was compelled to provide free medical care for indigents, secured his bus fare to Texas from Traveler's Aid, and organized an investigation of the camp's drinking water. But these smaller, frequent emergencies are less telling than a more dramatic tortilla crisis in which the Gomas powerfully affirmed the importance of family to migrant workers.

One summer, Joana Goma's husband's brother, his wife, and their five children could not find work. They were penniless and planned to stay for several months, hoping there might be employment in a later crop. Joana brought her husband's employer to their home in the middle of the night to see for himself all those little children sleeping on the floor, thinking that she might persuade him to offer her brother-in-law a job. The employer stalled, and she worked at securing public aid for the family. This process is a lengthy one, and she soon found her household with no money or food left but tortillas, which they lived on for several days while Joana visited local ministers to ask for loans. On the day the welfare check at last arrived, her father and mother were critically injured in an automobile accident in Texas; and Joana and her children traveled there immediately, financed by this check.

Migrant family life may appear chaotic as kin realign inside and outside the camps, travel when they need to give support, and share what they have down to the last tortilla. Joana and her husband will never be rich, for they are unwilling to cast off the demands of kin. They love them, and they also seem to know that they are happier and more secure in the long run if they embed their marriage in a larger family circle. Again, Joana appears the most submissive of wives, but as a sister, daughter, and in-law she is the most highly regarded member of the family.

RITUAL AND AFFIRMATION

Beyond the routine domestic order and beyond using food in emergencies as a metaphor for the ways in which person's lives are intertwined, migrants give food special significance in ritual. Some observers have noted that migrants' rituals seem both wasteful and tawdry, at best a mere release of tension for the poor.[13] From a certain perspective migrant ritual seems absurd: women waste valuable working time preparing a feast to commemorate a harvest which is not really theirs and which in fact signals a slack time between crops; or women cook extravagantly to celebrate a young girl's birthday in what appears to be a tragic display of false consciousness about the course of her future life. Further, migrant rituals are tainted by the unavailability in Illinois of their preferred foods and crops: sometimes women must substitute barbecued chicken and potato chips for the tamales, chili, and beans which have for centuries marked such occasions and are deeply rooted in an oral tradition shared by women through recipes. Even so, such feasting seems to testify to migrants' involvement with kin in ways that reach far beyond the ritual moment.

Susana Sangre is the youngest of five sisters dispersed throughout Texas and Illinois. She stays fairly permanently with her mother, father, and small nephews, whom she cares for when she is not working in the fields. As her fifteenth birthday approached, her sisters gathered in the camp bringing tamales from Texas. With the help of their mother and other women, the Sangre sisters spent almost a week digging great barbecue pits, soaking pinto beans to cook, and purchasing items such as cakes and potato chips in local stores. On the evening of Susana's birthday, almost everyone in the camp gathered to kiss and congratulate her, present her with inexpensive storebought gifts (most often handkerchiefs or jewelry), and feast and dance all night. She wore a long pink bridesmaid's dress, while the guests remained in their work clothes. Although her outfit seemed incongruous, it clearly reflected her honored status at the event, as did the great whoops and cheers which surrounded her as she opened each gift, initiated the dancing with her father, and graciously endured the evening's jolly courting. The effort and expense incurred by Susana's family were enormous, and one might argue that they should not delude her through such feasts about the significance or possibilities of her life.

The *quinceñiera* feast does signal the importance of her life to *them*, and the lavish ritual expressions which surround occasions such as this work to bind kin, recreate obligations, and promise reciprocity. Most persons know that they too will be commemorated at the appropriate times, and that their lives are significant to others as well. Further, through ritual, migrants dramatically defy the degrading "total institutions" in which they spend half their lives: the monotonous surroundings and crowded, unsanitary conditions which tacitly proclaim their worthlessness.[14] Celebrating the harvest proclaims their part in it and denies that they are its slaves. And to prepare their own foods when possible is to reaffirm the dignity of Tejano identity in an Anglo world which offers it little respect, as well as to root the celebrants in a long and great tradition mediated—made present—by the family.

STRANGERS AND FRIENDS

Tamales are distinct and unique by place: Texans prepare them differently from Californians, Salvadorian migrants to this country often disdain those made in Mexico. Tamales testify to rich oral tradition, for the most part women's tradition, about how to buy and cook them. Although many Anglos in the Southwest enjoy Mexican food and have in part transformed the tamale into a regional artifact, for Tejano migrants the real thing is deeply theirs, rooted in their homes, and kept alive by the women who prepare, distribute, and teach others about it.[15]

In Prairie Junction this distribution is critical not only in knitting together families, but in negotiating relations with outsiders as well. Such negotiations may be crucial to family life—as, for example, when migrants befriend Anglos who have the skills, power, or resources to help their kin in various ways. In these negotiations it is evident how misleading it is to proclaim family life an isolating, stultifying, belittling activity for women, as women use food to make friends and allies as well as to identify outsiders who will or will not commit themselves to the Tejano family's concerns. Women ply prospective friends with tamales and tacos, taking an acceptance of the hospitality they offer both as a show of respect for Tejano culture and as a tentative commitment to kin-like relations.

Ethnic boundaries, of course, remain important.[16] Migrant workers do not expect that prospective Anglo friends will relish these foods as Tejanos do. Migrants joke that "gringos' stomachs are too weak" and claim that they must smuggle chilies into Illinois restaurants so that they can season Anglo food properly. Many appreciated the respectful, self-deprecating remarks of a young poverty program lawyer who found that he could not eat the tacos women offered him without a healthy dose of ketchup. While potential friends should be open to traditional Tejano food, it is best appreciated by Tejanos themselves. Significantly, those Tejanos who ingratiate themselves to Anglos are labelled "Tio Tacos," the Spanish equivalent of Uncle Toms: thus, food becomes a metaphor for those who seem untrue to their ethnic identity.[17] Migrants use foodways to preserve a sense of who they are in an alien cultural setting just as they mobilize foodways to approach and appraise friends, and, again, it seems that women purposefully monopolize those skills necessary for plying and obligating others and for keeping ethnicity alive.

The most active cook in Prairie Junction is also married to the president of a self-help organization whose goal is to help those migrants who wish to "settle out," or leave the migrant stream and try to build a life in Illinois. Although Sra. Mezclado's husband wields the official community action power among Prairie Junction's Tejanos, she is the one who mobilizes several dozen women to cook the large benefit dinners on which the organization depends for funds. Sr. Mezclado's networking philosophy is consistent with the mutual assistance tenets of Tejano family life: he and his organization hold that no conjugal family can "settle out" without aid in procuring furniture, housing, and employment. Yet even in this context of outreach beyond the family, Sra. Mezclado continues to monopolize the foodways, and, with other women, to use food to identify and enlist the support of friends. Although she seems obsequious in the home, her husband acknowledges her authority and often speaks of women generally as living representations of the Lady of Guadalupe.[18] Sr. Mezclado is especially obedient to his own mother who, when she visits, rouses him early every day for church and insists that he keep a large statue of the Lady enshrined on his television set. Other men mock these traditional religious activities because they see Sr. Mezclado as an otherwise thoroughly modern man, but he argues that his mother is "*la jefa* [the boss]. I just can't say no to her." Again the marital paradox: while acknowledging the influence of women like Sr. Mezclado's mother, both spouses insist upon constructing a marital relationship which severely circumscribes sexual nuances, grants the husband seemingly whimsical authority, and offers the wife an unchallenged monopoly over domestic life.

GATHERING KIN: MEN, WOMEN AND MARRIAGE

Families and family foodways must be worked at, and among migrants it is women who most vigorously do so. Women are much more likely than men to be involved as liaisons among kin, in stretching networks to draw in kin-like persons who can be helpful, providing the props which allow persons to preserve their dignity in demeaning situations, and negotiating ethnic boundaries.

While young, women begin to build domestic convoys whose members will accompany and sustain them through life. Marriage is a crucial step in that process wherein women find both husbands and many more kin who will share their lives. Even very young and seemingly modern women uphold traditional roles when they marry. One such woman, Dolores Abierta, works in the migrant children's educational program as a teacher's aide. She feels flattered that her husband circles the school in his pick-up truck to watch over her when he can and that he forbids her to swim or wear shorts in public. He also "presses on my stomach when my period is late," "holds me in his lap and lets me cry like a baby," and "loves my cooking." Dolores takes great pride in the fact that "when we got married he was skinny and I was fat. Now it is the other way around." She also respects the limits he places on conjugal life and appreciates his concern that sexuality be confined by marriage: "Before we got married my brother-in-law's cousin used to come into my room and bother me. Now he leaves me alone."

Dolores makes it very clear that she will not allow any of her four brothers to marry women who will not obey them, cook their meals for them, and be ever ready for their sexual overtures. She polices her brothers accordingly, and she is especially wary of Anglo women, "who don't know how to be a good wife." At the same time, she gathers her kin around her, bringing her crippled mother from Texas to live in the migrant camp, giving her husband's cousin the car so "he'll have wheels," arranging for her husband's mother to change rooms so that they can be closer together and so that Dolores can learn from her how to cook tamales.

Within their convoys of kin, women's special nurturance of their husbands makes a good deal of sense. Not only do they bind men more and more closely, but also both women and men cooperate in setting marriage apart as something special within a wide circle of people sharing resources as well as the most intimate of concerns. Sexuality is no longer a larger issue. And while women cook often for many people, in marriage the obligation is immediate and forthright and binding: their husbands must have tamales.

NOTES

1. There is a great deal of ambivalence among scholars and the people themselves about the appropriate ethnic label for migrant workers from Texas and of Mexican descent. Many migrants refer to themselves as "Tejanos" (or Texans), others prefer the term "Mexicans," others "Mexican Americans," still others "Chicanos." "Tejano" is used here, because it seems to capture the migrants' sense of themselves, as bicultural with the caution that some migrants might prefer to be identified in other ways.

2. These incidents are reported from the author's personal participant-observation in Texas and Illinois.

3. Cf. Leo Grebler, Joan Moore, and Ralph Guzman, *The Mexican-American People* (New York: Free Press, 1970); William Madsen, *The Mexican-Americans of South Texas* (New York: Holt, Rinehart and Winston, 1973); Harlan Padfield and William Martin, *Farmers, Workers, and Machines* (Tucson: Univ. of Arizona Press, 1965).

4. Recently a number of scholars have begun to revise earlier views which held that the poor were virtually without culture, that the family life of the poor in particular was dysfunctional; cf. Carol Stack, *All Our Kin* (New York: Harper and Row, 1974), and Stanley West and June Macklin, eds., *The Chicano Experience* (Boulder, Col.: Westview Press, 1980). However, few scholars have used foodways to focus on the culture of the poor.

5. Cf. Judith K. Brown, "A Note on the Division of Labor by Sex," *American Anthropologist* 72 (1970): 1073–78; Louise Lamphere and Michelle Rosaldo, eds., *Woman, Culture, and Society* (Stanford, Calif.: Stanford Univ. Press, 1974); Peggy Sanday, "Toward a Theory of the Status of Women," *American Anthropologist* 75 (1973): 1682–1700.

6. See note 5 above.

7. Cf. W. Eberstein and W. P. Frisbee, "Differences in Marital Instability Among Mexican-Americans, Blacks, and Anglos: 1960 and 1970," *Social Problems* 23 (1976): 609–21; *Census of the US Population* 19 (Washington, D.C.: U.S. Department of Commerce, Bureau of the Census, 1970).

8. The name of the town and personal names are pseudonyms.

9. For more on this subject, see Ernesto Galarza, Herman Gallegos, and Julian Samora, *Mexican-Americans in the Southwest* (Santa Barbara, Calif.: McNally and Loftin, 1969); Lamar Jones, *Mexican-American Labor Problems in Texas* (San Francisco: R&E Research Associates, 1971); John Martinez, *Mexican Emigration to the US.: 1919–1930* (San Francisco: R&E Research Associates, 1971); Carey McWilliams, *North from Mexico* (New York: Greenwood Press, 1968); David North, *The Border Crossers* (Washington, D.C.: Department of Labor, 1970); Brett Williams, *The Trip Takes Us: Chicago Migrants on the Prairie* (Ph.D. diss. Univ. of Illinois at Urbana, 1975); Brett Williams, "Chicano Farm Labor in Eastern Illinois," *Journal of the Steward Anthropological Society* 7 (1976); Dean Williams, *Political and Economic Aspects of Mexican Immigration into California and the U.S. Since 1941* (San Francisco: R&E Research Associates, 1973).

10. Sra. Compartida has fostered almost a dozen children, most of whom were separated from their parents as infants. Recently, she has taken both her six-year-old grandniece and her very old and dying mother to live with her. One example of her kin-gathering activities occurred when she saw a young man in an orchard with, as she put it, "my husband's face," convinced him that he was her husband's nephew who had been separated from the family as a small child, took him home and reincorporated him in the family with great celebration and a tamale dinner.

11. See especially William Friedland and Dorothy Nelkin, *Migrant* (New York: Holt, Rinehart and Winston, 1971), treating Black migrants on the east coast.

12. He frequently threatens to "run off with a little `mojadita!' (the diminutive female term for `wetback')," she, to "throw him out and let him cook for himself, just like he did my cat." She also likes to boast about the time her doctor "played my legs, right in front of Pedro."

13. Friedland and Nelkin.

14. "Total institution" is a term used by Erving Goffman in *Asylums* (Garden City, N.J.: Doubleday, 1961). It refers to those institutions which are qualitatively more encompassing than most, segregating and degrading their inmates in dramatic ways, often by denying them ordinary access to the props and routines by which they build their lives.

15. For example, Gerald Ford was ridiculed by the San Antonio, Texas, press when, during his presidential campaign there, he attempted to eat a tamale without first removing the corn husk.

16. Cf. Frederik Barth, *Ethnic Groups and Boundaries* (Boston: Little, Brown, 1969), who argues that ethnic identity is realized most dramatically in the negotiation of boundaries among groups.

17. One such "Tio Taco" is criticized by others for avoiding his Tejano friends and trying very hard to align himself with his fellow (Anglo) factory workers. That he does this by taking big plates of tacos to the factory every day is especially offensive, for this is women's work. And that the Anglo workers do not reciprocate by attending the migrant organization's benefit dinners seems to indicate that "they don't care enough about our food to pay for it."

18. The Lady of Guadalupe is Tejanos' most beloved folk saint. She emerged in Mexico at the time of the Spanish Conquest, appears faintly Indian, and has been carried all over the world by Mexican migrants who turn to her frequently for help with many varied matters. As a saint, she is much like an earthly woman: she has no direct power of her own, but she has a great deal of influence as a liaison with Christ and because of this is both loving and approachable.

REFERENCES

Barth, Frederik. 1969. *Ethnic Groups and Boundaries*. Boston: Little, Brown.

Brown, Judith K. "A Note on the Division of Labor by Sex," *American Anthropologist* 72 (1970): 1073–78.

Census of the US Population 19. 1970. Washington, D.C.: U.S. Department of Commerce, Bureau of the Census.

Eberstein, W. and W. P. Frisbee, 1976. "Differences in Marital Instability Among Mexican-Americans, Blacks, and Anglos: 1960 and 1970," *Social Problems* 23: 609–21.

Friedland, William and Dorothy Nelkin. 1971. *Migrant*. New York: Holt, Rinehart and Winston.

Galarza, Ernesto, Herman Gallegos, and Julian Samora. 1969. *Mexican-Americans in the Southwest*. Santa Barbara, Calif.: McNally and Loftin.

Grebler, Leo, Joan Moore, and Ralph Guzman. 1970. *The Mexican-American People*. New York: Free Press.

Goffman, Erving. 1961. *Asylums*. Garden City, N.J.: Doubleday.

Jones, Lamar. 1971. *Mexican-American Labor Problems in Texas*. San Francisco: R&E Research Associates.

Lamphere, Louise and Michelle Rosaldo, eds., 1974. *Woman, Culture, and Society*. Stanford, Calif.: Stanford Univ. Press.

Madsen, William. 1973. *The Mexican-Americans of South Texas*. New York: Holt, Rinehart and Winston.

Martinez, John. 1971. *Mexican Emigration to the US.: 1919–1930*. San Francisco: R&E Research Associates.

McWilliams, Carey. 1968. *North from Mexico*. New York: Greenwood Press.

North, David. 1970. *The Border Crossers*. Washington, D.C.: Department of Labor.

Padfield, Harlan and William Martin. 1965. *Farmers, Workers, and Machines*. Tucson: Univ. of Arizona Press.

Sanday, Peggy. 1973. "Toward a Theory of the Status of Women," *American Anthropologist* 75: 1682–1700.

Stack, Carol. 1974. *All Our Kin*. New York: Harper and Row.

West, Stanley and June Macklin, eds., 1980. *The Chicano Experience*. Boulder, Col.: Westview Press.

Williams, Brett. 1975. *The Trip Takes Us: Chicago Migrants on the Prairie*. Ph.D. diss. Univ. of Illinois at Urbana.

Williams, Brett. 1976. "Chicano Farm Labor in Eastern Illinois," *Journal of the Steward Anthropological Society* 7.

Williams, Dean. 1973. *Political and Economic Aspects of Mexican Immigration into California and the U.S. Since 1941*. San Francisco: R&E Research Associates.

Uterine Families and the Women's Community

Margery Wolf

Margery Wolf is professor of anthropology and women's studies at the University of Iowa and is known especially for her fieldwork in Taiwan. Her research interests include feminist theory and gender studies, and she has published extensively on China.

Few women in China experience the continuity that is typical of the lives of the menfolk. A woman can and, if she is ever to have any economic security, must provide the links in the male chain of descent, but she will never appear in anyone's genealogy as that all-important name connecting the past to the future. If she dies before she is married, her tablet will not appear on her father's altar; although she was a temporary member of his household, she was not a member of his family. A man is born into his family and remains a member of it throughout his life and even after his death. He is identified with the family from birth, and every action concerning him, up to and including his death, is in the context of that group. Whatever other uncertainties may trouble his life, his place in the line of ancestors provides a permanent setting. There is no such secure setting for a woman. She will abruptly leave the household into which she is born, either as an infant or as an adult bride, and enter another whose members treat her with suspicion or even hostility.

A man defines his family as a large group that includes the dead, and not-yet-born, and the living members of his household. But how does a woman define her family? This is not a question that China specialists often consider, but from their treatment of the family in general, it would seem that a woman's family is identical with that of the senior male in the household in which she lives. Although I have never asked, I imagine a Taiwanese man would define a woman's family in very much those same terms. Women, I think, would give quite a different answer. They do not have an unchanging place, assigned at birth, in any group, and their view of the family reflects this.

When she is a child, a woman's family is defined for her by her mother and to some extent by her grandmother. No matter how fond of his daughter the father may be, she is only a temporary member of his household and useless to his family—he cannot even marry her to one of his sons as he could an adopted daughter. Her irrelevance to her father's family in turn affects the daughter's attitude toward it. It is of no particular interest to her, and the need to maintain its continuity has little meaning for her beyond the fact that this continuity matters a great deal to some of the people she loves. As a child she probably accepts to some degree her grandmother's orientation toward the family: the household, that is, those people who live together and eat together, including perhaps one or more of her father's married brothers and their children. But the group that has the most meaning for her and with which she will have the most lasting ties is the smaller, more cohesive unit centering on her mother, that is, the uterine family—her mother and her mother's children. Father is important to the group, just as grandmother is important to some of the children, but he is not quite a member of it, and for some uterine families he may even be "the enemy." As the girl grows up and her grandmother dies and a brother or two marries, she discovers that her mother's definition of the family is becoming less exclusive and may even include such outsiders as her brother's new wife. Without knowing precisely when it happened, she finds that her brother's interests and goals have shifted in a direction she cannot follow. Her mother does not push her aside, but when the mother speaks of the future, she speaks in terms of her son's future. Although the mother sees her uterine family as adding new members and another generation, her daughter sees it as dissolving, leaving her with strong particular relationships, but with no group to which she has permanent loyalties and obligations.

When a young woman marries, her formal ties with the household of her father are severed. In one of the rituals of the wedding ceremony the bride's father or brothers symbolically inform her by means of spilt water that she, like the water, may never return, and when her wedding sedan chair passes over the threshold of her father's house, the doors are slammed shut behind her. If she is ill-treated by her husband's family, her father's family may intervene, but unless her parents are willing to bring her home and support her for the rest of her life (and most parents are not), there is little they can do beyond shaming the other family. This is usually enough.

As long as her mother is alive, the daughter will continue her contacts with her father's household by as many visits as her new situation allows. If she lives nearby she may visit every few days, and no matter where she lives she must at least be allowed to return at New Year. After her mother dies her visits may become perfunctory, but her relations with at least one member of her uterine family, the group that centered on her mother, remain strong. Her brother plays an important ritual role throughout her life. She may gradually lose contact with her sisters as she and they become more involved with their own children, but her relations with her brother continue. When her sons marry, he is the guest of honor at the wedding feasts, and when her daughters marry he must give a small banquet in their honor. If her sons wish to divide their father's estate, it is their mother's brother who is called on to supervise. And when she dies, the coffin cannot be closed until her brother determines to his own satisfaction that she died a natural death and that her husband's family did everything possible to prevent it.

With the ritual slam of her father's door on her wedding day, a young woman finds herself quite literally without a family. She enters the household of her husband—a man who in an earlier time, say fifty years ago, she would never have met and who even today, in modern rural Taiwan, she is unlikely to know very well. She is an outsider, and for Chinese an outsider is always an object of deep suspicion. Her husband and her father-in-law do not see her as a member of their family. But they do see her as essential to it; they have gone to great expense to bring her into their household for the purpose of bearing a new generation for their family. Her mother-in-law, who was mainly responsible for negotiating the terms of her entry, may harbor some resentment over the hard bargaining, but she is nonetheless eager to see another generation added to *her* uterine family. A mother-in-law often has the same kind of ambivalence toward her daughter-in-law as she has toward her husband—the younger woman seems a member of her family at times and merely a member of the household at others. The new bride may find that her

husband's sister is hostile or at best condescending, both attitudes reflecting the daughter's distress at an outsider who seems to be making her way right into the heart of the family.

Chinese children are taught by proverb, by example, and by experience that the family is the source of their security, and relatives the only people who can be depended on. Ostracism from the family is one of the harshest sanctions that can be imposed on erring youth. One of the reasons mainlanders as individuals are considered so untrustworthy on Taiwan is the fact that they are not subject to the controls of (and therefore have no fear of ostracism from) their families. If a timid new bride is considered an object of suspicion and potentially dangerous because she is a stranger, think how uneasy her own first few months must be surrounded by strangers. Her irrelevance to her father's family may result in her having little reverence for descent lines, but she has warm memories of the security of the family her mother created. If she is ever to return to this certainty and sense of belonging, a woman must create her own uterine family by bearing children, a goal that happily corresponds to the goals of the family into which she has married. She may gradually create a tolerable niche for herself in the household of her mother-in-law, but her family will not be formed until she herself forms it of her own children and grandchildren. In most cases, by the time she adds grandchildren, the uterine family and the household will almost completely overlap, and there will be another daughter-in-law struggling with loneliness and beginning a new uterine family.

The ambiguity of a man's position in relation to the uterine families accounts for much of the hostility between mother-in-law and daughter-in-law. There is no question in the mind of the older woman but that her son *is* her family. The daughter-in-law might be content with this situation once her sons are old enough to represent her interests in the household and in areas strictly under men's control, but until then, she is dependent on her husband. If she were to be completely absorbed into her mother-in-law's family—a rare occurrence unless she is a *simpua*—there would be little or no conflict; but under most circumstances she must rely on her husband, her mother-in-law's son, as her spokesman, and here is where the trouble begins. Since it is usually events within the household that she wishes to affect, and the household more or less overlaps with her mother-in-law's uterine family, even a minor foray by the younger woman suggests to the older one an all-out attack on everything she has worked so hard to build in the years of her own loneliness and insecurity. The birth of grandchildren further complicates their relations, for the one sees them as new members for her family and the other as desperately needed recruits to her own small circle of security.

In summary, my thesis contends . . . that because we have heretofore focused on men when examining the Chinese family—a reasonable approach to a patrilineal system—we have missed not only some of the system's subtleties but also its near-fatal weaknesses. With a male focus we see the Chinese family as a line of descent, bulging to encompass all the members of a man's household and spreading out through his descendants. With a female focus, however, we see the Chinese family not as a continuous line stretching between the vague horizons of past and future, but as a contemporary group that comes into existence out of one woman's need and is held together insofar as she has the strength to do so, or, for that matter, the need to do so. After her death the uterine family survives only in the mind of her son and is symbolized by the special attention he gives her earthly remains and her ancestral tablet. The rites themselves are demanded by the ideology of the patriliny, but the meaning they hold for most sons is formed in the uterine family. The uterine family has no ideology, no formal structure, and no public existence. It is built out of sentiments and loyalties that die with its members, but it is no less real for all that. The descent lines of men are born and nourished in the uterine families of women, and it is here that a male ideology that excludes women makes its accommodations with reality.

Women in rural Taiwan do not live their lives in the walled courtyards of their husbands' households. If they did, they might be as powerless as their stereotype. It is in their relations in the outside world (and for women in rural Taiwan that world consists almost entirely of the village) that women develop sufficient backing to maintain some independence under their powerful mothers-in-law and even occasionally to bring the men's world to terms. A successful venture into the men's world is no small feat when one recalls that the men of a village were born there and are often related to one another, whereas the women are unlikely to have either the ties of childhood or the ties of kinship to unite them. All the same, the needs, shared interests, and common problems of women are reflected in every village in a loosely knit society that can when needed be called on to exercise considerable influence.

Women carry on as many of their activities as possible outside the house. They wash clothes on the riverbank, clean and pare vegetables at a communal pump, mend under a tree that is a known meetingplace, and stop to rest on a bench or group of stones with other women. There is a continual moving back and forth between kitchens, and conversations are carried on from open doorways through the long, hot afternoons of summer. The shy young girl who enters the village as a bride is examined as frankly and suspiciously by the women as an animal that is up for sale. If she is deferential to her elders, does not criticize or compare her new world unfavorably with the one she has left, the older residents will gradually accept her presence on the edge of their conversations and stop changing the topic to general subjects when she brings the family laundry to scrub on the rocks near them. As the young bride meets other girls in her position, she makes allies for the future, but she must also develop relationships with the older women. She learns to use considerable discretion in making and receiving confidences, for a girl who gossips freely about the affairs of her husband's household may find herself labeled a troublemaker. On the other hand, a girl who is too reticent may find herself always on the outside of the group, or worse yet, accused of snobbery. I described in *The House of Lim* the plight of Lim Chui-ieng, who had little village backing in her troubles with her husband and his family as the result of her arrogance toward the women's community. In Peihotien the young wife of the storekeeper's son suffered a similar lack of support. Warned by her husband's parents not to be too "easy" with the other villagers lest they try to buy things on credit, she obeyed to the point of being considered unfriendly by the women of the village. When she began to have serious troubles with her husband and eventually his family, there was no one in the village she could turn to for solace, advice, and, most important, peacemaking.

Once a young bride has established herself as a member of the women's community, she has also established for herself a certain amount of protection. If the members of her husband's family step beyond the limits of propriety in their treatment of her—such as refusing to allow her to return to her natal home for her brother's wedding or beating her without serious justification—she can complain to a woman friend, preferably older, while they are washing vegetables at the communal pump. The story will quickly spread to the other women, and one of them will take it on herself to check the facts with another member of the girl's household. For a few days the matter will be thoroughly discussed whenever a few women gather. In a young wife's first few years in the community, she can expect to have her mother-in-law's side of any disagreement given fuller weight than her own—her mother-in-law has, after all, been a part of the community a lot longer. However, the discussion itself will serve to curb many offenses. Even if the older woman knows that public opinion is falling to her side, she will still be somewhat more judicious about refusing her daughter-in-law's next request. Still, the daughter-in-law who hopes to make use of the village forum to depose her mother-in-law or at least gain herself special privilege will discover just how important the prerogatives of age and length of residence are. Although the women can serve as a powerful protective force for their defenseless younger members, they are also a very conservative force in the village.

Taiwanese women can and do make use of their collective power to lose face for their menfolk in order to influence decisions that are ostensibly not theirs to make. Although young women may have little or no influence over their husbands and would not dare express an unsolicited opinion (and perhaps not even a solicited one) to their fathers-in-law, older women who have raised their sons properly retain considerable influence over their sons' actions, even in activities exclusive to men. Further, older women who have displayed years of good judgment are regularly consulted by their husbands about major as well as minor economic and social projects. But even men who think themselves free to ignore the opinions of their women are never free of their own concept, face. It is much easier to lose face than to have face. We once asked a male friend in Peihotien just what "having face" amounted to. He replied, "When no one is talking about a family, you can say it has face." This is precisely where women wield their power. When a man behaves in a way that they consider wrong, they talk about him—not only among themselves, but to their sons and husbands. No one "tells him how to mind his own business," but it becomes abundantly clear that he is losing face and by continuing in this manner may bring shame to the family of his ancestors and descendants. Few men will risk that.

The rules that a Taiwanese man must learn and obey to be a successful member of his society are well developed, clear, and relatively easy to stay within. A Taiwanese woman must also learn the rules, but if she is to be a successful woman, she must learn not to stay within them, but to *appear* to stay within them; to manipulate them, but not to appear to be manipulating them; to teach them to her children, but not to depend on her children for her protection. A truly successful Taiwanese woman is a rugged individualist who has learned to depend largely on herself while appearing to lean on her father, her husband, and her son. The contrast between the terrified young bride and the loud, confident, often lewd old woman who has outlived her mother-in-law and her husband reflects the tests met and passed by not strictly following the rules and by making purposeful use of those who must. The Chinese male's conception of women as "narrowhearted" and socially inept may well be his vague recognition of this facet of women's power and technique.

The women's subculture in rural Taiwan is, I believe, below the level of consciousness. Mothers do not tell their about-to-be-married daughters how to establish themselves in village society so that they may have some protection from an oppressive family situation, nor do they warn them to gather their children into an exclusive circle under their own control. But girls grow up in village society and see their mothers and sisters-in-law settling their differences, to keep them from a public airing or presenting them for the women's community to judge. Their mothers have created around them the meaningful unit in their fathers' households, and when they are desperately lonely and unhappy in the households of their husbands, what they long for is what they have lost. . . . [Some] areas in the subculture of women . . . mesh perfectly into the main culture of the society. The two cultures are not symbiotic because they are not sufficiently independent of one another, but neither do they share identical goals or necessarily use the same means to reach the goals they do share. Outside the village the women's subculture seems not to exist. The uterine family also has no public existence, and appears almost as a response to the traditional family organized in terms of a male ideology.

Male and Female in Hopi Thought and Action

Alice Schlegel

Alice Schlegel holds a Ph.D. from Northwestern University, awarded in 1971. Currently a professor in the department of anthropology at the University of Arizona, she has carried out fieldwork in the southwestern United States among Native Americans; her research specialties include cross-cultural methods, adolescence, and gender.

When traditional Hopi women are asked "Who are more important, women or men?" a common reply is "We are, because we are the mothers," with the qualification that men are important, too, as the messengers to the gods.

This paper will examine some of the assumptions that have been made about female reproduction, separation of the sexes, and the position of women. In recently published literature on female status, the universally secondary position of women in society has been asserted, and it has been accounted for by women's role in bearing and rearing children (Chodorow 1974; Ortner 1974; Rosaldo 1974). It is furthermore implied that this secondary position becomes one of subordination when the sexes operate within separate domains, the public for men and the domestic for women (Rosaldo 1974, pp. 39–40). These assertions are contradicted by data from traditional Hopi society, where the sexes are divided into two domains of action, and women's role in the reproduction and maintenance of life is the conscious justification for the position of equality they enjoy.

We shall examine the separation of activity between the domestic organization of the lineage and household, under the control of a female head, and the religious and political organization of the village, under the control of male community leaders. We shall also note the level of the clan, midway between household and community, in which authority is shared between a brother and sister pair. We shall look at the Hopi concept of sexual interdependence—between male and female actors in the social scene and between principles of maleness and femaleness in ideology.

The key word here, I believe, is *balance*. Many societies operate with underlying concepts of ideological dualism. A widespread form of dualism either focuses upon or includes male-female relationships. Such notions are found both in tribal societies . . . and in literate civilizations such as China, where *yin-yang* is a core symbol for a range of binary oppositions. But dualism does not necessitate balance, or equality between the parts. It would require a lengthy excursion into Hopi metaphysics and cosmology to treat adequately the concept of balance as applied to man's nature and the universe, and that is beyond the scope of this paper. But the Hopi relationship of equality between the sexes, each with its own nature and social roles, will be examined in this light.

DOMESTIC LIFE

The Women in the Household

When a Hopi child is born, it is assured of a place within the matrilocal household and the matrilineal clan. If it is a boy, he will become a companion and helper to his father, who will teach him to farm, hunt, and herd. He is a potential heir to any of the religious-political positions held by his "uncles," or mothers' brothers. If it is a girl, she is welcomed as a source of continuity of the household and the clan. When she grows up, she or one of her sisters will inherit her mother's house and be responsible for the maintenance of her aged parents. As a mother and sister, she will have responsibility for many of the ceremonial objects used by her sons and brothers. She will "feed" the sacred masks by sprinkling them with cornmeal, thus assuring continual life and power to these necessary features of certain ritual performances. When asked, the Hopi insist that they wish for sons and daughters equally; however, women state that "you raise up a daughter for yourself, but you raise up a son for somebody else." Daughters remain at home, whereas sons are sent out upon marriage to become the providers and progenitors in the households of other women.

When a girl marries, she brings her husband into her household to work under the direction of her father and the ultimate authority of her mother. If she is not the heiress to the house, her husband will build her a house of her own, adjacent to or near her mother's house. Although he builds the house, it belongs to her and she can request him to leave at any time. Furthermore, all household goods, except the personal property of men, belong to her. Her husband farms fields assigned to her through her clan, and when the produce is brought in and she has formally thanked him, it is hers to allocate or dispose of as she sees fit. Of course, her husband is free to leave and move in with another woman or return to the house of his mother or sister, but in any event he lives in a house controlled by a female head. He moves into his wife's house as a stranger, and it is only after he has proven his worth through providing for her family that he earns a position of respect within it. The Hopi recognize this by saying that "a man's place is outside the house." All the long hours of labor in this dry and uncertain climate go to benefit a household and clan over which he has no authority beyond the authority he exerts over his young children, and his domestic satisfaction lies in the love and respect he earns as a good father and provider.

As might be expected, young men are none too eager to marry. To a woman, however, marriage is essential, as she needs a provider for herself and her children. While illegitimate children are not looked down upon, they are at a disadvantage in that they have no father to provide for them. A man who never married the mother of his child, or who has left her, is expected to contribute to his child's support, but rarely does so to the extent of fathers living in the home. A woman can turn to her brothers for some help, but this is usually burdensome for these men who have enough to do just taking care of their own families.

As a girl matures, she is under parental pressure to bring a husband into the house, for her father is eager for the help a son-in-law can give. In addition, her marriage is necessary for her life in the Afterworld: the wedding robes that her husband's male relatives weave for her become her shroud and the vehicle by which her spirit is transported into the world of the dead.

The boy, however, is under no such pressures. He enjoys his relatively carefree life as a young bachelor and is somewhat reluctant to take on the heavy responsibilities of marriage. Marriages are normally not arranged, and the burden of finding a spouse falls mainly upon the girl. Girls initiate a marriage by making the proposal, which may or may not be accepted. The transfer of labor and loyalty to the wife's household is symbolized by a ceremonial prestation [payment of money] of cornmeal to the groom's household, conceptualized by the Hopi as "paying for him," and by the short period of groom service that the bride performs by grinding corn and cooking for her husband's household while her wedding robes are being woven.[1] Once the wedding rituals are completed, the groom moves into the bride's house and "goes over to her side." Few men beyond their mid-twenties remain bachelors in spite of reluctance to marry, for the good Hopi is one who accepts the heavy duties of community responsibility, and fatherhood, highly valued by the Hopi, is one of the ways a man can contribute to the village.

Unlike the woman, the Hopi man has his responsibilities divided between two social units. To the household of his wife he owes his labor and his protectiveness as a father and a husband. However, he also owes loyalty to his natal household and clan. When clan matters arise, such as the assignment of clan lands or clan participation in ceremonies, male clan members are expected to take part. If a man holds a religious-political position, inherited through the clan, he must train one of his young clan mates, usually his sister's son, to succeed him. To a man who holds such a position, life is doubly busy—not only must he fulfill his domestic duties but he must also spend a great deal of time involved in ceremonial activities. Most of these leaders are middle-aged and old men, who are likely to have one or more sons-in-law in the house to help with farming and herding.

Women have no such potential conflict of loyalties. Once they have succeeded in marrying and bearing children, particularly daughters, they are established as responsible adults in the eyes of the clan and the community. They have produced life, and their role lies in the maintenance of physical life through feeding their families and others, and spiritual life through feeding the sacred objects. Most of this activity goes to benefit their own house and clan. Toward their husbands' natal house and clan they owe little beyond some contributions of food during periods of ceremonial activity, and a relationship of respect exists between them. Their greatest duties to households other than their own revolve around their roles as grandmothers and "aunts," or father's sisters, to the children of their sons and brothers, with whom they have an amiable joking relationship.

Hopi women appear to be in an enviable position when compared to women in male-dominant societies. Indeed, when the system works as it is designed to, these women are self-assured and confident of their place in the world. However, their very strength is also the source of their vulnerability. While they can make the final household decisions, they are dependent upon those men who have married into the house. They must have a husband or a son-in-law to provide for them. Fathers grow old and unable to work, brothers are busy with their own families, and sons marry and move out. It is critical for a woman to get and keep a husband, while men always have the alternative of moving in with their mothers or sisters. If a woman and her husband separate, her relatives are likely to urge her to forget the quarrel and take him back, saying: "One of your own people might be willing to plant for you, but only a husband will give you meat and clothes" (Forde 1931, p. 382). The Hopi emphasize the need for tact in marital relations, for they believe that love and the willing acceptance of responsibility cement the marital bonds. Even infidelity, said to be the most common cause of marital trouble, should be overlooked if possible, or at least dealt with by appealing to the errant partner's sense of marital and parental responsibility.[2]

The Woman and Her Male Kin

A woman is not under the authority of her husband, nor is she under the authority of her brother or mother's brother, as is the case in some other matrilineal societies (Schlegel 1972). It is true that an uncle (mother's brother) must be listened to with respect, and children are expected to obey him; and if parents are having difficulty with a recalcitrant child, the uncle will be called in to remonstrate or ultimately to punish him or her. Nevertheless, upon reaching adulthood the individual becomes his own master, and the uncle can only advise and remonstrate. While uncles are treated respectfully, this respect is tempered with a good deal of humor, and there is considerable reciprocal teasing and mild joking. . . .

Brothers and sisters are equals; if the brother has the right to criticize or advise his sister, so has she the right to do the same to him. Furthermore, although it is acceptable for a man to move into his sister's house upon separation from his wife, she can always refuse his request if she feels justified in doing so. In one case, the sister refused because she did not approve of her brother's reasons for leaving his wife (Nagata 1970, pp. 280–81).

In general, women are thought of as more emotional and headstrong than men, and therefore women are believed to be in need of advising by men more than men are by women. The role of adviser to a woman generally falls upon her close male kin—father, mother's brother, and brother. Husbands are reluctant to advise wives, and they should do it tactfully, as wives are thought likely to take offense. However, women do not hesitate to speak out and criticize or advise their fathers, uncles, and brothers if they feel the need to do so. They may point out to the kinsman that he is not behaving in proper fashion and thereby is not setting a good example for their own conduct. (Men may say the same to their fathers and uncles.) Older people of both sexes should be listened to respectfully by younger men and women, but they must earn this respect through their own good behavior.

Unlike many matrilineal societies, the mother's brother is not the kinsman who receives the greatest respect in this society. Rather, it is the *mö'wi*, or female in-law, the wife of a son, brother, or mother's brother. She is both addressed and referred to by this term, which connotes respect and deference, and there is the belief that using her name might bring harm to the one who does so. At the very least, using her name would be disrespectful. For no other status, kinship or otherwise, is the use of the name prohibited. The *mö'wi* is always treated with special courtesy by all those who address her husband as "son," "brother," or "uncle." The explanation given for this respect is that "she cooks for us [while her wedding robes are being woven] and brings food when she comes to visit." This is but one example of the high value placed upon women as feeders.

COMMUNITY LIFE

While most female authority is exerted within the sphere of household activities, women are not barred from participation in or influence over community activities. By withholding support they can informally exert the power of the veto (for an example, see below), although they rarely do so; for most of the community activities engaged in by men are for the benefit of women as much as for the benefit of men.

While household and community operate to a large degree as two separate areas of activity, they are not conceived of by the Hopi as two separate domains. The model of the house underlies the conception of the village; so to understand community authority and responsibility, one must understand the transformations of the concept of the house.

The house is, above all, the actual or symbolic structure that shelters the individual, that places and identifies him, and within which he is safe, whether in this life or the Afterworld. All creatures have houses, and to be without a house, as the spirit of the deceased is during his passage from the world of the living to the world of the dead, is to be in a state of danger to oneself and possibly others.

Each Hopi has a symbolic house, drawn for him when he is a newborn infant. One of the first actions of the Mudhead Clowns upon entrance into the plaza during ceremonial dances is to draw themselves a house upon the ground, for they are representing newly emerged beings.

The house of the family and matrilineage is the actual structure into which every Hopi is born and Hopi men marry. These are places for family privacy, and any adult caught spying into another house is believed to be up to no good, probably a witch looking at his or her victim. It is within these houses that women exert authority and men take a secondary place, as we have seen.

Each clan also has a house, one that is both actual and symbolic. It is actual in that it is the house belonging to the leading lineage of the clan, the lineage to which the Clan Mother and her brother the Clan "Big Uncle" belong. It is in this house that clan-owned ceremonial property is stored, and it is a duty of the Clan Mother to care for it. We can also think of the Clan House as symbolic, as the focal point of the entire clan under the joint leadership of a brother and sister pair. It is in the clan house in this sense that men and women share authority, in their roles as Mother and Big Uncle.

Finally, the entire village is conceived of metaphorically as a house: the term for village chief is *kikmongwi*, or leader of the house, the stem for house being *ki* and the word for leader being *mongwi*. The *kikmongwi* is addressed by all the villagers as "father," and his wife is addressed as "mother." It is at this level that authority over the "house" lies in male hands, the *kikmongwi* and his council. While an authority, the *kikmongwi* is by no means authoritarian; rather, like a father, his principal duty is to care for his children so that they may thrive. The father does this by providing food and clothing for them; the *kikmongwi* does this by acting as principal communicant with the rain-bringing, life-giving supernatural beings. It is through his prayers, coming from a pure heart and an untroubled mind, that the forces of blessing are released.

Women in Community Political Activity

While the political system can be studied as a structure of formal authority, it can also be examined as the process by which decisions are made that affect community life, and this must include noninstitutionalized power and influence as well as authority. This point of view is the more appropriate for the Hopi political system, in which authority over community action is dispersed rather than concentrated and decisions are appropriately arrived at by consensus rather than by decree. . . .

The Hopi do have a village chief, the *kikmongwi*, but his principal role is to maintain harmony between the village and the spiritual world. His council, composed of men who inherit their positions through their clans (having been selected and trained by the previous incumbent), serves more as an advisory group than as a legislative or judicial body. The focus of community life is the ceremonial system, and the individual ceremonies are under the control of *mongwi*, or leaders, who inherit their positions through their clans. (Some of these *mongwi* are on the council.) While some clans are more important than others, in that they "own" the more important ceremonies, there is no rigid hierarchy. As we have seen in the discussion of domestic life, authority is not a principle of social interaction of kin; similarly, it is not a

principle of social interaction within the community. The principles that are discussed by the Hopi and observable in action are the acceptance of duty and cooperation toward common goals. Whatever authority is exerted by community leaders is directed at the coordination of effort, not at enforcement of unilateral decisions. Resolution of conflicts is essentially a private matter between the parties involved; and conflicts that cannot be handled privately either break the village apart, as happened when Oraibi split in 1906, or simply persist for years or even generations.

To say, therefore, that women have no positions in the formal authority structure is to say very little.[3] As the mothers, sisters, and wives of men who make community decisions, the influence of women cannot be overestimated. These women, after all, control the houses that the men live in; and the man's position in the home is to a large extent dependent upon his relationship to its female head. Women do not hesitate to speak their minds, whether in the privacy of the home to male kin and their visitors or in public meetings. One example illustrates what is in effect the veto power of women: in one village the chief and his sister were divided over a political issue concerning the village, and she refused to play her role in the Soyal ceremony, led by the chief, until he capitulated. As Hopi men readily admit, women usually get their way.

Each village is politically autonomous, and alliances with other Hopi villages or with communities from other tribes exist only on an ad hoc basis. Trade is conducted between individuals; women do not generally go on trading parties, but they participate actively in any exchanges that occur when outsiders come into the village for that purpose. They also control any proceeds gained from trade goods, such as corn products or pottery, that they have processed or manufactured.

The one community activity from which women were excluded in earlier times, before the *pax Americana*, was warfare. For both practical and ideological reasons, war was a male activity. However, if a raid occurred when men were away on long-distance hunts, the women of necessity helped defend the village and the nearby fields. One of the favorite legendary figures in Oraibi is Hehe'wuhti, or Warrior Woman, who was in the process of pulling up her hair when the village was attacked. She led the women's defense with her hair up on one side, flowing down on the other, and thus is she portrayed.

Women in Community Ceremonial Activity

The Hopi have a complex ceremonial system, and it is the cycle of ceremonies that provides the rhythm of the yearly round. All children are initiated into the Kachina Society sometime between the ages of five and ten, after which they can take part in activities surrounding the kachina dances,[4] although only men actually dance as both male and female kachinas. In addition, some boys and girls are initiated at this time into the Powamu Society, which has the responsibility of caring for the kachinas.

In their late teens or early twenties, all men are initiated into one of the four men's fraternities: Wuwucim and Tao, which have a benevolent character concerned with reproduction and agriculture, and Al and Kwan, which have a fiercer character concerned with hunting (Al) and war (Kwan).

The ceremonial cycle contains four great ceremonies of village-wide involvement and some lesser ones put on by specific ceremonial groups. With the exception of the women's societies, control of all ceremonies is in the hands of male ceremonial leaders and most of the participants are men. Nevertheless, women play a vital role in ceremonial life. They grind the sacred cornmeal, the symbol of natural and spiritual life, that is a necessary ingredient in almost all ceremonies. When masked dances are held, the dancers are sprinkled with cornmeal by female members of the Powamu Society. Women provide the food that feeds the participants; in some of the ceremonies, this is distributed among onlookers, and this feeding is highly valued. Women as well as men may sponsor a kachina dance by providing, with the aid of their male and female relatives, the large quantity of food for the dancers to eat and to distribute to the audience. On such dance days the sponsor is said to "stand above the *kikmongwi*."

Women's Ceremonies

While most of the ceremonial societies are controlled by men, although they may have women members, there are three women's societies—Marau, Lakon, and Oaqül. These are optional: a woman need not enter any, or she can join any or all of them, although most women who belong to any belong only to one. Initiation can occur at any age, but most join as children or young girls or are brought in as infants by their mothers or other female kin. Each women's society has several male members as well, who act as assistants to the head priestess and make the *pahos*, or prayer sticks, required by the ceremonies. Like other societies, each women's society is "owned" by a clan, and the chief priestess and her male assistants belong to the owning clan.

The women's societies hold their major public ceremonies in the fall, after the termination of the men's portion of the ceremonial cycle in late summer.[5] All of them last for nine days, although in Hopi thinking they are eight-day ceremonies, as the first day is considered to be the last day of the preceding time of preparation rather than part of the ceremony itself. The major public performances are held on the last day. Most of the ceremonial activity takes place in a *kiva*, or ceremonial building, borrowed from the men who use it daily.[6] The chief priestesses move in for the duration of the ceremony, with other members spending as much time there as they can spare from their household duties.

While each of the women's societies has its own ritual and symbols, there are certain common elements. All include some representation of Muingwa, the god of germination and the protector of all wild and domestic plants. All use corn, actual or depicted, as the major ritual element. (It is a major ritual element in most other ceremonies as well.) All initiate new members by placing them inside a kind of hoop made of yucca, raising and lowering it four times to the accompaniment of prayers and blessings. The symbolism of birth is very clear.[7] In all the dances, the women form a semicircle with their backs to the spectators, while various activities occur within the circle. This is in contrast to the men's dances in which the dancers form straight lines. In the women's dances, unlike the men's dances, only the participants with special roles are dressed in costume, while the dancers in the semicircle wear traditional Hopi dress.

The most complex of these ceremonies is Marau, and it is the one with the most overtones of the male portion of the ceremonial cycle. Marau women are said to be "sisters" to the men of Wuwucim (and perhaps Tao), and there is much good-natured and bawdy bantering between these "siblings" at the time of the Marau dances. Three nights of burlesque plaza performances are included in the Marau ceremony, with women mocking the men's kachina dances and singing obscene or humorous songs about their "brothers."

The Marau ceremony itself contains elements that bring to mind elements of Wuwucim, the great winter ceremony of the four fraternities. (It takes its name from the Wuwucim Society, the largest of the fraternities.) As in Wuwucim, offerings are made to all the dead, and departed members of the society are called back to the ceremony. In the plaza performance on the last day, elements are included that seem to reflect some of the basic features of Wuwucim. After the dancers have formed their circle and begun dancing, two pairs of women in short men's kilts and headdresses come toward the circle. These are called *Marautaka*, or "Marau men." The first pair hold bows and arrows, and as they proceed they shoot the arrows into bundles of vines that they throw before them. These arrows are spoken of as "lightning arrows," and they symbolize fertilization, as lightning is thought to fertilize plants. Thus, they exhibit the benevolent, life-giving character of Wuwucim and Tao fraternities. However, by shooting arrows these women are also performing acts characteristic of hunting and warfare, related to the nature of the Al and Kwan fraternities. That this shooting has to do with more than germination is indicated by the fact that after the ceremony the arrows are deposited at the shrine of the war gods. The arrows, then, are a key symbol of two major, and contradictory, principles of Hopi relationship to their world—benevolence and predation. In the Wuwucim ceremony these principles are separated by allocating them differentially to two pairs of fraternities. In Marau, they are brought together.

The second pair of major performers carry long poles and rings wrapped in old buckskin, which is said to have come from the clothing of enemies slain long ago. As they proceed, they toss the rings to the ground and throw the poles at them. These poles bring to mind the lances carried by the Kwan society, and the association with enemies and the clothing of the dead parallel aspects of the Kwan society rituals. Thus, Marau seems to unite into a single set of rituals those rituals, and the principles underlying them, performed separately by men's groups during Wuwucim. It seems to be a condensation and transformation of the major symbolic elements of the men's ceremony.

Lakon and Oaqül are very much alike. They are both called basket dances because at the termination of each dance set in the major public performance, decorated baskets are thrown to the spectators. Men in the audience try to get them, shouting, pushing other men aside, and even grabbing them from each other's hands. Women and children, wisely, stand to the rear. At the end of the grabbing, both men and baskets are likely to emerge somewhat battered. It is said that all this aids men in their hunting, for the shouting attracts the curious deer and brings them close to the village.

There are symbolic and ritual features of Lakon that relate to hunting. Primary among these is the "sibling" relationship between Lakon women and Al (and possibly Kwan) men. Here again, as in Marau, male and female elements are brought together. This is most vividly depicted in the headdress worn by the two central performers in the Lakon dance, which has a bunch of feathers attached to the right side and a horn protruding from the left. These elements have been interpreted by one Hopi as representing masculinity (the horn) and femininity (the feathers as a replacement for flowers) (Titiev 1972, pp. 99–100, 293). There is a subtle relationship between women and game animals, especially antelopes (the major type of hunted game), that crops up in various rituals and even in jokes about extramarital sexual adventures: men talk about "hunting for two-legged deer." Outside of marriage, males are believed to be the sexual aggressors, and the predatory nature of male sexuality is revealed in the notion that a woman should be "paid" with a gift if she acquiesces. This is not prostitution but rather reflects the idea that one should give something in return for whatever has been taken.

Lakon and Oaqül seem to be harvest festivals as well, for effigies or other representations of Muingwa form an important element in the private kiva rituals, and seeds are used as a part of the altars in the kivas.

Decorated baskets, when not adorning the walls, are used for prestations of food at weddings and during Powamu, the spring festival of germination, so their use in these ceremonies seems to emphasize the feminine role of corn grinder and feeder. Oaqül, a recent introduction, is not so well integrated into the system as are the other two ceremonies.

The female portion of the ceremonial cycle, then, has a double role in the cycle. First, it emphasizes the distinctiveness of women by bringing in elements, such as baskets, that are specific to female activities. The birth-giving nature of the act of initiation is the most dramatic of these elements. Second, by incorporating, uniting, and transforming major elements that appear in male ceremonies, it transmits the message that women, like men, contribute to the Hopi community and universe. Men and women are separate and have distinctive functions and even characters, but they are both part of the total Hopi world and they work together for common goals. Through the women's ceremonies, the necessary interdependence of male and female is expressed.

MALE AND FEMALE IN HOPI IDEOLOGY

If we consider the women's ceremonies discussed above within the context of the total ceremonial cycle, particularly in relation to the men's ceremonies that immediately precede and follow them, we gain some insight into the way that male and female principles are conceptualized by the Hopi.

The major cycle, involving almost total village participation, ends in July with Niman, or the Home Dance. The kachinas, who made their first appearance shortly before Soyal in December, go after this dance to their home in the San Francisco Peaks, the sacred mountains to the southwest of the Hopi villages. In August, preceding the women's portion of the cycle, two men's ceremonies are held in alternate years. These are the Snake-Antelope Ceremony, conducted by the Snake and Antelope Societies, and the Flute Ceremony, conducted by the Flute Societies. They involve only the members of these societies and the clans that "own" them. These ceremonies can be thought of as complementary to one another, representing the two contradictory aspects of the masculine principle, benevolence and predation.[8]

The Flute Ceremony is replete with symbols of plant reproduction and the elements that foster it, such as water and the sun. This, I believe, is expressive of the male role as the germinator. As the farmer to his fields, the husband and father to his wife and children, the *kikmongwi* to his village, and the Great Spirit to his people, the male is needed to activate and care for life. In contrast, the Snake-Antelope Ceremony represents the predatory nature of males, who must also kill if life is to be maintained. Snake dancers wear war costume and refer to the snakes that they handle as "warriors." According to information given to Stephen (1936, p. 714) in 1843, the Snake Society members were the actual warriors in olden times, while the Antelopes were the old men who stayed home praying in the kivas for success. The duality of masculinity is represented in these two ceremonies, as it is represented in the two pairs of men's fraternities, Wuwucim and Tao, and Al and Kwan.

The Lakon ceremony, which is the first of the women's ceremonies, can be regarded as representing the different natures of male and female. Females are related to the elements that grow out of Mother Earth—edible plants in their natural form or as a medium of exchange, symbolized by baskets, and game animals. Males stand to females both as the farmer stands to his crops, a benevolent and protective relationship, and as the hunter stands to game animals. While this latter relationship is most obviously predatory, it contains an element of benevolence as well; for a hunter performs rituals that placate the dead animal by sending its spirit back to the animal world and thereby assuring the perpetuation of animal life. Men must activate the life force and they must protect it, but in protecting it they must also kill, both animals for food and enemies for safety. Women, however, do not partake of this dual role of life givers and life destroyers: their single nature is to give and keep life.

The Marau ceremony, which follows Lakon, can be regarded as the female counterpart to Wuwucim, as we have discussed above. The burlesque elements so prominent in this ceremony, which occur to a lesser degree in the Wuwucim ceremony, can be regarded as signifying the tension underlying the ambiguous relationship between men and women. On the one hand they are separate and have different characters; on the other they are the same, as members of the moral in contrast to the natural and supernatural worlds. That this joking is related to men and women as males and females is shown by the explicitly sexual nature of the songs and jokes exchanged and the vivid depictions of genitals used in the joking portions of the ceremonies. Wuwucim, the first ceremony in the male cycle, takes place in November.

The last of the women's ceremonies to be held is Oaqül, which is similar to Lakon. It seems to be the least important of the women's ceremonies and restates the message transmitted in Lakon.

The great cycle, involving four major community ceremonies plus a number of kachina dances, begins with Wuwucim and ends with Niman. This cycle expresses Hopi beliefs about the natural and social world and the progress of the Hopi people through time. The little cycle, which takes place between Niman and Wuwucim, consists of men's and women's society performances and transmits different messages. Taken all together, it is in part a symbolic statement about the nature of male and female and their roles in social life. It contrasts the double nature of men with the single nature of women. If I am correct in considering Marau to be a feminine transformation of Wuwucim, then this ceremony brings together the duality into an expression of unity.

THE FEMALE AS THE SOURCE OF LIFE

As the opening sentence of this paper indicates, Hopi women perceive their importance as lying in their reproductive role, and a good part of the role of men is to protect the women so that they can fulfill this role. When they act as guardians of the women and advisers to them, they are making it possible for women to have the physical and spiritual safety required if children, and the Hopi people, are to thrive. Health and life itself depend upon keeping harmony with other people and the spirit beings, and a troubled mind makes it impossible for a woman to care for herself and her children properly. If a woman is disturbed, she and her children are in danger.

Societal maintenance through the production and perpetuation of life is an important goal of any society, but it may become secondary if the immediate need of the society is focused around warfare or other specifically male activities. For the Hopi, who consider the taking of life in hunting and warfare a necessary evil, warfare is played down; productivity is the major social goal.[9] When the Hopi dance, they say that they are praying for rain; but this has to be understood not only realistically, as a desperate need in this dry climate, but also metaphorically. Rain, which the men induce through their harmonious relation with the spirit world, is a major symbol for the power that activates life. This power can also be dangerous—the lightning that fertilizes the fields can also kill, or torrential rains can wash away the young plants. The other major symbol of life activation, the sun, is potentially dangerous as well, for it can burn the delicate plants unless they receive the rain. So, the task of men is to control the life-activating force and permit it to operate beneficently through the bodies of women and within Mother Earth. Both sexes fulfill their necessary tasks within the natural and spiritual domains of promoting life.

The woman as the source of life itself is expressed by the feminine nature of corn, the dominant symbol of life and an ingredient in almost all ritual activity. Each newborn infant is given a perfect ear of corn, its Corn Mother, which will protect it as the symbolic house drawn for the infant protects it. It is not surprising that the god of plants, including corn, is a male, Muingwa, for it is a masculine duty to care for corn and all female life.

The life-giving nature of women is encapsulated in one of the Hopi witchcraft beliefs. In order to gain worldly power, a person bargains away his life, or "heart." In order to survive, he or she must magically steal the hearts of others, thus killing them. Children, being young and pure of heart, are the favored victims. It is said that the heart of a boy will give the witch four more years of life. The heart of a girl, however, will allow him or her to live eight more years.

CONCLUSION

We have examined some of the features of social organization and the ideological system that are related to the high evaluation of women among the Hopi and the equality they enjoy with men. In this integrated network of activities and beliefs, the social and subsistence roles of men and women form a model for the beliefs about masculinity and femininity. In turn, these beliefs provide the sense of "rightness" with which the Hopi perform their domestic and community activities. At every point along the path through life, traditional Hopi look to their beliefs to guide and justify their daily conduct, and the way in which they perform their daily activities influences their relationship with the spiritual world. When he tends his plants, or when he fulfills his marital and paternal duties, a Hopi man is not only performing subsistence and social activities but he is contributing to the maintenance of life as well; and his contribution takes on a sacred quality that permits him to stand in good relation to the spiritual world. When a Hopi woman grinds corn, she does so with the knowledge that she is providing food for her children and the people, and the very substance she handles is the sacred element of life. Corn grinding should not be regarded as the onerous and time-consuming task it would appear to be; rather, it is a sacred duty of women, to be done with a pure heart and untroubled mind. Women sing corn-grinding songs as they work to lighten the task and express its life-giving contribution.

Male and female are interdependent and equally important principles of Hopi social life and ideology. These principles are complementary rather than similar. The female sphere of activity is the household, and the male sphere of activity is the community. Men and women control different portions of the ceremonial cycle. Each sex has its own tasks—only men hunt, only women grind corn—although both may come together in caring for the fields or herds, even though this is primarily the duty of men. But the dichotomy of masculine and feminine that separates the sexes is bridged in their necessary interdependence at each point in the social and ideological systems. The separation of the sexes does not cause the subordination of one and superordination of the other; rather, it permits each sex to fulfill its necessary and equally valued role in the maintenance of the society. Where the ideological focus of a culture is life, and both sexes are believed to be equally necessary to the promotion of life, devaluation of either sex is unlikely. . . .

NOTES

1. For a discussion of wedding customs and the pressure on girls to marry, see Schlegel 1973.
2. One wonders why infidelity is at the same time so deplored and so common. It probably provides one of the few escapes from the tight regulation of social life, and even vicarious enjoyment of infidelity is apparent in the teasing and joking that goes on about "private wives" and "hunting for two-legged deer." Men are usually the initiators of sexual activity (although women sometimes do initiate sexual affairs), so infidelity may also be a means by which men express covert resentment against their wives for their relatively insecure position in the home. Furthermore, as there are strong sanctions against the overt expression of anger between men, the seduction of another man's wife may be a way of expressing hostility toward him.
3. Actually, there is one case in which women do enter the formal authority system: if a *mongwi* dies without naming an heir, it is up to the Clan Mother to name his replacement. . . .
    Today, there is even a woman who claims chieftainship of Oraibi, on the grounds that her brother, the designated chief, has not kept to the traditional Hopi way. There is considerable controversy over this: some Hopi claim that she is not a real chief, since, never having been initiated into a ceremonial fraternity, she cannot perform the chiefly rituals (see below); while others support her on the grounds that she has stepped in to provide necessary leadership. There is an earlier case of a woman chief of Moenkopi, a daughter village to Oraibi. Her position was never one of a true *kikmongwi*, as Moenkopi was included in the Oraibi ceremonial cycle: rather, she seems to have been a liaison between Moenkopi and the Anglo authorities in the nearby town of Tuba City. . . .
4. The term *kachina* refers both to a supernatural being whose primary role is to bring rain and to the man who impersonates him in the kachina dance. It is believed that when the dancer puts on the kachina mask, the spirit of the kachina enters his body and he becomes a kachina. There are well over 100 different kachina forms, some more popular than others.
5. Shorter ceremonies are held in winter months for the women's societies discussed here and the other societies discussed below. The major ceremony in each case is held in summer or autumn, and it is these ceremonies that are discussed in this paper.
6. Marau had its own kiva, owned by the Lizard Clan which owns Marau. In 1901 it was rebuilt and taken over by the men, who have since loaned it to the Marau Society for its ceremonies. Lakon and Oaqül use a different kiva, borrowed from the men. In addition to their ceremonial use, kivas serve as men's houses.
7. The hoop is used only for women's society initiation and the initiation of children into the Powamu and Kachina Societies, which are held in Marau Kiva at Oraibi. It is not used for initiation into other societies or the men's fraternities, even though the concept of rebirth is made explicit in the latter by treating the fraternity initiates like newborn infants.
8. Flute and Snake-Antelope ceremonies are complementary to one another in timing, and, as I indicate, in symbolic expression. According to Parsons (1940), there is archaeological and ethnohistorical evidence that the ceremonies were once the same ceremony, or at least more closely related than they are today.

Momtcit, a war ceremony comprising two sets of dancers like the Snake-Antelope Ceremony, is now defunct. Perhaps Momtcit was to Snake-Antelope as Oaqül is to Lakon, a restatement of the same message (see the discussion below).

9. Warfare themes are not central to the great cycle of ceremonies, even though they appear in the little cycle of summer and fall ceremonies. The Hopi have played down the prominence of warfare, and it was not the means by which manhood was achieved or validated—initiation into a fraternity accomplished that. Prowess in warfare was respected only in that it provided defense for the village and allowed the physical and spiritual activities dedicated to the maintenance of life to be pursued.

REFERENCES

Chodorow, Nancy. 1974. "Family Structure and Feminine Personality." In M. Z. Rosaldo and L. Lamphere, eds., *Women, Culture, and Society*, pp. 43–66. Stanford: Stanford University Press.

Forde, C. D. 1931. "Hopi Agriculture and Land Ownership." *Journal of the Royal Anthropological Institute of Great Britain and Northern Ireland* 61:357–405.

Nagata, Shuichi. 1970. *Modern Transformations of Moenkopi Pueblo.* Urbana: University of Illinois Press.

Ortner, Sherry B. 1974. "Is Male to Female as Nature Is to Culture?" In M. Z. Rosaldo and L. Lamphere, eds. *Woman, Culture, and Society*, pp. 67–88. Stanford: Stanford University Press.

Parsons, Elsie Clews. 1940. "A Pre-Spanish Record of Hopi Ceremonies." *American Anthropologist* 42:541–42.

Rosaldo, Michelle Zimbalist. 1974. "Woman, Culture, and Society: A Theoretical Overview." In M. Z. Rosaldo and L. Lamphere, eds., *Woman, Culture, and Society*, pp. 17–42. Stanford: Stanford University Press.

Schlegel, Alice. 1972. *Male Dominance and Female Autonomy: Domestic Authority in Matrilineal Societies.* New Haven: Human Relations Area Files Press.

———. 1973. "The Adolescent Socialization of the Hopi Girl." *Ethnology* 12:449–62.

Stephen, Alexander M. 1936. *Hopi Journal of Alexander M. Stephen.* Edited by E. C. Parsons. New York: Columbia University Press.

Titiev, Mischa. 1972. *The Hopi Indians of Old Oraibi: Change and Continuity.* Ann Arbor: University of Michigan Press.

9

Sex, Age, Common Interest, and Social Stratification

In all human societies, kinship and residence are important for the organization of people into groups that serve a variety of purposes. They are by no means the only **organizational principles**, however; others that are frequently used include sex, age, common interest and include stratification. In all societies, some division of labor by sex exists. In some societies, this is relatively flexible, in that tasks normally performed by one sex may be performed by the other, as circumstances dictate, without "loss of face." This is the case among the Bushmen, where many tasks are shared between men and women. In some other societies, though, the sexes are rigidly separated in what they do, as among the Iroquoian peoples of what now is New York State. Among them, the tasks of men took them away from their villages for purposes of hunting, warfare, and diplomacy (in the twentieth century, for high steel work in urban areas), while the work of women was carried out in and near the villages.

Grouping by age involves the concept of **age-grades** and **age-sets**: categories to which one belongs by virtue of age and cohorts of individuals who move through a series of age-grades together. The concepts should be familiar to any college student: A particular "class" (of '97, '98, or whatever) constitutes an age-set whose members pass through the first year, sophomore, junior, and senior age-grades together. Age-grades, with or without age-sets, are found in many human societies, with important ritual activity often marking the transition from one age-grade to the next.

Common-interest groups—formed for a specific purpose and to which one belongs by virtue of an act of joining (as opposed to automatic assignment by virtue of descent, age, sex, and so on)—are particularly characteristic of urban industrial societies, although they may be found in traditional agrarian societies as well. In the United States, they exist in profusion, ranging all the way from street gangs to civic groups like the Lions or Elks clubs. Common-interest associations are especially well suited to industrialized and developing societies, where new needs are constantly arising around which new associations can form.

Grouping by sex, age, or common interest may or may not involve a degree of inequality; after all, groups may exist for different purposes without being ranked as inferior or superior to one another. Among the Iroquoians, for example, the rigid separation of sexes was *not* associated with subordination of one sex to the dominance of the other. Rather, the tasks assigned each sex were regarded as of equal value, and neither sex could impose its will on the other. By contrast, stratification *always* involves inequality, as whole categories of people (**social classes**) are ranked high versus low relative to one another. **Stratification** is one of the defining features of **civilization** and is backed by the power of the state, which may use force to maintain the privileges of those most favored by the system. Needless to say, those in the uppermost class, the **social elite**, have prior claim to basic resources, whereas those at the bottom of the scale must make do with whatever those of higher rank leave them.

Although one may speak of sex, age, common interest, and stratification as if they were always discrete organizational principles, in reality things are not nearly so neat. Carol MacCormack provides a particularly good illustration of this; in Sierra Leone, sex, age, and common interest all are significant for membership in the Sande society, which is concerned with the physical and psychological well-being of women, especially where matters of sex and reproduction are involved. Restricted to female membership, all women are initiated into the society at about the time of onset of menstruation. An important point made by this article is its refutation of the notion, prominent among some Western intellectuals, that women are to nature as men are to culture.

Initiation into the Sande society for women, and the Poro society for men, marks the transition from adolescence to adulthood in Sierra Leone. In North America, this transition for many is marked by the four years of college. Here, an element of stratification enters in, for although some lower-class individuals are allowed in, middle- and upper-class people enjoy privileged access. In his article, Michael Moffatt looks at the coming of age of North American youth in college and how the experience has changed in the twentieth century.

The ultimate transition is, of course, from life to death, and in Sierra Leone, this marks the transition to a fourth age-grade, that of ancestors. In his article, Olatunde Lawuyi looks at obituaries published in Nigerian newspapers. He finds that these, along with congratulatory advertisements, serve the economic and political interests of the social elite in Nigerian society. Because these are costly to publish (they are an important source of revenue for the media), they are indicative by their mere existence of the wealth and power of their subjects. They further serve to advertise the particular concerns, interests, and accomplishments of the elite and allow other individuals to broadcast their association with prominent individuals.

The last article, by Brett Williams, is a neat illustration of social stratification in action. Two of the ways in which social classes are manifest is through **symbolic indicators**—activities and possessions indicative of one's status—and patterns of interaction—who interacts with whom and in what way. "Elm Valley" affords good illustrations of both and highlights the misunderstandings that stem from somewhat different worldviews held by members of different social classes.

Women and Symbolic Systems

Biological Events and Cultural Control

Carol P. MacCormack

Carol MacCormack received her Ph.D. from Bryn Mawr College in 1971, has taught in the department of social anthropology at Cambridge, England, and is presently Katharine P. McBride professor at Bryn Mawr. Her research interests include medical anthropology, theory, and gender, and a focal point of her study is West Africa.

The women come in from the fields and forest, laden with cocoyams and firewood, streaming with rain, screaming with fatigue at their husbands. They come from the wild, entering inside the village fence, inside house walls, within the boundaries that mark the domain of domesticated animals and the society of men. They come from nature to culture. In thus describing Bakweri women of Cameroon, Ardener continues with an analysis of their puberty rites, and concludes that these women have a model of the world which conceptually includes themselves with nature, while men bound mankind off from nature. Women's reproductive powers are their essence, and human reproduction is a thing of nature.[1]

Ardener's structural analysis rests upon Lévi-Strauss's hypothesis that it is the bounding off of culture from nature that accounts for our very humanity. Rather than mating within the consanguineal family as animals do, men at some point in evolutionary history renounced their sisters in the great gamble that some other men would also do the unnatural. By exchanging women, separate consanguineal groups became interwebbed with ties of affinity, and human society was born. Quite explicit in his structural analysis of society is the active role in exchange attributed to men and a passive role for women.[2]

Bakweri women's puberty rites symbolically confirm for Ardener the concept that Bakweri women see themselves within the domain of nature. While he mentions that each initiate has a sponsor to teach her women's "mysteries," he does not elaborate upon the social context of the teaching or the content of the lessons.[3] Yet in other women's initiation rites the very point of the rite of passage is to teach girls to bring the biological events of their lives under careful cultural control.[4]

For example, officials of the Sande society, a women's religious society in Sierra Leone, instruct their pubescent initiates during weeks or months of seclusion.[5] Following that period of liminality the newly knowledgeable women are reincorporated into society with the status of adults. Henceforth they do not have sexual intercourse in any place, at any time, with any person they wish, as animals do. Such "natural" behavior would be a grievous offense to ancestral spirits, whose wrath might rain disease and infertility on the people and the land. Successful bearing and rearing of children is informed by Sande knowledge about hygiene, nutrition, medicine, and myriad other practical techniques rather than being a careless matter of doing what comes naturally. Should a man look on voyeuristically at women while they bathe, as people look at animals, ancestral wrath might strike him down. His only salvation would be to go to the officials of the Sande society, publicly confess, and submit to a ritual cleansing. Not only men, but women who trespass against Sande laws are sanctioned by ancestors or Sande officials.

Rather than being uncontrolled reproduction machines, Sande women, with their secret knowledge, public laws, legitimate sanctions, and hierarchical organization, bring women's biology under the most careful cultural control. Those very laws, sanctions, and organizations give Sherbro and Mende women in Sierra Leone a solid base of conceptual thought, practical experience, and social cohesion from which to launch out still farther into the cultural domain of thought and technology, the stuff of national development.

SANDE ORGANIZATION

Sande is an acephalous system of corporate groups organized on the residence rather than the descent principle. Local chapters are not unified into an overarching hierarchy of officials. It derives its authority from the power and ongoing concern of founding ancestresses, made manifest on ritual occasions as masked figures.[6] In each local chapter, senior adult members, in a hierarchy of offices, provide leadership, and the sodality renews itself when a class of initiates is ritually "born" into the corporation which exists in perpetuity.[7] The most important corporate property which Sande owns is the secret knowledge transmitted to women at the time they are initiated. It also owns ritual objects and "medicine." Conceptually, "medicine" includes physical substances with effective pharmacological properties and physical substances which link persons with sources of power in the universe. If an initiated woman uses Sande knowledge and Sande medicine to treat an ill person, the fee she receives is not her own but is given to the officials of her local chapter. She has used corporate "capital," and the "profit" returns to the group, in the care of its officials.

Although a woman will most likely be initiated into her mother's Sande chapter, giving a matrilineal character to Sande organization, marriage usually follows quickly after initiation, and the woman will most likely go away to reside virilocally in her husband's town, transferring her active allegiance to the chapter where she lives. Initiation into Sande is just the beginning of a woman's lifelong active participation in her local chapter, where women gather for weeks or months during the initiation season. Initiations are held yearly in some towns and less frequently in sparsely populated areas. Officials of the chapter will spend a great deal of time in the initiation grove, while younger women, unless they are sponsoring a daughter's initiation, will spend less time in such activities. Aside from the initiation season, Sande women do not constitute a formal congregation, although they do interact informally and may dance together on public holidays.

A woman will, if possible, return to her natal village to give birth, maintaining a vital link with her mother's Sande chapter. Before hospitals provided an alternative, all Sande women gave birth in the Sande "bush," a cleared place in the forest, or in a house which only Sande women may enter. The woman in labor is given social support by her mother and other Sande women. She is given ritual protection by Sande "medicine," and the chapter headwoman attends her as midwife. The midwife, as headwoman, may be the very woman who supervised her transformation into responsible womanhood at initiation.

By residing with their husband's people following marriage, the women are "in between" their natal descent group in which they do not renounce membership and their husband's group into which they are not completely absorbed.[8] They also link their mother's Sande chapter with that of their mother-in-law. Contrary to the Lévi-Straussian model of women as passive objects transferred between groups of men, in Sande, women link corporate groups composed exclusively of women. Marriages are arranged with the consent of the bride and in consultation with male and female kin of both the bride's and groom's group. In the Sherbro ceremony of requesting a bride, the groom's group specifically consults the bride's mother, giving a gift "for the sake of the lappa," the garment in which a mother carries an infant on her back. "Carrying" is shorthand for nurturing the fetus through pregnancy and the child into maturity. Not only the mother but other ranking female kin of the bride are consulted and their approval sought before the marriage is finally contracted. In Sande, and in marriage, women physically move back and forth between groups, interpreting events, often in their own self-interest, to the other camp, generating information which ties corporate groups together in a bond of common interest.

The headwoman of a local Sande chapter is referred to in Mende by the title *majo*. She is ultimately responsible for the quality of each initiate's training in the skills of womanhood. As midwife and adviser on gynecological problems, she is instrumental in assisting women to fulfill their culturally defined adult role through childbearing. Headwomen link the separate chapters together in an informal fashion by moving about the country to assist in each other's initiation ceremonies. Some women, because of their demonstrated adeptness in guiding other women to sound physiological and psychological health, are known over a wide area. They may travel across linguistic and ethnic boundaries, making their rank known through personal testimonials and manipulation of the symbols of their office.

A woman destined for a commanding role in Sande will acquire more knowledge and demonstrate her growing adeptness in womanly skills. This is learned behavior, socially transmitted, and therefore by definition cultural, not natural. Increased knowledge and adeptness is acknowledged by rites which elevate some women to higher grades within Sande. A woman who dies before the rank has been ritually conferred will have it conferred posthumously as the first stage of the funeral ceremonies which Sande chapters conduct for their members. Although some women rise to higher grades within Sande, there is no automatic promotion based upon age alone, nor the kind of age grading of women in society at large, as there is among Nyakyusa men, for example.[9]

Poro is the male equivalent of Sande, concerned with religious belief, socialization of adolescent males, and adeptness in manly skills. It is more overtly political than Sande, functioning at the local level to counterbalance the largely secular power of chiefs, who may be men or women.[10] Sande women, as individuals or as officials of their sodality, also enter the political arena, exerting significant direct political force upon the larger society.[11]

It is important to stress that Sande is not a "counterinstitution" to men's authority. Poro and Sande complement rather than oppose each other. Poro officials perform such duties as seeing that wells are kept clean or that disputes do not escalate into fights. Sande officials perform other duties, for example, treating certain illnesses or enforcing a prohibition against sexual intercourse with lactating women, assuring some spacing of children. Each sodality has its own domain of social control, laying down explicit laws of behavior known to the entire community. If a law is breached, all parties in the crime are at fault. Sande and Poro provide their laws for the health and well-being of the entire community, not for their own group alone. When Sande begins an initiation season, Poro, out of respect, remains quietly in the background. When Poro is initiating, Sande women show their respect by remaining ritually quiescent.

INITIATION: A RITE OF PASSAGE

For analytical purposes, the female life cycle might be divided into four stages. The first is girlhood, from birth until the onset of menstruation. The second stage is that brief liminal period between the onset of menstruation and marriage when a female is no longer a girl but not yet by cultural definition a woman who might procreate. The third stage is adulthood, following Sande initiation and marriage or cohabitation with a man. The final stage is ancestorhood, following physical death.

The second stage is publicly marked when a group of girls, who have reached menarche, are ritually separated from the larger society for weeks or months. Under the sponsorship of their mother or other kinswoman, they enter through a portal into the Sande "bush," a cleared place in the forest or a secluded part of the town.[12] There the group of girls, in a classical liminal state, discard the clothing of childhood, smear their bodies with white clay, and dress alike in brief skirts and many strands of small beads.[13] Mature Sande women intensively train them to womanly responsibility, making them vividly aware of their incipient womanhood and their value to the larger society, especially as farmers, and bearers of children. In this institutional setting women dramatically pass on a strong, positive self-image to other women.

Shortly after entering the Sande bush, girls undergo the distinctive surgery of a Sande woman, in which the clitoris and part of the labia minora are excised. Sande women explain that excism helps women to become prolific bearers of children. Conceptually, it is the *majo* with "a good hand" who brings forth the procreative potential in a woman. Neither conception, childbirth, nor other biological matters such as hygiene are left to natural process.

Informants also said that the initial surgery made women clean. One might speculate along the lines Douglas has developed that by excising the clitoris, a rudiment

of maleness, all sexual ambiguity is removed from the incipient woman. She then fits purely and "safely" into the social structure, free from the impurity and "danger" of categorical ambiguity.[14]

In most societies with initiation surgery, the resultant visible scar or body modification is a sign that the initiated adult has been brought within a moral sphere. For a member of Poro, the pattern of scars on a man's back signify that he is one of "those who may procreate." In the Poro bush he was instructed in the social responsibilities that go with sexual intercourse and has sworn an oath to behave responsibly or suffer the consequences that an affront to the living and the ancestors would engender.

For a Sande woman, her scars and body modifications can only be known through intimate contact, by the partner with whom she is sharing a sexual relationship. He, upon knowing she is a Sande woman, can be confident that she is also trained in the moral and practical responsibilities of a potential procreator.

Initiation begins with a painful and dangerous ordeal, endured in a context of intense social support, a metaphor for childbirth which may occur in the same place among supportive Sande women. During the initiation period girls also experience intense positive gratification with abundant food, Sande songs, dancing, and storytelling, the stories often ending with an instructive moral linked to Sande laws. Those shared risks and pleasures help to bond the initiates into a cohesive social group. They swear an oath on Sande "medicine" before they leave the initiation grove, vowing never to reveal any fault in another Sande woman.[15] This solidarity training helps to mitigate co-wife rivalry and the potential divide-and-rule powers of polygynous husbands.

Most of the farming and household work girls do during initiation is not new to them. Since they have assisted their mothers from an early age, it is not new skills, but new attitudes toward work, that they learn. In childhood they worked in the role of daughter, but in Sande they begin to anticipate the role of wife in which they will have to work cooperatively with their co-wives and husband's kin. During the initiation period they work on the *majo's* farm, the *majo* being a nonconsanguine, just as their husband's kin who control farm land in their marital residence will be nonconsanguine authority figures. They also cook, wash clothes, and daub mud houses in the manner of a married woman working cooperatively with her co-wives. Although attitudes toward work change, the nature of work in girlhood and womanhood remains largely the same. The image of death and rebirth is not as prominent in Sande initiation ceremonies as it is in Poro, where boys give up a more carefree childhood in taking on adult tasks.

The initiation period concludes when a "medicine," made by brewing leaves in water, is used to wash the initiates ritually, removing the magical protection they enjoyed since entering the initiation grove. In their liminal state, under magical protection, they were dangerous to any man who approached them sexually. Following the washing and final rituals of status transformation, all ambiguity about their womanhood is removed. They have become mature women in knowledgeable control of their own sexuality, eligible for marriage and childbearing.

The time of initiation for most women is determined biologically by puberty. However, an older woman, perhaps an in-marrying stranger or trader who takes up residence within the geographical sphere of Sande influence, may be initiated at any time. Analytically, the belief system which underlies the Sande society might be explained with methods used by Lévi-Strauss in *Mythologiques* rather than those of more "humdrum ethnographic aim."[16] We might choose to see all human society structured in contrastive categories of female-male, nature-culture, passive-active, uncontrolled-controlled, and copier-creator. If we do, however, then there logically can be no place for women, except at the most menial levels of production and reproduction, in the development plans of nations.

NOTES

1. E. Ardener, "Belief and the Problem of Women," in *The Interpretation of Ritual*, ed. J. S. LaFontaine (London: Tavistock Publications, 1972), pp. 135–58.

2. C. Lévi-Strauss, *The Elementary Structure of Kinship* (1949; reprint ed., Boston: Beacon Press, 1969). U. Junus ("Some Remarks on Minangkabau Social Structure," *Bijdragen tot de Taal-, Land- en Volkenkunde* 120 [1964]: 293–326) questions the universality of Lévi-Strauss's assumptions, especially in matrilineal-matrilocal societies where men pass in marriage between descent groups. S de Beauvoir (*The Second Sex* [New York: Alfred A. Knopf, 1953], p. 239) and S. B. Ortner ("Is Female to Male as Nature Is to Culture?" in *Women, Culture, and Society*, eds. M. Z. Rosaldo and L. Lamphere [Stanford, Calif.: Stanford University Press, 1974], pp. 67–88) also speculate on the equation of women with nature and men with culture and on its consequences.

3. Ardener, pp. 149–50.

4. A. Richards, *Chisungu: A Girl's Initiation Ceremony among the Bemba of Northern Rhodesia* (London: Faber and Faber, 1956).

5. Information, unless otherwise specified, pertains to the Moyamba District of Sierra Leone. Sande occurs throughout Sierra Leone and in parts of neighboring Guinea and Liberia.

6. W. L. d'Azevedo ("Mask-Makers and Myth in Western Liberia," in *Primitive Art and Society*, ed. A. Forge [London: Oxford University Press, 1973], pp. 126ff.) briefly describes a male principle, manifest as the black masked figure in Liberian Sande. In the Sherbro and Mende areas of Sierra Leone that mask represents the spiritual power and serene beauty of womanhood.

7. In Lungi, Moyamba District, Sande women are buried in a great mound in the village. The mound reminds inhabitants of the power of women to bless and succor, their power existing in unbroken continuity from the living to the ancestors.

8. M. Strathern (*Women in Between* [London: Seminar Press, 1972]) gives a case study of women actively linking corporate descent groups.

9. M. Wilson, *Good Company* (London: Oxford University Press, 1951).

10. K. Little, "The Political Function of the Poro," pts. 1 and 2, *Africa* 35 (1965): 349–65 and 36 (1966): 62–71.

11. For political structures and strategies used by Mende and Sherbro women, see C. P. Hoffer (MacCormack), "Mende and Sherbro Women in High Office," *Canadian Journal of African Studies* 6 (1972): 151–64, and "Madam Yoko: Ruler of the Kpa Mende Confederacy," in Rosaldo and Lamphere (n. 2 above), pp. 173–87; and C. P. MacCormack, "Sande Women and Politics in Sierra Leone," *West African Journal of Sociology and Political Science* 1 (1975): 42–50.

12. Lest entry into the "bush" be interpreted as women's particular propensity to revert to nature, Poro men also enter a different clearing in the forest when they conduct initiations.

13. See A. Van Gennep (*The Rites of Passage* [1909 reprint ed., Chicago: University of Chicago Press, 1969]) and V. Turner (*The Ritual Process* [Chicago: Aldine Publishing Co., 1969]) for discussion of passage and liminality.

14. M. Douglas, *Purity and Danger* (London: Routledge and Kegan Paul, 1966).

15. This is the ideal. An occasional dispute between Sande women may go outside their moral community into the Native Administration court. In such cases, Sande "medicine" may be used for swearing an oath to tell the truth in court.

16. C. Lévi-Strauss, *The Raw and the Cooked* (Boston: Beacon Press, 1969; originally published in 1964 as *Le Cru et la Cuit*). The quote is from Ardener (n. 1 above), p. 145.

REFERENCES

Ardener, E. 1972. "Belief and the Problem of Women," in *The Interpretation of Ritual*, ed. J. S. LaFontaine. London: Tavistock Publications, pp. 135–58.

d'Azevedo, W. L. 1973. "Mask-Makers and Myth in Western Liberia," in *Primitive Art and Society*, ed. A. Forge. London: Oxford University Press, pp. 126ff.

de Beauvoir, S. 1953. *The Second Sex*. New York: Alfred A. Knopf.

Douglas, M. 1966. *Purity and Danger*. London: Routledge and Kegan Paul.

Hoffer (MacCormack), C. P. 1972. "Mende and Sherbro Women in High Office," *Canadian Journal of African Studies* 6: 151–64.

Hoffer, Carol MacCormack. 1974. "Madam Yoko: Ruler of the Kpa Mende Confederacy," in *Women, Culture, and Society*, eds. M. Z. Rosaldo and L. Lamphere. Stanford, Calif.: Stanford University Press, pp. 67–88.

Junus, U. 1964. "Some Remarks on Minangkabau Social Structure," *Bijdragen tot de Taal-, Land- en Volkenkunde* 120: 293–326.

Lévi-Strauss, C. 1969 [1949]. *The Elementary Structure of Kinship*, reprint ed., Boston: Beacon Press.

Lévi-Strauss, C. 1969. *The Raw and the Cooked*. Boston: Beacon Press.

Little, K. 1965. "The Political Function of the Poro," pt. 1. *Africa* 35: 349–65.

Little, K. 1966. "The Political Function of the Poro," pt. 2, *Africa* 36: 62–71.

MacCormack, C. P. 1975. "Sande Women and Politics in Sierra Leone," *West African Journal of Sociology and Political Science* 1: 42–50.

Ortner, S. B. 1974. "Is Female to Male as Nature Is to Culture?" in *Women, Culture, and Society*, eds. M. Z. Rosaldo and L. Lamphere. Stanford, Calif.: Stanford University Press, pp. 67–88.

Richards, A. 1956. *Chisungu: A Girl's Initiation Ceremony Among the Bemba of Northern Rhodesia*. London: Faber and Faber.

Strathern, M. 1972. *Women in Between*. London: Seminar Press.

Turner, V. 1969. *The Ritual Process*. Chicago: Aldine Publishing Co.

Van Gennep, A. 1969 [1909]. *The Rites of Passage*. Chicago: University of Chicago Press.

Wilson, M. 1951. *Good Company*. London: Oxford University Press.

Youth Culture and College Culture

Michael Moffatt

Michael Moffatt has a Ph.D. from the University of Chicago, which was awarded in 1976. He is now associate professor at Rutgers University. His regional research interests are in the United States and South Asia; besides youth and adolescence, his research interests include the relationship of anthropology to history.

In its nineteenth-century origins, college life was a specifically collegiate culture. And up through the middle of the twentieth century, less-privileged American youths knew it as the subculture of a college elite—of the more affluent undergraduates, typically from older WASP backgrounds. As Horowitz points out, college life did not just distinguish college students from the great masses of less-fortunate young women and men who did not attend college in those days. Many undergraduates were also excluded from it—from the "best" fraternities, for example. Horowitz calls these students "the outsiders," poorer undergraduates who were in college in order to achieve the middle-class status that the more-prosperous students who were enjoying college life took for granted. The outsiders tended to work hard at their studies and to view their professors with respect. Students in the college-life elite often stigmatized them as "grinds" (Horowitz 1987:56–81).

The original college-life culture slowly faded on American campuses during the twentieth century, however, and it virtually disappeared in the sea of change that swept over American youth culture in the late 1960s. Between about 1964 and 1968, the casually well-dressed college man (and woman) suddenly became archaic at Rutgers and at other American colleges. All at once the students were part of a common, classless, internationally defined youth culture. And in their new tastes in clothing and in music, they unmistakably stated their new antielitist sentiments. Blue jeans had once been working-class garb. Long hair and beards had distinguished cultural bohemians, as had casual drug use. Rock-and-roll music—supplanting collegiate musical tastes such as Peter, Paul, and Mary or "cool jazz"—was recently transformed black music. Army

jackets were the clothing of poor draftees into the unpopular Vietnam War (Moffatt 1985:174–176, 221–234, 241–243).

Students in the mid-1980s no longer looked like students from the late 1960s. But in the way in which a general youth culture rather than a specifically collegiate one dominated their lives, and in the way in which this youth culture was available to everyone, not just to an elite, they were still very much the children of the sixties. The old extracurriculum was almost gone. The most fundamental student pleasures were the pleasures of other adolescents: friendship and erotic fun. The students' musical tastes came directly to them out of popular culture, and they recognized the sixties, whose music they now revered as "classic rock," as the *fons et origo* of music as they knew it.

The nearest thing to the older collegiate look in clothing among the students in the 1980s was "preppie," named, with obvious irony, for prep school students rather than for college students. Preppie was one step more formal than "student casual": loafers rather than sneakers, slacks rather than blue jeans, and an Oxford shirt or an Izod shirt rather than a T-shirt or a sweatshirt. Undergraduates said that it was the look of student leaders and of academic straight-arrows. Other clothing fashions—"punk," "gay," "GQ," "jock"—had nothing to do with college; like music, fashions in clothes also originated in mass adolescent culture. College iconography was only incidentally visible on the walls of student rooms and on their clothing. Most Rutgers students guessed that no one in a crowd of strangers their own age would be able to guess that they were college students simply by looking at them.

There were some collegiate nuances in their otherwise mass-cultural-defined lives, however. Although the students did not show their college identity in any obvious way—that wouldn't be cool, they implied—

most of them guessed that other members of their own generation would probably be able to identify them as college students after talking to them for a few minutes. They were likely to sound more intelligent, they thought. They were likely to "talk better." The college transformation was a subtle, inward one, the students implied, not an outer identity to be flashed like a beacon. But almost all of them said that it was important to them that they were in college; privately, "college student" was an identity in which most of them took considerable pride.

Another type of collegiate nuance was exemplified by a category of popular music in the trend-defining periodical *Rolling Stone*: "college albums." College albums were the most sophisticated contemporary popular music—new wave, post–new wave, punk, hard core—the antithesis of Top 40. College albums received their biggest play on college radio stations. What marked them as collegiate was not some class-differentiated identity of their performers, however; they were not sung by buttoned-down preppies, for instance. It was their relatively difficult accessibility as art. Their actual content could be even raunchier than conventional popular music.

In *Campus Life*, Horowitz argues that American undergraduate culture in the 1980s is the product of two older student subcultures inherited internally on American campuses. Modern students are the "new insiders," she suggests—joyless workaholics like the old outsiders *and* nonintellectuals in their basic orientations toward higher education, like students in the old college-life elite (Horowitz 1987:263–288). As a summation of an average student attitude toward the life of the mind in American colleges in the late twentieth century, there is more than a grain of truth in Horowitz's typification . . . . She is dead wrong about the joylessness of the students, however. At Rutgers at least, in their own opinions at least, the students had lots of fun.

Moreover, though Horowitz is aware of the transformations in college youth culture that took place in the 1960s, she does not give enough weight to the impact that these changes have continued to have in the 1980s, of the degree to which contemporary popular youth culture continues to dominate the sensibilities of American undergraduates. The internal inheritance of campus traditions has not since the 1960s been the cultural force that she suggests it has been. Undergraduates at Rutgers—and elsewhere, on tangential evidence—only knew a few things about older college cultures. They knew that college was about adolescent autonomy. They knew that it was about fun and games: elaborate college pranks, and so on. They knew that they would find such typical college institutions as dormitories and fraternities on most campuses. Since the sixties, they had also expected to find political protesters and cultural radicals in college. But the images of "college" that the average undergraduate carried around in her or his head were probably conditioned much more by con-

temporary American mass culture in its adolescent version than by any of the older student traditions indigenous to American colleges. A short list of popular adolescent movies about American college life in the late 1970s and mid-1980s, for example, would begin with the type specimen *Animal House*, progress through favorites such as *Fraternity Vacation, Spring Break, The Sure Thing, Revenge of the Nerds, Real Genius,* and *Soul Man,* and culminate in Rodney Dangerfield's recent *Back to School*.

Otherwise, almost everything in the private lives of students on American campuses in the 1980s was in fact a projection of contemporary late-adolescent culture *into* the particular institutions of youth that colleges now represented—places where everyone else was fairly intelligent, places where you were on your own with a considerable amount of free time, and places where adult authorities had a minimum knowledge of and impact on your private life.

COMING OF AGE

The age grading that characterized most of American childhood and adolescence in the 1980s first developed for small numbers of middle-class college students a century and a quarter ago (see Kett 1977:126–128). And with age grading, college students also formulated stereotypical notions of their own physical and mental maturation in college. Drawing on older images of the Ages of Man, late-nineteenth-century undergraduates pretended that they progressed from infancy to maturity during their four short years in higher education. One typical image from Rutgers in the 1880s showed the freshman as a precocious baby, the sophomore as a drunken youth, the junior as a suave ladies' man, and the senior as a care-worn, middle-aged bourgeois (Moffatt 1985:57). And for two-thirds of a century, college class histories repeated the same conceits. Freshmen and sophomores were carefree, childish pranksters; juniors and seniors were more manly in body and in mind.

Rutgers students no longer drew such drawings or wrote such histories in the 1980s. But they still had similar concepts of the typical stages of their personal development in college, which they still enacted with some faithfulness. Freshmen were foolish and inexperienced. Sophomores were wild men (and women), the leading troublemakers in the dorms. Then, with a predictability that resembled that of some form of pupating insect, juniors almost always discovered that they had matured beyond the juvenilities of dorm culture. Dorm fun was now dorm foolishness. And the inescapable intimacies of collective living—everyone else knowing almost everything about you—had grown tiresome with time . . . .

Juniors usually decided that they were ready for something closer to an independent adult existence in the real world, usually an off-campus apartment. Seniors often wanted a maturer life-style still. Or they might typically consider themselves to be "burned out," victims of mild or severe cases of "senioritis," weary of college, apprehensive about what came next. Sexual maturity was no longer peculiar to college upperclassmen in the 1980s. Now it could characterize students in any of the four college classes. But the older you were, the more likely you were to be sexually active.

In student opinion, you were pushed through these stages of development in college in the 1980s by the various formal and informal learning experiences that characterized modern undergraduate college life. Students sometimes felt that college adults did have some impact on them in college. Four out of five students in a large class in 1987 said they thought that looking back twenty years after college they would remember a professor or two as people who had inspired them in college, who had made a real difference in what they were today as adults in the real world. But most of the time the students believed that they came of age in college thanks to what they learned among themselves on their own, student to student, or, paradoxically, thanks to what they learned from dealing with precisely the least personal, most uncaring sides of official Rutgers.

College from the students' point of view was a combination of academic and outside-the-classroom education. Academic learning gave you the credentials you needed to progress toward a good career, and perhaps it made you a broader, more knowledgeable person. Outside-the-classroom education, on the other hand, was often the greater influence on your personal development, many of the students believed. About half the same large class in 1987 said that academic and extracurricular education had been "different, but equally important" aspects of college learning for them so far. About one in five of the remaining students considered academic learning more important than extracurricular learning, and about four in five made the opposite judgment. So, for about 40 percent of these students, the do-it-yourself side of college was the most significant educational experience. And for all but 10 percent, extracurricular learning had been at least half of what had contributed to their maturation so far in college.

One form of outside-the-classroom education in college, according to the students, resembled academic learning in content but not in context: the extracurricular intellectual learning that they did among themselves. Like the rest of college life as the students enjoyed it in the 1980s, most of this intellectual fun took place in private, in long talks about philosophy, morality, politics, and other serious interests, usually with friends. Some of it also took place due to the extra-curricular programming available on campus, the students said, thanks to speakers, concerts, and other performances, thanks to an intellectual environment richer than anything they had typically known in their home-towns and high schools before college . . . .

The students sometimes referred to the rest of extracurricular learning in college as "social learning," as the things you had to know in order to be a competent adult in the real world as you would find it after graduation. And the students' college did prepare them for the real world as well, many of them firmly believed. Moreover, they added, a relatively cheap public college such as Rutgers often did a much better job of this than fancier private colleges were likely to do. You were, first of all, on your own in college, the students pointed out—much more so at Rutgers than at smaller, more personal colleges—and learning to take real responsibility for yourself helped you to grow up as an individual:

> Rutgers has helped me to learn what it is like to be on my own and take responsibility for my own actions. . . . The majority of college students find drinking to be of second nature . . . [but] I do not abuse the freedom obtained by living in college.
>
> —Freshman female

> It is up to the individual. No one else at Rutgers cares how he does.
>
> —Sophomore male

The academic work was more difficult than it had been in high school. Your teachers no longer knew you personally or cared about you. Guidance counselors were not tracking your every move any longer. Your parents were not sure what you were doing on a daily basis. You had a more flexible schedule and more free time than you had ever had in high school—and more distractions all around you. It was not easy under these circumstances to remember the serious purposes for which you had probably come to college in the first place. Learning to balance college work against college play was one of the tougher challenges of your college years, the students maintained.

Second, college, and Rutgers in particular, was more like the real world than hometown and high school had been. A century ago the student apologists for college life had claimed that the rich associational activities of the undergraduates had prepared them to be movers and shakers after college, to build business organizations and other voluntary organizations in adult life. Now, in the 1980s, student associations were in eclipse in college, but so, too, were similar activities in the real world beyond the groves of Academe. Now the real world, especially at the professional and middle-management levels toward which most Rutgers graduates were headed, was already highly organized. Now it was an impersonal and bureaucratically complicated place. And now, conveniently, thanks to Rutgers' impersonality and bureaucratic complexity, college prepared you for this aspect of life after college. Smaller, more elite colleges were cloisters compared to Rutgers, the students commonly argued. Rutgers, on the other hand, got you ready for the real world with a vengeance:

> How did Rutgers teach me to deal with the real world? The answer, as ironic as it seems, is through the "RU Screw" . . . through that tortuous, roundabout way of making everything three times more difficult to accomplish, I learned the skills of persistence and determination which I would need for the rest of my days. . . .
>
> —Junior female

Rutgers also mirrored the real world in the diversity of its undergraduate student body, the students often asserted. As a public institution, it brought students together from suburban hometowns and high schools that were often more homogeneous by class, by race, and by ethnic group. And here again, Rutgers resembled the real world much more than fancier colleges did:

> I have an old girlfriend from high school who now goes to Mt. Holyoke. It's all like "high-up Suzie Sorority" there. Like they're all just the *same.* My girlfriend is sheltered from life. I have to deal with more. Because this is a state university, they have to let in all kinds of people. You just can't imagine the *friends* you have at a place like this!
>
> —Sophomore male, 1985

The actual ability of Rutgers students to deal with real cultural diversity as I observed it in the dorms was often very limited. Many students could not tolerate it at all, but sealed themselves into little friendship groups of people as much like themselves as they could find. . . . Virtually all the undergraduates believed in the value of diversity, however. For "diversity"—like "friendship" and "community" as they were ideologically defined— was simply one more entailment of late-twentieth-century American individualism. . . . What was the point of being an individualist if everyone and everything was the same? Real choice required a diverse universe within which to choose.

Diversity, moreover, was an easily shared value because it was almost empty of content. Real cultural diversity to an anthropologist might mean the difference between an American middle-class youth from a white ethnic background raised in northern New Jersey and a student who had recently arrived in the United States from a small city in south Asia. To an undergraduate, on the other hand, it might mean a roommate who liked mellow music while you yourself liked punk, a nerdy roommate while you yourself were a jock, or

(somewhat more culturally) a friend whose third-generation white ethnic identity was different from yours—Italian versus Irish, for instance.

Nevertheless, undergraduate Rutgers was almost inevitably more diverse than anything most students had known to date, and was probably more diverse than the world in which most of the professors and other college adults lived. At the very least, the students at Rutgers had to learn to get along with people they did not like for reasons of cultural differences. "Archie Bunker would never make it as a Rutgers student," one student commented on a paper in 1987. At best, the students sometimes did learn valuable things at Rutgers about themselves and the world from other students who were really different from themselves.

> All in all I am very glad I came to Rutgers. Many people say it's too big. However, I really believe that is an advantage. There are so many different opportunities here . . . [Also,] being somewhat of a conservative, it was great being exposed to those "damn liberals."
>
> —Senior male

> In high school, everyone in my classes was either Irish, Italian or Polish. Here, I go to classes with Asians, Indians, Blacks, Puerto Ricans and many others, from whom I get different viewpoints.
>
> —Senior male

> Above all else, college is a breeding ground for interrelationships between students. If nothing else, a college student learns how to interact with his or her peers. The ability to form lasting relationships is of great value to the graduating adult. College is a step in the mental and psychological development of an individual.
>
> —Senior female

> One attribute of mine . . . that was well developed through the years I spent at Rutgers . . . is that of being a true partier. . . .
>
> —Senior female

> My social development [in college] seemed to help me as much, if not more, than my academic development into shaping me into what I am today. . . .
>
> —Senior male

In the end, the students claimed, even the fun of college life was a learning experience. And with this claim, the dichotomy between formal education (work, learning) and college life (fun, relaxation) collapsed entirely for the students. In the end, you learned from everything that happened to you in college, the students asserted. And, anthropologically speaking, they were not far from wrong. For they did spend those four hours a day in informal friendly fun, working on their real identities through such activities and practicing the "bullshit" necessary to the well-tuned American social self in the real world in the late twentieth century. And they did devote about the same amount of imaginative and real energy to "learning to pick up girls or guys" as they did to seeking out "meaningful relationships" during their college years. All these personal skills would undoubtedly continue to be useful to them long after they graduated from college. In their refinement, in their opinion—as much as in the intellectual learning that they acquired in college—they came of age, they progressed toward something like adult maturity during their four years at Rutgers.

But how and where did this all happen? How did particular students act out, negotiate, and modify these cultural conceptions and values at Rutgers in the 1980s? What sorts of variations were there among the somewhat variable late-adolescent youths who attended Rutgers? The best place to start looking for answers is back in the dorms.

REFERENCES

Horowitz, Helen Lefkowitz 1987. *Campus Life: Undergraduate Cultures from the Eighteenth Century to the Present.* New York: Knopf.

Kett, Joseph 1977. *Rites of Passage: Adolescents in America 1790 to the Present.* New York: Basic Books.

Moffatt, Michael 1985. *The Rutgers Picture Book: An Illustrated History of Student Life in the Changing College and University.* New Brunswick: Rutgers University Press.

Advertised Self in Obituaries and Congratulations in Some Nigerian Dailies

Olatunde Bayo Lawuyi

Olatunde Bayo Lawuyi received his Ph.D. in anthropology from the University of Illinois in 1985. He is now senior lecturer in social anthropology in the Department of General Studies at Oyo State University of Technology, Ogobomoso, Nigeria.

A conspicuous feature of the Nigerian dailies is the obituary[1] and congratulation advertisements. These advertisements, which altogether often take up more than a page, are considered to be among the less serious, less substantial and less important features of the dailies. Nevertheless, the advertisements—especially in papers with a wide circulation—appear to arouse considerable interest among the reading public. Some readers regard them, especially the obituaries, as "obnoxious" (Saro-Wiwa, 1990), as "junk journalism" (Abu, 1990) befitting a depraved society, as a form of communication (Obijiofor, 1989) or as money-making business (Dare, 1985a). These criticisms are related, no doubt, to the fact that the advertisements enter into popular culture as forms which relate the advertised with their socio-political community: specifically with its biography and personages and with its present social relations and members (Lawuyi, 1990).

The biographical approach helps to elucidate the complex ways by which self-definitions can be "translated" into public professional influence (Ben-Ari, 1987). But then it also dovetails into a larger framework of ceremonial and symbolism that pervades the lives of the elite in all sorts of situations meant to create or augment their status (Cohen, 1976; 1981). The ceremonial includes funeral ceremonies, chieftaincy title conferment festivities, and social parties where praise-music is played. These contexts are characterised by their special style of life (accent, dress, manners, patterns of friendship, exclusive gathering, and ideology) and by their symbols, which are either traditional but not popular, or popular but not traditional (Barber, 1987).

"Advertised Self in Obituaries and Congratulations in Some Nigerian Dailies" by Olatunde Bayo Lawuyi, from *Africa*, Vol. 61, No. 2, 1991. Reprinted with permisssion.

The identification with traditional symbols of status is not so much because the elite accept their values (Aluko, 1970; Achebe, 1966) as because they conceive of them as an adaptive, utilitarian tool in the mobilisation of support for their role. As Barber (1987) argued, the most important attribute of traditional symbols is not the power to communicate but the power to locate the elite within a specific social universe which is the ground of existence. Such symbols as are adopted therefore tend to be conservative, escapist or merely vacuous; "and in this way they work against the real interests of the people, accepting and reinforcing the values that maintain the *status quo*. They are instruments of ruling class hegemony in the Gramscian sense" (Barber, 1987: 7).

The expression "hegemony" means that the ruling class has shared values. But these values are not constant, they shift; each hegemony has a unique character of its own, and the process of making historical sense of them is inevitably hazardous—especially since we are dealing with vacuous symbols. If we wish then to approach the problem in a historical/anthropological fashion, "we have to identify processes that exemplify paradigm—transcendence, trains of events that open closed universes of meaning and make them comparable and accessible to each other" (Larsen, 1987: 4).

This article is concerned with the analysis of elite culture and the way it articulates the particular and the universal within an heterogeneous, stratified and dynamic system. The focus is on elite values in obituary and congratulation advertisements in the *Daily Times* (Lagos) and *Daily Sketch* (Ibadan), but careful consideration has been given to other newspapers. A remarkably similar pattern of publication is found nationally within Nigeria and regionally along the West African coast. Even elite residents abroad, with limited access to their national dailies, patronise regional publications like *West Africa* to advertise their concerns, interests and achievements. The accent is on the personal and institutional processes involved in the creation and maintenance of communities: for instance, career making, mobilisation of resources and personnel, and interaction of personalities. The thesis is that the obituary and congratulation advertisements are not only about power but are also attributes of status. Specifically, the power order and the economic order that inform their construction form a dialectic the essential manifestation of which is selfhood (Cohen, 1976). This selfhood, as a social construct, brings out not only the public nature of success, but also how it may be altered to define a new situation or status.

The analysis that follows is based on the examination of copies of the *Daily Times* (and *Sunday Times*) and the *Daily Sketch* (and *Sunday Sketch*), published since 1966 and stored, in the library of Obafemi Awolowo University—itself established in 1962. In addition, various interviews were conducted with the business managers of the *Daily Sketch* and the Broadcasting Corporation of Oyo State, with the *Guardian* (Lagos) and *Daily Times* correspondents in Ile-Ife, and with the newspaper vendors and advertisement agents in Ile-Ife. The interviews were conducted at various times between February 1989 and March 1990 on various issues which ranged from the history of the Nigerian press and the media's marketing strategy to public opinions about the publications. Still on public opinion, I conducted a survey of the "social marketing of the dead" by selecting three biographies of the deceased written in their "Order of Funeral Service"[2] for an analysis of how attitudes to criteria of success vary among the Yoruba according to religion, social origin and sex. The three biographies were selected on account of their "shortness," so that the respondent should not be subjected to a long essay that could be construed as a waste of time and hence discourage a positive response. Each of the three biographies was selected from the categories of (1) the uneducated, (2) public school teachers and (3) university lecturers. The only category left out in my collection of thirty "Orders of Funeral Services' is that of the businessmen and women—their write-ups are usually long.[3] The survey was administered to fifty lecturers who are Yoruba on the campus of Obafemi Awolowo University. The sample size was stratified by religion, urban/rural roots and sex. The survey was self-administered. The individual respondents were to identify significant events in each of the deceaseds' lives, to rate the events in the order they considered them significant, and to mention aspects which they thought were missing in the biographies but ought to be emphasised.

The analysis is organised in four sections: (1) an historical survey highlighting the evolution of marketing strategies; (2) a section on the structure of the obituary publications, highlighting career paths and social network; (3) a focus on the similarities and differences in obituary and congratulation publications, so as to present a consensual framework on the elite construction of selfhood, especially as mediated by forms of economic and political development; (4) the mode of celebrating the successes which inform the selfhood construction.

It would be difficult to appreciate the death symbolism, which is the central focus of attention, without understanding the emergence of modern individualistic morality and the new cultural premises that have resulted. Hence the attention paid to the merchant culture.

THE PRESS AND THE MERCANTILE CULTURE

The first newspapers in Nigeria were established in the 1850s and '60s. The aim was to increase the level of literacy; the emphasis was on literary content, politics was secondary. The early newspapers patterned their contents and style after the Sierra Leonean and Gold Coast (Ghana) papers, which were themselves products of British commercial influence. The *Sierra Leone Gazette*, published in Freetown during the first quarter of the nineteenth century, probably blazed the trail for others to follow. The decisive factor was to promote competence in the English language, though, in later years, the understanding of English was to serve the evangelical missions of the European Christian missionaries (Omu, 1978).

The foreign papers had obvious attractions for Nigerian readers. One was the increasing consciousness of the value of Western education. Another was the opportunities for trade and employment which the newspapers provided by their advertisements. Quite often jobs in Lagos were advertised in these foreign papers and the recruitment that followed provided incentives for the educated Nigerians of the diaspora to come to Lagos and exploit the opportunities for upward mobility and wealth. So great was the attraction of homecoming that Fred Omu noted:

> The trade of Lagos was characterised by what a newspaper was to call "suicidal competition among merchants." Business establishments which had begun to grow from the 1850s now proliferated and, in the absence of local newspapers, a few of these advertised their wares in the London-based *African Times*. The importance of the commercial situation lies not only in the fact that it stimulated further emigration but also because it heightened the demand for the type of news (shipping intelligence and market conditions, for example) that had fostered newspapers in England and other European countries. [1978: 22]

The advertisements made references to skills, education and experience. While these references do not essentially define success, they nevertheless enter into public discourse and arts as symbolic complexes which underlie and structure people's intellectual, academic and social careers. With their introduction the old and new symbols met, each competing for the attention of the public. The colonial intervention in local history, for instance, succeeded in transforming such symbols as education, Western dress, professional identity and property development into characteristics of the elite. But the Islamic and Christian interventions gave rise to symbols which include refinement of decorum, conspicuous piety, sympathy for the poor, and self-construction for job opportunities. These symbols mirror status differences, and found their way into the press in various modes of publication and advertisement.

How much revenue the early newspapers realised from advertisements is difficult to learn, as most publishers were reluctant to disclose the information (Omu, 1978). But Omu's work suggests that advertisements featured less prominently in the newspapers between 1880 and 1920. Many of the papers survived on the competence and managerial ability of their editors, on their political appeal, on the capital outlay of the publishers or on official patronage by local administrators. The *Nigerian Daily Times,* for example, survived through its ability to present a strong, healthy and vigorous public opinion (Omu, 1978: 61). But it had the advantage of being a "foreign capital supported daily" (Omu, 1978: 63). The *Nigerian Daily Times* had a virtual monopoly of European commercial advertising, and the revenue strengthened its ability to attract experienced technical staff who introduced popular techniques of presentation and general improvements in typography and distribution (Omu, 1978). All these enabled it to achieve a wide appeal and to undergo a process of expansion at a time when other papers were folding.

Between 1923 and 1930 no newspaper realised as much as £500 from sales. Quite a number depended on subscribers who often did not pay their dues, and on advertisers. The newspapers were forced to depend more on advertisers because, while they openly scolded subscribers for not paying (Omu, 1978), they could at least insist that advertisers should pay in advance. The space given over to advertisements fluctuated between 50 and 70 per cent of the type area of the newspapers. Indeed, in the 1920s some papers even averaged between 90 and 99 per cent. Very little portion of the advertisement pages was taken up by obituary or congratulation messages; most of them were on merchandise, household provisions and luxury goods, news of ships' movements and the activities of local administrators. Notable patrons were Paterson Zochonis, Pickering & Berthhould and Miller Brothers.

The proceeds from advertisements were still quite small. By the 1940s, conscious of the slow development of indigenous advertising, the press threw in a little bait to raise the revenue base (Dare, 1985b). Some introduced the cheap, but well patronised, classified advertisements common in British tabloids which rarely extended for more than a page or two and were charged per word. They were usually without the photographs of the advertised product. Others appealed to national sentiment which had built up since the nationalist movements began in the 1920s and consequently led to the birth of such politically motivated papers as the *West African Pilot* in 1939 and the *Nigerian Tribune* in 1949. In the attempt to broaden their revenue base the papers gave much space to personality profiles. In addition, obituaries took a more picturesque form with the display of passport size or full-length photographs indicating wealth (by dress and size of publication) and power (by insignia of the office the deceased held). The patrons were the civil servants, the private medical doctors and the businessmen.

The 1950s and '60s witnessed the establishment of many government newspapers such as the *Nigerian Outlook* (1960), *Morning Post* and *Sunday Post* (1961), *Daily Sketch* (1964) and *New Nigerian* (1966). It was an era that also saw the introduction of radio and television into the community (Dare, 1985b). Those who dominated the media advertisements were the government officials and the politicians canvassing for electoral support or haranguing the people to demonstrate their backing for ethno-regional interests and development. It was clear that:

> not only does the ruling elite make the news, it *is* the news—as endless verbatim reports of politicians' speeches, accounts of elite weddings and birthday parties, and the pages and pages of expensive obituaries testify. And if the poor are invisible, the very poor are a downright nuisance—some regimes have treated them literally as rubbish. [Barber, 1987: 3]

Governments, through their political activities and actors, were the major financiers of the papers, radio and television into the 1970s and early '80s. The patrons of advertisements widened, though, with the oil boom of the 1970s and the upward mobility fostered by it. By the late '80s, however, the total expenditure approved by the authorities for their papers and radio had taken a downward turn owing to a slump in the price of oil. The total expenditure for Federal Radio Corporation of Nigeria (FRCN) for 1988, for instance, was N13,147,392 as against N33,400,368 in the previous year. In 1986 the amount had been N51,182,056. "Without commercialisation and with the dwindling funding we are getting from the government," said Saka Fagbo, the director of commercials at Nigerian Television Authority (NTA), "we would have gone under" (*Newswatch*, 1989: 46). As of 1989 the FRCN had achieved 100 per cent of its targeted commercial activities, while the Broadcasting Corporation of Oyo State (BCOS) raised its revenue from a little over a million naira in 1988 to over 4 million naira in 1989.[4]

It is difficult to determine how much the Obituaries and Congratulations contributed to the companies' profits, since the authorities are unwilling to give the information.[5] But it is clear that the two advertisement forms represent a large chunk of the revenue. Most of the media (including the ones mentioned above) solicit congratulation messages and In Memoriams of famous people. They do so through their field agents, who receive a commission of between 5 and 15 per cent of sales, depending on the level of technical production involved, the nature of the advertised products (as shop windows or coverage of ceremony) and the variety of advertisements the agency can handle.[6] The rivalry also involves discounts on "group messages" especially for celebrated personalities on their installation as community heads or chiefs, on the award of honorary degrees at local and foreign universities, and on their birthdays. The discounts extend to paid advertisements to welcome the President, the governor of the state, or his officials, when on a visit to communities.

Generally, as in many cultures, it is felt to be somewhat distasteful to solicit obituaries. Yet "if you raise the price of obituary advertisements three-fold, there would always be takers" (Saro-Wiwa, 1990: 7). The patrons are the elite and they are served by a press unwilling to promote the sale of cadavers but nevertheless interested in advertising the achievements of the elite. The restrictions the media place on any advertisement depend upon the target audience. For instance, the *Concord* newspapers would not publish any advertisements of alcohol, since the religion of the publisher, a Muslim, forbids the sale of alcohol. Similarly, the *Guardian* newspaper once refused to publish any obituary advertisements. But by April 1989 the policy had changed as attempts were made to broaden the revenue base.[7] The company has since published obituaries of the wife of Professor A. E. Afigbo and of the wife of the proprietor, Chief M. Ibru. The focus is on the elite, in a paper that now says with pride that it is "the medium for Nigeria's top consumers, for the affluent and the influential, for the decision makers and opinion leaders, for those who value quality, and who spend money on themselves, families and homes" (*Guardian*, 11 November 1989: 4).

All papers in Nigeria now advertise the elite through their dead ones. In an attempt at calculating the revenue such publications could have yielded for the *Daily Times* and *Daily Sketch* in 1989, I noticed that the *Times* published an average of seven obituaries daily (ranging between four and ten) while the *Sketch* published an average of two obituaries (ranging between one and four). Of those published, there were more quarter-page advertisements than full-page or half-page ones in the two papers.[8] Most of the patrons were members of the business community and professional people. Generally, the *Times* had more full-page advertisements than the *Sketch*; in fact the full-page advertisements came to nearly a third of the total number published daily.

Between 1989 and January 1990 the *Daily Times* increased its charges by 10-20 per cent, while the *Sketch*'s charges rose by 10-15 per cent. I calculated that, on the basis of the total publications for the month of December 1989, the *Daily Times* achieved a revenue of not less than N750,000, while the *Sketch*'s total collection would amount to not less than N100,000. Further estimates for November 1989 and January 1990 (when the price rose) indicate that December 1989 brought in about 10 per cent less than November, but about 13 per cent more than January (i.e., apart from increase in price, there were more notices published). The margin of error would be plus or minus 5 per cent.

Radio and television are also involved in the business of marketing the elite. Their prices differ greatly for obituaries and congratulations, being much lower than those in the print media. The Broadcasting Corporation of Oyo State charges N30.00 for a radio announcement, N50.00 for a television announcement without a picture, and N60.00 for a television announcement with picture.[9] Generally, the various media tap the sentiments and financial abilities of various categories of people. The very wealthy patronise all the media. Those of middling income go for the use of the radio and the television. Those less well-off still patronise the radio mostly. Clientage differs because, firstly, the audio-visual media air their announcements within a few hours of the time the notices are put in. In contrast, most papers would require at least two weeks' notice. As a result the poor, who cannot afford mortuary costs for two weeks, or the Muslims, who are enjoined to bury their dead quickly, cannot use the print media. Secondly, the audio-visual media can be listened to or viewed by the illiterates, since some of the personal-paid announcements are in local, indigenous, languages. Thirdly, apart from their cheap prices, the audio messages do reach all the nooks and crannies of the nation.

The point, however, is not about obituaries and congratulations as documents contrived to portray wealth or somehow to order the complex reality in which Nigerians live and to give meaning to their lives. Rather, I suggest that an understanding of these publications entails taking into account a cultural context of commercial development and the definition of success.

THE STRUCTURE OF OBITUARY PUBLICATIONS

The obituaries are of two types: the "Obituary/Transition" released immediately after death and clearly similar to the "Notices" often pasted on house walls and electricity poles in rural and urban centres, and the "In Memoriam" which commemorates the duration of transition. The "In Memoriam" is reckoned in days, months or years and, with it, we examine textual phenomena as constitutive of social action (Mulkay, 1984: 547; Ben-Ari, 1987: 66), i.e., as reflexive of how people organise the social and cultural orders of their experience. An obituary goes thus:[10]

With great feelings of loss but in total
submission to the will of God, we announce
the transition into immortality of a
wonderful sister and mother

Mary Scott
which event occurred on Thursday—
28th December, 1989
Burial Arrangements
Funeral Mass at St. Dominic's Catholic Church, Yaba
at 12.00 on Friday, 05 January, 1990
Interment at Ikoyi Cemetery immediately after.
May Her Gentle Soul Rest In Peace
John A. V. Scott
for the family

[*Daily Times*, 3 January 1990: 19]

Contrast this with an In Memoriam which appeared in the same publication and on the same page:

In evergreen memory of our late
Father and Grandfather
Chief Amose Olatumbi Bamtefa
(The Baba Ijo of St. Peter's Anglican Church,
Sonyindo Sagamu)
who rested in the Lord on 3rd January, 1989
"To live in the hearts of those whom we love is never
to die"
Our most sincere appreciation goes to:
The Bishop of Remo Diocese, Chief (Mrs.)
H. I. D. Awolowo, Iya Ijo St. Saviour Church,
Ikenne, Chief (Mrs.) T. Ogunlesi, Iya Ijo
St. Paul's Church, Sagamu; Archdeacon Sewo,
Archdeacon Adewale, Canon Dr. & Mrs. Odumuyiwa
and the numerous well-wishers whose names we
cannot all possibly mention here for their
support and kindness during the funeral ceremony.
We thank you all
By Children and Grandchildren

[*Daily Times*, 3 January 1990: 19]

In the In Memoriam the writers allude to sources of support during bereavement and express their appreciation; they also convey their feelings on the role of the deceased in the development of self or collective maturity. There is, in addition, a photograph of the deceased and an indication of his social status as Baba Ijo (father of the congregation). As the day the deceased died is mentioned, we are thus afforded a glimpse of the mourning period. Elsewhere I have estimated that the mourning can last over fifty years (Lawuyi, 1988).

An "appreciation section" features In Memoriams published a year after death. All In Memoriams have a list of survivors or bereaved; some even mention their qualifications and place of residence. There is a hint of the genealogical link with the dead—as son, daughter,

nephew, cousin, etc. The line-up is indicative of seniority in the family structure. Thus even the deceased children of the deceased are not ignored; they are listed and assigned a proper rank. As an example of the list of survivors, the following children appeared as the bereaved of Mrs. Christiana Omoge Akagbosu:

Chief (Dr.) Joseph T. Akagbosu—(Son), Chairman/
Managing Director
Mr. Casimir T. Akagbosu—(Son), Commissioner of
Police, Benin State Command
Mr. Paul T. Akagbosu—(Son), Sales Manager,
Leventis Motors, Lagos

[*Daily Times*, 6 February 1986: 9]

The identification of surviving kin and their status is not uncommon for the relative ranking of the deceased's status within the community, especially among his peers. It is also important in order to establish the right of inheritance in situations where the deceased could possibly have begotten "illegal" children (e.g. those born by concubines). However, the practice of identifying kin and rank is much more common with the Bendelites and the Igbo than with the Yoruba. It is suggested that the Yoruba's overriding concern with malevolent forces, or *aye*, could have inhibited similar self expression.[11]

Within the obituary, attention is paid to such criteria of identity as the sex, age and place of birth of the deceased. These criteria are linked with references to a "career path," to the trajectory of self-promotion programmes which originate in a certain community and ethnic group and traverse various institutions of training and career development.

The criteria are distinct from, yet are linked to, the "appreciation" directed towards the elite by those below them: chiefs, military governors, politicians, academics, diplomats, service chiefs, bishops, etc. Mentioning these people clearly has to do with activities which underlie and structure the deceased's career. The elite career, heavily laced with opportunities for mobility and resource allocation and appropriation, consists of an inventory of roles which individuals have built up over time and is expressed in a small, but significant, reference to the emotions of those involved:

Your 1/6d [15k] school fees loan to your needy pupil in 1935 has already yielded abundant dividends from which many scholars today draw knowledge.

[*Daily Times*, 17 January 1986: 15]

Or:

Babe-Oke, we are grateful for the legacy of a good name, good education, exemplary upbringing and proud family tradition you have left for us; the imperishable services you gave to your community in inspiring the education of children and your generous disposition not only to your family, the less privileged within your community but also all those whose paths crossed yours!!

[*Daily Times*, 9 January 1990: 14]

In these descriptions of a "career" the individual is shown as having tried as much as possible to educate himself, his family and acquaintances. Within this career path role performance shifts from parenthood, community leadership or professional expertise to membership of religious organisations. The institutions to which the individuals are linked provide the recruitment area for their social networks. Hence for one who attended St. Peter's Anglican Church, Sonyindo, most of his friends had to come from his church, from Sagamu or from the Ijebu Yoruba (since Sonyindo is an Ijebu community). Similarly, for someone who served as director general of the department of local government in the military governor's office, Lagos State, the social network is urban in character:

> In particular we will remain forever indebted to His Excellency, Colonel Raji Rasaki the military governor of Lagos State; the entire members of the Lagos State Executive Council; the Honourable Commissioners of Lagos State; his former colleagues the Director-General of the various ministries and departments in Lagos State . . .
>
> [*Daily Times*, 6 January 1990: 17]

The individual as director general, as religious leader, as school principal or as army officer, would, while alive, have served in capacities in which he/she helped to recruit, to pay for and to contribute to the advancement of opportunities and jobs of others. Several roles do, of course, coexist in his/her network so that operationally emphasis must be placed on the institutional settings in which the network originated and was maintained.

Yet, even then, the individual's career on the one hand and the characteristic, both morphological and interactional, of the social network on the other are also related to obligations stemming from services previously rendered to the individual by his friends, relations and professional colleagues. In essence a multi-stranded network usually prevails, especially in a situation where the individual has enough room to manipulate the rules and situations to draw to himself a coterie of friends who could benefit from the manipulation. One then finds that a multi-stranded network is more distinctive of urbanites, and of public/private office holders, in contexts in which power relations are relatively unequal. In contrast, single-stranded networks characterise the relations of those without important public/private offices and who are rurally based: here, unlike in the urban centres, the individual is not involved in a loose-knit network organised by different ethnic, professional and national groups. He is intimately bounded to ru-

rally oriented loyalties and quite often those mentioned in the advertisement would be from the same rural background.

COMPARISON WITH THE CONGRATULATION PUBLICATIONS

But why publish congratulations? The answer lies in precisely the same thrust which motivates the publication of obituaries. In both attention is drawn to the achievements of a single individual with whom the writers identify. The preface to both texts begins with an "I," a "We" or a "The." For instance:

> The Chairman, Board of Directors and entire Staff of Jacco Pharmacy International Limited heartily rejoice with . . .
>
> [*Daily Sketch*, 19 March 1988: 14]

"The" projects a collective identity and so differs from "I":

> I, Architect J. A. Agunbiade On Behalf Of My Colleagues . . .
>
> [*Daily Sketch*, 5 March 1988: 13]

In dealing with the relationships constituted by the obituary or congratulation we should stress that the exercise of power by some people over others enters into all of them, on all levels. Certain economic and political relationships are crucial in that no matter what other functions the publication may perform, it must acknowledge the organisation of knowledge in a social unit, and then lead the reader to an uncomplicated appreciation of the social reality of debt and gratitude. This means that all interpersonal and intergroup relations projected in the publications must at some point conform to the dictates of economic or political power. Let it be said, however, that these dictates of power are but aspects of group relationships, mediated in this case through the forms of an economic or political organ.

Indeed, the congratulation advertisement merely expands on the economic process, on man and the relatively scarce resources available to him (Cohen, 1976: 22). It is about patronage, about economic power ultimately maintained by reward and deprivation. The advertisement celebrates a birthday (*Daily Times*, 8 January 1990: 23), the opening of a new business centre (*Daily Sketch*, 19 March 1988: 14), the conferment of a chieftaincy title (*Daily Times*, 24 January 1990: 11) or the receipt of an honorary degree (*Daily Times*, 13 January 1990: 19), to mention a few. In securing people's attention the writers focus on control of crucial resources and on those that exercise control, as well as on service to the nation, community or group. In one instance, it is appropriate to wish the celebrant:

more success in (his) contribution to the Pharmaceutical Industries in Nigeria and more years of service to the nation's health care system.

[*Daily Sketch*, 19 March 1988: 14]

In another instance the celebrant is wished more contributions to national development:

National Oil joins his (Major-General Hassan Usman Katsina's) admirers, family and friends in wishing him many more years of meaningful contribution to the development of one Great Nation.

[*Daily Times*, 20 January 1990: 4]

While undoubtedly underscoring a patronage relationship, the congratulation text, like that of the obituary, is heavily dependent on the social context in which men's ideas seek paradigmatic status (Darnell, 1971: 101, Ben-Ari, 1987: 67). Hence the promotion of the person of the advertiser and his business is not uncommon. This may be viewed as a strategy for gaining attention.

The Board, Management and Staff of
Globe Motors (Nig.) Limited
Rejoice with a bosom friend
Mr. Ime S. Umanah
On the award of an honorary doctorate degree
of Laws by the University of Calabar,
On the 13th of October, 1990
An apt acknowledgement of
your humble contributions
to finance and industry.
We are proud to be associated
With you.

[*Daily Times*, 13 January 1990: 19]

With the logo of the firm,[12] the address of the advertiser's place of business and the acknowledgement of a social debt the congratulation is used to improve the advertiser's economic chances. Usually an invitation goes to the reader to patronise the advertised and the advertiser's business. The strategy is one of using a stone to kill two birds: you praise, flatter, advertise your important client or boss, and improve your business or status as a result. Two things here are all-important: the first is that a person is not absolutely an individual. He is a means to an end. He is a "you" in a framework in which the "I," "We," "The" that mark the beginning of the texts are interchangeable and designate consuming interest. The second is that the "you" circle of society (however widely or narrowly this phrase may be understood) is a sort of loosely compacted person. Therefore, there are varied references to it in forms of age, place of birth, network of friends, and family structure and roles. This portrait of the self (as a flexible one) appear ideally suited to those who seek power and recognition outside their local communities in that they must learn to operate in an arena of continuously changing friendships and alliances, which form and dissolve in competition for scarce resources. This boils down to the fact that, as in obituaries, the individual must learn to function in a complex society by judicious manipulation of social ties and resources.

THE SYMBOLISM OF SUCCESS

The individuals who are able to operate both in terms of community-oriented and economically oriented expectations then tend to be selected out for mobility. They become the economic and political "brokers" of group-community relations: a function which carries its own reward within the merchant culture as increased publicity. The publicity is a delicate index of attitude, as the nature and style can reveal an underlying ideological orientation or significant changes.

So, how does death come into the picture? Ordinarily, death is not passed off as an achievement, as a success. But it nevertheless is one. In Nigeria it has become a more visible feature of social life when elevated in a burial ceremony or as an anniversary. A constellation of factors has produced this visibility. First, the political upheavals which marked the end of the First Republic in 1966 and involved arson, thuggery, mass destruction of life and property. These portrayed death as a symbol of power, as a victory for the destroyer (Achebe, 1966). Both the government and the opposition forces needed this power to legitimate their claims of superiority. They saw death not as a unifying symbol but as an expression of struggle either against injustice, inequality and exploitation or against lawlessness, unbridled ambition and arrogance. Death within this scheme was seen in terms not of self-completion or of the creation of symbolic immortality (as is critically bound into the way of dying in Japan: Litton, 1979). The deaths did not create a community of national heroes/heroines (Settar, 1989). Rather, the social response to these politically motivated deaths tends to imply that people see living/dying as a dynamic process characterised by competition (Togonu-Bickersteth, 1986).

Second, by the time of the oil boom, inequality within society had become distorted. The elite class had widened so rapidly and haphazardly that the symbolic line between rich and poor became blurred (Barber, 1987). There were more vehicles on the road and gradations within commercial culture were manifested in type of private vehicle and driving style, as well as in the profit motive. Careless driving, uncontrolled consumption of alcohol, speeding, and lack of expansion and maintenance of the transport routes caused accidents (Falola and Olanrewaju, 1986). On the roads were (and still are) damaged vehicles, burnt-out chassis, and lying as litter the bodies of men and animals. The universe of which driving is a part joins that of dynamism and power in being rooted in new-found wealth and guided by competition.

There is a third point. While occasions of death do provoke, in some instances, a sober mood, they are also in other instances the context for the celebration of success and competition. They create a joyful mood because the rites that follow exhibit structural features, symbolic motifs and performative patterns that recur in the same way that politicians celebrate their success over the opposition; i.e., the intention is to consume all that one had or use the celebration to demonstrate what one is not by adopting styles which contrast with everyday experience.

The demonstration of success may not, of course, be commonly shared within the heterogeneous, fluctuating conglomeration of ethnic, religious and class groups that make up Nigerian society but it is nevertheless linked with the world market economy to which every group is obliged to respond. Several objects used at burial ceremonies are thus the insignia of civic and political notables. These include garments or ornaments, the rare or laboriously produced materials of which symbolically distinguish the elite from the poor, the person of higher from those of lower rank or accomplishments. Among the Yoruba, these include expensive *aso oke*, lace materials and costly items of food and drink. Among the Igbo a Western-tailored suit shows class. With the Hausa-Fulani the individual is expensively dressed in "Babbarriga." In some ceremonies the entire family or a group of friends may even choose to wear the same colour and dress. But then there are subtle distinctions which mark status—for example, one type of lace material is cheaper than another. The symbolism of solidarity and independence (and, presumably, of dominance and hostility as well) between social ranks pervades the entire ceremony, even in the manner of conspicuous consumption. For food and drink are supplied in accordance with status and even here the rank of the receivers as well as that of the givers is granted recognition according to a minutely scrutinised order of precedence.

The obituary publications serve the useful purpose of calling people to such a "potlach." The specificity as well as generality of the response to the invitation is not only economically motivated (making it more apt for the merchant culture and its capacity to transmit messages and values across geographical, ethnic and even national boundaries) but also cultural.

The publicity given to the list of survivors, to the age of the deceased and to his/her social status accords well with the traditional Yoruba criteria of success which, according to Akiwowo (1983: 13–14), include: *ire aiku* (the value of good health till old age), *ire owo* (financial security) or *ire oko-aya*, the value of intimate companionship and love (*ire ife*), *ire o'mo'* (the value of parenthood)

and *ire abori o'ta* (the value of assured self-actualisation). The same publicity taps into the Igbo emphasis on individuality, achievement and status. A successful man in Igbo society is identified by the number of his children and wives, his social titles, his knowledge of other places, and the property he has accumulated (Uchendu, 1965). In addition, the publications convey values that are not in conflict with the Christian symbols of success, education, status mobility and professionalism. Most southern Nigerian Christians of the middle and upper classes, therefore, patronise them.

But while the northern Christians from Kwara, Benue, Plateau, Kaduna and Kaduna States also advertise the dead, their Muslim friends may not. Their objections touch on many factors, including *Mutumin Kirkii*, the concept of the good man (Kirk-Greene, 1974). Firstly, a *Mutumin Kirkii* highlights the outward civilities of human relations (patience, propriety, generosity, respect) of a kind not projected in the obituary or congratulation publications. Secondly, as Muslims bury their dead rather quickly, their demands for publication space cannot be sufficiently rapidly met. Thirdly, some Muslims would object to reproducing images of living or dead persons.

Essentially, variations do exist in ethno-regional attitudes to the publications. But there are also intra- and inter-group objections. Survey samples indicate that variations exist within the middle-class university community along lines of religion, social root and sex. This is because each group emphasises different criteria of success: the Christians focus on educational attainment (70 per cent of the sample, n = 20), and the Muslims on service to the community (60 per cent of the sample, n = 10). Those raised in urban centres highlight the fact that the obituaries serve as an inspiration to others (55 per cent of the sample, n = 30), while a considerably smaller number of those born in a rural community (40 per cent of the sample, n = 20) agree that it has inspirational value. More males (72 per cent) than females (65 per cent) think that such publications speak to success. Indeed, the females who were interviewed generally considered the obituary vulgar. Their opinion merges with that of Saro-Wiwa (1990), who actually believes that a paper should sell on the strength of its news coverage, its features, the quality of its editorial and the breadth and depth of coverage of social problems.

There is a general tendency among the educated to lay emphasis on the social responsibility theory of the press, assuming that the elite should not rule but serve. Their views of what the press should be are well summarised by Peterson (1979: 74), who has articulated the following features of the social responsibility theory: (1) service the political system by providing information, discussion and debate on public affairs; (2) enlighten the public so as to make it capable of self-government; (3) safeguard the rights of the individual by serving as a watchdog against government; (4) service the economic system, primarily by bringing together buyers and sellers of goods and services through the medium of advertising; (5) provide entertainment; (6) maintain its own financial self-sufficiency so as to be free from the pressures of special interests.

Obituaries and congratulations serve functions (4) and (6). The answer of the media to objections that they are promoting, through the vacuous symbol of death, the economic foundation of elitism is to argue for distinguishing between promoting the sale of death and the marketing of elitism.

CONCLUSION

The argument of this article is that obituary and congratulatory notices are part of the national culture but that attitudes to them vary across ethnic, religious and class groups. The acceptance or rejection of these publications is informed by cultural notions of success. Thus the material found in both obituaries and congratulations harp on the economic process and on the power created by reward and deprivation. Indeed, the construction of selfhood within each one of the publications is but an aspect of social relationships, mediated in this case through the various forms of economic or political development in Nigeria. The successful person, a member of the elite, is one who advances his career to a point that needs to be publicly acknowledged or celebrated. Death is just part of a symbolic complex of achievements that can be advertised.

NOTES

1. The word "obituary" is used here rather loosely to designate its various manifestations as "Transition," "In Memoriam," "Notice" or "Obituary." It is thus all-embracing and does not refer only to the specific form of the Obituary.

2. These are small pamphlets containing the order of worship both in the church and later at the burial ground. They contain the hymns to be sung, the prayers to be said and the Bible passages to be read on the occasion. Few of these "Orders of Funeral Services" contain biographies; many people consulted on the issue thought it either unnecessary or expensive—adding to the cost of production. The inclusion of a biography in the "order" is itself a recent phenomenon dating to the early 1970s. But it should be added that the Muslims also have their own pamphlets giving the Order of the Funeral Service. These rarely contain biographies, for the same reasons as those stated above.

3. The shortest in my collection has three pages of biographical sketch while the longest has five pages. The longest belongs to Chief S. Akinola, the Sawe of Ilesa, 1896–1988.

4. A radio announcement on BCOS in January 1990.

5. Neither Mr. Fola Awonusi, the advertisement manager of the *Daily Sketch*, nor Mr. Alawale, the Controller of Sales, BCOS, was willing to give information on this issue. In the case of Mr. Alawale it was because his company lumps together revenue from obituaries with that realised from other types of "Shop Windows" (birthday announcements, changes of name and adverts on the launch of a business). The effort to collect information on how much revenue the *Daily Times* realised failed too, despite the intervention of my friend Dr. Soremekun, a *Daily Times* columnist and former employee.

6. The BCOS agent in Ile-Ife supplied this information in an interview. The agent also mentioned that the individual advertiser inputs his material at the lithograph and typesetting stages, but that agents can write for illiterates who may not be familiar with the requirements of the media. The interview was conducted on 29 March 1990 in Oranmiyan shopping complex, shop B2.

7. I would like to thank the *Guardian* correspondent in Ile-Ife (name withheld on request) and Mr. Ayodele Jegede, also of the *Guardian*, for their useful insights into why the *Guardian* changed its stand. However, incidentally and ironically, the paper has been in the forefront of the debate on the value of the obituary advertisement to the publishers and to the reading public (see the references in the text).

8. In the *Daily Times* there are at least ten categories of advertisement. These are full-page, half-page, 13 in. x four columns, 13 in. x three columns, 6 1/2 in. x four columns, 6 1/2 in. x three and a half columns (i.e. quarter-page), 6 1/2 in. x three columns, 15 cm. x two columns, 7.5 cm. x two columns and "SCI." The cheapest is "SCI." It is about one-ninth the price of the full page.

9. All prices are relative to 1989. Information was supplied by Mr. Alawale, who also hinted at the value attached to the various media. Mr. Gbenga Fayemiwo, the editor of *Kowe*, an Ejigbo-based newspaper, was also of much help in discerning the attitudes of the public to the obituary and congratulation publications.

10. Those broadcast on radio and television contain the same information as published in the print media.

11. Dr. Toyin Falola, personal communication, 15 February 1990.

12. The logo is placed either at the top or at the bottom of the advertisement. In addition there would be a picture of the celebrant or advertiser, and not just a photo of the person being celebrated.

REFERENCES

Abu, Sully. 1990. "All the news that's fit for the trash-can," *Guardian*, 4 March, p. 7.

Achebe, Chinua. 1966. *A Man of the People*. London: Heinemann. Akiwowo, Akinsola. 1983. *Ajobi and Ajogbe: Variations on the Theme of Sociation*. Ile-Ife: University of Ife Press.

Aluko, T. M. 1970. *Chief the Honourable Minister*. London: Heinemann.

Barber, Karin. 1987. "Popular arts in Africa," *African Studies Review*, 30 (3), 1–78.

Ben-Ari, Eyal. 1987. "On acknowledgment in ethnographies," *Journal of Anthropological Research*, 43 (1), 63–84.

Cohen, Abner. 1976. *Two-Dimensional Man*. Berkeley: University of California Press.

———. 1981. *The Politics of Elite Culture*. Berkeley: University of California Press.

Dare, O. 1985a. "The art of the obituary," *Guardian*, 22 October, p. 9.

———. 1985b. "Press: 126 years of patchy service," *Newswatch* (Lagos), October.

Darnell, R. 1971. "The professionalization of American anthropology: a case study in the sociology of knowledge," *Social Science Information*, 10, 85–103.

Falola, T., and Olanrewaju, S. A. 1986. *Transport Systems in Nigeria*. Syracuse, N.Y.: Syracuse University Press.

Kirk-Greene, A. H. M. 1974. *Mutumin Kirkii: The Concept of the Good Man in Hausa*. Bloomington: Indiana University Press.

Larsen, Tord. 1987. "Action, morality, and cultural translation," *Journal of Anthropological Research*, 43 (7), 1–28.

Lawuyi, Olatunde B. 1988. "Obituary and ancestral worship: analysis of a contemporary cultural form in Nigeria," *Sociological Analysis,* 48 (4), 372–79.

———. 1990. "The story about life: biography in the Yoruba obituaries," *Diogenes,* forthcoming.

Litton, R. J., et al. 1979. *Six Lives, Six Deaths: Portraits from Modern Japan.* New Haven: Yale University Press.

Mulkay, M. 1984. "The ultimate compliment: a sociological analysis of ceremonial discourse," *Sociology,* 18 (4), 531–49.

Obijiofor, Levi. 1989. "Obituaries as communication," *Guardian,* 8 April, p. 9.

Omu, Fred. 1978. *The Press and Politics in Nigeria, 1880–1937.* London: Longman.

Peterson, Theodore. 1979. "The social responsibility theory," in F. S. Siebert et al. (ed.), *Four Theories of the Press,* pp. 73–103. Urbana: University of Illinois Press.

Saro-Wiwa, Ken. 1990. "In pursuit of excellence," *Daily Times,* 11 February, p. 7.

Settar, S. 1989. *Inviting Death: Indian Attitudes Towards the Ritual Death.* New York: Brill.

Togonu-Bickersteth, F. 1986. "Obituaries: conception of death in the Nigerian newspapers," *Ife Social Sciences Review,* 9 (1–2), 83–93.

Uchendu, V. C. 1965. *The Igbo of South-Eastern Nigeria.* New York: Holt, Rinehart and Winston.

Owning Places and Buying Time

Class, Culture, and Stalled Gentrification

Brett Williams

Brett Williams is associate professor of anthropology and director of American studies at American University, Washington, D.C. She received her Ph.D. from the University of Illinois in 1975. Her fieldwork has been done in the United States, among migrant workers of Mexican descent from Texas, in a mixed ethnic neighborhood of a northeastern city and among waitresses. She has written on all of these topics, as well as on southern folklife and on the African-American hero, John Henry. Her research interests include poverty, the media, folklore, and politics and culture.

Gentrification allows ethnographers a rare glimpse of the interplay of class and culture in everyday life. But because dramatic displacement generally follows, we seldom find the chance to observe this process in detail. In the last few years, however, economic hard times have stalled gentrification, so that people who may not have intended to be neighbors have come to share problematic communities. They bring to these communities different resources, visions of neighborhood, expectations for neighbors, and patterns of everyday interaction. The limits and opportunities of class shape varied neighborhood traditions at the same time that these traditions stretch and enliven the constraints of class. Stalled gentrification thus makes everyday life a rich arena for exploring the interaction of passions, economics, habits, and ways of carving out a life.

My research, six years of participant-observation and structured interviews, took place in a neighborhood that I will call Elm Valley, where class divisions tend to coincide with renting and owning. A streetcar suburb in a northeastern city, Elm Valley lost many of its white residents in the 1950s and 1960s. After a period when its population was mostly Black American, Elm Valley—like other areas undergoing gentrification—has been rediscovered by white middle-class settlers (Allen, 1980; Goldfield, 1980; Hennig, 1982; McCaffrey, 1982). Other new immigrants have come as well, able, because of the city's strict rent control laws, to crowd into small apartments. Today the population of this

neighborhood of about 5000 people is approximately 50% Black American, 20% Latin American, 20% white, and 10% immigrants from other parts of the world, especially Southeast Asia, East Africa, and the Caribbean. If the gentrification that began in the mid-1970s had continued, most of the Black owners would have been displaced by higher taxes and pressure from speculators; the tenants, too, would have been forced out by renovations and condominium conversions. Instead, city legislation and high interest rates have, since 1980, stalled gentrification. Thus, Elm Valley is surprisingly diverse, and home ownership crosses lines of race. Black families make up the majority of both owners and renters. Almost all non-Anglo immigrant groups rent, however; and most of the young, newer, white residents own their homes.[1]

In spite of the disruption of gentrification and displacement, the neighborhood might be a model of class and cultural integration. Distinctly bounded by a park and two avenues, it has a lively main street and many small businesses that allow neighbors to build contacts (Jacobs, 1961). The architecture of Elm Valley stresses the front porch, and its wide, deep alleys encourage informal, disclosing interaction from kitchens, around gardens, and over clotheslines out back. Finally, the Black families who bought houses in the 1950s, together with the core of white families who chose to stay, have given Elm Valley an unusual cross-racial bridge that until recently stretched out a tradition of civic activism.[2]

These neighborhood qualities have shaped passionate attachments to Elm Valley, but with gentrification these attachments have failed to cross the barriers of social class. Neighborhoodwide organization has folded after 100 years. New owners wage an escalating memo and bulletin war against the men on the street. In the large apartment buildings that preserve Elm Valley's class diversity, tenants discriminate among themselves as they negotiate with their landlords about renovation and control. Elm Valley is a crumbling community of lost possibilities, even though people there are trying to resist chaotic change and take control of their lives. Yet they bring to these efforts disparate, sometimes distracting visions of neighborhood and of neighbors. This article explores the conflicts that have erupted from those perceptions, as well as the clues those conflicts hold to the interaction of class and culture.

RENTERS FACING OWNERS

On one block in Elm Valley a large dilapidated apartment building that I call The Manor faces attractive rowhouses across the street. Renters and owners do not enter one another's homes, but looking across the street allows them glimpses of others' lives. Renters see owners engaged in optional, honorable tasks such as carpentry, painting, and gardening. This renovation and tinkering ironically mirrors the deterioration of The Manor. In addition, most of tenants' domestic duties are defensive, fighting back filth in their overcrowded apartments. When families postpone washing dishes, let food sit out overnight, or fail to mop their floors after meals, they invite pests that are especially problematic if the families sleep where they eat. Many one-bedroom apartments shelter from four to a dozen people, who sleep in the living/dining room area and, for example, store their shoes under the coffee table. Such intensive use means recleaning the same small space each day to reap the largely negative rewards of relatively fewer roaches and mice. The puttering, *offensive* tasks renters observe across the street cast these circumstances into sharp relief.

These same tasks also signal to tenants owners' control over the physical facades of their houses. By contrast, tenants feel strongly their own lack of control over a facade. For example, they are not allowed to use the grass in front of their building to play games or mind children. If they do, the resident manager may emerge from the building with a shrill public reprimand. This lack of control is obvious in other ways as well. Tenants would like a say about such strategic decisions as installing a security system, controlling pests, permanently repairing the elevator and the boiler. Many feel at the mercy of machines that swallow money more reliably than they dispense goods and services. The erratic support system of The Manor makes everyday life a gamble: A person might return home loaded with groceries and a child in a stroller to discover a broken elevator and face a four-floor walkup, or put off washing his or her hair

until morning only to find that there will be no hot water for three days. The laundryroom is a source of special indignities; residents have to stand in line for the few machines that work, jealously defend their places between loads, and negotiate the treacherous transition from washers to even scarcer, often cold driers.

Even when tenants are inside their apartments, conversations and quarrels, the smell of meals, and the sounds of music and television seep through the walls and out into the halls; embarrassing substances drip through the floors and ceilings. As one woman put it, "I know everybody hears our little family things." And they did: This woman's husband was a notorious drinker who enjoyed playing Dr. King's "I Have a Dream" speech at top volume when high. Other families' secrets erupted as well, as a bathtub might overflow, smoke filter out, or a woman chase her husband into the hall.

Finally, tenants find telling the places where they see owners—outdoors but in charge, on their porches, in their yards, shovelling the snow from a small patch of sidewalk. These transitional spaces highlight the easy movement outdoors and back inside that tenants lack, for they must negotiate buffer zones such as hallways, elevators, and stairwells. Although they enjoy meeting neighbors in these places, tenants feel vulnerable there as well (Jacobs 1961; Reed, 1974). The annexes to a house also bear witness to greater space inside (which families can use to separate eating, sleeping, and recreational activities), and to a more negotiable domestic organization (as families can divide themselves up in ways that parents who must lug small children with them to the laundry room cannot). Thus, these glimpses of owners' lives reflect varied features of life in a house and the rights and privileges that accompany owning one: easy access, choices about tasks and companions, negotiable space, taking the domestic offensive, and orchestrating a flexible family.

When owners look across the street at the dwellings of tenants, they see an impersonal shared facade with no options for outdoor tasks beyond fixing and washing cars. Some complain that the building blocks the sun. Some comment on what they consider to be an astonishing parade of foot traffic and a great deal of hauling. Rather than cars, most tenants depend on the multipurpose pull-along cart that is a centerpiece of low-income urban life. Those tenants who prefer the public laundromat to The Manor's whimsical machines join others who tow groceries and small children. All of these sights seem embarrassing as they testify to a less-controlled presentation of self, a perception shared by some tenants who complain about having to display their dirty laundry and who line their carts with plastic garbage bags to preserve what privacy they can. Finally, from the vantage point of owners, renters seem to engage in widespread, inappropriate use of the outside, a matter at the center of conflict in Elm Valley. Because owners know little beyond what they see at places like The Manor, the people who use the street seem to have become emblematic of renters. Their activities outdoors testify to contrasting strategies for living in a neighborhood.

THE WORK OF THE STREET

Elm Valley's tenants choose tremendous financial sacrifice to stay in a neighborhood they prefer to those suburbs rapidly swelling with the displaced poor. Some do not see this as a choice, citing the "time and trouble it takes to move" or "the money we'd spend commuting back into town," and claiming "I'd be back over here everyday anyway." Others, however, are explicit about opting for a neighborhood. What I will call "the work of the street" reflects, encourages, and rewards that decision to stay.

The work of the street reflects in part the small, hot apartments, in which people feel they cannot entertain, and the sparse financial resources that prevent renters from traveling freely. Although women use the street freely during the day, and although there are women on the street and linked to the street at night as well, they do not gather there in the clear and dramatic ways that men do. Their networking strategies seem more varied and more likely to be inside, whether at work, at church, or inside their buildings. The work of the street seems to be largely the preserve of men.

On the street men bolster family economies. They network and they pool. They swap services such as rides, repairs, and hauling; exchange goods such as clothing, small appliances, furniture, food stamps, and things from work such as crabs, tostados, pesticides, and cleaning fluids. Men often trade goods for favors—souse meat or "gas money" for a ride; pirated or home-grown vegetables for babysitting; playing a number in exchange for "a taste"; help with moving in exchange for a crib; homemade soup for a watch. Sometimes men organize small cooperatives for a trip to a suburban farmers' market to shop in bulk. The pooling and swapping that is so important to the poor and so often the concern of women is in this situation an activity that men also share.

Some men earn their living by streetwork. One man owns a truck, which he uses for harvesting the surplus vegetables of suburban gardeners, moving furniture, delivering appliances, and salvaging trees to sell for firewood. Another man sells dresses, coats, and jewelry on the street and is generally available there to sweep and run errands for shopkeepers, help mind children for passersby, or deliver them to nursery school. Men like these two are conscientious and self-conscious custodians of the street, keeping careful track of what goes on during the day and often sharing information and delivering messages and warnings.

Other men do not live from streetwork but look to it to solve routine problems: to find information about a city bureaucracy, to look for jobs, to have appliances repaired, to locate help with moving, to fill ordinary, everyday needs. The street as *work* looms large in family negotiations; men stress its financial benefits when they bargain for time away from their homes: "I have to try to run into Ben so that I can tell him Maria needs firewood"; "I have to deliver these greens to Harper so that I can tell Jimmy to come around and fix the stereo"; "How do you expect me to find a job if you won't let me go to the tavern?" But the men of Elm Valley, like their counterparts in other cities, love the street (Hannerz, 1969; Liebow, 1967; Suttles, 1968; Williams, 1981). It is fruitless to untangle the financial benefits of streetwork from the other attractions of streetlife, and the men of Elm Valley would not do that, for finances are interwoven with a great deal of trust and talk, lasting social relationships, and the detailed knowledge that works just as well to manage stigma as to cook up deals.

In the intricate world of the street men do all they can to understand the details of one another's biographies. Because they memorize others' reputations, they tolerate a great deal of deviance and diversity. I was first struck by this early one morning when a slightly tipsy man approached me with a big sharp chisel. I was grateful when another man chorused, "Just getting off work, Curly?" and proceeded to tell me that Curly worked all night cleaning and repairing office buildings. I particularly appreciated this exchange because the second man had tried to make me feel safe on the street, but there are many other examples. One man is well liked but known to be a pickpocket; those whose pockets he picks generally blame themselves because they know, and know that he knows they know he does that. Another man is known as a soft touch but a terror "when he's drinking," yet another as a soft touch when he's drinking. Others are known to be "not drinking," a personal career linked to problems of health, family conflict, alcoholism, or probation.

The street is also an arena for preserving the culture of the Carolinas, through foodways (souse meat, greens, and many parts of the pig, including tails, ears, and knuckles); remedies (junction weed boiled with a penny for chicken pox, wild onion roots boiled with butter and Calvert whiskey for a cold, ear wax for chapped lips); expressions (to be pleasantly tipsy on Calvert is to be "high as a Georgia pine"). Men also identify real friends as "from Carolina" or "from my home town." On the street they share urban lore as well, organizing complicated neighborhood lotteries around football games, sharing stories about the numbers, playing strategies, lucky wins, narrow losses ("That's how the numbers get you"). Many residents agree that the more dire their straits, the more obliged they are to play. Beyond financial possibilities, however, numbers strategies and lore are much more than work; one's regular number, evolving tactics for choosing one and deciding where to play it, biography of wins and narrow losses are important parts of personal identity. Each person is a complex weave of vivid everyday detail acted out on the street.

The world of the street draws in its shopkeepers and muddles divisions between shopper and seller. One man, for example, claims that in 18 years he has done no shopping outside Elm Valley. He has long-term relationships with some of the older shopkeepers, relations which may involve credit or part-time employment. As new stores open, he entrenches himself in each, coming to be known by name and to entangle and complicate relationships, crossing all the usual boundaries of urban consumption. He arranges layaway at the drugstore, barter at the thrift shop (whose owner watches for and saves clothes that fit him and his family), charitable contributions for his children's nursery school from the new grocery store. He defines his needs so that they can be satisfied in Elm Valley and then redefines and stretches what it offers.

It is on the street that we see most clearly the passion for texture that is central to the renters' neighborhood world, a passion that emerges from the interplay of financial constraints and cultural traditions. This passion for texture is much like the thick description valued by folklorists and ethnographers (see Geertz, 1973). It includes a decided preference for depth over breadth, an interest in rich, vivid, personal, concrete, entangled detail. It involves repetition, density, mining a situation from many faces and angles. A joke, a story, a teasing line can be retold and rephrased many times, as long as the emphasis varies just slightly. Inside apartments I saw a love of texture in a desire to fill empty spaces with artifacts and objects and to manage the density of domestic life by weaving through it the sounds and colors and rhythms of television. It emerged in renters' interest in programs such as *Dallas* and *Dynasty*, which offer vivid, concrete, detailed entanglements. It is clear in many residents' preference for local over national news, for stories that can be followed from beginning to end. It is clearest on the street in the intimate knowledge men build of one another, in the ways that roles, institutions, and relationships are complicated and rewoven, the formal and informal sectors muddled, interaction intimate and multifaceted.

THE METROPOLITAN VISION

Owners have also chosen a community in the face of other options. New owners' reasons for choosing Elm Valley vary. Some like the convenient commute, but keep more cosmopolitan personal attachments; some are fond of the lovely streetscapes and fine, historic architecture; some are nostalgic, even utopian in their hope of rooting themselves in an old-fashioned urban neighborhood; some are activists tackling international problems there. Many value the personal growth that they feel accompanies confronting diversity. Their perceptions of neighborhood life generally differ from renters, and these perceptions again reflect some of the complex class cultures, including varied resources for travel and indoor activities as well as radically different visions of what a neighborhood offers and how it should be used.[3] Looking at some of owners' strategies for handling family needs should make this difference clear.

As a result of stalled residential gentrification, the commercial gentrification of Elm Valley is also incomplete (see Hennig, 1982). Although the commercial strip boasts an art and an antique store, there is no PLANTS, Etc. or California Café. Thrift shops, dry cleaners, and liquor stores rely on large numbers of clients rather than wealthy ones. Most owners find them uninteresting and inadequate and therefore shop outside the neighborhood, often while driving to and from work.

For child enrichment, many owners look outside Elm Valley for pools, schools, playgrounds, violin and ballet lessons. Few owners avoid the neighborhood completely; most use mixed strategies.[4] One woman, for example, devoted many hours of volunteer time to a local nursery school, for she felt that it offered her daughter an important multicultural experience. Now, however, she sends her child to elementary school outside the neighborhood. A strong advocate of hiring local people for domestic work, repairs, and childcare, she shops in remote parts of the metropolitan area and does not walk through Elm Valley because she considers it unsafe. (To some extent gender crosscuts class in limiting women's movement at night; however, cars do provide shells of sorts for metropolitan travel for those who own them.)

Another woman, active in a bid to have Elm Valley named a historic district, has led a fight to stop the local Korean grocery store from placing advertising leaflets under windshield wipers. It developed during a meeting on the topic that she had no idea that this store underpriced local supermarket chains, or that the owner had hired all local workers ("winos" in some versions) to cement neighborhood relations. It had not occurred to her to shop there. Her assumptions would be incomprehensible to many tenants; they had learned as much as they could about the new store as soon as it had opened, in part through the new workers, who gave the owners an immediate pipeline to the street.

Other owners juggle buffering and involvement in a number of ways; but strategies that may be appropriate for families can create problems for the community. Elm Valley already houses institutions inherently segregated by class: buses, church basement daycare centers, laundromats. Other places that might jumble people across class lines and encourage small contacts are segregated by default (see Jacobs, 1961; Love, 1973; Merry, 1980, 1981; Molotch, 1969). These range from the local elementary school to shops, taverns, and parks. That owners leave the neighborhood to find more elaborate toddler parks is especially hard on female tenants with small children. Women work parks to build contacts with other parents so that they can organize play groups, carpools, babysitting coops, birthday parties and everyday friendships (see Swartley, 1983). Most women are wary of Elm Valley's one rather inadequate park, which therefore remains in the hands of men, many of whom do take their children there, but most of whom hardly need another arena for building contacts.

Thus, the greater financial resources, shopping, and child enrichment strategies as well as the more metropolitan vision of many new owners deprive them of access to the street. To just hint at the complex interplay of race, ethnicity, and residence here, the more extended and established Black households are nearly always tied through at least one male member to the street. The few longer-term white residents of Elm Valley either work the streets or the alleys. Those tenants in group houses or small apartments, even if they are white and new to Elm Valley, are less likely to own cars, more likely to walk and to know at least some of the shopkeepers who are tied into street talk. But few of the newer white owners pursue these arenas.[5]

"HOW CAN WE GET THE BUMS OFF THE STREET?"

The various groups involved perceive one anothers' strategies differently. One day several men prominent on the street explained their vision of the situation: The newer owners are different from the older, "racial whites," who are "stuck in (Elm Valley) with its cheap beers and cheap (Black people) because they're too old or too poor to move." The newer residents "move in but don't associate." In part they may be afraid: "They hear a lot of garbage when they go outside the neighborhood to associate." This "garbage" is not challenged because those who hear it do not get to know the details of their neighbors' personalities. But mostly they do not associate because "they just don't know how—they weren't raised up that way." Although these men feel strongly that the newer residents should "learn how to speak on the street," their assessment is fairly benign in its stress on cultural background.

Their attention to detail also contributes to these men's feelings about the new owners. Some of the men on the street cite neighborhood history as a reason to feel benign: Whites have always lived in Elm Valley; integration was fairly painless; prejudiced individuals stand out and can be known. Some of these individuals, how-

ever, are regarded with affection simply because they are known. For example, one of the tavern owners is an 82-year-old native Kentuckian who freely uses racial epithets, organized hard for John Connelly's presidential campaign, and tries to persuade Blacks that they should support the party of Lincoln. She is widely considered a cheap and temperamental employer and a vindictive, erratic hostess. Nonetheless, many details of her life are known: Her concern for alcoholics; her personal rescue of a popular retarded man; the joy she takes in children. (Her case demonstrates, I believe, the extent to which a passion for detail and texture is ultimately a forgiving world view.)

Other men cite the fallout effects of class privilege as grounds for their relatively benign feelings toward the new owners. Property owners demand and receive decent city services, so that Elm Valley's streets, traffic lights, and curbs are better repaired and its trash more reliably hauled away than in the past. New owners also bring volunteer time, money, and knowledge to neighborhood activities; they organize block parties, renovate the local library, and heal the elm trees.[6]

Owners for the most part do not reciprocate this good will; their feelings seem to vary from indifference to tolerance or compassion to vague unease or active dislike. They lack many of the tenants' inclinations to build detailed cross-class portraits: Tenants (and certainly not the men on the street) do not bring tangible class resources into Elm Valley life; new owners do not call on neighborhood memories in evaluating biographies; many have a broader, more metropolitan vision rather than an eye for local detail. In any event, new owners are not often motivated to explore the texture of Elm Valley life. Their feelings toward tenants in general are not at issue here; my concern, like theirs, is the way in which some owners' more extreme feelings about the men on the street (as standing for tenants) are splitting Elm Valley apart.

Late in 1983 a cluster of angry residents organized a committee they called "Elm Valley's Corridor Committee." During their early months they distributed memos and handbills attacking the men on the street and citing particular abuses such as loitering, littering, drinking and using profanity. "What can we do about public urination?" queried one flier. Eventually this group circulated a letter to Elm Valley households with a list of demands, including one for foot patrols with guard dogs.

The city's charter establishes for each neighborhood an elected neighborhood council, composed of five members representing small districts within the neighborhood. Hearing murmurs of support for the Corridor Committee, this council invited city officials to a public meeting to air the complaints. The Corridor Committee's chair set the tone, asking in her introductory remarks, "How can we get the bums off the street?"

The committee's paper war had gone unnoticed by tenants, for it occurred outside the social system of personal exposure and talk which they see as structuring neighborhood life. The meeting was another matter. Few tenants attended, for they feel that the neighborhood council is a property owners' preserve. What most considered to be the vicious contents of the letter, however, had leaked out. Several of the more central and flamboyant men from the street therefore attended the meeting out of anger and curiosity. Also, the more politically active but usually distracted residents came to argue against what they saw as racist rabble-rousing, as did some of the men from established Black households with ties to the street. For the first time Elm Valley had a forum where people could talk and interpret acts across class.

At the meeting the owners made momentary alliance with feminists who did not want to be harassed on the street. Trying to reconcile these two interests, a white renter who also works as a nursery school social worker suggested that when walking the street a person "salute each man." She argued that the men on the street feel that they make it safer, because they watch out for their friends and they also know what goes on. They know who is likely to mug, and after the mugging they will hear about it. Some of the Black householders commented that outdoor toilets might address the public urination problem and that large trash cans might help with litter. A Latino leader argued that the men on the street "don't have homes." The only man to talk from the street complained that "the police always come down on us but not the Spanish people." The outcome of this long, angry and complicated meeting was the triumph of a liberal solution: Elected officials repeated their reluctance to "enforce manners"; the police chief cited "people's right to use the street"; beat officers explained the difficult logistics of arresting someone urinating outdoors; and the council was charged to explore available social services.

The wide appeal of the Corridor Committee is puzzling, however, especially since it grew among people who had chosen to live in a varied urban community. To some extent class cultures can help to explain this appeal: We have seen that the interplay between traditions and resources that expresses class cultures encourages owners to choose breadth over depth in everyday life. The virtues of this choice are obvious, as these families preserve access to those facilities that they feel enrich and broaden their lives, and that offer them continuing advantages in school and at work. Yet probing for depth, texture, and intricacy seems to be a more successful strategy than buffering and juggling density if one wants to carve out a comfortable life in Elm Valley. Grasping the neighborhood's texture depends on a rich public life of inspection and exposure for at least the male members of renting families. Yet this occasion for building and exploring texture stigmatizes those who have figured out how well it works to build a community.

"YOUR BUILDING IS GOING DOWN, DOWN . . ."

The second arena of conflict is between landlords and renters irritated by the deterioration of their buildings. The Manor provides one example: A network of women tenants began to organize in winter, a time of intense sociability within the building and a time when tenants felt the building's problems more harshly. The women were angry about the malfunctioning machines, the erratic heat and hot water, and especially concerned about the stairs and hallways, which were emerging as popular places to socialize, smoke, and drink. They initiated a campaign of petition signing and letter writing. The most telling feature of the women's written complaints was the way they were framed. These frames reveal a sense of having paid with rent money and time for a home, a place where one belongs and feels secure. These women added a moral dimension as they called up a relationship between building a home and the kinds of people they are. They cited personal qualities to legitimize their requests. For example, each woman noted in her letter how long she had lived in The Manor: "I have lived here for 18 years," or "This is the first time in 13 years I have had to complain," or "We have been here $8\,^1/_2$ years and have cooperated with the Agency in every way." This matter of ethos seems crucial in legitimizing their demands. The women asked for more say about transitional places and the mechanical support system. Their demands did not appeal to universal human rights or even to local law. They demanded particular privileges because they were particular sorts of people: moral, concerned, and settled. Ironically, the glimpses they have managed of owners' lives seem to have encouraged them to identify with owners as a kind of people.[7]

These personal letters offered details of the women's everyday lives ("I am often home alone in the afternoons and it is very cold") and tried out names rumored to attach to officers of the management corporation. The corporation response, however, was a less personal, masterful mass memo. Beginning "Dear Tenant," it mentioned the tenants' complaints as well as the grievances of owners across the street about litter on the lawn. It grouped hallways, stairwells, the laundry room, and the lawn as "public areas," and used them as evidence that tenants of the Manor were *not* like homeowners after all: They dumped trash on the floor, they left graffiti in the laundry room, they used the stairwell as a bathroom. Tenants should improve themselves, for "It's your home." Lumping all tenants denies the exceptional homeowning qualities the women attributed to themselves. The message is that these kinds of discriminations are inappropriate; while the women had invoked the cultural attributes surrounding connections and commitments to a place, management responded by lumping them by class.

Tenants offered varied explanations for the rapid and distressing decline of the building. One theory held that management was allowing it to deteriorate on purpose so that long-term tenants would leave. Turnovers allowed the landlords to raise rents; and if the building deteriorated enough to be condemned, the owners could gut it and convert into condominiums. Few of the renters believed that management would collaborate in the building's decline; many felt that owners would want to keep homeowning-like people in the building and would certainly want to keep the property up.

Another view suggested that a recent change in resident managers was responsible. Like many other mediators, resident managers give owners a face; they personalize landlords to tenants at the same time that they are known as tenants themselves. In theory they are neutral and fairly powerless mediators, there as go-betweens for owners and tenants to everyone's mutual benefit. In practice they are rarely neutral enough to jeopardize their jobs. As one manager put it (in response to a tenant's complaint that his negligence had meant that her friend's ceiling had collapsed and almost killed a baby), "I only got one friend and that's the man who gave me my job."

This manager, Mr. Ironsides, was a problem drinker who rarely responded to tenant requests for repairs. Coincident with stalled gentrification and the movement of Latino tenants into the building, he had died. He was replaced by a woman who proved to be competent and prompt at managing repairs. Mysteriously, tenants began to mutter within a few weeks that she was "too nice," "too weak," and "too soft." Mr. Ironsides reemerged in the public memory as a hero, a man who "roamed the halls with a blackjack" keeping order. Ms. Johnson's unpopularity was partly a matter of timing and partly a matter of gender. Some of the hostility reflected ethnicity—a Jamaican labeled "African" by the custodial staff, she was seen as too lenient toward other "foreigners." This hostility that Black renters felt toward her illuminates the third divisive arena in Elm Valley.

"THE DO DROP IN" OR HOME AS SANCTUARY

Many Black renters placed the bulk of the blame for the building's problems on the "Spanish people," a half-dozen extended families recently arrived from El Salvador. The complaints of women and men tenants against these families varied in revealing ways. Women tenants complained many times that "Spanish people use the hall like a porch." The young men liked to congregate in the halls, and they often failed to manage the stigma of public life in time-honored local ways, for example, by moving discreetly away from a woman approaching or by offering a wholesome-sounding greeting to signal benevolent intent. In addition, they cheerfully broke

bothersome rules: One group, for example, simply commandeered the service elevator whenever the one designated for tenants was stuck somewhere else.

Most striking about Black women's antagonisms toward these young Latino men, however, was their use of labels emphasizing ethnicity rather than gender and age. Most of us are leery of groups of young men hovering in an ambiguous place, but what tenants stressed in encoding these groups was that they were "Spanish." Perhaps the stress on ethnicity reflected Latino families' general transformations of domestic life space. As large, extended families in desperate straits, they crowded many people into their small apartments. Other tenants claimed that "one might sign the lease and then they sneak all kinds of others in." Not knowing exactly who or how many occupied a unit disoriented other tenants, and their confusion was compounded by irritation at the efficient dispersal of Latino family members to manage tasks such as laundry. Those tenants who had developed ways to beat the laundry room rush soon found that there was never a time when several elderly Latinas were not in the laundry room minding infants and washing many loads of clothes. Even more annoying was the houselike use to which Latino families transformed their apartments. On two floors domestic networks spread out over several apartments, but because they shared many tasks and responsibilities, the families flowed between these units, left their doors open, and encouraged their children to play in the halls. They did, in fact, use the hall as a porch.

A hall is the closest thing to a porch that tenants have. It is an important transitional area for storing trash on the way to the trash room, packing urban carts, and chatting. Informal dress and even night clothes seem to be acceptable in the hall (see Reed, 1974). Latino families were drawing a fairly appropriate analogy between hall and porch that was consistent with the living arrangements most had known at home. But to other tenants this use of the hall as porch highlighted all its contradictions: This great, shared, indoor porch in which there was neither privacy nor say so demanded some sort of cooperation in limiting interaction. Families who used it detracted from others' right to have it not used.

Women saw these behaviors as proof that the Latino tenants were not like homeowners. Some were concerned about the preponderance of men in these families, and argued, "Women make an apartment more like a home." Others stressed transiency: "They think this is the `Do Drop In,' they're like college students; they don't care about keeping it up because they don't want to make it a home."

Men phrased the problem a little differently. Many male tenants felt that Latinos "use the hall like the street," and that they did not make the appropriate overtures for sharing public space. In turn, they attributed all anonymous troubles to Latinos, including the trash room fires that grew common during the winter of 1983 and one episode in which 50 tires were slashed. As one man put it, "Spanish people only come out at night, because they think they're white then. Black people do what they want during the day."

There is an irony in this process that seems to parallel what is happening outdoors. Black renters' passion for texture and detail is thwarted by a language and set of customs they do not understand. Most of the refugees define home differently than Elm Valley's long-term tenants because they have radically different priorities for it. Many want to offer shelter to fellow refugees and, in fact, to use the promise of shelter to encourage kin and friends to migrate. They are not so interested in keeping up the property or necessarily in building ties. They want to use home as a sanctuary. Even those who may want more privacy soon face a choice between cutting off fellow refugees and doubling up. Their desperation has created scenes in several apartments featuring rows of cots and numbers of depressed and displaced people.

None of these things is particularly clear to other tenants, who know little of the circumstances in Central America that have propelled these refugees north. The theory they have built to explain The Manor's decline relies heavily on the immediate and concrete details of building life that they can observe every day. Whenever one family moves out, it is replaced by another of lesser quality. This gradual substitution of good tenants by worse ones means that the building inevitably deteriorates. Management is complicit "because they don't screen new tenants," but the problem is essentially one of tenant mobility. If tenants move out, there is likely to be something wrong with the building anyway; those who come in are by definition not settled or committed, and if they are willing to move into a declining building, they are doubly suspect. Speaking a different language and bringing culturally distinct and inappropriate traditions for inhabiting space further complicate the problem. In The Manor women argue that by settling in and taking an active, moral interest in a building one can act like a homeowner. This ethos then frames the rhetoric through which they demanded particular privileges and services. The frame turns out to be a divisive one that leads to blaming other tenants for problems with the landlord and for the decline of the building.

CONCLUSION

Stalled gentrification brings together residents who ordinarily would not be neighbors and who have disparate options, constraints, perceptions, and traditions that are expressed in varied, easily misunderstood strategies for urban life. New owners buy a piece of a place and feel that through property they have put down roots in the community. Acquiring the responsibility and concerns attached to property values makes them less sympathetic to the men on the street, who seem to endanger those things. Their more cosmopolitan attachments and broader visions place them to some extent outside Elm Valley's cultural system.

Unable to buy houses, Elm Valley's renters have bought time and used that time to dig in and build ties. Entangled in a rich weave of local ethnographic detail, renters have expressed their anger over the threat of displacement in part through efforts to align themselves with the qualities that seem to characterize owners: settledness, commitment, connections, control. They have thus built difficult divisions among themselves. Owners distance themselves from the characteristics that seem to stick to renters: inappropriate display, misuse of public space and time, immersion in immediate time and place.

Ironically, a rich, diverse community with many possibilities for truly intricate integration is torn apart by conflicts rooted in the constraints of class, the traditions through which people link themselves to ethnic and racial groups, and the playing out of those constraints and traditions in everyday life strategies.

NOTES

1. For many reasons that will become apparent, the name of this neighborhood is a pseudonym, the location disguised, the statistics rounded out, and the description of my research abbreviated. The research has involved a complicated constellation of residential patterns and community organizing activities as well as formal research strategies such as taped interviews and participant observation. Because I was the mother of two infants during the research, I have been worried about distorted findings, particularly regarding male-female relations and in describing such arenas as the laundry room. I have found Rosaldo's (1984) discussion of "the positioned observer" reassuring.

2. Some of these friendships continue on the integrated residential blocks. Because they are cross-racial and longstanding, they are an important kind of neighborhood glue.

3. To stress the circumstances of renting and owning is not to deny the importance of race and ethnicity. There is some evidence that the passion for texture has deep roots in Black culture, seen, for example, in urban street epics, children's clapping, rhyming and jumprope games, and blues music. The circumstances of renting thus encourage and bolster the emergence of a cultural form that has been expressed in other times, places, and media as well. It is significant in Elm Valley that many Black householders seem to entexture their alley communities or residential blocks and to link themselves to the street through at least one male family member. However, renting as a class constraint is still important in encouraging people to probe for depth. White renters are generally much more tied to the shops, schools, and sidewalks of Elm Valley than their counterparts who own. It is too soon to tell exactly what the strategies of the new, renting refugees from Southeast Asia and Central America will be: Early observations indicate that Latin men have begun to embrace the life of the street; Southeast Asian families may be building a public life around one apartment building.

4. In one unusual but representative situation, two men with two toddlers apiece grew to know each other when one was assigned to be the other's doctor and noted from his patient's file that they were neighbors. The children began to play together, but their paths soon split. The doctor had bought a house in Elm Valley before it was fashionable and he enjoys its international variety. He was, however, determined that his children not suffer culturally because of his decision. When the doctor was in charge of the children, they went to a park in a wealthy neighborhood, to swimming lessons in the suburbs, or to a museum. The patient minded his own children frequently, but he saw their early developmental tasks differently. Although he took them regularly to Elm Valley's seedy park, he also let them play right on the sidewalk while he talked to his friends, and he took them shopping and into taverns with him. He patiently herded them to the store, allowing them to inspect every plant and animal specimen, vehicle, pothole, stairwell, and construction site that caught their attention along the way. He taught them to greet and joke with all the shopkeepers, bus drivers, and people on the street. He wanted them to learn details, nicknames, reputations, stories and histories, what to expect and predict, how to capture texture for themselves.

5. Many of the owning families do seem to seek texture in particular places, revisiting, for example, a special park, a small museum, or the downtown dinosaurs. They bring to these places the same ethnographic affection that for many renters is an encompassing, definitive strategy for living in a neighborhood.

6. Hennig (1982) writes of gentrification that although planners expected it to boost cities' financial resources by increasing tax revenues and decreasing demand for social services, this has not been the case. New owners demand more, back up those demands, and dislike contributing to the public sector in exchange for services they are more likely to find elsewhere. This appreciation of class privilege in a multicultural situation is similar to what Rosen (1977, 1980) found in his research at a preschool: Middle-class parents stressed a desire to expose their children to cultural differences; poorer parents stressed the status of a school that middle-class children attended and a desire to reap the benefits in skills and resources that would help their children excel in schools later on.

7. The house is a well-worn centerpiece of the American Dream, in which it usually stands for happiness and success. Constance Perrin's (1978) interviews with people in the housing and banking industries revealed that they read a great deal into houses and in particular into owning one. Her informants easily painted owners as more independent, responsible, and rooted than tenants, whom they believed to be poor providers and decision makers, socially marginal, and uncommitted to a community. The mortgages that banks grant owners certify that they are properly climbing the ladder of life; and owning a house further encourages good character and valued behaviors, in part by liberating residents from the problematic relations that stem from tenants' shared use of common facilities. Realtors seem to have carried these associations even further, as their promotional materials refer to houses as "homes." "Home" to stand for even an empty house has crept into popular usage almost metaphorically, with all the nuances of connections, commitments, and roots that "home" used to pose in contrast to house.

REFERENCES

Allen, I. (1980) "The ideology of dense neighborhood development." *Urban Affairs Q.* 15, 4: 409–428.

Geertz, C. (1973) *The Interpretation of Cultures.* New York: Basic Books.

Goldfield, D. (1980) "Private neighborhood redevelopment and displacement." *Urban Affairs Q.* 15, 4: 453–468.

Hannerz, U. (1969) *Soulside.* New York: Columbia University Press.

Hennig, J. (1982) *Gentrification in Adams Morgan.* Washington, DC: George Washington University Press.

Jacobs, J. (1961) *The Life and Death of Great American Cities.* New York: Random House.

Liebow, E. (1967) *Tally's Corner.* Boston: Little, Brown.

Love, R. (1973) "The fountains of urban life." *Urban Life and Culture* 2, 2: 161–209.

McCaffrey, P. (1982) "The gentry are coming." *Perspectives* (Winter): 22–27.

Merry, S. (1980) "Racial integration in an urban neighborhood." *Human Organization* 39, 1: 59–69.

——— . (1981) *Urban Danger: Life in a Neighborhood of Strangers.* Philadelphia: Temple University Press.

Molotch, H. (1969) "Racial integration in a transition community." *Amer. Soc. Rev.* 34: 878–893.

Perrin, C. (1978) *Everything in Its Place.* Princeton, NJ: Princeton University Press.

Reed, P. (1974) "Situated interaction: normative and nonnormative bases of social behavior in two urban residential settings." *Urban Life and Culture* 2, 4: 460–487.

Rosaldo, R. (1984) "Grief and a headhunter's rage," in E. Bruner (ed.) *Text, Play, and Story.* Washington, DC: AES.

Rosen, D. (1977) "Multicultural education: an anthropological perspective." *Anthropology and Education Q.* 8: 221–226.

——— . (1980) "Class and ideology in an innercity preschool." *Anthro. Q.* 53: 219–228.

Suttles, G. D. (1968) *The Social Order of the Slum.* Chicago: University of Chicago Press.

Swartley, A. (1983) "If this were any other job, I'd shove it." *Mother Jones* 8 (May): 33–55.

Williams, M. (1981) *On the Street Where I Live.* New York: Holt, Rinehart & Winston.

10

Political Organization and Social Control

Political organization and **social control** are about the ways in which power is distributed and embedded in society. Power is found in all social relationships. Even in seemingly innocuous places like Disney World, Clifford Shearing and Philip Stenning show the subtle and not so subtle ways in which people are controlled. Power is not about physical force alone, as was shown by the way the Ayatollah Khomeini defeated the Shah of Iran with neither troops nor equipment or, as was shown more recently, by the dramatic collapse of the Soviet Union. This is what makes the study of it so fascinating. An insightful perspective on these events can be gained from the world traditionally studied by anthropologists.

Undoubtedly, one of the most profound events to have set the parameters for the political structures under which the poor majority of the world's population live came with the Colonial Era. This was a short, intense period from about 1884 to 1960 when the European powers, at the height of the Industrial Revolution, acquired large amounts of colonial real estate in Africa and Asia.

Judith Van Allen's essay is a representative study of how this colonial intrusion had an impact on "traditional" society. She shows how **colonialism** undermined women's traditional autonomy and argues that colonial authorities were largely oblivious to what they were doing because the way in which they saw the world and asked questions was shaped by their Victorian outlook. To consolidate their position, the British and the other colonizers used remarkably similar strategies. They created a class of **subalterns**, local indigenes who were propelled into positions of petty power and who ruled on the colonizers' behalf.

In this regard, they were aided by missionaries who provided these subalterns with the minimal educational skills and who played a further important role in legitimating colonial rule. At the same time, missionaries also provided the seedbed for the later anticolonial movements.

Van Allen's study provides a graphic illustration of the process that concerns Jason Clay, namely, the wars between **nations** and **states**. Most of the states in the contemporary world are the product of colonialism.

Van Allen's subalterns, or warrant chiefs and clerks, became the source of the Third World elite or *petite bourgeoisie* whom Clay castigates for using the state to enrich themselves. As Archie Mafeje, a leading African anthropologist, put it: "They think that the way to fish is by emptying the pond." There are a number of reasons for such a predatory worldview, which is intimately tied into how they view the state. Certainly, they do not see the state the way Western political theorists see it, as some sort of neutral umpire protecting and caring for its citizens in exchange for its taxes. As a Papua New Guinean put it to one of this book's editors: "The State is a money box in a tent which is controlled by the senior officials." This intellectual legacy is still very much with us and indeed will probably grow as Africa and the other Southern Hemisphere countries become increasingly marginalized and hence less subject to public scrutiny.

Clay, like Van Allen, sees autonomy as the crucial issue and how **cultural pluralism** is tolerated within the state as the major issue facing the close of this century. This issue is perhaps slightly overstated to make the point. Consider Papua New Guinea as an example: It is a country of some 3 million people with over 700 different nations of which the largest language group has less than 200,000 speakers. Ask any Papua New Guinean what they regard as the major achievement of their Australian colonizers (Papua New Guinea rather reluctantly became independent in 1975), and they will say the creation of **law** and order. Prior to colonization, they will say everyone fought but the Australians brought peace to the country. Papua New Guineans are renowned for their **egalitarian ethos**. Politically, they have no strongly developed **hierarchies** with chiefs or kings. This meant that if they had a dispute, they had to settle it between themselves largely through "self-help," typically in the form of warfare and related compensation payments. The Australians brought peace by creating overarching third-party dispute management forums for the hearing of disputes. (In short, they said, if you have a problem, do not make a war but bring it to the district commissioner to hear it.) This principle of **dispute management** was not new. Indeed, it forms one of the rationales for the creation of the World Court of International Justice. What is important, though, is why were these triadic structures successful during the colonial heyday but not in the post–independence era? Here, a complex array of factors revolving around power and legitimacy come into play. Some of these are brilliantly analyzed in Simon Harrison's article on Armageddon in a small New Guinea village. Conflict, as Harrison points out, can serve constructive ends in certain circumstances. He arrays the number of techniques—some magical, some kinship related, and some economical—that come into play in conflict and conflict management and stresses the role of symbolic violence and how imagined dangers can be used as a technique of social control. Now that the United States no longer has the "Evil Soviet Empire" to fear, who will be imagined as dangerous?

"Sitting on a Man"

Colonialism and the Lost Political Institutions of Igbo Women

Judith Van Allen

When this article was written in 1972 Judith Van Allen was an instructor of political science at the University of California at Berkeley. Since that time, she has written a book with Gene Marine entitled *Food Pollution: The Violation of Our Inner Ecology,* which was published by Holt, Rinehart and Winston.

In the conventional wisdom, Western influence has "emancipated" African women—through the weakening of kinship bonds and the provision of "free choice" in Christian monogamous marriage, the suppression of "barbarous" practices, the opening of schools, the introduction of modern medicine and hygiene, and, sometimes, of female suffrage.

But Westernization is not an unmixed blessing. The experience of Igbo women under British colonialism shows that Western influence can sometimes weaken or destroy women's traditional autonomy and power without providing modern forms of autonomy or power in exchange. Igbo women had a significant role in traditional political life. As individuals, they participated in village meetings with men. But their real political power was based on the solidarity of women, as expressed in their own political institutions—their "meetings" (*mikiri* or *mitiri*), their market networks, their kinship groups, and their right to use strikes, boycotts and force to effect their decisions.

British colonial officers and missionaries, both men and women, generally failed to see the political roles and the political power of Igbo women. The actions of administrators weakened and in some cases destroyed women's bases of strength. Since they did not appreciate women's political institutions, they made no efforts to ensure women's participation in the modern institutions they were trying to foster.

Igbo women haven't taken leadership roles in modern local government, nationalist movements and national government and what roles they *have* played have not been investigated by scholars. The purpose in

"'Sitting on a Man': Colonialism and the Lost Political Institutions of Igbo Women" by Judith Van Allen, from *Canadian Journal of African Studies,* Vol. VI, No. ii, 1972, pp. 165–181. Reprinted with permission.

describing their *traditional* political institutions and source of power is to raise the question of *why* these women have been "invisible" historically, even though they forced the colonial authorities to pay attention to them briefly. We suggest that the dominant view among British colonial officers and missionaries was that politics was a man's concern. Socialized in Victorian England, they had internalized a set of values and attitudes about what they considered to be the natural and proper role of women that supported this belief. We suggest further that this assumption about men and politics has had a great deal to do with the fact that no one has even asked, "Whatever happened to Igbo women's organizations?" even though all the evidence needed to justify the question has been available for 30 years.

IGBO TRADITIONAL POLITICAL INSTITUTIONS[1]

Political power in Igbo society was *diffuse.* There were no specialized bodies or offices in which legitimate power was vested, and no person, regardless of his status or ritual position, had the authority to issue *commands* which others had an obligation to obey. In line with this diffusion of authority, the right to enforce decisions was also diffuse: there was no "state" that held a monopoly of legitimate force, and the use of force to protect ones' interests or to see that a group decision was carried out was considered legitimate for individuals and groups. In the simplest terms, the British tried to create specialized political institutions which commanded authority and monopolized force. In doing so they took into account, eventually, Igbo political institutions dominated by men but ignored those of the women. Thus, women were shut out from political power.

The Igbo lived traditionally in semi-autonomous villages, which consisted of the scattered compounds of 75 or so patri-kinsmen; related villages formed "village-groups" which came together for limited ritual and jural purposes. Villages commonly contained several hundred people; but size varied, and in the more densely populated areas there were "village-groups" with more than 5,000 members.[2] Disputes at all the levels above the compound were settled by group discussion until mutual agreement was reached.[3]

The main Igbo political institution seems to have been the village assembly, a gathering of all adults in the village who chose to attend. Any adult who had something to say on the matter under discussion was entitled to speak—as long as he *or she* said something the others considered worth listening to; as the Igbo say, "a case forbids no one."[4]

Matters dealt with in the village assembly were those of concern to all—either common problems for which collective action was appropriate ("How can we make our market `bigger' than the other villages' markets?") or conflicts which threatened the unity of the village.[5]

Decisions agreed on by the village assembly did not have the force of law in our terms, however. Even after decisions had been reached, social pressure based on consensus and the ability of individuals and groups to enforce decisions in their favour played a major part in giving the force of law to decisions. As Green[6] put it:

> [O]ne had the impression . . . that laws only establish themselves by degrees and then only in so far as they gain general acceptance. A law does not either exist or not exist: rather it goes through a process of establishing itself by common consent or of being shelved by a series of quiet evasions.

Persuasion about the rightness of a particular course of action in terms of tradition was of primary importance in assuring its acceptance and the leaders were people who had the ability to persuade.

The mode of political discourse was that of proverb, parable and metaphor drawn from the body of Igbo tradition.[7] The needed political knowledge was accessible to the average man or woman, since all Igbo were reared with these proverbs and parables. Influential speech was the creative and skillful use of tradition to assure others that a certain course of action was both a wise and right thing to do. The accessibility of this knowledge is indicated by an Igbo proverb: "If you tell a proverb to a fool, he will ask you its meaning."

The leaders of Igbo society were men and women who combined wealth and generosity with "mouth"— the ability to speak well. Age combined with wisdom brought respect but age alone carried little influence. The senior elders who were ritual heads of their lineages were very likely to have considerable influence, but they would not have achieved these positions in the first place if they had not been considered to have good sense and good character.[8] Wealth in itself was no guarantee of influence: a "big man" or "big woman" was not necessarily a wealthy person, but one who had shown skill and generosity in helping other individuals and, especially, the community.[9]

Men owned the most profitable crops such as palm oil, received the bulk of the money from bridewealth, and, if compound heads, presents from the members. Through the patrilineage, they controlled the land, which they could lease to non-kinsmen or to women for a good profit. Men also did most of the long-distance trading which gave higher profit than local and regional trading which was almost entirely in women's hands.[10]

Women were entitled to sell the surplus of their own crops and the palm kernels which were their share of the palm produce. They might also sell prepared foods or the products of special skills, for instance, processed salt, pots and baskets. They pocketed the entire profit, but their relatively lower profit levels kept them disadvantaged relative to the men in acquiring titles and prestige.[11]

For women as well as for men, status was largely achieved, not ascribed. A woman's status was determined more *by her own achievements* than by the achievements of her husband. The resources available to men were greater, however; so that while a woman might rank higher among women than her husband did among men, very few women could acquire the highest titles, a major source of prestige.[12]

At village assemblies men were more likely to speak than were women; women more often spoke only on matters of direct concern to them.[13] Title-holders took leading parts in discussion, and were more likely to take part in "consultation." After a case had been thoroughly discussed, a few men retired in order to come to a decision. A spokesman then announced the decision, which could be accepted or rejected by the assembly.[14]

Apparently no rule forbade women to participate in consultations but they were invited to do so only rarely. The invited women were older women, for while younger men might have the wealth to acquire the higher titles and thus make up in talent what they lacked in age, younger women could not acquire the needed wealth quickly enough to be eligible.[15]

Women, therefore, came second to men in power and influence. While status and the political influence it could bring were achieved and there were no formal limits to women's political power, men through their ascriptive status (members of the patrilineage) acquired wealth which gave them a head start and a life-long advantage over women. The Igbo say that "a child who washes his hands clean deserves to eat with his elders."[16] But at birth some children were given water and some were not.

WOMEN'S POLITICAL INSTITUTIONS

Since political authority was diffuse, the settling of disputes, discussions about how to improve the village or its market, or any other problems of general concern were brought up at various gatherings such as funerals, meetings of kinsmen to discuss burial rituals, and the marketplace, gatherings whose ostensible purpose was not political discussion.[17]

The women's base of political power lay in their own gatherings. Since Igbo society was patrilocal and villages were exogamous, adult women resident in a village would almost all be wives, and others were divorced or widowed "daughters of the village" who had returned home to live. Women generally attended age-set gatherings (*ogbo*) in their natal villages, performed various ritual functions, and helped to settle disputes among their "brothers."[18] But the gatherings which performed the major role in self-rule among women and which articulated women's interests *as opposed to* those of men were the village-wide gatherings of all adult women resident in a village which under colonialism came to be called *mikiri* or *mitiri* (from "meeting").[19]

Mikiri were held whenever there was a need.[20] In *mikiri* the same processes of discussion and consultation were used as in the village assembly. There were no official leaders; as in the village, women of wealth and generosity who could speak well took leading roles. Decisions appear often to have been announced informally by wives telling their husbands. If the need arose, spokeswomen—to contact the men, or women, in other villages—were chosen through general discussion. If the announcement of decisions and persuasion were not sufficient for their implementation, women could take direct action to enforce their decisions and protect their interests.[21]

Mikiri provided women with a forum in which to develop their political talents among a more egalitarian group than the village assembly. In *mikiri*, women could discuss their particular interests as traders, farmers, wives and mothers. These interests often were opposed to those of the men, and where individually women couldn't compete with men, collectively they could often hold their own.

One of the *mikiri's* most important functions was that of a market association, to promote and regulate the major activity of women: trading. At these discussions prices were set, rules established about market attendance, and fines fixed for those who violated the rules or who didn't contribute to market rituals. Rules were also made which applied to men. For instance, rowdy behavior on the part of young men was forbidden. Husbands and elders were asked to control the young men. If their requests were ignored, the women would handle the matter by launching a boycott or a strike to force the men to police themselves or they might decide to "sit on" the individual offender.[22]

"Sitting on a man" or a woman, boycotts and strikes were the women's main weapons. To "sit on" or "make war on" a man involved gathering at his compound, sometimes late at night, dancing, singing scurrilous songs which detailed the women's grievances against him and often called his manhood into question, banging on his hut with the pestles women used for pounding yams, and perhaps demolishing his hut or plastering it with mud and roughing him up a bit. A man might be sanctioned in this way for mistreating his wife, for violating the women's market rules, or for letting his cows eat the women's crops. The women would stay at his hut throughout the day, and late into the night, if necessary, until he repented and promised to mend his ways.[23] Although this could hardly have been a pleasant experience for the offending man, it was considered legitimate and no man would consider intervening.

In tackling men as a group, women used boycotts and strikes. Harris describes a case in which, after repeated requests by the women for the paths to the market to be cleared (a male responsibility), all the women refused to cook for their husbands until the request was carried out.[24] For this boycott to be effective, *all* women had to cooperate so that men could not go and eat with their brothers. Another time the men of a village decided that the women should stop trading at the more distant markets from which they did not return until late at night because the men feared that the women were having sexual relations with men in those towns. The women, however, refused to comply since opportunity to buy in one market and sell in another was basic to profit-making. Threats of collective retaliation were enough to make the men capitulate.

As farmers, women's interests conflicted with those of the men as owners of much of the larger livestock—cows, pigs, goats and sheep. The men's crop, yams, had a short season and was then dug up and stored, after which the men tended to be careless about keeping their livestock out of the women's crops. Green reports a case in which the women of a village swore an oath that if any woman killed a cow or other domestic animal on her farm the others would stand by her.[25]

A woman could also bring complaints about her husband to the *mikiri*. If most of the women agreed that the husband was at fault, they would collectively support her. They might send spokeswomen to tell the husband to apologize and to give her a present, and, if he was recalcitrant they might "sit on" him. They might also act to protect a right of wives. Harris describes a case of women's solidarity to maintain sexual freedom:

> The men . . . were very angry because their wives were openly having relations with their lovers. The men . . . met and passed a law to the effect that every woman . . . should renounce her lover and present a goat to her husband as a token of repentance . . . The women held . . . secret meetings and, a few mornings later, they went to a neighboring [village], leaving all but suckling children behind

them... [The men] endured it for a day and a half and then they went to the women and begged their return ... [T]he men gave [the women] one goat and apologized informally and formally.[26]

Thus through *mikiri* women acted to force a resolution of their individual and collective grievances.

COLONIAL PENETRATION

Into this system of diffuse authority, fluid and informal leadership, shared rights of enforcement, and a more or less stable balance of male and female power, the British tried to introduce ideas of "native administration" derived from colonial experience with chiefs and emirs in northern Nigeria. Southern Nigeria was declared a protectorate in 1900, but it was ten years before the conquest was effective. As colonial power was established in what the British perceived as a situation of "ordered anarchy," Igboland was divided into Native Court Areas which violated the autonomy of villages by lumping many unrelated villages into each court area. British District Officers were to preside over the courts, but were not always present as there were more courts than officers. The Igbo membership was formed by choosing from each village a "representative" who was given a warrant of office. These Warrant Chiefs were also constituted the Native Authority. They were required to see that the orders of the District Officers were executed in their own villages and were the only link between the colonial power and the people.[27]

It was a violation of Igbo concepts to have one man represent the village in the first place and more of a violation that he should give orders to everyone else. The people obeyed the Warrant Chief when they had to, since British power backed him up. In some places Warrant Chiefs were lineage heads or wealthy men who were already leaders in the village. But in many places they were simply ambitious, opportunistic young men who put themselves forward as friends of the conquerors. Even the relatively less corrupt Warrant Chief was still, more than anything else, an agent of the British.[28]

The people avoided using Native Courts when they could do so. But Warrant Chiefs could force cases into the Native Courts and could fine people for infractions of rules. By having the ear of the British, the Warrant Chief could himself violate traditions and even British rules, and get away with it since his version would be believed.[29]

Women suffered particularly under the arbitrary rule of Warrant Chiefs, who were reported as having taken women to marry without conforming to the customary process, which included the woman's right to refuse a particular suitor. They also helped themselves to the women's agricultural produce, and to their domestic animals.[30]

Recommendations for reform of the system were made almost from its inception both by junior officers in the field and by senior officers sent out from headquarters to investigate. But no real improvements were made.[31]

ABA AND THE WOMEN'S WAR

The Native Administration in the years before 1929 took little account of either men's or women's political institutions. In 1929, women in southern Igboland became convinced that they were to be taxed by the British. This fear on top of their resentment of the Warrant Chiefs led to what the British called the Aba Riots, and the Igbo, the Women's War. The rebellion provides perhaps the most striking example of British blindness to the political institutions of women. The women, "invisible" to the British as they laid their plans for Native Administration, suddenly became highly visible for a few months, but as soon as they quieted down, they were once again ignored, and the reforms made in Native Administration took no account of them politically.[32]

In 1925 Igbo men paid taxes, although during the census count on which the tax was based the British had denied that there was to be any taxation. Taxes were collected without too much trouble. By 1929, the prices for palm products had fallen, however, and the taxes, set at 1925 levels, were an increasingly resented burden.[33] In the midst of this resentment, an overzealous Assistant District Officer in Owerri Province decided to update the census registers by recounting households and household property, which belonged to women. Understandably, the women did not believe his assurances that new taxes were not to be invoked. They sent messages through the market and kinship networks to other villages and called a *mikiri* to decide what to do.

In the Oloko Native Court area of Owerri Province, the women decided that as long as only men were approached in a compound and asked for information, the women would do nothing. They wanted clear evidence that they were to be taxed before they acted.[34] If any woman was approached, she was to raise the alarm and they would meet to discuss retaliation.

On November 23, the agent of the Oloko Warrant Chief, Okugo, entered a compound and told a married woman, Nwanyeruwa, to count her goats and sheep. She retorted angrily, "Was your mother counted?" Thereupon "they closed, seizing each other by the throat."[35] Nwanyeruwa's report to the Oloko women convinced them that they were to be taxed. Messengers were sent to neighboring areas. Women streamed into Oloko from all over Owerri Province. They massed in protest at the district office and after several days of protest meetings succeeded in obtaining written assurances that they were not to be taxed, and in getting Okugo arrested.

Subsequently he was tried and convicted of physically assaulting women and of spreading news likely to cause alarm. He was sentenced to two years' imprisonment.[36]

News of this victory spread rapidly through the market *mikiri* network, and women in 16 Native Court areas attempted to get rid of their Warrant Chiefs as well as the Native Administration itself. Tens of thousands of women became involved, generally using the same traditional tactics, though not with the same results as in Oloko. In each Native Court area, the women marched on Native Administration centers and demanded the Warrant Chiefs' caps of office and assurances that they would not be taxed. In some areas the District Officers assured the women to their satisfaction that they were not to be taxed and the women dispersed without further incident. But the British in general stood behind the Warrant Chiefs; at that point they interpreted the women's rebellion as motivated solely by fear of taxation, and Oloko was the only area in which a Warrant Chief had directly provoked the women's fears of taxation by counting their property.

Women in most areas did not get full satisfaction from the British, and, further, some British district officers simply panicked when faced by masses of angry women and acted in ways which made negotiation impossible.

In most of the Native Court areas affected, women took matters into their own hands—they "sat on" Warrant Chiefs and burned Native Court buildings, and, in some cases, released prisoners from jail. Among the buildings burned were those at Aba, a major administrative center from which the British name for the rebellion is derived. Large numbers of police and soldiers, and on one occasion Boy Scouts, were called in to quell the "disturbances." On two occasions, clashes between the women and the troops left more than 50 women dead and 50 wounded from gunfire. The lives taken were those of women only—no men, Igbo or British, were even seriously injured. The cost of property damage estimated at more than £60,000, was paid for by the Igbo, who were heavily taxed to pay for rebuilding the Native Administration centers.[37]

The rebellion lasted about a month. By late December, "order" was somewhat restored but sporadic disturbances and occupation by government troops continued into 1930. In all, the rebellion extended over an area of six thousand square miles, all of Owerri and Calabar Provinces, containing about two million people.[38]

The British generally saw the rebellion as "irrational" and called it a series of "riots." They discovered that the market network had been used to spread the rumor of taxation, but they did not inquire further into the concerted action of the women, the grassroots leadership, the agreement on demands, or even into the fact that thousands of women showed up at native administration centers dressed in the same unusual way: wearing short loincloths, their faces smeared with charcoal or ashes, their heads bound with young ferns, and in their hands carrying sticks wreathed with young palms.[39]

In exonerating the soldiers who fired on the women, a Commission of Enquiry spoke of the "savage passions" of the "mobs," and one military officer told the Commission that "he had never seen crowds in such a state of frenzy." Yet these "frenzied mobs" injured no one seriously, which the British found "surprising."[40]

It is not surprising if the Women's War is seen as the traditional practice of "sitting on a man," only on a larger scale. Decisions were made in *mikiri* to respond to a situation in which women were acutely wronged by the Warrant Chiefs' corruption and by the taxes they believed to be forthcoming. Spokeswomen were chosen to present their demands for the removal of the Warrant Chiefs and women followed their leadership, on several occasions sitting down to wait for negotiations or agreeing to disperse or to turn in Warrant Chiefs' caps.[41] Traditional dress, rituals and "weapons" for "sitting on" were used: the head wreathed with young ferns symbolized war, and sticks, bound with ferns or young palms, were used to invoke the powers of the female ancestors.[42] The women's behavior also followed traditional patterns: much noise, stamping, preposterous threats and a general raucous atmosphere were all part of the institution of "sitting on a man." Destroying an offender's hut—in this case the Native Court buildings—was clearly within the bounds of this sanctioning process.

The Women's War was coordinated throughout the two provinces by information sent through the market *mikiri* network. Delegates travelled from one area to another and the costs were paid by donations from the women's market profits.[43] Traditional rules were followed in that the participants were women—only a few men were involved in the demonstrations—and leadership was clearly in the hands of women.

The absence of men from the riots does not indicate lack of support. Men generally approved, and only a few older men criticized the women for not being more respectful toward the government. It is reported that both men and women shared the mistaken belief that the women, having observed certain rituals, would not be fired upon. The men had no illusions of immunity for themselves, having vivid memories of the slaughter of Igbo men during the conquest.[44] Finally, the name given the rebellion by the Igbo—the Women's War—indicates that the women saw themselves following their traditional sanctioning methods of "sitting on" or "making war on" a man.

Since the British failed to recognize the Women's War as a collective response to the abrogation of rights, they did not inquire into the kinds of structures the women had that prepared them for such action. They failed to ask, "How do the women make group decisions? How do they choose their leaders?" Since they saw only a "riot," they explained the fact that the women injured no one seriously as "luck," never even contemplating that perhaps the women's actions had traditional limits.

Because the women—and the men—regarded the inquiries as attempts to discover whom to punish, they did not volunteer any information about the women's organizations. But there is at least some question as to whether the British would have understood them if they had. The market network was discovered, but suggested no further lines of inquiry to the British. The majority of District Officers thought that the men organized the women's actions and were secretly directing them. The Bende District Officer and the Secretary of the Southern Province believed that there was a secret "Ogbo Society" which exercised control over women and was responsible for fomenting the rebellion.[45] And the women's demands that they did not want the Native Court to hear cases any longer and that all white men should go to their own country, or, at least, that women should serve on the Native Courts and one be appointed District Officer—demands in line with the power of women in traditional society—were ignored.[46]

All these responses fall into a coherent pattern: *not* of purposeful discrimination against women with the intent of keeping them from playing their traditional political roles, but of a prevailing blindness to the possibility that women had *had* a significant role in traditional politics and should participate in the new system of local government. A few political officers were "Of the opinion that, if the balance of society is to be kept, the women's organizations should be encouraged alongside those of the men."[47] Some commissioners even recognized "the remarkable character of organization and leadership which some of the women displayed" and recommended that "more attention be paid to the political influence of women."[48] But these men were the exception: their views did not prevail. Even in the late 1930's when the investigations of Leith-Ross and Green revealed the decreasing vitality of women's organizations under colonialism, the British still did not include women in the reformed Native Administration. When political officers warned that *young men* were being excluded, however, steps were taken to return their traditional political status.[49]

"REFORMS" AND WOMEN'S LOSS OF POWER

In 1933 reforms were enacted to redress many Igbo grievances against the Native Administration. The number of Native Court Areas was greatly increased and their boundaries arranged to conform roughly to traditional divisions. Warrant Chiefs were replaced by "massed benches"—allowing large numbers of judges to sit at one time. In most cases it was left up to the villages to decide whom and how many to send.[50] This benefitted the women by eliminating the corruption of the Warrant Chiefs, and it made their persons and property more secure. But it provided no outlet for collective action, their real base of power.

As in the village assembly, the women could not compete with the men for leadership in the reformed Native Administration because as individuals they lacked the resources of the men.[51] In the various studies done on the Igbo in the 1930's, there is only one report of a woman being sent to the Native Court and her patrilineage had put up the money for her to take her titles.[52]

Since the reformed Native Administration actually took over many functions of the village assemblies, women's political participation was seriously affected. Discussions on policy no longer included any adult who wished to take part but only members of the native courts. Men who were not members were also excluded, but men's interests and point of view were represented, and, at one time or another, many men had some chance to become members; very few women ever did.[53]

The political participation and power of women had depended on the diffuseness of political power and authority within Igbo society. In attempting to create specialized political institutions on the Western model with participation on the basis of individual achievement, the British created a system in which there was no place for group solidarity, no place for what thereby became "extra-legal" or simply illegal forms of group coercion, and thus very little place for women.

The British reforms undermined and weakened the power of the women by removing many political functions from *mikiri* and from village assemblies. In 1901 the British had declared all jural institutions except the Native Courts illegitimate, but it was only in the years following the 1933 reforms that Native Administration local government became effective enough to make that declaration meaningful. When this happened, the *mikiri* lost vitality,[54] although what has happened to them since has not been reported in detail. The reports that do exist mention the functioning of market women's organizations but only as pressure groups for narrow economic interest[55] and women's participation in Igbo unions as very low in two towns.[56]

The British also weakened women's power by outlawing "self-help"—the use of force by individuals or groups to protect their own interests by punishing wrongdoers. This action—in accord with the idea that only the state may legitimately use force—made "sitting on" anyone illegal, thereby depriving women of one of their best weapons to protect wives from husbands, markets from rowdies, or coco yams from cows.[57]

The British didn't know, of course, that they were banning "sitting on a man"; they were simply banning the "illegitimate" use of force. In theory, this didn't hurt the women, as wife-beaters, rowdies and owners of marauding cows could be taken to court. But courts were expensive, and the men who sat in them were likely to have different views from the women's on wife-beating, market "fun" and men's cows. By interfering with the traditional balance of power, the British effectively eliminated the women's ability to protect their own interests and made them dependent upon men for protection against men.

Since the British did not understand this, they did nothing to help women develop new ways of protecting their interests within the political system. (What the women *did* do to try to protect their interests in this situation should be a fruitful subject for study.) What women did *not* do was to participate to any significant extent in local government or, much later, in national government, and a large part of the responsibility must rest on the British, who removed legitimacy from women's traditional political institutions and did nothing to help women move into modern political institutions.

MISSIONARY INFLUENCE

The effect of the colonial administration was reinforced by the missionaries and mission schools. Christian missions were established in Igboland in the late 19th century. They had few converts at first, but their influence by the 1930's was considered significant, generally among the young.[58] A majority of Igbo eventually "became Christians"—they had to profess Christianity in order to attend mission schools, and education was highly valued. But regardless of how nominal their membership was, they had to obey the rules to remain in good standing, and one rule was to avoid "pagan" rituals. Women were discouraged from attending *mikiri* where traditional rituals were performed or money collected for the rituals, which in effect meant all *mikiri*.[59]

Probably more significant, since *mikiri* were in the process of losing some of their political functions anyway, was mission education. English and Western education came to be seen as increasingly necessary for political leadership needed to deal with the British and their law—and women had less access to this new knowledge than men. Boys were more often sent to school, for a variety of reasons generally related to their favored position in the patrilineage.[60] But even when girls did go, they tended not to receive the same type of education. In mission schools, and increasingly in special "training homes" which dispensed with most academic courses, the girls were taught European domestic skills and the Bible, often in the vernacular. The mission-

aries' avowed purpose in educating girls was to train them to be Christian wives and mothers, not for jobs or for citizenship.[61] Missionaries were not necessarily against women's participation in politics—clergy in England, as in America, could be found supporting women's suffrage. But in Africa their concern was the church, and for the church they needed Christian families. Therefore, Christian wives and mothers, not female political leaders, was the missions' aim. As Mary Slessor, the influential Calabar missionary, said: "God-like motherhood is the finest sphere for women, and the way to the redemption of the world."[62]

VICTORIANISM AND WOMEN'S INVISIBILITY

The missionaries' beliefs about woman's natural and proper role being that of a Christian helpmate, and the administration's refusal to take the Igbo women seriously when they demanded political participation, are understandable in light of the colonialists having been socialized in a society dominated by Victorian values. It was during Queen Victoria's reign that the woman's-place-is-in-the-home ideology hardened into its most recent highly rigid form.[63] Although attacked by feminists, it remained the dominant mode of thought through that part of the colonial period discussed here; and it is, in fact, far from dead today, when a woman's primary identity is most often seen as that of wife and mother even when she works 40 hours a week outside the home.[64]

We are concerned here primarily with the Victorian view of women and politics which produced the expectation that men would be active in politics, but women would not. The ideal of Victorian womanhood—attainable, of course, by only the middle class, but widely believed in throughout society—was of a sensitive, morally superior being who was the hearthside guardian of Christian virtues and sentiments absent in the outside world. Her mind was not strong enough for the appropriately masculine subjects: science, business and politics.[65] A woman who showed talent in these areas did not challenge any ideas about typical women: the exceptional woman simply "had the brain of a man," as Sir George Goldie said of Mary Kingsley.[66]

A thorough investigation of the diaries, journals, reports, and letters of colonial officers and missionaries would be needed to prove that most of them held these Victorian values. But preliminary reading of biographies, autobiographies, journals and "reminiscences," and the evidence of their own statements about Igbo women at the time of the Women's War, strongly suggest the plausibility of the hypothesis that they were deflected from any attempt to discover and protect Igbo women's political role by their assumption that politics isn't a proper, normal place for women.[67]

When Igbo women with their Women's War forced the colonial administrators to recognize their presence, their brief "visibility" was insufficient to shake these assumptions. Their behavior was simply seen as aberrant. When they returned to "normal," they were once again invisible. Although there was a feminist movement in England during that time, it had not successfully challenged basic ideas about women nor made the absence of women from public life seem to be a problem which required remedy. The movement had not succeeded in creating a "feminist" consciousness in any but a few "deviants," and such a consciousness is far from widespread today; for to have a "feminist" consciousness means that one *notices* the "invisibility" of women. One *wonders* where the women are—in life and in print.

Understanding the assumptions about women's roles prevalent in Victorian society—and still common today—helps to explain how the introduction of supposedly modern political structures and values could reduce rather than expand the political lives of Igbo women. As long as politics is presumed to be a male realm, no one wonders where the women went. The loss of Igbo women's political institutions—in life, and in print—shows the need for more Western scholars to develop enough of a feminist consciousness to start wondering.

NOTES

1. The Igbo-speaking Peoples are heterogenous and can only be termed a "tribe" on the basis of a common language and contiguous territory. They were the dominant group in southeastern Nigeria, during the colonial period numbering more than three million according to the 1931 census. The Igbo in Owerri and Calabar Provinces, the two southernmost provinces were relatively homogenous politically and it is their political institutions which are discussed here. Studies in depth were done of the Igbo only in the 1930's, but traditional political institutions survived "underneath" the native administration, although weakened more in some areas than in others. There were also many informants who remembered life in the precolonial days. The picture of Igbo society drawn here is based on reports by two Englishwomen Leith-Ross and Green, who had a particular interest in Igbo women; the work of a government officer, Meek; a brief report by Harris, and the work of educated Igbo describing their own society, Uchendu and Onwuteaka. See M. M. Green, *Igbo Village Affairs* (London: Frank Cass and Co., Ltd,. 1947; page citations to paperback edition, New York: Frederick A. Praeger, 1964); J. S. Harris, "The Position of Women in a Nigerian Society," *Transactions of the New York Academy of Sciences*, Series II, Vol. 2, No. 5, 1940; Sylvia Leith-Ross, *African Women* (London: Faber and Faber, 1939); C. K. Meek, *Law and Authority in a Nigerian Tribe* (London: Oxford University Press, 1957, orig. pub. 1937); J.C. Onwuteaka, "The Aba Riot of 1929 and Its Relation to the System of Indirect Rule," *The Nigerian Journal of Economic and Social Studies*, November 1965; Victor C. Uchendu, *The Igbo of Southeast Nigeria* (New York: Holt, Rinehart and Winston, 1965).

2. Daryll Forde and G. I. Jones, *The Ibo- and Ibibio-Speaking Peoples of South-Eastern Nigeria* (London: International African Institute, 1950), p. 39; J. S. Harris, *op. cit.*, p. 141.

3. Victor C. Uchendu, *op. cit.*, pp. 41–44.

4. *Ibid.*, p. 41; M. M. Green, *op. cit.*, pp. 78–79.

5. J. S. Harris, *op. cit.*, pp. 142–43; Victor C. Uchendu, *op. cit.*, pp. 34, 42–43.

6. M. M. Green, *op. cit.*, p. 137.

7. The sources for this description are Uchendu and personal conversations with an Igbo born in Umu-Domi village of Onicha clan in Afikpo division who, however, went to mission schools from the age of seven and speaks Union Igbo rather than his village dialect.

8. Victor C. Uchendu, *op. cit.*, p. 41.

9. *Ibid.*, p. 34; C. K. Meek, *op. cit.*, p. 111.

10. M. M. Green, *op. cit.*, pp. 32–42.

11. Sylvia Leith-Ross, *op. cit.*, pp. 90–92, 138–39, 143.

12. C. K. Meek, *op. cit.*, p. 203; Victor C. Uchendu, *op. cit.*, p. 86.

13. M. M. Green, *op. cit.*, p. 169.

14. Victor C. Uchendu, *op. cit.*, p. 41.

15. C. K. Meek, *op. cit.*, p. 203.

16. Victor C. Uchendu, *op. cit.*, p. 19.

17. C. K. Meek, *op. cit.*, p. 125; M. M. Green, *op. cit.*, pp. 132–38.

18. M. M. Green, *op. cit.*, pp. 217–32.

19. Sylvia Leith-Ross, *op. cit.*, pp. 106–108.

20. M. M. Green, *op. cit.*, pp. 178–216.

21. *Ibid.*, p. 180; Sylvia Leith-Ross, *op. cit.*, pp. 106–107.

22. J. S. Harris, *op. cit.*, pp. 146–47.

23. *Ibid.*, pp. 146–48; M. M. Green, *op. cit.*, pp. 196–97; Sylvia Leith-Ross, *op. cit.*, p. 109.

24. J. S. Harris, *op. cit.*, pp. 146–47.

25. M. M. Green, *op. cit.*, pp. 210–11.

26. J. S. Harris, *op. cit.*, pp. 146–47.

27. Daryll Forde, "Justice and Judgment Among the Southern Ibo Under Colonial Rule," unpublished paper prepared for Interdisciplinary Colloquium in African Studies, University of California Los Angeles, pp. 9–13.

28. *Ibid.*, pp. 9–13; J. C. Anene, *Southern Nigeria in Transition, 1885–1906* (New York: Cambridge University Press, 1967), p. 259; C. K. Meek, *op. cit.*, pp. 329–30.

29. Daryll Forde, *op. cit.*, p. 12.

30. J. C. Onwuteaka, *op. cit.*, p. 274.

31. C. K. Meek, *op. cit.*, pp. 329–30; Harry A. Gailey, *The Road to Aba* (New York: New York University Press, 1970), pp. 66–74.

32. Information on the Women's War is derived mainly from Galley and Perham, who based their descriptions on the reports of the two Commissions of Enquiry, issued as Sessional Papers of the Nigerian Legislative Council Nos. 12 and 28 of 1930, and the Minutes of Evidence issued with the latter. Gailey also used the early 1930's Intelligence Reports of political officers. Meek and Afigbo also provide quotations from the reports, which were not, unfortunately, available to me in full. See Margery Perham, *Native Administration in Nigeria* (London: Oxford University Press, 1937); Idem, *Lugard: The Years of Adventure; 1858–1898* (London: Collins, 1956); Idem, *Lugard: The Years of Authority, 1898–1945* (London: Collins, 1960); A. E. Afigbo, "Igbo Village Affairs," *Journal of the Historical Society of Nigeria*, 4: 1, December 1967.

33. Harry A. Gailey, *op. cit.*, pp. 94–95; C. K. Meek, *op. cit.*, pp. 330–31.

34. Harry A. Gailey, *op. cit.*, pp. 107–108.

35. Margery Perham, *Native Administration in Nigeria, op. cit.*, p. 207.

36. Harry A. Gailey, *op. cit.*, pp. 108–13.

37. S. O. Esike, "The Aba Riots of 1929," *African Historian*, Vol. 1, No. 3 (1965): 13; J. S. Harris, *op. cit.*, p. 143; Margery Perham, *Native Administration in Nigeria, op. cit.*, pp. 209–12.

38. Harry A. Gailey, *op. cit.*, p. 137; Margery Perham, *Native Administration in Nigeria, op. cit.*, pp. 209–12.

39. J. S. Harris, *op. cit.*, pp. 147–48; Margery Perham, *Native Administration in Nigeria, op. cit.*, pp. 207ff.; C. K. Meek, *op. cit.*, p. ix.

40. Margery Perham, *Native Administration in Nigeria, op. cit.*, pp. 212–19.
41. *Ibid.*, pp. 212ff.
42. Harris reports a curse sworn by the women on the pestles: "It is I who gave birth to you. It is I who cook for you to eat. This is the pestle I use to pound yams and coco yams for you to eat. May you soon die!" See J. S. Harris, *op. cit.*, pp. 143–45.
43. Harry A. Gailey, *op. cit.*, p. 112.
44. Margery Perham, *Native Administration in Nigeria, op. cit.*, pp. 212ff; J. C. Anene, *op. cit.*, pp. 207–24; S. O. Esike, *op. cit.*, p. 11; C. K. Meek, *op. cit.*, p. x.
45. Harry A. Gailey, *op. cit.*, pp. 130ff.
46. Sylvia Leith-Ross, *op. cit.*, p. 165; Margery Perham, *Native Administration in Nigeria, op. cit.*, pp. 165ff.
47. Margery Perham, *Native Administration in Nigeria, op. cit.*, p. 246.
48. A. E. Afigbo, *op. cit.*, p. 187.
49. C. K. Meek, *op. cit.*, p. 336.
50. Margery Perham, *Native Administration in Nigeria, op. cit.* pp. 365ff.
51. C. K. Meek, *op. cit.*, p. 203.
52. *Ibid.*, pp. 158–59. She was divorced and had to remain unmarried as a condition of her family's paying for her title as they wanted to be sure to get their investment back when future initiates paid their fees to the established members. If she remarried, her husband's family, not her own, would inherit her property.
53. Sylvia Leith-Ross, *op. cit.*, pp. 171–72; Lord Hailey, *Native Administration in the British African Territories, Part III, West Africa* (London: H. M. Stationary Office, 1951), pp. 160–65.
54. Sylvia Leith-Ross, *op. cit.*, pp. 110, 163, 214.
55. Henry L. Bretton, "Political Influence in Southern Nigeria" in Herbert J. Spiro (ed.), *Africa: The Primacy of Politics* (New York: Random House, 1966), p. 61.
56. Audrey C. Smock, *Ibo Politics: The Role of Ethnic Unions in Eastern Nigeria* (Cambridge: Harvard University Press, 1971), pp. 65, 137.
57. Sylvia Leith-Ross., *op. cit.*, p. 109.
58. *Ibid.*, pp. 109–18; C. K. Meek, *op. cit.*, p. xv. Maxwell states that by 1925 there were 26 mission stations and 63 missionaries (twelve of them missionary wives) in Igboland. The earliest station was established in 1857, but all but three were founded after 1900. Fifteen mission stations and 30 missionaries were among Igbo in Owerri and Calabar Provinces. See J. Lowry Maxwell, *Nigeria: The Land, the People and Christian Progress* (London: World Dominion Press, 1926), pp. 150–52.
59. Sylvia Leith-Ross, *op. cit.*, p. 110; J. F. Ade Ajayi, *Christian Missions in Nigeria, 1841–1891: The Making of a New Elite* (Evanston, Ill.: Northwestern University Press, 1965), pp. 108–109.
60. Sylvia Leith-Ross, *op. cit.*, pp. 133, 196–97, 316.
61. *Ibid.*, pp. 189–90. According to Leith-Ross, in the "girls' training homes . . . the scholastic education given was limited, in some of the smaller homes opened at a later date almost negligible, but the domestic training and the general civilizing effect were good." Evidence of these views among missionaries can be found in J. F. Ade Ajayi, *op. cit.*, pp. 65, 142–44; G. T. Basden, *Edith Warner of the Niger* (London: Seeley, Service and Co., Ltd., 1927), pp. 13, 16, 33, 55, 77, 86; Josephine C. Bulifant, *Forty Years in the African Bush* (Grand Rapids, Mich.: Zondervan Publishing House, 1950), pp. 163 and *passim*; W. P. Livingstone, *Mary Slessor of Calabar* (New York: George H. Doran Co., n.d.), pp. iii–vi; J. Lowry Maxwell, *op. cit.*, pp. 55, 118.
62. W. P. Livingstone, *op. cit.*, p. 328.
63. Page Smith, *Daughters of the Promised Land* (Boston: Little, Brown and Co., 1970), pp. 58–76; Doris Stenton, *The English Woman in History* (London: George Allen and Unwin, Ltd., 1957), pp. 312–44.
64. Eva Figes, *Patriarchal Attitudes* (New York: Stein and Day, 1970); Ruth E. Hartley, "Children's Concepts of Male and Female Roles," *Merrill-Palmer Quarterly*, January 1960.
65. Walter E. Houghton, *The Victorian Frame of Mind, 1830–1870* (New Haven: Yale University Press, 1957), pp. 349–53. Numerous studies of Victorian and post-Victorian ideas about women and politics describe these patterns. In addition to Houghton, Smith and Stenton, see, for example, Kirsten Amundsen, *The Silenced Majority* (Prentice Hall, 1971); Jessie Bernard, *Women and the Public Interest* (Aldine-Atherton, 1971); John Stuart Mill and Harriet Taylor Mill, *Essays on Sex Equality* (University of Chicago Press, 1970); Martha Vicinus (ed.), *Suffer and Be Still: Women in the Victorian Age* (Indiana University Press, 1972); Cecil Woodham-Smith, *Florence Nightingale, 1820–1910* (McGraw-Hill, 1951). It was not until 1929 that all English women could vote; women over 30 who met restrictive property qualifications got the vote in 1918.
66. Stephen Gwynn, *The Life of Mary Kingsley* (London: Macmillan and Co., Ltd., 1932), p. 252. Mary Kingsley along with other elite female "exceptions" like Flora Shaw Lugard and Margery Perham, all of whom influenced African colonial policy, held the same values as men, at least in regard to women's roles. They did not expect ordinary women to have political power any more than the men did, and they showed no particular concern for African women.
67. See, for non-missionary examples, J. C. Anene, *op. cit.*, pp. 222–34; W. R. Crocker, *Nigeria: A Critique of British Colonial Administration* (London: George Allen and Unwin, Ltd., 1936); C. K. Meek, *op. cit.*; Mary H. Kingsley, *Travels in West Africa* (London: Macmillan and Co., Ltd., 1897); Idem, *West African Studies* (London: Macmillan and Co., Ltd., 1899); Margery Perham, *op. cit.*; A. H. St. John Wood, "Nigeria: Fifty Years of Political Development Among the Ibos" in Raymond Apthrope (ed.), *From Tribal Rule to Modern Government* (Lusaka, Northern Rhodesia: Rhodes-Livingstone Institute for Social Research, 1960).

REFERENCES

Ade Ajayi, J. F. 1965. *Christian Missions in Nigeria, 1841–1891: The Making of a New Elite.* Evanston, Ill.: Northwestern University Press, 1965.

Afigbo, A. E. 1967. "Igbo Village Affairs," *Journal of the Historical Society of Nigeria,* 4: 1, December.

Amundsen, Kirsten. 1971. *The Silenced Majority.* New York: Prentice Hall.

Anene, J. C. 1967. *Southern Nigeria in Transition, 1885–1906.* New York: Cambridge University Press.

Basden, G. T. 1927. *Edith Warner of the Niger.* London: Seeley, Service and Co., Ltd.

Bernard, Jessie. 1971. *Women and the Public Interest.* New York: Aldine-Atherton.

Bretton, Henry L. 1966. "Political Influence in Southern Nigeria" in Herbert J. Spiro (ed.), *Africa: The Primacy of Politics.* New York: Random House.

Bulifant, Josephine C. 1950. *Forty Years in the African Bush.* Grand Rapids, Mich.: Zondervan Publishing House.

Crocker, W. R. 1936. *Nigeria: A Critique of British Colonial Administration.* London: George Allen and Unwin, Ltd.

Esike, S. O. 1965. "The Aba Riots of 1929," *African Historian,* Vol. 1, No. 3: 13.

Figes, Eva. 1970. *Patriarchal Attitudes.* New York: Stein and Day.

Forde, Daryll. n.d. "Justice and Judgment Among the Southern Ibo Under Colonial Rule," unpublished paper prepared for Interdisciplinary Colloquium in African Studies, University of California Los Angeles.

Forde, Daryll and G. I. Jones, 1950. *The Ibo- and Ibibio-Speaking Peoples of South-Eastern Nigeria.* London: International African Institute.

Gailey, Harry A. 1970. *The Road to Aba.* New York: New York University Press.

Green, M. M. 1964. *Igbo Village Affairs*. London: Frank Cass and Co., Ltd., 1947; page citations to paperback edition, New York: Frederick A. Praeger.

Gwynn, Stephen. 1932. *The Life of Mary Kingsley*. London: Macmillan and Co., Ltd.

Hailey, Lord 1951. *Native Administration in the British African Territories, Part III, West Africa*. London: H. M. Stationary Office.

Harris, J. S. 1940. "The Position of Women in a Nigerian Society," *Transactions of the New York Academy of Sciences*, Series II, Vol. 2, No. 5.

Hartley, Ruth E. 1960. "Children's Concepts of Male and Female Roles," *Merrill-Palmer Quarterly*, January.

Houghton, Walter E. 1957. *The Victorian Frame of Mind, 1830–1870*. New Haven: Yale University Press.

Idem, 1899. *West African Studies*. London: Macmillan and Co., Ltd.

Idem, 1956. *Lugard: The Years of Adventure, 1858–1898*. London: Collins.

Idem, 1960. *Lugard: The Years of Authority, 1898–1945*. London: Collins.

Kingsley, Mary H. 1897. *Travels in West Africa*. London: Macmillan and Co., Ltd.

Leith-Ross, Sylvia. 1939. *African Women*. London: Faber and Faber.

Livingstone, W. P. n.d. *Mary Slessor of Calabar*. New York: George H. Doran Co.

Maxwell, J. Lowry. 1926. *Nigeria: The Land, the People and Christian Progress*. London: World Dominion Press.

Meek, C. K. 1957 (1937). *Law and Authority in a Nigerian Tribe*. London: Oxford University Press.

Mill, John Stuart and Harriet Taylor Mill. 1970. *Essays on Sex Equality*. Chicago: University of Chicago Press.

Onwuteaka, J. C. 1964. As quoted in *Igbo Village Affairs*, Green, Margaret M. London: Frank Cass and Co., Ltd., 1947; page citations to paperback edition, New York: Frederick A. Praeger.

Onwuteaka, J. C. 1965. "The Aba Riot of 1929 and Its Relation to the System of Indirect Rule," *The Nigerian Journal of Economic and Social Studies*, November.

Perham, Margery. 1937. *Native Administration in Nigeria*. London: Oxford University Press.

Smith, Page. 1970. *Daughters of the Promised Land*. Boston: Little, Brown and Co.

Smock, Audrey C. 1971. *Ibo Politics: The Role of Ethnic Unions in Eastern Nigeria*. Cambridge: Harvard University Press.

St. John Wood, A. H. 1960. "Nigeria: Fifty Years of Political Development among the Ibos" in Raymond Apthrope (ed.), *From Tribal Rule to Modern Government*. Lusaka, Northern Rhodesia: Rhodes-Livingstone Institute for Social Research.

Stenton, Doris. 1957. *The English Woman in History*. London: George Allen and Unwin, Ltd.

Uchendu, Victor C. 1965. *The Igbo of Southeast Nigeria*. New York: Holt, Rinehart and Winston.

Vicinus, Martha (ed.). 1972. *Suffer and Be Still: Women in the Victorian Age*. Bloomington, Ind.: Indiana University Press.

Woodham-Smith, Cecil. 1951. *Florence Nightingale, 1820–1910*. New York: McGraw-Hill.

What's a Nation? Latest Thinking

Jason W. Clay

Jason Clay, who received his Ph.D. from Cornell in 1979, is an associate in social anthropology at the Peabody Museum, Harvard University. His primary position is as research and editorial director for Cultural Survival, Inc., an advocacy group for indigenous people founded by David Maybury-Lewis (see Chapter 2). Clay is also director of marketing for Cultural Survival and has played a major role in developing markets for goods produced in sustainable ways by indigenous peoples (Rain Forest Crunch is one example). He has published extensively on issues involving the rights of indigenous peoples.

Eastern Europe's revolts and the Soviet Union's unraveling are part of a worldwide call to redefine the relationship of the *state* to the *nations* each contains.

There are about five thousand nations in the world today. What makes each a nation is that its people share a language, culture, territorial base, and political organization and history. The Kayapó Indians are but one nation within the state called Brazil. The Penan people of Sarawak are but one nation within the state called Malaysia. To nation peoples, group identity matters well beyond state affiliation. The five thousand nations have existed for hundreds, even thousands of years. The majority of the world's 171 states have been around only since World War II. Very few nations have ever been given a choice when made part of a state. Some states have far better records than others, but overall, no ideology, left or right, religious or sectarian, has protected nations or promoted pluralism much better or worse than any other. In fact, the twentieth century has probably seen more genocides and ethnocides than any other.

All modern states are empires, and they are increasingly seen as such by nations. From Lithuania to Canada, the movement by nations pushing for power sharing and autonomy demands that the world evolve a creative new kind of geopolitics—call it "decentralized federalism"—or be gripped by worse and worse cycles of violence.

Clearly, the Palestinians who live within Israel's borders will not soon identify themselves as Israelis. But did you know that the Oromos in Ethiopia have more members than three-quarters of the states in the United Nations, and that they do not think of themselves as Ethiopians? The twenty million Kurds don't consider themselves first or foremost Turks, Iranians, Iraqis, or Syrians. The Efe Pygmies barely know what Zaire is. There are about 130 nations in the USSR, 180 in Brazil, 90 in Ethiopia, 450 in Nigeria, 350 in India. That so many nations are squeezed into so few states is, in fact, the nub of the problem.

Three-quarters of the 120-odd shooting wars in the world today are being fought between nations and the states that claim to represent them. With very few exceptions, these wars are not about the independence of nations, but rather their level of autonomy: who controls the rights to resources (land, water, minerals, trees), who provides local security, who determines the policies that affect language, laws, and cultural and religious rights. While states can exist regardless of the answer to these questions, nations cannot.

In most states, power is in the hands of a few elites, who operate by a simple credo: Winner take all. They control foreign investment and aid, and use both to reinforce their power. They set local commodity prices, control exports, and levy taxes. The result, on average, is that powerless nations provide most state revenues and receive few services in return. "Development" programs usually allow a state to steal from its nations, whether it be Indian land throughout North and South America, Penan timber in Malaysia, pastoralists' land throughout Africa, or oil from the Kurds in Iraq. Naturally, most nations attempt to resist this confiscation of their resources, which leads to open conflict.

Nearly all debt in Africa, and nearly half of all other Third World debt, comes from the purchase of weapons by states to fight their own citizens. Most of the world's 12 millon refugees are the offspring of such conflicts, as are most of the 100 million internally displaced people who have been uprooted from their homelands. Most of the world's famine victims are nation peoples who are being starved by states that assimilate them while appropriating their food supplies. Most of the colonization, resettlement, and villagization programs are sponsored by states, in the name of progress, in order to bring nation peoples to their knees.

A vicious circle forms. The appropriation of a nation's resources leads to conflict, conflict leads to weapons purchases, weapons purchases lead to debt, and debt leads to the appropriation of more resources—and the cycle intensifies.

As the cold war ends, new relationships will evolve, not only between the United States and the USSR, but also among their allies and the nonaligned states. Seeing fewer Third World countries as proxies in an ideological war, the superpowers are pulling back on aid. That means cutting the umbilical cords of Third World elites. The consequent weakening of their power may unleash more struggle between state rulers and nations who sense an opportunity to win more control over their futures. The number of shooting wars in states is likely to increase, at a time when arms makers and NATO and Warsaw Pact countries are trying to dump obsolete weapons and find markets for new ones. Nation-state conflicts, when intensified, will spawn legions of refugees—*this* is likely to be the growth field of the 1990s.

Yet it is clearer in 1990 than in recent decades that cultural identity is alive and well. In Africa, for example, to justify dictatorships and one-party rule, local elites and foreign interests have long proclaimed the evils of tribalism. Lately, some self-described "liberators for life" have apparently concluded that they can only survive by opening up their political systems. Dictators in Benin, the Ivory Coast, Zaire, and Zambia have moved to allow opposition parties and elections. But simply allowing tribes to form political parties won't necessarily defuse pressures, because it won't change the fact that these are nations within states. There is intriguing talk in Uganda of a confederation of tribes, based on the League of Iroquois, where local power would be left to the tribes and state politics would be decided by a joint council in which each tribe, regardless of size, has an equal vote. Under such a system, larger tribes are likely to resent not being able to wield proportional power. Yet it does address the vulnerability of small nations, which insist that they have the right to exist, as long as they do not deny others those same rights.

If nations and states are to find a peaceful coexistence, a system of decentralized federalism will have to evolve. By this I mean a political system that is built from the bottom up, one that gives autonomy and power to nation peoples, who in turn empower the state to act on their behalves.

Beyond this guiding principle, there is no one model. Weak states with strong nations may break themselves into new states. Newly independent nations, after trying to make a go of it for a while, may later decide it is to their advantage to be part of a larger political unit. Many nations may use independence as a negotiating stance and settle for more local control within a state. To date, because the political processes in most states are not open, the only way nations have been able to push for their rights is to take them by force. The next twenty years will likely be bloody if the world cannot find a new and better way to answer the demands of its now emboldened nations.

Armageddon in New Guinea

Simon Harrison

Simon Harrison, a Briton, did fieldwork in Papua New Guinea and now lectures at the University of Ulster.

The technology to destroy ourselves, we suppose, is something that people have never had to live with before. It makes the Nuclear Age different from all other periods in history. But in fact, among tribal societies there were, and are, some that believed they had quite equivalent powers, and that their social conflicts could bring about the end of the world. This perceived danger is not an especially new problem for society, or something that people have never had to face before, but one which they have lived with in different parts of the world probably for thousands of years. It might be instructive to see how those "simpler" societies coped with the power, as they saw it, to bring about their own extinction and compare the ways they adapted to it with the way we have.

What I should like to describe are the methods a Papua New Guinea people called the Manambu have for trying to resolve conflict. They live mostly in a single village of about thirteen hundred people divided into a number of intermarrying kin groups, and they make their living mainly by fishing and by cultivating yams.

The two dominant kin groups in the village can be called the Blacks and the Reds, because they claim those two colours as their special emblems. Both groups own many different techniques of magic which they believe give them powers over their natural environment: over the weather, the fertility of crops and animals, and so on. Most importantly, the Blacks are the owners of the surrounding lagoons which the people depend on for fish, and they carry out all the magic and ritual to do with fishing and with ensuring that fish are plentiful. The Reds, for their part, own all the magic and ritual to do with the growing of yams, and all the main stages in the yearly yam-growing cycle have to be inaugurated by

their hereditary magicians. In their magic and ritual, the two groups represent themselves as using all their powers for each other's welfare and sustenance. But this magical reciprocity also has a kind of sinister side as well. Both groups have greatly feared powers of sorcery capable, so the villagers believe, of destroying their society. The Blacks own two such weapons of magical mass destruction: one for infesting the community with plagues of poisonous insects and snakes, the other for destroying everyone's livelihoods by silting up the fishing lagoons. The Reds, likewise, own two. One is magic for calling up storms and destroying the community with thunderbolts, which the villagers believe hurl down fist-sized stones. The second is magic to cause the total collapse of the sky, which their ancestors are said to have separated from the earth in mythical times and shored up in its present position on posts. The two groups are equal both in their destructive powers and in their life-giving ones. As one of the magicians told me:

> We Blacks control the things of the earth, while the Reds control the things of the sky. The Reds could destroy the village from the air. But we could destroy it from the ground.

The political leaders in this society are the magicians and sorcerers, and their spells tend to be inherited in certain lines of descent. These magical powers are both an hereditary privilege and a kind of family curse as well. The actual knowledge of magic is dangerous, and illnesses and death are supposed to run in the families which own the spells. There are many legends about the gruesome fates that sorcerers and their close kin are generally supposed to have. One storm-sorcerer, for instance, was supposedly driven insane and eventually killed by his own magical powers and, so the story goes, bit off his own fingers and ate them as he was dying. The powers of a magician or sorcerer can turn him eventually into something not quite human, and

"Armageddon in New Guinea" by Simon Harrison, from *Anthropology Today*, Vol. 1, No. 1, 1988. Royal Anthropological Institute. Reprinted with permission.

leaders in this society are figures of ambiguous legitimacy, because their destructive powers are inseparable from their positive ones.

Among other things, it is their role to maintain the balance of power which, as the villagers see it, keeps order in their society. If the Blacks sent a plague of snakes, the Reds could retaliate with thunderbolts. If the Blacks destroyed the fishing lagoons, the Reds would collapse the sky. It is a kind of New Guinean version of Mutual Assured Destruction. But the possibility of that mutual destruction actually happening is a spectre that men raise often, especially in disputes between the groups. Even quite small disputes are usually magnified to cosmic proportions in the political rhetoric of this society. An ordinary argument over a land boundary, for instance, may lead quite quickly to the two sides conjuring up images of annihilation and to a kind of magical brinkmanship as each tries to force the other to back down. Men threaten to obliterate each other with floods and earthquakes. Elderly sorcerers point menacingly into the sky at strange cloud-formations, warning everyone that unnatural signs are beginning to appear, that the world is on the verge of coming apart.

The obvious and, I think, least interesting difference between their brinkmanship and ours is, of course, that we actually can destroy our world; they only imagine they can destroy theirs. If one of their disputes really did get completely out of hand, nothing would happen. Enraged sorcerers might command the sky to fall but, presumably, it would stay where it is. They are only shadowboxing in New Guinea, unlike ourselves who play for real. Actually, it does sometimes happen that sorcerers try to summon up storms or other disasters, and if the disasters do not materialize, they can always claim magnanimously to have let their rivals live after all. Whether his storms appear or not, a sorcerer can find a way to turn events to his credit.

The interesting point is as follows. This New Guinea society seems to present something of a contradiction. They are a small, quite intimate community of kin and neighbours, who depend on one another for their livelihoods and live much of the time on good terms. But when they do have disputes, they readily use levels of threatened aggression against each other which even our most militaristic, bomb-them-back-into-the-stone-age sorts of modern political figures might hesitate at. Diplomacy in this society has little to do with exchanging benign assurances of goodwill. It is more a kind of competitive display of apocalyptic visions. Men react to conflict by overplaying its dangers, not by underplaying them, and they try to extract from a dispute the greatest possible sense of threat and catastrophe.

There seem to me, then, to be two questions here. Firstly, why this close-knit, and in most ways cohesive, society should carry out its disputes in such violent imagery. And, secondly, how that symbolic violence is able to resolve conflict at all, rather than simply aggravating it. Part of the answer, I think, can be provided by the argument of Mary Douglas (1966, 1975, 1986): that culturally perceived risks to the environment or to society, whether real or not, operate as a means of social control. Actual or imagined dangers are ideas that people can use to coerce and put pressure on each other, to constrain one another's behaviour and, among other things, maintain order.

If I can try to illustrate how this argument might be applied to the New Guineans: the capacity which the two sides imagine they have to destroy each other is only the negative, dark side of a social relationship that is also constructive and cooperative. Between them, they are responsible in magic and ritual for the natural environment: for the changing of the seasons, the growth of plants and animals, and so on. The proper functioning of all of nature, as they see it, is their own handiwork and depends entirely on collaboration among men in what Morauta (1973) calls a magical division of labour. And so they assume they are able to undo that handiwork as well. They think they can control nature in destructive ways, only because they also conceive of themselves as controlling it for one another's benefit and well-being. And so they can habitually threaten each other with Armageddon in their conflicts in a way that modern states could not risk doing, because the basic premise in their society—which we lack—is that the rival groups are indispensable to each other and completely interdependent for their existence. It is because that interdependence is taken for granted so totally, that the idea of the end of the world can work as a powerful symbol for men to use effectively to resolve or limit disunity among themselves. The apocalyptic threats which are part of the normal language of political diplomacy in that society, are actually not in any simple sense acts of hostility but, among other things, appeals for reconciliation. The elderly sorcerers threatening each other with cataclysmic battles that never happen, are bringing disputes under control, not escalating them out of control.

The New Guineans' belief that they have these grandiose magic powers probably developed in a context similar to the one that has produced the arms race in our society: namely, in processes of competition between rival groups for prestige and power. But a puzzle is that they seem to be able to put the threat which such powers signify to social uses which we do not. What I mean is that they have not invented their version of Mutual Assured Destruction in order simply to keep a stalemate in existence between their two rival sides, or what we call a balance of terror. Among other things, it is a way of creating a heightened sense of responsibility for one another and a kind of mutual indebtedness. They do not perceive an estrangement or a political standoff in the ability to destroy each other, but draw quite the opposite lesson. As they see it, the possession of that power intensifies their accountability to each other, and ties them all the more closely to one another.

This is not a contrast I should like to overdraw. Similar ideas of mutual accountability are of course available to us as well, and exist as a potential resource that the language of political confrontation can draw on. Perhaps one might discover, implicit in our own cold war rhetoric, comparable appeals to notions of shared responsibility.

The idea that conflict can have constructive effects as well as destructive ones, and can produce cohesion instead of disorder, is associated most closely in social anthropology with Max Gluckman (1955, 1977). Gluckman argued that in simple societies particularly, where the material conditions of life make for a homogeneity of values and beliefs, the consensus of values gives those societies an especial resilience and stability. Whatever else people in those societies may dispute, they share an unshakeable sense of the rightfulness of their own social order. And so their conflicts work in the end to reproduce that social order instead of destroying it. But what we might nowadays say is that if the conflict can have constructive effects, it is not only because it is occurring within a common moral universe, but perhaps more basically because it is taking place in a common communicative universe. It is less perhaps the taken-for-granted legitimacy of the social order, than the taken-for-granted conventions of discourse that make it possible for conflict to produce order. It seems to me that the key to the explanation of order in this New Guinea society is Gluckman's apparently paradoxical insight, that where there is first a consensus among people, conflict can recreate and reinforce that consensus. If we rephrase him, he may perhaps also be able to provide a means of understanding those societies, such as this one in New Guinea, where the consensus only tenuously and ambiguously concerns legitimacy, and where legitimacy seems less clear-cut than among the African peoples whom Gluckman studied. What is continuously reproduced through the disputes, I think, is primarily an effective intersubjectivity among political actors, a certainty as to cultural conventions they must follow to be intelligible to each other. The consensus that forms the backdrop to their conflicts is less like moral unanimity than what Dell Hymes (1972) calls communicative competence.

I can try to illustrate my point by making a comparison with our own society for a moment. A problem we often seem to have in our debates over our version of Armageddon is that, in comparison with the New Guineans, we lack a publicly agreed, culturally standardized set of images for describing our version of Armageddon.

Some of our predictions of a post-World-War-Three world are more optimistic and reassuring than others. On the pessimistic side, there are predictions of a nuclear winter and the complete extinction of life. A good example of optimism, on the other hand, is the American report by the Stanford Research Institute on the effects of a nuclear war on the United States' economy. Among its many detailed forecasts, was that a nuclear attack would seriously affect the manufacture of Coca-Cola only for a few weeks, and would apparently have little impact on the availability of potato crisps. A conference of the Defense Atomic Support Agency reassures us that any shortages would in any case be eased considerably by there being a rather smaller population to feed (Bodley 1983: 198). Part of the problem here, of course, in trying to decide whether statements such as those actually have meaning, is that the effects of a nuclear war cannot in fact be accurately calculated. But in all the apparently technical arguments over the possible consequences, over whether such a war might be survivable, or feasible, and so on, what is being contested is what the prevailing idioms of public discourse are going to be: whether that possible future can be described more credibly in images of a new Ice Age and the end of the world, or of supply inelasticities and the contraction of consumer markets. It is each other's languages the two sides are trying to put out of action. Implicitly what is at issue is what communicative conventions are going to count as real. It is not simply that we disagree whether we should have nuclear arms or not: we are unsure whether to use the language of econometrics or of eschatology when we discuss them. Or rather, the choice of codes tends itself to be a political one.

A difference with New Guinea is that there, there is a communicative consensus. People at least agree on the imagery in which to describe annihilating each other. Or to put it slightly differently, a much narrower range of imagery counts as credible. To them, a radical breakdown in their cooperation with one another could only have one outcome, not several possible ones. There is only one conceivable scenario, and only one idiom in which to discuss it, rather than a range of possible worlds and possible languages competing with one another for dominance of public discourse. There is only one imaginable future that all escalating conflicts converge towards and that all unchecked disputes would run out of control into. Their brinkmanship can work to restrain conflict and reestablish order, because, whatever else may be negotiable in a dispute, its implications are not negotiable. There are no disputes about what lies over the brink. And so the threats men make to destroy each other, however divisive they are at one level, cannot jeopardize men's sense of dependence upon each other: they can only signify their interdependence. A sorcerer threatening to bring down the sky is not disrupting social unity but emphasizing the need for it. The more graphic and aggressive the threats, the more powerfully they convey the idea of that interdependence. What men come away from their conflicts sharing with one another is a reaffirmed certainty, not necessarily perhaps that their world is rightful, but more importantly, that it is real. Besides their powers to make the crops grow, the seasons change and so on, men also have destructive powers: and whether or not that is the way the world ought to be, it is the way the world is.

Partly, then, what enables them to use threats of destroying each other to bring order out of conflict, is that it is only against a whole background of shared assumptions about what is real, that the men can accurately grasp the intentions behind one another's rhetorical aggression and properly interpret the meaning of their opponents' acts. A man can see an appeal for conciliation implicit in his opponent's threats, or perceive the act of appeasement that comes disguised as a provocation. The two sides in a dispute share entirely the same understanding of what exactly the actual stakes are and, although they may very much doubt each other's goodwill, they never doubt each other's rationality. I do not think any of their conflicts could reach a point where the two sides start to be mutually unintelligible or to suspect they are. Perhaps then, to return to my rephrasing of Gluckman, we might say that the order they regenerate out of their conflicts is first of all a shared communicative competence before it is shared moral sentiments.

In a sense it is quite incongruous to try to compare our society with theirs, our conflicts between states with their small-scale, face-to-face confrontations between groups of kinsmen. But a difference which seems to me worth pointing out between the New Guineans with their imaginary weapons of mass destruction, and us with our real ones, is that their culture gives them a single, consensual symbolism in which to convey to each other the reality of those powers. The Manambu do not always control their disputes effectively, any more than we do. But to the extent that they do control their disputes, it is perhaps because that symbolism makes their imaginary technology of destruction at least as real to them as our real technology is to most of us.

REFERENCES

Bodley, J. H. 1983. *Anthropology and Contemporary Human Problems.* Palo Alto: Mayfield.

Douglas, M. 1966. *Purity and Danger.* London: Routledge.

Douglas, M. 1975. *Implicit Meanings.* London: Routledge.

Douglas, M. 1986. *Risk Acceptability According to the Social Sciences.* London: Routledge.

Douglas, M. and Wildavsky, A. 1982. *Risk and Culture: An Essay on the Selection of Technological and Environmental Dangers.* Berkeley: University of California Press.

Gluckman, M. 1955. *Custom and Conflict in Africa.* Oxford: Blackwell.

Gluckman, M. 1977. *Politics, Law and Ritual in Tribal Society.* Oxford: Blackwell.

Hymes, D. 1972. On communicative competence. In J. B. Pride and J. Holmes (eds.) *Sociolinguistics.* Harmondsworth: Penguin.

Morauta, L. 1973. Traditional Polity in Madang. *Oceania,* 44: 127–155.

Say "Cheese!"

The Disney Order That Is Not So Mickey Mouse

Clifford D. Shearing and Philip C. Stenning

Clifford Shearing, a criminologist at the University of Toronto, is currently attached to the Community Law Center at the University of the Western Cape, South Africa. His coauthor Philip Stenning of the Center for Criminology, University of Toronto, has published primarily on policing, prosecutions, firearms control, and criminal law topics.

One of the most distinctive features of that quint-essentially American playground known as Disney World is the way it seeks to combine a sense of comfortable—even nostalgic—familiarity with an air of innovative technological advance. Mingled with the fantasies of one's childhood are the dreams of a better future. Next to the Magic Kingdom is the Epcot Center. As well as providing for a great escape, Disney World claims also to be a design for better living. And what impresses most about this place is that it seems to run like clockwork.

Yet the Disney order is no accidental by-product. Rather, it is a designed-in feature that provides—to the eye that is looking for it, but not to the casual visitor—an exemplar of modern private corporate policing. Along with the rest of the scenery of which it forms a discreet part, it too is recognizable as a design for the future.

We invite you to come with us on a guided tour of this modern police facility in which discipline and control are, like many of the characters one sees about, in costume.

The fun begins the moment the visitor enters Disney World. As one arrives by car one is greeted by a series of smiling young people who, with the aid of clearly visible road markings, direct one to one's parking spot, remind one to lock one's car and to remember its location and then direct one to await the rubber-wheeled train that will convey visitors away from the parking lot. At the boarding location one is directed to stand safely

behind guard rails and to board the train in an orderly fashion. While climbing on board one is reminded to remember the name of the parking area and the row number in which one is parked (for instance, "Donald Duck, 1"). Once on the train one is encouraged to protect oneself from injury by keeping one's body within the bounds of the carriage and to do the same for children in one's care. Before disembarking one is told how to get from the train back to the monorail platform and where to wait for the train to the parking lot on one's return. At each transition from one stage of one's journey to the next one is wished a happy day and a "good time" at Disney World (this begins as one drives in and is directed by road signs to tune one's car radio to the Disney radio network).

As one moves towards the monorail platform the directions one has just received are reinforced by physical barriers (that make it difficult to take a wrong turn), pavement markings, signs and more cheerful Disney employees who, like their counterparts in other locations, convey the message that Disney World is a "fun place" designed for one's comfort and pleasure. On approaching the monorail platform one is met by enthusiastic attendants who quickly and efficiently organize the mass of people moving onto it into corrals designed to accommodate enough people to fill one compartment on the monorail. In assigning people to these corrals the attendants ensure that groups visiting Disney World together remain together. Access to the edge of the platform is prevented by a gate which is opened once the monorail has arrived and disembarked the arriving passengers on the other side of the platform. If there is a delay of more than a minute or two in waiting for the next monorail one is kept informed of the reason for the delay and the progress the expected train is making towards the station.

Once aboard and the automatic doors of the monorail have closed, one is welcomed aboard, told to remain seated and "for one's own safety" to stay away from open windows. The monorail takes a circuitous route to one of the two Disney locations (the Epcot Center or the Magic Kingdom) during which time a friendly disembodied voice introduces one briefly to the pleasures of the world one is about to enter and the methods of transport available between its various locations. As the monorail slows towards its destination one is told how to disembark once the automatic doors open and how to move from the station to the entrance gates, and reminded to take one's possessions with one and to take care of oneself, and children in one's care, on disembarking. Once again these instructions are reinforced, in a variety of ways, as one moves towards the gates.

It will be apparent from the above that Disney Productions is able to handle large crowds of visitors in a most orderly fashion. Potential trouble is anticipated and prevented. Opportunities for disorder are minimized by constant instruction, by physical barriers which severely limit the choice of action available and by the surveillance of omnipresent employees who detect and rectify the slightest deviation.

The vehicles that carry people between locations are an important component of the system of physical barriers. Throughout Disney World vehicles are used as barriers. This is particularly apparent in the Epcot Center, the newest Disney facility, where many exhibits are accessible only via special vehicles which automatically secure one once they begin moving.

Control strategies are embedded in both environmental features and structural relations. In both cases control structures and activities have other functions which are highlighted so that the control function is overshadowed. Nonetheless, control is pervasive. For example, virtually every pool, fountain, and flower garden serves both as an aesthetic object and to direct visitors away from, or towards, particular locations. Similarly, every Disney Productions employee, while visibly and primarily engaged in other functions, is also engaged in the maintenance of order. This integration of functions is real and not simply an appearance: beauty *is* created, safety *is* protected, employees *are* helpful. The effect is, however, to embed the control function into the "woodwork" where its presence is unnoticed but its effects are ever present.

A critical consequence of this process of embedding control in other structures is that control becomes consensual. It is effected with the willing cooperation of those being controlled so that the controlled become, as Foucault has observed, the source of their own control. Thus, for example, the batching that keeps families together provides for family unity while at the same time ensuring that parents will be available to control their children. By seeking a definition of order within Disney World that can convincingly be presented as

being in the interest of visitors, order maintenance is established as a voluntary activity which allows coercion to be reduced to a minimum. Thus, adult visitors willingly submit to a variety of devices that increase the flow of consumers through Disney World, such as being corralled on the monorail platform, so as to ensure the safety of their children. Furthermore, while doing so they gratefully acknowledge the concern Disney Productions has for their family, thereby legitimating its authority, not only in the particular situation in question, but in others as well. Thus, while profit ultimately underlies the order Disney Productions seeks to maintain, it is pursued in conjunction with other objectives that will encourage the willing compliance of visitors in maintaining Disney profits. This approach to profit making, which seeks a coincidence of corporate and individual interests (employee and consumer alike), extends beyond the control function and reflects a business philosophy to be applied to all corporate operations (Peters and Waterman, 1982).

The coercive edge of Disney's control system is seldom far from the surface, however, and becomes visible the moment the Disney-visitor consensus breaks down, that is, when a visitor attempts to exercise a choice that is incompatible with the Disney order. It is apparent in the physical barriers that forcefully prevent certain activities as well as in the action of employees who detect breaches of order. This can be illustrated by an incident that occurred during a visit to Disney World by Shearing and his daughter, during the course of which she developed a blister on her heel. To avoid further irritation she removed her shoes and proceeded to walk barefooted. They had not progressed ten yards before they were approached by a very personable security guard dressed as a Bahamian police officer, with white pith helmet and white gloves that perfectly suited the theme of the area they were moving through (so that he, at first, appeared more like a scenic prop than a security person), who informed them that walking barefoot was, "for the safety of visitors," not permitted. When informed that, given the blister, the safety of this visitor was likely to be better secured by remaining barefooted, at least on the walkways, they were informed that their safety and how best to protect it was a matter for Disney Productions to determine while they were on Disney property and that unless they complied he would be compelled to escort them out of Disney World. Shearing's daughter, on learning that failure to comply with the security guard's instruction would deprive her of the pleasures of Disney World, quickly decided that she would prefer to further injure her heel and remain on Disney property. As this example illustrates, the source of Disney Productions' power rests both in the physical coercion it can bring to bear and in its capacity to induce co-operation by depriving visitors of a resource that they value.

The effectiveness of the power that control of a "fun place" has is vividly illustrated by the incredible queues of visitors who patiently wait, sometimes for hours, for admission to exhibits. These queues not only call into question the common knowledge that queuing is a quintessentially English pastime (if Disney World is any indication Americans are at least as good, if not better, at it), but provide evidence of the considerable inconvenience that people can be persuaded to tolerate so long as they believe that their best interests require it. While the source of this perception is the image of Disney World that the visitor brings to it, it is, interestingly, reinforced through the queuing process itself. In many exhibits queues are structured so that one is brought close to the entrance at several points, thus periodically giving one a glimpse of the fun to come while at the same time encouraging one that the wait will soon be over.

Visitor participation in the production of order within Disney World goes beyond the more obvious control examples we have noted so far. An important aspect of the order Disney Productions attempts to maintain is a particular image of Disney World and the American industrialists who sponsor its exhibits (General Electric, Kodak, Kraft Foods, etc.). Considerable care is taken to ensure that every feature of Disney World reflects a positive view of the American Way, especially its use of, and reliance on, technology. Visitors are, for example, exposed to an almost constant stream of directions by employees, robots in human form and disembodied recorded voices (the use of recorded messages and robots permits precise control over the content and tone of the directions given) that convey the desired message. Disney World acts as a giant magnet attracting millions of Americans and visitors from other lands who pay to learn of the wonders of American capitalism.

Visitors are encouraged to participate in the production of the Disney image while they are in Disney World and to take it home with them so that they can reproduce it for their families and friends. One way this is done is through the "Picture Spots," marked with signposts, to be found throughout Disney World, that provide direction with respect to the images to capture on film (with cameras that one can borrow free of charge) for the slide shows and photo albums to be prepared "back home." Each spot provides views which exclude anything unsightly (such as garbage containers) so as to ensure that the visual images visitors take away of Disney World will properly capture Disney's order. A related technique is the Disney characters who wander through the complex to provide "photo opportunities" for young children. These characters apparently never talk to visitors, and the reason for this is presumably so that their media-based images will not be spoiled.

As we have hinted throughout this discussion, training is a pervasive feature of the control system of Disney Productions. It is not, however, the redemptive soul-training of the carceral project but an ever-present flow of directions for, and definitions of, order directed at every visitor. Unlike carceral training, these messages do not require detailed knowledge of the individual. They are, on the contrary, for anyone and everyone. Messages are, nonetheless, often conveyed to single individuals or small groups of friends and relatives. For example, in some of the newer exhibits, the vehicles that take one through swivel and turn so that one's gaze can be precisely directed. Similarly, each seat is fitted with individual sets of speakers that talk directly to one, thus permitting a seductive sense of intimacy while simultaneously imparting a uniform message.

In summary, within Disney World control is embedded, preventative, subtle, co-operative and apparently non-coercive and consensual. It focuses on categories, requires no knowledge of the individual and employs pervasive surveillance. Thus, although disciplinary, it is distinctively non-carceral. Its order is instrumental and determined by the interests of Disney Productions rather than moral and absolute. As anyone who has visited Disney World knows, it is extraordinarily effective.

While this new instrumental discipline is rapidly becoming a dominant force in social control . . . it is as different from the Orwellian totalitarian nightmare as it is from the carceral regime. Surveillance is pervasive but it is the antithesis of the blatant control of the Orwellian State: its source is not government and its vehicle is not Big Brother. The order of instrumental discipline is not the unitary order of a central State but diffuse and separate orders defined by private authorities responsible for the feudal-like domains of Disney World, condominium estates, commercial complexes and the like. Within contemporary discipline, control is as fine-grained as Orwell imagined but its features are very different. . . . It is thus, paradoxically, not to Orwell's socialist-inspired Utopia that we must look for a picture of contemporary control but to the capitalist-inspired disciplinary model conceived of by Huxley who, in his *Brave New World,* painted a picture of consensually based control that bears a striking resemblance to the disciplinary control of Disney World and other corporate control systems. Within Huxley's imaginary world people are seduced into conformity by the pleasures offered by the drug "soma" rather than coerced into compliance by threat of Big Brother, just as people today are seduced to conform by the pleasures of consuming the goods that corporate power has to offer.

The contrasts between morally based justice and instrumental control, carceral punishment and corporate control, the Panopticon and Disney World and Orwell's and Huxley's visions is succinctly captured by the novelist Beryl Bainbridge's observations about a recent journey she made retracing J. B. Priestley's celebrated trip around Britain. She notes how during his travels in 1933 the centre of the cities and towns he visited were defined by either a church or a centre of government (depicting the coalition between Church and State in the production of order that characterizes morally based regimes).

During her more recent trip one of the changes that struck her most forcibly was the transformation that had taken place in the centre of cities and towns. These were now identified not by churches or town halls, but by shopping centres; often vaulted glass-roofed structures that she found reminiscent of the cathedrals they had replaced both in their awe-inspiring architecture and in the hush that she found they sometimes created. What was worshipped in these contemporary cathedrals, she noted, was not an absolute moral order but something much more mundane: people were "worshipping shopping" and through it, we would add, the private authorities, the order and the corporate power their worship makes possible.

REFERENCES

Bainbridge, B. (1984) Television interview with Robert Fulford on "*Realities*" Global Television, Toronto, October.

Foucault, M. (1977) *Discipline and Punish: The Birth of Prison.* New York: Vintage.

Peters, T. and R. H. Waterman, Jr. (1982) *In Search of Excellence: Lessons from America's Best-Run Companies.* New York: Warner.

Priestley, J. B. (1934) *English Journey: Being a Rambling but Truthful Account of What One Man Saw and Heard and Felt and Thought During a Journey Through England the Autumn of the Year 1933.* London: Heinemann and Gollancz.

11

Religion and Magic

What does it mean to be religious? Is belief rational? Can we have faith in science? Why do we wear appropriate clothing on ritual occasions? What foods go with which meals? The greater part of our existence is devoted to making sense of the world rather than telling the truth about it. Indeed, French anthropologist Claude Lévi-Strauss argues that the distinctive characteristic of humans is precisely their capacity to make meanings in order to make sense of ourselves. In such projects, he argues, humanity has an **a priori** classification system that is ingrained before practical utilization of knowledge. The analysis of this deeply structured classification system is by **structural analysis**. Thus, the reason why we eat certain food on certain occasions and dress appropriately for certain rituals or activities is based on this classification system. The more basic this system of classification, the more difficult it is for us to reconcile activities involving mutually incompatible categories. For example, the distinction between human and animal is fundamental, and this would explain why bestiality is still viewed with horror in most societies.

Our day-to-day knowledge is built on and supported by a prior system of knowledge that is gratuitous (in opposition to the Western notion that systems of thought always have practical ends in view). This is why in our day-to-day life we operate on a mass of assumptions and partial understandings and accept authority of our society as mediated through physicians, electricians, and lawyers. Actions are based on a mixture of faith and experience. If we fail to achieve our ends, then we might seek alternative explanations. Thus the failure of a light bulb might eventually be attributed to "chance," which would be the structural equivalent of "God" in another society.

One of the ways in which we accentuate difference between ourselves and others is by exaggerating *their* propensity to have "weird" beliefs and practices in contrast to our own eminently rational and logical beliefs and actions. *They* are always held to be guided and influenced by magic and superstition. Nowhere is this expressed more strongly than in the realm of **magic** and **religion**. We have a strong faith in the "technological fix" for solving our problems. The problems of famine, starvation, and even AIDS, we believe, rhetoric notwithstanding, will be solved by science. Science will provide us with the technological means of neutralizing the problem, thereby al-leviating us from the necessity of changing our behavior.

Tanya Luhrmann shows how witches are alive and active as a subculture even in highly industrialized countries like Britain and the United States. She shows how they construct "tradition" to legitimize their activities and points to the fallacy that "we" are so different from "them."

That our beliefs frequently override technology is shown in Silvia Rodgers' paper in which she subjects ship-launching ceremonies to a classic structuralist analysis. She shows how the religious beliefs (superstitions?) of sailors (including even senior officers), their symbolic classification of the ship, the extensive reincarnating power of a ship's name, and the relationship between women and ships all play an important role in how sailors believe and act. Unlike the people in Simon Harrison's New Guinea village (see Chapter 10), these are sailors with high educational qualifications and experience, who literally control earth-shattering means of destruction in the form of nuclear weaponry.

This theme is further explored in the selection by Nigel Rapport on Canadian Sargeant Hibbs and his blind faith in his polygraph machine. In this article, Rapport compares it to that classic case of **poison oracle** used by the Azande and finds some strikingly similar strategies and techniques in the way Sargeant Hibbs mesmerized his audience into treating his construction of the truth as irrefutable.

231

The Goat and the Gazelle
Witchcraft

Tanya Luhrmann

Tanya Luhrmann received her Ph.D. in 1986 from Cambridge University, England, and has since taken a position as assistant professor at the University of California in San Diego. Her regional interests lie in England and India, whereas her topical interests include psychological anthropology, rationality, and morality. Her work in psychological anthropology won her the prestigious Sterling Award for best paper in this field.

Full moon, November 1984. In a witches' coven in northeast London, members have gathered from as far away as Bath, Leicester and Scotland to attend the meeting at the full moon. We drink tea until nine—in London, most rituals follow tea—and then change and go into the other room. The sitting room has been transformed. The furniture has been removed, and a twelve foot chalk circle drawn on the carpet. It will be brushed out in the morning. Four candlesticks stake out the corners of the room, casting shadows from the stag's antlers on the wall. The antlers sit next to a sheaf of wheat, subtle sexual symbolism. In spring and summer there are flowers everywhere. The altar in the centre of the circle is a chest which seems ancient. On top an equally ancient box holds incense in different drawers. On it, flowers and herbs surround a carved wooden Pan; a Minoan goddess figure sits on the altar itself amid a litter of ritual knives and tools.

The high priestess begins by drawing the magic circle in the air above the chalk, which she does with piety, saying "let this be a boundary between the world of gods and that of men." This imaginary circle is then treated as real throughout the evening. To leave the circle you slash it in the air and redraw it when you return. The chalk circle is always drawn with the ritual knife; the cakes, wine and the dancing always move in a clockwise direction. These rules are part of what makes it a witches' circle and they are scrupulously observed. On this evening a coven member wanted us to "do" something for a friend's sick baby. Someone made a model of the baby and put it on the altar,

at the Minoan goddess' feet. We held hands in a circle around the altar and then began to run, chanting a set phrase. When the circle was running at its peak the high priestess suddenly stopped. Everyone shut their eyes, raised their hands, and visualized the prearranged image: in this case it was Mary, the woman who wanted the spell, the "link" between us and the unknown child. We could have "worked" without the model baby, but it served as a "focus" for the concentration. Witches of folklore made clay and waxen effigies over which they uttered imprecations—so we made effigies and kept a packet of plasticene in the altar for the purpose. By springtime, Mary reported, the child had recovered, and she thanked us for the help.

Modern witchcraft was essentially created in the forties—at least in its current form—by a civil servant, Gerald Gardner, who was probably inspired by Margaret Murray's historical account of witchcraft as an organized pre-Christian fertility religion branded devil-worship by the demonologists, and more generally by the rise of interest in anthropology and folklore.[1] Gardner had met Aleister Crowley, knew of the Golden Dawn, and may have been a Freemason. (Indeed his rituals show Crowleyian and Masonic influence.[2]) In the early fifties, Gardner published fictitious ethnographies of supposedly contemporaneous witches who practised the ancient, secret rites of their agrarian ancestors and worshipped the earth goddess and her consort in ceremonies beneath the full moon.[3] He claimed to have been initiated into one of these groups, hidden from watchful authorities since the "burning times."[4] In his eyes, witchcraft was an ancient magico-religious cult, secretly practised, peculiarly suited to the Celtic race. Witches had ancient knowledge and powers, handed down through the generations. And unlike the rest of an alienated society, they were happy and content. This paragraph gives the flavour of his romanticism:

> Instead of the great sabbats with perhaps a thousand or more attendants [the coven] became a small meeting in private houses, probably a dozen or so according to the size of the room. The numbers being few, they were no longer able to gain power, to rise to the hyperaesthetic state by means of hundreds of wild dancers shrieking wildly, and they had to use other secret methods to induce this state. This came easily to the descendants of the heath, but not to the people of non-Celtic race. Some knowledge and power had survived, as many of the families had intermarried, and in time their powers grew, and in out of the way places the cult survived. The fact that they were happy gave them a reason to struggle on. It is from these people that the surviving witch families probably descend. They know that their fathers and grandfathers belonged, and had spoken to them of meetings about the time of Waterloo, when it was an old cult, thought to exist from all time. Though the persecution had died down from want of fuel, they realized that their only chance to be left alone was to remain unknown and this is as true today as it was five hundred years ago.[5]

The invention of tradition is an intriguing topic: why is it that history should grant such authority, even in so rational an age? Witches speak of a secretive tradition, hidden for centuries from the Church's fierce eye, passed down in families until the present generation. There is no reason that such claims could not be true, but there is very little evidence to support them. The most sympathetic scholarship that speaks of an organized, pre-Christian witchcraft has very shaky foundations[6]—although there is more recently work that suggests that there were at least shared fantasies about membership in witch-related societies.[7] But those accused of witchcraft in early modern Europe were very likely innocent of any practice.[8]

Witches have ambivalent attitudes towards their history. . . . They share, however, a common vision of their past, differing only on whether this past is myth or legend. Many of them say that the truth of the vision is unimportant: it is the vision itself, with its evocative pull, that matters. The basic account—given by someone who describes it as a myth—is this:

> Witchcraft is a religion that dates back to paleolithic times, to the worship of the god of the hunt and the goddess of fertility. One can see remnants of it in cave paintings and in the figurines of goddesses that are many thousands of years old. This early religion was universal. The names changed from place to place but the basic deities were the same.
>
> When Christianity came to Europe, its inroads were slow. Kings and nobles were converted first, but many folk continued to worship in both religions. Dwellers in rural areas, the "Pagans" and "Heathens," kept to the old ways. Churches were built on the sacred sites of the old religion. The names of the festivals were changed but the dates were kept. The old rites continued in folk festivals, and for many centuries Christian policy was one of slow cooptation.
>
> During the times of persecution the Church took the god of the Old Religion and—as is the habit with conquerors—turned him into the Christian devil. The Old Religion was forced underground, its only records set forth, in distorted form, by its enemies. Small families kept the religion alive and in 1951, after the Witchcraft Laws in England were repealed, it began to surface again . . .[9]

It is indeed an evocative tale, with secrecy and martyrdom and hidden powers, and whether or not witches describe it as actual history they are moved by its affect.

Witchcraft is meant to be a revival, or re-emergence, of an ancient nature-religion, the most ancient of religions, in which the earth was worshipped as a woman under different names and guises throughout the inhabited world. She was Astarte, Inanna, Isis, Cerridwen—names that ring echoes in archaeological texts. She was the Great Goddess whose rites Frazer and Neumann—and Apuleius—recorded in rich detail. Witches are people who read their books and try to create, for themselves, the tone and feeling of an early humanity, worshipping a nature they understand as vital, powerful and mysterious. They visit the stone circles and pre-Christian sites, and become amateur scholars of the pagan traditions behind the Easter egg and the Yule log.

Above all, witches try to "connect" with the world around them. Witchcraft, they say, is about the tactile, intuitive understanding of the turn of the seasons, the song of the birds; it is the awareness of all things as holy, and that, as is said, there is no part of us that is not of the gods.[10] One witch suggests a simple exercise to begin to glimpse the nature of the practice:

> Perhaps the best way to begin to understand the power behind the simple word *witch* is to enter the circle . . . Do it, perhaps, on a full moon, in a park or in the clearing of a wood. You don't need any of the tools you will read about in books on the Craft. You need no special clothes, or lack of them. Perhaps you might make up a chant, a string of names of gods and goddesses who were loved or familiar to you from childhood myths, a simple string of names for earth and moon and stars, easily repeatable like a mantra.
>
> And perhaps, as you say those familiar names and feel the earth and the air, the moon appears a bit closer, and perhaps the wind rustling the leaves suddenly seems in rhythm with your own breathing. Or perhaps the chant seems louder and all the other sounds far away. Or perhaps the woods seem strangely noisy. Or unspeakably still. And perhaps the clear line that separates you from bird and tree and small lizards seems to melt. Whatever else, your relationship to the world of living nature changes. The Witch is the change of definitions and relationships.[11]

The Goddess, the personification of nature, is witchcraft's central concept. Each witch has an individual understanding of the Goddess, which changes considerably over time. However, simply to orient the reader I will summarize the accounts which I have heard and have read in the literature. The Goddess is multi-faceted, everchanging—nature and nature's transformations. She is Artemis, virgin huntress, the crescent moon and the morning's freshness; Selene, Aphrodite and Demeter, in the full bloom of the earth's fertility; Hecate and axe-bearing Cerridwen, the crone who destroys, the dying forests which make room for new growth. The constant theme of the Goddess is cyclicity and transformation: the spinning Fates, the weaving spider, Aphrodite who each year arises virgin from the sea, Isis who swells and floods and diminishes as the Nile. Every face of the Goddess is a different goddess, and yet also the same, in a different aspect, and there are different goddesses for different years and seasons of one's life.

The Goddess is very different from the Judaeo-Christian god. She is in the world, of the world, the very being of the world. "People often ask me whether I *believe* in the Goddess. I reply, 'Do you believe in rocks?'"[12] Yet she is also an entity, a metaphor for nature to whom one can talk. "I relate to the Goddess, every day, in one way or another. I have a little chitchat with Mommy."[13] Witches have talked to me about the "duality" of their religious understanding, that on the one hand the Goddess merely personifies the natural world in myth and imagery, and that on the other hand the Goddess is there as someone to guide you, punish you, reward you, someone who becomes the central figure in your private universe. I suspect that for practitioners there is a natural slippage from metaphor to extant being, that it is difficult—particularly in a Judaeo-Christian society—genuinely to treat a deity-figure as only a metaphor, regardless of how the religion is rationalized.[14] The figure becomes a deity, who cares for you.

Gardner began initiating people into groups called "covens" which were run by women called "high priestesses." Covens bred other covens; people wandered into the bookstore, bought his books and then others, and created their own covens. By now there are many types of witchcraft: Gardnerian, Alexandrian, feminist, "traditional" and so forth, named for their founders or their political ideals. Feminist covens usually only initiate women and they usually think of themselves as involved with a particularly female type of spirituality. Groups stemming from Gardner are called "Gardnerian," Alexandrian witchcraft derives from Alex Sanders' more ceremonial version of Gardnerian witchcraft. Sanders was a charismatic man who deliberately attracted the attention of the gutterpress and became a public figure in the late sixties. Some of those who read the sensationalistic exposés and watched the television interviews were drawn to witchcraft, and Sanders initiated hundreds of applicants, sometimes on the evening they applied. Traditional witches supposedly carry on the age-old traditions of their families: whether by chance or otherwise, I met none who could substantiate their claim to an inherited ritual practice.

Covens vary widely in their style and custom, but there is a common core of practice. They meet on (or near) days dictated by the sky: the solstices and equinoxes and the "quarter days" between them, most of them fire-festivals in the Frazerian past: Beltane (1 May), Lammas (1 August), Halloween (31 October), Candlemas (2 February). These are the days to perform seasonal rituals, in which witches celebrate the passage of the longest days and the summer's harvest. Covens also meet on the full moons—most witches are quite aware of the moon's phases—on which they perform spells, rituals with a specific intention, to cure Jane's cold or to get Richard a job. Seasonal ritual meetings are called "sabbats," the full moon meetings, "esbats."[15] Membership usually ranges between three and thirteen members, and members think of themselves—or ideally think of themselves—as "family." In my experience, it usually took about a year of casual acquaintance before someone would be initiated.[16] The process took so long because people felt it important that a group should be socially very comfortable with each other, and—crucially—that one could trust all members of the group. As a result, covens tended to be somewhat socially homogeneous.[17] In the more "traditional" covens, there are three "degrees." First degree initiates are novices, and in their initiation they were anointed "witch" and shown the witches' weapons.[18] Second degree initiates usually take their new status after a year. The initiation gives them the authority to start their own coven. It consists in "meeting" death—the initiate acts the part of death if he is male; if she is female, she meets death and accepts him. The intended lesson of the ritual is that the willingness to lose the self gives one control over it, and over the transformations of life and death. Third degree initiation is not taken for years. It is essentially a rite of mystical sexuality, though it is sometimes "symbolic" rather than "actual." It is always performed in privacy, with only the two initiates present.[19] Behind the initiation lies the idea that one becomes the Goddess or God in one of their most powerful manifestations, the two dynamic elements of the duality that creates the world.

Witchcraft is a secretive otherworld, and more than other magical practices it is rich in symbolic, special items. Initiates have dark-handled knives they call "athames," which are the principal tools and symbols of their powers: they have special cups and platters and incense burners, sometimes even special whips to "purify" each other before the rite begins. There is always an altar, usually strewn with herbs and incense, with a statue of the Goddess, and there are always candles at the four directions, for in all magical practice the four directions (east, south, west, north) represent the four ancient elements (air, fire, water, earth) which in turn represent different sorts of "energies" (thought; will power; emotion; material stability).[20] Then, another symbol of the secrecy and violation of convention, most covens work in the nude. This is ostensibly a sign of freedom, but probably stems from the evocative association of witchcraft and sexuality, and a utopian vision of a paradisial past. There are no orgies, little eroticism, and in fact little behaviour that would be different if clothes were being worn. That witches dance around in the nude probably is part of the attractive fantasy that draws outsiders into the practice, but the fantasy is a piece with the paganism and not the source of salacious sexuality. Or at least, that seemed to be the case with the five covens I met.

I was initiated into the oldest of these witches' groups, a coven which has remained intact for more than forty years. It was once Gardner's own coven, the coven in which he participated, and three of the current members were initiated under his care. It pleases the anthropologist's heart that there are traces of ancestor worship: the pentacle, the magical platter which holds the communion "mooncakes," was Gardner's own, and we used his goddess statue in the circle.

The coven had thirteen members while I was there. Four of them (three men and one woman) had been initiated over twenty-five years ago and were in their fifties: an ex-Cambridge computer consultant, who flew around the world lecturing to computer professionals; a computer software analyst, high priest for the last twenty years; a teacher; an ex-Oxford university lecturer. The high priestess was initiated twenty years ago and was a professional psychologist. Another woman, in her forties, had been initiated some ten years previously. She joined the group when her own coven disbanded; another man in his fifties also came from that coven. He was an electronic engineer in the music industry. By the time I had been in the group several months, Helga and Eliot's coven had disbanded (this was the coven associated with the Glittering Sword) and Helga at any rate preferred to think of herself as a Nordic Volva rather than as a Celtic witch. So she abandoned witchcraft altogether, though she became deeply engaged in the other magical practice, and Eliot and another member of his coven, the young Austrian who was also in the Glittering Sword, joined the group. The rest of the younger generation included a woman in her thirties who was a professional artist but spent most of her time then raising a young child. Another member was a middle-level manager of a large business. He was in his late thirties and was my "psychic twin": we were both initiated into the group on the same night. Another man, thirtyish, managed a large housing estate. The computer consultant and the teacher had been married twenty-five years, the high priest and high priestess had lived together for twenty. Four other members had

partners who did not belong to the group, but two of them belonged to other magical groups. Three members of the group were married to or closely related to university lecturers—but this was an unusually intellectual group.

This coven, then, had a wide age range and was primarily composed of middle-class intellectuals, many of whose lovers were not members of the group. This was not particularly standard: another coven with whom this group had contact had nine members, all of whom were within ten years of age, and it included three married couples and three single individuals. A Cambridge coven had a similarly great age span, and as wide a range of professions. But one in Clapham was entirely upper working class, and its members were within about fifteen years of age. For the meetings, the group relied upon a standard ritual text. Gardner (with the help of Doreen Valiente, now an elder stateswoman in what is called the "Craft") had created a handbook of ritual practice called the "Book of Shadows," which had supposedly been copied by each initiate through the ages. ("Beltane special objects: jug of wine, earthenware chalice, wreaths of ivy . . . High priestess in east, high priest at altar with jug of wine and earthenware chalice . . .") The group performed these rites as written, year in and year out: they were fully aware that Gardner had written them (with help) but felt that as the original coven, they had a responsibility to tradition. In fact, some of them had been re-written by the high priest, because Gardner's versions were so simple: he felt, however, that he should treat them as Gardner's, and never mentioned the authorship.

The seasonal rituals were remarkable because in them, the priestess is meant to incarnate the Goddess. This is done through a ritual commonly known as "drawing down the moon." The high priestess' ritual partner is called the "high priest," and he stands opposite her in the circle and invokes her as the Goddess; and as Goddess, she delivers what is known as the "Charge," the closest parallel to a liturgy within the Craft. Gardner's Book of Shadows has been published and annotated by two witches, and it includes this text.

The high priest: Listen to the words of the great Mother; she who of old was called among men Artemis, Astarte, Athene, Dione, Melusine, Aphrodite, Cerridwen, Dana, Arianhod, Isis, Bride, and by many other names.

The high priestess: Whenever ye have need of anything, once in the month, and better it be when the moon is full, then shall ye assemble in some secret place and adore the spirit of me, who am Queen of all witches. There shall ye assemble, ye who are fain to learn all sorcery, yet who have not won its deepest secrets; to these will I teach things that are yet unknown. And ye shall be free from slavery; and as a sign that ye be really free, ye shall be naked in your rites; and ye shall dance, sing, feast make music and love, all in my praise. For mine is the ecstacy of the spirit, and mine is also joy on earth; for my law is love unto all beings. Keep pure your highest ideal; strive ever towards it; let naught stop you or turn you aside. For mine is the secret door which opens up the Land of Youth, and mine is the cup of the wine of life, and the Cauldron of Cerridwen, which is the Holy Grail of immortality. I am the gracious Goddess, who gives the gift of joy unto the heart of man. Upon earth, I give the knowledge of the spirit eternal; and beyond death, I give peace, and freedom, and reunion with those who have gone before. Nor do I demand sacrifice; for behold, I am the mother of all living, and my love is poured out upon the earth.

The high priest: Hear ye the words of the Star Goddess; she in the dust of whose feet are the hosts of heaven, and whose body encircles the universe.

The high priestess: I who am the beauty of the green earth, and the white Moon among the stars, and the mystery of the waters, and the desire of the heart of man, call unto thy soul. Arise and come unto me. For I am the soul of nature, who gives life to the universe. From me all things proceed, and unto me all things must return; and before my face, beloved of Gods and men, let thine innermost divine self be enfolded in the rapture of the infinite. Let me worship be with the heart that rejoiceth; for behold all acts of love and pleasure are my rituals. And therefore let there be beauty and strength, power and compassion, honour and humility, mirth and reverence within you. And thou who thinkest to seek for me, know that seeking and yearning shall avail thee not unless thou knowest the mystery; that if that which thou seekest thou findest not within thee, thou wilt never find it without thee. For behold, I have been with thee from the beginning; and I am that which is attained at the end of desire.[21]

The nature-imagery, the romantic poetry, the freedom—this is the style of language commonly heard within these ritual circles. The point of this speech is that every woman can be Goddess. Every man, too, can be god. In some Gardnerian rituals—like Halloween—the high priestess invokes the stag god in her priest, and he gives similar speeches.

When the coven I joined performed spells, no ritual form was prescribed because no spell was identical to any other. The idea behind the spell was that a coven could raise energy by calling on their members' own power, and that this energy could be concentrated within the magical circle, as a "cone of power," and directed towards its source by collective imagination. The first step in a spell was always to chant or meditate in order to change the state of consciousness and so have access to one's own power, and then to focus the imagination on some real or imagined visual representation of the power's goal. The most common technique was to run in a circle, hands held, all eyes on the central altar candle, chanting what was supposedly an old Basque witches' chant:[22]

Eko, eko, azarak
Eko, eko, zamilak

Eko, eko, Cernunnos
Eko, eko, Aradia[23]

Then, the circle running at its peak, the group suddenly stopped, held its linked hands high, shut its eyes and concentrated on a prearranged image.

Sometimes we prefixed the evening with a longer chant, the "Witches' Rune":

Darksome night and shining moon
East, then South, then West, then North;
Hearken to the Witches' Rune—
Here we come to call ye forth!
Earth and water, air and fire,
Wand and pentacle and sword,
Work ye unto our desire,
Hearken ye unto our word!
Cords and censer, scourge and knife,
Powers of the witch's blade—
Waken all ye unto life,
Come ye as the charm is made!
Queen of Heaven, Queen of Hell,
Horned hunter of the night—
Lend your power unto the spell,
And work our will by magic rite!
By all the power of land and sea,
By all the might of moon and sun—
As we do will, so mote it be;
Chant the spell, and be it done![24]

The tone of the poem captures much about witchcraft; the special "weapons" with special powers, the earthly power and goddess power used within the spell, the dependence of the spell upon the witches' will.

Most of the coven meetings I attended in England—in all I saw the rituals of some six Gardnerian-inspired groups—were similar in style. However, there were also feminist covens, a type of witchcraft relatively rare in England but quite important in the States. Witchcraft appeals to feminists for a number of reasons. Witches are meant to worship a female deity rather than a male patriarch, and to worship her as she was worshipped by all people before the monotheistic religions held sway: as the moon, the earth, the sheaf of wheat. Members of feminist covens talk about witchcraft and its understanding of cyclic transformation, of birth, growth and decay, as a "woman's spirituality," and the only spirituality in which women are proud to menstruate, to make love, and to give birth. These women (and sometimes also men[25]) are often also compelled by the desire to reclaim the word "witch," which they see as the male's fearful rejection of a woman too beautiful, too sexual, or past the years of fertility. The witches of European witch-craze fantasies were either beautiful young temptresses or hags.

Feminist covens emphasize creativity and collectivity, values commonly found in that political perspective, and their rituals are often quite different from those in Gardnerian groups. Perhaps I could offer an example, although in this example the women did not explicitly describe themselves as "witches" but as participating in "women's mysteries."

On Halloween 1983 I joined a group of some fifteen women on top of a barrow in Kent. One of the women had been delegated to draw up a rough outline of the ritual, and before we left for the barrow she held a meeting in which she announced that she had "cobbled together something from Starhawk and Z Budapest [two feminist witchcraft manual authors]." (Someone shouted, "don't put yourself down.") She explained the structure of the rite as it stood and then asked for suggestions. Someone had brought a pot of red ochre and patchouli oil which she wanted to use, and someone else suggested that we use it to purify each other. Then it was suggested that we "do" the elements first, and people volunteered for each directional quarter. The person who had chosen earth asked if the hostess had any maize flour which she could use. We talked about the purpose of the rite. The meeting was like many other feminist organization meetings: long on equality, emotional honesty and earthiness, short on speed.

When we arrived on the barrow some hours later, we walked round in a circle. Four women invoked the elements, at the different directions, with their own spontaneously chosen words. It was an impressive midnight: leafless trees stark against a dark sky, some wind, an empty countryside with a bull in the nearby field. Then one woman took the pot of red ochre and drew a circle on the cheek of the woman to her left, saying, "may this protect you on Halloween night," and the pot passed around the circle. Then the woman who had drafted the ritual read an invocation to Hecate more or less taken from Starhawk, copied out in a looseleaf binder with a pentacle laminated on the front:

> This is the night when the veil that divides the worlds is thin. It is the New Year in the time of the year's death, when the harvest is gathered and the fields lie fallow. The gates of life and death are opened; the dead walk, and to the living is revealed the Mystery: that every ending is but a new beginning. We meet in time out of time, everywhere and nowhere, here and there, to greet the Death which is also Life, and the triple Goddess who is the cycle of rebirth.

Someone lit a fire in a dustbin lid (the cauldron was too heavy to carry from London) and each of us then invited the women that we knew, living or dead, to be present. We then chanted, the chant also taken from Starhawk, in which we passed around incense and each person said, "x lives, x passes, x dies"—x being anger, failure, blindness, and so forth. The chorus was: "it is the cold of the night, it is the dark." Then someone held up a pomegranate (this was found in both Starhawk and Z Budapest) and said, "behold, I show you the fruit of life." She stabbed it and said, "which is death" and

passed it around the circle, and each woman put a seed in the mouth of the woman to her left, saying, "taste of the seeds of death." Then that woman held up an apple—"I show you the fruit of death and lo"—here she sliced it sideways, to show the five pointed star at its centre—"it contains the five pointed star of life." The apple was passed around the circle, each woman feeding her neighbour as before and saying, "taste of the fruit of life." Then we passed a chalice of wine and some bread, saying "may you never be hungry," pulled out masks and sparklers, and danced around and over the fire. Many of these actions required unrehearsed, unpremeditated participation from all members present, unlike the Gardnerian coven, where those not doing the ritual simply watch until they are called to worship or to take communion (members often take turns in performing the rituals, though). There was also the sense that the group had written some of the ritual together, and that some of the ritual was spontaneous.

There are also "solo" witches, individuals who call themselves witches even though they have never been initiated and have no formal tie to a coven. I met a number of these women (they were always women). One had an organization she called "Spook Enterprises" and sold candles shaped like cats and like Isis. Another called herself a witch but had never been initiated, although she was well-established in the pagan world. Another, the speaker at the 1983 Quest conference, gave talks on "village witchcraft": on inquiry, it appeared that she had been born in Kent, and was an ex-Girtonian.[26]

Mick, the woman of this sort whom I knew best, owned a Jacobean cottage where she lived alone on the edge of the Fens, the desolate drained farmland outside Cambridge. She managed a chicken farm. She told me that she discovered her powers at the age of ten, when she "cursed" her math teacher and he promptly broke his leg in two places. It was clear that witchcraft was integral to her sense of self, and she took it seriously, albeit with theatre. She called her cottage "Broomstick Cottage," kept ten cats and had a cast iron cauldron near the fire place. In the corner of the cottage she had a small statue of Pan on an altar, alongside a ritual knife stained with her own blood. Many of the villagers knew her and in Cambridge I heard of the "Fen witch" from at least four different sources. Once, when I was sitting in her garden (her Elizabethan herb garden), two little boys cycled past. One shouted to the other, "*that's* where the witch lives!" Mick got "collected" for her personality, she told me: people seem to think it exotic to have a witch to supper. And this may have been one of the reasons she cherished her claims. She was a very funny, sociable woman, always the centre of a party, but a bit lonely, I think, and a bit romantic: witchcraft served a different function for her than fervent Christianity might have done, but like all religions, the witchcraft reduced the loneliness, lent charm to the bleak landscape, and gave her a social role.

There is a certain feel to witchcraft, a humour and an enthusiasm, often missing in other groups. Witchcraft combines the ideal and the mundane. It blends spiritual intensity and romanticism with the lovable, paunchy flaws of the flesh. Fantasies of elfin unicorns side comfortably with bawdy Pans. The high priest of the coven I joined described this as "the goat and the gazelle": "all witches have a little of each." Part of this is the practice itself. People can look slightly ridiculous standing around naked in someone's living room. One needs a sense of humour in order to tolerate the practice, as well as enough romanticism to take it seriously. And witches are perhaps the only magicians who incorporate humour into their practice. Their central invocation, the declamation of the priestess-turned-goddess, calls for "mirth and reverence." Laughter often rings within the circle, though rarely in the rites. One high priestess spontaneously explained to me that "being alive is really rather funny. Wicca [another name for witchcraft] is the only religion that captures this."

NOTES

1. *In Witchcult in Western Europe* (1921), Murray argued—much influenced by Frazer—that an organized pre-Christian fertility cult lay behind the witchcraft persecutions. The religion centred on the cycle of the seasons and their crops, and deity was incarnate in a horned male god, who had a female form, Diana. Murray proposed that the male god had superseded the female deity, and that the Inquisition had twisted the symbolism into a cult of devil-worship. Murray described her researches as anthropological, and compared witches to shamans: just as shamans understand themselves to leave their bodies, so witches believed themselves to leave their bodies to "fly"—when they participate in certain rituals. It was a commendable approach, because it interpreted the witchtrials as concerning genuine popular belief—not as the collective delusion historians often assumed.

    Other influential books in the development of modern witchcraft were Leland (1899) *Gospel of Aradia*; Frazer (1890; the twelve volumes were slowly published, and the abridged volume appeared in 1922, when Frazer's influence was at its peak—Cohn (1975: 107) *The Golden Bough*; Evans-Wentz (1911) *The Fairy Faith in Celtic Countries*; and later, Graves' (1968; first edition 1948) *The White Goddess*.

2. There seems to be no hard evidence that Gardner actually was a Mason. However, there are some striking similarities in ritual structure between the two practices: an initiatory hierarchy of three "degrees" (Masonry of course has many higher degrees in addition to the three basic ones); an initiation ceremony in which an initiate is presented blindfolded, with a garter around one leg, then presented to the different directional quarters, and presented both the "weapons" or "tools" of what is known as the "Craft."

3. He claimed that he had only published then because of the repeal of the Witchcraft Laws in 1951, which proclaimed the practice of witchcraft illegal. They were replaced by the Fraudulent Mediums Act. See Farrar and Farrar (1984: 277).

4. Gardner may well have been initiated into a practising group. He claimed that he had been initiated in 1939 by one Dorothy Clutterbuck. Some members of the group I joined had actually known him, and one at least—the most senior member—was persuaded that the group had existed, and that "Old Dorothy" was not a fictitious character. Gardner talked about her, he said, as if she had been alive. Valiente, Gardner's close associate, was also persuaded of this woman's reality, and searched for the traces of her in county records. She produced evidence of a Dorothy Clutterbuck born and buried at a suitable time, in suitable places. See appendix in Farrar and Farrar (1984: 283–300). However, there is no reason to suppose that if such a group existed, it necessarily predated the publication of Murray's book.

5. Gardner (1954: 46).

6. While the attempt to examine the sixteenth- and seventeenth-century witchcraft persecutions as the product of popular belief was laudable, Murray took the apparent beliefs of the accused for their actual practice, and she drew her evidence from literary accounts of trials and from confessions exacted under torture. Certainly many confessions attest to the existence of sabbats, flying and the like, and there were those who believed that they were witches and confessed freely. However, there is little evidence to indicate the existence of an organized pagan fertility cult. Macfarlane, for example, found no evidence for an underground pagan religion in his thorough study of witchcraft prosecutions in Essex, nor did the language of the prosecutions include descriptions of the sabbat, the diabolic contract, and so forth (1970: 10). Thomas, drawing on a formidable knowledge of the period, concludes that "in England there can be little doubt that there was never a 'witch-cult' of the type envisaged by contemporary demonologists or their modern disciples" (1971: 516). The "Murrayite thesis" is rarely taken seriously, in its full form, today.

7. The relative ease with which people confessed to practice in itself indicates a widespread popular belief in witchcraft: whatever political purpose the persecution may have served, it depended upon common folk belief. In addition, there seems to have been popular medieval European belief in a Diana (Herodias, Holda) figure, who travelled through the night accompanied by souls of the dead and by female devotees. These "ladies of the night" visited households with benevolent care; there were also beliefs of "night-witches," cannibalistic women who devoured babies (Cohn, 1975: 206–19). Ginzburg presents evidence from late sixteenth-century Friuli of a belief in the "benandanti," "good walkers," who left their bodies at night and, armed with fennel stalks, set out to battle witches over the crops, the livestock, or other desired goods. This fantasy seems to have its roots in a pre-Christianity fertility religion. However, it is not clear that the benandanti ever met in the flesh, or that the fantasy was anything but that. "On the basis of the available documents, the existence or non-existence of an organized set of witches in fifteenth- to seventeenth-century Europe seems to be indeterminate" (Ginzburg, 1983: xiv). Further evidence of a pre-Christian belief in witchcraft is given by Le Roy Ladurie (1987).

8. Explanations of the "witchcraft craze" of early modern Europe are rife. Accounts include: Trevor-Roper (1956), Cohn (1975), Thomas (1971), Macfarlane (1970), Henningsen (1980), Ginzburg (1983), Larner (1981, 1984), Estes (1983), Le Roy Ladurie (1987), Ben-Yehuda (1980). Accounts of the Salem trials include Boyer and Nissenbaum (1974) and Demos (1982). The corpus of this work is one of the best illustrations of the complex causality of any particular historical events, for the different accounts—admittedly handling different events in varied contexts—point to the interdependency of psychological fantasy, small-scale social tension, and larger political and economic developments: the fear of a being who subverts the fertility of body and land, with unrestrained perverted sexuality, the cannibalistic, incestuous "bad mother"; the child-rearing customs particular to a given society; the availability of criminal proceedings which made prosecutions available; the rise of a commercial ethic, a new individualism and the demise of the small face-to-face

community; the collapse of a magic-like Catholicism for a stern, unforgiving Protestantism and the rise of a post-Galenic medicine, able to differentiate between the natural and non-natural cause for a disease; the political tensions within a given community; and then, Reformation and Counter-Reformation tensions, the rise and tenure of a notion of the "godly state" in which Christianity held political significance. This blend of personally salient fantasy, cognitive shift, and political ideology probably precipitated the outbreak of witchcraft fear as Europe crossed the boundary from early modernism into secularized nation-states, heightening and creating social tension in its wake. But it is a phenomenon with many explanations and many causes, a typically messy transformation.

The accounts of African witchcraft are as numerous, but tend to be more homogeneous in their explanation, pointing primarily to witchcraft's role in relieving social tension—a social "strain gauge," as one author puts it. Nevertheless, authors sometimes mention the psychodynamic elements of witchcraft fantasy, and point to some of the larger political elements of a rash of witchcraft accusations. The primary collections of essays, which include papers or book-excerpts from most of the scholars in the area, include: Marwick (1970), Douglas (1970), Middleton and Winter (1963), and Middleton (1967).

9. Adler (1986: 45–6).
10. This is a phrase taken from Crowley's Gnostic Mass (1929: 345–61). It sometimes appears in witchcraft rituals or in writings about the practice.
11. Adler (1986: 43–4).
12. Starhawk (1979: 77).
13. Witch, Z. Budapest, quoted in Adler (1986: 105).
14. Gombrich's (1971) study of Sinhalese Buddhism draws a related conclusion, that devotees tend to treat the Buddha-figure as a god, not—as doctrine would have it—an enlightened man.
15. The terms are probably drawn from Margaret Murray, although "esbat" appears in a sixteenth-century French manuscript (Le Roy Ladurie, 1987: 7). "Sabbat" is a standard demonologist's term.
16. I was fortunate: there was a feeling in the group I joined that my time in the country might be limited, and certainly that my stay in London was relatively brief (fifteen months). In consequence I was initiated only six months after my initial contact with the members.
17. This may be an exaggeration. Social ease with the applicant was clearly pertinent to the coven's decision to initiate someone, and personality style seemed more crucial than socioeconomic standing. I knew an applicant turned down by one coven, despite the fact that he was of a similar age and background as most of the members, and despite the fact that their coven needed more men to have an even balance of the sexes—which is thought desirable. This was probably because he seemed too independent to the high priestess; there was at least some personality conflict between them.
18. As already mentioned, this portion of the ritual resembles the first degree initiation in Freemasonry.
19. The role and nature of this "third degree" initiation has been, not surprisingly, a source of some controversy within witchcraft, and different participants have differing views about whether it should be "actual" or "symbolic" or held at all.
20. Air, earth, water and fire were recognized constitutive elements in the ancient world and their role and nature was a matter of considerable debate. The attribution of directional definition and human capacity may be a later accretion.
21. Farrar and Farrar (1981: 42–3).
22. Pennethorne Hughes corroborates this attribution, but it is not clear that other historians would substantiate the claim.
23. Farrar and Farrar (1984: 17).
24. Farrar (1971: 20).
25. There was at least one group of this ilk that was mixed: they would probably argue for the importance of integrating the male divine principle into a goddess-centred religion, and so justify the men's presence in a context usually focused on "women's mysteries."
26. Girton is the oldest women's college at Cambridge.

REFERENCES

Adler, M. 1986. *Drawing Down the Moon*. Boston: Beacon.

Ben-Yehuda, N. 1980. "The European Witch-Craze of the 14th to 17th Centuries: A Sociologist's Perspective." *American Journal of Sociology*, 86(1), pp. 1–31.

Boyer, P. and S. Nissenbaum. 1974. *Salem Possessed*. Cambridge: Harvard University Press.

Cohn, N. 1975. *Europe's Inner Demons*. New York: New American Library.

Crowley, A. 1976 [1929]. *Magick in Theory and Practice*. New York: Denver.

Demos, J. 1982. *Entertaining Satan*. Oxford: Oxford University Press.

Douglas, M. (ed.). 1970. *Witchcraft: Confessions and Accusations*. London: Tavistock.

Estes, L. 1983. "The Medical Origins of the European Witch-Craze." *Journal of Social History*, 17, Winter, pp. 271–84.

Evans-Wentz, E. 1911. *The Fairy Faith in Celtic Countries*. Oxford: Oxford University Press.

Farrar, J. and S. Farrar. 1981. *Eight Sabbats for Witches*. London: Robert Hale.

Farrar, J. and S. Farrar. 1984. *The Witches' Way*. London: Robert Hale.

Frazer, Sir J. G. 1922. *The Golden Bough*. Abridged version. London: Macmillan.

Gardner, G. B. 1982 [1954]. *Witchcraft Today*. New York: Magickal Childe.

Ginzburg, C. 1983 [Italian 1966]. *The Night Battles*. Trans. J. and A. Tedeschi. Baltimore, Md.: John Hopkins University Press.

Gombrich, R. 1971. *Precept and Practice*. Oxford: Clarendon.

Graves, Robert. 1968 [1948]. *The White Goddess*. New York: Farrar, Strauss and Giroux.

Henningsen, G. 1980. *The Witches' Advocate: Basque Witchcraft and the Spanish Inquisition (1609–1614)*. Reno: University of Nevada Press.

Larner, C. 1981. *Enemies of God*. Oxford: Basil Blackwell.

Larner, C. 1984. *Witchcraft and Religion*. Oxford: Basil Blackwell.

Le Roy Ladurie, L. 1987. *Jasmin's Witch*. Aldershot: Scolar Press.

Leland, C. 1899. *Aradia: Gospel of the Witches*. New York: Samuel Weiser.

Macfarlane, A. 1970. *Witchcraft in Tudor and Stuart England*. New York: Harper and Row.

Marwick, M. (ed.). 1970. *Witchcraft and Sorcery*. Harmondsworth: Penguin.

Middleton, J. (ed.). 1967. *Myth and Cosmos*. Austin: University of Texas Press.

Middleton, J. and E. H. Winter (eds.). 1963. *Witchcraft and Sorcery in East Africa*. London: Routledge and Kegan Paul.

Murray, M. 1921. *The Witchcult in Western Europe*. Oxford: Oxford University Press.

Starhawk, 1979. *The Spiral Dance*. New York: Harper and Row.

Thomas, K. 1971. *Religion and the Decline of Magic*. New York: Scribner's.

Trevor-Roper, H. R. 1956. *The European Witchcraze*. New York: Harper and Row.

Z. Budapest, quoted in Adler, M. 1986. *Drawing Down the Moon*. Boston: Beacon, p. 105.

Feminine Power at Sea

Silvia Rodgers

Silvia Rodgers was awarded her doctorate in anthropology at Oxford University for her research on the symbolism of ship launching in the Royal Navy.

The ceremony that accompanies the launch of a Royal Navy ship is classified as a state occasion, performed more frequently than other state occasions and to an audience of thousands. But until now it has never been the subject of research, either historical or anthropological.

If the ceremony of launching looks at first sight like the transition rite that accompanies the ship as she passes from land to water, it soon becomes clear that the critical transition is from the status of an inanimate being to that of an animate and social being. From being a numbered thing at her launch, the ship receives her name and all that comes with the name. This includes everything that gives her an individual and social identity, her luck, her life essence and her femininity.

My research into the ceremony sheds light not only on the nature and development of the ceremony itself but also on the religious beliefs of sailors, on the symbolic classification of a ship by sailors, on the extensive and reincarnating power of the ship's name, and on the relationship between women and ships and mariners. It is the last aspect on which I want to concentrate here.

Most of us know that sailors refer to a ship by the feminine pronoun. But the extent of the metaphor of the ship as a living, feminine and anthropomorphic being, is not, I think, appreciated. Furthermore, it is this metaphor that shows up the quintessential and extraordinary nature of the launching ceremony. I say "extraordinary" because this ceremony is unique in our society and any of its auxiliary societies in that it symbolically brings to life an artefact. It looks more like a case of animism than of personification. Its status in the Royal Navy as a state occasion makes all this even more remarkable, particularly as it is accompanied by a service of the established Church.

"Feminine Power at Sea" by Silvia Rodgers from *Royal Anthropological Institute News*, Vol. 64, 1984. Royal Anthropological Institute. Reprinted with permission.

There are of course other new things that are inaugurated by secular or sacred means. But in none of these instances does the artefact acquire the properties of a living thing, let alone a feminine person. There is the proclivity to personify virtues and institutions in the feminine, but these are not conceptualized as living and human beings. Personal articles are given human attributes, with a name and even a gender. But this is not a social rule, nor a rule of grammar, as in the case of the personified ship. Nor is life, name and gender instilled through the public enactment of a prescribed ceremony.

Members of the Royal Navy, and indeed the merchant navies, talk about a ship as having a life, a soul, a spirit, a personality and a character of her own. These notions are not necessarily differentiated, and the terms are used interchangeably. Whether the word "soul," "life" or "spirit" is used depends on the informant. What is constant is the gender of the ship. In the English language, which allows gender only to human beings and animals of determinate sex, it is the rule to refer to a ship as "she" or "her." While reflecting the strength of the metaphor, the rules of grammar also indicate its limit. The linguistic boundary lies in the region of the relative pronoun. According to Fowler it is correct to say: "The ship that lost her rudder" and the "*Arethusa* that lost her rudder" or "*Arethusa* who lost her rudder." Sailors frequently drop the "the" in front of the name of a ship. They explain that if I went to see a friend I would not say "I am going to see the Sally" but "I am going to see Sally" and that this applies to a ship.

The image of the ship as a fictive woman is established in diaries and chronicles, is legally encoded in naval and legal documents, and celebrated in poetry and prose. It survives masculine names, figureheads and the labels East-Indiamen and men-of-war. In the current Royal Navy, as I have indicated, the metaphor is as strong as ever. But what kind of woman is she? A ship is represented as possessing the attributes of more than one category of woman. All are stereotypes that are idealized by sailors.

Two images predominate: the all-powerful mother who nurtures and offers womb-like protection; and the enchantress of whom a man can never be certain. Other images intrude, but all inspire romantic and consuming love, awe and constant devotion. When Conrad writes of "the mysteries of her (the ship's) feminine nature" and how the love of a man for his ship "is nearly as great as that of man for a woman, and often as blind" he expresses the sentiments of modern sailors.

Conrad not only depicts vividly the ship as a woman, but brings out the whole environment of being at sea. My informants frequently explain to me, with some emotion and with interesting detail, the reality at sea. It is disorienting, frightening as well as awe-inspiring. This environmental context is crucial when we look for reasons for the feminine nature of the ship. In an environment which is not the natural habitat of human beings, a man may feel himself to be especially vulnerable if as a species he is incompletely represented. That vulnerability could well account for the partnership of an all-male crew with a feminine ship. It is significant that the male and secular principle is complemented not by a secular and natural woman, but by her metaphysical and metaphorical manifestation. Needham has gathered enough ethnographic evidence from diverse and land-based societies to suggest that the complementary opposition men:women::temporal:mystical is widespread if not archetypal. It is easy to understand that the oceanic environment exacerbates the need for mystical protection that emanates from women. In addition, in circumstances where uncertainty and the likelihood of sudden death is increased, the symbol of rebirth in the form of the mother would be particularly welcome. Nor should we omit to look at the metaphor from the point of view of the archetypal figure of the mother and the mother goddess which according to Neumann is deep within the human psyche. Neumann (1974) also explains how the ship has served as the symbol of the mother, of rebirth, and salvation for many cultures over many periods; and not only for people that go to sea.

It comes as a surprise to find that unlike the life essence of the ship, the universality of the ship as a symbolic woman is undermined by some ethnographic data. Nevertheless it is very widespread and historical, and cross-cultural material helps to underline the supernatural power of women in the oceanic domain. Hornell finds that from the Mediterranean to the Pacific Ocean, and from Ancient Greece to that the 20th century, "ships are generally considered to be feminine." He believes the feminine principle is often introduced when the ship is dedicated to her tutelary goddess at the launch. He describes such cases from the coast near Madras. Hornell points out that sometimes there is an identifiable icon of the deity. Malinowski relates how the Trobriand canoes are closely associated with the Flying Witches, whose Power is on occasion concentrated in the carvings at the prow.

In western societies, from the coasts of Preclassical Mediterranean to Catholic Europe, patron saints of mariners are usually feminine. Figureheads, now no longer extant on British ships, were particularly efficacious if the image was a woman, especially if she was bare-breasted (Kemp 1976). There is some ground for concluding that this icon symbolized the mother who suckled the infant god, and that this made her a powerful intercessor especially against the devil. However one hardly needs this evidence to recognize the existence of a special relationship between women, ships and mariners in British fleets.

First and foremost is the irrefutable feminine nature of the ship. Then there is the launch at which the two most important personages are both feminine: the ship and her sponsor. It is the role of the sponsor, a woman of high rank by ascription, to exercise her mystical powers to imbue the ship with luck and life by naming her in strict adherence to the ritual detail: the bottle must move, the ship begin to move, the name (the generator of the luck and life) be pronounced—all at the same moment. Anything else augurs bad luck for the ship. Unfortunately, a ship at her launch is hypersensitive towards her sponsor and may react with self-destructive wilfulness to any lapse by the sponsor in her manner of dress or rendition of the formula. There are many accounts of instances when a ship has refused to move or moved too soon, making it impossible for the bottle to break at the right moment. When a ship behaves in this way she puts her own luck at risk, but it is always the sponsor who is blamed. The sponsor's power to bless has inadvertently turned into the power to curse.

There are several ethnographic examples where positive power coexists with negative power in one and the same person: a coexistence that had been spotted earlier by Jacob Grimm (in Briffault 1927). But negative power, where ships of the Royal Navy are concerned, usually emanates from ordinary women. Strict taboos attempt to restrict this harmful influence. A woman on board a ship at night is regarded with particular misgiving. She is bound to bring bad luck, and sophisticated technology is no proof against this. On the contrary, it may itself be a target. This is nicely demonstrated by the true story of the Rolls-Royce engine of a destroyer that blew up when a woman computer programmer had spent the night on board. It was perfectly true that the manufacturers had omitted to drill a critical hole, and the engine could have blown up at any time. But why, the officers wondered, had it blown up on the one night that a woman was on board? (The reasoning is Azande, the granary is waterborne.) The taboos excluding women from critical areas extend to the part of the dockyard where ships are under construction. We know that equivalent taboos are described in a host of ethnographies. They also operate on oil rigs and down coal mines in Britain, and are very stringent in fishing communities here and across the world.

With modern technology no match for the vicissitudes of luck, it is not surprising to find that the ceremony of the launch is as indispensable as ever, and part of the regulations of the Royal Navy. Nor is it surprising that it is still believed that if the bottle fails to break at exactly the right time, the fate of the ship is in doubt.

At the launch of a destroyer in 1975, a distinguished naval officer was alarmed when he thought that the sponsor had failed to break the bottle across the bow. "After all," he told me, "I might be in command of her one day." The role of the sponsor has if anything increased. Advanced technology has made it possible for her to be seen to control not only the mystical but also the technical part of the launching. From 1876, engravings in the *Illustrated London News* portray Royal sponsors setting the ship in motion and releasing the bottle with just a touch of the finger. It may have been coincidental that this overall control mechanism was installed at the same time as the Christian service was added to the ceremony.

But the very existence of a Christian service presents a puzzle. The critical part of the launching ceremony is concerned with imbuing the ship, an artefact, with luck and the soul and personality of a feminine entity—hardly in accord with Christian doctrine. Although this naming ritual has always been called a "christening," the term is misleading: the subject of the ritual is not a human being but an artefact; the liquid is not water but wine; the celebrant is neither ordained nor male. The duties of the sponsor (or godmother as she is sometimes referred to) are in any case not consistent with that of a Christian godmother, apart from the secular obligations that start after the launch.

The puzzle comes no nearer to solution when one looks at the varying attitudes of ministers of the Church to this ceremony. Some clergymen in the 19th century voiced strong disapproval of the naming ritual and of its being called a baptism. Today, incumbents of parishes local to the shipyards are happy to conduct the service at a launch. The only aspect that continues to baffle them is that no higher ranking ministers are ever invited to officiate, not even when the Queen Mother is the sponsor. Although the service was inaugurated by the Archbishop of Canterbury in 1875, since then it has been the rule for the local incumbent to conduct it. But if the ceremony of the launch seems to bother the main body of the Church, for naval chaplains the problem is even more complicated. Among the duties of the Chaplain of the Fleet is the keeping up to date of the launching service, and approving the minister chosen to conduct it. Yet, as a senior naval chaplain was at pains to point out to me, according to the Naval Chaplaincy no naval chaplain should himself ever take part in a launching. Incidentally, this same chaplain shares, and with conviction, the view of sailors that the ship is a living and feminine entity, though he does deny the ship her soul, that hallmark of a Christian being.

To understand the religious beliefs of sailors one has to look beyond the tenets of Christianity. The power of a ship's name, the naming ceremony, the metaphor of the ship as a fictive woman, the taboos relating to women: all are part of the beliefs of sailors which they themselves call "superstitious." It is well known in our own society that sailors are superstitious. What is not appreciated is that when sailors describe themselves as being superstitious, and they do so frequently, it has none of the usual pejorative connotations. They explain it as a natural consequence of life at sea, which makes them see things in a different way. An acceptable part of their syncretic religion, it comes near to the sense that adhered to *superstitio* in early Classical Rome: a valued and useful quality (Benveniste 1973).

Historical investigation shows that this so-called superstition has always existed in British navies, though specific manifestations may have changed. A ceremony to mark the launch of a new ship seems to have been imperative for centuries. But it has undergone such transformations that it is unrecognizable from, for example, the one performed in Pepys's time. The ship has always been feminine, but the relationship between women and ships had shifted over time. That the power of women has remained confined to the supernatural plane will come as no surprise.

With so much emotion invested in a ship, one may well ask why the demise unlike the launch, of a Royal Navy ship, is marked only by routine, and not by ritual. The answer must surely lie in the name through which the life, luck and personality survive the body of any one ship. The choice of names is vast, but the same names recur time and again: the present *Ark Royal* is the fifth ship of that name; the first belonged to Elizabeth I. If a name is outstandingly lucky and illustrious, it is reincarnated more frequently than others. The name as the keeper of life, as integrator into society and its history, has ethnographic parallels. Mauss draws on North American Indian material to show that the name of a person is part of the stock of the tribe, and that it reincarnates the original ancestor (1950, 1979). When Gronbech describes the power or the names in *The Culture of the Teutons* (1931) he could be writing about names of Royal Navy ships. But unlike the societies studied by Mauss and others, the Fleet, or the society of Royal Navy ships, consists entirely of feminine personages.

REFERENCES

Benveniste, Emil. 1973. *Indo-European Language and Society*. London: Faber.

Briffault, Robert. 1927. *The Mothers: A Study in the Origins of Sentiments and Institutions*. New York. 3 vols.

Conrad, Joseph. 1960. *The Mirror of the Sea*. London: Dent.

Gronbeck, V. 1931. *The Culture of the Teutons*. London: Oxford University Press.

Hornell, James. 1946. *Water Transport*. Cambridge: Cambridge University Press.

Kemp, Peter. 1976. *The Oxford Companion of Ships and the Sea*. London: Oxford University Press.

Malinowski, Bronislaw. 1932. *Argonauts of the Western Pacific*. London: Routledge.

Mauss, M. (1950) 1979. *Sociology and Psychology* (trans. B. Brewster). London: Routledge.

Needham, Rodney. 1980. *Reconnaissances*. Toronto: Toronto University Press.

Neumann, E. 1974. *The Great Mother* (trans. R. Manheim). Princeton: Princeton University Press.

A Policeman's Construction of "The Truth"

Sergeant Hibbs and the Lie-Detector Machine

Nigel Rapport

Nigel Rapport, who received his Ph.D. from the University of Manchester, is a Fellow of the Institute of Social and Economic Research, Memorial University of Newfoundland. His fieldwork has been carried out in rural England and has focused on the use of English in society and the individual construction of meaning.

I

It is 7.30 p.m., and Sergeant Hibbs faces his class of budding criminology students. There are the hopefuls, intent upon a future in the Royal Newfoundland Constabulary, or the RCMP, or the Correctional Service of Canada. There are the Sisters of Mercy preparing for a pastoral vocation at Her Majesty's Penitentiary. There is the woman from the Military Police, and the man from the Lightship Community Rehabilitation Centre for Probationers and Parolees.

It is a large lecture-theatre, steeply sloping, and Sergeant Hibbs stands at the front, a small metallic box on the table before him. The sergeant seems a rather sad man. He fixes his audience in his gaze and speaks methodically:

The polygraph is a machine which determines the truth and untruth in suspects, victims and informants. The word "polygraph" comes from the Greek language where it means "many writings." The polygraph machine measures physiological changes in a person being examined in response to the asking of certain questions. The rate of respiration, the blood-pressure, the pulse rate, and the galvanic skin response—the resistance of the skin to an electric current, which lessens as perspiration increases—these are recorded simultaneously by the instrument. *The Sergeant fingers the metal box, and then lightly traces the aeroplane stickers on its leather valise—proud souvenirs of missions accomplished far and wide.*

"A Policeman's Construction of 'The Truth': Sergeant Hibbs and the Lie-Detector Machine" by Nigel Rapport, from *Anthropology Today*, Vol. 4, No. 1, 1988. Royal Anthropological Institute. Reprinted with permission.

The history of civilization is filled with attempts to verify the truth and detect lies. Traditionally in Africa they'd apply a hot iron nine times to an individual's tongue, and if it burnt he was guilty. Because his mouth went dry when he was tense. So it was the same as China when they put dry rice into a person's mouth, and if it was dry when he spat it out he was guilty. They still use that there today. And it was the same in India: if a donkey brayed when the victim was holding its tail then he was guilty. That was called the Ordeal of the Sacred Ass. But see, it's easy psychology. And these ancient tests—and the Ordeal of the Red-hot Stones, or the Boiling Water—they sometimes showed a shrewd understanding, but they weren't reliable or scientific.

Coming closer in time, there were fore-runners of the polygraph techniques thought-up by an Italian, Cesare Lobrose, in 1885. And then the first American on the scene was William Marston, in 1915; and then another in 1921, John Larson; and then Leonarde Keeler in 1930, who's the real father of the polygraph we have today. And the pioneer. Keeler applied the instrument to police work, and also refined it for war-time and for using it in business and security work and industry. This model of mine is the Ambassador and it goes where I go. It's no crock! *The Sergeant surveys the room, warning off any impertinent challenge.* Here are the pens. This measures blood pressure. And this measures sweat. And these buttons here are intensifiers, so that an obese person's breathing can be made equivalent to a thin person's. The first thing I was taught in College was not to touch the machine before the course was completed or else there was a $2 fine every time you did it! *The Sergeant laughs at the reminiscence* And people soon learn! *and fondles his instrument panel.* So, we ask a question, and then wait twenty seconds for reaction time, and then mark the effects of the body when the man answers. It works 'cause of the fear of punishment. [. . .]

More than two million polygraph, or lie-detector, tests are conducted annually in the U.S.A.; and all over North America use of the machine, whether to screen prospective spouses, employees, or felons, is growing rapidly. In an American society of great normative multiplicity, I find it sociologically significant that a means of garnering fundamental truths is increasingly popular. It is also pertinent that the accredited arbiter is technological.

In 1985, in the guise of a student of criminal procedure, I attended a lecture on the polygraph given by a Sergeant Hibbs of the R[oyal] C[anadian] M[ounted] P[olice]. I was in the process of researching how the word "violence" informed conversation in the city of St. John's,[1] but the sergeant's lecture, and his fetish for detail, prompted the following: thoughts on the detailed construction of inescapable truth.[2]

II

It is through details and their arrangements that a culture is to be understood, Leach explains.[3] The continuum of the external world is culturally carved into the details of classes and categories, with which symbolic games of object and boundary are then played. These games create "information," according to Bateson, and the details of cultural reality are found replicated in a world which would otherwise appear to be without intelligible character; congruence is achieved between cognitive expectations and events.[4] But what of the fetishization of detail? The cultural practice of detailing the world with seemingly reverent regard for facts, numbers and procedures? Here I shall explore the use which Sergeant Albert Hibbs makes of this practice: the cognitive game he plays as he constructs a world of detailed order and achieves "the truth."

The more detailed and segmented the cognitive construction of an environment, the more passage through that environment may be controlled, routed and predictably predetermined. When people and events are pedantically classified, and behaviour pedantically itemized and categorized, impropriety can be easily spotted and potential disorder stopped. Adapting Foucault, I shall call such pedantry *disciplinary detail*.

Foucault analyses the rise of what he calls "disciplinary time" in seventeenth century France.[5] Such discipline entails an increasingly detailed partitioning of time into more subdivisions. With more available moments, he argues, the less exhaustible time can be seen to become; and the more precisely, elaborately and intensively use can be extracted from each segment. Moreover, the more segmented time is, the more it can be administered, and individual behaviour timetabled. And with increasingly minute intervals, the governing of individual activity can be regulated in more detail.

Rhythms can be imposed, repetition controlled, acts sustained and constrained through an entire succession, as the non-repetitive onward march of continuous time is carved-up and subordinated to the experience of repetitive movement within a grid composed of regular intervals and stationary categories.

Disciplinary detail is the practice of extending the above construction of time to a wider mode of construing the world. Details are marshalled like cohorts in battle. For the policeman, they provide the definite knowledge by which the criminal is caught and convicted and his flight thwarted. It is like the lowering of an archaeologist's site-grid on an environment otherwise entropic. By applying a grid of precise, disciplined, factual categories to a case, each category replete with a detailed enumeration of proper procedures and improper behaviours, the criminal is easily pinpointed; his flight slowed by every detail he causes to be misplaced. Indeed, the more closely-knit the grid, the denser the categories of order, the more likely the hemmed-in criminal will be to trip, and the less likely to escape. Once the policeman's grid is lowered, then, and the contents of the environment enumerated and sorted, the truth is self-evident. The order of the grid fulfills itself.

However, such an imposition of order and imprisonment of disorder may still be disputed; especially in a world of criminal noise. Thus it is that in the lecture Sergeant Hibbs offers proof: the polygraph. Here is simultaneously the culmination of disciplined police procedures and their verification. Now the polygraph provides scientific corroboration of the truth which the police procure. Explaining this police mastery in detail, Sergeant Hibbs invites his audience to recognize and celebrate its oracular infallibility. Having introduced the machine, then, the sergeant continues like this:

> Now, there are fifteen full-time polygraphists in Canada with the RCMP, and we have one co-ordinator in Ottawa. My responsibility, B-division, is all of Newfoundland and Labrador. In Canada, polygraph operations are used by the RCMP and the provincial police in Ontario and Quebec, and the Armed Forces, and CP Rail, and some corporations for periodical examinations of their employees, and by several municipalities. As we use it in the RCMP it's voluntary, and the person signs a consent-form. But first the investigator on a case writes a report, a brief, of why he's suspicious and wants me to test someone. Then my Detachment Commander makes sure the investigator is up to date, and isn't just wanting to use the instrument as a crutch. Then it goes forward to the officer in charge of the three island areas within B-division—that's St. John's and Gander and Corner Brook. And then it's approved by the Head Officer in St. John's, and then if it passes all that, I step in and complete any other necessary details to assist the future test. And make sure the machine is always ready to work.

So, the suspect comes, or some witness they want to see if what he believes is the truth, and I give him a Police Caution, and explain what he's doing is voluntary and of his own free will and then he signs the release form. Then, before I start, I find out about the person. Is he fit, mentally and physically? Like I don't do pregnant women till they've given birth, and I don't do it if he's got a flu, or been physically abused. Or if he's exhausted, or he's seeing his doctor about his mental health, or if he's got a possible heart-complaint. So I ask what he likes and doesn't like, and his ambitions, and how he feels society treats him, and how he got on with his parents and brothers and sisters. Last year 7% of my tests weren't completed because I stopped and advised them to get a medical, 'cause like their blood pressure was way out of whack and they'd not seen a doctor for twenty-seven years or something. And maybe they felt fine, but one woman who went to a doctor after she saw me got hospitalized!

So I do a background information form. Then I ask what does he or she know about the charge. If nothing at all, then I send them home, because the police officer hasn't done his work. Then I explain how the machine works, and we review together what I'm gonna ask him so nothing comes as a surprise. 'Cause this machine tells me what a person believes to be true. It's like an extension of the unconscious system of the individual. So it's like mums don't need a machine, and they can detect when a youngster is lying. 'Cause we're all brought up not to lie so when we do it affects us. And it's just psychology, using the same ways as mothers when we lied to her. Like when you're dealing with juvenile delinquents, nine times out of ten they're the ones who did it before and keep on doing it, right? Or know who did it. And most of them won't change. But they'll stand there and never look you in the eye. They look down and wiggle a foot, and it's only the good liars you can't detect who can look you in the eye, and ignore all the positive reinforcement of getting found out all the time in the end.

It's a shame. But I was burned once, sucked in all the way by some juveniles who lied, and next time you go looking for them. Because it's like a stimulus: you put your hand on the oven and get burned, and then you don't do it again! So you get to be hard, and not listen to excuses, and you get to recognize guilt reactions. Like you get to know a drunk car too, 'cause buddy looks down and won't look at you when you pass, and that shows he's hoping that if he doesn't look at you then you won't see him. But you get to recognize the swervy turns in the road, and the wide corners he's taking. And the dome light's on and windows open and broken taillight and lower socio-economic class, generally. I know that's a tough thing to say, but 50–60% of the time the guilty drunks have these characters, and beat-up cars and living in shacks and no jobs and poor, and they still afford $20 to $30 night on booze . . .

So you have buddy [colloquial Newfoundland English = *the bloke*] in the room ready for the test, on his own chair so you don't catch herpes off him: I mean some of the sorts I get in you don't even wanna touch 'em! And it's about one-and-a-half hours for the interview, like to allay the fears of the innocent and increase them for the guilty. Then I ask the questions. First I ask a known truth question. Next I check his trust and ask whether he thinks I'll ask him questions which we've not reviewed before. Then the third and fourth questions are on outside issues, and if the case is about a family theft I may slip in the word "hurt" or "cheat" in those questions.

Then the fifth question is one of the important and relevant ones about the case. Then sixth is a control question. A control question is a safeguard in the examination, and it's designed so buddy will probably lie to it. So not all that relevant or important to the case, but just to compare the response to that question to the relevant ones, to see if they respond the same as the lie. Like if buddy is accused of a theft, I could ask him if he was charged with shoplifting before he was sixteen. Like a question that's almost certain to be right, so when he says "No," it's bound to be a lie.

Anyway, moving along, the seventh question is another relevant one, after the control question. Number eight is a known truth question. Number nine is another control question and number ten another relevant one. Buddy just answers "Yes" or "No" all the time, and it takes fifteen minutes or something to complete the examination. Then if I ask say seven questions altogether, and buddy scores +6 then he's truthful. If it's –6 then he's lying. And if it's between then the test isn't definite, and I set up one for another time. But it's usually indefinite 'cause buddy's had drugs, like marijuana within the past twenty-four hours, and that dries the skin and affects his responses.

There's a doctor in Utah who found 100% success with his polygraph, although there's one in Minnesota who said it was only 50%, but he's against using it anyway. But no science is 100% accurate ever. And not everyone I say are lying are always caught. Last year, 30% of the tests I did were truthful people, 7% were not definite and 63% were lying. I did 123 examinations. And when I said someone was lying, in 85 to 90% of the cases they made admissions of guilt later, or they admitted it when I confronted them and said they were! And I'm nice to people too! *The sergeant chuckles.* Then once buddy is charged and before the courts, polygraphs' analysis usually aren't allowed. But I've given evidence in court lots of times and it's been accepted. Because though the polygraph isn't admissible as proof anything else buddy says to me in the interview, before or after, *is* admissible.

But I've taken formal courses, and had practical experience too, on being nice to everyone. 'Cause my attitude would affect you. Like if I was barking at you, and you were innocent, it could render the test invalid. On the other hand the Law has to contain real teeth to shock those people still expecting the old kid-glove treatment. And it's no use at all if you're gullible when you're dealing with criminally inclined people with social and psychological problems, and maybe violent, too. And some of them you get are just out-and-out liars. Most of them are prone to lie more about the further past than the recent past 'cause it's harder to prove. But one case I remember, no one had heard of buddy. Not even employers he claimed in the past. And then we found he had two names and sixty-five convictions under his old one! And he'd told nothing but a network of lies and tissue of untruths. That one's gone blind now 'cause him and a few other inmates in the pen drank Gestetner fluid. So he won't be writing any more bum cheques! But even when it's like that, I can't let my heart rule my head, if you like, and I got to leave behind me all the case reports I read every day as a policeman, and just go in with an open mind. I mean I know we're bad, but we aren't that bad! We aren't sadists, eh? Not unless they really screw up!

So I get a high admissions rate. Very high. Another case I had in 1982 or '83 was buddy suspected of stealing a money bag. And I said he was innocent, and eighteen months later they found it stuck in the bank night-deposit mechanism. So I was proved right, though no one else believed my machine at the time. And at the opposite extreme, every murder we get lots of people admitting to it, 'cause they're depressed or something. One guy here in Newfoundland admits to everything, like even downing a helicopter eh, and we get him at the station and prove he doesn't know anything about it. So it works two ways, eh?

Now, the course they run at the Canadian Polygraph School is also considered one of the best in the world. The English come to it, and if the Americans came too it could be full time. And you only get twelve students there at a time, so you're sure of good calibre students always. And then they do well and present papers in American seminars after. Well now, *the sergeant plants his hands proprietorially on either side of his machine* come and take a closer look if you want, 'cause that's about all I wanna say. So look but, again, please don't touch.

The lecture ends.

III

For Sergeant Hibbs, the polygraph pronouncements, scientific and detached, validate police categories, and vindicate their detailed application. I should like to describe his perception of them as oracular; and I have in mind comparison with the Azande poison oracle, *benge*. Before I turn to an analysis of the detail in Sergeant Hibbs' speech, then, I juxtapose certain features from Evans-Pritchard's ethnography, to be kept in view.[6]

Benge is the Azande name of a poison administered to chickens. The poison is inanimate, not a personal being. However, under certain ritual conditions, *benge* becomes dynamic; a mystical agent. It can answer questions "Yes" or "No" by killing or sparing the chickens.

Benge is an activity which adult Zande males take pride in. It is used to corroborate preliminary evidence of witchdoctor sleuths or lesser oracles, and empowers men to act against the machination of Evil and Disorder.

Benge is consulted in secret, and at a distance from the polluting effects of the mundane: women, sex, tabued food. The poison is kept potent in hidden caches, and is often administered by adolescent boys who are not concerned with the problems the adults are addressing.

The men sit politely before the oracle. The poison is administered and is followed by an expert harangue of five or ten minutes duration, with traditional imagery and question-formulations. There is a long elucidation of fact and inference, suggesting "Yes" or "No" answers in alternating fashion: "if this is so, *benge*, kill the fowl; if this is so, spare it," and so on. Only when all details have been heard, and judgement well-considered, should *benge* respond through the body of the chicken—a response whose every minor twitch is significant to the expert eye. Then a second testing corroborates the first.

Benge is infallible. Any mistakes or contradictions in pronouncements are due to human weakness, or the interference of other mystical power. Finally, the veracity and reliability of the oracle and official operators of the prince are indisputable. The prince's *benge* decisions have the force of law.

Now, with the Azande in mind, I return to Sergeant Hibbs' performance.[7]

I suggest that it is constructed from eight separable themes, eight classes of fact. Each theme establishes in terms of its own routinized gradations an inexorable progression towards truth. As detail follows detail, the order which the sergeant seeks to replicate becomes more and more inevitable. And as theme marches with theme, the sergeant's cognitive construction of world order is lowered into position.

Theme 1 is the progress of civilization. The polygraph machine is found at its zenith: through Africa to China to India to Italy, we finally get Americans on the scene in 1915. From hot irons to dry rice, donkeys' tails, red-hot stones and boiling water, we get the first really reliable truth-test in the 1930 polygraph; culminating in 1985 with the Ambassador model. The machine is now infallible. And even if this science is sometimes less than 100% accurate, which, nevertheless, an unbiased American doctor claimed, then the interference of an evil science, such as cheating by the use of the chemical marijuana, is responsible.

Theme 2 is the operator who officially invokes the machine's dynamism. He, too, has a pedigree: Leonarde Keeler is now father to a lineage of polygraphists. He pioneered its use, and today, many are the organizations which recognize the munificence of his bequest: for example, the RCMP, where Sergeant Hibbs decided to give his help, together with fourteen other collaterals. Coordinating with an elder in Ottawa, each gives his principal efficient and honest service: in 85–90% of cases wrongdoers admit their guilt after Hibbs' pronouncement; even if it sometimes takes years for the RCMP to catch up and admit his veracity in their courts of law.

Sergeant Hibbs achieved this status through a long apprenticeship, theme 3. At one of the world's best polygraph academies, a school bringing neophytes

3,000 miles, he changed from a boy not even allowed to touch the machine, under threat of a fine, to a master fluent even in the word's Greek etymology. Now it is he who holds seminars and occasionally removes the machine from its cache.

For the machine must be approached with proper respect, theme 4, its ministry available only to those who have shown themselves worthy. First, the police constables must diligently work at their own investigations. Then their brief must pass a Detachment Commander, then an Area Commander, and then finally the Head of RCMP "B" Division passes the suit on to Sergeant Hibbs, and makes his supplications on the constable's behalf. And if Sergeant Hibbs is not satisfied with the strength or sincerity of the request, then the case is rejected. For poor police work merely means that not every officer whom the polygraph empowers to act fulfills the order, and convicts a liar. That is time wasting and worse, an affront to the whole proceedings.

In fact, there was a time when Sergeant Hibbs *was* gullible and *could* be duped, but no longer, theme 5. Nowadays he knows that 70% of the people he meets on his beat will probably be liars: juvenile delinquents or drunks or dope-freaks or shoplifters or burglars; and while not sadistic, he enjoys seeing them shocked by the law's teeth as they pass from the stage of felon to convict and prisoner; he has successfully prosecuted many, the juridical maze notwithstanding. Criminals cannot now elude him.

However, this is to pre-empt the case. For, first, the fitness of prospective participants must be ascertained, theme 6. The suspect who is enabled to enjoin the rite, and contest his innocence, will suffer physiological and psychological strain; but all such change must be wrought by the machine from an initial parity: the ordeal must begin with equilibrium. Thus, it is insulting to suggest that the machine abuse its sensors through contact with the already polluted: the physically or mentally ill, the drunk, the pregnant. Then, from this equilibrium a lying man will feel fear of punishment in measurable proportion to the extent of his lies. And every physiological reaction is captured. For the machine becomes an extension of the participant's psyche. It is the rational counterpart of the intuition which mothers possess. And since even criminals are strained when they lie, Sergeant Hibbs can now detect them all.

Having vetted the supplicants, Sergeant Hibbs proceeds with preparatory ablutions, theme 7. First, the participant must sign a consent form, a voluntary laying-down before the power of the machine, its heritage and its officiant. Then a background information form is completed: together the officiant and the participant prepare an offering in which no room is left for confusion, or secrets, or the play of chance; all relevant details must be provided so that the machine's rumination is total. Moreover, all mundanities must be excluded, and heart and mind open and quietly receptive to the

machine's probings. Finally an impartial Sergeant Hibbs encourages participants to feel nice and relaxed. Only the guilty, realizing their impotence, then flee the lists.

Lastly, theme 8, the address comes, and in formulaic fashion the sergeant and the suspect spell the issues out for the machine. A question of known truth, then trust, then marginal issues, then pertinent ones, then a control question, and then the same over again. Is this a criminal or not? Through traditional refrains, the lie is stalked, and then a verdict awaited. And last year the Sergeant achieved clarity in 93% of his cases. But if for some reason the offering was not wholly acceptable, then a second ceremony is easily arranged.

IV

I have been classifying the details of Sergeant Hibbs' narrative into various themes, and likening these to some of the facets of ritually consulting an oracle. In the body of his lecture, these themes may be seen to have proceeded more or less *in harmony*; to be heard as what Lévi-Strauss would describe as a *melody*, a syntagmatic chain; the analogy with his mythic analysis is obvious. Moreover, in mythic narration it is this melody which elicits the participation of auditors in the performance and causes them to collaborate in its consummation. It is the structure of the narrative which draws narrator and listener together as co-celebrants, with the audience becoming part of the world to which the myth gives form.[8]

This also holds true for Hibbs' lecture. The melody of his delivery is especially intricate, detail building on detail, theme buttressing theme; and his audience responds by becoming an intent congregation, annotating, grinning and nodding in chorus. The situation is reminiscent of John Berger's account of "myth"-telling in the idioms of the English village. There, he tells us, as the intimacies of intricate genealogies and personalities and the histories of ancient car engines and football matches are painstakingly discussed, so participants meet in a rich and vibrant, local landscape. The minutiae of the topics examined and the details shared bring the interactants closely and publicly together.[9] Here, disciplinary detail serves Hibbs as both a medium and a message.

As a medium of communication, the details in the Sergeant's performance act as a binding rhetoric. His precise exposition and intricate examination are means of including the audience within the bounds of his lecture, his myth, his worldview—even if the audience's part in the interaction involves more gesture than vocalization. The process is similar to that which Jack Goody ascribes to the scriptorial device of listing.[10] In a list is to be found an ordering of items. But through a multiplication of categories, often abstract, and a relocating within a distinct and bounded conceptual space, that order is one possibly ascribed by the list itself, whatever the items' prior relations. Thus Goody suggests that listing involves a different mode of thought, a different reflective capacity, to oral discourse. In the Newfoundland environment, a culture still largely oral, the disciplinary detail of such police listing is perhaps specially significant: so much more a mark of position, and an even greater enticement to an audience of respectful and hopeful neophytes. As a medium of communication then, I suggest that Sergeant Hibbs' listing of detail helps effect a replacement of his audience's universes of conceptual discourse by his own. In the welter of detail, alternative arguments, alternative categories and relations proffering larger-scaled canvases, come to be dissected and replaced; their inexactness is made to seem very amateurish and clumsy.

Sergeant Hibbs' message also speaks of detail. It proclaims that the details of police order are correct and the Sergeant's use of them as the RCMP's polygraphist proper and consistent. Furthermore there is now scientific proof that this is the case. For just as regularly as the police make judgements in terms of their categories of innocence and guilt, informant and criminal liar, ripe for prosecution, so the polygraph machine provides independent corroboration that the terms of this cognitive construction are the true ones. Sergeant Hibbs affords the disciplinary detail of police procedure irrefutability.

V

Lévi-Strauss describes myths and symphonic songs as machines for the suppression of time, and Leach extends his statement to include all ritual sequences; their rhythms regulate and constrain.[11] Moreover, the sequences are "unitary": their end is implicit in their beginning, and their beginning pre-supposes their end. Their message is tautological, already contained within them; and any alteration is ideally suppressed.

Sergeant Hibbs' lecture, whose narrative I have likened to a mythic performance, is a machine for the fulfillment of a worldview, and for the suppression of noise. It follows a unitary sequence: proper procedure is implicit from the beginning; a beginning which presupposes the end of the deviant criminal. The lecture is tautological; it is composed of arguments, details, which eventually lead one back to one's beginning: the polygraph corroborates the worldview whose gradations of knowledge culminate in the polygraph. And yet the circularity is obscured by the mass of encyclopaedic detail which one is led to apprehend *en route*. Engorged on a surfeit of information, an eager audience is mesmerized into treating the sergeant's conception of the truth as irrefutable, and the issue of inexorable scientific progress.

In an entropic world, full of competing definitions of truth, Sergeant Hibbs, like Zande males, has a means of habitually transcending the lie.[12] He can enter an ethereal realm, and engage the assistance of an omniscient mystical agent—Science. And not only does his mode of cognitive construction trap the criminal, it also provides a resource for the successful management of meaning: convincing others, as well as himself, of the legitimacy of the order thus gained.[13]

NOTES

1. See *Talking Violence: An Anthropological Interpretation of Conversation in the City*; ISER, St. John's, Newfoundland, 1987.
2. For his comments on this article, my thanks to Robert Paine. An extended version will appear as "The rite of oracular lie-detection in St. John's: Sergeant Hibbs and the details of truth; *ISER Research and Policy Papers*, Memorial University of St. John's, Newfoundland, 1987.
3. pp. 33–36: *Culture and Communication*; Cambridge University Press, 1976.
4. pp. 177–179: *Communication: The Social Matrix of Psychiatry;* Norton, New York, 1951 (with J. Ruesch).
5. pp. 149–160: *Discipline and Punish*; Pantheon, New York, 1977.
6. Passim: *Witchcraft, Oracles and Magic Among the Azande*; Oxford University Press, 1950.
7. I did not meet Sergeant Hibbs again, after this lecture, which perforce delimits my analysis and "idealizes" this reproduction of his form of life.
8. Cf. Lévi-Strauss: "The Effectiveness of Symbols," pp. 187–204 in *Structural Anthropology*; Basic Books, New York, 1963; also R. Bauman: *Verbal Art as Performance*, p. 16. Newbury House, Rowley, Mass., 1978.
9. p. 100: *A Fortunate Man*; Writers and Readers, London, 1981.
10. pp. 81, 111: *The Domestification of the Savage Mind*; Cambridge University Press, 1977.
11. Op. cit. p. 44.
12. For further discussion of such diversities of meaning, see Rapport: *Are Meanings Shared and Communicated? A Study of the Diversity of Worldviews in an English Village*; Ph.D. Thesis, University of Manchester, 1983.
13. Perhaps the most vital resource informing political life—cf. Anthony Cohen: *The Management of Myths: The Politics of Legitimation in a Newfoundland Company*; ISER, St. John's Newfoundland, 1975.

REFERENCES

Bateson, Gregory and J. Ruesch. 1951. *Communication: The Social Matrix of Psychiatry*. New York: Norton.

Bauman, R. 1978. *Verbal Art as Performance*. Rowley. Mass.: Newbury House.

Berger, John. 1981. *A Fortunate Man*. London: Writers and Readers.

Cohen, Anthony. 1975. *The Management of Myths: The Politics of Legitimation in a Newfoundland Company*. ISER, St. John's, Newfoundland.

Evans-Pritchard, E. E. 1950. *Witchcraft, Oracles and Magic Among the Azande*. Oxford: Oxford University Press.

Foucault, Michel. 1977. *Discipline and Punish*. New York: Pantheon.

Goody, Jack. 1977. *The Domestification of the Savage Mind*. Cambridge University Press.

Leach, R. E. 1976. *Culture and Communication*. Cambridge University Press.

Lévi-Strauss, C. 1963. *Structural Anthropology*. New York: Basic Books.

Rapport, Nigel. 1987. *Talking Violence: An Anthropological Interpretation of Conversation in the City*. ISER, St. John's, Newfoundland.

Rapport, Nigel. 1987. "The Rite of Oracular Lie-Detection in St. John's: Sergeant Hibbs and the Details of Truth." *ISER Research and Policy Papers*, Memorial University of St. John's, Newfoundland.

Rapport, Nigel. 1983. *Are Meanings Shared and Communicated? A Study of the Diversity of Worldviews in an English Village*. Ph.D. Thesis, University of Manchester.

12

Culture Change

Cultures change all the time, but the most dramatic instances are to be found in the confrontation between small-scale and large-scale societies. By 1900 hardly any autonomous tribal people were left on the globe because most had been conquered and subjugated by powerful forces of Western technology and ideology. This take-over changed political relationships profoundly. *It was not Western culture per se that confronted these people but a worldwide economic system that made use of this inexpensive labor administered usually by some form of colonialism. It was in this economic exploitation in which these people were transformed.*

The results of this transformation were hardly uniform. Industrialization or colonialism did not shape new household or other cultural forms; rather, these were the product of how so-called tribal people *interpreted* their colonial experiences and acted on the basis of these interpretations. Some cultures are clearly more amenable to culture change than others, and explanations of culture change have been sought in a variety of interlocking factors including relative deprivation, exploitation and economic inequality, and congruence of cultural elements. Frequently, culture change is manifested in terms that are the antithesis of the colonial situation. Thus, for example, if the colonized are treated in a hierarchical way, the culture change movement might stress **egalitarianism**. This is known, following the anthropologist Victor Turner, as a form of antistructure or **liminality**.

Perhaps the most dramatic form of these **revitalization movements** are those known as **Cargo Cults** or **Millenarian movements**—typically "religiously based" movements that promote social change. They are also movements to make sense of what is a bewildering and frustrating experience for many of the colonial underdogs. Much interesting work has been done on this subject, and some anthropologists have even gone so far as to apply these models to their own society. The rise of Christianity, for example, shows many similarities with Melanesian Cargo Cults. Both are very much the products of an oppressive colonial system and led to the formulation of an alternative lifestyle and ideology. The major difference is, of course, that Christianity went on to become a successful movement whereas most of these movements are rather shortlived.

What one is to make of these movements depends on whose point of view is taken. The Mau Mau, for example, was a movement in Kenya that the colonial authorities saw as a terroristic movement, which used "sick" rituals like the slaughter of goats and people to intimidate the local populace. Later analyses, however, showed it to be not a fanatical cult but a highly effective anticolonial movement. Outsiders' preoccupation with the esoteric, and lack of basic communication because of language barriers, has often resulted in them projecting their own fantasies onto such movements—a situation abetted by the need of such movements to maintain some secrecy.

That such movements need not only be of short duration is well illustrated by the independent church movement in southern Africa; these churches, often with Millenarian overtones, are significant factors there. For example, in 1992 at Easter, the major political leaders including President F. W. deKlerk, Nelson Mandela, and Mangusothu Buthelezi went to the Zion City of Morija, a dusty town transformed into a mass camp. In Morija live some one-half to a million followers of the Zion Christian Church of Bishop Edward Leganjane, who alone boasts some 6 million followers. The article by James Kiernan provides a useful grounding in how some of these contemporary Zulu Zionist churches operate, providing members not only with an important sense of identity but also with numerous other social services. Indeed, many development experts now see these churches as examples of successful grass roots–generated "development projects" based on self-help whose success contrasts very sharply with projects imposed from above by the state in the form of development projects.

After gaining independence, many Southern Hemisphere countries were given massive foreign aid, which was meant to help develop the countries. Much of this aid is believed to be misplaced. Originally, when financial aid was provided to these countries, anthropologists were rarely consulted for a number of reasons: They were believed to favor "traditional culture" and thus were against change; moreover, they took too long to do their studies because they insisted on field-

work. But after some particularly dismal failures of foreign aid, anthropologists are increasingly being called on to provide the local perspective because they are believed to be well qualified to serve as bridge personnel who understand both the worlds of the local people and that of the planners. They are supposed to help identify the unanticipated consequences of large development projects. Such unanticipated consequences can often be disastrous for the local people as A. L. Spedding's case study of the coca eradication project in Bolivia, part of President Reagan's War on Drugs, shows.

Anthropologists are by no means unanimous as to what their role should be in these **social engineering projects**. *Their attitudes range from seeing them as simply another form of recolonization to disillusionment to damage control and accepting that such projects are inevitable.* The papers by James Brain and Alexander Robertson provide a sense of the range of concerns that anthropologists have in this regard.

Coca Eradication

A Remedy for Independence? — With a Postscript

A. L. Spedding

A. L. Spedding did fieldwork in Bolivia between 1986 and 1988 for her London School of Economics Ph.D. She now works as a free-lance writer, novelist, and researcher.

. . . Tratar de quitar la coca es querer que no haya Peru . . . es, finalmente, imaginacion de hombres que por sus intereses, pensando que hacen algo, destruyen la tierra sin la entender.

. . . To try to get rid of coca is to wish that there be no Peru . . . it is, finally, the dream of men who for their interests, thinking they are doing something, destroy the earth without understanding it.

—Juan de Matienzo (1567) *Gobierno del Peru*

If development is something which occurs in programmes funded by aid, there is not much development in Bolivia. The region of Bolivia I am concerned with is Sud Yungas, a section of the eastern slopes of the Andes, with a subtropical climate and an economy based on the cultivation of coca by Aymara peasant farmers. By local standards, it is a long way from being a backward area; since the price of coca began to rise in the 1970s, branch roads have been constructed into most districts, there is considerable commercial activity, many communities have piped water supplied to all houses except those next to springs, and some have even installed a domestic electricity supply, tapping into the network carrying hydroelectricity from a distant dam. All this has been achieved through self-help and community labour projects, organized by the peasants themselves, and using the windfall profits of the great coca boom which ran from about 1970 and took off between 1980 and 1986. The only programme funding economic development, as opposed to medical aid, is the UN's Agroyungas project. Its aim is development through crop substitution, which is a euphemism for coca eradication. Yet the properties of coca make it a development economist's dream. So why does it have to be eradicated and replaced by coffee for the export market?

"Coca Eradication: A Remedy for Independence? — With a Postscript" by A. L. Spedding, from *Anthropology Today*, Vol. 5, No. 5, 1989. Royal Anthropological Institute. Reprinted with permission.

Coca is a woody, slow-growing shrub, with a straggling habit of growth and a maximum height of about 1.50m. The part of the bush which is harvested is its leaves, borne in pairs, bright green, resembling bayleaves but smaller and thinner. If they are not stripped off the bush, after three or four months they turn brown and fall off, to be replaced by a new crop. In practice the leaves are harvested before they turn brown, dried in the sun and packed into sacks for transport and sale. Many adults in Bolivia consume coca, as an infusion or by "chewing" it. In fact the leaves are not chewed, but placed in the side of the mouth between gum and cheek, with a small quantity of *llujta*, an alkaline paste made from vegetable ashes. In combination with saliva, this releases some of the fourteen alkaloids which the leaves contain. The consumer sucks on the wad from time to time to absorb them in the juice it produces.

The effect is rather like a strong cup of coffee, without the tremors and headaches overindulgence in caffeine can produce. Swallowing the coca juice suppresses appetite and reduces thirst. It contains appreciable quantities of vitamin A, and the llujta provides calcium. An accustomed chewer can extract enough stimulants from it to stay awake all night, so it is used not only for all-night rituals but by long distance lorry and bus drivers. An infusion of coca is a cure for the stomach problems due to high altitude, and coca tea is consumed by upper and middle class Bolivians, although chewing it is restricted to people considered ethnically Indian, most of whom are peasants. Coca is an ingredient in a variety of herbal cures in the Andean medical system, and is essential in indigenous ritual and divination.[1]

Until the collapse of tin prices in the 1980s, mining was the principal export sector of the Bolivian economy, as it had been when Bolivia was the province of Upper Peru in the Spanish Empire. The first great coca boom occurred in response to the sixteenth-century mining boom. The Spanish provided Indian forced labourers with coca because it meant they could work longer hours with less food, but even had the shifts been short, people would have refused to mine without coca. A mine lies in the territory of the earth spirits and coca is indispensable as offering to and protection from them.[2] Spaniards bought up coca estates and dominated the lucrative trade which supplied the mines; they had a vested interest in preserving coca.[3] The Catholic Church, however, recognized coca chewing as a rite of indigenous religion, and combated its use. The quote which heads this essay is from a Spanish colonial administrator of the sixteenth century; it is plain that the debate between those who benefit from coca, and those who want to eradicate it, was already active in 1567.

Opponents of coca claim that it damages the health and renders the habitual user thoughtless and apathetic. Coca use is thought to be a consequence of poverty: people cannot afford food and chew coca to dull their hunger. This, in turn, is thought to stupefy them so that they are even less able to overcome their disadvantages. It is true that—for instance—a homeless person in the Bolivian capital, or a poor peasant parent with seven children to feed, will obtain an ounce of coca to keep themselves going while they give what food they have to their children; but I encountered just as many habitual, and even heavy, users of coca among the rich peasants who had plenty to eat. The true importance of coca is religious and ritual; it is an essential mediating agent in Andean culture. The exploitation which native Andeans have been subjected to has produced a situation where many of the people most committed to the Andean cultural tradition are very poor, but coca is not used because of poverty, although it does provide a much appreciated solace in the lives of the dispossessed; if people give up coca when they become rich, this is because the social system obliges middle class people to shun Andean customs. In this sense any attack on coca amounts to a direct attack on the Andean tradition, and this is exactly why the Catholic Church opposed its use. The recent use of coca to produce a prohibited drug has only provided secular grounds for this continuing assault on indigenous values.

From the point of view of a peasant family, coca is a superb crop. It grows at altitudes up to 2,000m above sea level (which is rather low in Andean terms), needs no irrigation, resists drought and disease, and provides three harvests a year. In Yungas it is planted in terraces of pounded earth, which require a huge investment of labour to create, but once the field has been planted, it will start to yield in its second year. If it is well maintained it will go on yielding three harvests a year for thirty years or more. It needs weeding regularly, and the harvest is extremely labour-intensive, but it can be harvested by anyone aged eight to eighty, and labour is the one resource which the peasant family can produce in ample supply. In Sud Yungas, every peasant man is expected to make a coca field when he marries. By the time the coca is in full production, the children will be old enough to start helping with the harvest. This new coca is called *wawa kuka*, "child coca."

When yields start to decrease, the plants are pruned back to stumps and allowed to regenerate. This can be repeated almost indefinitely, although the plants start to thin out after a while. Each harvest is called *mita*. This comes from the Inka term *mit'a*, a turn in the state labour draft. It was adapted as *mita* by the Spaniards to provide drafts of labourers for mines, weaving shops, and public service. The mature coca is called *mit'ani*, "owns a mita"; during the days of labour service on the hacienda, the mit'ani was the woman obliged to perform domestic services in the landlord's house. As the coca plants die off, they are replaced by manioc, then citrus saplings and coffee, and the field eventually becomes a mixed plot of these and other crops. If wished it can be made over into another coca field. By this time the couple who planted the original field will be dead or in retirement, and a new generation will be working the land. If any coca plants from the old field still survive, they are not grubbed out when the land is cleared, but left sticking out of the new terraces. They are called *awicha*, "grandmother"; the integration of coca into the cycle of the domestic group is paralleled in the names it receives at various stages.

During times when coca is in boom, as it was in the sixteenth as well as the twentieth century,[4] it is planted in fields carved directly out of the forest. The usual use of these fields is for subsistence crops, such as maize, walusa (an Andean variety of taro), beans and vegetables. After some years of repeated cropping the soil is "tired," and it is at this point that coca should be planted, it responds well on exhausted soils. Bolivian consumers prefer the small-leaved and aromatic coca which grows on the hillsides of degraded red slate which is all that is left in the traditional coca regions, some of which have been producing coca in the same place since the fifteenth century and earlier.[5] These regions lie between 1,000 and 2,000m above sea level. In recent years people from the Andean highlands have migrated in number to the colonization schemes in the tropical lowlands (below 600m above sea level). The soil in these areas is very poor once the forest has been cleared, and people do not hold enough land for them to be able to clear a new field every two years as the original indigenous population did. They fell and burn the forest, sow maize the first year and rice the next; after this the soil is good for nothing, so they plant coca, which will grow when nothing else will.[6] In these conditions it provides four harvests a year, bearing big leaves which have a bitter taste when chewed and are unusable for divination. The alkaloid content, however, is the same (some sources claim that it is higher than the mid-altitude product, but my evidence does not support this) and this lowland coca is mainly used for processing into cocaine base. Badly planned colonization projects have thus given a major fillip to the cocaine trade. Sud Yungas, however, is an old-established (Inka and before) coca region, and most of its production is of a quality suitable for the "traditional" Bolivian market.

The complex process by which cocaine is extracted from the leaves (some four hundred pounds of which are needed to provide a pound of relatively pure cocaine) was discovered in 1880, but cocaine only became the "drug of choice" for extensive sectors of the US bourgeoisie from about 1975 onwards. It has gone out of fashion in the middle classes of California (whose preferred diversion is now going to Narcotics Anonymous meetings) but the British government continues to predict an avalanche of "snow" and its new derivative, crack, which, it claims, is about to swamp Britain's cities. Crack appears to be cocaine carbonate, very similar in properties to cocaine sulphate, the crude base produced in primitive forest "factories" for later conversion to the soluble (and hence snortable) cocaine hydrochloride.

Like crack, this base can be mixed with tobacco and smoked. It is highly addictive. Yungas peasants who go to work treading coca in these "factories" are given it as part of their wages. If they use it at all (many just sell it) it is to "quit oneself the drunkenness" so as to prolong even further the sessions of festive drunkenness which are indispensable to every ritual and social occasion in the Andes. They use base in the same way as they use alcohol: smoke or drink to excess, pass out, suffer a hangover and go back to work, with no further recourse to intoxicants—apart from the daily chew of leaves—till the next special occasion. A few individuals do develop a habit, but most have relatives and friends who soon put a stop to it. Most of the people who manufacture or deal in base in Bolivia do not consume it, which contrasts with the situation in the West, where the majority of cocaine dealers became involved in the business as consumers. I was familiar with various small-scale peasant base makers, but their activities did not lead to violence, theft, or addiction; the social structure of the rural community is strong enough to restrain anti-social activities.

Contrast this to the ravages reportedly wrought by cocaine and crack addiction in the United States: for the proletarian there who takes up crack, the drug provides a direct escape from boredom and an urban environment which is all too often hideous and decaying. Crack and cocaine dealing offer a chance to make money, not only to those whose race and class restricts their access to the formal job market, but also to financiers prepared to take a risk for high gain; while the proprietor of a Bolivian base factory barely makes a living, the individuals who finance international smuggling can reap vast rewards. The potential benefits of the drug trade

are not combated by effective means such as punitive damages for banks found to be laundering funds, while the activity of government agencies supposed to be combating the trade are at times equivocal; witness the evidence in the recent Cuban cocaine smuggling trial that US agents had infiltrated the operation, but allowed it to continue shipping drugs into the States because this could be used to smear Cuba.[7] Hysterical denunciations of "the pushers," who usually come from disadvantaged and disaffected social groups, provide an excuse for more expenditure on mechanisms of social control, not only domestic police and customs but extending to military and paramilitary incursions in producing countries, under the guise of attacking the problem at its source. Support for neoliberal economic policies is often combined with demands for political and economic interference in this form. No-one suggests that the answer to alcoholism is uprooting the vineyards of France and California, but the answer to cocaine addiction is military campaigns in the Andes, aerial spraying with poisonous herbicides (which is now being carried out in Peru), and programmes such as Agroyungas.

Agroyungas began to function in Sud Yungas from 1985 onwards. It is funded by the UN, with contributions from Italy and other EEC countries including Britain (Conservative politician Timothy Raison visited Bolivia in 1987). The UN appointed a Spaniard as overall director, backed up by other international technocrats. The salaries of this directorate and the staff in project's funds [sic]. A second portion is absorbed by the rather lower salaries paid to Bolivian engineers, agronomists, and sociologists, who are the active interface between the technocrats and the peasants. Their pay is generous by local standards, but they resent being paid less than the "gringos" on the senior staff. Some crumbs are left to pay the local people hired as cooks, drivers and field assistants. All this money is paid out as salaries, not loans, and the recipients are free to do what they like with it; which is not the case with the funds disbursed to peasant producers.

The UN makes available US$2,000 dollars per hectare of coca eradicated. This is a loan, not a payment. Most peasants do not have as much as one hectare under coca, and receive correspondingly less. The money is paid out over a period of three years. Just as the poor in the United States are given part of their welfare benefits in food stamps to prevent them spending money on anything else, only a part is disbursed in cash, at a level calculated to cover the day-wages for extra labour needed to fulfill the project's demands. The rest of the payment is in the form of tools and seedlings for the crop which is to replace coca. This is an improved form of coffee known as catura coffee. In return the peasant has to deposit some kind of land title as security for the loan. If the loan is not repaid, this will be used to seize the land—which sounds brutal, but this sanction is the only one strong enough to get most peasants to pay back loans to someone not personally known to them. It has to be paid back within seven years, plus interest of three to five per cent on the outstanding sum. This is very cheap, since ten per cent a month is considered a fair rate of interest on loans from local moneylenders.

When Agroyungas arrived in Sud Yungas, it was headed by an enthusiastic engineer who I will call "Guillermo." He ran around making all sort of promises; apart from improved coffee, people would have roads built into every recess of their communities, and would receive help with chicken and duck breeding, mules for transport and better water supply so that they could grow irrigated vegetables. None of these promises ever materialized, apart from catura coffee and the roads. Road building consisted of driving a JCB through the community—in at least one case, undermining the foundations of a house which collapsed as a result—and calling the resulting earth track a road. People were initially attracted by these offers and by the cheap loans. Guillermo played down the coca eradication aspect— "it depends on you," he would say. Actually uprooting coca is unthinkable within the customary system of land use, and people were encouraged to sign up for the project without its being emphasized that if they did they would in due course have to pull up their coca. The sociologists who were working on the project in 1987 said that Guillermo had made a lot of careless promises and had eventually been dismissed, after which things had proceeded more sensibly. The peasants' explanation of his overenthusiasm and subsequent dismissal is rather different:

> That engineer Guillermo? My cousin used to drive his jeep for him. He was a dealer! When they drove to the capital they had to stop a few kilometres before the police checkpoint. The base was hidden in the engine. Guillermo opened it up and sprinkled it with petrol so that it wouldn't smell, then they just drove on through.

Agroyungas is part of the Bolivian government's Three Year Plan to do away with the *narcotrafico*. The inception of this plan coincided with the arrival of US troops in Bolivia in July 1986. 1986–7 was to be the year of Voluntary Eradication, 1987–8 of Forcible Eradication, and 1988–9 of Interdiction, with the construction of new prisons for unregenerate growers and traffickers. The first years of Agroyungas, then, corresponded to Voluntary Eradication; clients of the programme were shocked when, in 1987, the project started to demand that they actually dig up their coca, since the catura coffee was supposed to be coming into production to replace it.

Coffee does have advantages as a smallholding crop. Its disadvantages are, firstly, it needs either reasonably good soil or fertilizers in order to yield well, and secondly, it only gives one harvest a year. Since the nineteenth century coffee has been a secondary cash crop in Sud Yungas. The local variety is an arabica known as criollo coffee; it has adjusted to local soils and climate and though it does not bear much, what it does yield is better quality than catura coffee. Like coca, when it gets too straggling it can be pruned back to a stump and then regrows. It is cultivated in a mixed plot of citrus, bananas and other crops, protected by tall shade trees which are also pollarded for firewood. In these conditions it yields adequately and seeds itself within the thicket; to grow more coffee one simply transplants these young plants. Catura coffee plants fruit loaded with berries and look wonderful when they stand next to the sparse criollo coffee. However they do not seed themselves, need a special nursery, and must be fertilized and sprayed if they are to realise their superior potential. After a number of years they are exhausted and must be replaced; apparently they do not survive pruning. The coffee harvest is already the worst labour bottleneck of the year and were there to be still more coffee produced it would be even harder to get enough people to pick it: I have seen catura coffee left unharvested, admittedly when its owners were not peasants, for this reason. People are used to coca, which provides money almost all year round from a series of small fields with staggered harvests, and do not want to depend on a large once-a-year harvest with the inevitable period of penury preceding it.

Annual harvests also encourage debt bondage to buyers who advance money in the months before the crop comes in. In addition people are not used to investing much time or money in coffee—in contrast to coca. Coca does not self-sow and has to be propagated in a nursery for up to two years before it can be transplanted; at this stage it is still only six inches high. It is the only crop for which firebreaks are constructed round its fields, and the only one for which insecticides are used. It is not sprayed, since the grower expects to be able to chew it, but ground insecticides are used against root infestation and leaf-cutter ants. Coca has a symbolic value which means that people are prepared to go to all this trouble for it, since they take a lot of pride in producing a crop which is considered desirable according to the traditional criteria. It should have small leaves, of a size to fit comfortably in the mouth, and be "sweet"— contain a large amount of oil of wintergreen and other aromatics. These aromatics, rather than the alkaloid content, are what coca chewers value. The crop should have regularly shaped leaves, without discolouration or misshapes, and be carefully dried so that it preserves a good green colour: discoloured coca signifies disease in the system of divination, and has an unpleasant taste. Coca growers dispense quantities of coca to their guests on ritual occasions and there is a lot of prestige to be lost if one dispenses a poor quality coca. Conversely, there is no prestige at all to be gained if one produces a good crop of catura coffee.

During boom years, new coca fields are created everywhere, but when prices collapse, as they did in 1986, these speculative fields are rapidly abandoned to bush. The mechanisms of the global market—which is now saturated and declining—will deal with the excess production generated in response to the temporary fashion for cocaine in the West. Coca eradication is measured by area cleared, not the fall in production, so a huge field with a few exhausted plants in it counts for more than a small but highly productive one. Most of the fields offered for eradication are already choked by weeds or are too old to be of any value. At times the grower takes the loan for eradicating such a field and uses it to plant a new coca field in an area out of sight of the authorities, but the growers who do this are peasant farmers for whom coca is the only practical cash crop; speculators who got into coca when its price was rising no longer find it economic, the low price does not pay for the labour necessary. The fields which continue in cultivation are those managed by peasant families who cannot afford to abandon their investment, have to occupy their family members somehow, and do not find catura coffee an adequate alternative.

The directors of Agroyungas also failed to take into account the structure of the peasant community. Each family owns several plots, usually scattered throughout the extension of the community, and may also exploit plots in common land; in the latter case these plots are used for subsistence annuals, not for perennial crops. If legal titles are held, they give the owners the standing of smallholder; although in Peru the peasant community is a legal entity, communal landholding has no standing in Bolivian law. In practice, however, the *sindicato* (gathering of household heads) exercises jurisdiction over the community as a whole. It acts as guarantor of land titles, decides disputes over boundaries, and decides if outsiders shall be allowed to cultivate or buy land within the community. This jurisdiction extends to deciding if a new crop which would alter the system of land use—as would the replacement of coca by catura coffee—should be introduced. If it is to be introduced, then a majority of the community will do so at the same time.

Agroyungas was misled by the formal status of peasant communities as bundles of smallholders and approached individuals to see if they would join the project. The more united communities discussed this in the syndicate and in the majority of cases decided not to join; their members abided by this decision. Some communities were already divided, however, and certain individuals joined the project while others did not (it seems that there were no cases of entire communities which decided to abandon coca). In at least one such community the subsequent activities of Agroyungas exacerbated the divisions to the point where those who were with the project violently assaulted those who were not. The peasant commentary on this interprets it

as a sign that those who had joined the project, when they found that they did not just get money to grow coffee but had to pull up their coca, realized that they were losing out. Out of jealousy they attacked those who had stayed with the customary economy based on coca. This only encouraged the communities which had not yet joined the project to stay out of it. By 1987 Agroyungas would only take on new clients if they subscribed in groups of at least twelve households. Most communities in Sud Yungas have between thirty and sixty households, so if twelve are prepared to come out in public for Agroyungas, it is likely that they will be able to drag a sufficient majority in their wake. Agroyungas admitted that they had entered the area totally ignorant of local conditions and that much of the project had failed as a result.

This relative lack of success is the only really good thing about Agroyungas: it didn't do much harm because it didn't do much anyway, at least for the peasantry. Another example which I encountered during fieldwork was a European-based "appropriate technology" group, represented by several young people on generous EEC grants. They spent a year climbing Andean peaks and canoeing down tropical rivers, as well as consuming "Bolivian marching powder,"[8] and then, when they realised that they had not actually done anything to justify their grant, wrote a laudatory report on a series of "appropriate technology" water pumps designed by an engineer with a grant from Oxfam. They did not actually sponsor the installation of any of these pumps, which could be used in irrigation and small-scale mining. Meanwhile the peasants continue "scratching the earth" (as they themselves describe it) with implements which have not changed since the eighteenth century. Should they decide independently to produce a new crop instead of coca, they receive no support. One man in Sud Yungas had the idea of producing strawberries, a luxury crop which enjoys a high price in the city, but which needs specially prepared fields and a lot of care. He had heard on the radio that the government offered loans to petty producers, so he applied to the local branch of the Banco Agrafio for a loan, only to be repeatedly fobbed off with the claim that they had not received authorization from the capital. In the end he planted a few strawberries with family labour and the help of an old woman working in *ayni* (mutual aid); with a loan he would have been able to employ wage labourers and plant an area large enough to be profitable, and when he made money from it the demonstration effect would have encouraged many other people to try the new crop. A government which was sincerely interested in coca eradication should have jumped at the chance to support local initiatives like this.

How would it benefit the people of Sud Yungas if, instead of coca, they depended on coffee as their main cash crop? Aymara came to Sud Yungas perhaps in the twelfth century, to grow coca, cotton, hot peppers and tobacco, to send up the mountain to the Altiplano (around 4,000m above sea level) where their political capital was and is. In return they received supplies of meat, fish and dried tubers which they could not produce in Yungas. This interchange continues to be the basis of the economy in Sud Yungas. The recent insertion of coca producers in the international economy via clandestine trade has introduced merely superficial changes in the region. The same traders who buy coca for the traditional market also buy it for base makers. Many intermediaries compose the chain between peasant producer and the barons who ship coke to Miami, and this insulates growers to some degree. After the inflated prices of the boom collapsed in 1986 (in response to the arrival of US troops in the lowlands and the simultaneous departure of the major drug traffickers) the market returned to the annual cycle determined by regional supply and demand. This market is static, but reliable, and allows some of the surplus value generated to be retained within the region. Not so with coffee.

The three export houses which sell Bolivian coffee abroad have depots in Sud Yungas, which buy coffee direct from producers or from local intermediaries. The 1987 price offered to producers was a quarter to a third of the price which had been paid two years before. This was due to the breakup of the world coffee cartel which had maintained prices. Coffee prices are subject to speculation and depend on the state of negotiations between the major consumer, the USA, and the major producers, Brazil and Colombia. The Brazilian harvest is a major determinant of price in the South American region. If the peasants were to depend on coffee for their cash income, they would be tied directly to these unpredictable fluctuations in the world coffee market, which have no relation to the state of their own harvests or anything else in their regional or national economy. The religious and ritual uses of coca are attacked in the Bolivian press with claims that *aculli* (traditional coca chewing) is "drug addiction," "one of the most basic signs of the backwardness of our peasant population" and a cause of "introversion, submission, cowardice, lesser mental and physical development."[9] This barely veiled racism typifies the attitude of the upper classes in Bolivia towards the rural Andean masses. These upper classes are already dependent on US aid handouts and the fluctuations of world commodity markets; perhaps this is why they see the destruction of the still resilient peasant economy through "development" as a form of progress.[10]

POSTSCRIPT

The current escalation of violence in the Colombian "drug wars" and the concomitant announcement of "further increases in US spending on drug-control programmes in the Andean countries" (Guardian, 6.9.89) has brought particular salience to the subject of this article. It is depressing to see that much of this spending will be in the form of "military aid" and the provision of aircraft and vehicles to assist the armed repression of the cocaine trade, when it is well known that repression only weeds out the small and unprotected traders while encouraging the large "cartels" to purchase more arms and militarize their operations. Commentators admit that "there has been less violence in Bolivia, where . . . governments have resisted US pressure to begin forcible eradication of coca fields" (Guardian, 5.9.89) while in Peru the government's heavy-handed tactics in the coca region of the Huallaga valley have led to coca growers accepting the presence of Sendero Luminoso guerillas, who regulate the trade, levying a "revolutionary tax" and obliging buyers to pay a fair price to local producers of coca and base.

The Bolivian government has not so much resisted US pressure as been too weak to do anything to prevent coca growing, but even there the militarized narcotics force known as the "Leopardos" has been extending its operations throughout 1988 and 1989. The only way to reduce the amount of coca grown in the Andes—given that the demand for cocaine in the West does not seem to be decreasing—is to fund a programme of genuine capital investment in the local economy.

In Sud Yungas, one possibility would be the construction of large-scale irrigation systems allowing people to cultivate crops requiring quantities of water: coca does not need irrigation. In other regions, the building of roads would allow people to produce crops which need motor transport to be brought to the cities: coca has a high value per unit weight and is not very perishable, so it is one of the few cash crops that can be grown in places with poor communications. It is to be hoped that the publicity being given to coca will provide an opportunity to consider the many alternatives to armed repression.

NOTES

1. An account of the many uses of coca is given in Carter, William and Mauricio Mamani, *Coca en Bolivia*, La Paz, 1986. As well as being "chewed," coca is burnt or buried in ritual offerings, applied as a plaster or an infusion in medicine, and used for divination, where the leaves are scattered and the patterns they fall into observed. Apart from the medical use as tea, all these uses of coca are strongly associated with Indian ethnicity and serve as one of the diagnostic markers of ethnic affiliation.

2. Nash, June. 1979. *We eat the mines and the mines eat us: dependency and exploitation in Bolivian tin mines.* New York.

3. Ruggiero, Romano and Genevieve Tranchard, 1983. Una encomienda coquera en los yungas de La Paz (1560-6) HISLA 1.

4. Matienzo, Juan de. 1967. *Gobierno del Peru.* [1567]. Paris.

5. Albo, Xavier. 1978. El mundo de la coca en Coripata, Bolivia. *America Indigena* 38.4.

6. Flores, G. and Blanes, F. 1084. ¿Donde va el Chapare? La Paz.

7. *The Independent*, 4 July 1989.

8. McInerney, J. 1985. *Bright lights, big city.* New York.

9. Quotes from *Documento Responsibilidad*, a sensational magazine devoted to cocaine scandals: issue 2, La Paz, May 1987.

10. Galeano, Eduardo. 1973. *Open veins of Latin America. Five centuries of the pillage of a continent.* New York and London, 1973.

REFERENCES

Albo, Xavier. 1978. El mundo de la coca en Coripata, Bolivia. *America Indigena*.

Carter, William and Mauricio Mamani. 1986. *Coca en Bolivia*. La Paz.

Flores, G. and F. Blanes, 1984. ¿Donde va el Chapare? La Paz.

Galeano, Eduardo. 1973. *Open veins of Latin America. Five centuries of the pillage of a continent*. New York and London.

Matienzo, Juan de. 1967. *Gobierno del Peru*. [1567]. Paris.

McInerney, J. 1985. *Bright lights, big city*. New York.

Nash, June. 1979. *We eat the mines and the mines eat us: dependency and exploitation in Bolivian tin mines*. New York.

Quotes from *Documento Responsibilidad*, a sensational magazine devoted to cocaine scandals: issue 2, La Paz, May 1987.

Ruggiero, Romano and Genevieve Tranchard. 1983. Una encomienda conquera en los yungas de La Paz (1560) HISLA 1.

The Independent, 4 July 1989.

The Ugly American Revisited

James L. Brain

James Brain first experienced Africa, where he has done fieldwork, as a welfare officer for the British Colonial Service. He went on to study anthropology at Syracuse University, which granted him a Ph.D. in 1968. He is now emeritus professor of anthropology at the State University of New York College at New Paltz, and his research specialties include social organization, social change, sex roles, and Swahili.

In 1958 the publication of the novel *The Ugly American* by William J. Lederer and Eugene Burdick caused a great furor. In that year alone there were twenty printings. Its emotional and political impact were instrumental in the founding of the Peace Corps and perhaps the establishment of the National Defense Education Act. A sense of shame and dismay was aroused among most liberal-minded educated Americans by the idea that our State Department representatives abroad could be so naive and gullible, so isolated in a cocoon of air-conditioned American technological culture, so lacking in any knowledge of alien cultures and languages, that they would do more harm than good to American real interests. Many of us felt guilty and even outraged that the ignorance and ethnocentrism of our aid administrators were getting us hated in the world.

Many people never read the novel and assumed from its title that it was about the ugliness of the American image abroad; indeed, it became common to say "He's a real ugly American." In one sense this idea correctly identified the message of the book; in another, it is ironic that one of the book's few heroes was the person referred to: a small ugly modest man who understood the real needs of the people and wanted to initiate schemes such as the construction of simple water pumps using a bicycle as the power unit. The snag that the little man discovered was that such schemes were of no interest whatever to anyone in the State Department. The reasons can be simply stated and they are just as strong today: (1) they are not spectacular even though they might revolutionize people's lives; (2) they would only cost a few thousand dollars; nothing that costs less

"The Ugly American Revisited" by J. L. Brain. Reprinted by permission of the author.

than several millions is even considered; (3) no American institution—companies, contractors, universities—would make a big profit.

I recently saw the book in a flea market, bought it and re-read it. It was horribly resonant to me as I recently worked for US AID on a two-year contract in Tanzania. I resigned after one year filled with dismay. Nothing has changed: we are still making the very same mistakes, spending huge sums of our tax money, and getting ourselves cordially hated for it.

Tanzania has been the recipient of perhaps more non-military aid than any other country in Africa, taking it from all kinds of sources, both east and west. Like every Third World country, its economy has suffered severely from the massive rise in oil prices and from the low prices for the kind of crops on which it depended in the past for its foreign exchange—coffee, cotton, sisal, tobacco. At the same time it is very shocking for someone like myself who went there first some 32 years ago to see the depths of poverty, inefficiency, and squalor to which it has been reduced. The reasons are many and complex. Chief among them are undoubtedly: (1) the nationalization of the wholesale and retail sector of the economy: shops have virtually nothing in them most of the time; bare requirements of sugar, flour, rice, cooking oil, etc. arrive at irregular intervals—sometimes weeks or months apart—and are sold out immediately (the majority of the people live by subsistence agriculture so although they can no longer get any luxury goods (sugar, margarine, luxuries!) they don't starve, otherwise the country would collapse in a month); (2) the nationalization of the highly effective producer cooperative movement started under the British in the nineteen fifties: the government is now the sole buying agent and pays poor prices, pays late, or even in IOUS; (3) the omnipresent party which really runs the country and which together with the huge bureaucracy constitutes an exploitative regime that makes the former colonial period look benign indeed; (4) the policy of compulsory "villagization" carried through in the seventies which has left a legacy of bitterness, cynicism, and passive resistance among the peasants.

Leaving this all aside—hard but just possible if we really want to help the people—what sort of things are being done in the way of international aid? There seems to be a correlation between the size of the country and the effectiveness of its aid program: the smaller the better; the larger, the poorer—with us, of course, the largest. For instance, Norway trains forestry experts—essential for a country with no other fuel resources as yet tapped. Denmark trains veterinarians—crucial for a country that has millions of cattle, sheep and goats, yet where meat and dairy products are almost unobtainable. Even the Republic of Ireland has a useful little scheme running a carpet factory to make carpets from the sisal it is hard to sell (the man running it was a gem: he had started a darts club at the local bar and was totally one of the boys). If you visit the West German aid organization you will find it very modest, yet it is doing an excellent job and is very popular. The Dutch have a good scheme constructing small village wells and pumps. There is no Dutch aid office; it is part of the embassy.

Contrast this with the United States. The AID office occupies two air-conditioned floors of a large office block and is considerably larger than the embassies of most countries. The U.S. Embassy is some three miles away in a mini-fortress (originally made for the Israelis until they had to leave the country) inconveniently located for everyone except perhaps the ambassador. Outside the AID office is a large sign which includes the logo of two clasped hands. It used to have one black hand and one white—the latter representing the United States—until someone finally realized that all Americans are not white and all aid recipients are not black. The hands are now both the same neutral color. (Incidentally, a few blocks away is the USIS office which has everything captioned in English for a population of whom perhaps ten percent know English. Why? "We are only interested in the educated elite," I was told by the officer in charge. As far back as 1965 I was protesting to the ambassador that American projects had notice boards describing them to the public only in English, and even volunteered to translate them into Swahili, which is known to the entire population, unlike most African countries where there is a multiplicity of languages. When the Chinese were giving aid to Tanzania a few years ago all their projects had large signs in Chinese, English and Swahili. In that same year, I now recall, a highly intelligent young woman whom I had trained in Swahili and who came out as an officer in the information service, was hurriedly removed to another country after pressure from the State Department community who were outraged that she should be friendly with one of the most important Tanzanian ministers. She was white.)

Inside the AID office one is met by a massive photograph of the incumbent president, the floors are carpeted, a pretty receptionist and glamorous secretaries all add to the impression of a huge organization. The impression is only too correct. Two busy floors of highly salaried officers are dreaming up six-million-dollar schemes. Nothing less is ever considered—as someone once said: "The paper work alone costs that much."

The process goes something like this. Someone has an idea for a project. Since it is going to be very expensive a lot of work has to go into preparing it. The preparation of a contract can take a long time and the final resultant document has all the size of a family bible. All kinds of congressional conditions have to be met—many of them concerned with certifying that the country to whom the aid will be given is not hostile to the U.S. It is very easy to evade these conditions, but the amount of paper required is almost incredible. Doubtless some of the schemes proposed and which have been carried out in the past have been of value to Tanzania; many have not. Why, one might ask, does a country like Tanzania accept such schemes? The answer, as one might expect, is that there is something in them for a lot of people. Usually every scheme will mean some free vehicles, some new buildings, salaries for some staff positions, and perhaps most importantly, some scholarships for Africans to go to the U.S. for advanced degrees. Why do we get involved? The answer is much the same: there is something in it for a lot of people.

When a scheme has been processed through Washington and agreed to by the country concerned, it is put out for tender—perhaps the most bizarre system of any aid system. The bidders are usually land-grant universities. They claim to make no profit out of such a deal; on the other hand, many of their faculty members get free trips out as consultants, salaries for faculty and staff members at the home university are met, other faculty members can be shipped off for a few years at the government's expense (who will then become "experts"), and the university will get the students who have been awarded scholarships. One might question the value of involving agricultural institutions in this country committed to an "agribusiness" approach in the agriculture of countries at a largely subsistence level; or the sense of sending students to such institutions where they will learn almost nothing of any practical value to them at home. Moreover, one often wonders what on earth anyone from, say, Colorado or Utah has to contribute as a consultant on a three-week visit.

The persons recruited to go out for two or three years (like myself) are called "contract staff." They are the second-class citizens of the AID hierarchy. The real mandarins are the career officers of the State

Department—and I hasten to add that many of them are decent, hardworking people, but caught in a system that is absurd. As I said, their job is to dream up new schemes—never less than six million dollars, remember—and, of course, to be "project officers" to keep a vague eye on the hatched chicks that actually make it through the astounding jungle of regulations in Washington. To do this they received—in 1981—a minimum salary of $50,000 plus a substantial post allowance, commissary privileges (including duty-free liquor), travel allowances for home leave annually for themselves and their families, a large house surrounded by a chain-link fence and guards. In effect they live at a level far above what most would expect in jobs in this country, far, far above the level of any of the previous colonial service officers. They are totally out of contact with the ordinary people. None that I met spoke more than a few words of any local language. Their social contacts are confined to the upper elite of the government and the diplomatic corps. Many of them are able to retire in their forties on a pension. As I said before, many of them are good, kind people, but they are trapped into a crazy, expensive, wasteful and largely useless system that gets us no credit and a lot of hatred.

Not only are most of the career officers totally out of contact with the people of the countries in which they are working; they are also astonishingly ignorant of the cultures of those countries. Peace Corps Volunteers usually get a good training in the language, history, political development and culture of the country. They are only there for two years. Career officers of the State Department are often in a country for many years but know nothing of it beyond the capital and the game parks.

To someone like myself who was involved in the Peace Corps from its first inception, the ironies of contrast are constant. Whereas Peace Corps Volunteers really know a lot about the country where they are going and have to have some proficiency in the language, AID personnel have no preparation other than a pamphlet about the cost of living and what to take. There is no language requirement on them even though they may stay in a country for several years. Peace Corps Volunteers live not too differently from the local people, travel by local transportation, have to speak the language. They have done a great deal to change the image of rich Americans. Even contract AID officers (and this included me) are supplied with a large house, a refrigerator and large freezer, have to purchase a car, and have salaries considerably larger than they would get in the U.S.—enormous by local standards. Perhaps it is necessary to get qualified people; volunteers are just starting their careers; most AID contract officers are taking an unpaid leave of absence. There is usually some antagonism between the Peace Corps and the AID organiza-

tion—the former feeling sometimes a little holier than thou and the latter feeling guilty about the stark contrast between themselves and the local people.

What kind of schemes am I talking about? Let us take a couple: first, the one with which I was connected. I have to backtrack a little to explain my connection. I worked in extension work in Tanzania and Uganda from 1951–63. In 1971, as an anthropologist, I returned for the summer to do research on belief systems. The dean of the agricultural college, who had known me for many years, instantly coopted me to give a series of lectures to the students on extension work because nowhere in their technically-oriented syllabus did they learn how to put over what they had learnt. It seemed to me to be a very useful idea and so in 1980 I applied for and was to be given a Fullbright fellowship to do this for a whole year. At this juncture I was approached by AID and asked wouldn't I like to do the same thing for two years at a high salary ($36,000 as compared to the $16,000 of the Fullbright)? Greed won out and I turned down the Fullbright: a decision I deeply regret. To my astonishment I found that the college had gone from the sublime to the ridiculous, with the establishment of an entire academic department devoted to agricultural education and extension. My idea is that students need perhaps two courses: an introduction to cultural anthropology to help them to understand how communities function, and a course on how to teach a practical subject. They certainly do not need courses on the philosophical and psychological foundations of education. Part of the scheme was to supply three faculty members, part to send Tanzanians to the States to do doctorates, part to build a large training center for courses, workshops, conferences and the like. Admirable, one might think, but there are dozens of idle buildings around where one could do any of these things without spending a large sum of money.

As I was about to leave, a new project was shaping up in which a big western state university would send out about twenty researchers with Ph.D.s to carry out research on the latest buzz-word—farming systems. Obviously, such a scheme will be very costly—each officer in the field costs $100,000 a year for a start—and I constantly voiced two major criticisms. First, most of the information required is already well known if someone were to do a little reading of the archives. Second, it would be quite possible for a trained anthropologist with a good knowledge of Swahili to obtain all that is needed in a few weeks at most; in many cases a few days would be enough. To bring in American farming experts with no background in East Africa, with no knowledge of the language or culture, unfamiliar with the history, is like throwing American taxpayers' money down the drain. But, of course, the university concerned will make a lot of money, all kinds of lucrative contracts will result, instant experts will be created—and then they will be able to be called in to advise on similar problems elsewhere.

In Africa in general and Tanzania in particular one major cultural matter of supreme importance has so far escaped the experts' notice, just as it escaped the notice of the colonial regimes of the past: that the farmers of Africa are usually the women. At the very least the women work on the farms as much as the men—they also fetch the water, cut and fetch the firewood, pound corn in a mortar, do the cooking, take care of the children. The only politician in all Africa to realize this fact is the often maligned Hastings Banda of Malawi, one of the only countries in Africa to be self-supporting in food. How? Dr. Banda invites the women from a particular area to the capital, gives them a big dance with lots of beer and food and a present, and then exhorts them to go back home and do everything the extension officers tell them.

The impression that I constantly got was that most AID people mentally perceived a "farmer" to be a tall white man, wearing blue jeans, boots and a Stetson staring out over his wide acres. Ronald Reagan receiving the Queen of England at his ranch would be a good model. The idea that a farmer might be a woman was not something that had really sunk in. Given the sharply divided sex roles of African society, a man cannot deal with women; on the other hand, a well-educated woman—African or American—can be accepted by both men and women. Plainly, we should send women experts and train more African women.

What should we do then? We might take a lesson from the smaller countries and think small. Abolish the wasteful AID offices and their career persons whose task it is to produce these expensive and largely useless schemes. One or two officers attached to the embassy should be entirely sufficient to act as liaison with the government and the contract workers. Get involved in small-scale schemes which don't need large buildings and vehicles. The kind of training that extension workers might get in India, Egypt, Israel, or even China

would be of far more use than anything they could get in this country. Must we always make a profit? Would it be too much to pay for people to go elsewhere, to admit that we don't have all the agricultural answers, especially for small-scale peasant agriculture that is likely to remain the mode for the foreseeable future? If the millions poured into the present schemes were channelled into research in intermediate technology it would be much more useful. Simple hand grinding machines and small-scale wells and pumps could make life less burdensome for the real producers of food— the women.

An even more radical idea was propounded in 1966 by Charles Hynam when he wrote an article with the intimidating title of "The Disfunctionality of Unrequited Giving." He pointed out that long ago in anthropology it was noticed that the principle of reciprocity is one of the most basic in human social organization. If you continually give things to someone which he cannot return he will feel a sense of obligation to you which in time will inevitably turn to dislike, hatred even. The application of this to the international aid scene is obvious. The more aid we give the more we shall be hated. His solution is one of supreme simplicity. Instead of all the bilateral aid agreements, everyone should channel funds to the World Bank which would then set up local branches all over the Third World like savings and loan associations. One of the major hindrances to development is often lack of initial capital on a small scale. By having a local bank it would be possible for individuals, or even cooperatives or whole villages, to obtain loans to finance projects which would be repaid with reasonable rates of interest. No one would be obligated to anyone and a lot of development would result. The beauty of the idea is that it does not prescribe a capitalist mode of development or a socialist one but could assist both individuals or groups.

It is sad enough that we should be wasting such astronomical sums on crazy weapons. Should we not make sure that the money we do spend to help Third World countries does in fact help them?

The New Zion

James Kiernan

James Kiernan, an ex-patriate Irishman, teaches at the University of Natal, Durban. As an ex-priest, he has a long-term interest in different forms of expression of spirituality.

God help the poor who live in depressed and depressing cities like Soweto and KwaMashu without the benefits of a welfare state. It would appear, however, that He does help them. This is what Zulu Zionists, among others, preach and they themselves are the living proof of such divine intervention.

Certainly it is this belief that motivates their ministry to the African poor. Their activities enliven and give fresh meaning to the tired old cliché that God helps those who help themselves. Of course, there is always the possibility that some are in a better position to help themselves and that they use such advantage to better themselves at the expense of others. This allegation is often levelled at the leaders of such African independent churches.

Readers may be forgiven for thinking that this is the norm rather than the exception, bearing in mind how often our newspapers inform us of glaring and objectionable incidents of this kind.

One recalls in particular the case of an African pastor in Umlazi some years ago who took delivery at Durban Harbour of one of a limited order of foreign luxury cars for which he paid the then princely sum of R16,000. From where did he derive such a large sum of money? From the contributions of his flock, we were assured, some of who were pictured, impoverished and exiguous in appearance, surrounding their happy pastor.

However this may stretch the limits of our credulity, it is a common stereotype of independent African churches and their leadership and evokes the familiar image of religious exploitation: that of venal men playing upon the susceptibilities of simpleminded followers

and extracting from them their very means of survival, instead of being primarily engaged in making a meaningful contribution to their spiritual welfare.

Is this how we view the African churches? In fact it would be false and misleading to represent them in this way. Undoubtedly, every new religion attracts its share of charlatans.

There are a number of genuine religious leaders who have done well for themselves, notably Lekhanyane (near Pietersburg), Shembe (near Durban) and Nzuzu (Hammersdale), who once owned a fleet of busses. Yet the vast majority of these churches, and there are several thousand of them, belong in a much lower league, have a smaller membership, and most cannot be regarded as a business.

Few church leaders can hope to garner an annual income approaching R1,000 from subordinate congregations for the support of headquarters, so the possibility of building up capital reserves is out of the question; constituent congregations are small and do not command remotely the means of erecting permanent church buildings even on a modest scale; ministers must contribute more to congregational undertakings than they receive by way of financial rewards and are more likely to be out of pocket than to realise even the most marginal profits; consequently they must rely on full-time employment for their own support. Clearly, then, it is not a general characteristic of these African churches that leaders live off their followers, much less exploit them financially.

Yet there is something to be learned from the stereotype. If it is false, it is because it grossly exaggerates a fundamental feature of these African religious groups. This is a religion which sets its sights on this world, the here and now.

Ultimately, one may look beyond the grave for final justification but, more realistically, religious probity should bring more tangible benefits in one's lifetime. It

"The New Zion" by James Kiernan, from *Leadership*, Vol. 4, No. 3, 1985. Reprinted with permission.

is these "short-term" secular rewards delivered in this world, rather than those deferred to the next, which become the major focus of religious striving.

If these tangible blessings are the immediate objective of religious activity, it follows that they are an external index of inner spiritual power. Hence the religious status of groups and their leaders depends to a large extent on the display of visible signs of success in achieving these rewards. More than purely economic rewards are involved here; health and harmony feature prominently. Nevertheless, economic success is an important ingredient so that the more prosperous a church is, the more attractive it becomes spiritually.

For most struggling churches this is only an ideal, but it can give rise to certain anomalies. If "we" can provide a large car for our pastor to drive around in, even if we deprive ourselves in doing so, it speaks eloquently of our spiritual prowess.

Such anomalies aside, the perceived like between spiritual and material well-being is by no means an idiosyncracy symptomatic of a modern materialistic society. It is continuous with a long tradition in the indigenous religion of Africa, in terms of which the maintenance of a good relationship with deceased ancestors is a guarantee of protection, stability, good health, fecundity and prosperity.

The more a church exhibits signs of material success or the better its members are convinced that their adherence to it will eventually give them secular rewards, the more it attracts new members.

While the myriad small churches battle to maintain and expand their membership in a highly competitive situation, others build on modest gains and steadily become bigger. Yet the growth process has inbuilt limitations and very few churches make it into the big league without being arrested, even several times, by internal schism.

HISTORY OF SECESSIONS

This happens so frequently that it is almost a general rule. At a certain stage of its growth a church becomes ripe for fragmentation. It has outgrown its own simple organisation and is becoming unmanageable; its leader at his central headquarters can no longer maintain regular contact with his outlying congregation, particularly those at some distance away, let alone discipline and control them, and because the church is not recognised by the state and its leaders do not qualify for railway travel concessions, touring the outposts is prohibitively expensive.

The inevitable breakdown in management becomes difficult to deal with if growth is concentrated in a region or area at some remove from the centre. The drift away from the centre can be arrested by elevating a prominent minister from the area at risk to the position of deputy leader or vice-president. At best, this can be only a temporary measure. After a time, ambition usually gets the better of allegiance, the deputy cuts the knot and establishes himself as an independent leader.

If the manner in which these churches has developed is to some extent due to the opportunism of rising leaders, in a more general sense, their very existence can be partly accounted for by the corresponding dearth of leadership opportunities for Africans in society at large. Things may have improved somewhat recently, but for a long time Africans with innate leadership ability were blocked from exercising responsible leadership in almost all spheres of life: industrial, commercial, political and administrative.

STEADY SUBDIVISION

This was also true of religious organisations until very recently. While the mission churches employed an educated African ministry, white control was not threatened by even a token black presence in the higher echelons of leadership. Over the years, the African clergy in these white-dominated churches took this exclusion to be based on discrimination and reacted against it by setting up churches of their own.

The first of these, the "Ethiopian" Church, was formed in Johannesburg in 1892. Most subsequent collective defections of this kind adopted the Ethiopian reference as part of the title of the resultant new separatist bodies, so that it became convenient to give the label "Ethiopian" to this movement as a whole.

In the same way, the term "Zionist" is used to cover a similar range of variations but on a different motif. Most churches of the Zionist variety were not offshoots of mission churches, but initially sprang spontaneously from the inspiration of an African visionary or charismatic person.

The earliest of these Zionist manifestations were partly the outcome of Pentecostal influences imported from America at the turn of the century. The first "Zion church" was established by Büchler in Johannesburg in 1895; Mahon in the Free State followed in 1902. In 1904 at remote Wakkerstroom, Le Roux, a Dutch Reformed minister who was frustrated by white rejection of his Pentecostal leanings, resigned his ministry to set up the Christian Catholic Church in Zion among the Zulu.

These three South African whites, under the supervision of an American missionary, Daniel Bryant, were instrumental in conveying to blacks a belief in Christian healing and the practice of adult baptism by full immersion. Of these three departures, it was Le Roux's impetus which was the most decisive for the development of black Zionism. His Zulu converts rapidly became independent, establishing their own Zionist churches and communicating the received message in a distinctively African mode.

While both Ethiopians and Zionists have provided opportunities for aspirant African leaders in an apartheid society, only the Ethiopian societies can be called separatist in that each originally hived off as a unit from a Christian denomination. Zionists have independently rallied around certain unorthodox Christian ideas or have responded to the call of an African prophet with his own religious vision. The Ethiopian separatists have retained the doctrine, worship and organisation of their parent bodies, merely swopping white for black management. The Zionists have adapted Christianity to African requirements by intricately blending it with elements selected from indigenous African religion. Whereas, at least until the Fifties, the Ethiopians actively and vocally supported black political aspirations, Zionists have always scrupulously avoided any suggestion of political flirtation.

Both types of independent church have been subjected to the inexorable and steady process of subdivision, but the number of Zionist churches has been further augmented by the continual creation of new self-styled Zionist groups imperfectly aping the standard model. There is no shortage of charismatic individuals willing to adopt the basic Zionist blueprint and re-fashion it to their own design. Approximately since the Fifties, Zionists have increasingly outnumbered Ethiopians, who appear to suffer stagnation, and have continued to expand at a faster rate, their strongest growth points now being in the cities.

Accurate figures are not available to back this claim of Zionist ascendancy, but one indication of it is to be found in observed instances of Ethiopian churches adopting a Zionist style of worship. Certainly, it can be said that it is in the Zionist churches that the full creative force of religious innovation is most vigorously at work among the black population.

The full spectrum of this movement to religious independence now accounts for at least 29 per cent of Africans (39 per cent of church-going Africans), far greater support than any single missionary church can command and (although again enumeration must defy accuracy) it is estimated that there may be as many as 4,000 such independent churches in South Africa alone, without taking into account their plentiful presence in neighbouring African countries.

How can we account for this astounding growth? Where does the appeal lie? Not in the promise of a distant but blissful future, but in the provision of genuine rewards in the present. What are these attractions? They are many, but the most obvious and outstanding drawcard of Zionist churches is their healing activity. Ask any Zionist why he or she joined one of these churches and healing will almost certainly be one of the reasons provided, if not the only one.

A typical meeting consists of a prayer-and-bible service followed by healing. Of the two, the second is easily the more gripping and spectacular—a session in which sound and movement, drumming, singing, clapping and dancing are intensified. A circular space is created by a ring of healers singing loudly and constantly in motion, alternating from clockwise to anti-clockwise. Individuals in need of treatment step into this healing space one by one and submit passively to a controlled and moderate physical assault; healing hands are impressed upon them, they are spun around, their backs and shoulders vigorously pummelled and their bodies caressed and brushed-down by the wooden staves that all Zionists carry.

This is not the sado-masochism that it might seem to be. As one observer recently commented: "If you find yourself at the centre of this, you won't feel forgotten." Those who experience this caring attention exude a serenity and calmness which is palpable yet defies description. Not everybody gets the full treatment; it rather depends on the severity of his condition and many are attended to in a casual and summary fashion.

In fact there is a great deal more to Zionist healing than is immediately apparent. A Zionist prophet is equipped to see beneath the surface of the patient's symptoms by inspiration and vision and, on the common understanding that an illness or misfortune is ultimately caused by some social disturbance, he will interrogate the patient and probe into his or her personal circumstances until he has located the cause in some deficiency or deviance in moral behaviour. Once the diagnosis has been reached, a remedy can be prescribed—the use of specially designated water as a cleanser and expellent, the wearing of a particular item of religious apparel as a protection and, of course, continued attendance for further treatment.

PURITAN ETHIC

These conceptions and procedures are thoroughly African but the power which renders them effective is essentially Christian. It is the power generated by communal prayer and its source is the Holy Spirit.

Anyone, even a non-Zionist, can avail himself of this healing service and it has the great advantage of being virtually free. A small thanksgiving offering is expected if the treatment is considered successful, but there is no fee as such. For this reason it has a special appeal for the poor for whom the alternatives (consulting a medical doctor or a traditional practitioner) are relatively expensive.

Of course, there is a hidden cost: the likelihood of becoming so dependent upon Zionist treatment as to have no recourse but to join their ranks. Although Zionists do not make it a condition of the service they offer, they naturally hope to capture adherents in this way.

The other major incentive for Zionist affiliation is an economic one, although it has its basis in morality. It can be summed up by saying that Zionists conduct their lives according to a puritan ethic. Not given to reflection on the meaning of religion and lacking any pretence of a theological framework, they wholly devote their energies to the practice of religion according to strict but simple moral rules. These rules will be familiar to anyone with a puritan upbringing. They prohibit drinking, smoking, gambling, bad language, gossiping, marital infidelity and sexual promiscuity. Dabbling in sorcery is forbidden and playing football or engaging in any other recreational pursuit is also frowned upon. Not only do all these activities squander time and energy that might be otherwise devoted to religious development, but they entail spending money and are, therefore, economically draining.

Zionist moral rules are therefore rules of not spending but of saving. On the other hand, all the prohibited activities are perfectly "normal" among the population at large, particularly so among men. The fact that Zionists are odd in this respect sets them apart from the others.

PROCESS OF GROWTH

Their colourful uniforms serve the same purpose except in the work situation where they are easily distinguished by their austere behaviour, their seriousness and their refusal to be drawn into the bantering and innuendo of workfellows during breaks. On the job, they tend to be diligent and industrious, not given to wasting time, willing to undertake responsibility and generally displaying the characteristics of boss's men. They are therefore ideally suited for promotion to positions such as supervisors and drivers, in which their singularity and reliability are assets.

It is not to be expected that individuals, immediately on becoming Zionists, conform to type. It is a process of growth, an accumulation of experience, a gradual absorption of Zionist values such as thrift and diligence and an increasing application of these to daily living. It is a fact, however, that those who attain positions of leadership within Zionism, after long service, are also those who have significantly improved their occupational status.

The self-disciplined Zionist, austere, thrifty and industrious, succeeds in bettering his life-style and in improving his occupation and income, on a modest rather than a spectacular scale. The appeal to the poor and struggling urban African is obvious. Acceptance of the Zionist code holds out the prospect of reasonable prosperity, the promise of economic success and of a measure of upward mobility.

Zionism offers other less tangible rewards which derive in part from those described, in particular, fellowship and mutual support. Zionists meet weekly or more frequently in very small groups. The unit of worship rarely exceeds 30 adults with their dependent children and is usually much smaller.

The size of the group is restricted by the favoured meeting-place, a single room in a township house, although groups gather on patches of waste-ground, along rivers, railways, and roadsides. Space is therefore not the only restriction on numbers. The small group has an intimacy not normally felt in larger church gatherings. Each person is known to all the others, his domestic arrangements and general life-style an open book, and interaction can be conducted on a closer and more personal basis. When a genuine problem is experienced, however slight, it can be aired in the certain knowledge that it will receive a sympathetic hearing, that the burden will be shared and that if anything can be done to ease the situation a concerted attempt will be made to help.

In effect, an individual difficulty becomes a collective responsibility. Nobody need feel that he or she struggles alone. Any life-crisis such as the birth of a child, the loss of a job, the incurring of funeral expenses or the imprisonment of a son, is the occasion for a collection to be taken up, in which each gives according to his or her means, knowing that one can count on the same support if in a similar bind.

The fruits of economic success are not hoarded but redistributed to some extent and everybody contributes. This concrete expression of concern gives substance to the sentiments of caring and sharing which are the sinews of the Zionist group. The small group recognises that the welfare of one is the welfare of all and that co-operation and mutual support is a potent instrument in the unceasing battle against grinding poverty.

In dispensing these common benefits, Zionist churches also cater for the sectional interests of men and women and for their sometimes divergent needs. Why women should in general be more attracted to religion than men remains an open question, though much ingenuity and guesswork are needed to answer it.

COMPLEMENTARITY OF THE SEXES

There are about three times as many women as men in these African churches. In itself, this is not remarkable, as most other churches display the same imbalance. But collectively, Zionist women make up a formidable pressure group, not only because they meet together apart from the men but because, in so doing, they join forces with the women of other congregations and Zionist churches. Such regular concentration of women on specifically female interests must mean that Zionism somehow makes provision for their special needs.

Leaving aside the more obvious distinctions, there are two ways in which Zionist men and women differ significantly from each other. Firstly, men virtually monopolise positions of leadership. It is true that there are many groups and churches on the margins of the movement in which women hold high office as ministers and even bishops, but the mainstream of Zionism withholds the exercise of office from women.

A woman may share in her husband's office to some extent but she does not hold it in her own right. The wife of a preacher, for instance, would be ordained with him. She would thereafter be accorded the status of "preacher's wife," she could even preach at a meeting of women but not in the presence of men. While most men occupy some office or other, women act very much in the shadow.

The second difference is that, while Zionist women mix easily with other women, Zionist men keep very much to themselves. Zionist women are well aware of the life-style of neighbours; they know the problems they experience and can identify with them. The problems are all too familiar to women living in the townships: how to keep a home going on inadequate income, how to preserve children from malnutrition and ill-health, how to ensure that they grow up uncontaminated by the corruption of township living.

Zionist women know the solutions to such problems: wean your husband away from the financially draining path of being a man among men and concentrate his resources on his home and family; take advantage of the healing services offered by Zionism and bring its moral influence to bear on the upbringing of children. Zionist women are aware that among women they enjoy certain advantages and, in general, they tend to radiate a sense of security which is the envy of most other women.

The distinct advantage that Zionist males possess is access to positions of leadership and to carving out a career in the Zionist organisation. There is a sense in which this represents a trade-off between men and women, as we shall see.

While the image that Zionists have of themselves is that of coping well with adversity and may involve an element of complacency and self-congratulation, the black population as a whole tends to despise them and this is particularly true of Christians and the educated. The great majority of Zionists are indubitably poor and relatively uneducated, a large proportion being virtually illiterate. The educated look down on them, not simply because they are Zionists, but social inferiors. Besides, their worship is noisy, full of enthusiasm and it displays a measure of what might be taken for wild abandon; not the sort of people a respectable middle-class African would choose as neighbours.

Christians, too, look askance at them because of their healing methods, by which they do battle with sorcery, and in the course of which they draw upon the techniques of the African diviner, sorcery and divina-tion being anathema to Christians. Yet it is not unknown for those who despise them to seek their help in a crisis. Contempt is tempered by need when an illness defies the best efforts of Western medicine and does not respond to the remedies of traditional specialists. Zionists then become the only alternative and rejection, at least for a time, gives way to dependence.

On the other hand, Zionists are generally feared because their claim to overcome and rout evil spirits is taken seriously. When spirits are driven out of the Zionist procreate, they must find a home somewhere and the credulous would argue that if Zionists have the power to send spirits away, they have the ability to direct them to other targets. Consequently, Zionists are accorded a widespread measure of wary and grudging respect and people tend to keep their distance.

This reticence accords with the Zionists' proclivity towards minding their own business and feeds their exclusiveness and social isolation. Yet, if they are cut adrift in this fashion, how can they win converts? How explain their growth? The answer lies in the complementarity of the sexes. Women retain the domestication of their men by according them uncontested roles of leadership. But to climb the leadership ladder, men must attract converts. They are unable to do so because of their extreme social isolation. Consequently, their wives must procure converts for them from the only pool in which they are socially involved, that is, among other women. These female converts must then endeavor to domesticate their own men by drawing them into Zionism and thus the circle is complete. In this manner, Zionism converts Christian and non-Christian.

These gentle, peace-loving people are not engaged in a crusade of social reform. They are not intent on moving the earth by social upheaval. Nor are they in the least interested in bringing about political change. At one time, the Ethiopian churches aligned themselves with the aims of African nationalism, but Zionists have never espoused any political cause. They are unaware of their numerical and organisational strength, which in any case is splintered into small enclaves. It never occurs to them that they have social or political means at their disposal and, for their purposes, politics is like football, chasing a bag of wind, a sheer waste of valuable time.

WELFARE SOCIETY

Zionists specialise in the employment of religious means to alleviate suffering. Religious values are invoked to motivate sentiments of sharing and mutual support and to realise significant gains against poverty. One should not underestimate the power of this complex arrangement. Zionism does not destroy the status quo, but quietly shapes society by transforming the individual and by offering him an alternative social mould.

The intense social life of the small group is the key to this transformation; the small group offers both internal intimacy and outward anonymity. What emerges is a religiously imbued welfare society which uncompromisingly tackles the existential problems of poor urban blacks by the ingenious management of available human resources. In order to work efficiently, the Zionist group demands the total allegiance of its members; it leaves no aspect of their lives unscrutinised or unregulated and it usually succeeds in captivating their hearts and minds.

In the end, what is really significant is that so many are ready to pay that price—40 per cent of church-going Africans and 30 per cent of the total African population is a difficult argument to refute. And Zionism is still growing.

The Dal Lake

Reflections on an Anthropological Consultancy in Kashmir

Alexander F. Robertson

Alexander Robertson studied at Edinburgh University in Scotland, where he was granted the Ph.D. in 1967. Now a professor at the University of California in Santa Barbara, he was formerly director of the Centre for African Studies and assistant director of development studies at Cambridge in England. He has a number of books to his credit based on research in Africa and Asia.

In 1985 I found myself between academic jobs for several months, and when the opportunity of an anthropological consultancy arose I took it with alacrity. In such tasks one does not expect great amenity, and it is not often that one is invited to ply one's anthropological craft in such a spectacularly beautiful place as Kashmir. Moghul Emperors and modern tourists alike have regarded the Dal Lake as the closest earthly approximation to paradise.

Nevertheless, having recently pontificated on the Anthropology of Planned Development in my *People and the State* (CUP, 1984), the prospect of a return to practical tasks was sobering. In the book I expressed anxieties about the role of the anthropologist as *vox populi*: how can we properly adduce the "interests of the people" to the essentially technical processes of contemporary development planning? How can we deal with the moral dilemmas of acting as a cheap substitute for democracy, of trying to discover and translate the motley perceptions and desires of the victims of planning into terms which render them more readily manipulable by those in positions of power?

It is probably easier for an academic moonlighter than the professional consultant to reflect critically on these matters. Before the memories fade I would like to record my participation in the Dal project team, especially how, in the eight fleeting weeks at my disposal, I set about discovering the "interests of the residents,"

conveying these authoritatively to my nine technical colleagues, and ensuring that they were adequately expressed in our final report.

Preliminary inspection of the terms of reference for the job indicated that in such matters my conscience would be exercised very thoroughly at the Dal Lake. A northern suburb of the city of Srinagar, the Lake was subject to mounting population pressure. Not only were its waters becoming polluted, they were shrinking. The project involved mainly technical advice on "conservation and development" (in itself a somewhat contrary notion): the improvement and monitoring of water quality, the evaluation and modification of current land use plans; the prospects and policies for tourism; and how the bureaucracies responsible for the Lake should be reorganized. My own commission was to "examine the social implications of development options," which would enable the team to "suggest development policies which take account of the interests of the residents." The rhetoric was familiar, and I felt I could resist the temptation to over-rate either my influence or the humanitarian virtues of my role. If there was a genuine wish to incorporate the diverse and competing views of the local people in the design of development, a foreign anthropologist could be no substitute for direct consultation with the Lake dwellers. It seemed more realistic to assume that my commission reflected official anxiety that the people who lived and worked on the Lake might thwart plans which were already in hand for its development as the region's principal tourist resort. But the inescapably political aspects of my role would surely bring me into conflict with those who were pursuing essentially technical solutions to the problems of the Lake.

THE TEAM AND THE TASK

The Dal Lake, about eight square miles of open water, lotus gardens, willow-shaded channels and islets, set against the spectacular Himalayan foothills, beggars the description of tourist brochures. The Moghul Emperors ornamented this natural beauty with their famous formal gardens at Shalimar, Nishat and Chashmashahi. The British rulers of India were likewise entranced by the Lake, but were debarred by Kashmiri law from acquiring land and building houses. Instead they bought or rented houseboats, which soon became little floating palaces, combining Edwardian English amenity with evocations of Moghul grandeur. Today most of the 10–15% of foreigners among the quarter million annual visitors to Kashmir spend a few nights on the thousand or so houseboats. The preference of Indian tourists for terra firma has encouraged the proliferation of hotels around the south of the Lake. However, the tourist trade has suffered serious reversals in recent years, partly because of protracted hostilities with India's neighbours in the north-west, and more immediately because of internal tensions in Kashmir and Punjab. . . .

A special High Power Board had been created in 1981 to oversee development of the Dal, but it was seldom convened, depending instead on its overworked executive body, the Srinagar Urban Environmental and Engineering Department (UEED). These lively and conscientious engineers had assumed a wide range of functions, from digging ditches to prosecuting encroachers. Inevitably they became our most immediate collaborators on the consultancy.

Against this formidable bureaucratic array, the interests of the people of the Dal Lake itself seemed all the more remote. A somewhat candid account of the superordinate concerns of the project might go like this: in a sluggish domestic economy, the British consulting firms were anxious to take a firm grip on overseas aid projects, which implied building up an efficient and complaisant reputation with the ODA and the Indian authorities. The possibility of involvement in a subsequent phase of the Dal project emphasized this interest. For my part, as a freelance anthropologist I had no wish to alienate these, or any other potential employers, by pressing some uncongenial vision of the Lake's future. The Indian Ministry of Works and Housing could doubtless have suggested a dozen alternative uses for the price of our project. In accepting the offer of British aid for a sensitive border area, they would have nothing to gain from alienating a Kashmiri government which is, currently, sympathetic towards Delhi. A beleaguered Kashmiri government would wish devoutly to revive its flagging tourist trade, but not at the expense of stirring up controversy in its own capital city. For their part, the engineers and administrators of Srinagar would be very reluctant to cede control of their Lake to outsiders: apart from being a source of tourist revenue, it is a communications system and a vital component of the city's water and food supply.

I asked for at least a week prior to departure to read about Kashmir. Although I was not challenged, I think my colleagues regarded this as a luxury: it seems that history has little relevance in development consultancy, empirical observation being the order of the day. In my brief survey of the literature I was struck by how often Kashmir had been subjected by outsiders, and by their repeated descriptions of the physical squalor and moral turpitude of Kashmiri people. This shed an interesting light on our own commission to investigate pollution. Wondering how I might be received by the Lake dwellers, I took heart from the grudging admission of earlier travellers that the people were cheerful, garrulous and unbowed, and ingenious in extracting material benefits from outsiders. . . .

DISCOVERING THE LAKE

Our first important discovery was that the Lake was not nearly so dirty as we had been led to believe. In the constricted channels on the city side, pollution was gross, but the rest of the water body was mostly clean and well-oxygenated. Neither the farmers, who valued night soil, nor even the houseboat operators with their suspected flush toilets, were responsible for measurable fecal or other contamination. Evicting farmers and fishermen would plainly have little effect on the real problem, which was how to control the huge volume of untreated sewage emanating from the hotels and city houses, some of which washed back into the Lake. Our sanitary engineers were much exercised suggesting improvements, while the limnologist proposed monitoring systems which would provide accurate evidence of changes in the water quality.

The issue of encroachment was more complicated. The Lake was very evidently shrinking, and the resident population was obviously culpable. The water level was in fact controlled very precisely at one major sluice, but the flow and displacement within the Lake were affected by innumerable factors, ranging from silting to the very visible construction of solid building land. The UEED was making a determined attack on both these processes, but while the Lake dwellers were being rigorously prevented from adding to, or even repairing their houses, more influential people were encroaching and building very blatantly, trucking in huge quantities of soil and rocks to create new land. Legislation against such abuses had to be tightened up and policed with greater rigour and impartiality. Some of the engineers' approaches to these problems seemed misguided, notably their efforts to use new roads as barriers against encroachment: to us it seemed clear that new lines of communication would only encourage the sprawl of peri-urban settlement. Since these "dykes" were also interfering with the flow of fresh water through the Lake, we recommended the removal or drastic realignment of the newest of them.

More fundamental was the centuries-old process of horticultural encroachment which was simultaneously destroying the Lake and creating its unique character. We were surprised first by official ignorance of how this process worked, and then by our own difficulties in trying to understand it. Very largely through my conversations we arrived at the following synoptic view of the dynamism of the Lake's topography.

In anticipation of its physical and economic transformation, open water (now about half the total area of the Lake) is owned, bought and sold, the most valuable stretches being the houseboat moorings. Fishing rights remain in the public domain. With minimal cultivation, beds of reed can be established, and are used extensively in building, thatching, mat-making and other crafts. Water lily too needs little encouragement, and is harvested for mulch or sold in the city as fodder. Lotus needs more care; its seeds and rhizomes are great delicacies, and its flowers and leaves are collected in the late summer for decorative and ceremonial uses. The lotus gardens which so entrance the visitors are not, as many suppose, "just natural"; they are owned, highly valued, and—a symptom of the encroachment process—they are cultivated.

A more remarkable but less obvious feature of the Lake is the floating gardens. These are dense mats made of reed clumps, about two metres wide and up to eighty metres long. They are treated with weed and silt from the Lake bed, and used for growing mainly tomatoes and cucurbits. They can be poled from place to place and, by providing shade and a downwash of mulch, help to prepare lotus beds. Over time—as much as forty years—the floating garden becomes very ponderous, perhaps a metre thick, at which stage it is poled to a suitable place, loaded with weed and silt, and sunk as the basis of solid land.

These strips of new land (called dembs) set among the hamlets, lotus gardens and reed beds, give the western side of the Lake its special character. They are also constructed by in-fill, without recourse to floating gardens, and they create a maze of channels, shaded by the willows which are used to secure their foundations. They are regularly watered, mulched and treated with fertilizers, and bear up to four crops a year—much more productive than the floating gardens. Dal is the main source of vegetables for Srinagar and also for the Indian frontier forces, a major consideration in planning alternative uses for the Lake.

The most consolidated land is indicated by mature trees and substantial brick-built houses clustered tightly on islets strung out across the Lake. Lake farmers like to have a portfolio of land and water holdings—lotus gardens interspersed with dembs, floating gardens and stretches of open water close to their established village land. The image of encroachment advancing as a solid, perceptible frontier across the surface of the Lake is thus a false one. Because the process is gradual, emanating from numerous growth nodes, it is very difficult for the outsider to discern. The official legal understanding of the Lake is still a cadastre (register for taxation) compiled by a British official more than seventy years ago. Farmers are well aware of the outsiders' ignorance of the technicalities of their way of life; for example, they deride the city-dweller's notion that "we throw mats onto the water and tomorrow they have become solid land." This process which creates such an attractive land- and water-scape is gradually eliminating the Lake. We found it necessary to argue forcefully that there is nothing passive about the beauty of Lake Dal: it is sustained by the economic activities of the people who live and work there, cultivating lotus, maintaining the channels, clearing the water lily, dredging for silt. The remedy which is now in hand, the eviction of the people and re-landscaping of the Lake precincts, will produce broad stretches of shallow open water, indistinguishable from recreational lakes all over the world. Even if it were practicable to arrest the process of encroachment, the inevitable consolidation of undifferentiated vegetable plots would have much less tourist appeal. It seemed that the best we could recommend was some moderation of the pressures to encroach, which might prolong the present characteristics of the Lake.

It was here that enquiry into the lives and interests of the Lake dwellers became crucial. In objective designation, they are all "Hanjis," water people. This has residual caste connotations and is considered pejorative by the people themselves, especially upwardly mobile landholders and houseboat proprietors. Moreover, there are marked distinctions in occupation, habitation, custom and even language among the "Hanjis," differences which are sustained by endogamy, religious affiliation and other kinds of group solidarity. An undiscriminating official view of the Lake dwellers has led to the assumption that their interests are uniform, and that plans for their future need not be distinguished. A few hours in the very different worlds of the farmers, the fishermen or the houseboat owners made it plain to me that such reckoning could be disastrous. A sanguine recommendation of the team was that avenues of communication should be opened up with each of these groups, not simply the most vocal or influential.

Over two or three centuries a division of labour has been established in which the limited resources of the Lake are shared with remarkable mutual forbearance. Although aware of the attrition of the water surface, the fishermen had no serious quarrel with the horticulturalists, whose gardens provided sheltered areas for fish. They were not perturbed by pollution, claiming that they fished even in the dirtiest areas. More troublesome was the fisheries department, with its relentless policing of licences, net gauges and closed waters. The fishermen were evidently poor, living (in huts and boats) very much on the Lake margins, and with little to gain from the tourist trade—thus a minority plainly threatened by plans for the Dal. The bargees, shifting timber and other commodities between the Lake and the river Jhelum, were likewise at risk.

The farmers and others supplemented their incomes with craft work: the Lake hamlets are hives of artisanal activity, with even the tiny children at work making carpets, shawls, papier maché boxes or woodcarvings. Although they are at the end of a drastic chain of exploitation they have at least a foothold in the tourist economy. It is tourism which has established a new and potent category on the Lake, a rising class of affluent "Hanjis." The most obvious beneficiaries, and the most criticized, are the hoteliers and houseboat owners, people of very considerable wealth and political influence. The notion of pollution attaches itself very readily to such class antagonism, the rich decrying the squalor of the fishing communities and the dirty habits of villager or bargee; and these in turn criticizing the garbage and raw sewage disgorged every day from hotels and houseboats.

Surprisingly, no-one I spoke to challenged the need for plans to conserve and develop the Lake, or even the desirability of tourism; having lived for so long under threat of eviction it was the delay in the making and implementing of clear decisions which people found most irksome. Perhaps because of their aquatic heritage and the fluidity of the landscape, they were less insistent about their local roots than the peasants I have encountered elsewhere. They were ready to move, so long as they could be relocated in the vicinity of the Lake ("we are like ducks") and be guaranteed a livelihood. They were not perturbed by the need to change occupations, so long as they suffered no hardship.

They were, however, acutely concerned about adequate compensation. UEED officials complained that local estimates of property values were soaring outrageously. More pointedly, the evacuees proposed that they be settled on the east of the Lake—in prime locations which are rapidly being acquired and built on by the Kashmiri bourgeoisie. Meanwhile the UEED is constructing three resettlement colonies to the west, at some distance from the Lake shore, and has already placed fifteen evicted families in one of them. These pioneers have as yet few amenities and have been obliged to build their own houses to rigid specifications on very cramped lots, with little material assistance. Their hardships have made the resettlement colonies notorious and evacuees who can get enough compensation have preferred to settle independently in the city.

My visit to the resettlement colony, and my candid disappointment with what I had seen, occasioned a lively debate with the UEED staff, who concluded that as a social work person, I was too susceptible to exaggerated tales or woe. The Dal people, I was warned, were ruthless and calculating, only too quick to cash in on the humanitarian instincts of the planners. In trying to moderate the utilitarian argument that the interests of a handful of Lake dwellers should not override the welfare of Kashmir as a whole, I suggested that the very sizable social benefits of the Lake realized by tourism should be matched by generous concern for the costs which the displaced population was being obliged to bear. This point had been put to me very adroitly by the people of one village who had compiled a list of every man, woman and child, together with claims for compensation for future lifetimes of benefit from the Lake which they were being asked to forgo. Everywhere, my UEED assistant and I were lectured pointedly on the advantages of choice and mobility which our education and social privileges had given us, and reminded us that their own options were much more constricted.

PROPOSING A POLICY

It became increasingly apparent to us, as a team, that the policy of wholesale eviction made little sense. The plan was limited to residential, not horticultural land, where the process of encroachment was most active. Moreover, with the limited cash at their disposal, it would take the UEED forty or fifty years to buy out the Lake dwellers, even at present rates of compensation. In the meantime, it would be wholly unreasonable to subject people to restrictions on housebuilding and the expansion of economic resources. Population pressure on the Lake was not caused by immigration but by natural growth, and this could not be contained by brute force. Farmers in particular—half of the Lake population—complained that marriages and the natural cycle of family growth were already in abeyance, a source of much discontent among the rising generation. It seemed that the most plausible way to alleviate population pressure, and thus the encroachment process, was to intervene constructively in the process of family development.

Armed with a number of sorry tales on tape, we decided to make this central to our remedy for the problems on the Lake. Arguing that the inhabitants were essential to the amenity of the Lake as a tourist asset, not a rival use of its resources, we proposed that the funds now being used to buy them out should be diverted to providing housing and alternative occupations in and around Srinagar for the frustrated rising generation.

Comparative experience of resettlement schemes suggested that younger people would be more ready to move and invest in a new life. With continued legal constraints on encroachment and new building, the Lake population could be more or less stabilized within existing resources. This compromise of conservation and development could only be temporary. It seemed apparent to most people that the tide of change could not be held back indefinitely, but fifty years is an eternity to the development planner.

Our decision-making was galvanized by presentation of an outline of our report to our UEED colleagues, an afternoon of mild drama in which we closed ranks against their current building, dredging and evicting programme, but reaffirmed their key role in the management of the Lake. Although we formed a consensus about the organization of our report in a series of discussions before we left Kashmir, the team was once again fragmented after our return to Britain. I worked in Cambridge, telephoning and exchanging drafts of the socio-economic sections with my land-use colleague; meanwhile the limnologist laboured in his cottage in the distant Welsh hills, while the staff of the two consulting firms in London, Glasgow and Edinburgh edited, collated, and polished the policy document.

On reading the final report of our mission several months after my involvement in the project had ceased, I was somewhat disappointed to see that we were advocating the reanimation of the "High Power Board" for the Dal, a body which had been dormant since its establishment four years previously. This, I thought we had agreed, would be inviting bureaucratic sprawl and further inertia. It was clear that whatever solution we proposed would require a frame of reference which transcended the shores of the Lake, and a managerial arena in which the diverse interests of municipal and state departments, and of the public, could be convened authoritatively. But in our discussions we had in mind a regrouping of the agencies which were already actively involved in the affairs of the Lake, not some lofty and dissociated body. The new decision, I was told, emanated from a senior legal counsellor in Britain, who had not actually visited Kashmir.

Nevertheless, I was pleased to see how vividly the report conveyed our experiences of the Lake, and how clearly the practical solutions which our team had devised resonated with my own account of what the people had told us. Of course, we were merely counsellors, not decision-makers, and it remains to be seen whether our arguments will prevail among the more exalted and potent interests which must determine the future of the Lake.

13

The Future of Humanity

The philosopher Kierkegaard once wrote that there were two ways. The one was to suffer, and the other was to be a professor of the fact that another is suffering. In this sense, we are all potential professors. Anthropologists, who are largely drawn from the affluent middle class and have made a career out of studying "others" who are typically lesser privileged, especially have a special obligation to profess.

The fact is, the "others" have suffered in the past, are suffering in the present, and will continue to suffer in the future. Sometimes the suffering is so unpleasant that we do not want to hear about it. This is one reason why **genocide** is a topic hardly ever discussed. Yet the implications for understanding the banality of evil are awesome. It is for this reason that we include the short article by Jared Diamond on genocide in this anthology. It is also for this reason that the piece on **AIDS** by Ronald Frankenberg is included. While genocides still do occur, Iraq and the Kurds being the most notorious recent example, AIDS runs the risk of similarly becoming "invisibilized" even though **pandemic**.

It is important to address these issues. Many years ago, before World War II, the anthropologist Everett C. Hughes studied a small German village that was so close to one of the concentration camps that the villagers could literally see the smoke from the stacks. After the war, he returned to the village to discover that the villagers were hardly touched by their proximity to the death camps. He wrote a classic essay entitled "Good People and Dirty Work" on how people could symbolically tune out such disturbing aspects of living. In this increasingly globally interdependent world, we cannot afford such luxuries. Part of the problem is not that we do not want to see, but that we do not know *how* to see.

One of the key ways in which we see and understand phenomena is by use of metaphor. For example, physicians did not know how the heart functioned until a pneumatic pump was invented; then, by using the pump as metaphor, they started understanding how the heart functioned. It is for this reason that we include the essay by Gernot Köhler entitled "Global Apartheid." What Köhler does is take **apartheid** as a metaphor and apply it to global society. Whether we agree with it or not, the metaphor does enable us to view the world differently. It also provides us with a recipe for possible action.

Since Köhler wrote his paper, important and optimistic changes have occurred in South Africa, but globally the situation has become much worse. The gap between rich and poor and white and people of color has increased substantially. In 1960 the gap between the richest fifth was some thirty times greater than the poorest fifth. By 1989 it had increased to 60 times, and now it is estimated to be over a 150 times greater. Currently, it is estimated that the rich (white) countries, which have about only one-quarter of the world's population, consume more than 70 percent of the world's energy, 75 percent of its metals, 85 percent of its wood, and 60 percent of its food.

Even among countries receiving aid, there are major discrepancies. Thus, the richest 40 percent of Southern Hemisphere countries receive more than twice as much aid as the poorest 40 percent. This proves the old adage that development aid is like champagne: In success you deserve it, and in failure you need it. And like the South African government being accused of providing the more affluent Zulus of Buthelezi with weaponry, we find that globally countries that spent heavily on arms—

more than 4 percent of their gross national product—received twice as much aid as more moderate military spenders (*Weekly Mail*, 1992).

In this era where selfishness and egoism have been elevated to a virtue in the form of "Yuppiedom," it is important to take **global interdependency** not as a source of potential shame but as a source of moral responsibility. The political philosopher Robert Goodin (1985) does this by developing a comprehensive theory of responsibility based on the concept of vulnerability. More people are vulnerable to us—individually or collectively—than we have made commitments to in any sense, but we have the same sort of strong responsibilities toward all those who are vulnerable to our actions and choices. While we should try to protect the vulnerable, we should also strive to reduce their vulnerability. This approach fits particularly well with anthropology precisely because the people we "traditionally" study are especially vulnerable.

There are many ways in which we can protect and aid the vulnerable on this globe. One collective form in which this takes place is through **anthropological advocacy groups** like Cultural Survival, but there is also the possibility of individual personal action. One anthropologist who is involved in such an exercise is Megan Biesele, who is working with those whom we label the Bushmen. The Bushmen are famous in the anthropological literature for being a prime example of "the original affluent society" insofar as they did not have to work much to achieve their basic level of subsistence. Their image has further been influenced by the runaway successful movie *The Gods Must Be Crazy*. Much of this mystique and our fascination with them has been fed by **ethnographies**, which have been misinterpreted by a public eager to project our own fantasies on to another people. The truth of the matter is that far from being some band of "beautiful people," the Bushmen have been the most brutalized and exploited peoples in southern Africa's bloody history and almost genocided out of existence. Biesele provides a fascinating contemporary account of Bushman society (focused on the place where *The Gods Must Be Crazy* was filmed) based on extended field participation and linguistic fluency. She lets her people almost speak for themselves. Such forms of self-critical advocacy ethnography, we are convinced, are one of the most important waves of the future.

REFERENCES

Goodin, Robert. 1985. *Protecting the Vulnerable*. Chicago: University of Chicago Press.

Hughes, Everett C. 1984. *The Sociological Eye: Selected Papers*. New Brunswick, N.J. Reprint: originally published by Aldine-Atherton, Chicago 1971.

Weekly Mail. 1992. "North v. South: The Great Divide." May 22.

AIDS and Anthropologists

Ronald Frankenberg

Ronald Frankenberg is the director for medical social anthropology at the University of Keele in the United Kingdom. His research has been carried out in such diverse places as Zambia, Tuscany, and Wales.

Some years ago, a commission was formed for urgent anthropology, and Claude Lévi-Strauss and others sought to save Amazonian groups who were not merely threatened here and now but whose whole future was in jeopardy. AIDS requires urgent anthropology on an even greater scale, for if the pandemic is not checked it is as capable of virtually destroying human life on earth as nuclear radiation or other ecological disasters. However, there is every hope of checking its progress, and for once there is no argument but that, as has slowly come to be realized, anthropology (social, ecological and through the study of the culture of risk) could and must be of major importance in stopping all three separate but related epidemics which WHO has recognized as making up a global pandemic.

AIDS itself is not a disease but a complex of symptoms and diseases which some (up to now about 80,000 known to WHO) if not all of the persons (between five and ten million worldwide—Mann 1988) infected with a virus called HIV are no longer able to resist because of damage to their immune system. ("HIV may cause neurological disease in infected patients in whom immune defence remains intact. This observation raises the possibility that neurological features may eventually come to dominate the clinical perception of HIV related disease." OHE 1988.) There is as yet no cure nor vaccine against HIV in sight and even the most optimistic predictions of either—ten years' time—would be too late to avert catastrophe. Prevention is not merely better than cure, it is the cure: prevention of transmission of the virus (epidemic one), prevention of the development of the AIDS syndromes which HIV makes possible (epidemic two) and prevention of unnecessary suffering for

the general population including the HIV seropositive and people with AIDS caused, not by biological, but by socially determined factors (epidemic three).

HIV is spread worldwide in the same ways through sexual intercourse (homosexual or heterosexual), through transfer of blood (transfusions, sharing or reuse of injection needles), and from mother to child (Acheson 1988).

THE FIRST PATTERN

Industrial West, Australia, Latin America

As is now well known AIDS was first identified as a problem amongst Gay men in certain cities in the United States who began to present to medical institutions with rare cancers and a form of pneumonia. [Because of] The presence and often co-presence of these conditions, it gradually became apparent (despite institutional resistance from those, especially in the National Institutes of Health, opposed to transmission theories of malignant disease—Shilts 1987), must arise from damage to the immune system and from a transmissible virus disease. Gay men paid and continue to pay a terrible price for this knowledge; but everyone, Gay or not, is given the possibility of salvation by the chance of the virus's identification among those people at that place and at that time. For the United States, despite all the faults of its health care system, has a medical infrastructure which makes it possible quickly to identify new medical disorders and to discover the categories of people affected and thus to identify causative mechanisms and modes of transmission and what needs to be done to prevent or cure them. Given the political will, it also has the financial means to cope with new epidemics. Second, there is in San Francisco a self-conscious, more or less solidary, articulate and politically active Gay community, which, after an unsurprisingly faltering

"AIDS and Anthropologists" by Ronald Frankenberg, from *Anthropology Today,* Vol. 4, No. 2, 1988. Royal Anthropological Institute. Reprinted with permission.

beginning (Shilts 1987), took stock of the situation and demonstrated to other Gays and to the rest of the world what could be done humanely to care for those already infected, and to slow down or stop further transmission. Unfortunately, through no fault of theirs, it was already too late for many of their friends and lovers. Professor M. W. Adler, one of Britain's leading experts, has pointed out that the symptomless nature of HIV infection, and the long latent period (5–8 years) before its effects, including those on the immune system, become apparent, meant that the first cases of AIDS emerged in 1980 when nearly a quarter of a cohort of Gay men were HIV seropositive (*The Independent* 17 February 1988). Also unfortunately Gays elsewhere in the world were less well-placed to respond, although self-help organizations like the Terrence Higgins Trust and Body Positive did a major task in Britain; and non-Gays were not disposed to listen or to learn from people whom at best they saw as other than themselves and at worst feared and hated for the challenge they seemed to represent to accepted social and family order and their own hardly (in both senses) suppressed temptations and desires. Even anthropologists failed to react constructively; as I reported in my A. T. article (February 1987) on the 1986 AAA meetings, AIDS was left to the Gay Caucus and put at the most unpopular time. When, at last, it became a prominent topic at the 1987 meetings, many still saw it as a purely Gay issue. Despite the negative reactions, we now know—as Hafdan Mahler, Director of WHO has forcibly pointed out—that it is possible to check the spread of even an intractable and insidious disease by health promotion at a societal or communal level even when biological methods seem to offer little help. This knowledge, where before was merely hope, holds out new and exciting potentials for what is coming to be called social epidemiology, epidemiology reciprocally enriched by the social and cultural understandings of anthropology and sociology.[1]

The tendency to associate modes of transmission by means of body fluids with "risk groups" instead of the more epidemiologically useful "risk behaviours," led to "drug addicts"—as, in popular parlance, non-legitimated intravenous drug users are unhelpfully called—being added to Gays as scapegoats. The wish to see AIDS as a problem for the other, non-respectable, the out-of-control, was intensified. It was further reinforced by the notion of the "innocent victim," the haemophiliac infected with Factor 8 and the HIV-positive baby. Thus the Pope showed his rational lack of fear of biological contagion by embracing a person with AIDS; to the approval of some Catholics and the dismay of others, his message was made ambiguous in relation to the fear of moral contagion by the fact that he chose a child with haemophilia. I felt that he might have reassured my Orthodox Jewish aunt who, when I was a child, warned me against Christianity whose Founder's best friend Mary Magdalene, she said, was a prostitute.

Especially since, as in earlier epidemics of sexually transmitted disease (Brandt 1987), prostitutes and the promiscuous (people with more sexual experience than us) were singled out for blame together with people from outside the metropolitan Industrial West.[2]

THE SECOND PATTERN— AFRICA AND THE CARIBBEAN

The reaction to the discovery of AIDS and HIV infection among Gay men and intravenous drug users was, as I have already suggested, at best distanced but reproving pity. They had scored an "own goal" as Princess Anne put it, more in sorrow than in anger, and at worst a theologically perverse, at least by New Testament standards, theory of divine anger and retribution was favoured in Britain by some Chief Constables and Rabbis. The reaction to the discovery in one part of Africa of developed AIDS, and of widespread HIV positivity spread for the most part heterosexually and therefore equally prevalent among men and women, only just escaped from being catastrophic. Western ignorance of geography, and stereotypes of African promiscuity, together with hasty suggestions of still greater immigration and travel control over black (and sometimes poor) Africans in sharp contrast to the absence of such suggestions in relation to white (and often rich) Americans led, at first, understandably to outright denial of the problem. Careful diplomacy by WHO and others and the good sense and experience of African politicians and statesmen with President Kaunda characteristically giving a courageous lead, very quickly overcame this denial.[3]

Particularly in urban areas of South Central Africa, up to 25% of the population between 20 and 40 years old may be HIV positive, and in some areas also 5–15% or even more of pregnant women are. The implications of these figures are staggering. The urban elite, on whom further development and national economic recovery depend, may be more than decimated. The productive and skilled workers and educators may be rendered ineffective and a whole generation made virtually unable to reproduce itself. Orphans and the elderly may be left without support, and achievements in the field of health may be made impossible to maintain. This is also a danger in poor areas of Southern Europe and in parts of Latin America, and even ultimately Asia.

THE THIRD PATTERN

In Asia, most of the Pacific, the Middle East and much of Eastern Europe, there are very few cases of AIDS, and even HIV seems to have appeared more recently than in other parts of the world. In most of these countries it is believed that HIV came from outside either from sexual intercourse with foreigners or by the import of infected blood products. However there is now evidence of internal transmission in the usual ways, and even if these nations succeed, in fact, in carrying out the policies of isolation and control to which some of them, including India, China and the Soviet Union are, in part, committed, they will not entirely halt the spread of HIV. Fortunately despite their reservations they attended the recent WHO summit and are signatories of the London Declaration and thus pledged to world co-operation.

THE ROLE OF ANTHROPOLOGY

The first objective of WHO's Global AIDS strategy is to prevent HIV infection, but this cannot be done in isolation from, or with indifference towards, either the development of AIDS among those already infected or the social experience of people, rightly or wrongly, believed to be at special risk, as well as the HIV seropositive and persons with AIDS.

Surprisingly little is known about specific individual sexual behaviours or about culturally approved practices of groups and subgroups. Straightforward questionnaire techniques are difficult to apply and produce data of arguable validity. Among British sociologists, Coxon (1988) has developed an ingenious self-reporting diary technique to study sexual behaviour of Gay men. Social or cultural anthropologists have already specialist knowledge of, as well as the necessary skills to discover, patterns of sexual behaviour in different societies and sub-groups. They are unlikely even to be tempted to the view that *"we have our regulated sexual patterns, you are a bit odd but understandable, they are just promiscuous."* They can understand the social circumstances in which desires become practices and in turn symbolic markers of either individual or cultural and social identity. Their knowledge and study of other kinds of behaviour change can help them to see how changes of practice can be instituted from within a society in such a way as to leave cultural and personal identity unthreatened.

How valuable such a skill may be and how urgent its application is, can be demonstrated by the difference between say Danish and British television advertising aimed at young people, which deserves comparative analysis. The British seems based on an assumption that the culture of young people can be at once ignored and condemned as bad or at least amoral, and that decisions (about risk-taking for example) are purely personal or at most dyadic. Even if the disco culture portrayed has been researched and is accurate, the wider social context of sought-for approval and avoidance of disapproval by important others, especially among peers and coevals, is just not there. The Danish advertising, on the other

hand, begins by accepting that there are adolescent hedonistic values, and while leaving the choice of fundamental change open to young people themselves, shows how existing patterns can be modified to make them safer. An even sharper contrast may be seen between the Australian Government's "fear of death based" TV campaign, which was aimed at the whole population, and that (presented as an example of "how to do it" at the London Summit) which Aboriginal health promoters devised in co-operation with local people and which aimed not at instilling terror but at the enhancement of life with reduced danger. Clearly, involving groups in self-help health promotion is one of the more effective strategies for preventing the transmission of HIV, and one in which anthropologists have much to offer as facilitators.

Anthropologists have sometimes been criticized in the development field for being better at analysing failure than helping to create success. As regards AIDS, this may be a useful fault. Health educators are aware that while smoking in Britain, for example, has in general decreased, smoking amongst working-class young people and women has risen. Anthropologists again have the skills, both theoretical and practical, to examine the meanings and practices which make such crucial differences occur.

There is a world of difference between talking of a disease that has hitherto mainly affected Gays, and talking of a "Gay disease," or still more if "queer" or even "homosexual" is substituted for Gay. Anthropologists have learned, what they may not themselves even recognize as being a rare, sensitivity to partly concealed linguistic elisions like using Lapp for Sami, or Eskimo for Inuit, which may be perceived by those named as adding a latent symbolic communication of lack of esteem to the use of surface signs.

Anthropologists study *disease* as manifested in its particular social context of *sickness* as well as carrying an individual meaning of *illness*. They are thereby both less surprised and better prepared to analyse situations where danger and sickness are attributed prematurely or even falsely to those identified as being at risk. The knowledge that healing, whether by shaman, surgeon or sacerdote, is a social process, laden with specifiable cultural meanings, gives anthropologists an important possible role in understanding and investigating how, for example, traditional healers may be encouraged within their own society and culture to do the sick no harm and to continue to protect the well. The anthropological literature on natural and especially body symbolism (Douglas 1973) has prepared its students to understand such cultural taboos and non-taboos as the ability of British television audiences to tolerate (even before nine in the evening) the pictorial representation of the unnatural breach of body boundaries by (illegitimate) needles in contrast to the impossibility of the explicit depiction (unlike elsewhere in Northern Europe) of, not necessarily per se disapproved, sexual penetration.

Furthermore, anthropological study of the myriad different cultural meanings of death (Frankenberg 1987, Bloch et al. 1982) puts its practioners in a strong position to help in the social adjustment already faced by many Gays and their relatives to a changing demographic pattern in which people are dying in their reproductively, productively and socially most active years, an actual and potential shift in the modal age of death upwards in the developing world, downwards in industrial society.

The advent of HIV and its mode of transmission have taken not only medicine and epidemiology by surprise, but have also found both the social and cultural anthropology of risk perception and behaviour, and cultural ecology theories in anthropology, as yet insufficiently developed. Health promotion is central in countering the pandemic arising from HIV infection as well as future global pandemics. There is also a renewed realization of the social implications of measured mortality in terms of both changing age distributions of individual dying and the possibility that the future of human society is once again in question through potential ecological disaster. These developments have given a new potential importance not just to virology and immunology within core medical specialties, but also to the study of anthropology in general and medical anthropology within it. When WHO gathered together more Health Ministers than ever before at the London Summit in January last, the handful of invited independent observers included at least three anthropologists, and anthropologists also played a prominent part at the First International Conference on the Global impact of AIDS in March. We are presented with a challenge which we are despite our deficiencies uniquely qualified to meet, and which for our own sakes and for the sake of the general good we cannot afford to shirk.

NOTES

1. For examples in other fields see the work on developing societies of Patrick Vaughan, Carol MacCormack, Kris Heggenhougen and others at the London School of Hygiene and Jean La Fontaine's recent report on Child Abuse in Britain for ESRC (see *Anthropology Today*, October 1987, p. 1).

2. The London fieldwork and comparative analysis of LSE anthropologist Sophie Day has shown how simplistic and unjust this is in relation to prostitute women.

3. As is so often the case there remain contrary views; see Chirimuta and Chirimuta 1987 and *The Guardian* 5 February 1988 for a favourable review of this book which in my personal view is wrong. It has also been argued, without evidence strong enough to convince most epidemiologists or WHO, that both African and Gay prevalence of AIDS are synergistically affected by other sexually transmitted diseases. Poverty is, of course, even more prevalent in Africa.

REFERENCES

Acheson, Sir D. 1988. Modes of Transmission: The Basis of Prevention Strategies. Paper to World Summit of Ministers of Health for AIDS Prevention. London WHO/UKG, January.

Bloch, M. and J. Parry. 1982. *Death and the Regeneration of Life*. Cambridge University Press.

Brandt, A. 1987. *No Magic Bullet* with additional chapter on AIDS. Oxford University Press.

Chirimuta, R. C. and R. J. 1987. *AIDS, Africa and Racism*. Chirimuta, Bretby, Derbyshire.

Coxon, A. P. M. 1988. The sexual diary as a research method in the study of sexual behaviour of gay males. *Sociological Review*. 36, 2, May (forthcoming).

Douglas, M. 1970 (1966). *Purity and Danger*. Penguin.

Douglas, M. 1973 (1970). *Natural Symbols*. Penguin.

Frankenberg, R. 1987. Life: Cycle, Trajectory or Pilgrimage? A Social Production Approach to Marxism, Metaphor and Mortality. Chapter XII, pp. 122–140 in Alan Bryman et al. *Rethinking the Life Cycle*. Macmillan.

LaFontaine, J. 1988. *Child Sexual Abuse*. An ESRC Research Briefing.

Mann, J. 1988. Global AIDS: Epidemiology, Impact, Projections and the Global Strategy. Paper to World Summit... (as under Acheson above).

Office of Health Economics. 1980. HIV and AIDS in the United Kingdom. Briefing no. 23, January, London.

Shilts, R. 1987. *And the Band Played On*. Penguin.

In Black and White

Jared Diamond

Jared Diamond teaches physiology in the medical school of the University of California, Los Angeles, but has spent much time studying birds in New Guinea. Although not an anthropologist, he frequently writes on anthropological topics for such magazines as *Natural History* and *Discover*.

How have ordinary people so often throughout human history, brought themselves to commit genocide?

While the anniversary of any nation's founding is taken as cause for its inhabitants to celebrate, Australians have special cause in this, their bicentennial year. Few groups of colonists faced such obstacles as those who landed with the first fleet at the future site of Sydney in 1788. Australia was still terra incognita: the colonists had no idea of what to expect or how to survive. They were separated from their mother country by a sea voyage of 15,000 miles, lasting eight months. Two and a half years of starvation would pass until a supply fleet arrived from England. Many of the settlers were convicts who had already been traumatized by the most brutal aspects of brutal eighteenth-century life. Despite those beginnings, the settlers survived, prospered, filled a continent, built a democracy, and established a distinctive national character. It's no wonder that Australians feel pride as they celebrate their nation's founding.

Nevertheless, one set of protests has marred the celebrations. White settlers were not the first Australians. Australia had been settled at least 40,000 years before by the ancestors of the people now usually referred to as Australian aborigines and also known in Australia as blacks. In the course of English settlement, most of the original inhabitants were killed by settlers or died of other causes, leading some descendants of the survivors to stage protests this year. The bicentenary celebrations focused implicitly on how Australia became white. This column focuses instead on how Australia ceased to be black and how courageous English settlers came to commit genocide.

Lest white Australians take offense at this piece, I should make it clear at the outset that I am not accusing their forefathers of having done something uniquely horrendous. My reason for discussing the extermination of the aborigines is precisely because it isn't unique: it's a well-documented example of a common event in human history. Genocide is such a painful subject that either we'd rather not think about it at all or else we'd like to believe that nice people don't commit genocide, only Nazis do. But our refusing to think about it has consequences: we've done little to halt the numerous episodes of genocide since World War II, and we're not alert to where it may happen next. Hence I'll indicate briefly how frequent it is, why people do it, and what I learned from a friend of mine who joined in a genocidal massacre thirty years ago. Let's begin by recalling the founding of white settlement in the state of Tasmania.

Tasmania, an island slightly larger than West Virginia, lies 200 miles off Australia's southeast coast. When it was discovered by Europeans in 1642, it supported about 5,000 hunter-gatherers related to the aborigines of the Australian mainland and with perhaps the simplest technology of any modern peoples. Tasmanians made only a few types of simple stone and wooden tools. Like the mainland aborigines, they lacked metal tools, agriculture, livestock, pottery, and bows and arrows. Unlike the mainlanders, they also lacked boomerangs, dogs, nets, knowledge of sewing, and ability to start a fire.

Since the Tasmanians' sole boats were rafts capable of only short journeys, they had had no contact with any other humans since the rising sea level cut off Tasmania from Australia 10,000 years ago. Confined to their private universe for hundreds of generations, they had survived the longest isolation in modern human history—an isolation otherwise depicted only in science fiction. When the white colonists of Australia finally ended that isolation, no two peoples on earth were less equipped to understand each other than were Tasmanians and whites.

The tragic collision of these two peoples led to conflict almost as soon as British sealers and settlers arrived in about 1800. Whites kidnapped Tasmanian children as laborers, kidnapped women as consorts, mutilated or killed men, trespassed on hunting grounds, and tried to clear Tasmanians off their land. Thus, the conflict quickly focused on Lebensraum, which throughout human history has been among the commonest causes of genocide. As a result of the kidnappings, the native population of northeast Tasmania in November 1830 had been reduced to seventy-two adult men, three adult women, and no children. One shepherd shot nineteen Tasmanians with a swivel gun loaded with nails. Four other shepherds ambushed a group of natives, killed thirty, and threw their bodies over a cliff remembered today as Victory Hill.

Naturally, Tasmanians retaliated, and whites counter-retaliated in turn. To end the escalation, Governor Arthur in April 1828 ordered all Tasmanians to leave the part of the island already settled by Europeans. To enforce this order, government-sponsored groups called roving parties, and consisting of convicts led by police, hunted down and killed Tasmanians. With the declaration of martial law in November 1828, soldiers were authorized to kill on sight any Tasmanian in the settled areas. Next, a bounty was declared on the natives: five British pounds for each adult, two pounds for each child, caught alive. "Black catching," as it was called because of the Tasmanians' dark skins, became big business pursued by private as well as official roving parties. At the same time a commission headed by William Broughton, the Anglican archdeacon of Australia, was set up to recommend an overall policy toward the natives. After considering proposals to capture them for sale as slaves, poison or trap them, or hunt them with dogs, the commission settled on continued bounties and the use of mounted police.

In 1830 a remarkable missionary, George Augustus Robinson, was hired to round up the remaining Tasmanians and take them to Flinders Island, thirty miles away. Robinson was convinced that he was acting for the good of the Tasmanians. He was paid 300 pounds in advance, 700 pounds on completing the job. Undergoing real dangers and hardship, and aided by a courageous native woman named Truganini, he succeeded in bringing in the remaining natives—initially by persuading them that a worse fate awaited them if they did not surrender, but later at gunpoint. Many of Robinson's captives died en route, but about 200 reached Flinders, the last survivors of the former population of 5,000.

On Flinders Island Robinson was determined to civilize and christianize the survivors. His settlement—at a windy site with little fresh water—was run like a jail. Children were separated from parents to facilitate the work of civilizing them. The regimented daily schedule included Bible reading, hymn singing, and inspection of beds and dishes for cleanness and neatness. However, the jail diet caused malnutrition, which combined with illness to make the natives die. Few infants survived more than a few weeks. The government reduced expenditures in the hope that the natives would die out. By 1869 only Truganini, one other woman, and one man remained alive.

These last three Tasmanians attracted the interest of scientists, who believed them to be a missing link between humans and apes. Hence when the last man, one William Lanner, died in 1869, competing teams of physicians, led by Dr. George Stokell from the Royal Society of Tasmania and Dr. W. L. Crowther from the Royal College of Surgeons, alternately dug up and reburied Lanner's body, cutting off parts of it and stealing them back and forth from each other. Crowther cut off the head, Stokell the hands and feet, and someone else the ears and nose, as souvenirs. Stokell made a tobacco pouch out of Lanner's skin.

Before Truganini, the last woman, died in 1876, she was terrified of similar postmortem mutilation and asked in vain to be buried at sea. As she had feared, the Royal Society dug up her skeleton and put it on public display in the Tasmanian Museum, where it remained until 1947. In that year the museum finally yielded to complaints of poor taste and transferred Truganini's skeleton to a room where only scientists could view it. That, too, stimulated complaints of poor taste. Finally, in 1976—the centenary year of Truganini's death—her skeleton was cremated over the museum's objections, and her ashes were scattered at sea as she had requested.

While the Tasmanians were few in number, their extermination was disproportionately influential in Australian history because Tasmania was the first Australian colony to solve its native problem and achieve the most nearly final solution. It had done so by apparently succeeding in getting rid of all its natives. (Actually, some children of Tasmanian women by white sealers survived, and their descendants today constitute an embarrassment to the Tasmanian government, which has not figured out what to do about them.) Many whites on the Australian mainland envied the thoroughness of the Tasmanian solution and wanted to imitate it, but they also learned a lesson from it. The extermination of the Tasmanians, carried out in settled areas in full view of the urban press, had attracted some negative comment. Hence the extermination of the much more numerous mainland aborigines was effected at or beyond the frontier, far from urban centers. The colonial governments' instrument of this policy, modeled on the

Tasmanian government's roving parties, was a branch of mounted police termed Native Police, who used search-and-destroy tactics to kill or drive out aborigines. A typical strategy was to surround a camp at night and to shoot the inhabitants in an attack at dawn. White settlers also made widespread use of poisoned food to kill aborigines. Another common practice was round-ups in which captured aborigines were kept chained together at the neck while being marched to jail and held there. The British novelist Anthony Trollope expressed the prevailing nineteenth-century British attitude toward aborigines when he wrote, "Of the Australian black man we may certainly say that he has to go. That he should perish without unnecessary suffering should be the aim of all who are concerned in the matter."

These tactics continued in Australia long into the twentieth century. In an incident at Alice Springs in 1928, police massacred thirty-one aborigines. The Australian parliament refused to accept a report on the massacre, and two aboriginal survivors (rather than the police) were put on trial for murder. Neck chains were still in use and defended as humane in 1958, when the Commissioner of Police for the state of Western Australia explained to the *Melbourne Herald* that aboriginal prisoners preferred being chained.

The mainland aborigines were too numerous to exterminate in the manner of the Tasmanians. However, from the arrival of British colonists in 1788 until the 1921 census, the aboriginal population declined from about 300,000 to 60,000.

Today the attitudes of white Australians toward their murderous history vary widely. While government policy and many whites' private views have become increasingly sympathetic to the aborigines, other whites deny responsibility for genocide. For instance, in 1982, *The Bulletin,* one of Australia's leading news magazines, published a letter by a lady named Patricia Cobern, who denied indignantly that white settlers had exterminated the Tasmanians. In fact, wrote Ms. Cobern, the settlers were peace loving and of high moral character, while Tasmanians were treacherous, murderous, warlike, filthy, gluttonous, vermin infested, and disfigured by syphilis. Moreover, they took poor care of their infants, never bathed, and had repulsive marriage customs. They died out because of all those poor health practices, plus a death wish and lack of religious beliefs. It was just a coincidence that, after thousands of years of existence, they happened to die out during a conflict with settlers. The only massacres were of settlers by Tasmanians, not vice versa. Besides, the settlers only armed themselves in self-defense, were unfamiliar with guns, and never shot more than forty-one Tasmanians at one time.

I have already mentioned that the fate of Australian aborigines was typical of many episodes of genocide throughout human history in having been precipitated by a conflict over Lebensraum. In addition, Ms. Cobern's letter is a classic example of the usual response of a people charged with genocide. Typically, killers deny most responsibility for group murders; invoke self-defense or provocation, insofar as they acknowledge any responsibility at all; attribute ultimate responsibility to the victims, and denigrate the victims as subhumans implicitly deserving of death, whatever death's actual cause.

To appreciate that the fate of the Australian aborigines was hardy unique, we have only to recall our own not-quite-complete extermination of American Indians, another struggle over Lebensraum. History books usually portray this struggle as a series of military conflicts in our distant past between groups of armed adult males: the U.S. Army versus mounted Indian warriors. In fact, much of the struggle consisted of sneak attacks and isolated murders in which white civilians killed Indians of any age and either sex. It was only in 1916 that the last "wild" Indian in the United States (the Yahi Indian known as Ishi) died, and frank and unapologetic memoirs by the killers of his tribe were still being published as recently as 1923. For instance, a rancher named Norman Kingsley explained how, in shooting a group of more than thirty unarmed Yahis that he had cornered in a cave, he exchanged his .56 caliber Spencer rifle for a .38 caliber revolver when it came to shooting the babies, because "the rifle tore them up so bad." When Robert Anderson wrote about his dawn attack on a Yahi village, he mentioned that his friend Hiram Good suggested sparing the women while killing every man or well-grown boy, but "it was plain to me that we must also get rid of the women," who were then killed with some particular savagery not described in detail.

It used to be thought that humans were unique among animals in killing members of their own species. However, recent field studies have documented murder or group murder by many other species, including ants, hyenas, wolves, lions, monkeys, gorillas, and chimpanzees. Genocide by humans is at least as old as the oldest preserved written records. We all know the biblical account of how the walls of Jericho came tumbling down at the sound of Joshua's trumpets. Less often quoted is the sequel: Joshua obeyed the Lord's command to slaughter Jericho's inhabitants, as well as those of Ai, Makkedah, Libnah, Hebron, Debir, and many other cities. This was considered so ordinary that the Book of Joshua devotes only a phrase to each slaughter, as if to say: of course he killed all the inhabitants, what else would you expect? The sole account requiring elaboration is of the slaughter at Jericho itself, where Joshua did something really unusual: he spared the lives of one family (because they had helped his messengers).

We find similar episodes in accounts of the wars of the ancient Greeks, Crusaders, Pacific islanders, and other groups. Obviously, I'm not saying that slaughter of the defeated irrespective of sex has always followed crushing defeat in war. But that outcome, or else milder versions like the killing of men and the enslavement of women, happened often enough that they must be considered more than a rare aberration in our view of human nature. Since 1950 there have been nearly twenty episodes of genocide, including two claiming more than a million victims each (East Pakistan in 1971, Cambodia in the late 1970s) and four more with more than a hundred thousand victims each (the Sudan and Indonesia in the 1960s, Burundi and Uganda in the 1970s). A few cases attracted some international attention, but who protested the slaughter of Zanzibar's Arabs in 1964 or of Paraguay's Aché Indians in the 1970s?

What are the situations in which genocide is most likely? Historically, perhaps the commonest situation has involved one people attempting to usurp another people's Lebensraum, as exemplified by the fate of Australian aborigines and Native Americans. Another common type of situation involves power struggles within a pluralistic society, as when Rwanda's Hutu people killed Tutsi people in 1962–63 and when Burundi's Tutsi killed Hutu in 1972–73. As for scapegoat killings of a helpless minority blamed for frustrations of their killers, one immediately thinks of slaughters of Jews by many peoples over many centuries and of Stalin's killings of several ethnic minorities in Russia at the height of World War II. Most of these types of genocide also involved racial or religious persecution.

All human societies have sanctions against murder, which must somehow be overcome for genocide to happen. Overriding principles commonly invoked include self-defense, revenge, manifest rights to land, and possessing the correct religion or race or political belief. These are the principles that fan hatred and transform ordinary people into murderers. A further universal feature of genocide is an "us/them" ethical code that views the victims as lower beings or animals to whom laws of human ethics don't apply. For instance, Nazis regarded Jews as lice; French settlers of Algeria referred to local Moslems as *ratons* (rats); Boers called Africans *bobbejaan* (baboons); educated northern Nigerians viewed Ibos as subhuman vermin; and Ms. Cobern expressed a low opinion of Tasmanians.

Many books have been written on the psychology of genocide. It's hard not to go numb while reading them. It remains hard to imagine how we, and other nice ordinary people that we know, could bring ourselves to look helpless people in the face while killing them. I came closest to being able to imagine it when a friend whom I had long known told me of a genocidal massacre at which he had been a killer.

Kariniga is a gentle Tudawhe tribesman who worked with me in New Guinea. We shared life-threatening situations, fears, and triumphs, and I like and admire him. One evening after I had known Kariniga for five years, he described to me an episode from his youth. There had been a long history of conflict between the Tudawhes and a neighboring village of Daribi tribesmen. Tudawhes and Daribis seem quite similar to me, but Kariniga had come to view Daribis as inexpressibly vile. In a series of ambushes the Daribis finally succeeded in picking off many Tudawhes, including Kariniga's father, until the surviving Tudawhes became desperate. All the remaining Tudawhe men surrounded the Daribi village at night and set fire to the huts at dawn. As the sleepy Daribis stumbled down the steps of their burning huts, they were speared. Some succeeded in escaping to the forest, where Tudawhes tracked down and killed most of them during the following weeks. But the establishment of Australian government control ended the hunt before Kariniga could catch his father's killer.

Since that evening, I've often found myself shuddering as I recalled details of it—the glow in Kariniga's eyes as he told me of the dawn massacre; those intensely satisfying moments when he finally drove his spear into some of his people's murderers; and his tears of rage and frustration at the escape of his father's killer, whom he still hoped to kill some day with poison. That evening, I thought I understood how at least one nice person had brought himself to kill. The potential for genocide that circumstances thrust on Kariniga lies within all of us. As the growth of world population sharpens conflicts between and within societies, humans will have more urge to kill each other, and more effective weapons with which to do it. To listen to first-person accounts of genocide is unbearably painful. But if we continue to turn away and to not understand it, when will it be our own turn to become the killers—or the victims?

Global Apartheid

Gernot Köhler

Gernot Köhler was connected to the Center of International Studies at Princeton University at the time he wrote this article in 1978.

The concept of apartheid has significance far beyond the situation in South Africa which coined the term. Indeed, the concept can be generalized to apply to the present world situation. It provides both a better understanding of the present human condition and more effective guidelines to change it. The processes of interdependence, interpenetration and intercommunication in the present era have made the entire humanity into one global society. The present nation-state system, which obscures the appearance of this society, fails miserably in responding to the concerns and needs of the global community. The concept of global apartheid provides a more realistic and comprehensive view of the world and suggests appropriate ways of so acting as to make a beginning toward realizing a just, participatory, peaceful and humane global society.

This paper presents the view that Global Society is an apartheid system. The purpose of this paper will be to define and describe global apartheid, analyse some of its most striking features, and suggest some broad strategy lines for overcoming its worst aspects.

STRUCTURAL SIMILARITIES WITH SOUTH AFRICAN APARTHEID

It would be useful for our present discussion to distinguish between apartheid as a policy and apartheid as it is practiced within specific societies. Policies of apartheid are programs or measures that aim at the creation or maintenance of racial segregation. Supporters of such policies claim that segregated development of two racial groups does not imply dominance of one over the other. Apartheid, in this view, permits the possibility of separate but equal, or equivalent, life chances for each of the separated races. The logic of this argument apart, its

validity has been disproved in fact wherever such a policy has been professedly tried. Apartheid policies just cannot be pursued and sustained except in the context of structural apartheid.

When we speak of apartheid as a structure, we refer to the social, economic, political, military, and cultural constitution of a society. Whenever a minority race dominates a majority composed of other races in a society, that society exhibits a structure of apartheid.

South Africa is a classic example of this. In South Africa, the dominance of the white minority over the black majority takes different forms—from the denial of political representation to the black majority to brutal repression to an enormous differential in living standards to many others.

Condemnation of South African apartheid has been almost universal. The UN General Assembly has condemned racism and apartheid in South Africa on numerous occasions, with majorities bordering on unanimity, despite the well-known reluctance of member-states to have the organization intervene in the domestic jurisdiction of any state. If on few issues in international politics there has been such a massive agreement, it is because policies of racial segregation, which assure the dominance of the white stratum of society, flagrantly violate the aspirations of a majority of humanity for liberation from dominance and are in sharp conflict with the norms of equality of all human beings, and because apartheid constitutes the most repugnant form of human rights violation.

It is argued below that the apartheid structure of the global society has important similarities with that of South Africa. Indeed, the global society is a mirror reflection of South African society. One can go a step further and say that global apartheid is even more severe than South African apartheid. There seems to be no other system that is more "apart," in the sense in which apartheid is. Let us, then, look at the macrostructure of the global society.

THE STRUCTURE OF GLOBAL SOCIETY

The world is commonly seen as a multitude of countries or nation-states. World politics and world economics are commonly understood as a set of relations between sovereign nation-states. This view, though not wrong, is limited. It is true that nation-states issue passports and visas, show national flags, organize military forces, make national laws, conduct foreign policy, make trade agreements with other nation-states, and so on. World affairs can be comprehended by what nations and their governments do to each other, be it in the military, economic, cultural, or other domains. Such intergovernmental and interstate exchanges and relations today seem all-important, although their importance in relation to the activities of non-governmental actors and in relation to supranational organizations are changing. In recent years, an increasing awareness of interdependence has led to some questioning of the manner in which the nation-state system operates. Numerous observers have become sensitive to the phenomenon of transnationalism, which implies a diminution in the sovereignty of individual states. Nevertheless, the prevailing view still is that the most useful way of understanding global politics is through the prism of the nation-state system.

Without questioning the validity of these views, we now propose an alternative—namely, to view the world as a macrosociety. This view is reinforced by pictures of the earth as seen from outer space, by an increased sense of economic interdependence between countries, by the emergence of world conferences for the airing of views on diverse subjects of global interest, by intellectual endeavors and scientific models which treat the world as a single system. The notions of meeting the basic needs of four to eight billion people, establishment of minimal levels of decency with regard to civil and political liberties of all individuals and groups, notions of pollution and resource depletion and of quality of life are becoming more commonplace in the rhetoric of academics, policy-makers and knowledgeable and responsible individuals around the globe. Perhaps the most forceful illustration of this approach is a recent article by Nathan Keyfitz in which he analyzes the social structure of the world as if the globe was a single society.[1] We believe that these trends capture a part of reality not adequately comprehended by the paradigm of the nation-state system, and it is in that spirit that we wish to speculate about world society.

When we view the world society as a macrosociety, we begin to ask questions that we normally ask only with regard to national societies—e.g. is it nice to live there? What is the political system of this society? What is its economic system and how does the world society allocate its resources? How is this society stratified? What is the role of women in world society? How does world society treat its children? What are the race relations in the world society? How does the world society protect its members from murder and mass murder? How does it provide for

social security? Is it a happy society? These questions are different from those dealt with in the study of international politics and international economics, if only because they relate to the world society rather than to the nation-state.

The literature that comes closest to dealing with global structure in this sense is to be found in the writings on imperialism, dependency, and center-periphery relations. These see the world society as a highly stratified macrosociety which is characterized by exploitation and relations of political, economic, military, and psychological domination and dependence between the center and the periphery of the world. This modern world system, which emerged in the fifteenth and sixteenth centuries, transcends national boundaries, cripples the economic circuits of peripheral societies, generates artificial underdevelopment, and affects both center and periphery countries in various domains other than economic.

While this mode of analysis is very valuable, it could be even more so if it stressed the important fact of racial stratification on a world scale and the attendant racist attitudes and behaviors, which are still with us although the formal empires have all but withered away. We therefore propose to use the concept of "global apartheid" for the interpretation and analysis of the present structure of world society.

As indicated above, our contention is that the structure of the world is very similar to the structure of South Africa and that both are equally appalling. The similarity manifests itself in all major dimensions of analysis—political, economic, military, cultural, psychological, social, racial and legal. A formal definition of "global apartheid" though capturing only the skeleton of a concept, might read thus: Global apartheid is a structure of world society which combines socioeconomic and racial antagonisms and in which (i) a minority of whites occupies the pole of affluence, while a majority composed of other races occupies the pole of poverty; (ii) social integration of the two groups is made extremely difficult by barriers of complexion, economic position, political boundaries, and other factors; (iii) economic development of the two groups is interdependent; (iv) the affluent white minority possesses a disproportionately large share of world society's political, economic, and military power. Global apartheid is thus a structure of extreme inequality in cultural, racial, social, political, economic, military and legal terms, as is South African Apartheid.

SOME DATA ON GLOBAL APARTHEID

In South Africa, the population ratio between the nonwhite majority and the white minority is about 4.7 to 1. In the world society, about two-thirds of the population is nonwhite and one-third white. Both in South Africa and in the world society, being "white" and belonging to the upper stratum tend to go together, although there are also poor whites and rich nonwhites. The upper stratum—both in South Africa and the world—is not a homogeneous group. There exist linguistic-ethnic-cultural cleavages within this stratum (notably, Afrikaner versus English in South Africa and "West" versus "East" in global society). The whites in South Africa and in the world alike enjoy a higher standard of living and have more power than the nonwhites. The world income tree (Figure 1) ... shows the economic stratification of the world. It shows the rich countries at the top and the poor countries at the bottom according to their per capita gross national product, and countries with similar wealth are grouped together. The length of the bars shown in the figure indicates how many people belong to each income group. Figure 1 thus shows how about two-thirds of humanity live at, or close to, the bottom, of the socioeconomic pyramid of the world, while one-third of humankind live in middle and top positions. The West (or, the "First World") and the East (i.e. the "Second World") occupy the top and middle ranks of this tree. They happen to be predominantly "white," Japan being the major exception. They are the upper crust of the world society in much the same way as Afrikaner and English whites in South Africa are the upper stratum of that society.

When we treat the world as a single society and compare its inequality to situations of inequality *within* certain countries, we find that *global* inequality of income is even more severe than the income inequality within national societies (Table 1).

Table 1. Income Shares

Segment of population	Bulgaria	USA	India	South Africa	World
	Percentages of gross national product (or gross global product) received by the three segments of population				
Top 20%	33.2	38.8	52.0	58.0	71.3
Middle 40%	40.0	41.5	32.0	35.8	23.5
Lowest 40%	26.8	19.7	16.0	6.2	5.2

Sources: 1. Roger D. Hansen, *The U.S. and World Development: Agenda for Action 1976* (New York: Praeger, 1975), pp. 148–149 for Bulgaria (1962), USA (1970), India (1964), and South Africa (1965); 2. World Bank, *Population Policies and Economic Development* (Baltimore: John Hopkins University Press, 1974), p. 37 for World (1971).

As Table 1 shows, the income inequality of the world is even worse than that of South Africa. In South Africa, the poorest 40% of the population receive only 6.2% of the national product, while the poorest 40% of the world receive an even smaller share (5.2% of the world product). At the other end of the spectrum, the richest 20% of South Africa's population take 58.0% of the income, while the richest 20% of the world take even more (71.3% of the world income.)

Life expectancy is also an index of global apartheid. The members of the affluent, predominantly white societies of the "North" live longer than the members of the poor, predominantly nonwhite societies of the Third World (see Figure 2). It shows that life expectancy is lowest for the poorest countries and tends to rise in

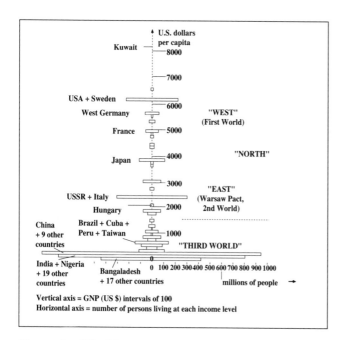

Figure 1.   World Income Tree

Source: Ruth Legot Sivard, *World Military and Social Expenditures 1976* (Leesburg. Virg. WMSE Publications), pp. 21–31. The grouping of data by intervals of $100.00 per capita done by the author.

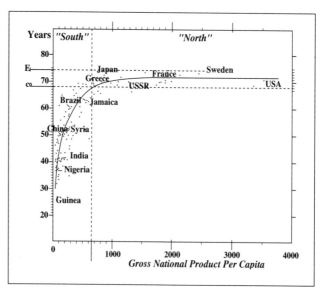

Figure 2.   Relationship of life expectancy with per capita GNP

Source: Adapted from G. Köhler and N. Alcock, "An Empirical Table of Structural Violence." *Journal of Peace Research 13*, 4, 1976.

proportion to a country's wealth until a certain threshold is reached. Above that threshold of wealth, life expectancy tends to change very little. The countries of the "North" enjoy a similar, high life expectancy. Eastern Europe is, in this respect, as privileged as the Western affluent societies.

It should be noted, too, that most of the world's weapons of mass destruction are owned by the white societies of the "North"—the United States, USSR, France, and England. World Wars I and II and the possibility of a future nuclear war between the United States and the Soviet Union have so much occupied the minds of some of us in the affluent countries that we fail to see that *actual* international violence (resulting from international wars and intervention) and *actual* civil violence (from revolutions, riots, massacres, etc.) and actual structural violence[2] (from miserable socioeconomic conditions) are all related to global apartheid. Estimates for the year 1965 show how all three forms of large-scale violence are unequally distributed in a manner that is consistent with global apartheid (see Table 2).

Table 2 shows the enormous inequality of death and suffering from war and other forms of violence. If violence were equally distributed, the North, with 30% of the world's population, would suffer 30% of all forms of violence and the South, with 70% of world population, would suffer 70% of all violent deaths. The data indicate, however, that the South has suffered much more than "its fair share" of violent death—namely, over 90% in all categories—and that the North has had correspondingly low shares.

While comparable up-to-date estimates are not available, preliminary calculations suggest the following developments since 1965:

a. The world total of deaths due to structural violence seems to have declined slightly despite the rise in world population. It can be assumed that the distribution of fatalities between the North and the South remains as unequal since 1965 as it was in 1965.

Table 2.   The Inequality of Global Violence

A. Estimated world totals, 1965 deaths from:	
international violence	11,500–23,000
civil violence	92,000
structural violence	14,000,000–18,000,000

B. Distribution of violent deaths, 1965 (World = 100% in each category)		
Affluent "North"	population	30.6%
	international violence	9.1%
	civil violence	.1%
	structural violence	4.2%
Poor "South"	population	69.4%
	international violence	90.9%
	civil violence	99.9%
	structural violence	95.8%

Source: Gernot Köhler and Norman Alcock, "An Empirical Table of Structural Violence," *Journal of Peace Research,* 4. The percentages for structural violence are based on the so-called Swedish Model.

b. The world total of deaths due to large-scale armed violence, both international and domestic, does not exhibit a steady trend but fluctuates considerably from year to year and period to period. Between 1965 and 1976, a peak was reached in 1971 when the Pakistan-Bangladesh-India war and the war in Vietnam sent the annual world total of deaths in this category to about 1.5 million or more. From 1973 to 1976, the corresponding world figure may have been around 100,000 deaths, with the inequality between the North and the South remaining undisturbed.[3]

THE NEED FOR REFORM OF THE INTERNATIONAL SYSTEM

Most observers agree that the international system is currently in a phase of major changes although there is a wide range of views both on the nature and on the most desirable direction of this transformation. In our view, the world society, structured like global apartheid, clearly requires reforms in order to make the society more suitable for living in for most of its members. Just as the world community opposes apartheid in South Africa, it should also oppose global apartheid. Ideally, reform should lead to the abolition of global apartheid. This is not merely a moral demand; for two-thirds of this world society, it is urgent and necessary to enable this multiracial majority to live a life of dignity.

For the more affluent societies of the North, the abolition of global apartheid may not seem urgent, but it is in their own interest no less than in the interest of the South to actively press for a world without apartheid. This view is dictated by political and economic prudence. As the examples of Zimbabwe (Rhodesia) and South Africa amply illustrate, the maintenance of an apartheid system is costly in political, military, social, economic, and psychological terms.

But as long as the apartheid system is not challenged from below, the self-interest of the upper stratum, defined in narrow wealth and power terms, is tied to the perpetuation of the status quo. As soon as it is effectively challenged from below, the costs of maintaining it begin to rise. When the lower stratum of the system becomes highly self-assertive and permanently "unruly" in the perspective of the predominantly white upper stratum, the self-interest of the upper stratum is no longer served by the defense of the status quo. Prudent upper-stratum statesmanship then feels inclined to doubt its usefulness in terms of the costs of maintaining apartheid. The following is a short list of such costs.

1. *Economic health.* The world economy cannot unfold its full productive potential because global apartheid impedes the productivity of the Third World and, thereby, keeps the North's income from trade with the South far below what it could be. This, in turn, contributes to slow growth, inflation, and unemployment in the North.

2. *Economic security*. The affluent countries require oil, minerals, and other goods from the Third World. Lack of North's responsiveness to Third World interests increases South's inclination to disrupt oil and resource flows to the North.

3. *Military security*. Deep economic conflicts in the world system contribute to the world's military instability. This is dangerous for the affluent countries in view of the fact that even those armed conflicts which are seemingly "peripheral" from the viewpoint of the North can lead to a breakdown of deterrence and to a large-scale war between the two major alliances of the North, as World War I illustrated.

4. *Liberty*. Massive poverty breeds authoritarianism of the Right or the Left. To the extent that the affluent countries cherish the world-wide presence of liberty, the lack of liberty in the world, linked to global apartheid, must be counted as a cost.

5. *Human growth*. For many people in the affluent societies who have a humanistic or spiritual orientation, the present world situation which stunts human growth and development on such a large scale is a cost.

The development of race relations in the United States provides an interesting illustration both of the opportunities and of the difficulties encountered in the abolition of an unfair racial situation. It shows that it is quite possible that major segments of the dominant white stratum come to support desegregation policies. On the other hand, the example also shows that progress in this direction is slow and that, even after the society's attitudes and laws on race have begun to change, the problem continues in terms of class differences.

MAJOR DIMENSIONS OF REFORM

It is not enough to set out to abolish global apartheid; there ought to be a fair idea of where to go—i.e. there ought to be an image of an alternative world structure. Such an alternative would, in my opinion, have to satisfy the following criteria: (1) basic needs for all individuals are satisfied and abject poverty is eradicated; (2) racial discrimination is eliminated; and (3) international and intranational income differences are significantly reduced.

For this purpose, it is necessary to make a realistic assessment of the present structure and its dynamics. As noted above, there are two competing paradigms which claim to provide an accurate view of the world: the classical nation-state paradigm and the center-periphery paradigm. It is now generally recognized that a pure nation-state paradigm does not sufficiently correctly conceptualize the enormous economic and racial stratification of the world. The center-periphery paradigm, on the other hand, though a valuable contribution to the understanding of the dynamics of the global political economy, is found to be rather constrictive when attempts are made to apply it to political and social action in all the regions of the world. The example of South Africa is very instructive in this regard. When we apply the center-periphery analysis to the South African situation, all members of the white minority have to be considered as members of the "center," and all members of the black majority as members of the "periphery." While this interpretation seems plausible, one of its inferences does not hold for South Africa. The center-periphery analysis assumes or predicts that all members of the center have an interest in maintaining the unfair status quo. In South Africa, however, as Steve Biko pointed out, white opposition to the status quo has been at times very strong and was, on occasion, stronger than the black opposition to it.[4] The center-periphery analysis is thus—for the South African situation—not as "realistic" as one might think. I am contending that, at the global level, the center-periphery paradigm is likewise too rigid and less realistic.

At the world level, we find many members in the "center of the center," i.e. elites in the North, who oppose global apartheid and global militarism. We also find many elites in the Third World who do not behave as lackeys of the global center, as assumed or predicted by the center-periphery theory. Furthermore, the "periphery of the center," i.e. workers, housewives, employees, etc. in the countries of the North, do not unequivocally support the "center of the center" in efforts to maintain the global status quo. The activities of the lay members of churches in North America and Europe in voluntary aid to the Third World and in opposition to South African apartheid are a clear illustration of this point. Nor do the "masses" in Third World countries necessarily oppose collaboration between their leaders and Northern countries. In short, the center-periphery paradigm is partly true, but it is far from an accurate description of the reality.

If we view the world as structured on the lines of global apartheid, the role of the Northern, white opponent to global apartheid—"elite" or "mass"—makes sense. Similarly, the Southern, nonwhite moderate collaborator with the North—"elite" or "mass"—can be seen under the paradigm of global apartheid, as a shrewd politician on behalf of underdog interests or a traitor to those interests—depending on circumstances and behavior—whereas he is made out to be invariably a traitor of underdog interests in the center-periphery paradigm.

The world is thus most realistically depicted as a society which is "apart" and stratified, i.e. global apartheid, and which encompasses armed nation-states as administrative districts. Policies for world reform can mobilize support not only in the "periphery of the periphery," as center-periphery analysis assumes, but throughout the North and the South, both among "elites" and "masses." As in any large-scale political movement, different sectors of the movement may support even a drastic reform movement for somewhat different reasons and on the basis of a combination of different interests.

Socioeconomic issues are obviously central to the abolition of global apartheid. At the same time, other dimensions—military, political-legal, ecological, and cultural-psychological—are related to the socioeconomic issues and must undoubtedly be attended to in any attempt to abolish that system. Thus, we believe that it can be shown that the prospect of progress toward disarmament would be vastly improved by a movement directed toward abolishing global apartheid. Similarly, modification of the institutional structures at the global level (e.g. in the World Bank, international commodity markets, and others) should be enhanced to permit racial balance and fair representation of the world's multiracial majority. Thirdly, ecological considerations might be given serious attention by persons in the Third World if the movement for an ecologically sane world took recognition of the world's apartheid. Finally, in the cultural-psychological realm, we must learn cognitions and attitudes which combine positive communal and national identifications with positive attitudes toward a common world society and which entail a respect for common global concerns and interests as opposed to particularistic national interests.

TOWARD A JUST, PARTICIPATORY, PEACEFUL AND HUMANE GLOBAL SOCIETY

It is generally recognized that social theory and the major concepts of an era arise out of, and respond to, the underlying material and social conditions which have a bearing on political action and the establishment of normative orders. Thus, for example, both Adam Smith and Karl Marx would probably agree that the notions of the marketplace and of class antagonism were products of empirical situations which favored the use of such concepts and the values they imply. Concepts which are able to combine a grasp of the ongoing behavioral world and provide a normative thrust become the basis, then, for determining what is considered as "knowledge," "information," and "data" about the world, and how we are to behave towards it. We have attempted to articulate the concept of global apartheid because we believe that the processes of interdependence, interpenetration, and the communicative era in which we live are making the planetary dimension of human society the most significant new prism through which to view social processes and the social organization of humanity. We believe further that the state system fails miserably in meeting the concerns and needs of this emerging global community. It is our contention that the concept of global apartheid— even in the limited form in which we have presented it here—provides us with a more comprehensive and realistic way of viewing the world, and thus enables us to suggest ways of behaving and acting in the political, economic and social realm so as to begin to realize a just, participatory, peaceful, and humane global society.

NOTES

1. Nathan Keyfitz, "World Resources and the World Middle Class," *Scientific American* 235, 1, July 1976, pp. 28–35.
2. "Structural violence" is a term used in contemporary peace research and is to be distinguished from armed violence. While armed violence is violence exerted by persons against persons with the use of arms, structural violence is violence exerted by situations, institutions, social, political and economic structures. Thus, when a person dies because he/she has no access to food, the effect is violent as far as that person is concerned, yet there is no individual actor who could be identified as the source of this violence. It is the system of food production and distribution that is to blame. The violence is thus exerted by an anonymous "structure." The measurement of the number of persons killed through structural violence uses statistics of life expectancy. By comparing the life expectancy of affluent regions with that of poor regions, one can estimate how many persons died in the poor region on account of poverty and poverty-related conditions (e.g. lack of doctors, clean water, food, etc.), which can be interpreted as "structural violence."
3. Trends in global structural and armed violence in the twentieth century are being investigated by William Beckhardt and Gernot Köhler. The research is in progress.
4. An interview with Steve Biko, conducted by Bernard Zylstra and published in the *Christian Science Monitor*, 10 November, 1977, pp. 18–19, contains the following passages.

    Question: What is black consciousness?

    Biko: By black consciousness I mean the cultural and political revival of in oppressed people ... So black consciousness says: "Forget about colour!" But the reality we faced 10 to 15 years ago did not allow us to articulate this. After all, the continent was in a period of rapid decolonization, which implied a challenge to black inferiority all over Africa.

    This challenge was shared by white liberals. So for quite some time the white liberals acted as the spokesmen for the blacks ...

    ... Society as a whole was divided into white and black groups. This forced division had to disappear; and many nonracial groups worked toward that end. But almost every nonracial group was still largely white, notably so in the student world ... So we began to realize that blacks themselves had to speak out about the black predicament ...

    At this time we were also influenced by the development of a black consciousness movement in the United States ...

REFERENCES

Keyfitz, Nathan. 1976. "World Resources and the World Middle Class," *Scientific American* 235, 1, July, pp. 28–35.

Zylstra, Bernard. 1977. "An Interview with Steve Biko." *Christian Science Monitor*, 10 November, pp. 18–19.

The Bushmen of Today

Megan Biesele

After receiving her Ph.D. in anthropology from Harvard in 1975, Megan Biesele worked in Botswana on land rights and economic self-determination. She has taught at both the University of Texas and Rice University, but since 1987 she has been foundation director and project director of the Nyae Nyae Foundation of Namibia.

Until the 1950's several thousand Bushman people were still hunting large game with poisoned arrows and gathering wild food in the westward extension of the Kalahari basin in Namibia. This area provided a last refuge for the Bushman people, hunted as vermin since the first arrival of Dutch settlers at the Cape in 1652. In the Kalahari basin they were able to continue their ancient way of life, living in small, mobile bands of about 40 people, each one centered on and supported by the resources of a *n!ore*, the Ju/'hoan Bushman word meaning "the place to which you belong," or "the place which gives you food and water." Bushmen have lived around these *n!ores* for as long as 40 000 years, practicing one of the most ancient and simple human technologies on earth.

In the past 40 years, however, life has changed drastically for Namibia's Bushmen. In the mid-1960's the Odendaal Commission recommended to the South West African government that the West Caprivi and Bushmanland be designated as "homelands" for all the people classified as "Bushman" in Namibia. Ironically the proclamation of "homelands" has meant the loss of vast areas of land traditionally used by the Bushmen. The process of "legal" dispossession, which predates the decision to establish homelands, signalled the end of the hunter-gatherer way of life for the vast majority of Namibian Bushmen. Beginning in the 1950's the Department of Nature Conservation began to expropriate large sections of the traditional hunting lands for game and nature reserves. The process began with the Hai//'om Bushmen being driven from their lands to make way for the Etosha Game Reserve. Around the same time the Kxoe Bushmen lost their land on the Kavango River

when it was proclaimed a nature reserve. In 1968 the Department of Nature Conservation expropriated the West Caprivi for a game reserve. About 6000 Ju/'hoan people were evicted from the land they had lived on for centuries.

In 1970 Bushmanland was established. For the Ju/'hoan Bushmen it meant the loss of 90% of their traditional land of Nyae Nyae, and all but one of their permanent waterholes. Southern Nyae Nyae, about 32000 sq km, was expropriated by the administration and given to the Herero as Hereroland East.

Northern Nyae Nyae, about 11000 sq km was first incorporated into the Kavango homeland and then proclaimed the !Kaudum Game Reserve in 1982. One of the last acts of the Interim Government of National Unity was to confirm the expropriation of the !Kaudum Game Reserve.

Today 33000 people classified as "Bushman" in Namibia have no land on which to hunt, gather or produce food and are increasingly without work. Without land they have resorted to employment in the army or to ill-paid work for white and black farmers. The vast majority who have been unable to get employment squat near places of work, dependent on the wage earners. This has been the pattern for so long now that new generations have grown up without the skills to hunt and gather. Malnutrition and disease led to a 5% decline in the population classified as "Bushman" in the 1970's. . . .

The Ju/'hoan people of Eastern Bushmanland, called Nyae Nyae, have been more fortunate. Some 3000 out of the total population of 33000 Bushmen have retained ties to a fragment of their land. For the past generation they have been the only people in Namibia who have hunted and gathered for their living while learning new farming skills. They are also the only people classed as "Bushman" who still have real residential ties to their foraging territory.

"The Bushmen of Today" by Megan Biesele, from *Shaken Roots*, Enviromental & Development Agency.

Nyae Nyae stretches north to south along the Namibia-Botswana border between the Kavango River and the Eiseb Valley. Originally it extended over approximately 50000 sq km. Hunter-gatherers need more than 37 sq km per person to sustain a stable population in this area. An uplift in the rock formation brings water to the surface in Nyae Nyae. Clearly visible on a geological map, the uplift makes Eastern Bushmanland rise like an island in a sea of sand. Twelve permanent and nine semi-permanent waterholes make the communal land habitable. . . .

In contrast to Nyae Nyae, Western Bushmanland—two thirds of the homeland created in 1970—lies in the deep sand sea. Water must come from deep boreholes requiring expensive pumping engines. The cost of fuel for pumping makes subsistence farming impossible. Bush foods and game are scarce. *Gifblaar*, a plant poisonous to cattle, is very common.

It was in Western Bushmanland that the South African Defence Force (SADF) chose to locate its "Bushman" battalion headquarters and bases. Bushmen from Namibia and those displaced by the Angolan civil war were recruited into the army as trackers and infantrymen for the offensive against Swapo in Angola. Thousands of Bushman people lived in Western Bushmanland until the elections in November 1989, supported by the relatively high salaries of war. Now with the war over, people have nowhere to turn. Some are reportedly trying to eat grass in a desperate struggle to survive. . . .

Most of the Bushmen who made a career of army life over the last decade are Barakwengo, Hai//'om and Vasekela people from the northern areas and from Angola. Now, as the wages of war dry up the soldiers and their families squat in a kind of numbness. They have no land and no homes.

"My future?" one man said, "I don't see a future."

Other ex-soldiers are more fortunate. Ju/'hoan Bushmen from Eastern Bushmanland around Tium!kui have land to return to, and families who have stayed on the land to develop and possess it. /Kaece /Kunta, whose people live at the permanent waterhole at /Aotcha settled by ≠Oma Stump, welcomed the end of life in the army when the war ended. /Kaece /Kunta has no regrets as he recalls his war experiences.

"They told us we would be getting on a plane in Rundu. We had to fly at night because when you fly into Angola in the daytime they shoot you down. The flight is about 1000 km. When we arrived there, they told us to be very careful of going out in the open, because planes were flying over and shooting from the air. It was here that we saw fighter planes for the first time in our lives. The white people lined us up and we stood there and looked at them. Then the white people said, 'Hey, Bushmen, you must watch out for those planes: if they see you they'll shoot you dead—'and after that we knew.

"When we were on the ground later, we were very much afraid, because the planes were searching for us up in the sky above. They shot at us terribly, pursuing us relentlessly. . . .

"People were also throwing handgrenades. These bombs are certain death and even to speak of them is to speak badly. The only reason we lived through it is we were taught how to be careful. If this had not happened, none of us Bushmen would have returned. All our thoughts were put to living through it.

"We saw the villages of the dead, those who had been killed, and their dead children. We saw the skulls of dead people, and those of children who had died. When you walked through these villages, you were stepping on death, the corpses of dead people. It was horrible. You had to step on them and they just crumbled to dust.

"If hunger gripped your middle while you were on these 'ops' and you hadn't seen food for three days, and then you had a chance to eat, you couldn't eat the food because it all tasted like death. If you were too weak to work, they'd prick your one shoulder with a needle, then prick your other shoulder, so you'd have strength to work well. . . .

"My parents didn't agree when I first wanted to go into the army. But I went in anyway—I thought it was just plain work. It was only later that they began killing people. The whole time I was in Angola, all I thought about was staying alive long enough to get back to my family."

DEATH BY MYTH

> There are two kinds of films. One kind shows us as people like other people, who have things to do and plans to make. This kind helps us. The other kind shows us as if we were animals, and plays right into the hands of people who want to take our land.
>
> —Tsamkxao ≠Oma

One of many pernicious myths about Bushman people, exacerbated by films like "The Gods Must Be Crazy," is that they still live in a desert never-never land without unfulfilled desires. The reality is that all but about 3% of the Bushman people in Namibia are completely dispossessed and must struggle unremittingly to survive. Whether they do so on white-owned farms, on Herero or Kavango cattle posts, squatting at the edges of towns, or living in dependence on police or the army, their ability to control their own lives is very limited. As a people with a long history as hunter-gatherers, everything in their background conditions them for dependency on people they perceive as stronger.

Traditionally, the Bushmen had no leaders, believing that a person who set himself up as better than another was without shame and harmful to group life. Nurturant and undemanding of their children, they promoted tolerance and downplayed ambition. Thus they suffer today not only from exploitation at the hands of more arrogant peoples, but also from the social legacy of a life that once worked when land was limitless and competing people few. Bushman people can be fairly characterized as those who have again and again stood aside as stronger forces muscled in. . . .

A n!ore IS A PLACE YOU DO NOT LEAVE

The trees are ours, and the elephants are ours. This is our land. Our things we make and wear come from it—our ostrich beads, our bows and arrows.

We Ju/'hoansi are people who have lived in our *n!oresi* for a long time. We didn't know the thing called a horse, and we made fires and did all our work without burning the tortoises and other tiny things. There were no white people's trucks driving around in our *n!ore*, here on our land. When these things came, their people saw us as nothing-things. So they shut off the land with fences and the eland died against the fences so that today our children are dying of hunger. There are no eland left, the wire has killed them all. And that fence between here and Botswana has also killed many animals. This was the work of governments. We once had our own government which kept us alive but this new government which has come in has killed us.

—/Kaece Kxao, N//haru≠'han, Eastern Bushmanland

Isolation from the outside world ended abruptly for the Ju/'hoansi when Native Administration of their area began in 1960. There was a migration of all bands to a single administrative centre called Tjum!kui, where they were given a school, a clinic, a church, a large jail, and some small jobs.

Some 900 Ju/'hoan people believed the administration's promises to teach them gardening and subsidize stock-raising, and an area which once supported 25 people by hunting and gathering was overwhelmed. A government-subsidized bottle store, unemployment, and the local disappearance of bush foods under heavy human pressure combined to turn Tjum!kui into a rural slum. The Ju/'hoansi called it "the place of death."

In the late 1970's a movement began among some families in Tjum!kui to return to the *n!oresi* from which they came. Tsamkxao ≠Oma and his father ≠Oma "Stump" took their people back to /Aotcha, location of the only permanent waterhole now left within the shrunken borders of Bushmanland. Black /Ui took his family to N≠aqmtjoha, and Kxao "Tekening," the artist,

took his to N≠anemh. They began to work in earnest to hold onto their land. Now 25 new communities have returned to their families' old places. "We must lift ourselves up, or die!" people tell each other.

The Ju/'hoansi in Nyae Nyae have started a new life as farmers. They still rely a great deal upon hunting and gathering as they make the difficult transition to small-scale stock-raising. But they know the land left to them does not permit a return to hunting and gathering alone. Life in such a transition is not easy and they struggle against many things: against lions that kill their cattle, and elephants that trample their gardens and wreck their water pumps; against unhelpful or hostile officials who believe them incapable of development. They also struggle within themselves to adapt the cultural rules and values that underwrote the old foraging way of life to the very different one of agriculture.

Ju/'hoansi know that without more intensive food production they are doomed to remain wards of some government, dependent and vulnerable. Tsamkxao ≠Oma is the chairperson of the newly-formed Nyae Nyae Farmers' Cooperative, a body which ties all the communities together to support the farming effort. Since 1986 Tsamkxao and the representatives from the 25 new communities have worked to make the cooperative a democratic organization responsible for many decisions about development. But as Tsamkxao said, "The Farmers' Coop is coming into government things much later than everyone else: the Boers took hold of things first. Now it's very late and we have to get going." . . .

At the time of the November 1989 election in Namibia, the Nyae Nyae Farmers' Cooperative was ratifying its first constitution, ≠*Hanu a N!an!a'an*. Representatives from the 25 villages travelled the rutted dirt tracks of Eastern Bushmanland to hold informational meetings and explain the new document. Written by a committee of Ju/'hoansi and hired scribes in English and the Ju/'hoan language, the constitution is intended to inject legal strength into ancient Ju/'hoan concepts of communal land holding. . . .

Representatives of the Farmers' Cooperative know that media coverage of what they are now trying to do is essential. They want to make the point in Southern Africa that there are similar groups of people in other parts of the world. Australian Aborigines, and North and South American Indians are also struggling for land rights and self-determination. Tsamkxao ≠Oma, the coop chairman welcomed a journalist recently saying, "We're glad you're here because newspapers are very important to us. I went to a conference in Cape Town last year and I found that many people there had never even heard about us. Newspapers will help us inform people, and they may be a way to help end discrimination. These days we cannot accept that our children have to hear words like 'bobbejaan' and 'kaffir.'"

Easily mythologized, Bushman people have captured the interest of popular media like film, TV, and glossy magazines. But their real voices have been obscured by the loud clamour of the myths in which they are enshrined. Silenced by the voice-overs, not only of film narrators, but also of neighbours and governments and even of well-meaning friends, they have gone on communicating to each other but not to the world outside. Bushmen have been seen both as a sort of fairy-folk, floating over the landscape with no concept of property and no need for solid resources, and as blood-thirsty poachers with a killer instinct. Romanticisation and denigration can amount to the same thing in the end, a kind of death by myth . . . or by misinformation.

The Nature Conservation forces of what was once the South West African government were succeeding in taking Bushman land right up until the last days before UN Resolution 435 was implemented. Dreaming of a future revenue-generating tourist industry, the conservationists have sequestered huge swatches of what once was the well-known and reliably productive n!ores of the Ju/'hoan and Kxoe Bushmen. Tsamkxao spoke of an area of Nyae Nyae where Ju/'hoansi have lived for as long as anyone can remember, the permanent waterhole of Gura, where Nature Conservation and the Department of Government Affairs have joined forces to promote safaris and trophy hunting at the expense of Farmers' Coop plans for the area.

"Something we've known for a long time is that the antelopes of Gura were ours, our fathers' fathers' sustenance. And the water there has been our source of life. Even I, when I was small, washed myself at Gura and drank the water there when I was thirsty. At that time I didn't know of a single European or Afrikaner who had been there. This government which calls itself `Bushmanland' is talking about my things! Why should other people make money here from our animals? We have been here a long time: don't the Nature Conservation officials know they are just small children?"

Officials do seem to be neglecting an important source of information about the environment by not listening to the Ju/'hoan hunters. These people, with their long history of stability in the area have a great deal to contribute to conservation planning. Many generations of information about animal and plant species and their interactions should not be discounted simply because they have been passed on orally. The written tradition of scientific study in this area is young by comparison, and could profit from an infusion of older wisdom. Bushman folklore and religion contain evidence of a very ancient and healthy respect for natural resources, and an ethic of conservation which is thorough-going and socially sound. In fact, seeing these people as natural conservators may be a good way to appreciate what they can contribute. As a /Gwi Bushman, Compass Matsoma, of neighbouring Botswana said recently, "We are the only ones who can live with animals without killing them all."

Not only tourists and hunters but also eager pastoral peoples now wait at the shrunken borders of "Bushmanland" for opportunities to move in. Descendants of survivors of the German Herero Wars at the beginning of this century, when General Von Trotha issued his famous genocide order to kill all men, women and children, have been living as refugees in Botswana. With the coming of independence, many now hope to return across the border and settle on the rich pastures and relatively abundant waters of the Nyae Nyae area, one of the last areas not yet overgrazed in Namibia.

But the Nyae Nyae people say "People shouldn't think they can ruin one area by grazing too many cattle and then move onto someone else's land and ruin that too. We will keep the numbers of our cattle small. We think not only of today but of tomorrow and the day after that."

As new cattle herders, Ju/'hoansi face many challenges. The primary one is the confrontation with their own tried-and-true means of organizing their work. While hunting with poisoned arrows is a most individualistic pursuit, sharing of all food was customary. Keeping cattle and planting dryland gardens involves a new negotiation of labour processes and products. Ju/'hoansi spend a lot of time talking about this.

A dark side coexists with the exultation and excitement of new beginnings. Alcohol undermines Ju/'hoan spirit as it does that of so many African communities. People in Eastern Bushmanland do not seem to be chronic alcoholics at this stage. Distance from bottle stores and poverty have protected most of them. But many brew beer from sugar and yeast on pension day, and when the bottle store was still open in Tjum!kui it caused immense social disruption.

Just after the independence election, Ju/'hoan people took their first public stand acknowledging that excessive drinking is a community problem. At a meeting of the Nyae Nyae Farmers' Cooperative, strong feeling arose over the issue of the social disruption caused by home-brewed beer.

"Those who drink are the ones who cause anger and fighting. Those who don't drink just sit quietly . . . We're not saying don't drink at all, but just drink slowly and wisely . . . I think we should say to ourselves, I have work to do before I drink. First I'm going to do my work.

"When you drink, you shouldn't go around thinking like a Boer and telling people that you are a big shot. If you do that, someday people will become angry with you and their hearts will grow big against you. You don't go saying you're a chief. Instead, you sit together and understand each other. None of us is a chief, we're all alike and have our little farms. So when you drink, just think clearly about it and talk to each other about being careful. We've been told now, so let's be smart about drinking. Let's not fight. Let's start today to talk to each other about drinking and help each other." (Dabe Dahm.)

The bottle store at Tjum!kui, which once did big business on army pay day, has been closed.

Back on their land after living in town with the problems of alcoholism and unemployment, Ju/'hoansi can once more be dignified examples for their children. "We are people who have our work," they say. Children see their mothers and fathers engaged again in productive activities they know well.

A sense of purpose again pervades life in Eastern Bushmanland. Enthusiasm to take part in building a new Namibia runs through the meetings of the Nyae Nyae Farmers' Coop. . . .

NOT KNOWING THINGS IS DEATH

The importance of knowledge in obtaining a living is very much present in the minds of the Ju/'hoan Bushmen. Once they had to be able reliably to tell the difference between poisonous and non-poisonous plants and to judge the likelihood of crossing paths with a worthwhile animal at a given season of the year. They had to know how to make riems, rope, string, sinew thread, carrying bags and nets, stamping blocks, aerodynamically effective arrows, and much more, all from natural materials. The word for "owner" (kxao) in Ju/'hoan most deeply means "master," in the sense of one who knows, or knows how to use. To own property is to be its steward; to own an area of land, a n!ore, is not to possess it exclusively but to use it well.

"A big thing is that my food is here and my father taught me about it. I know where I can drink water here. My father said to me, `These are your foods and the foods of your children's children.' If you stay in your n!ore you have strength. You have water and food and a place." . . .

When things change greatly in one generation, sometimes older people teach children, and sometimes children are in a position to teach adults. Kxao/Ai!ae of N≠anemh says to his boys that the way to keep your n!ore is to develop it.

"I hold my cattle in my left hand, and my garden in my right hand, and together they give me life." . . .

New ideas and new concepts have flooded into Nyae Nyae in one generation. Has there been enough time for Ju/'hoansi themselves to change sufficiently to participate in the coming independence? Events like UN Resolution 435 and free elections and the final end of apartheid have suddenly overtaken them with many of them not knowing what is really in store.

Like other Namibians, Ju/'hoan Bushmen have had their geographical isolation deepened by the apartheid policies of South Africa and before that, as long as a century ago, by the original German colonial administration of Südwest. They have lived through decades of administrations whose communications have somehow missed them because, being egalitarian, they did not have identifiable chiefs. . . .

Suddenly, now, Ju/'hoansi face both the challenge and the opportunity of taking part in a political process watched eagerly by the eyes of the world. But can a small minority with a hunting and gathering heritage, a recent history of isolation and exclusion from affairs that concern them, and a problematic present situation of economic underdevelopment and militarization transform itself quickly enough? Can the Ju/'hoansi hold on to what remains of their ancient territory and also take advantage of the new opportunities of freedom? An egalitarian culture which has always underplayed leadership is faced with the necessity of selecting leaders to participate in the new politics. As at the South African Cape three centuries ago, when leaders were called into being among Bushman groups warring for their lives with the Dutch colonists, Ju/'hoansi are now creating leaders to meet the challenges of the present. . . .

In 1988, news of the implementation of UN Resolution 435 and the promise of free elections in 1989 startled the Ju/'hoansi into a realization of the magnitude of possible changes. Since September of 1988 the Nyae Nyae Farmers' Cooperative, a grassroots community organization in Eastern Bushmanland, has been holding informational meetings about Namibian independence at far-flung villages. Black /Ui at N≠aqmtjoha welcomed the arrival of the discussion team: "I thank you all. I thank you for this talk which comes from far away to us. But one thing that gives me pain is that long ago I never heard anything like this, but only today am hearing it. Today my heart is happy with what I have heard. News is life."

Before the effects of the UN election information process were felt in Bushmanland, the Farmers' Coop tried to explain elections to people who had no word for them in their language. Many had never even heard the Afrikaans word verkiesing.

"An election means to come to an understanding about a n!ore."

"An election means that you give praise to the person who will sit in the chair of leading, the head person."

"An election is where you plant your feet and stop."

The talks about elections and other democratic concepts were held in villages of grass or mud houses with no protected public gathering place. The sun beat down at the edges of whatever patch of shade could be found large enough to shelter the village people and the bakkie-load of travellers. Children bounced on their mothers' laps and people of all ages sat close together, often with their legs crossing those of their neighbours. The chairperson of the Farmers' Cooperative, Tsamkxao ≠Oma, constantly encouraged others besides himself to speak.

Issues as small as how to keep tourists from swimming in the drinking water dams to ones as large as securing legal title to their land have been under long discussion at these meetings.

The Nyae Nyae area communities are preoccupied with how to ensure that they are included in talks about conservation and other issues concerning them. Great resentment is felt toward government officials who travel all the way from Windhoek to Tjum!kui, a distance of 750 kilometres, ostensibly to consult with the Ju/'hoan communities, but actually only to meet with the white officials at the comfortable Nature Conservation rest camp, and then go home. The public nature of communication has become a vital issue, and it came to a head in early March 1989 with the arrival of an SADF public relations team at /Aotcha.

Huge armoured vehicles swept into the tiny village of mud houses. Uniformed men with submachine guns silenced the usual hubbub. The army was pulling out of northern Namibia, campaigning as it went for the Democratic Turnhalle Alliance (DTA), Swapo's main opposition. "Watch out for the Hyena" (Swapo) and "Vote for the Eland" (DTA) were the condescending folktale slogans the soldiers offered. "The eland is the animal without deceit: you are the eland."

The Ju/'hoan hunters' sign for eland antelope horns is a "V" made with the first and second fingers. This also happens to be the adopted hand sign for the DTA. In a further twist of irony, which the soldiers couldn't have known about, but which made an even harder puzzle for the Ju/'hoansi to unravel, "Eland" is an ancient clan name for many Ju/'hoansi in the area. Hyenas, on the other hand, are thought of as outcast animals who are always up to no good. Some people were taken in by this overwhelming symbolism, but others remained skeptical. "Swapo has never done anything to us; why should anyone call them hyenas before hearing what they have to say?" said one man.

Ultimately, the public relations meeting at /Aotcha was a bit of a rout because the officer in charge refused the people's request to tape the session. The message brought by the SADF that day was hardly secret, but since it could not be taped, the people regarded the communication as a "theft." Unfortunately for the army it didn't know that the Ju/'hoansi call tape cassettes ≠xusi, their word for oracle disks. Oracle disks are thrown down on the ground like dice and are said to reveal the future by the pattern they make. These disks are traditionally made from eland hide and are thus associated with the eland's herd sociability and supposed guilelessness.

Playing with strong symbolism can ultimately backfire, as it did resoundingly during the last feverish days of election campaigning in Bushmanland. Dabe Dahm, a Farmers' Cooperative representative at the village of //Auru, had thought for a year about the DTA's use of the eland to represent its party. Having observed violent drunkenness and clear intimidation of potential voters by the DTA campaigners, he said, "Today my shame is piled high. My people's name

from long ago, `the people of the eland,' has been rubbed in the dirt and stolen by politicians who will never do anything for us. All they want is to give other people our land."

The same day at Dabe Dahm's village people spoke of the loss of the actual eland on which they once depended. Many adults remembered a time when eland were abundant in their area.

Most Ju/'hoansi believe that the drastic reduction in eland numbers is due to the game fences. . . . Regardless of their decline in numbers, eland live in folklore and inhabit people's minds and a move to try eland domestication in Nyae Nyae is gaining support. Ju/'hoansi see eland farming as a sensible alternative to the kind of abuse of grazing resources they have seen destroy the productivity of adjacent areas such as Eastern Hereroland. The eland is adapted to the area, it does not suffer from the effects of *gifblaar*, and it can sustain itself on water-bearing plants such as desert cucumbers and juicy roots when water is scarce. Some Ju/'hoan people have worked on the farms of Afrikaner people in the Grootfontein area who keep eland and other game on their farms, and they know what a fine candidate the eland is for management as a herd animal. . . .

"Trucks with hunters shooting from them have chased away the animals we had here, trucks and the fences that have been built. Long ago you saw all the animals here, even eland. But today there's not a single eland. Even ostrich eggs you don't see, because the ostriches too are stopped by the fences. We don't want this, we want the fences taken down so that wild animals will come back and be close to us as before."

"If Ju/'hoansi had strength, maybe they could think of catching lots of eland, and maybe roan antelopes, and farming with them. But until after the election we will have no strength. The white people still have all the strength in this land. Maybe after the election we could do it . . . Long ago the eland used to cross Nyae Nyae according to the season, but one season the fence was closed on them and on their calves, and they haven't returned."

It's clear that the policies of the South West African state with their paternalism and emphasis on separation have angered the Ju/'hoansi for a long time. In particular they resent being left out of communications. Ju/'hoansi call themselves "the owners of argument," and "the people who talk too much." For them, it's important that issues be discussed and debated by everyone so that ill-will doesn't fester in someone left out of the talk. . . .

The idea of representation for their voices in government is catching on among the Ju/'hoansi at the same time as they are realizing the power of the printed word. As Tsamkxao told one group meeting under a thorn tree, "One problem is that we have no scribe. We have no-one who is the 'owner of the mail.' So let the children help us. Let the children go to school, learn, and know. Let's make a plan. Let's let everyone know that we have someone with a writing-stick. Let's have a scribe, a writer, a translator. Let's not be without these."

None of the language of democracy, in fact, seems terribly new among the Ju/'hoansi, rather it is age-old. These are the people who gravely said to anthropologist Richard Lee over a decade ago: "We have no headman, each one of us is a headman over himself." The concept of "one person, one vote" fits right in with Ju/'hoan ideology, and among these sexually egalitarian people one doesn't even have to add, as would be necessary in many parts of the world, "and a woman's vote is just like a man's."

Tsamkxao illustrated democracy at one meeting, at a place called //Xa/oba, talking about collective strength and the responsibilities of the people's representatives: "I thank the old people who have spoken, but we also need to begin to hear from the young people about their *n!ores*. Everyone must work together. Do you see these sticks in my hand? If you pick up lots of sticks, you can't break them. But one stick alone breaks easily. So we want things from now on to be done on paper, legally, beginning with meetings where everyone comes together to listen. We don't want a Ju/'hoan representative who just stuffs news into his own ears and doesn't speak to us. If you speak for a group of people to a government, and if you speak badly, it doesn't just affect one person. It affects everyone. When you do something, all your people should have a way of learning about it. Political parties are for letting people know things."

One of the things Ju/'hoansi are letting people know now is that they suggest legal institutionalization of something like their old *n!ore* system. They know it has been successful over a long span of time, and see it as the basis for something that could work in Namibia's future. It would mean a new kind of survival for them, too, not the traditional one, but a creative one, their own special contribution to nation-building.

In 1989 Namibia had good rains. By March, Bushmanland was lush and green. One evening, as lilac-breasted rollers tumbled after insects against cumulus clouds lit with a pink glow by the setting sun, an historic meeting began at Nyae Nyae. After generations without meaningful talk with outside political forces, representatives of the Nyae Nyae Farmers' Coop met with officials of Swapo, the party which will construct the Namibian land tenure systems to come. With the two

groups sitting on the grass in a rough circle of about forty people, including onlookers, the Coop presented a document stating its goals with regard to land and representation. Written in the Ju/'hoan language and translated into English, the statement calls for a democratic national system with regional autonomous government in Nyae Nyae based on current and longterm residence.

Ju/'hoansi know they are the last Bushman people in Namibia to have an unbroken contact with even the small fragment of land that is still theirs. And they know these ties to land are their main resource: "Where your mother and father are buried is where you have your strength."

The Ju/'hoansi of Eastern Bushmanland are the lucky ones. But they are planning carefully to share their land and a chance to make an independent living with other Bushmen in Namibia. The election and the talk that preceded it has begun to give these isolated people a sense of the altruism needed to create a nation.

"I said to the Administrator General, 'Will you help us since our *n!ore* is small? Hereros have taken part of it and !Kaudum is another part gone.'

"I also told him, 'The people who once worked in the army today have no work and no other strength. How will we help those people?'

"I said, 'The people called Vasekela—we still haven't met together to talk with them. I understand that they may be allowed to stay in Western Bushmanland and make gardens. We must ask how they are going to do that without water.'

"We want to help everyone we can. It's important that we who are the Ju/'hoansi have our own government and do our own work. We have only a small place, but we want to go to the Gobabis farms and find our people who long ago were taken away. We want to get them and bring them here. Can we find a way to help everyone?

"We have received money from the 'owners of helping' [aid funds] and we have dug boreholes for more water in our small land. The !Kaudum people are many, and many others are on police-posts that will now die, or in Gobabis. We who are representatives of the Nyae Nyae Farmers' Cooperative are like people planting a tree. We should realize that we are not just one small thing but are starting something big. The work will go on, even beyond our deaths. The boreholes will be there." (Tsamkxao ≠Oma.)

Glossary

a priori In logic, working from the general to the particular; deductive reasoning.

age-grade A category determined by age; each person goes through many categories of age during life.

age-sets A group of persons initiated into an age-grade at the same time and who move together through successive age-grades thereafter.

agrarian society One in which food is produced by farming the land.

AIDS Acquired immunodeficiency syndrome; a fatal disease transmitted sexually, through contaminated blood products, and from a mother to child during pregnancy and/or through breast milk. Now pandemic.

anthropological advocacy group Group formed to advance the rights of indigenous peoples.

anthropological perspective The practice of viewing customs and institutions in their holistic and evolutionary context.

anthropology The study of humankind, in all times and places.

apartheid The separation of races within a single society, with whites monopolizing positions of power and having favored access to valued resources.

applied anthropology The use of anthropological techniques and knowledge in order to solve "practical" problems.

autonomy Self-government.

balanced reciprocity Where goods are exchanged, those that are given and those that are received are of equal value.

cargo cults A type of revitalization movement common in parts of the Pacific; adherents believe the ancestors will arrive in a ship loaded with white peoples' cargo and will drive whites out.

civilization A type of society marked by the presence of urban settlements, social inequality, and a state type of political organization.

clan A noncorporate group in which each member claims descent from a common ancestor without necessarily knowing the genealogical links to that ancestor.

code switching The process of changing from one level of language to another.

colonialism The unilateral assertion of political jurisdiction over a people and their territory by some other people.

common-interest group A group formed for a specific purpose with membership based on an act of joining, rather than age, kinship, marriage, or territory.

communication The transmittal of information from one individual to another, whether it be a hunger cry from an infant, words of a language, or flirtatious behavior.

cultural anthropology The branch of anthropology concerned with human behavior (as opposed to physical, also known as biological, anthropology).

cultural arrogance The ethnocentric notion that one's own culture is superior to another.

cultural pluralism Interaction socially and politically within the same society of people with different ways of living and thinking.

culture The values and standards of a people that enable them to make sense of the world and to shape every aspect of their behavior.

development economist An economist who studies or works with peoples or cultures whose lives are in the midst of cultural change.

dispute management How a society handles disagreements such as ownership of land, marital rights, or dowry.

economic exploitation Exploitation of one population's labor and resources by another population for the latter's benefit, at the expense of the former.

economics The study of the production, distribution, and consumption of goods and commodities.

egalitarian ethos The expectation that all should share equally in valued resources and have an equal say in making important decisions.

egalitarian redistribution The redistribution of resources so that all members of the society share equally.

egalitarianism A social system in which as many valued positions exist as there are persons capable of filling them.

enculturation The process by which a people's culture is transmitted from one generation to the next.

endogamy Marriage within a specified category of individuals.

ethnocentrism The belief held by all people that one's own culture is superior in every way to all others.

ethnographies Studies of particular cultures based on firsthand observation.

ethnology The study of cultures from a comparative or historical point of view.

exchange The reciprocal giving of things, whether it be camels for wives, bananas for meat, money for manufactured goods, or whatever.

exogamy Marriage outside of a specified group.

extended family A family composed of two or more married couples with their dependent offspring, the core members of which are related by ties of blood, who live together in one household.

family A residential kin group minimally composed of a woman, her dependent children, and at least one adult male joined through marriage or blood relationship.

fieldwork The study of a society, or some segment thereof, carried out in that society itself.

foraging The finding of food in nature, as opposed to food production through farming or herding.

generalized reciprocity Exchange in which the value of the gift is not calculated nor is the time of repayment specified.

genocide The extermination of one people by another, either as a deliberate act or as the accidental outcome of activities carried out by one people with little regard for their impact on others.

global interdependency The interdependency between all of the peoples of the world that has come to exist in the twentieth century.

globalization The development of global interdependency; the process by which the world's peoples become increasingly interdependent.

hierarchy An organizational structure in which high-ranking elements subsume lower-ranking ones.

historical linguistics The study of linguistic change and the relationships between different languages.

holistic A perspective by which anthropologists view things in the broadest possible context, in order to understand their interconnections and interdependence.

homosexuality A sexual preference for members of one's own, rather than the opposite, sex.

hunter-gatherer One who lives on foods either hunted or gathered in the wild; preferred term now is food-forager, which incorporates hunting, gathering, fishing, and scavenging.

incest Sexual relations between individuals, normally declared "off-limits," usually between parents and children or siblings of opposite sex; in some cultures, however, other relationships may be considered incestuous.

kindred The maternal and paternal relatives of a particular individual to whom he or she can appeal for assistance and who gather together on important occasions in the life of the individual.

kinesics "Body language"; system of postures, facial expressions, and body motions that convey messages.

language Communication by means of sounds that are put together in meaningful ways according to a set of rules.

law Social norms, the neglect or infraction of which is regularly met by the threatened or actual application of physical force on the part of an individual or group possessing the socially recognized authority to do so.

liminality Being at the point of change, from one status to another.

lineage A corporate group, membership in which is based on demonstrable descent from a common ancestor.

linguist One who studies languages, their structure, and use.

linguistic anthropology A branch of cultural anthropology that studies the linguistic behavior of humans.

magic The idea that there are ritual formulas that, if followed precisely, manipulate supernatural powers for desired ends.

male initiation rite See *Rite of passage.*

market exchange The buying and selling of goods and services with prices set by forces of supply and demand. In non-Western societies, usually occurs in a marketplace.

marriage A transaction and resulting contract by which a woman and a man establish continuing rights of sexual access to one another and in which the woman involved is eligible to bear children.

matrilineal descent Ancestry traced to a common ancestor exclusively through women.

matrilineal society A society in which matrilineal descent is an important organizing principle.

millenarian movement In a colonial or multicultural society, a revitalization movement that attempts to resurrect a group, with its own subcultural ideology, that has long suffered in an inferior social position.

multiculturalism The doctrine that accepts the validity of groups within a larger society operating according to their own distinctive standards and values.

nation A people who share a common language, culture, territorial base, political organization, history, and (often) religion.

natural selection An evolutionary process by which individuals with characters best suited to a particular environment survive and reproduce with greater frequency than do those without them.

negative reciprocity Contrasts with balanced reciprocity in that one party to the exchange tries to get the better of it.

nuclear family Consists of husband, wife, and dependent children, living together in a single household.

Oedipus complex In psychoanalysis, the term for the child unconsciously to be attracted to the parent of the opposite sex while being hostile to the same-sex parent.

organizational principle A principle, such as descent from a common ancestor, by which individuals are organized into groups within a society.

pandemic Epidemic over large regions; for example, AIDS is pandemic globally.

paralanguage The extralinguistic noises such as grunts, cries, or laughter that accompany language.

patrilineal descent Ancestry traced to a common ancestor exclusively through men.

patrilineal society A society in which patrilineal descent is an important organizing principle.

physical anthropologist An anthropologist who studies humans as biological organisms.

poison oracle The use of poison to summon the supernatural to find the truth of a matter.

political organization The means by which decisions are made, conflicts resolved, and order maintained within a society.

polygamy A form of marriage in which one may have multiple spouses, that is, one man with two or more wives (polygyny) or one woman with two or more husbands (polyandry).

prehistorian One who studies ancient societies for which there are no written records.

psychoanalytic theory The theory of personality developed in the late nineteenth century by Sigmund Freud.

psychological anthropology The branch of cultural anthropology that studies the interface between culture and the individual.

redistributive exchange The collection of goods by some central agent, be it a "big man" or the state, for subsequent redistribution.

religion Rituals, with explanatory myths, that mobilize supernatural powers for the purpose of achieving or preventing transformations of certain events.

revitalization movements Social movements, commonly of a religious nature, that seek to totally reform a society.

rite of passage A ritual that marks changes in the lives of individuals, such as birth, puberty, marriage, and death.

social anthropologist An anthropologist who studies the social life of human beings.

social class In a nonegalitarian society, a class of individuals who enjoy equal or nearly equal prestige according to the system of evaluation.

social control The control exerted on individuals by the institutions of their society.

social elite In a nonegalitarian society, those who occupy important positions of power and have preferred access to valued resources.

social engineering project A project designed specifically to change some aspect of a society.

social group Any socially recognized group within a society.

society A people who share a common territory and who share common cultural traditions.

sociolinguistics The study of how language is used in particular social settings.

state A country with a centralized political system having the power to coerce.

stratified society The division of society into two or more groups of people (social classes) who do not share equally in the basic resources that support life, influence, and prestige.

structural analysis Analysis of the underlying structure of a myth or activity.

structural linguistics The scientific study of the structure of a language.

subaltern Subordinate.

subculture The standards and values of a group of people within a larger society.

subsistence Means of support of way of life.

symbolic indicator Activities and positions indicative of one's position in a class-structured society.

variable Something that changes; in science, a factor that is varied while all others are held constant.

Index